THE LIBRARY
ST. MARY'S COLLEGE OF MARYLAND
ST. MARY'S CITY, MARYLAND 20686

72504

W9-ASL-267

The BERLIN CRISIS of 1961

Robert M. Slusser

THE BERLIN CRISIS OF 1961

Soviet-American Relations and the Struggle for Power in the Kremlin, June-November 1961

The Johns Hopkins University Press

Baltimore and London

Copyright © 1973 by The Johns Hopkins University Press
All rights reserved
Manufactured in the United States of America

The Johns Hopkins University Press, Baltimore, Maryland 21218
The Johns Hopkins University Press Ltd., London

Library of Congress Catalog Card Number 72–4025
International Standard Book Number 0–8018–1404–9

Library of Congress Cataloging in Publication data will be found
on the last printed page of this book.

In memory of

Paul Eric Slusser

1949—1971

Introduction

For a long time historians have been loath to study the recent past, citing inadequate perspective or the alleged lack of documentation as reasons to justify their reluctance. When it comes to the recent history of the Soviet Union, their reluctance has been greatly strengthened by the obstacles which the Soviet regime puts in the path of historical research.

A sound understanding of recent Soviet history is, nevertheless, a vital necessity for mankind, and the task of studying it must be undertaken, notwithstanding the difficulties which it entails. Fortunately, the systematic investigation of recent Soviet history is not impossible. Documentation of various kinds exists in abundance, to an extent which would probably surprise people who have not looked into the matter. In particular, there is a veritable wealth of material available on Soviet internal and foreign policy during the years of Khrushchev's dominance (1957–64).

Three factors have contributed to this favorable situation: first, the ideological conflict between the Soviet Union and Communist China, which generated a vigorous and often revealing polemical literature on both sides; second, the continuing struggle for power in the Communist party of the Soviet Union, which produced much valuable documentary evidence, though often of an oblique kind; and third, the personality and policies of Khrushchev himself— ebullient, loquacious, impulsive, and at times calculatedly indiscreet—which in a number of ways helped greatly to ease the historian's task.

For the study of Soviet-American relations in the Khrushchev period, the situation is also unusually favorable. One of the consequences of the assassination of President Kennedy was the early publication of a number of historically valuable memoirs by participants in his administration, as well as books by observers and critics. The internal debate in the United States over the Vietnam war has produced a flood of studies and documentary compilations on the period, of a kind historians seldom have access to so soon after the event. Thus materials have become available which make it possible to study the American side of the Soviet–U.S. relationship in far greater depth than would ordinarily be true for events of the recent past, and evidence from the American side often casts a revealing light on Soviet actions and policies.

The result of all these factors, and others contributing toward the same end, is that the study of recent Soviet history and of Soviet–U. S. relations in the Khrushchev–Kennedy era is a task which the historian may undertake with a well-founded hope of achieving worthwhile results. It goes almost without saying, of course, that the task is beset by formidable difficulties of interpretation and analysis, that there are many points on which documentary evidence is not available, that there are some important questions which must remain unanswered, and that the conclusions reached must sometimes be stated in provisional form. But to a greater or lesser degree, the same things could be said of work in any other historical period. Here, as elsewhere, the historian's basic problem is to devise suitable methods for making the available sources yield their fullest significance.

In the present study I have tried to work in accordance with three basic principles: first, observance of strict chronological order and careful dating in the succession of events and their interrelation; second, attention to the close and continuous interaction between Soviet internal and foreign policy; and third, recognition of the wide-ranging scope of recent Soviet history, regarding which no a priori exclusions of possibly relevant areas of concern can safely be made.

The present study deals with an episode—probably the major episode—in Soviet–U.S. relations, and in Soviet (and U.S.) foreign policy in general, during the first year of the Kennedy administration. History, however, is a continuous never-ending stream of interrelated events and processes, and it is impossible to achieve an adequate understanding of any given episode in isolation from its larger historical context, no matter how intensively one may scrutinize the evidence. I have already published an essay dealing with Soviet foreign policy during the entire Khrushchev period (1957–64), which constitutes a kind of pilot project for the series of linked studies of which the present volume has been conceived as an integral part.[1] The conclusions I reached in that essay have been in part confirmed, in part modified, and in part enriched by entirely new insights as the result of the more detailed research which underlies the present volume. In particular, my concept of the Soviet policy-making process in the Khrushchev period and of Khrushchev's position vis-à-vis his colleagues in the collective leadership has been radically altered

[1]"American, China, and the hydra-headed opposition: The dynamics of Soviet foreign policy," in Peter H. Juviler and Henry W. Morton, eds., *Soviet Policy-Making: Studies of Communism in Transition* (New York, Praeger, 1967), pp. 186–269.

as a result of the almost microscopic enlargement of the field of study which followed my decision to devote an entire volume to the brief six-month period of the Berlin crisis of 1961.

The dominant view among Western scholars who investigated the problem of Soviet policy-formation in the period before Khrushchev's overthrow in October 1964 was that Khrushchev wielded the same kind of unlimited power as, in their time (in the view of these same scholars), did his predecessors Stalin and Lenin.[2] A challenge to this view was offered by a minority of scholars who held that Khrushchev, powerful though he might be, was nevertheless forced to take into account the views and wishes of others in the Soviet leadership group. Some of the minority scholars tended to view this process as one of interaction on the personal level, others thought of it in terms of socio-economic interest groups in the Soviet population, with which individual Soviet leaders tended to identify themselves and for which they served as spokesmen.[3]

My own preference lay with the minority, but even their explanation seemed to me to require further analysis. It was partly to achieve a more satisfactory understanding of the problem that I embarked on the research project of which the present volume forms a part. What emerged from the study surprised even me: it was the discovery that neither of the two opposing schools of interpretation of recent Soviet political history had found a completely satisfactory answer to the problem of policy-formation, though both had grasped part of the complex reality. What I found was evidence of a power struggle more intense, more violent, and more divisive than had previously been suspected, a situation in which power lay at times in the hands of a single leader, at times was shared by a collective leadership, and at times seemed to be up for grabs, with whoever could grasp the levers of power entitled to operate them.

Once I had recognized the significance of the evidence pointing to this unorthodox conclusion, confirmatory details turned up in the most varied contexts. The real test of the hypothesis, I realized, would be the record of the Twenty-second Congress of the Communist Party of the Soviet Union in October 1961. It was only after I had subjected the protocols of the congress to a detailed day-by-day, session-by-session, speech-by-speech analysis, integrated with the simultaneous events taking place in Berlin, Washington, Peking, and elsewhere, that I felt confident that the hypothesis I had formulated would stand the test of any desired degree of factual verification. The evidence, to

[2]For the classic statement of this approach see Merle W. Fainsod, *How Russia Is Ruled* (Cambridge, Mass., Harvard University Press, 1953; 2nd rev. ed., 1963).

[3]For a debate on the problem, see a series of articles in *Problems of Communism:* Thomas H. Rigby, "How strong is the leader?", vol. XI, no. 5, Sept.–Oct. 1962, pp. 1–8; Carl Linden, "Khrushchev and the party battle," ibid., vol. XII, no. 5, Sept.–Oct. 1963, pp. 27–35; and Thomas H. Rigby, "The extent and limits of authority (A rejoinder to Mr. Linden)," ibid., pp. 36–41.

a surprising extent, was there, once one approached the congress as an event unfolding in time and space rather than as a kind of Platonic abstraction related solely to its own genre, that of Communist party congresses.

The analysis of recent Soviet history presented in this book thus differs in some important respects from any previously offered. It is based on a detailed matrix of factual evidence organized on chronological principles, but at certain key points it substitutes analysis and inference for concrete documentary evidence. To that extent its conclusions must be regarded as hypotheses, subject to modification as additional sources become available. But I am convinced that it is essentially correct, and I therefore feel justified in presenting it as a contribution to historical understanding and as the basis for further investigation. Of any alternative explanation of the facts I would ask only that it demonstrate a comparable capacity to organize and explain the detailed evidence which is now available.

A valuable by-product of the conclusions reached on the basis of an intensive analysis of Soviet foreign policy in the Khrushchev–Kennedy period is that they put in a new and more revealing light the foreign policy of the Kennedy administration. Several attempts have recently been made to depict John F. Kennedy as a dogmatic anti-Communist, a Cold War-monger whose actions helped create the very crises with which his administration tried to cope.[4] It is not necessary to make an extensive analysis of Soviet foreign policy in order to refute oversimplified and inaccurate analyses of this kind; the evidence of Kennedy's patient search for a basis for negotiations with the Soviets over Berlin during the 1961 crisis is part of the historical record, and it is only by ignoring the plain facts that the authors in question have managed to construct their image of Kennedy as a Cold Warrior.

What emerges from intensive study of the Soviet side in the Berlin crisis of 1961, however, is the recognition that the Soviet threat to vital U.S. interests was in actuality even more direct and dangerous than anyone in Washington at the time realized. The prevailing view in the Kennedy administration, reflecting and based on the consensus of American scholars, was that Khrushchev dominated the process of Soviet foreign policy formation and that he was, in the final analysis, a rational and responsible statesman who might flirt with brink-of-war policies but who could always be relied on to draw back well short of the brink itself.

By contrast, the picture of the Soviet leadership which emerges from the present work is that of a group so badly split by nearly unbridgeable differences over fundamental policy questions that at times it was subject to no

[4]See Louise Fitzsimons, *The Kennedy Doctrine* (New York, Random House, 1972) and Richard F. Walton, *Cold War and Counterrevolution: The Foreign Policy of John F. Kennedy* (New York, Viking Press, 1972), as well as the laudatory review of both volumes by David Schoenbrun, *New York Times Book Review*, March 19, 1972, pp. 6–7.

single unifying force. It is the picture of a process of foreign policy formation in which an opposition faction could play Russian roulette with the peace
of the world by taking actions which deliberately risked nuclear war, and in
which a struggle for internal political power was successfully masked from
the outside world, only to erupt in disguised form as a major schism in the
international Communist movement.

The Soviet–Western conflict over Berlin in 1961 has a long history of its
own. Its origins date back to World War II and the arrangements drawn up
at that time by the principal nations of the Grand Alliance—Britain, France,
the Soviet Union, and the United States—for the postwar administration of
defeated Germany and its capital, Berlin. Under four-power agreements
reached in 1944 and 1945 Germany was divided into four zones of administration, each to be administered by one of the four Allied powers. Berlin was
also placed under four-power control, despite the fact that it was entirely
surrounded by territory assigned to the Soviet Zone of Administration and lay
some 110 miles east of the zones administered by the Western Allies.

Since the Soviet Union and its wartime partners frequently differed in the
postwar years, sometimes sharply, over policy to be pursued in Germany
and Berlin, it is not surprising that this complex and cumbersome administrative structure has provided frequent opportunities for Soviet–Western conflict. It is not necessary to summarize here the principal stages in that conflict.[5] Suffice it to say that when the Soviets and the Western powers
clashed over Berlin in 1961, they were replaying a long-familiar scenario. In
particular, the Soviet demand for the conclusion of a peace treaty with Germany, which was to form a dominant theme in the Berlin crisis of 1961, had
previously been raised in the most insistent way by Soviet Premier Nikita
Khrushchev in November 1958. At that time Khrushchev demanded that a
German peace treaty be signed within six months, though when the deadline
actually came, in May 1959, he let it pass without protest.

Obviously, this earlier "Berlin crisis" constitutes part of the immediate
historical background of the subject of the present study, since everyone
concerned in the crisis of 1961 was vividly aware that Khrushchev had recently
tried the same gambit and had failed to achieve his objective.

It is relatively easy to sketch the general background of the Berlin crisis of
1961 in international events and to provide references to works dealing with

[5]For excellent summaries of the development of the Soviet–Western conflict over Germany
and Berlin, see Jack M. Schick, *The Berlin Crisis 1958–1962* (Philadelphia, University of
Pennsylvania Press, 1972) and Chapters 2–11 of Jean Edward Smith, *The Defense of Berlin*
(Baltimore, The Johns Hopkins Press, 1963).

the subject in its broader aspects. It is a more difficult problem, however, to provide background concerning the recent internal history of the Soviet regime. Fortunately, a number of excellent analyses bearing on various aspects of the subject have recently appeared.[6] These and similar studies will help the reader gain an understanding of the general character of Soviet politics in the Khrushchev era.

One vitally important episode which helped set the stage for Soviet policy during the Berlin crisis of 1961 was a meeting of the Communist Party Presidium (the party's ruling policy-making body) which I believe took place in mid-February 1961, just six months before the onset of the major phase of the Berlin crisis. This meeting, and the decisions it reached, are the subject of an essay I recently published.[7] I have summarized the findings of the article in the present study where they bear on its immediate subject, however, and in general have tried to make the book as self-contained as possible, even while recognizing the unending flow of historical change and development.

Und somit fangen wir an.

---

[6]See especially the works of Michel Tatu, Carl Linden, Sidney I. Ploss, and Robert Conquest mentioned in the List of Works Cited.

[7]"The Presidium Meeting of February 1961: A Reconstruction," in Alexander and Janet Rabinowitch, with Ladis K. D. Kristof, eds., *Revolution and Politics in Russia; Essays in Memory of B. I. Nicolaevsky* (Bloomington, Indiana University Press, 1972), pp. 281–92.

Contents

The BERLIN CRISIS of 1961

1 The Opening Phase: The Soviets Stake Their Claim

Players and rules of the game

The international crisis over the status of Berlin, which occupied the center of the world's attention in the second half of the year 1961 and which brought the great powers within hailing distance of an all-out nuclear war, can best be understood as a kind of game played by a small number of nations and their political leaders for certain definite stakes. The ground rules of the game and its principal phases were determined by the Soviet leadership, who deliberately initiated the crisis at a time of their own choosing, continued it as long as they saw a chance of winning, and beat a camouflaged but unmistakable retreat when they were no longer willing or able to match the raises of their adversaries.

The principal players in the game formed two major groups: (1) the Western (NATO) alliance, comprising the United States, Great Britain, France, Western Germany (the Federal Republic of Germany, abbreviated FRG), and the smaller nations of the NATO alliance (of which two, Italy and Belgium, were to play leading roles at certain moments during the crisis), and (2) the Soviet Union and its ally-satellites, the East European nations which were members of the Warsaw Pact. In this group, one Soviet satellite, the East German regime (officially known as the German Democratic Republic, abbreviated GDR), under its party boss Walter Ulbricht, was not only directly involved by reason of its immediate interest in the fate of Germany and Berlin, but pursued at times an independent policy of its own, in the well-founded expectation that its initiatives would find support among some members of the Soviet leadership. Forming part of the Soviet alliance system in theory but increasingly divergent in practice were the system's largest state, next to the Soviet Union itself, Communist China (the Chinese People's Republic, abbreviated CPR), and its smallest, Albania, both joined in an increasingly close ideological opposition to the Soviet leadership—an opposition which was to make steady progress during the Berlin crisis.

It was one of the rules of international relations which the Soviets had succeeded in forcing on the other nations of the world that the principles on which relations between the two groups were conducted were marked by a striking degree of asymmetry. The nations of the Western alliance, while they tried with varying degrees of success to reach an agreed policy among themselves, insisted on preserving a considerable area of individual freedom of maneuver as sovereign powers, able at times to enter into direct bilateral negotiations with the leader of the opposite group, the Soviet Union. The Soviet leadership thus had as one of its operating capabilities the possibility of working on the hopes or fears of the individual states entering into the Western alliance in an effort to undermine its unity or influence its policies.

No reciprocal opportunities existed for members of the Western alliance to deal directly with the subordinate members of the Soviet-led group, since the Soviets maintained a tight control over the foreign policies of the members of the Warsaw Pact.

Significantly, none of the Western powers maintained formal diplomatic relations with the Soviet client state most directly involved in the crisis, the GDR—in fact, nonrecognition of the Ulbricht regime, as an artificial Soviet creation lacking international validity, was one of the points of principle on which the Western alliance took its stand. Below the formal diplomatic level, it is true, there were many and varied contacts between East and West Germany, and to a lesser degree between the GDR and the three Western nations —the United States, Britain, and France—which occupied the western sectors of the former German capital, Berlin, located deep within the territory of the GDR. The general assumption in the Western alliance, however, was that the GDR was of negligible importance in the formation of Soviet policy in the Berlin crisis, which it was generally believed was formulated in Moscow by Khrushchev personally. Not surprisingly, the Western allies found themselves caught off guard when the Soviets took a step dictated primarily by the urgent needs of their East German client state, or when the Ulbricht regime acted on its own initiative.

By contrast, the Soviet Union maintained formal diplomatic relations with West Germany and sought actively to influence its policies. It was a Soviet note to the FRG (that of February 17, 1961) which marked the start of the Soviet campaign on Berlin in 1961, and continuous Soviet pressure on the Federal Republic was maintained throughout the crisis. Never absent from the minds of all Germans, East and West, was the fact that the key to Germany's fate—eventual reunification or the final formalization of division—was held by the Soviet Union, as the consequence of the territorial arrangements which had been established at the end of World War II.

The short-lived "spirit of Vienna"

Even before Khrushchev and Kennedy met in Vienna, efforts were being made by Soviet news media to create an atmosphere in which agreement by the West to Soviet demands would appear as the triumph of good will and reasonableness. On the day the Vienna conference opened the *New York Times* noted that "some Soviet commentators were already talking last week of a 'Spirit of Vienna' while simultaneously preparing to blame Mr. Kennedy if a relaxation of world tension did not ensue. Their view was that the Soviet government had made a whole series of proposals for solving world problems and it was now up to the United States to accept them."[1]

Despite the almost total lack of substantive agreement between Khrushchev and Kennedy at Vienna, Soviet propaganda media immediately after the encounter of the two leaders made an effort to continue this campaign. Khrushchev himself set the tone in a brief farewell speech in which he called for "the peaceful solution of controversial international questions by means of negotiations" and for "good relations with all countries." "I would like to believe," he said, ". . . that the meetings and conversations which we had here with the President of the U.S.A., Mr. Kennedy, will contribute to the attainment of these goals, to the establishment of a stable peace among nations."[2]

New York Times correspondent Seymour Topping reported from Vienna:

> Less than an hour after Mr. Khrushchev said good-bye to President Kennedy at the Soviet Embassy, the Moscow radio broadcast the view that the Vienna conference represented "a good beginning."
>
> Soviet officials in Vienna were more eager than their United States colleagues to picture the conference as a success. They appeared to be motivated by a desire to prepare the ground for further high-level talks and to increase Mr. Khrushchev's personal stature in the Communist world. Mikhail A. Kharlamov [Soviet press chief] . . . represented Mr. Khrushchev as "very satisfied" with his initial encounters with the President.[3]

The "spirit of Vienna" campaign came to an early halt, however, not only because of the lack of any concrete foundation on which to base it but also because it encountered no support within the Soviet leadership when Khrushchev returned to Moscow. On his arrival at the Moscow airport on June 5 he was met by members of the Presidium, including Frol R. Kozlov, "appearing in public for the first time since he suffered a heart attack in late April."[4]

In his report on Khrushchev's return Osgood Carruthers noted that: "There was no great fanfare in the Moscow press—no talk of any 'spirit of Vienna' or victories for Mr. Khrushchev's policies."[5]

For a few days after Khrushchev's return, nevertheless, Adzhubei's *Izvestiia* made an effort to continue the "spirit of Vienna" campaign. An article on June 6, entitled "Make way for common sense," maintained that: "In Vienna

[1]*New York Times*, June 4, 1961, sect. 4, p. 1 (hereinafter cited as *NYT*).

[2]N. S. Khrushchev, *Kommunizm—mir i schast'e narodam*, 2 vols. (Moscow: Gospolitizdat, 1962) 1:140–41 (hereinafter cited as Khrushchev, *Kommunizm*).

[3]*NYT*, June 5, 1961, p. 1.

[4]Osgood Carruthers, *NYT*, June 6, 1961.

[5]Ibid.

the basis was laid for an exchange of views on a wide range of problems with which the whole world is concerned—the cessation of nuclear testing, disarmament, the German question, and the situation in Laos. Many observers agree that a good basis was laid in Vienna, one that raises hope in the hearts of all people who cherish peace."[6]

Two days later an *Izvestiia* editorial entitled "Follow the path of peace" made a last effort to keep the campaign alive. "The Vienna meeting," it said, ". . . is a reminder that there are no insuperable obstacles to tackling the settlement of unresolved international problems around a table, in a business-like atmosphere. Vienna is a beginning that demands continuation."[7]

Publication in *Pravda* on June 9 of the full text of Kennedy's June 6 report to the nation on the Vienna meeting can be regarded either as the final echo of the "spirit of Vienna" campaign or as its quietus, since the campaign could scarcely survive the revelation to the Soviet public of the "somber" view of the meeting taken by the U.S. leader.

The first skirmish: pressure on West Germany

An important aim of Soviet strategy was to cut off West Berlin from West Germany. On June 8 this phase of the campaign got under way with notes from the Soviet Foreign Ministry to the three Western powers protesting an announced plan of the Federal Republic to hold a session of the Bundesrat, the upper house of the FRG legislature, in West Berlin on June 16. Calling the West German plan "a major new provocation against the USSR, the GDR, and the other socialist states," the notes continued with the assertion that West Berlin "is located on the territory of the German Democratic Republic and, by general agreement, has never formed and does not now form part of the FRG." An even more strongly worded note to the same effect was delivered to the Federal Republic's embassy in Moscow.[8]

Basing itself on historical precedent and the four-power agreements on Berlin, the Federal Republic promptly rejected the Soviet protest. "Such meetings," its reply on June 9 stated,

> . . . are in full accord with the four-power status of Berlin and the constitutional links between the Federal Republic and Berlin. This is why the allied Kommandatura, the body which is responsible for the observance of the four-power status of the city, has never raised any objections to meetings of the Bundestag [lower house] and Bundesrat in Berlin. The fact that for many years numerous meetings of the Bundestag and Bundesrat have

[6]K. Perevoshchikov and N. Polianov, "Make way for common sense," *Izvestiia*, June 6, 1961 (hereinafter cited as *Izv.*); *Current Digest of the Soviet Press*, XIII/23, p. 3 (hereinafter cited as *CDSP*).

[7]*Izv.*, June 8, 1961; *CDSP*, XIII/23, pp. 3–4.

[8]*Pravda*, June 9, 1961; *CDSP*, XIII/23, p. 17; *Vneshniaia politika Sovetskogo Soiuza i mezhdunarodnye otnosheniia. Sbornik dokumentov, 1961 god* (Moscow: Izdatel'stvo Instituta Mezhdunarodnykh Otnoshenii, 1962), pp. 141–43 (hereinafter cited as *VPSS, 1961*).

taken place in Berlin, without the Soviet Government in any way objecting to them until 1959, shows how contrived and unjustified the Soviet charges are. In 1959 the Soviet Government for the first time protested against such a meeting in Berlin, without, however, advancing a pertinent reason for its assertion that such meetings were incompatible with the four-power status.[9]

Not content with rejecting the Soviet charge, the West German note called attention to the inconsistent behavior of the Soviet Union with regard to its satellite, the GDR:

> The Soviet Government's protest is even harder to understand if the fact is taken into account that for a long time it has permitted the "Volkskammer" of the Soviet Zone to hold its sessions in the Soviet sector of Berlin. Again and again events are being organized in the Soviet sector which are in clear contravention of the four-power status of the city. This holds true in particular for the repeated military demonstrations of the People's Army [the East German Volkspolizei] against which the three western powers have had to protest on many occasions.[10]

West German firmness was matched in Washington, where State Department spokesman Lincoln White issued a statement on June 9 defending the proposed meeting. "We continue to find it difficult to understand," White said, "how the routine meeting of a free, democratic parliament can, by any stretch of the imagination, be characterized as a 'new, major provocation against the Soviet Union.'"[11]

So far, the dispute appeared to be local in character and of limited scope. To increase the pressure and widen the arena of action, TASS on June 9 published the full texts of the two memoranda which Khrushchev had given Kennedy at Vienna, thereby for the first time disclosing publicly the full range of the Soviet campaign. (According to a report in the *New York Times*, Rusk had made nondisclosure of the notes "a test of Soviet seriousness in negotiations with the West."[12])

The shock effect of the publication of the Soviet notes produced its intended result. Not yet certain just how serious the threat to their position was, the Western allies considered it prudent to yield the point without a struggle. In the words of the *Survey of International Affairs*, "it was essential to avoid anything likely to provoke Mr. Khrushchev in his current mood of over-confidence, and pressure was brought to bear on the West German

[9]U.S. Senate, Committee on Foreign Relations, *Documents on Germany, 1944–1961* (Washington, D.C.: G.P.O., 1961), pp. 651–52 (hereinafter cited as *Documents on Germany*).

[10]Ibid., p. 652.

[11]*NYT*, June 10, 1961, p. 1; Jean Edward Smith, *The Defense of Berlin* (Baltimore: The Johns Hopkins Press, 1963), p. 236 (hereinafter cited as Smith, *Defense of Berlin*).

[12]*NYT*, June 12, 1961, p. 13; Arnold Horelick and Myron L. Rush, *Strategic Power and Soviet Foreign Policy* (Chicago: University of Chicago Press, 1966), p. 123 (hereinafter cited as Horelick and Rush).

government to abandon the annual meeting of the Bundesrat in West Berlin, pressure lent point to by a Soviet note on 9 [8] June. The West German government yielded to this on 11 June and cancelled the meeting."[13]

It is hard to see how accepting an unjustified Soviet claim and thereby seriously weakening the Western position could help moderate Khrushchev's "mood of over-confidence." Obviously the Western action could have only the reverse effect.

Khrushchev reports to the Soviet people on Vienna

On June 15 Khrushchev spoke to the Soviet people via radio and television on the results of the Vienna meeting. It was nine days since President Kennedy had presented his accounting to the American people, a week since the Soviets had published the text of his address, five days since the Soviet press had disclosed the full text of the memoranda presented at Vienna. There had thus been ample time for a further development of Soviet thought on the problems at issue. Khrushchev's address, however, contained nothing new, nothing not familiar from scores of earlier Soviet speeches and statements. Both in structure and content it followed the Vienna meeting closely, devoting its major attention to disarmament and the German question.

By way of preamble Khrushchev dwelt with satisfaction on the harmonious relations allegedly existing between the Soviet Union and its allies, seeking to convey at the outset the image of a strong, united, harmonious group of socialist states proceeding undaunted and purposefully toward a glorious future. To do so he was forced to ignore certain disquieting developments which were already threatening to shatter the unity of the communist bloc: in Albania, the execution of the leaders of a pro-Soviet faction on May 31;[14] in Czechoslovakia, well-advanced preparations for the overthrow of Khrushchev's ally, Czechoslovak Minister of the Interior Rudolf Bárák (his dismissal was announced on June 24);[15] in China, ominous signs of a hardening of attitude toward the Soviet Union, which would erupt into undisguised hostility early in July.

On disarmament, Khrushchev touched on familiar Soviet positions without developing or modifying them. The only novelty in this portion of his speech was a noncommittal reference to the forthcoming bilateral talks with the United States: "On June 19 negotiations between the Soviet Union and the United States on disarmament questions will begin in Washington. One would like to hope that this time we shall at least meet with a constructive approach on the part of the United States."[16]

[13]D. C. Watt, *Survey of International Affairs, 1961* (London: Oxford University Press, 1965), p. 232 (hereinafter cited as *SIA, 1961*); Smith, *Defense of Berlin*, p. 236.

[14]*NYT*, June 2, 1961, p. 45.

[15]William E. Griffith, *Albania and the Sino-Soviet Rift* (Cambridge, Mass.: M.I.T. Press, 1963), p. 75 (hereinafter cited as Griffith, *Albania*); *NYT*, June 25, 1961, p. 14.

[16]*Pravda,* June 16, 1961; *CDSP*, XIII/24, p. 4.

Turning to Germany, Khrushchev again covered familiar ground, stressing the urgent need for a peace treaty and the changes which the treaty would cause in the situation in West Berlin. The general tone was moderate:

> It has always been recognized that after a war a peace treaty should be concluded among the states. This has already become a custom and, if you will, a rule of international law. Examples of it can be found in international practice after the second world war too. Peace treaties were signed more than 14 years ago with Italy and other states that fought on the side of Hitlerite Germany. The United States, Britain and other countries concluded a peace treaty with Japan in 1951. Yet the governments of these same countries will not even hear of concluding a peace with Germany.[17]

In several passages, however, Khrushchev let the naked threat of force show through. Having explained that control of the access routes to West Berlin would be turned over to the GDR after conclusion of a German peace treaty, he warned: "If any country violates the peace and crosses another's borders—land, air or water—it will bear the full responsibility for the consequences of aggression and will be duly repulsed."[18]

The six-month deadline for an agreement on Berlin laid down in the Vienna memorandum was restated: "We ask everyone to understand us correctly: The conclusion of a peace treaty with Germany cannot be put off any longer; a peace settlement in Europe must be achieved in Europe this year."[19]

Khrushchev went on to imply a change in the world balance which left the West no choice but to accept Soviet demands:

> Some people in the West are threatening us, declaring that if we sign a peace treaty, it will not be recognized and that armed force will even be employed to prevent its implementation. They seem to forget that the times have now changed. If the position-of-strength policy in regard to the Soviet Union was useless even before, today it is all the more doomed to fail. The Soviet Union is against the use of force in relations between states. We are for peaceful settlement of issues between states. Nevertheless, we are in a position to meet any resort to force with a fitting repulse, and we have the means to defend our interests.[20]

Having disposed of the two major issues, Khrushchev devoted the remainder of his talk to a number of the minor questions taken up at Vienna, in the process artfully distorting the record. On Laos he reaffirmed the Vienna agreement on establishment of an independent, neutral state, but made it clear that the Soviet Union would in fact do nothing to curb the communist guerrilla forces which were threatening the precarious cease-fire: "If the United States government is really eager for peace in Laos, it should contribute to the earliest success of the negotiations in Geneva. No one should obstruct these nego-

[17]*CDSP*, XIII/24, p. 4.
[18]Ibid., p. 6.
[19]Ibid.
[20]Ibid., p. 7.

tiations on various contrived pretexts that the cease-fire arrangement is purportedly being violated in Laos. If such cases have actually occurred, the national patriotic forces are not to blame. The American side and its military advisers in Laos are well aware of this."[21]

On the differences between his and Kennedy's concepts of peaceful co-existence, Khrushchev portrayed U.S. policy as being blindly opposed to any changes in the status quo and claimed that the movement of national liberation was identical with the historically inevitable spread of communism.

Khrushchev concluded his speech with a positive evaluation of the Vienna meeting and of Kennedy: "I must note that all in all I came away pleased with these talks. If I were to be asked, 'Was it worth while making arrangements for the meeting, was it worth while holding it?', I would answer without a moment's hesitation—the holding of such a meeting was worth while, and, more than that, it had to be held."[22] As to the President, Khrushchev said: "I formed the impression that President Kennedy appreciates the great responsibility that rests with the governments of two such mighty states. I should like to hope that awareness of that responsibility will continue to exist, so that urgent international problems can be solved, the stones removed that are blocking the road to lasting peace, to the improvement of relations between the Soviet Union and the United States of America."[23]

It was no accident that Khrushchev ended his speech with a tribute to the soberness and sense of responsibility of the American President. An essential element in Soviet strategy in the 1961 Berlin crisis was the calculation that it was an acceptable risk to raise the tension to a point at which the West would yield to Soviet demands rather than accept the alternative of war. To run this risk it was essential that the leader of the opposing alliance should be known to be a man of reason and soberness of purpose. Sounding out Kennedy in this respect had therefore been a principal aim in Khrushchev's trip to Vienna, and he was stating no more than the truth when he said, "the holding of such a meeting was worth while, and, more than that, it had to be held."

Ulbricht's press conference of June 15

Khrushchev's June 15 speech harked back to the Vienna meeting; its purpose was to convince the Soviet people that the policy being pursued by their government in the impending test of strength over Berlin was a reasonable one, based on a sincere desire for peace and the reduction of international tension. Aspects of conflict and discord were played down, and the final passages paying tribute to the sobriety and sense of responsibility of the American President were designed to reassure Khrushchev's listeners that no risk of war was involved.

[21]Ibid., p. 8.
[22]Ibid.
[23]Ibid.

On the same day that Khrushchev delivered his report, East German party boss Walter Ulbricht held a news conference at which, by contrast, strident emphasis was placed on the positive results which the communist states would achieve as the result of their confidently anticipated triumph over the Western powers in the struggle over Berlin. Ulbricht went out of his way to disavow any plans for sealing off West Berlin by the construction of a wall:

> ... there are people in West Germany who would like us to mobilize the building workers of the GDR capital to put up a wall. I am not aware of any such intention, since the building workers in our capital are chiefly engaged in the housing program, and their time is fully occupied. Nobody intends to put up a wall. As I said before, we are in favor of a contractual settlement of relations between West Berlin and the GDR Government. This is the simplest and most normal way to solve these questions.[24]

Ulbricht thus explicitly ruled out recourse to the minimum objective of the Soviet campaign in Berlin. His statements later during the press conference, however, showed that his and Khrushchev's maximum objectives diverged significantly. For Khrushchev the West Berlin question, together with the demand for a German peace treaty, was a lever which could be used to force the West to acknowledge a shift in the international balance in favor of the Soviet Union. For Ulbricht, West Berlin was not so much a means to an end as an end in itself, or rather to a cluster of related goals: elimination of a dangerous drain on the vitality of the GDR, enhancement of the international prestige of the GDR, stabilization of the regime's shaky economic and political position. The international aspects of the Berlin problem were of secondary interest to Ulbricht; his eye was fixed on a definite target—absorption of the Western sectors of Berlin.

Ulbricht therefore brushed aside contemptuously any suggestion of Western rights in Berlin: "As regards the state frontier—our frontier runs along the Elbe and so on, and the territory of West Berlin forms part of the territory of the G.D.R."[25] Conclusion of a German peace treaty, Ulbricht said, echoing Khrushchev, would leave the Western powers no choice but to negotiate directly with the GDR over access routes to West Berlin: ". . . if a peace treaty is achieved, then those states interested in communications with West Berlin have no other course but to conduct negotiations of that kind with the G.D.R. Government. . . . That is to say, nobody can avoid negotiating on this problem with the G.D.R."[26] The peace treaty would finally establish Germany's boundaries along the lines agreed to at the end of World War II: "The existing frontiers will remain. The peace treaty does not alter the frontiers and it cannot alter them. And if the Western powers do not conclude a peace treaty, the frontiers will be altered still less."[27]

[24]*Documents on Germany*, p. 652.
[25]Ibid., p. 653.
[26]Ibid., p. 654.
[27]Ibid., p. 655.

As to the suggestion, advanced in the Western press, that the Western powers might undertake a show of force to defend their position in West Berlin, Ulbricht professed to find it unbelievable:

> What nonsense all this is. We simply do not want to believe and cannot believe that it is the desire, the ambition, of the United States to appear before the whole world as an aggressor. I don't think I need to say any more about this. We would be pleased if certain people were to refrain in the future from answering our many peace offers time after time with foolish saber-rattling of other weapons. We would like to tell them amicably: stop that noise with your weapons, stop the rattling, and wait until we have reasonable negotiations on equal terms.[28]

The most ominous statements made at Ulbricht's press conference—statements which helped contribute to a growing sense of panic among many citizens of East Germany—concerned the future of West Berlin after the anticipated Soviet victory. Tempelhof, the big airfield linking the city with West Germany, Ulbricht implied with heavy irony, would be closed down in the interests of air safety: ". . . if such arrangements are made for air traffic, the inhabitants of the central boroughs of Berlin will benefit greatly. There will not be so much noise in the central boroughs, and there will no longer be the danger that planes will hit them on the head. Everything will be settled in an orderly manner."[29]

More forthright were passages in which Ulbricht indicated what his concept of neutrality would mean for the beleaguered city:

> . . . the free city of West Berlin, after the conclusion of the peace treaty, will not be disturbed either by occupation forces or by agents' centers, or by radio stations of the organizers of the cold war, or by other measures which might serve the preparation of war. That is to say, West Berlin must not be utilized, either against the interests of the G.D.R. and the socialist states, or against the United States, Britain, France, the German Federal Republic, or other Western states. West Berlin is truly to be a neutral city.[30]

Khrushchev's military speech of June 21: the Soviets initiate the bidding

In a formal setting which bore evidence of careful preparation, Khrushchev on June 21 delivered a major speech to a public meeting in the Kremlin marking the twentieth anniversary of Hitler's attack on the Soviet Union. Khrushchev himself appeared wearing the uniform of a Soviet lieutenant general, the rank he had held as political adviser on the Stalingrad Front during World War II. Behind him were ranged political and military leaders, four of whom—Minister of Defense Marshal R. Ya. Malinovsky, Commander-in-Chief of

---

[28] Ibid., p. 657.
[29] Ibid., p. 658.
[30] Ibid., p. 660.

Soviet Ground Forces Marshal V. I. Chuikov, Commander of Troops of Moscow Military District General of the Army N. I. Krylov, and Major General
A. N. Saburov, former commander of a partisan unit in the Ukraine—also
delivered speeches. The meeting was evidently designed to give the impression of close unity between the communist party and the Soviet army and to
lend Khrushchev the added prestige of overt support by the army. In return,
Khrushchev presented the armed forces with a number of concessions in the
course of his speech, evidently for the purpose of ensuring their support in
the forthcoming Berlin crisis.

Even before the June 21 meeting there had been a number of actions calculated to enhance Khrushchev's personal stature. On June 11 *Izvestiia* reported the opening in Moscow of a documentary film, "Our Nikita Sergeevich," concerning which it said: "Always and in all things side by side with the
people, in the thick of events—that is how Soviet people know Nikita Sergeevich Khrushchev, that is how they see him in the documentary film."[31]

A week later *Pravda* reported the award to Khrushchev of the Order of
Lenin and his third gold hammer and sickle medal for "outstanding services"
in "guiding the creation and development of the rocket industry, science and
technology and in the successful accomplishment of the world's first manned
space flight, made by a Soviet citizen in the space ship-satellite 'Vostok,'
which opened a new era in the conquest of space."[32]

Along with Khrushchev, but not named by *Pravda*, over seven thousand
"designers, executive officials, scientists, and workers" who had contributed to the success of the April 12 flight received awards. Among the unnamed thousands were two of Khrushchev's closest political associates, his
ally Leonid Brezhnev and his adversary F. R. Kozlov, both of whom received
the Order of Lenin and the hammer and sickle gold medal with the title,
"Hero of Soviet Labor."[33]

Major Gagarin, the cosmonaut whose flight was the occasion of these
awards, contributed a glowing testimonial to Khrushchev's leadership in the
Soviet space program:

> We Soviet cosmonauts and the scientists, engineers and workers who cre-
> ated the space ships constantly feel Nikita Sergeevich Khrushchev's
> tremendous concern for the development of space technology. Soviet
> cosmonautics is Nikita Sergeevich's beloved child. He devotes a great deal
> of energy, work and care to this new matter. The Party Central Committee
> First Secretary and Soviet government head knows by their names and
> deeds the scientists, workers, technicians and engineers, all who are cre-
> ating the mighty space ships. They turn to the Party Central Committee, to
> Nikita Sergeevich Khrushchev, with their joys and concerns, they get sup-
> port and counsel, they meet with Nikita Sergeevich in the laboratories

[31]*Izv.*, June 11, 1961, p. 3.
[32]*Pravda*, June 18, 1961, p. 1; *CDSP*, XIII/23, p. 15.
[33]Radio Moscow, June 19, 1961.

and the factory shops and at the cosmodromes. "Nikita Sergeevich Khrushchev is the pioneer explorer of the cosmic age," our cosmonauts and builders of space ships rightly declare. It is with a feeling of filial gratitude and love that I, my parents and our fellow-townsmen congratulate Nikita Sergeevich wholeheartedly on the high award and wish him good health and further successes in the struggle for the welfare of the people and for peace on earth.[34]

The spotlight cast on the Soviet premier by these demonstrations and statements was not merely an indication of self-flattery and vanity, but was designed to enhance Khrushchev's prestige at home, in preparation for the risky test of strength in the international arena which the Soviets were about to undertake.

Praise by military men for Khrushchev's war-time record accompanied these testimonials and awards. On June 20 the Soviet army newspaper *Red Star* published a review by Marshal A. I. Yeremenko, one of the leading Soviet commanders in World War II, of the second volume of the official *History of the Great Patriotic War of the Soviet Union 1941–1945*. In his review Yeremenko sharply criticized Stalin for his "incorrect evaluation of the military and political situation" at the outbreak of the war and gave credit to Khrushchev, then a member of the Military Council of the Southwestern Front, for advice which, had it been followed by the General Staff, might have averted the mass encirclement of Soviet troops at Kiev in September 1941.[35]

Marshal Yeremenko's own book, *Stalingrad: Notes of a Front Commander*, was reviewed in *Pravda* on June 24 by Major General I. Rukhle. The reviewer quoted a passage in which Yeremenko praised Khrushchev's "ebullient energy, his ability to work with people and form a correct idea of their positive qualities and shortcomings, and his high party spirit."[36]

The author, in the words of the reviewer, "shows great warmth in much of his book in describing N. S. Khrushchev's work at the front, and he recounts striking episodes showing how, in the midst of a complex combat situation, Nikita Sergeevich decisively and unflaggingly discarded everything that was of no help to the cause and supported everything that helped make progress toward the goal. He took an active part in working out specific forms for operations and in deciding the directions the main army thrusts would take."[37]

Similar praise for Khrushchev's military record and strategic ability was contained in several of the speeches delivered by Soviet army leaders at the June 21 meeting. Recalling Khrushchev's war-time service as a member of the Military Council of the Stalingrad Front, Marshal Chuikov paid glowing tribute to his qualities as a leader:

[34]*Pravda*, June 18, 1961, p. 1; *CDSP*, XIII/23, p. 15.
[35]*Krasnaia Zvezda*, June 20, 1961; *CDSP*, XIII/25, pp. 12–14.
[36]*Pravda*, June 24, 1961, p. 4; *CDSP*, XIII/25, p. 14.
[37]*CDSP*, XIII/25, p. 14.

We had many heroes in Stalingrad. But it must be stressed that it was not individual heroes who defended Stalingrad. This was accomplished by the entire glorious collective of Stalingraders, and an enormous role in creating this friendly collective united in one family belonged to the faithful Leninist Nikita Sergeevich Khrushchev, a member of the Military Council [*stormy applause*]. He was the soul of the Stalingraders. The skill of persuasion and high Party and fighting exactingness were wonderfully combined in him. He skillfully studied people and, after studying them, trusted them without unnecessary petty tutelage.[38]

In his account of the final battles in the West, Chuikov made his own contribution to the campaign to force the Western powers out of West Berlin:

... the historic truth is that during the assault on Berlin there was not a single American, British or French armed soldier around it, except for the prisoners of war, whom we freed [*applause*]. Therefore the claims of the U.S., British and French ruling circles to some kind of special rights in Berlin are entirely unfounded. They did not take it. They came there to fulfill the conditions of surrender, and on the basis of the fulfillment of these conditions the occupation of Berlin should long since have ended [*applause*].

General Saburov, in his speech, singled out for emphasis Khrushchev's talent as a strategist of the partisan movement operating behind German lines:

The partisans of the Ukraine well remember the enormous role played by you, Nikita Sergeevich, in the development of the partisan movement. I recall December of 1941 and your first radiogram, when you congratulated our partisans on their successful operations in the capture of Zernovo Station and the district center of Suzemka. You cannot imagine what this radiogram meant to us. It strengthened our desire to fight the enemy even more vigorously, even more courageously. From that time we have always heeded your voice and felt support and help.

I also recall June of 1942, when you sent us a radiogram in which you proposed that we consider and inform the Central Committee about the possibility of shifting our unit to the right bank of the Dnieper. We interpreted your radiogram as a major strategic plan for the disposition of partisan forces.

Your plan, Nikita Sergeevich, was later embodied in a well-known raid by two units—ours and Kovpak's—on the right bank of the Dnieper. This raid had great strategic importance and was fully justified. With the arrival of our units in Zhitomir and Rovno Provinces and part of Kiev Province, an enormous Partisan Territory was formed that became the main base for development of the partisan movement on the right bank of the Dnieper.[39]

Thus Khrushchev's merits as a strategist, able to evaluate correctly the intentions and probable course of action of an enemy and to form a sound plan

[38]*Pravda*, June 22, 1961; *CDSP*, XIII/25, p. 5.
[39]*CDSP*, XIII/25, p. 5.

of action, were praised by leading army commanders at the outset of a new campaign, in which the armed forces would be a prime asset in the strategic plans of the Soviet leadership—one played for high stakes against a powerful adversary.

Not all the military leaders at the June 21 meeting, it is true, indulged in such outspoken panegyrics for Khrushchev's strategic ability. In his speech, Defense Minister Marshal Malinovsky, no friend of Khrushchev despite his earlier service alongside him at Stalingrad and elsewhere, dwelt mainly on the alleged misdeeds of the Western powers, in 1941 and currently. Denying that the Soviet Union bore any responsibility for the outbreak of World War II, Malinovsky declared that "it is the governments of the Western Powers that were guilty of unleashing World War II." After sketching the military history of the war on the Russian front, Malinovsky advanced the claim that the Soviets would have won even without the help of the Western allies: "Only when the allies clearly realized that fascist Germany would be defeated by the Soviet Union even without their help did they hasten to open up a second front in Europe, landing their troops in Normandy. These are the facts and you can't escape them. Thus the decisive role in the defeat of fascist Germany and its allies belongs to the U.S.S.R."[40]

The relevance of all this to the immediate occasion was that, in Malinovsky's view, the Western allies had changed neither their methods nor their goals since 1941. "Blinded by class hatred for socialism, they are trying to carry out the same policy that led mankind to World War II."[41] The major danger at present, Malinovsky asserted, was American imperialism:

> The American imperialists, who lay claim to world domination, are the principal force of reaction and aggression. Together with their allies, they have created a gigantic military apparatus and a ramified system of aggressive blocs like NATO, SEATO and CENTO and of military bases around the borders of the U.S.S.R. and other socialist states, are stockpiling nuclear and rocket arms and are creating centers of international tension in Algeria, the Congo, Laos, and Cuba. Nor can one fail to be alerted by the fact that the bellicose American generals are persistently demanding the implementation of new military doctrines. The notions of "the ultimate weapon" and "the strategy of intimidation" they advance, the doctrine of "massive retaliation" they preach, the principles of "shield and sword," the strategy of "flexible reaction" or "limited" and "local" wars—all these are the outward forms that give pseudo-theoretical grounds to the aggressive substance of the wild schemes for unleashing a new war, the sharp edge of which is directed first and foremost against the U.S.S.R. and the other countries in the socialist camp.[42]

The Soviet people, however, Malinovsky warned, "will be able to defend our homeland from the encroachments of any aggressor, we have the where-

[40] Ibid., p. 4.
[41] Ibid.
[42] Ibid.

withal to defend ourselves, and we can put a strait jacket on any madman who unleashes a new nuclear war."[43]

Like Malinovsky, Khrushchev in his speech at the June 21 meeting combined historical examples with current applications. He followed the Defense Minister in laying the blame for the outbreak of World War II on the Western powers: "The scheme of the Western Powers was a far-reaching one—to destroy the Soviet Union and at the same time weaken Germany in order themselves to rule undivided in the world and dictate their conditions to all."[44]

Like Malinovsky, Khrushchev asserted a direct continuity between Western policy in 1939 and in 1961: "Even today these ideas have not died in the minds of the aggressive imperialist circles of the West. They would not be loathe to try to put this to the test once again today if they could find a force that they could incite against the Soviet Union."[45]

If the aspirations of the Western powers had not changed, however, the conditions within which their policy was framed had altered drastically: "The might of the Soviet Union and the entire socialist camp has grown to such an extent that if the Western Powers mobilized all their forces in a senseless attempt to destroy the achievements of the peoples of the socialist countries, this time, too, they would suffer complete failure."[46]

Assuring his listeners that his words were not meant as a threat but as "an appeal for common sense," Khrushchev continued, "It is necessary at long last to understand that the land of Soviets has now changed, the world has changed, the correlation of forces and armaments has changed."[47]

Strengthening peace, not war, Khrushchev maintained, was the reason for the Soviet determination to sign a peace treaty with Germany: "The Soviet people do not want war, and for this very reason we are striving to eliminate the causes of its outbreak. For the sake of this, *we and other peace-loving states will sign a peace treaty with the German Democratic Republic at the end of this year.*"[48]

With regard to the future status of West Berlin, Khrushchev asserted the reasonableness of the Soviet position while at the same time insisting on the very point which was the principal source of tension in the crisis—transfer of control over access routes to the GDR:

> We propose giving West Berlin the status of a free city. We do not at all intend to change West Berlin's social and political system. This is the internal affair of its population. Neither the Soviet Union nor the German Democratic Republic intends to restrict West Berlin's ties with all countries of the world. But in accordance with international law, the sovereign rights of the

---

[43] Ibid., p. 5.
[44] Ibid., p. 7.
[45] Ibid.
[46] Ibid.
[47] Ibid.
[48] Ibid., emphasis supplied.

German Democratic Republic, through whose territory the communications linking West Berlin with the outside world pass, must be respected.[49]

A lengthy section of Khrushchev's speech was devoted to an exposition and defense of the familiar Soviet position on disarmament. Strikingly new, however, was a passage in which he took up the question of the resumption of nuclear tests—the first occasion on which a Soviet spokesman had broached this subject in a public address for a long time. Khrushchev had assured Kennedy at Vienna that the Soviet Union would not resume testing unless the West did so first, giving the impression of goading the West into resumption of testing. This theme was now taken up, expanded, and given a sharply increased sense of urgency:

> The Soviet Union has not been conducting tests of nuclear weapons for almost three years now, although we have no agreement on this matter with the Western Powers. We can continue abstaining from nuclear weapons tests and propose to the Western Powers that we reach agreement both on the entire disarmament problem and on its component aspects, including the testing of nuclear weapons.
>
> Some American leaders are urging the U.S. Government to resume testing nuclear weapons if the Soviet Union does not accept the demands of the Western Powers. What can be said about such threats? They do not frighten anyone and only show the unreasonableness of those who resort to them. We must warn these gentlemen: The moment the U.S.A. resumes nuclear explosions, the Soviet Union will immediately begin testing its nuclear weapons. The Soviet Union has developed many devices that require practical verification. Such verification will of course increase the fighting capacity of our armed forces, make it possible to create even better atomic and hydrogen bombs and enable us to improve the process of their production. If in reply to the resumption of nuclear tests by the Western Powers we did not begin testing our weapons, we would weaken the defenses of our country and the entire socialist commonwealth.
>
> Thus the entire responsibility for resumption of the testing of nuclear weapons will rest with the governments of the Western Powers.[50]

The implications of this passage were clear: If the Western powers resumed nuclear testing as a way of raising the stakes in the struggle over Berlin, the Soviets were fully prepared to meet this challenge. Since the setting and context of the speech indicate that it represented a bid by Khrushchev for the support of the armed forces in the Berlin crisis, this passage carried the further implication of a promise to the military leaders that they would not have long to wait before being given authorization to resume nuclear testing. It is noteworthy, incidentally, that in the week before the speech Radio Moscow carried a number of reports on alleged U.S. plans to resume nuclear testing in the near future.

[49] Ibid.
[50] Ibid., p. 9.

To understand the significance of this, and other concessions by Khrushchev to the military leaders, it is necessary to take into account the fact that a number of deep-seated disagreements over military policy had developed in recent years between Khrushchev and certain military and political leaders. Two areas in particular had aroused dissension: the share of national budgetary resources which should be allocated to the armed forces and the balance within the armed forces between the conventional arms and the newer branches of service, especially the missile (rocket) troops.

By his policy of cutting back on appropriations for the armed forces in order to free budgetary resources for the civilian economy (notably in his troop reduction proposal of January 1960), Khrushchev had offended party and army protagonists of top priority for the armed forces. In his search for a strategic doctrine which would combine budgetary economies with unimpaired or even enhanced fire power, Khrushchev had shown a marked predilection for the rocket troops and a corresponding tendency to downgrade the role allotted to the traditional arms. On both counts, Khrushchev's June 21 speech contained significant concessions to the demands of those whose special interests he had previously opposed.

Speaking on a military anniversary and appearing in uniform as a sign of his personal identification with the armed forces, Khrushchev promised that these forces would be given whatever they needed for defense: "Our armed forces must always be ready to ensure in a reliable manner the security of the Soviet Union, they must have everything necessary in order immediately to smash any opponent who encroaches on the liberty of our Motherland [*stormy, continuous applause*]. Let those who are hatching aggressive plans with regard to the Soviet Union know what fate awaits them if they unleash war and commit aggression [*stormy applause*]."[51]

As to the relative share of allocations among the various branches of the armed services, Khrushchev promised to pursue a balanced policy: "The strengthening of the defense of the Soviet Union depends on the perfection of *all* the types of troops of our Armed Forces—infantry and artillery, engineer troops and communications troops, tank units and the Navy, the Air Force, and the rocket troops."[52]

Acutely aware, however, of the inescapable strategic realities of 1961, and anxious to convey a clearcut threat of retaliation, Khrushchev immediately followed this statement with a tribute to the special tasks assigned to the rocket troops:

In our times exceptionally great responsibility lies on the rocket troops, especially on the units which service the ballistic rockets of various ranges, from tactical to intercontinental. Their fighting preparedness and training must be at the peak, because a great deal depends on the rocket troops. It is their devastating power which deters in the first instance any potential

[51]Khrushchev, *Kommunizm*, 1:185.
[52]Ibid., p. 186; emphasis supplied.

aggressor from attacking us and our allies. Their capacity to strike a retaliatory blow is the force which will inevitably punish an aggressor if he
nevertheless decides on an act of folly and unleashes a new war [*prolonged
applause*].[53]

With this challenging affirmation of Soviet military strength Khrushchev
deliberately cast the forthcoming test of strength in military terms, associating
the armed forces with Soviet strategy in the Berlin crisis and asserting a unity
of purpose between the party and the military. The June 21 speech represented
the Soviets' opening bid in the contest over Berlin.

Khrushchev reverts to the theme of economic rivalry:
Alma Ata, June 24 and 25

Three days after his demonstrative show of solidarity with the Soviet
armed forces, Khrushchev delivered a speech at Alma Ata, capital of the
Kazakh SSR, in which he reverted to his favorite theme of the great future
which awaited the Soviet economy and the inevitability with which it would
one day outstrip that of the United States. Like his speeches in Yerevan and
Tbilisi in May, the Alma Ata speech was one of a series delivered at ceremonial meetings marking the fortieth anniversaries of the establishment of
Union Republics.

Following the pattern established in his May speeches, Khrushchev was
lavish in praise of local heroes and full of optimism for the economic future of
the given republic as part of the Soviet Union. A special theme taken up in the
Alma Ata speech of June 24 was the relations between the native Kazakhs and
the immigrants in their land—Russians, Ukrainians, Belorussians, and others.
This was a highly delicate subject since, as Khrushchev and his listeners
were both well aware, the 1959 census had shown that as the result of massive
population shifts and immigration to Kazakhstan (particularly in connection
with the Virgin Lands program), the Kazakhs now found themselves a minority in their own republic.

Khrushchev's speech did little to ease the situation in this respect: he even
quoted the advice given the Kazakhs by one of their leading writers, Abai:
"Learn the language and culture of the Russians. That is the key to life."[54]

Khrushchev's heavy-handed and not particularly tactful emphasis on the
need for the Kazakhs to acquiesce gracefully to Russian dominance reflected
the confidence of a man who feels sure of his welcome. The Kazakh party apparatus, which had been overhauled at a party plenum in early February, was
in fact solidly behind the Soviet leader under its first secretary, D. A. Kunaev,
an old associate of Khrushchev who, after Khrushchev's fall, at a Central

[53]Ibid.
[54]*Pravda* and *Izv.*, June 25, 1961; *CDSP*, XIII/25, p. 15.

Committee plenum in March 1965, was to show his regard for the ex-leader by still according him the honorary accolade of "comrade."[55]

In his June 24 speech Khrushchev touched only briefly on international events, contenting himself with expressing confidence that the policy followed by the Soviet Union on "the most important problem of the day—the problem of disarmament and for the conclusion of a German peace treaty in the near future" was a "sound, well-founded stand" to which the Soviet Union intended to hold firmly.

Noteworthy is the vaguely defined time limit—"the near future"—instead of the specific six-month deadline laid down at Vienna. Taken in the overall context of the Alma Ata speech, this milder variant suggests that Khrushchev on this occasion, far from the pressures of Moscow and feeling himself among friends, was permitting himself to relax and give expression to his own deeper convictions. A jumbled and nearly incoherent passage in the speech on the tastiness of horseflesh, a native Kazakh delicacy, strongly suggests that Khrushchev was somewhat inebriated.[56]

The impression that the real Khrushchev was breaking through is strengthened by those portions of the speech which dealt with Soviet economic growth. Citing the adoption of the new draft party program by a Central Committee plenum on June 19, Khrushchev restated his cherished but controversial thesis of balanced growth between heavy industry and those branches of the economy producing goods for the consumer: "Speedy growth has been charted for all branches of the national economy. Light industry and the food industry—that is, the branches directly concerned with meeting the needs of the population—will undergo speedy development along with heavy industry."[57]

Khrushchev was not satisfied, however, merely with optimistic forecasts of Soviet economic growth; what gave him special satisfaction was the prospect of overtaking and surpassing the United States. "Old Russia was among the economically backward countries to which foreign oppressors played the boss. But today the Soviet Union, having outstripped all the well-developed capitalist states, is already drawing right up to, treading on the heels of, the very leader of the capitalist world—the United States. When a little time has passed

---

[55] *Plenum Tsentral'nogo Komiteta Kommunisticheskoi Partii Sovetskogo Soiuza 24–26 marta 1965 goda. Stenograficheskii otchet* (Moscow: Izdatel'stvo Politicheskoi Literatury, 1965), p. 104; Michel Tatu, *Power in the Kremlin, From Khrushchev to Kosygin* (New York: Viking Press, 1968), p. 422 (hereinafter cited as Tatu).

[56] Radio Moscow, June 24, 1961. For evidence of the thoroughness with which the Soviet censors worked over this passage in order to conceal the evidence of Khrushchev's condition, compare the text as delivered with two published variants: (a) Khrushchev, *Kommunizm*, 1:294, and (b) N. S. Khrushchev, *Stroitel'stvo Kommunizma v SSSR i razvitie sel'skogo khoziaistva* (Moscow: Gospolitizdat, 1962–64) 5:412–13 (hereinafter cited as Khrushchev, *Stroitel'stvo*).

[57] *CDSP*, XIII/25, p. 19.

we shall say to them, 'Step aside, gentlemen, we are moving out ahead, and you'll never catch up with us now'."[58]

On the following day, still in Alma Ata, Khrushchev delivered a second speech covering much the same ground but in a less formal manner. Particularly striking in the June 25 speech were the passages dealing with Soviet–U.S. economic rivalry:

> We can move, can move mountains, and therefore, in spite of our lag behind the western countries, in spite of the twenty years that we lost because of the wars that were imposed upon us and the reconstruction that followed, we have been able in 44 years to reach second place in the world. Britain, the ruler of the seas, which had Africa and Asia, we have left it behind. France we have left behind [*applause*]. . . . Now only America is left for us. It is like an already aged runner, you know: he has had, so to speak, both prizes and first prizes. Then others were born and trained, and he is still running—he lives on yesterday's glory, but he is short of wind; and therefore it is a young, fresh, strong one who will reach the finish line first. . . . By now the scientists of America are studying and reporting to the government that the Soviet Union will have caught up with America in 1970. That is also our figure, so they are in complete agreement with us, with our calculations [*applause*].[59]

Taken as a whole, the Alma Ata speeches constitute a striking anomaly in the Berlin crisis of 1961. Delivered at the outset of the Soviet campaign, just as the Soviets were staking their position in military terms, they form an incongruous interlude in which Khrushchev stressed his own vision of a Soviet victory in peaceful economic competition with the United States. Viewed in the context of the Berlin crisis the Alma Ata speeches were not merely irrelevant but inconsistent; viewed in the longer perspective of Khrushchev's statements they are recognizable as an expression of his deeper long-term concerns and views. Away from the Kremlin, away from the controls exercised over him by the other members of the collective leadership, Khrushchev was a different man from the Khrushchev who had addressed the June 21 meeting. The net effect of the contrast is to reveal the artificiality, the contrived and forced character of the whole Soviet campaign on Berlin and to hint strongly that Khrushchev's heart lay not with the military whose uniform he had donned on June 21 but with the agricultural specialists whom he addressed three or four days later.

[58] Ibid., p. 20.
[59] Radio Moscow, June 25, 1961.

2 Framing a Western Position

While the Soviets were unfolding their strategy in the Berlin campaign, the Western allies were undergoing a period of anxiety and self-questioning. The general assumption among them was that a time of testing lay ahead, but that its onset was not yet imminent. The President's parting words to Khrushchev at Vienna—"It will be a cold winter"—were an indication that he expected only a gradual build-up of tension in the conflict over Berlin. The President and his advisers assumed they had ample time to frame a counterstrategy. At worst, it was thought likely that Khrushchev would make good on his threat to call a peace conference on Germany immediately after the Communist Party Congress in October.[1]

The cautious pace in Washington was the product of several factors, of which the most important were the existence of conflicting views within the administration as to how best to respond to the Soviet challenge and the need to coordinate any response with America's major allies. It was not until mid-July, for example, that a reply to the Soviet memorandum on Germany handed to the President at Vienna was ready. The slowness in replying to this memorandum is all the more striking when it is contrasted with the prompt U.S. reply to the companion Soviet memorandum on disarmament, which was sent on June 17. As a spirited, if provocative statement of the Western position and a critique of the Soviet proposals, the note deserves careful attention.[2]

---

[1]Theodore C. Sorensen, *Kennedy* (New York and Evanston: Harper & Row, 1965), p. 586 (hereinafter cited as Sorensen).

[2]U.S. Arms Control and Disarmament Agency, *Documents on Disarmament, 1961* (Washington, D.C.: G.P.O., 1962), pp. 189–95 (hereinafter cited as *Documents on Disarmament, 1961*).

The U.S. note on disarmament of June 17

Central to the U.S. June 17 note was an analysis of the Soviet position on a test ban agreement. Point by point the note took up the proposals set forth in the Soviet memorandum of June 4, as well as earlier in the test ban talks at Geneva, and rejected them as unworkable. After consideration of the Soviet demands for a three-man head to the control body ("involves a built-in veto over the operation of the control system"), a limit of three on-site inspections per year ("a completely inadequate sampling"), the use of Soviet nationals to head any control post established on Soviet territory ("fundamentally contrary to the aim of objective international surveillance"), and a majority of Soviet nationals on the staff of on-site inspection teams ("would frustrate completely the purpose of on-site inspection of suspicious events"), the note criticized as scientifically unfounded the Soviet refusal to accept Western proposals for a three-year moratorium on small underground nuclear tests ("amounts to a demand for a permanent unpoliced ban").

Turning to the Soviet demand that the test ban talks be merged in comprehensive negotiations on disarmament, the note dismissed it curtly as "unacceptable." In explaining this stand the note alluded significantly to pressure on the United States government to end the de facto test ban moratorium by resuming nuclear testing:

> The delay in reaching a test ban agreement which would result from merging the test ban negotiations into the comprehensive disarmament negotiations suggests that the Soviet Union is attempting to continue a situation in which the United States accepts an unenforced commitment not to test. This would leave the Soviet Union, with its closed society, its government unaccountable either to a parliament or to an informed public opinion, and its actions shrouded in a veil of secrecy, free to conduct nuclear weapons tests without fear of exposure. For almost three years, the United States has been willing to assume the risk of not testing nuclear weapons without the certainty that the Soviet Union has likewise stopped its testing. The national security and defenses of the free world do not allow this risk to be assumed indefinitely.[3]

Failure to move forward from the unpoliced de facto test ban to one provided with adequate controls, in the U.S. view, "would mean the further proliferation of nuclear weapons and the testing of such weapons by an ever-greater number of countries. In view of the ease of clandestine nuclear testing under an unpoliced ban, it means that each government will face an increasing need to take whatever steps may be necessary in its own defense, including nuclear testing."[4]

Taking a wider view, the note saw in the Soviet position evidence of a retrograde attitude toward its responsibilities as a great power for the peace and security of the international community:

[3]Ibid., p. 194.
[4]Ibid., p. 195.

. . . the Soviet Government apparently desires to return to a period of history when the sovereign state admitted no limitation to its actions. The positions maintained by the Soviet Union at Geneva appear to mean that, even with all that is at stake, the Soviet Union is not ready to abate in some small degree its regime of secrecy and jealously-guarded sovereignty.

This attitude offers small prospect for a constructive outcome of the Geneva test ban negotiations. It also offers little hope for the development of the kind of world, under an international rule of law, in which general disarmament can take place.[5]

Important in itself, conclusion of a test ban treaty, the note maintained, would "brighten the prospects for agreement in other areas of conflicting interests."[6]

However one may judge the soundness of the arguments set forth in the June 17 note, it must be recognized that its self-righteous attitude and sweeping condemnation of the Soviet position were bound to sting the Soviets into a retort for which, objectively regarded, the note provided ample ground. More significant, the passages in the note referring to the mounting pressure on the United States to resume testing fitted perfectly into the Soviet strategy of goading the United States into precisely this step, and may well have served as the immediate occasion for the counterthreat of a Soviet resumption of testing in Khrushchev's speech of June 21. It is understandable, perhaps, that no one in Washington recognized the link between the disarmament negotiations and the on-rushing Berlin crisis, but it remains surprising that at a time when caution was the watchword of the day and every word directly relating to Berlin and Germany was being carefully weighed, a statement on disarmament which was almost certain to provoke the Soviets and to generate a strong counteraction should have been dispatched so promptly and with so little apparent realization of its probable consequences.

Tightening the Western alliance

The Berlin crisis of 1961, as we have noted, was a contest not merely between the United States and the Soviet Union but between the two opposing alliance systems grouped around them. Recognizing that the ties linking the nations of the Western alliance faced a period of intense strain, Kennedy took a number of steps during the initial phase of the crisis designed to strengthen them.

Immediately after his Vienna meeting with Khrushchev, the President flew to London for a discussion with British Prime Minister Harold Macmillan. Far more than the tentative encounter between the two men at Bermuda in April, this stopover on Kennedy's homeward journey marked the start of what, in Schlesinger's phrase, was to be "Kennedy's closest personal relationship with

[5]Ibid.
[6]Ibid.

a foreign leader."[7] The "considerable temperamental rapport"[8] which the two men were to develop was all the more valuable in that their basic views on policy toward the Soviet Union often diverged rather widely. The British leader, with his roots in the pre-1914 Edwardian past and his deep horror of war resulting from the experience of two world holocausts, felt strongly that virtually no possible gains were sufficiently vital to justify the risk of nuclear war.

The discussion at No. 10 Downing Street, conducted on a personal and informal basis at Macmillan's suggestion, ranged widely, with special attention being devoted to the nuclear test ban talks and disarmament. Uppermost in the minds of both men, nevertheless, was the looming threat to the Western position on Berlin. On this subject a partial meeting of minds was achieved. Macmillan, despite his preference for negotiations with the Soviets, agreed that a proposal to initiate East–West talks now would be taken in Moscow as a sign of weakness. He therefore fell in with Kennedy's urging of the immediate need for accelerated military planning on Berlin and for the adoption of contingency plans to counter possible Soviet actions.[9] In the words of the joint communiqué issued at the end of their meeting: "The situation in regard to Germany was reviewed and there was full agreement on the necessity of maintaining the rights and obligations of the allied governments in Berlin".[10]

U.S.–British contacts were extended with the arrival in Washington on June 14 of Lord Home, British foreign secretary. Finding that U.S. officials were as yet only in the opening phase of what seemed likely to be a prolonged discussion on the policy to be pursued in Berlin, Lord Home turned matters over to a subordinate and flew on to Chicago, where on June 17 he gave a speech affirming Western resolution.[11] As the Berlin crisis developed, a perceptible shade of difference was to emerge between the views of Lord Home and those of his chief, Prime Minister Macmillan.

A foreign visitor who was to play a significant role at a later stage in the Berlin crisis, Italian Prime Minister Amintore Fanfani, paid a visit to the White House on June 12–13 as the result of an initiative within the White House staff which deliberately bypassed the professional diplomats in the State Department, distrustful of the Italian statesman's professed willingness to collaborate with the Italian socialists and other parties to the left of center (the "opening to the left").[12] Balancing cautiously between East and West, the Italian government had signed a three-year trade agreement with the Soviets just before Fanfani left for the United States.[13]

[7]Arthur M. Schlesinger, Jr., *A Thousand Days: John F. Kennedy in the White House* (Boston: Houghton Mifflin; Cambridge, Mass.: The Riverside Press, 1965), p. 376 (hereinafter cited as Schlesinger).

[8]Ibid.

[9]Ibid.

[10]Department of State, *American Foreign Policy: Current Documents, 1961* (Washington, D.C.: G.P.O., 1965), p. 547 (hereinafter cited as *AFP, 1961*).

[11]*SIA, 1961*, pp. 232–34.

[12]Schlesinger, pp. 876–77.

[13]*Pravda*, June 8, 1961.

Fanfani's visit served to strengthen U.S.–Italian relations, increase Italy's stature as a partner in NATO, and deepen its commitment to the goals of the Western alliance.

A state visit not directly related to the Berlin crisis but of cardinal importance in strengthening the Western position within the overall context of international relations was the meeting at the White House on June 21–22 between the President and Prime Minister Hayato Ikeda of Japan. Whether by coincidence or design, the visit occurred just over a year after an episode which marked an abysmal low in U.S.–Japanese relations—the cancellation by the Japanese government of a projected visit to Tokyo by President Eisenhower in the wake of widespread anti-American riots in Japan. As if to make amends for the past and to underline the resurgence of U.S.–Japanese amity, the gathering at the White House for Ikeda's visit included former President Eisenhower.

The joint communiqué issued at the end of the Japanese Premier's visit emphasized the common security problems faced by both nations in Southeast Asia and the Pacific area and their support for the United Nations as an instrument for peace and international security. Of immediate significance in the context of the Berlin crisis was a passage affirming a common stand on disarmament and a nuclear test ban: "The President and the Prime Minister recognized the urgent need for an agreement on a nuclear test ban accompanied by effective inspection and control measures, agreeing that it is of crucial importance for world peace. They also expressed their conviction that renewed efforts should be made in the direction of general disarmament."[14]

As the nation most intimately acquainted with the horrors of atomic warfare, Japan's position on these questions was a matter of particular significance. The close understanding resulting from the visit by Ikeda was, therefore, a valuable contribution to the strengthening of the Western position as the showdown over resumed nuclear testing drew closer.

The President's underlying concept of the way in which the United States could most effectively use its manpower and resources to combat communist subversion and aggression found expression in an address to the Eighth National Conference on International Economic and Social Development on June 16. Sustained and intelligently administered foreign aid, Kennedy argued, was the indispensable key to countering the communist tactics of support for and identification with the national liberation movement in underdeveloped nations:

> In 1952, the Communists were seeking to expand their influence primarily through military means. In 1952, the United States was concerned about Korea-type control and invasions with actual military forces. Now, however, we have seen an entirely different concept, which the Communists have very frankly and generously explained to us at great length: Mr. Khrushchev's speech in January—he reiterated it again in Vienna—the so-called

---

[14]U.S., Office of the Federal Register, *John F. Kennedy. Containing the Public Messages, Speeches, and Statements of the President, January 20 to December 31, 1961* (Washington, D.C.: G.P.O., 1962), p. 471 (hereinafter cited as *JFK, 1961*).

war of liberation, which is not the Korean type of war, where an armed force of one side passes across en masse the frontier of another country, but instead the seizure of power internally by what he considers the forces of liberation but which are, as we know in many cases, forces which are Communist controlled and which are supported from outside the country, but which are internal in their operation. It is for these reasons and because of this change in the Communist strategy which they believe offers them the best hope of success that this work [foreign aid] is more important today than it's ever been before.[15]

The U.S. contribution, Kennedy urged, should be material support for governments intent on improving the well-being of their people:

I think that we should recognize that the efforts to seize power in these countries, particularly those that are bordering the periphery of the Communist bloc, can be stemmed only—particularly in those countries where poverty and ignorance and illiteracy are the order of the day—can be stemmed only by one thing. And that is governments which are oriented and directed towards assisting the people and identified with causes which mean a better life for the people of those countries. Quite obviously we cannot stem any tide which is inevitable. But I do not believe it inevitable that the governments in those areas should adopt policies which are reactionary. I think it's inevitable that they will adopt policies which are progressive and I think we should assist them. If we're not prepared to assist them, then quite obviously they cannot carry this burden, in many cases, by themselves. And if we're not prepared to assist them, whatever efforts they make will be doomed to failure. So I think that what we want to see in these areas are governments which are concerned with the life of their people, which are making a genuine effort, which are making and putting forward programs which over a period of time promise a better life for the people. And then we should be prepared to play our part and that is what we are suggesting in this program, and that in my opinion is in the best interest of our country at this time.[16]

As for military support to weak governments fighting subversion, the sound course, in the President's opinion, was to "train and equip the local forces upon whom the chief burden of resisting local Communist subversion rests."[17]

Another occasion effectively used by the President to expound his ideas on East–West relations was the entry into force on June 23, 1961, of the multilateral Treaty on Antarctica. With obvious application to the stalemated test ban talks in Geneva, Kennedy said:

This is a significant treaty in several respects. First and foremost it provides that the vast Antarctic continent shall be used for peaceful purposes only. Accompanying this provision is the important provision whereby the parties have the right to send observers anywhere in Antarctica at any time to see

15Ibid., p. 461.
16Ibid., pp. 461–62.
17Ibid., p. 463.

that the Treaty is not being violated, and the right of overflight of all areas of Antarctica. It could very well provide valuable experience in the field of international inspection in other situations.[18]

In these and similar statements the President refrained from direct comment on recent speeches by Khrushchev, Ulbricht, and other communist spokesmen. It fell to Secretary of State Dean Rusk at his news conference on June 22 to discuss and rebut some of the charges and claims made by Khrushchev in his speech of the preceding day.[19] Brushing aside Khrushchev's distortions of the historical record—"Chairman Khrushchev's description . . . of the alleged origins of World War II will scarcely impress any serious historian"—Rusk directed the major part of the conference to a clarification of U.S. policy on Germany. "The essential thing," he said, "is that the three Western Powers, as the President put it, are in Berlin not by sufferance but by right, and those rights can't be terminated by unilateral action taken by the Soviet Union. You start from there. And our commitments to the people of West Berlin are very strong and very far-reaching."[20]

As to Khrushchev's claim that in announcing plans for signing a separate peace treaty with East Germany the Soviets were doing nothing more than to follow the U.S. example with regard to the peace treaty with Japan, Rusk provided a succinct and inclusive rejoinder to this frequently voiced Soviet complaint:

> There are several important differences between the Japanese Peace Treaty and this proposal to sign a treaty with the so-called East German Republic. In the case of Japan, there was a representative, elected government representing a unified nation with which to sign a peace treaty. There were 49 nations, I believe, which did in fact sign that peace treaty. The Soviet Union was consulted by the then Ambassador [sic], John Foster Dulles, in the early stages and had an opportunity to consult freely prior to the meeting of the Japanese Peace Conference in San Francisco. They did not avail themselves of the full opportunity that was there for them for consultation.
>
> At the conference itself the Russians attended, and the conference proceeded to sign a treaty. That treaty did not purport to, nor did it, affect any tangible rights of the Soviet Union in Japan. The situation in Berlin involves quite a different situation, with the United States and France and the United Kingdom exercising very specific rights and obligations in West Berlin. There was nothing like that in the Japanese situation at all. Nor did we have a representative government in Germany to decide for all of Germany and certainly not a representative government in the so-called East German Republic. I think the situations are quite different.[21]

* * *

[18]Ibid., p. 472.
[19]*Department of State Bulletin*, 45 (1961): 51–57 (hereinafter cited as *DSB*).
[20]Ibid., p. 55.
[21]Ibid., pp. 56–57.

Khrushchev's challenging speech of June 21 had the effect of accelerating Western efforts to reach agreement on a common policy with regard to Berlin, but the pace still remained painfully slow, primarily because the U.S. administration itself was engaged in an extensive internal debate over what course to pursue. Without waiting for a resolution of the debate, two Western leaders voiced their nations' firm commitment to defense of the Western position in Berlin at this time. Speaking in the House of Commons on June 27, Macmillan indicated a willingness to negotiate with the Soviets over West Berlin, but not at the expense of the freedom of the inhabitants of the city:

> Her Majesty's Government, in concert with their allies, have over the years made a number of comprehensive proposals for the just and equitable solution of the problem of Germany and Berlin. . . . All these proposals have been rejected by the Soviet Government, who prefer instead to manufacture an artificial crisis for the purpose of gaining their own ends. We and our allies have certain obligations in Germany, and we do not intend to abandon them. Among these obligations is the preservation of the freedom of the people of West Berlin. The Soviet Government must come to realise that we intend to defend this, and that we cannot countenance proposals inconsistent with it. If they wish to discuss the issue with us, we are prepared to do so, but they must understand that it can only be on the basis that I have described. The House will appreciate from what I have said that there is no question whatever of any modification of British commitments in Berlin.[22]

If the Soviets had seriously desired negotiations on Berlin at this time, Macmillan's statement would have provided them with an opening, for he included among the Western proposals one advanced in 1959, which, as the *Survey of International Affairs* points out, "had contained an element of conversations if not of negotiations between the two German governments."[23] The Soviets, however, let the opportunity slip past.

Macmillan's emphasis, as usual, was on the need for a reasonable approach and on the willingness of the British government to undertake negotiations, once their fundamental commitment to West Berlin was recognized by the Soviets. Characteristic too was his description of the Berlin crisis as "artificial," with the implication that it need not be taken too seriously.

A far more alarmist note was sounded on June 29 by British Foreign Secretary Lord Home in a speech in London, in which he warned that the British people faced an "extremely dangerous" world situation as the result of the Berlin crisis and predicted that the next six months "are going to be one of the most difficult and dangerous periods through which this country has passed since the last war."[24] Lord Home's statement, which was clearly intended to prepare British public opinion for a period of heightened inter-

---

[22]Royal Institute of International Affairs, *Documents on International Affairs, 1961* (London: Oxford University Press, 1965), p. 302 (hereinafter cited as *DIA, 1961*).

[23]*SIA, 1961*, p. 236.

[24]*NYT*, June 30, 1961, p. 2.

national tension, provided a revealing indication of the still prevailing view in the West, even among those who feared the worst, that a fairly extensive period lay ahead before the crisis reached its climax. Macmillan himself, speaking before a Conservative party meeting at Bowood on July 1, took a line considerably closer to that of Lord Home than was customary for him. The West, he said, "cannot countenance interference with Western rights" in Berlin, and he hinted at the possibility of war if the Soviets forced the issue: "Let there be no mistake. This is an issue on which the peoples of the Western world are resolute. It is a principle which they will defend."[25]

In France, President de Gaulle was meanwhile exhorting his nation and its allies to achieve unity in the face of the impending threat. At Verdun on June 28, he said: "It is by remaining united, first among Frenchmen and then between free peoples, our friends, our allies, that we have all the chances of turning aside the storm."[26] The following day he repeated the advice in varied terms: "Clouds are piling up over Europe. It is time for the West to close ranks."[27] At a rally in Épinal on June 30 he spelled out his warning even more clearly: "We are on the eve of a serious international crisis. . . . in the face of this danger there is no better guarantee for France than unity and no better guarantee for the free world than solidarity."[28]

Washington searches for a policy

Shortly after he returned from Vienna, Kennedy, in accordance with a standard practice in his administration, established a "task force" to help frame policy and develop initiatives on the Berlin problem. The Berlin task force's immediate assignment was to prepare a reply to the Soviets' Vienna note on Germany, a task which occupied most of its attention during June and early July.[29] Meanwhile, under the mounting pressure from abroad, the internal debate in the U.S. administration grew sharper, reaching its first major climax toward the end of June. On the morning of June 28 the President at his regular press conference presented a statement which summed up the administration's thinking on the legal aspects of the Berlin issue. "It is of the greatest importance," Kennedy said, "that the American people understand the basic issues involved and the threats to peace and security of Europe and of ourselves posed by the Soviet announcement that they intend to change unilaterally the existing arrangements for Berlin."[30]

Calling the crisis over Berlin "Soviet-manufactured," the President identified three major Soviet objectives in their drive: first, "to make permanent the

[25]*NYT*, July 2, 1961, p. 1.

[26]*NYT*, June 29, 1961, p. 2.

[27]*Washington Post*, June 30, 1961, p. A-1.

[28]*NYT*, July 1, 1961, p. 2.

[29]Schlesinger, p. 383.

[30]*JFK, 1961*, p. 476.

partition of Germany"; second, to "bring an end to Allied rights in West Berlin and to free access for that city"; and third, to create a situation "in which the rights of the citizens of West Berlin are gradually but relentlessly extinguished."[31] "This is not just a question of technical legal rights," he continued, ". . . It involves the peace and the security of the peoples of West Berlin. It involves the direct responsibilities and commitments of the United States, the United Kingdom, and France. It involves the peace and the security of the Western world."[32]

Notably absent from the President's summing up of the Western position was any direct reference to the West German government, its vital stake in West Berlin, its interest in German reunification, and its role in the Western alliance. A consistent neglect of this aspect of the task of tightening the Western alliance runs through this entire phase of the Berlin crisis. A certain degree of personal incompatibility between the young President and the venerable West German chancellor, Dr. Konrad Adenauer, and between the Washington administration and West German ambassador to the United States, Dr. William Grewe, may account in part for this oversight, the consequences of which were to make themselves felt during the crisis.

Reverting to one of his major concerns at the Vienna meeting, the President warned against misjudging the unity and resolve of the Western nations: "There is danger that totalitarian governments not subject to vigorous popular debate will underestimate the will and unity of democratic societies where vital interests are concerned. . . . The Soviet Government has an obligation to both its own people and to the peace of the world to recognize how vital is this commitment."[33]

In a second prepared statement at the June 28 press conference the President expressed disappointment over what he termed "the Soviet Union's refusal to negotiate seriously on a nuclear test ban at Geneva," and warned that the stalemate there "raises a serious qestion . . . about how long we can safely continue on a voluntary basis a refusal to undertake tests in this country without any assurance that the Russians are not now testing."[34] He had accordingly, he continued,

> . . . directed that the President's Science Advisory Committee convene a special panel of eminent scientists to take a close and up-to-date look at the serious questions involved, including two questions in particular. First, what is the extent of our information on whether the Soviet Union has been or could be engaged in secret testing of nuclear weapons?
>
> Second, to the extent that certain types of tests can be concealed by the Soviet Union, what technical progress in weapons could be under way in that area without our knowledge?[35]

[31]Ibid., pp. 476–77.
[32]Ibid., p. 477.
[33]Ibid.
[34]Ibid.
[35]Ibid.

The panel, to be headed by Stanford physicist W. K. H. Panofsky, was given the mandate

> . . . to consider whether or not the Soviet Union could be conducting clandestine nuclear tests during the moratorium, and what progress the U.S.S.R. could make through such tests. The group was also asked to consider what progress the United States could make if it resumed nuclear testing, and what would happen if both sides resumed testing. In connection with the last question the panel was specifically asked to estimate the possibility of the Soviet Union's overcoming the United States' lead in nuclear weapons.[36]

In answer to a question later on in the press conference the President acknowledged that he had not seen ". . . any information, nor did the previous administration have any knowledge, which would state that the Soviet Union has been testing—information either by seismography or by any other means."[37]

It appears, however, that as of this date reports from scientists in other countries told a different story. According to the *Survey of International Affairs*: "At the end of June reports were beginning to come in from the seismographic research institutes of Japan, Finland and Sweden of seismic events within Soviet territory which the Japanese and the Swedes at least believed to be nuclear, of low-yield nuclear weapons."[38]

Turning to a third area in which Soviet and American rivalry was manifesting itself, the President provided a statement on peaceful economic competition. As we have seen, this was a theme which Khrushchev had stressed in his speeches at Alma Ata on June 24 and 25, and in addressing himself to it the President showed a shrewd ability to recognize and encourage an aspect of Soviet policy which, if pursued, might serve to divert it from more dangerous issues. Kennedy maintained that this was a form of international competition in which the United States had nothing to fear: "I believe that we can maintain our productive development and also our system of freedom. We invite the U.S.S.R. to engage in this competition which is peaceful and which could only result in a better living standard for both of our people."[39]

Among the questions which the President parried at the June 28 press conference was one concerning possible plans for "a partial mobilization to meet the threat in Berlin."[40] Both the President and his questioner were well aware, no doubt, that in its July 3 issue, which appeared on the newsstands on June 26, two days before the press conference, *Newsweek* had published a story de-

---

[36]Harold K. Jacobson and Eric Stein, *Diplomats, Scientists and Politicians. The United States and the Nuclear Test Ban Negotiations* (Ann Arbor: University of Michigan Press, 1966), pp. 277–78 (hereinafter cited as Jacobson and Stein).

[37]*JFK, 1961*, p. 483.

[38]*SIA, 1961*, p. 258, citing *Sunday Times* (London), July 2 and Sept. 3, 1961, and *Le Soir*, Sept. 5, 1961.

[39]*JFK, 1961*, p. 478.

[40]Ibid.

tailing the alleged contingency plans of the Department of Defense for the Berlin crisis, including partial mobilization. In a report on the incident on June 30, the *Washington Post* attributed to administration officials a description of the *Newsweek* story as being "accurate enough to cause grave concern about the disclosure of future and more important recommendations from the Joint Chiefs [of Staff] to the President," adding that the President had called on the FBI to investigate what was termed a "critical leak" of the nation's contingency plans for Berlin.

While disavowing official cognizance of the partial mobilization plan, the President indirectly acknowledged its validity by referring directly to its immediate source, a report on Berlin prepared at his direction by a task force headed by former Secretary of State Dean Acheson. It was the Acheson report which formed the central item in a meeting of the National Security Council which took place on June 29, a meeting which can be regarded as the formal opening of high-level U.S. planning for the Berlin crisis. Detailed and apparently accurate accounts of the meeting were published in the American press almost immediately,[41] and, in addition, fairly extensive summaries of the meeting have been provided by Sorensen and Schlesinger.

The best summary of the Acheson report is provided by Schlesinger. "Acheson's basic thesis," he writes,

> was that West Berlin was not a problem but a pretext. Khrushchev's *démarche* had nothing to do with Berlin, Germany or Europe. His object, as Acheson saw it, was not to rectify a local situation, but to test the general American will to resist; his hope was that, by making us back down on a sacred commitment, he could shatter our world power and influence. This was a simple conflict of wills, and, until it was resolved, any effort to negotiate the Berlin issue per se would be fatal. Since there was nothing to negotiate, willingness on our part to go to the conference table would be taken in Moscow as evidence of weakness and make the crisis so much the worse.[42]

The basic cause of such Soviet daring, Acheson maintained, was Khrushchev's belief that all-out war had become an increasingly remote possibility:

> Khrushchev had only dared precipitate the crisis . . . because his fear of nuclear war had declined. Our problem was to convince him that this complacency was misplaced and that we would, in fact, go to nuclear war rather than abandon the status quo. This called for the build-up—prompt, serious and quiet—of both our conventional and nuclear forces. If Khrushchev signed his treaty with East Germany, we should not quibble about this or about changes in access procedures. But, the moment there was interruption of access itself, we must act: first an airlift—and then, if that could not be sustained against Soviet counter-measures, a ground probe in force too large to be stopped by East German troops alone. Acheson cited a Joint

[41]*NYT*, June 30, 1961, p. 1; Joseph Alsop, *Washington Post*, July 3, 1961.
[42]Schlesinger, p. 381.

Chiefs of Staff estimate that two Allied divisions could hold out indefinitely inside East Germany against an enemy of three or four divisions. The point would be, not to defeat the communist forces in the field, but to persuade Moscow that we had the resolve to go on, if necessary, to nuclear war. There was a substantial chance, Acheson said, that the necessary military preparations would by themselves cause Khrushchev to alter his purpose; but he added frankly that there was also a substantial possibility that nuclear war might result.[43]

Almost as an afterthought Acheson conceded the possibility that negotiations, under certain circumstances, might be useful: "He even sketched the outlines of a settlement, suggesting that Khrushchev's treaty be accompanied by an exchange of declarations assuring the western position in Berlin, along with certain western concessions—perhaps guarantees against espionage and subversion from West Berlin, perhaps even recognition of the Oder–Neisse line—thrown in to make the result more palatable to Moscow."[44]

But the major emphasis in the report and in what Schlesinger describes as Acheson's "brilliant and imperious oral presentation" was on the need to stand firm in the test of wills precipitated by Soviet action. The Acheson report, Schlesinger adds, "helped fix the debate for a time in terms of a clear-cut choice between negotiation and a military showdown."[45]

As a major policy step, to prepare for the test of strength and to convince Khrushchev of the seriousness of the national purpose, Acheson recommended that the President should proclaim a national emergency under which he could move toward full combat status by calling up one million reserves, extending terms of service in the armed forces, and bringing back dependents from Germany, thereby putting the troops there in a state of battle preparedness.[46]

Within the administration, according to Sorensen, Acheson's recommendations were initially supported by the Departments of State and Defense.[47] Schlesinger provides a more precise analysis of the State Department's internal divisions and notes that some of the administration's top experts on Soviet policy, including Ambassadors Thompson and Harriman, disagreed with Acheson, arguing that Khrushchev's goals might well be more limited than was envisaged by Acheson, and that a "quiet military buildup," accompanied by the preparation of specific proposals on Berlin, would probably be more effective.[48]

As to the President himself, Schlesinger and Sorensen agree that he tended to side with the critics of the Acheson report. Favoring a policy of negotiation, Kennedy recognized at the same time the wisdom of building up Western mili-

[43]Ibid., pp. 381–82.
[44]Ibid., p. 382.
[45]Ibid., p. 385.
[46]Sorensen, p. 589.
[47]Ibid.
[48]Schlesinger, p. 383; Sorensen, p. 589.

tary strength in Berlin and West Germany, not only in order to convince the Soviets of Western firmness but to avoid the dangerous dilemma posed by the existing U.S. and NATO contingency plans for Berlin. As Sorensen puts it: "In the event of blocked access [to West Berlin], under these plans, a series of military 'probes' down the *Autobahn* would be attempted. But with the West lacking both the intention and the capacity to wage a conventional war on the ground, these probes were too small to indicate a serious intent and would surely be quickly contained by the Soviets or even by the East Germans alone. Then the plans called for nuclear weapons."[49]

Regarding the strategy underlying these plans as "weak and dangerous," Kennedy advocated instead "a rapid buildup of combat troops in Central Europe,"

> . . . with a contingent large enough to convince Khrushchev that our vital interests were so deeply involved that we would use any means to prevent the defeat or capture of those forces. This required a force large enough to prevent any cheap and easy seizure of the city by East German guards alone, which would weaken our bargaining power—and large enough to permit a true "pause," a month instead of an hour before choosing nuclear war or retreat, time to bring up reserves, to demonstrate our determination, to make a deliberate decision and to communicate at the highest levels before the "ultimate" weapons were used.[50]

To guard against the possibility that Khrushchev might be tempted to speculate on Western disunity, Kennedy advocated a similar military increase by other Western nations.[51]

Kennedy and Khrushchev: efforts toward contact

While the Western alliance and the Soviets were girding themselves for a showdown, unofficial explorations were taking place with regard to the possibility of direct but informal contact between the top men on each side. The explorations grew out of the working level agreement at the Vienna meeting to arrange a joint television debate in the United States and the Soviet Union.

The debate itself (or rather its American phase, since the Soviets subsequently reneged on their promise to reciprocate), took place over the National Broadcasting Company television network on June 24, on the program, "The Nation's Future." Adzhubei and Kharlamov represented the Soviet side, Harrison Salisbury and Pierre Salinger the American. Since all four participants were closely linked with the press it was natural that much of the sixty-minute program should be spent debating the position of journalism in the United States and the Soviet Union. The U.S. team reproached their Soviet counterparts with lack of freedom to criticize their government, while the

[49]Sorensen, p. 587–88.
[50]Ibid., p. 588.
[51]Ibid.

Soviet spokesmen retorted with charges of journalistic sensationalism in the United States. Salinger, who as White House press secretary spent much of his time trying to persuade U.S. newspaper editors not to publish stories which the administration considered damaging to the nation's security, taxed the Soviets with the secrecy which surrounded major events in their country, for example, the preparations for the Gagarin flight on April 12.

At the close of the program Kharlamov summed things up gracefully: "I think we have had a good discussion here. Regardless of our differences on particulars, partly due to mutual ignorance or misunderstanding, it is better to seek mutual understanding than to seek war. It is better to seek cooperation in order to prevent war than to emphasize the differences that exist among us."[52]

Though it reached a large audience in the United States, the television debate was less significant for future U.S.–Soviet relations than the personal contacts it helped to foster. On the day following the debate, when the Russian team were guests at Pierre Salinger's home, Kharlamov made use of the occasion to report the "grave concern" felt in the Soviet Union over the lack of progress in the disarmament negotiations. Reflecting the budgetary pressures on the Soviet leadership, he told Salinger: "We are both spending too much on missiles. It is time we spent more on goods the people can use. But your new President is even harder to bring to the bargaining table than Eisenhower. Our patience is great but not inexhaustible."[53] In reply Salinger assured the Russian that "President Kennedy was most eager to break the disarmament stalemate, and his negotiator, John J. McCloy, had instructions to explore the widest possible area of agreement."[54]

One of the Soviet guests at the party, Georgi M. Bolshakov, editor of the English-language Soviet magazine *USSR*, proffered some gratuitous advice on American foreign policy: "You Americans have too many [allies] and they're always fighting among themselves. You ought to decide which ones are important and get rid of the rest of them."[55]

The comment is interesting for its implied contrast between the two opposing power blocs as they approached the test of strength over Berlin and for its tacit—and erroneous—assumption that the Soviets in this respect enjoyed a more favorable position than the United States.

The most significant result of the television debate came on the following day, Monday, June 26, when Adzhubei, Kharlamov, and Bolshakov were guests at the White House for an hour-long discussion with the President. Taking his cue from Khrushchev's June 25 speech in Alma Ata, Kennedy adroitly steered the conversation around to the subject of U.S.–Soviet eco-

---

[52]Pierre Salinger, *With Kennedy* (New York: Doubleday, 1966), p. 186 (hereinafter cited as Salinger).

[53]Ibid., pp. 186–87.

[54]Ibid., p. 187.

[55]Ibid.

nomic rivalry. Khrushchev, as we have seen, had compared the United States to an "aged runner" and had predicted that the Soviet Union would overtake it in economic output by 1970.

Having first stressed that he wished Adzhubei to convey his remarks to his father-in-law, Khrushchev, the President said: "I don't think you can do that [outstrip the U.S. by 1970] at your present rate of growth. You're like the high-jumper. He can raise the bar a foot at a time until he reaches a certain height, say six feet. But for the next foot he must raise it by inches, and after that by fractions of inches."[56]

When Adzhubei retorted that "you use one set of figures to measure our growth and we use another," the President clinched his point: "I'm not minimizing your effort. You've made remarkable economic advances. This is the kind of peaceful competition I would like to see us have. But you must do more than you are to see that the peace is kept. Do that and we'll all be around in 1978 [sic] to find out whether Mr. Khrushchev's estimates are correct."[57]

When Adzhubei questioned Western peaceful intentions because of the presence of American troops in West Berlin (conveniently overlooking the twenty-two Soviet divisions in East Germany), the President took advantage of the opening to define American policy on this point: "Our force of 10,000 is token in nature. It is a symbol of our commitment to West Berlin—a commitment we fully intend to maintain."[58]

In the course of the discussion Kennedy asked Adzhubei to convey a personal message to Khrushchev reaffirming the American policy stand outlined at the Vienna meeting.[59]

The discussion between Kennedy and Adzhubei evidently made a strong impression on Khrushchev, who was always acutely sensitive to questions of personal prestige and the recognition by foreign leaders of what he considered the respect due Soviet officials. In a speech on June 28, which was otherwise highly belligerent in tone, Khrushchev included a passage toward the end expressing appreciation for the President's gesture in arranging the meeting with Adzhubei and his colleagues (more of this presently). Later, when the first climax of the Berlin crisis was past, Khrushchev was to tell Kennedy, in his first personal letter to him, that he had planned to write to him shortly after the Kennedy–Adzhubei meeting, but had been temporarily discouraged from doing so by the "belligerence" of Kennedy's July 25 speech.[60]

[56]Ibid.

[57]Ibid. Salinger evidently mistook the date postulated by Khrushchev for overtaking the United States.

[58]Ibid., p. 188.

[59]*Washington Post*, June 28, 1961, p. A–15. Salinger, who was present at the White House discussion, does not confirm this report, but it is inherently probable in view of Kennedy's overriding concern to convey his position to Khrushchev with the utmost clarity. It was in all likelihood his chief reason for arranging to see Adzhubei and his colleagues. See also the account of the meeting in Hugh Sidey, *John F. Kennedy, President* (New York: Atheneum, 1963), p. 213 (hereinafter cited as Sidey).

[60]Sorensen, p. 552.

Even before the initiation of the private correspondence between the two statesmen, therefore, a kind of dialogue had been established between them, as a result of their intense curiosity about each other and the concern each felt for the security of the nation with which he was entrusted. The availability of virtually instantaneous newspaper, radio, and television reports of the public utterances of the two leaders and their associates made it possible for them to engage in an indirect but effective exchange of ideas, in which a theme stated by one would be picked up by the other, developed, then tossed back for further elaboration. Khrushchev's introduction of the economic competition theme in his Alma Ata speeches is an excellent example of this process. Noting the theme, Kennedy at once recognized its potential as a means of steering U.S.–Soviet rivalry into peaceful, nonmilitary channels. Having prepared himself by obtaining statistics on the U.S. and Soviet rates of economic growth,[61] he introduced the subject in his discussion with Adzhubei on June 26 and had a formal written statement on it ready for his news conference on the 28th. As we shall see, Khrushchev in turn responded to Kennedy's overture, even at a time when he was otherwise at his most belligerent (speech of July 8). Though the economic-rivalry theme was to be temporarily drowned out by the increasing stridency on both sides, the effort had not been wasted, for it helped keep alive the prospect of a turn away from threats of war, toward a more genuinely peaceful world.

[61]Sidey, p. 213.

3 The Soviets Increase the Pressure

While the United States was deep in the throes of internal debate over policy in the Berlin crisis, and while its allies were waiting with mounting impatience for it to make up its mind, the Soviets were stepping up their pressure against the Western position in Berlin. Khrushchev's visit to Alma Ata had marked a temporary breathing space in the Soviet campaign; on his return to Moscow it was resumed in full force. On June 27 *Pravda* published the text of a telegram from Khrushchev and Brezhnev to party and government officials in East Germany which linked Hitler's "perfidious attack" on the Soviet Union with the allegedly revenge-seeking and militarist policies currently being pursued by West Germany. These it contrasted sanctimoniously with "the consistent struggle of the G.D.R. to create a single democratic peace-loving Germany and to strengthen peace and safety in Europe."[1]

Though it reiterated the demand for a German peace treaty—"The interest of peace in Europe makes it imperative to conclude a peace treaty with Germany and to normalize the situation in West Berlin on this basis"—the telegram showed some signs of wavering on the end-of-1961 deadline by stating that "the Soviet Union and all other peace-loving countries will *do all they can* so that it is signed by the end of this year."[2]

The apparently more moderate formulation contained in the telegram to the GDR leaders, however, signified no let-up in the Soviet pressure. On the following day the Soviet press published the first generally available photographs of a new Soviet delta-wing bomber claimed to have a capacity of intercontinental missions. Western observers were permitted a glimpse of the big plane as it took off for a rehearsal of a Soviet air show—the first in five years —scheduled to be held at Tushino, near Moscow, on July 9. Marshal Sergei I.

[1] *Documents on Germany, 1961*, p. 671.
[2] Ibid.; emphasis supplied.

Rudenko, deputy commander of the Soviet air force, was reported as saying, "Our main object is to demonstrate the might of Soviet aviation."[3]

Khrushchev addresses the North Vietnamese

On June 28 Khrushchev addressed a ceremonial meeting devoted to Soviet–North Vietnamese friendship in the Great Hall of the Kremlin. The occasion was the visit to the Soviet Union of a governmental delegation from North Vietnam (the Democratic Republic of Vietnam, abbreviated DRV), headed by DRV Premier Pham Van Dong. (The delegation had been greeted by Khrushchev on its arrival in Moscow on June 26[4] and was to remain in the Soviet Union until July 5.)[5]

The June 28 speech marked the vigorous resumption of the Soviet campaign on Berlin, but it dealt with a number of other significant topics in international relations as well. Much attention was devoted to the situation in Southeast Asia, particularly the rising tide of conflict in Vietnam and the precarious cease-fire in Laos. Khrushchev drew a stark contrast between the "socialist" policy of the "work-loving and talented" people of the DRV and the "puppet authorities' policy, alien to the people" which he claimed was being pursued in South Vietnam. He affirmed Soviet solidarity with the DRV: ". . . the Soviet government fully supports the policy of the government of the Democratic Republic of Vietnam aimed at consolidating peace in Southeast Asia and throughout the world. We stand resolutely with the government of the Democratic Republic of Vietnam for the earliest solution of the problem of the peaceful reunification of Vietnam."[6]

Aid by the United States to the Republic of Vietnam (South Vietnam), however, was roundly denounced as imperialism: "In violation of the Geneva agreements [of 1954], the U.S. has been supplying South Vietnam with thousands of tons of military equipment and materiel. It is continuing to outfit and train the army of South Vietnam and has been sending many military advisers there. It has in fact involved the South Vietnamese authorities in the military adventures of SEATO [the South-East Asia Treaty Organization]."[7]

Although he had frequently advocated Soviet support for "wars of liberation," Khrushchev denied any responsibility for the guerrilla conflict in South Vietnam: "The struggle of the people of South Vietnam is not the handiwork of Moscow, not the intrigues of the communists. It is an expression of popular rage; it represents the fervent resolve of the people to have done with poverty and lack of rights; it is a struggle against the colonialist despoilers and

[3]*NYT*, June 29, 1961, p. 14.
[4]Khrushchev, *Kommunizm*, 1:212–13.
[5]Ibid., pp. 237–38.
[6]*Pravda*, June 29, 1961; *CDSP*, XIII/26, p. 10.
[7]*CDSP*, XIII/26, p. 10.

against their henchmen, who follow an even crueler policy than do the coloni-alists themselves."[8]

Turning to Laos, Khrushchev laid full responsibility for the continuing con-flict there on the United States and its allies: "There would be no Laotian question if the United States and its SEATO-bloc allies were not interfering in the internal affairs of that country and trying to convert Laos into a base for their aggressive policy in Southeast Asia."[9]

As to the continuing Geneva conference on Laos, Khrushchev hailed the recent (June 20) agreement between the three Laotian princes (Souvanna Phouma, Souphanouvong, and Boun Oum) on a program to establish a govern-ment of national unity and expressed the hope that it would adhere to a policy of neutrality and would soon be set up.

Having paid due attention to the problems which were uppermost in the minds of his Vietnamese guests, Khrushchev now shifted to the larger areas of Soviet policy, taking up first the question of disarmament. His emphasis here was on the Soviet proposals for sweeping, all-inclusive disarmament: "We have proposed to solve the problem of disarmament in a basic way—disperse all national armies, destroy all existing stocks of weapons, stop the production of armaments everywhere, in other words, carry out general and complete disarmament under international control."[10]

With regard to a nuclear test ban agreement, Khrushchev varied slightly his usual formula that such an agreement could be reached only within the framework of an agreement on general and complete disarmament, claiming that the Soviets wanted such an agreement but that the Western powers were holding up the test ban talks by opposing the Soviet demand for a three-man control board: "Our government has been and remains an advocate of an international nuclear test ban agreement under strict international control involving equality of rights. Conclusion of an appropriate agreement is being obstructed by the unwillingness of the American and British negotiating part-ners to take Soviet interests into consideration."[11]

The basic reason for the stalemate in the disarmament negotiations, ac-cording to Khrushchev, was "the unwillingness of certain circles in the West . . . to give up the policy of the arms race and the preparation of new military adventures."[12]

From here it was an easy and natural step to the question of Berlin: "This is also the only explanation there can be for the unwillingness of the Western powers to promote a peace settlement with Germany that would reliably en-sure stability and security in Europe."[13]

[8]Ibid.
[9]Ibid.
[10]Khrushchev, *Kommunizm*, 1:222.
[11]*Pravda*, June 29, 1961; *CDSP*, XIII/26, p. 11.
[12]*CDSP*, XIII/26, p. 11.
[13]Ibid.

Khrushchev then outlined the Soviet position on Berlin and Germany, adding a new and significant disclosure to the familiar Soviet proposals for a German peace treaty: "We propose to settle in an international document the obligation of the Germans never to encroach on the independence, freedom and sovereignty of other nations and to live in peace and friendship with them, *not resorting to force or the threat of force.*"[14]

Khrushchev next took up various proposals being advanced in the West for countering the Soviet pressure on West Berlin, noting particularly the contingency plans currently under consideration in Washington and NATO. He dismissed out of hand the possibility that economic sanctions could swerve the Soviets from their fixed course: "Threats of breaking off trade relations will not, of course, keep us from signing a German peace treaty."[15] Rupture of diplomatic relations would fare no better: "The West has already tried getting along without diplomatic relations with us, and has even tried refusing to recognize the Soviet state. At the time this venture foundered. It is not hard to see that an even more scandalous fiasco is in store for the authors of a venture of this kind these days."[16]

As to military measures, Khrushchev warned that the Soviet armed forces were fully capable of overcoming any threat, just as they had beaten back the Nazi invaders: "If the opponents of peace and peaceful coexistence declare mobilization anyway, we shall not let ourselves be caught napping. *We are taking necessary measures, and if need be we will take additional steps, to reinforce our security.*"[17]

As in the case of the resumption of nuclear testing, Khrushchev thus tried to shift the blame for the escalation of the conflict onto the Western powers, equating discussion in the West of possible countermeasures with the equivalent actions. Taken in conjunction with the June 21 speech, in which he had promised the armed forces whatever they needed for the defense of the Soviet Union, Khrushchev's June 28 speech indicates that a decision had been taken in principle to strengthen the Soviet armed forces.

The basic question at issue, Khrushchev implied, was the relative balance of power between the Soviet Union and the Western alliance: "Western statesmen maintain that the military power of the capitalist and socialist camps is now balanced. But in that case a balanced international policy must be pursued—that is, relations must not be exacerbated and there must be no resort to threats. Unfortunately, the good sense that should derive from recognition of the correlation of forces that has taken shape in the world is not in evidence in the policy of the Western powers."[18]

[14]Khrushchev, *Kommunizm*, 1:223; emphasis supplied.

[15]*Pravda*, June 29, 1961; *CDSP*, XIII/26, p. 11.

[16]*CDSP*, XIII/26, p. 11.

[17]Ibid., p. 12; emphasis supplied. Note Khrushchev's evident awareness of the substance of the policy debates in Washington.

[18]*Pravda*, June 29, 1961; *CDSP*, XIII/26, p. 12.

But Khrushchev was not content merely to assert a parity of power between the Soviets and the West (recognition of which he adroitly ascribed to "Western statesmen," thus making it appear that the Soviet claims for parity were officially accepted in the West). He went on to claim that in *total* power the Soviet bloc was already preponderant:

Furthermore, the forces are not equal: We consider the forces of socialism and peace a good deal mightier than the forces of imperialism and war [*prolonged applause*]. We are relying not only on our economic and military power; behind us is the righteous cause of our people, the righteousness of all peoples and all countries that take their stand for peaceful coexistence and the peaceful settlement of all issues in relations between states. And the conclusion of a German peace treaty is the most peaceful of peaceful solutions.[19]

This being the case, the efforts of the Western powers, and particularly of West Germany, to block Soviet intentions were short-sighted and doomed to failure. Rejecting Western proposals for all-German elections to decide on reunification, Khrushchev insisted that only by direct negotiations between the two German governments could this goal be achieved: "Unification of the German Democratic Republic and the Federal German Republic into a single state can be achieved only as a result of negotiations and cooperation between the governments of these states themselves. Other countries must not interfere in this internal affair of the Germans."[20]

As to the status of West Berlin after conclusion of a German peace treaty, Khrushchev strove to give the appearance of reasonableness: "I want to say once more that West Berlin will have the social and economic order its population wishes. We propose the establishment of reliable international guarantees of noninterference in the affairs of West Berlin: Let the guarantors be the four great powers, which could keep a contingent of their armed forces in the free city; or the armed forces of neutral countries, or of the United Nations, could be such guarantors."[21]

Beneath the smooth assurances, however, lay the unyielding demand for recognition by the Western powers of the GDR's right to control the access routes to the city:

There will be no blockade of West Berlin, no barriers will be put in the way of access to the city. West Berlin will be able to maintain free relations with all states at its own discretion. But since the communications to West Berlin run through the territory of the German Democratic Republic, according to established international traditions and laws an agreement with the government of that state is required for making use of them. No one is permitted to violate the ground, air or water frontiers of a sovereign state. Any attempt to disregard generally accepted standards of international intercourse has always met with, and it will meet with, a fitting rebuff.[22]

[19]*CDSP*, XIII/26, p. 12.
[20]Ibid.
[21]Ibid.
[22]Ibid., p. 15.

Far from wishing to upset the balance of power in Europe, Khrushchev argued, Soviet policy was designed to stabilize the existing status quo: "Some organs of the Western press maintain that the Soviet Union wishes with its proposals on the German question to upset the balance that has formed in Europe. One has but to take even a cursory look at the Soviet proposals to see that such assertions do not correspond to the facts. What we are proposing is precisely to confirm what has come about as a result of the war, to recognize the situation that actually exists in Europe and to conclude a peace treaty with the two German states."[23]

At the very end of the substantive portion of his speech Khrushchev paid tribute to the policy of personal contacts between officials of different nations, citing as a particularly encouraging example Kennedy's interview with Adzhubei and his press colleagues: "We highly appreciate the fact that President Kennedy received our journalists and had a talk with them, just as he had somewhat earlier talked with another large group of Soviet journalists. All these contacts are contributing to better understanding and the normalization of relations between our countries, and we would like this policy to continue."[24]

Although Khrushchev in his June 28 speech explicitly ruled out the possibility of a new Berlin blockade, the East German government on the same day took a move calculated to test Western willingness to resist interference with the access routes to the city. In a decree published in the official GDR gazette, Ulbricht's regime announced that beginning August 1 it would impose restrictions on foreign air traffic across its territory. Foreign aircraft would be required to register with a GDR "safety center" on entering and leaving the airspace over East German territory, and radar-equipped foreign aircraft would be required to obtain permission before flying over the GDR.[25] If this action was intended as a probe of Western attitudes, the response was swift and clearcut: on June 29, State Department spokesman Lincoln White categorically rejected the demands contained in the GDR decree, citing the four-power agreements on access to Berlin under which Western aircraft were authorized to use specific access routes "without prior notice."[26]

The first nuclear threat against the West

The GDR decree was a low-level feint which the West had no difficulty in parrying. If Soviet strategy in Berlin was to be successful, more direct pressure would have to be applied, and by the Soviets themselves, not by the GDR. A heightened phase of the war of nerves accordingly got under way early in July. At a reception in the Kremlin on July 2 Khrushchev sought out the British ambassador, Sir Frank Roberts, and, in the words of the *Survey of*

[23]Ibid.

[24]Ibid. Kennedy's earlier meeting with a group of Soviet journalists, headed by B. S. Burkov, chairman of the board of the "Novosti" press agency, took place on May 22, 1961: Radio Moscow, May 22, 1961.

[25]*NYT*, June 29, 1961, p. 1.

[26]*NYT*, June 30, 1961, p. 1.

International Affairs, "indulged in one of his characteristic outbursts of passion."[27] Available press reports on the conversation [28] agree in general outline on what was said. Sir Frank is reported to have stated at the outset his government's view that the Soviet offensive on Berlin was "artificial and illegal," and that the Soviets were striving to create unilaterally a "new situation" in Central Europe and Berlin. Countering Khrushchev's advocacy of a German peace treaty as a "logical step," Sir Frank stressed the responsibilities for Berlin vested in the four occupying powers by the Potsdam Agreement and the need for free elections in all of Germany as a basis for eventual reunification.

Khrushchev, according to Alsop, brushed aside these positions as "unreal, legalistic arguments irrelevant to the present situation," and stressed "the futility of any attempt to resist him." The addition of ground forces by the Western powers to their existing troop strength in Germany—one division to the NATO forces, for example—could be countered a hundredfold on the Soviet side, he said. Raising the threat to a higher level, Khrushchev pointed out the vulnerability of Britain to nuclear attack: "Only six of his H-bombs, he declared, would be quite enough to annihilate the British Isles, and nine would take care of France."[29]

According to the somewhat divergent *New York Times* account, Khrushchev did not "directly threaten the West with nuclear extinction," but if armed conflict broke out over Berlin, "the early use of nuclear weapons . . . was regarded by Khrushchev as inevitable."

Whatever the exact terms employed, the interview with Sir Frank Roberts initiated a new phase of Soviet policy in which the direct or veiled threat of Soviet nuclear attack on one or another member of the Western alliance was used as a means of intimidation.

Foreshadowings of a shift in the Soviet budget

In his speeches of June 21 and 28 Khrushchev had hinted at forthcoming measures to strengthen the Soviet armed forces. An article in *Pravda*, on July 2, defending the Soviet space program against critics of its high cost provided evidence of high-level debates on budget priorities at just this point. The immediate subject with which the article dealt was one of the components of the Soviet space ship, its jet nozzle, and the contention of the author, Vladimir Orlov, was that this device offered the prospect of finding important application in the field of the conducting of electricity through plasma. Ostensibly directing his remarks to unnamed foreign critics of the Soviet space program, Orlov vigorously defended it as a vital contribution to the Soviet economy:

> How we would like to bring these foreign supporters of the "unpracticality" and "unprofitableness" of space research into this laboratory! They would

[27]*SIA, 1961*, p. 237.
[28]Joseph Alsop, *Washington Post*, July 12, 1961, p. A–17; *NYT*, July 14, 1961, p. 6.
[29]*Washington Post*, July 12, 1961.

be visually convinced that today the jet nozzle is becoming a part of modern technology not only as an important part of the rocket engine but also as an element with a much broader, more universal significance than were the wheel or propeller in the history of technology; that space science is pointing out ways to construct terrestrial machines; and that the whole complex of scientific and technological research in space is a very important link to which the Soviet government and Communist Party are raising to an unprecedented height all the other links in this great chain of technical progress and all sections of the material base to improve the life and well-being of the workers.[30]

A sign that announcement of a major Soviet decision was impending was a mysterious appearance by Georgi Kornienko, counselor of the Soviet embassy in Washington, who visited Arthur Schlesinger, Jr., on July 5. The discussion centered around Berlin, with Kornienko expressing himself as

... puzzled by the American attitude toward Berlin, much as he had expressed puzzlement about our policy toward Cuba two months before. This led to a long and fruitless discussion of juridical and political issues. Finally he said, "The real trouble is that you don't believe that we are sincere when we say that we honestly wish to keep things as they are in West Berlin within the new context." I [Schlesinger] said that I feared that this was true, that experience had made us wary, and that the so-called guarantees which Russia offered guaranteed nothing. To this he replied, "Well, if you do not consider these guarantees adequate, why don't you propose your own guarantees? All we want to do is to have a chance to discuss these things."[31]

Comparison of several episodes in which Kornienko was involved provides the basis for resolving this minor enigma in Soviet–U.S. relations. The evidence provided by Schlesinger indicates that this relatively low-level diplomatic official was used at times by Khrushchev for informal probes of U.S. intentions as a kind of last-minute check before taking a major policy step—in April, the unveiling of Soviet plans for Berlin in the Walter Lippmann interview, in July the announcement of an increase in the Soviet military budget. Cautious as always on the eve of major policy moves, and perhaps hoping that by direct person-to-person contact he might be able to avoid taking an irrevocable and risky step, Khrushchev used Kornienko (as he was later to use other Soviet officials) as a personal though unacknowledged emissary to ascertain American intentions, as a kind of last-minute insurance against unpleasant surprises, and possibly even—if his luck was running—as a means to open the way to a quick-fix settlement of contentious issues.

Schlesinger, however, could make nothing of the visit and evidently did not attempt either to follow it up or to report it to the President. Its chief effect was to stimulate him to prepare, in collaboration with several like-minded

[30]*Pravda*, July 2, 1961.
[31]Schlesinger, p. 385.

administration officials, a memorandum for the President criticizing the Acheson report on Berlin for "shaping policy along restrictive and potentially dangerous lines."[32] The paper evidently helped shift the debate in Washington away from the stark alternatives outlined in the Acheson report and the military contingency plans onto a broader basis.[33] To this extent, then (though it must be remembered that Kennedy's mind was already moving in the same direction), the Kornienko mission, while it failed in its primary purpose, did help to modify U.S. policy in the Berlin crisis and thus to strengthen the possibility for its peaceful resolution.

The Soviet note on disarmament of July 5

During the evening of July 4, Khrushchev, together with other Soviet leaders, put in an unexpected appearance at the U.S. embassy's reception for Independence Day—the first time in three years that he had done so. He was in a jovial mood, playing with Ambassador Thompson's seven-year-old daughter and staying to the end of the ninety-minute reception.[34] Any hopes that a thaw in U.S.–Soviet relations had set in, however, were dashed on the following day when Soviet Foreign Minister Gromyko gave Ambassador Thompson the Soviet reply to the U.S. note on disarmament of June 17.

The Soviet note was an effective, though highly slanted document, portraying Soviet policy as one of sincere and persistent striving for genuine disarmament and taking skillful advantage of openings provided by the American note. Seizing on the passage in the June 17 note concerning pressure on the United States to resume nuclear weapons testing, the Soviet note charged that the United States had in reality already decided to break the test moratorium and was therefore stalling at the Geneva talks:

> . . . the American note gives the impression that the U.S. government is now concerned with only one thing: how to justify before public opinion the planned renewal of nuclear weapons tests in the U.S.A. and to find an excuse for burning the bridges leading to an agreement on the banning of such tests. After all, the American press does not conceal the fact that the U.S. Defense Department—the Pentagon—and the American Atomic Energy Commission are just waiting for the signal to resume nuclear tests.[35]

To justify the Soviet stand, the note then offered a brief résumé of the history of the test ban negotiations since 1958, dwelling with particular satisfaction on the shift in U.S. policy after the 1958 conference of experts. As to the three-year moratorium on underground tests proposed by the United States, the Soviet note saw in it only a pretext for espionage.

---

[32]Ibid., p. 386.

[33]Ibid., pp. 387–88.

[34]*NYT*, July 5, 1961, p. 1 (UPI dispatch from Moscow), reported, "He appeared to enjoy every minute of it."

[35]*Izv.*, July 7, 1961; *CDSP*, XIII/27, p. 7.

A lengthy passage in the note attacked the Western powers for their refusal to accept the Soviet proposal for a three-man head for the control body, acceptance of which was portrayed as an indispensable step to progress in the disarmament negotiations.

In an unusually bitter passage the demand for a *troika* was linked directly with current events in the strife-torn Congo, where U.N. Secretary-General Dag Hammarskjöld was trying to carry out policies which had earned him the unrelenting hostility of the Soviets. "The tragedy of the Congo," the note said,

> . . . clearly showed the world how dangerous it is to entrust to one person the task of fulfilling important decisions. Only the politically blind could fail to see that it was precisely Hammarskjöld, who says he is a neutral man, who helped the colonialists and is still helping them to commit monstrous crimes on Congolese soil. It is none other than Hammarskjöld who, to please the colonialists, turned inside out the Security Council's decisions aimed at defending the Congo's national independence. The colonialists are using Hammarskjöld and the U.N. officials he sponsors to stifle the liberation forces in the Congo and to finish off the Congolese patriots. Can one call Hammarskjöld's behavior in the Congo neutral when he jeers at elementary justice and protects the murderers of Patrice Lumumba, that ardent fighter for the independence of the Congo?
>
> No, Hammarskjöld is not neutral in the matter of the Congo or in any other international affairs, although he is a representative of neutral Sweden. In fact, he has been and remains a person who carries out the policies of a single group of states, namely the capitalist states. And after all this, the U.S. government is trying to impose a person like Hammarskjöld as the single administrator of an agency called upon to exercise control over the cessation of nuclear weapons tests.[36]

The continuing nuclear tests by France provided a convenient basis for another attack on the U.S. position:

> In its note the U.S. government says that for the past three years the U.S.A. has been taking the "risk" of abstaining from nuclear weapons tests while there is no international agreement on the matter, and that it cannot take this "risk" forever.
>
> If the question is put in these terms, it must be said that the risk is being borne by the Soviet Union and not the U.S.A. It is well known, after all, that during the time the Soviet Union has been abstaining from experimental explosions of nuclear weapons, an ally of the United States in the NATO bloc—France—has been testing nuclear weapons and is thus in a position to improve these weapons in the interests of the United States of America as well as its ally in this bloc.[37]

Perhaps the most effective passage in the July 5 note, from a propaganda point of view, was one which took up the challenge in the U.S. note of June 17 on the nature of Soviet society:

[36]*CDSP*, XIII/27, p. 7.
[37]Ibid., pp. 8–9.

It is a matter of regret that the U.S. government deems it appropriate in its note to enter on the slippery course of attacks on the social system of the Soviet Union. What is this, a manifestation of hostility toward communism or an attempt to draw attention away from the weakness of the U.S.A.'s stand on disarmament questions?

The Soviet government has no intention at this point of entering into a discussion with the U.S. government about which society, the socialist or the capitalist, is "open" and which is "closed." The government of the U.S.S.R. thinks that if in the course of considering disarmament, the banning of nuclear tests, or in general any problem of relations between states, free rein were to be given to each side's feelings about the other side's social system, it would have to be admitted that any basis for agreement would be eliminated from the outset. The Soviet government has always held to this point of view and considers it the only correct one. However, since the U.S. government has brought up this question, we would like to say with all possible emphasis that Soviet society is indeed firmly and reliably closed to the activities of exploiters or oppressors of any kind who feed off the blood and sweat of the people; it is closed to those who are enemies of the social and state system of the U.S.S.R. But it gives limitless scope for the satisfaction of the needs and desires of the working people, who enjoy full power in the Soviet Union and have complete dominion over the fruits of their labor.

And for whom is American society open? It is open only for the exploiters, for the handful of monopolies that have placed the entire power of the state at the service of their narrow interests. It ill befits a country with a system based on the cruel exploitation of man by man to give lessons in democracy to the Soviet people. If there is truth in the statements American leaders are fond of repeating to the effect that in the U.S. all secrets are common knowledge, that the people are informed about every step the government and other official institutions take, how would the U.S. government reply to the following questions:

Did the American people, or even so highly placed an agency as the U.S. Congress, know about the provocational flights by American U–2 aircraft over the U.S.S.R.? Apparently they did not know until these flights were exposed and the guilty parties were caught red-handed.

Was it with the approval of the American people that atomic bombs were dropped on Hiroshima and Nagasaki? No, the American people knew nothing about the preparations for this inhuman act, and as far as is known they condemn it.

Finally, were the American people consulted about the recent aggression against Cuba that was prepared and organized on U.S. territory with U.S. support? No, it was kept a deep secret from the American people.[38]

The disputed question of the number of on-site inspections was alluded to briefly, with the usual Soviet charge that the figure on which the Western powers insisted was merely a cloak for espionage.

[38]Ibid., p. 9.

In conclusion the Soviet note made a bold bid to appropriate one of the stock Western positions, the insistence on verified controls during the actual process of disarmament: ". . . the Soviet government states that it will never agree to any disarmament measures without effective control over the implementation of these measures. The Soviet government will not enter upon a disarmament program without control because bitter experience has taught it not to rely on the word of its Western partners in agreements."[39]

As to what kind of control measures it envisioned, however, the Soviet note was silent. Like the U.S. note to which it was a reply, it represented a sharp escalation in propaganda bitterness, without any substantive progress toward agreement. Its confident prediction that the United States was moving full-speed ahead to the resumption of nuclear testing was perhaps its most significant contribution to the growing international tension.

In what looked like a deliberate move in the war of nerves, Radio Moscow on the same day (July 5) announced the demolition of a mountain in the Caucasus by a "powerful peaceful explosion," without indicating, however, whether the blast was a nuclear or conventional explosion.[40]

The Soviet military chiefs confer

It could be expected that on the eve of a major policy announcement concerning the armed forces, Khrushchev would feel the need to consult with his senior military advisers. It is therefore not surprising to find indirect evidence that just such a consultation took place in Moscow on July 4–6.

On the morning of July 4, Soviet Defense Minister R. Ya. Malinovsky, who had returned to Moscow the preceding day from a ten-day visit to Finland, took his place on the presidium of an all-army conference of Komsomol workers in the Kremlin. With him on the platform were most of the armed service chiefs: Marshal M. V. Zakharov, chief of the General Staff; Marshal A. I. Yeremenko, Malinovsky's deputy in the Defense Ministry; Marshal K. S. Moskalenko, head of the Soviet rocket forces; Marshal V. I. Chuikov, chief of ground forces and newly appointed head of Soviet civil defense; Marshal K. A. Vershinin, head of the Soviet air force; and two senior advisers to the Department of Defense, Marshal K. K. Rokossovsky and Marshal S. M. Budënny. The conference presidium also included two leading officials of the army-political apparatus: Marshal F. I. Golikov, head of the Main Political Administration (the branch of the Party Central Committee charged with supervision of the political loyalty of the armed forces), and Major General N. R. Mironov, head of the Department of Administrative Organs of the

[39]Ibid., p. 22.

[40]*NYT*, July 6, 1961 (Reuters dispatch from London). For a statement by the U.S. Atomic Energy Commission disclaiming knowledge of the blast, see *NYT*, July 7, 1961, p. 2.

party Central Committee (which supervises, among other things, the state security police).[41]

Following the opening session the Komsomol conference carried on its business without the assistance of the service chiefs, until its final session on the evening of July 6, when Malinovsky returned to deliver an important address. It is highly probable that the service chiefs spent part of the intervening period of July 4–6 conferring together, as a group and with Khrushchev, working out the final details of the military reorganization which he was preparing to announce.[42]

Malinovsky addresses the Komsomol conference, July 6

While details of the service chiefs' conference must remain a matter of speculation, their most important conclusions were promptly made known in the form of two speeches, one by Malinovsky, the other by Khrushchev. Malinovsky's speech to the closing session of the Komsomol conference was deliberately shaped as the counterpart to Khrushchev's military speech of June 21.[43] Khrushchev had identified himself with the armed forces and had promised them significant concessions; in return Malinovsky associated the armed forces with Khrushchev's economic policies and lavished praise on Khrushchev personally. Malinovsky's speech was therefore a composite product in which pro-Khrushchev passages were incongruously grafted on to the main subject—an exposition of current Soviet military doctrine.

At the outset Malinovsky espoused Khrushchev's line on economic competition with the United States: "In just a few years the Soviet Union will become the first industrial country in the world, which approximately in 1970 will surpass the most developed capitalist countries in industrial production per capita."[44] He went on to laud the January 1961 plenum of the party Central Committee for its directives on economic policy, singling out for special attention Khrushchev's speeches at the plenum and at the zonal agricultural meetings which followed it.

Having paid tribute to the party leader and his policies, Malinovsky turned to the more familiar and congenial field of military policy. His major point here was the greatly increased weight of the rocket troops in the overall balance of the Soviet armed forces: "Notwithstanding significant reductions, the defensive strength of our Motherland has been in no way weakened. The party and government have adopted all necessary measures to ensure that the combat strength and fire power of our Armed Forces should increase. The

[41] *Krasnaia Zvezda*, July 5, 1961, p. 1.

[42] *SIA, 1961*, p. 337, states that shortly after Khrushchev's interview with Sir Frank Roberts on July 2, Khrushchev "convened a meeting of his senior military advisers . . ." (no source cited).

[43] Text of Malinovsky's speech in *Krasnaia Zvezda*, July 8, 1961, pp. 1–2.

[44] Ibid., p. 1.

basic condition for this has been the creation of the rocket troops, equipped with the most effective weapons for carrying out the main tasks in contemporary warfare."[45]

Not merely had a separate branch of the services been established for the rocket troops; rocket weapons were being incorporated in units throughout the armed forces, and training and tactics were being modified to correspond.

> The most important fact is that all branches of the armed forces are being converted to rocket equipment. Thus the rocket units and formations are becoming the basic fighting strength of all branches of the armed forces. In this connection a number of new tasks confront us. Under modern conditions we must learn to wage war in a new way. If the imperialists unleash a war, there will be no unbroken front lines. We shall have to act boldly and decisively, often without sensing any support from neighboring units, advancing towards our target with exceptional speed, always remembering that in modern battles the victory will often be won by small but bold detachments. Therefore all tactical training, all exercises, must be approached on the basis of the new demands by all, from small sub-units to large units.[46]

Since the forthcoming struggle over Berlin would be first of all a test of nerves on both sides, Malinovsky devoted part of his speech to contrasting the combat morale of the Soviet and the Western soldier, and in his peroration he ladled out generous helpings of praise for Khrushchev, while still managing to stress the role of the rocket forces.

Khrushchev's speech to the military graduates, July 8

The climax of the first phase of Soviet strategy in the Berlin crisis of 1961 was the announcement by Khrushchev on July 8 of a one-third increase in the budget of the Soviet armed forces. The announcement came in the course of a speech which he delivered at a reception honoring graduates of the military academies of the Soviet armed forces. It was embedded in a text which rather awkwardly combined a review and restatement of Soviet policy in Germany with the favorite Khrushchevian theme of economic competition between the Soviet Union and the United States.

After a preamble congratulating the military cadets and praising the role of the armed forces in defending the Soviet Union, Khrushchev touched briefly on the new draft Party Program which had been approved by the June 19 Central Committee plenum. The standard Soviet position on disarmament was next outlined in a few brief paragraphs, leading to a restatement of the claim that East and West were now approximately equal in power: "Today it is acknowledged in the West that the forces of the Soviet Union and other so-

---

[45]Ibid.

[46]Ibid. For a partial translation of this passage of Malinovsky's speech, see *NYT*, July 15, 1961, p. 2.

cialist countries are not inferior to the forces of the Western powers. However, the proper conclusions are not drawn from this fact: given equal forces, there must also be equal rights and equal opportunities. Yet our partners, acknowledging that the balance of power has not tilted in their favor, nevertheless want to dominate in international agencies and impose their will there."[47]

Indulging in a little deliberate obfuscation, Khrushchev briefly revived the moribund Polish (Rapacki) proposal for a nuclear-free zone in Central Europe, only to return at once to the larger theme of disarmament.

Thus far Khrushchev had said nothing of substance; the opening sections of his speech had been mere props, designed to provide a sense of anticipation and build-up for the real subjects. Getting down to business, Khrushchev next restated at considerable length Soviet policy with regard to a German peace treaty and the future of Berlin. The emphasis, as usual, was on the reasonableness of the Soviet position.

Contrasted with Soviet reasonableness, Khrushchev maintained, were the bellicose statements of Western leaders such as General de Gaulle, Macmillan, and Adenauer. The latter was the object of special attention:

> Replying to our proposals for the conclusion of a peace treaty, proposals which, it would seem, are perfectly natural, the West begins to count divisions. And Chancellor Adenauer is shouting himself hoarse for nuclear weapons. What does Adenauer need nuclear weapons for? Twice German militarism has engineered world wars. Now, when the wounds of the Second World War are still being felt, he calls for nuclear weapons. The Bundeswehr [West German army] needs them not for peace but for unleashing a third world war.[48]

As always, it was when he came to defining the proposed future status of West Berlin that Khrushchev revealed most clearly the real significance of the Soviet proposals:

> West Berlin is an island inside the German Democratic Republic, an island where the capitalist order has been preserved. We do not want to intervene in the domestic affairs of the city's population or do anything to affect the prestige of the United States, the United Kingdom and France.
>
> Is it possible to find a solution such as would satisfy all countries that fought against Germany and would not disturb the established way of life in West Berlin? Yes, it is possible, and we propose such a solution—to grant West Berlin the status of a free city, to give it a guarantee, either by the four great powers—the United States, the United Kingdom, France, and the Soviet Union—or by neutral countries, or by the United Nations Organization.

---

[47]*DIA, 1961*, p. 308; complete text, pp. 307–19, citing *Soviet News* (London), July 10, 1961. Russian text in *Pravda*, July 10, 1961, and Khrushchev, *Kommunizm*, 1:257–76.

[48]*DIA, 1961*, p. 310.

If the Western powers have a better version of guarantees, let them propose it.*

However, it is only natural that any West Berlin solution must take into consideration that the city lies in the center of a sovereign state and that all communications of West Berlin with the outside world pass across the territory of that state. It is accepted in international relations that access to one country or other across the territory of another state has always required appropriate agreements with the authorities of that state.[49]

Khrushchev was firm with regard to the question of access rights to Berlin after signature of a Soviet–GDR peace treaty: "After the conclusion of the treaty, the Soviet Union will lay down all the obligations it has hitherto discharged on the communications lanes with West Berlin. In short, the government of the German Democratic Republic will enjoy full sovereignty over all its territory, just like any other independent state."[50]

The refusal of the Western powers to accept the Soviet proposals and their threats to use force to defend the status quo, Khrushchev maintained, were nothing but an attempt to repeat Hitler's war of aggression against the Soviet Union:

Remember how Hitler pushed the world to the brink of war and then unleashed war. He advanced gradually, step by step, methodically towards this goal; he extorted concessions from the western powers. He was encouraged by the ruling circles of Britain, France and America. They believed that with the help of fascism they would be able to defeat the Soviet Union, to destroy communism. . . .

Evidently the frantic monopolists and the West German revenge-seekers would not be averse to embarking once again on this road with a view to settling disputed questions through war. The monopolists regard the question of communism, its development, as the main issue. Their reason is obscured by hatred of communism, of the countries of socialism. They may lose all self-control and the imperialists may unleash a new war. Adenauer is repeating what Hitler did in his day when preparing for war. And actually the same countries that encouraged Hitler are now encouraging Adenauer.[51]

Having carefully fostered the seeds of distrust of West Germany among her allies, Khrushchev now turned to drawing a contrast between the situation in 1941 and that twenty years later:

The situation has changed radically since then. In those days the Soviet Union and People's Mongolia were in the midst of capitalist encirclement.

*Note the similarity to Kornienko's statement to Schlesinger (above, p. 45).

[49]Ibid., pp. 310–11.
[50]Ibid., pp. 313–14.
[51]Ibid., p. 314.

Now the mighty socialist camp, a camp which unites over one billion people, is growing and becoming stronger. The colonial system is collapsing and ever more new and independent states are emerging and embarking upon the road of a peaceful policy.

Today it is not the forces of imperialism but the forces of peace and socialism that determine the main laws, the main direction of international and social development.[52]

Khrushchev concluded this section of his speech with a categorical commitment to sign a German peace treaty, regardless of possible Western countermeasures (though without specifying any definite time period): "We shall sign the peace treaty and order our armed forces to administer a worthy rebuff to any aggressor if he dares to raise a hand against the Soviet Union or against our friends."[53]

Khrushchev was now ready to tackle the central theme of his speech. He had maintained that the Soviets and their allies were equal in power to the Western alliance and that they would "administer a worthy rebuff" to any attempt to block their announced policy in Germany. "The Soviet armed forces today," he assured his listeners, "have everything necessary in order to carry out successfully the responsible tasks set before them. They possess the necessary quantities of thermonuclear weapons and the most efficient means of delivering them—close combat, intermediate and intercontinental missiles."[54]

His emphasis was on the certain doom of the capitalist system if war broke out: "It is best for those who are thinking of war not to imagine that distances will save them. No, if the imperialists unleash a war, it will end with imperialism's complete collapse and ruin. Mankind will end, once and for all, the system which gives rise to wars."[55]

All of this was obviously intended to cushion the shock of the disclosure that Soviet military power, far from being equal to that of the West, was in imminent danger of being decisively outstripped. "The government of the Soviet Union," Khrushchev continued,

> is attentively following the military measures taken recently by the United States of America and its NATO allies. We cannot ignore such facts as the building up of armed forces in the western countries, the steps to increase considerably the number of strategic nuclear bombers, which are constantly kept in the air. The forces of Western Germany are being equipped with the latest weapons and increased numerically.
>
> The United States President, Mr. Kennedy, has proclaimed in his recent messages to Congress a so-called "new course." It provides for stepping up the program of developing rocket-missile strategic weapons and an increase

[52]Ibid.
[53]Ibid., p. 315.
[54]Ibid.
[55]Ibid.

in the military preparedness of all services. For this purpose President Kennedy has proposed that military allocations be increased as compared with the draft budget submitted by the previous President by more than three and a half billion dollars. This means that the military expenditures in the fiscal year of 1961–62 will exceed 53 billion dollars. The military expenditures in the Federal Republic of Germany have increased by 18 per cent this year. A considerable growth of military expenditures is characteristic of Britain, France, and other NATO countries. This is how the Western powers are replying to the Soviet Union's unilateral reduction of armed forces and military expenditures carried out over several past years.[56]

We have seen how Marshal Malinovsky, in his speech to the Komsomol conference on July 6, dealt with the problem of staking a claim for the unimpaired or even increased fire power and overall strength of the Soviet armed forces in the face of reorganization and numerical cuts. Khrushchev, in his July 8 speech, took a different line. "Would it be correct for us in these conditions," he asked rhetorically, "to continue to reduce our armed forces unilaterally?", and immediately supplied the answer: "Taking into account the existing situation, the Soviet government has been compelled to instruct the Ministry of Defense to suspend temporarily, pending special orders, the reduction of armed forces planned for 1961. In view of the growing military budgets in the NATO countries, the Soviet government has taken a decision to increase defense expenditures in the current year by 3,144 million rubles, thereby raising the total military expenditures in 1961 to 12,399 million rubles."[57]

Betraying a certain embarrassment, Khrushchev immediately added, "These are forced measures, comrades. We are taking them owing to the emerging circumstances, because we cannot neglect the interests of the Soviet people's security."[58]

This was the closest Khrushchev had yet come, in a public utterance during the Berlin crisis, to a frank admission that Soviet policy in Germany involved a risk to the peace and security of the Soviet people themselves. The announcement of a one-third increase in the Soviet military budget constituted both a public confession of the price Soviet policy in Germany would exact from the Soviet people and a raising of the stakes in the international game being waged over the future of Germany and Berlin.

With the hardest and most awkward part of his task behind him, Khrushchev turned with an unmistakable sense of relief to the more congenial topic of peaceful economic competition between the Soviet Union and the United States. Picking up the statement on this theme in the President's news conference of June 28, Khrushchev said: "We appreciate such an approach. This, of course, is much better than competing in the development of ever

[56]Ibid., pp. 315–16.
[57]Ibid., p. 316.
[58]Ibid.

more destructive types of weapons. We have always said this and we go on repeating it."[59]

Citing statistics on growth rates in the two countries, Khrushchev elaborated on his earlier predictions:

> I shall not enter into polemics with Mr. Kennedy. Simple calculations will be sufficient. The volume of the Soviet Union's industrial production was equal to 60 per cent of American output in 1960. The average annual rates of industrial growth in our country have amounted to 10.6 per cent during the past 16 years. If Soviet industrial output continues to grow annually by 10 per cent, in 1966 the Soviet Union will be producing 106 per cent of the present American output and in 1970 it will be producing 156 per cent.
>
> In order to increase by 56 per cent in 10 years, United States industrial output must increase by 4½ per cent annually. However, even if the Americans succeed in ensuring an annual increment of 4½ percent, as Mr. Kennedy would like it to be, we shall overtake them just the same in 1970. If the Americans retain the rate of their industrial output at 2 per cent, which they have averaged in the postwar years, the Soviet Union will outstrip America already in 1967. If American industrial output increases by 3 per cent annually, we shall leave them behind in 1968. Approximately the same figures could be adduced with regard to the prospects of agricultural development in our two countries.[60]

The underlying basis for his confidence in Soviet success, Khrushchev asserted, was the inherent superiority of socialism over capitalism: "Under the capitalist system economic development depends very little on the President. Every capitalist disposes of his capital himself and throws workers out into the street if that benefits him. . . . Such are the laws of capitalism— draconic laws, but laws which still operate. The socialist system, of course, does not and cannot have all this."[61]

Good relations with the United States, Khrushchev maintained, were being impeded by U.S. restrictions on trade with the Soviet Union. Not that the Soviets needed U.S. goods: "I should like to be understood correctly. We stand for the development of trade with the United States of America, but not because we cannot do without it. The Soviet Union will not only keep going, but will continue its rapid advance, fulfilling and overfulfilling the economic plans that are drafted."[62] But increased Soviet–U.S. trade would be a valuable contribution to a general improvement in international relations:

> . . . is it possible to speak seriously about the improvement of relations and the creation of an atmosphere of confidence between the two strongest powers in the world if one of them is pursuing a policy of economic discrimination in relation to the other? Of course not. If the United States had displayed good common sense and given up the policy of artificially re-

[59]Ibid.
[60]Ibid., p. 317.
[61]Ibid.
[62]Ibid., p. 318

stricting trade relations with the Soviet Union, that would have promoted the improvement of friendly relations, an improvement in the international climate.[63]

All of this, of course, was strikingly out of key in a speech the primary purpose of which was to raise the Soviet military stakes in the tense struggle over Berlin. Perhaps in no other single document were the underlying incompatibility and irreconcilability between Khrushchev's conflicting policy aspirations more nakedly set forth than here. As though in recognition of this discrepancy, Khrushchev brought this portion of his speech to a close with a rather lame attempt to combine its two major themes—increased military spending and peaceful economic competition—into a single vision of the future à la Khrushchev:

> Soviet policy is a policy of peaceful coexistence. That is why we tell President Kennedy, General de Gaulle, Mr. Macmillan: Let us compete in this sphere. This would be sensible. If we were to conclude a peace treaty with Germany, shake hands and declare that we would devote our efforts to economic competition, all the people of the world would heave a sigh of relief. This would be a good prologue for further talks and for the realization of mankind's age-old dream of lasting peace on earth. We are ready for this and we offer our hand to the Western governments.[64]

With the sketching of this utopian dream, Khrushchev had concluded the substantive portion of his address to the military graduates. In its brief concluding passages he addressed them directly, exhorting them to be models of "political maturity and high morality," to master the technical side of their rapidly changing profession, and to maintain unbroken ties with the people and the party.

Significance of the increase in the military budget

As Sidney Ploss has shown, during the summer of 1961 Khrushchev and his supporters were engaged in a stubborn struggle with economic and political conservatives in the party and government over investment priorities. Khrushchev's goals, as set forth in the draft Party Program submitted to the Central Committee plenum on June 19, included a scaling down of the preponderant role of heavy industry in favor of consumers' goods and agriculture. "In the new period of the Soviet Union's development," the draft program stated, ". . . the growth and technological progress of heavy industry must ensure the expansion of consumer goods industries to meet ever more fully the requirements of the people."[65] On this basis the draft made the definite forecast

---

[63]Ibid.

[64]Ibid.

[65]Sidney I. Ploss, *Conflict and Decision-making in Soviet Russia: A Case Study of Agricultural Policy 1953–1963* (Princeton: Princeton University Press, 1965), p. 229 (hereinafter cited as Ploss), citing supplement to *Moscow News*, Aug. 5, 1961.

that by 1971: "The demand of all sections of the population for high-quality consumer goods—attractive clothes, footwear, and goods improving and adorning the daily life of the Soviet people, such as comfortable modern furniture, up-to-date domestic goods, a wide range of goods for cultural purposes, etc.—will be amply satisfied."[66]

Closely linked with the internal economic targets set forth in the draft program was the goal of overtaking the United States in industrial output by 1970, which we have seen Khrushchev expounding in his Alma Ata speeches of June 24 and 25 and in his July 8 speech to military graduates.

What effect would the increase in the military budget have on these aspirations? As we have seen, Khrushchev himself, in his July 8 speech, appeared to feel no apprehension that the Soviet Union's rate of economic growth would be slowed down as a result of the increase in the arms budget, and he emphasized the "forced" and—by implication—temporary nature of the military increase.[67]

In the Soviet press discussion of the draft program, which followed its publication on July 30, 1961, supporters of the Khrushchev line continued to predict an unbroken tempo of advance toward the goals it set forth, even though the draft itself, as Ploss has pointed out, contained an escape clause "which made the achievement of welfare goals contingent on a more or less stable world atmosphere."[68]

This apparent confidence in Soviet economic prospects, even in the face of increased military expenditures, would be understandable if the budget shift was less impressive than it appeared to be. Doubt has been expressed by some analysts as to the reality of the budgetary increases announced by Khrushchev. According to Abraham S. Becker, a senior economist with the RAND Corporation: "A suspicion has been expressed . . . that much, if not all, of this 45 per cent increase in the level of 'defense' expenditure, comparing the 1962 plan with the original 1961 plan, represents reclassification of military outlays formerly concealed in the residuals discussed above. The motivation for such a reclassification was, presumably, political—a response to the increase in the U.S. military budget."[69]

In contrast, another leading analyst of the Soviet economy, Abram Bergson, concluded that the actual increase in the Soviet military budget might be considerably larger than the announced figures would indicate: "By implication, the projected increase in the Soviet defense budget might amount not to

[66]Ibid.

[67]Carl A. Linden, *Khrushchev and the Soviet Leadership 1957–1964* (Baltimore: The Johns Hopkins Press, 1966), p. 115 (hereinafter cited as Linden). The same point is made by Matthew P. Gallagher, "Military Manpower: A Case Study," *Problems of Communism*, vol. 13, no. 3 (May–June 1964): 56.

[68]Ploss, p. 231.

[69]Abraham S. Becker, "Soviet Military Outlays Since 1955" (Santa Monica, RAND Corporation, 1964), p. 50.

$3.5 billion [the equivalent at the standard exchange rate of the increase announced by Khrushchev], but possibly to about $8 billion."[70]

In an analysis of Soviet military expenditures in relation to disarmament policy carried out at the Massachusetts Institute of Technology, a study group concluded that the military budget rise announced by Khrushchev on July 8 represented a genuine increase in outlays, but that it probably did not directly cause a slowdown in *overall* Soviet economic growth.[71] The MIT team did not, however, attempt to differentiate between the impact of the arms build-up on the heavy industry sector and on those branches of the economy—consumers' goods and agriculture—favored by Khrushchev, beyond the general observation that "the burden of defense spending was impeding Soviet advance in what Khrushchev designated in 1959 as the main arena of East–West competition: economic growth."[72]

Two other RAND Corporation analysts, Arnold L. Horelick and Myron Rush, accepted the increase in Soviet arms spending as genuine, but concluded that its primary purpose was to increase the pressure on Berlin: "Since such an increase could not be spent on a rational program within that year, a major purpose of the announcement must have been to demonstrate the seriousness of Soviet intentions in regard to Berlin."[73]

There is evidence from several areas, however, to indicate that the increased weight of armament spending had an adverse effect on other sectors of the Soviet economy in 1961. One example among several is the rate of Soviet economic aid to developing nations. According to Marshall I. Goldman, Soviet foreign aid commitments in 1961 dropped from the 1960 level of over $1 billion to about $300 million, while "no new aid agreements have been signed since November 1961, despite some golden opportunities."[74]

In a comprehensive study of the Soviet economy prepared by a group of scholars for the Joint Economic Committee of the U.S. Congress, Martin J. Kohn reached the conclusion that "industrial investment was sharply cut back" in 1961, and linked this evidence directly with the Soviet military build-up: "The comprehensive nature of the cutbacks gives added weight to the evidence that economic plans were revamped in 1961 to step up current production for immediate defense needs at expense of other goals."[75]

---

[70]Abram Bergson, "Letter to the Editor," *NYT*, July 25, 1961, p. 26.

[71]Lincoln P. Bloomfield, Walter C. Clemens, and Franklyn Griffiths, *Khrushchev and the Arms Race: Soviet Interest in Arms Control and Disarmament 1954–1964* (Cambridge, Mass.: M.I.T. Press, 1966), pp. 109–13.

[72]Ibid., p. 107.

[73]Horelick and Rush, p. 124.

[74]Marshall I. Goldman, "Letter to the Editor," *NYT*, June 9, 1962, p. 24.

[75]U.S. Congress, Joint Economic Committee, 87th Congress, 2nd session, *Dimensions of Soviet Economic Power* (Washington, D.C.: G.P.O., 1962), p. 231. It should be noted that the burden of Soviet spending for armaments in 1961 was substantially increased by actions announced at the end of August of that year. See Chapter VII, below.

Light on the motivations and implications of Khrushchev's July 8 announcement can be obtained by comparing his speech with that of Marshal Malinovsky two days earlier. Malinovsky, as we have seen, said nothing about increased allocations to the military, but asserted instead that the armed forces were successfully maintaining their overall combat strength within a *reduced* budget. Since the decision to increase the military share of the budget must already have been taken at the time Malinovsky spoke, it follows that he was deliberately leaving public announcement of this dramatic step for Khrushchev. Thus the decision to increase the military budget was *directly* related to the Berlin campaign and, in a larger sense, to Khrushchev's efforts to achieve a diplomatic victory over the West. His evident reluctance to dwell on the budget announcement, however, and his unrealistic forecast immediately thereafter of unchecked Soviet economic growth show that the decision was an uncongenial one for him. The strong implication is that it was forced on him at his meeting with the service chiefs, between July 4 and 6, as the price of their support for Soviet policy in the Berlin crisis.

On the basis of this analysis we can hazard a tentative reconstruction of the process of policy formulation in the period between Khrushchev's military speech of June 21 and his budget announcement on July 8. In the June 21 speech Khrushchev made certain conciliatory gestures to the military and implied that further concessions would be forthcoming. In the spirit of release and euphoria which characterized his expedition to Alma Ata a few days later he indulged in the luxury of golden dreams of future abundance surpassing that of the United States. Back in Moscow, Khrushchev reacted to the growing evidence of Western military preparations for a showdown over Berlin by the bluster and threats of his stormy interview with Sir Frank Roberts on July 2. Then came the conference with the service chiefs, at which the bill for this policy was presented. Khrushchev the political leader could threaten the British Ambassador with the spectre of one hundred Soviet divisions for every one the West could put into Germany, but it was the service chiefs who would inform him of the specific cost this kind of action would entail. Real and substantial raises in the appropriations for the armed forces, not empty gestures and threatening words, were the price they exacted for going along with Khrushchev in his Berlin policy.

For a man of less unquenchable optimism than Khrushchev, the meeting with the service chiefs would have come as a sobering revelation of the price a foreign policy of bluster and intimidation would exact. On Khrushchev this experience had, at least temporarily, no visible effect: we have seen how his announcement of the "forced" increase in military appropriations was followed immediately by a detailed, circumstantial prediction of early Soviet victory in economic competition with the United States.

It would only be a matter of time, however, before the weight of the new military expenditures would make themselves felt in other sectors of the budget. The first casualty of the Soviet Union's Berlin strategy was, therefore, Khrushchev's own cherished economic program. For the Western alliance, however, and particularly for the U.S. leadership, the internal significance of the arms budget increase was of secondary importance; the immediate point which concerned them was that by this step the Soviets had sharply raised the stakes in the contest over Berlin.

Backing up Khrushchev's bid, July 9–16

During the week following Khrushchev's speech to the military graduates a number of Soviet spokesmen, including Khrushchev himself, did their best to maintain the heightened pace of the Soviet offensive on Berlin. The Soviet air force made a significant contribution with an impressive display of air power, including new types of fighters and bombers being shown publicly for the first time, at Tushino Airport near Moscow on July 9. The moral to be drawn from the show was spelled out by a Radio Moscow commentator: "The impressive and, I should say, majestic spectacle of the might of the Soviet Air Force acts as a sobering factor on even the most unruly heads, and is capable of penetrating the skulls of the diehards among the warmongers."[76]

Soviet Air Force Commander-in-Chief Marshal Vershinin, in an article in *Pravda* on the same day, devoted special attention to the role of rockets in the Soviet armed forces, and did not fail to offer his congratulations to Khrushchev, "the inspirer of the work on the mastery of space," for the high awards recently granted him in this connection. The increased importance of rockets, Marshal Vershinin said, had caused a shift in some of the tasks assigned to aviation, but its overall role "has remained large. . . . Therefore our party and government show concern for the development of rocket technology. Our Air Force is now equipped with supersonic and high-altitude planes of all types. Instead of guns, they are armed with 'air to air' rockets, and instead of bombs they have 'air-to-ground' rockets. The controls of planes and the methods for using them in combat have also undergone substantial changes on the basis of the newest technology."[77]

One of the reasons for Khrushchev's confidence in the worldwide victory of communism was his conviction, based ultimately on Lenin's analysis of imperialism, that the end of colonialism would greatly strengthen the forces of communism and fatally undermine the position of the Western powers. An official visit to the Soviet Union at this time by Dr. Kwame Nkrumah, chief of state of Ghana and one of the leading advocates of black nationalism in Africa, strengthened Khrushchev's conviction and provided an opportunity to expound his views on the place of the anti-imperialist movement in the world balance.

At a luncheon in the Kremlin honoring Dr. Nkrumah, on July 11, Khrushchev postulated a virtual identity of interests between the Soviet Union and the peoples of the former colonies emerging into independence. The conse-

[76]Radio Moscow, July 9, 1961.
[77]*Pravda*, July 9, 1961; *CDSP*, XIII/27, p. 32.

quences of this tacit alliance, he predicted, must necessarily be a fundamental shift in the world balance of power which would find expression in major changes in the structure of the United Nations. Citing the "tragedy in the Congo" as a "stern verdict on the U.N.," Khrushchev issued a virtual defiance of the United Nations as presently constituted:

> The imperialist powers wish to prolong their dominance of the United Nations Organization. But it is completely clear that the dominance of any group of states in an international organization deprives it of the possibility of fulfilling its functions. For example, *even if all the nations of the world took a decision which did not correspond to the interests of the Soviet Union, which endangered its security, the Soviet Union would not recognize such a decision and would defend its rights, based on force.* And we have what is needed for this.[78]

Khrushchev complained that "during the entire existence of the United Nations" the "imperialist" powers had never once had the idea of allowing a communist, a member of the socialist states, to hold the post of general secretary. The Soviet Union has no wish to dominate the United Nations, Khrushchev said, but it demanded equality; for this, ". . . We consider that in the first place it is necessary to create an executive organ of the U.N. composed of three persons, representing the three basic groups of nations which exist in the contemporary world."[79]

Thus, just as the Soviet campaign on Berlin was entering its major phase, Khrushchev reiterated the Soviet position on the restructuring of the United Nations in the most uncompromising terms. He was not yet willing to moderate his demands on this point.

*   *   *

The speech honoring Nkrumah marked the temporary end of Khrushchev's presence in Moscow; for the remainder of the month of July he was on vacation in Sochi, awaiting the response of the West to his challenge on Berlin and devoting his attention to the more congenial task of drawing up plans for Soviet agriculture. On July 20 he sent the Presidium of the Central Committee a memorandum outlining "several urgent tasks in the field of agriculture," in which he proposed "significant increases in the production and procurement of grain" as well as other measures to improve farm output.[80]

Other Soviet spokesmen, however, continued the campaign of pressure. Frol R. Kozlov, in a speech on July 11 at a reception at the Mongolian embassy marking the fortieth anniversary of the establishment of the Mongolian People's Republic, hailed the ties of friendship between the Soviet and Mon-

[78]Khrushchev, *Kommunizm*, 1:279–80; emphasis supplied.
[79]Ibid., p. 280.
[80]Khrushchev, *Stroitel'stvo*, 5:418–41.

golian peoples and delivered a stern warning to the Western powers: "If . . . the aggressive imperialist forces, contrary to good sense, try to push the world into the gulf of a new war, they will receive a crushing rebuff, and, as Comrade N. S. Khrushchev has emphasized, no distance will save them."[81]

Foreign Minister Andrei Gromyko added to the tension on the following day with a calculated outburst of temper against West German Ambassador Hans Kroll, who had come to deliver the Federal Republic's long overdue answer to the Soviet note of February 17. According to Kroll's own account, Gromyko, after a quick glance through the German note, read to him a declaration on behalf of the Soviet government reiterating the fixed Soviet intention of signing a peace treaty with the GDR unless the Western powers accepted Soviet proposals for an all-German peace treaty and the conversion of West Berlin into a "free city."

As an ominous addition to the standard Soviet position, however, the declaration read by Gromyko included the following passage:

> After conclusion of the treaty all the rights of the Western powers stemming from the capitulation of Germany will be ended. *At appropriate points on the boundary between the G.D.R. and the Federal Republic, Soviet troops will be deployed and the Soviet Union will, if necessary, fulfill all its obligations with regard to the G.D.R.*
>
> In case the Western powers make an attempt to employ force, it will be answered with force. In other words: in case the Western powers and the Federal Republic dare to unleash a war against us, they will get the war with all its consequences.[82]

In his accompanying oral presentation, which Kroll describes as "unusually wrought-up," Gromyko sharply attacked the policies of the West German government, particularly its relations with the GDR and its alleged desire for atomic weapons. He ridiculed the pledges by Western leaders of "firmness" in the Berlin crisis, warning that if war broke out, Germany itself would be destroyed in a matter of hours.

Gromyko's intemperate outburst, which bore all the earmarks of a carefully staged display (Kroll emphasizes that Gromyko barely glanced at the lengthy West German note before launching into his tirade), can be recognized as another move in the Soviet campaign of crude physical threats against individual powers in the Western alliance, which had begun with Khrushchev's interview with Sir Frank Roberts on July 2.[83]

* * *

[81] *Pravda*, July 12, 1961.

[82] Hans Kroll, *Lebenserinnerungen eines Botschafters* (Cologne and Berlin: Kiepenheuer & Witsch, 1967), p. 500 (hereinafter cited as Kroll); emphasis supplied.

[83] A substantially accurate report of the Gromyko–Kroll interview appeared in the *New York Herald Tribune*, July 23, 1961 (hereinafter cited as *NYHT*); cited in *SIA, 1961*, p. 238.

To back up Khrushchev's July 8 speech and the general Soviet pressure, Soviet Ambassador to the United States Mikhail Menshikov at about this time launched his own campaign of intimidation. According to James Reston, "Menshikov has been, if anything, even more extreme and menacing than anybody else. Menshikov has been saying to diplomats in Washington that the decision to make a separate peace treaty with Communist East Germany has been taken in Moscow; that he was present when it was taken; that such a peace treaty would end all Western rights in Berlin; and that any attempts by the West to enforce its rights there would start a nuclear war."[84]

On the same day on which Reston's report was published, the *New York Herald Tribune* front-paged a sensational story concerning the publicly expressed views of the Soviet Ambassador. In the course of a cocktail party at the Iraqi embassy on July 14, according to the story by Warren Rogers, Jr., the Soviet Ambassador disclosed that he was planning to return home for a six-week vacation. One of the Americans present thereupon said to him:

"Mr Ambassador, you could perform a great service for your country, our country, and perhaps for history if you would tell Mr. Khrushchev that we are determined to fight for Berlin. What you report may have a lot to do with whether or not we have war."

"We don't want war," the Ambassador said. "But there is a buildup. On both sides. You are going to arm the Germans with nuclear weapons. You talk about reunification, and the German people do not want to reunify." The American said he was concerned that there might be a miscalculation by Mr. Khrushchev—strong Soviet steps based on the misconception that the American people would not fight.

"I do not believe this," Mr. Menshikov said. "I've talked to many people in this country. My reports are objective. They have to be. Many of the Americans I've talked to do not want to fight. They don't feel the way you do."

The American insisted that, in the final analysis, the American people would go to war over Berlin.

"The American people are not ready," Ambassador Menshikov said. "They don't want to fight. In the final analysis, when the chips are down, the American people won't fight for Berlin."[85]

Six days later, in an interview in New York, as he was about to embark on his homeward voyage, Menshikov gave his own version of the incident:

What actually happened, the Soviet Ambassador said, was that at a Washington party in the course of a supposedly off-the-record conversation, "a gentleman kept saying that he would fight for Berlin." "I said," Mr. Menshikov continued, "What do you want to fight for?" He said, "We want West Berlin to have freedom." I said nobody wanted to do anything against West Berlin. The gentleman kept insisting: "Please report to your govern-

---

[84]*NYT*, July 16, 1961, sect. 4, p. 8.
[85]*NYHT*, July 16, 1961, pp. 1, 18.

ment that we will fight for Berlin." I said: "Nobody can keep you from committing suicide if you want to."[86]

Asked by the reporter his opinion of the willingness of the American people to fight for Western rights in Berlin, Menshikov hedged, but then, in substance, confirmed the accuracy of the earlier story by adding: "I don't think it is in the interest of the American people to fight for the interests of West German militarists, revanchists and fascists."[87]

It was this view, evidently, which the Soviet Ambassador had been reporting to Moscow and which he delivered to the Soviet leadership on his return. The fact that he was returning by boat, however, rather than by air, and that his leave of absence from his Washington post had been set at six weeks, only served to underline the calculated nature of the Soviet strategy on Berlin and the absence of any real expectation of Khrushchev's part that war was a possibility seriously to be reckoned with.

Similar conclusions were reached by a Western correspondent in Moscow, noting the lack of any visible preparation for nuclear attack in the Soviet Union. In a report filed from Moscow on July 8, in the immediate wake of Khrushchev's speech to the military graduates, though not published until July 16, Osgood Carruthers stated: "*There are no outward signs of even the most elementary preparations for civil defense against nuclear blasts or fallout. . . .* one gets the feeling that the Soviet leaders and their military chiefs, while keeping their forces and weapons at constant peak readiness, are steeped in confidence either that their first retaliatory blow against any surprise attack would be effective or, probably more likely, that there will not be any such attack."[88]

It was during the month of July, nevertheless, that Marshal Chuikov was placed in charge of the Soviet civil defense program, and to judge by the evidence of Soviet preparations in this field by the spring of 1962, serious work on civilian shelters and other preparations got under way in the summer of 1961.

*   *   *

It was an integral part of Soviet strategy in the Berlin crisis to attempt to disrupt the common front of the Western alliance. The dire threats directed against individual Western nations (so far, the United Kingdom and Western Germany), were calculated to produce this result. A related tactic was to hold out to individual members of the Western alliance the hope of avoiding war by entering into negotiations with the Soviets on disputed issues. The first positive response to this latter aspect of Soviet strategy came in the second

[86]Harrison Salisbury, *NYT*, July 21, 1961, p. 12.
[87]Ibid.
[88]*NYT*, July 16, 1961, p. 7; emphasis supplied.

half of July. According to the *Survey of International Affairs*, an invitation to visit Moscow had been extended to the Italian premier, Signor Fanfani, in mid-June, ". . . but the date suggested, 13 July, had proved impossible. The new invitation came on 16 July, and envisaged a visit taking place at the beginning of August. After some heart-searchings, the Italian Premier accepted for himself and the Foreign Secretary, Signor Segni. . . . It was made clear that the purpose of the visit was to discuss Germany and Berlin."[89] The Soviet–Italian discussions for which this acceptance paved the way were to prove a touchstone of the genuineness of Soviet interest in serious negotiations on Berlin and Germany.

East German contributions to the Soviet campaign in Berlin

In support of the Soviet pressure on Berlin, the communist regime in East Germany faithfully mimicked the threatening gestures and menacing words of its powerful ally, in the process sometimes exceeding Soviet spokesmen in stridency. For the record, the East German rubber-stamp legislative body, the Volkskammer, discussed a "German peace plan" at its session on July 6. "Conclusion of a uniform peace treaty with both German states," according to the plan, was "the supreme task of the German nation."[90]

GDR propaganda official Gerhart Eisler, in a statement two days later, warned that Western efforts to block signature of a peace treaty by curtailing trade between West and East Germany might result in an unintended but effective new Berlin blockade: "After all, the West German economy sends goods worth several million dollars to West Berlin through our territory. It uses our communication links on land, water and air. Blockade against the German Democratic Republic therefore could easily lead to a self-inflicted blockade for Bonn."[91]

According to an announcement by the GDR news service on the same day, an all-German Protestant Church congress scheduled to be held in East Berlin on July 19–23 had been banned by the East Berlin police chief, "in the interests of preserving law and order."[92] Finding that the East German authorities had prohibited the use of the railroads for delegates to the congress, Protestant Church leaders announced the cancellation of the congress on July 12, a result which a State Department spokesman characterized as "a deplorable violation of religious liberty."[93]

At a press conference in Rostock on July 10, Otto Winzer, deputy foreign minister of the GDR, boasted that the GDR would assume full control over

[89]*SIA, 1961*, p. 239, citing *Corriere della Sera*, July 18, 22, and 25, 1961, and *Neue Zuercher Zeitung*, July 22 and 26, 1961. Note that the original invitation came just before Fanfani's visit to Washington.

[90]Text in *Documents on Germany*, p. 833, from East Berlin television, July 6, 1961.

[91]*Washington Post*, July 9, 1961, p. A–14.

[92]Ibid.

[93]Ibid., July 12, 13, and 14, 1961.

land and air access routes to Berlin from West Germany after it had signed a peace treaty with the Soviets. The GDR, Winzer said, "has full sovereignty and its authorities will not act as the agents of any other power."[94]

These were mere pinpricks, which might irritate but which did not fundamentally alter the situation. More ominous, because it took the form of a routine administrative announcement, was the appearance in *Neue Justiz*, the official organ of the East German Ministry of Justice, on July 16, of plans for the administration of West Berlin after conclusion of a Soviet–GDR peace treaty. The treaty, it was stated, would take effect "for the entire territory of the G.D.R., on which West Berlin is situated."[95]

The rising tide of refugees from East Germany

As the Soviet–GDR pressure on Berlin gained in intensity, thousands of the inhabitants of East Germany made the weighty decision to abandon their homes and jobs and try their luck in the West. In the three days following Khrushchev's July 8 speech 2,600 refugees poured into the reception centers in West Berlin; their reasons for fleeing, a *New York Times* interviewer reported, included fear of a military showdown over Berlin, the growing shortages of food, and general economic hardship in East Germany.[96]

In response to communist threats, the refugee tide was running well ahead of the level attained in preceding years: 8,231 East Germans fled to the West during the first twelve days of July 1961, as compared with 5,061 during the similar period in 1960. For the first six months of 1961, Western officials reported a total of 103,159 refugees.[97]

Faced with this steadily accelerating drain of their citizens and manpower (the refugee flood included a disproportionately high number of the young, the able-bodied, and the technically trained), GDR officials began to display definite signs of disquiet. Early in July a member of the East German party Politburo, Hermann Matern, criticized party officials for inadequate political leadership in blocking the flights and said that the party as a whole should wage a struggle against them "in open discussions among party members and with the people."[98]

The long-term implications of the refugee flight for the East German economy and for the political stability of the communist regime were analyzed in an article in the June 10, 1961, issue of the *Economist* (London). Since 1949, when the GDR was established, the *Economist* reported, over two and a half million people had left the GDR for the West, reducing the total population to approximately 17 million and badly crippling the East German economy.[99]

[94]*NYT*, July 11, 1961, p. 7.
[95]*NYT*, July 17, 1961, p. 3; *SIA, 1961*, pp. 238–39.
[96]*NYT*, July 11, 1961, p. 1.
[97]*NYT*, July 13, 1961, p. 3.
[98]*Washington Post*, July 5, 1961, p. A–12.
[99]"Waiting Game in Berlin," *Economist*, June 10, 1961, pp. 1118–19.

Virtually certain of finding jobs in West Germany, which had a chronic labor shortage, doctors, teachers, engineers, skilled mechanics, and apprentices from East Germany had shown special eagerness to make the move to the West. The focal point of this unending flow of humanity from East to West Germany was the city of Berlin, where one could still move freely between the Soviet sector and the three sectors occupied by the Western allies. Once he reached West Berlin the refugee, if his credentials and bona fides were satisfactorily established, could be certain of being flown out to West Germany and finding a job.

The refugee situation thus constituted an ever-present goad to Soviet and East German officials to undertake concrete measures to choke off this debilitating drain on the vitality, the viability, and the prestige of the East German regime.

China and the Soviet Union move closer to an open break

It is a striking fact that at the very moment when the Soviet campaign in Berlin was being launched, relations between the Soviet Union and communist China and between the Soviets and China's only European ally, Albania, plummeted to a new low.

Despite intensive scrutiny by a number of scholars, the underlying reasons for this development have remained obscure. Donald Zagoria notes that China at just this time was "in the midst of a severe economic crisis which threatened mass starvation,"[100] and suggests that by the autumn of 1961, "the struggle over Albania had acquired a momentum of its own."[101] But little attention has been devoted to the coincidence in time between the decline in Soviet–Chinese and Soviet–Albanian cordiality and the Berlin crisis, nor has any explanation of these developments been offered in terms of the policy-formulation processes in the Soviet leadership.

If the reasons for the deterioration of Soviet–CPR (Chinese People's Republic) and Soviet–Albanian relations in the summer of 1961 remain obscure, the facts pointing to these developments are not in doubt. In the first half of July in particular, i.e., just when Khrushchev was staking his military bid on Berlin, there came a cluster of events indicating a sharp increase in Sino-Soviet and Soviet–Albanian tension. It was from this period also that the first general Western recognition of the split can be dated. It would take a considerably longer time, however, before official Western institutions and individuals grasped the meaning of these developments and an even longer time before their implications for Soviet and Western policy would be explored.

In analyzing this phenomenon it will be convenient to group the evidence under major headings, within the general time period from mid-June through mid-July 1961.

[100]Donald S. Zagoria, *The Sino–Soviet Conflict 1956–1961* (Princeton: Princeton University Press, 1962), p. 374 (hereinafter cited as Zagoria).

[101]Ibid., p. 382.

Economic tensions

Given the economic crisis in China to which Zagoria has called attention, it would be natural to expect Chinese eagerness for Soviet economic aid and Soviet recognition of the Chinese plight manifested in measures of aid. There are, in fact, several indications pointing in this direction, e.g., a Soviet article on June 10 which presented a generally favorable picture of CPR economic progress, but which noted that: "The Chinese people have to overcome considerable difficulties resulting from the national calamities that did great damage to agriculture."[102]

On June 19 two Soviet–CPR agreements were signed in Moscow covering economic and scientific cooperation. The *Pravda* report on the signing emphasized "the atmosphere of mutual understanding and fraternal cooperation" which, it said, had characterized the negotiations, and went on to say: "Both sides expressed mutual satisfaction with results achieved in the negotiations on economic cooperation in the belief that the agreements signed on these questions will promote a further strengthening of economic cooperation between the U.S.S.R. and the C.P.R. and a further development of the national economies of both countries."[103]

A discordant note, however, was struck early in July when the May issue of *Vneshniaia Torgovlia* [*Foreign Trade*] was belatedly released, with the first published details of the sizable (288 million rubles) debt owed the USSR by China for earlier trade deficits.[104] The same source provided the first official report of the signature, on April 5, 1961, of a Soviet–CPR agreement on measures for the liquidation of this debt over the period 1961–65 by the delivery of Chinese goods.

Doctrinal differences

The long-standing rivalry between Khrushchev and the Chinese Communist leadership headed by Mao Tse-tung over the interpretation of basic Marxist-Leninist doctrine and its application to current policies contributed to the increase in Sino–Soviet tension at this time. In the Soviet draft Party Program approved by the Central Committee plenum on June 19 it was maintained that the Soviet experience of "building socialism" was binding for all other communist parties, including the Chinese. It was therefore a calculated affront by the Chinese when their party theoretical journal published an article in its July 1 number which took direct issue with the Soviet claim. "In analyzing social problems," the article maintained, "the absolute demand of Marxist theory is to place the problem within a definite historical limit. In addition, if a certain country (or, for example, the national program of this country) is referred

[102]I. Popov and L. Tomashpolsky, "The Chinese People Are Building Socialism," *Ekonomicheskaia Gazeta*, June 10, 1961, p. 4; *CDSP*, XIII/26, pp. 7–8.

[103]*Pravda*, June 23, 1961, p. 3; *CDSP*, XIII/25, p. 23.

[104]*Vneshniaia Torgovlia* 5 (1961): 11–12, 17–18; Harry Schwartz, *NYT*, July 5, 1961, p. 7.

to, the concrete characteristics of this country that distinguish it from other countries in the same historical era must be taken into account."[105]

The clash over foreign policy issues

Sharply varying estimates of the international situation as seen from Moscow and Peking helped fuel the growing Sino–Soviet dispute at this time. Of paramount importance here was the interpretation to be placed on U.S. policy under the Kennedy administration. Despite the fact that the Soviets were engaged in a contentious and risky controversy with the Western alliance over Berlin, the virulence with which Peking spokesmen denounced the United States far surpassed anything being heard from Moscow. The differences in approach became sharply apparent when one of the two centers commented on statements with regard to the United States emanating from the other. For example, Zagoria notes that: "Even Khrushchev's militant speech on the twentieth anniversary of the German invasion of the U.S.S.R. . . . was not enough for Peking. A *Jen-min jih-pao* [Peking daily] editorial on June 28 praised that speech and then went on to add criticism of the U.S. administration that went far beyond Khrushchev."[106]

Even more revealing of the basic difference in attitude toward the United States was the Soviet treatment of an interview on June 29 granted by CPR Foreign Minister Chen Yi to two correspondents of the Canadian Broadcasting System in Geneva (where Chen was attending the international conference on Laos). The version of Chen's remarks broadcast by Peking Radio on July 2 included sharp criticisms of U.S. policy at the Laos conference which were completely eliminated from the Soviet version published five days later in *Izvestiia*.

Significantly, Chen confirmed the widespread reports of the setbacks which had hampered Chinese economic growth: "In the past three years . . . natural calamities have taken place in China such as had not occurred in the preceding 100 years. This has indeed inflicted serious hardships upon us. But at the same time it should be noted that despite the serious natural calamities, we have escaped famine."[107]

As reported by *Izvestiia*, Chen conspicuously failed to state that the Soviet Union was coming to the assistance of the Chinese in their distress, but he dwelt with suspicious emphasis on the alleged solidarity which existed between the two nations:

Chen Yi also refuted the inventions of the bourgeois press concerning Soviet–Chinese relations. Relations between China and the Soviet Union, as well as relations among all the socialist countries, he said, are fraternal international relations of a new type. These relations are built on a common

---

[105] *Hung Ch'i*, July 1, 1961, cited in Zagoria, p. 372.
[106] Zagoria, p. 449.
[107] *Izv.*, July 7, 1961, p. 6; *CDSP*, XIII/28, p. 23.

basis of Marxism–Leninism and on the principles of proletarian internationalism. These are relations of unbreakable solidarity.

China and the Soviet Union always support one another, which serves as convincing proof of this solidarity. . . . The great solidarity between China and the Soviet Union is an important contribution to peace the world over and to the progress of mankind, Chen Yi said in conclusion. No provocations or intrigues are capable of shaking this unbreakable solidarity to the slightest degree.[108]

No wonder that Harrison Salisbury, analyzing the Soviet version of Chen's interview, called it "virtually without precedent," and added: "It was regarded by specialists in Soviet affairs as strong evidence of the seriousness of the strain on relations within the Communist world."[109]

The struggle for allegiance of the Asian communist parties

As the Sino–Soviet dispute deepened, the communist parties of the world faced the awkward choice between Moscow and Peking. Particularly exposed to this agonizing dilemma were the smaller communist parties of Asia, in North Vietnam, North Korea, and the Mongolian People's Republic (Outer Mongolia), all of whom shared borders with China. During late June and the first part of July, Khrushchev and the Soviet leadership played host to well-publicized visits to Moscow by party and government leaders from North Vietnam (June 26–July 3) and North Korea (June 29–July 10), while a party delegation headed by senior Presidium member Mikhail Suslov attended a party congress in the Mongolian capital (July 1–4). In Moscow, on July 11, Frol Kozlov made a speech at a reception given by the Mongolian Ambassador to mark the fortieth anniversary of the establishment of the Mongolian People's Republic.[110]

Valuable results in the strengthening of ties between the Soviet Union and its Asian ideological allies resulted from these contacts, for example, a Soviet–North Korean military aid pact signed in Moscow on July 6 and a Soviet–Mongolian exchange of notes on July 17 concerning aid in the development of virgin lands. (North Korean Premier and party leader Kim Il-sung shrewdly hedged his bets by proceeding directly to Peking after his Moscow sojourn, where, on July 11, he signed a military aid agreement "almost identical" with the one he had signed in Moscow the preceding week.)[111]

Soviet relations with Yugoslavia and Albania

Always a sensitive barometer of the state of Sino–Soviet relations, Soviet governmental and party relations with Albania went from bad to worse at this

[108]*CDSP*, XIII/28, p. 23.
[109]*NYT*, July 9, 1961, p. 21.
[110]*Pravda*, July 12, 1961.
[111]*NYT*, July 12, 1961, p. 1.

time, while Soviet–Yugoslav ties were being systematically strengthened. A turning point was the dispatch on July 6 of a letter from the Albanian party Central Committee to its Soviet counterpart warning the Soviets that bilateral talks between the two parties would be impossible as long as the Soviets continued their political, economic, and military pressure on Albania. (An example of what the Albanians had in mind, no doubt, was the withdrawal at the end of May of all Soviet submarines from the naval base on the island of Sazan [Sasseno], off the Albanian mainland.)[112]

From July 7 to 13 Yugoslav Foreign Minister K. Popović was in the Soviet Union, in accordance with plans first announced on April 26. (The invitation to Popović, significantly, had come at a time when Khrushchev's influence in the formulation of Soviet foreign policy was paramount.) The final Soviet–Yugoslav communiqué, issued on July 14, stressed the closeness of Soviet and Yugoslav foreign policy interests in a way "which must have infuriated the Albanians still further."[113] As an indication that the good relations between the Soviet Union and Yugoslavia would be still further improved in the future, the communiqué noted that: "In the course of the talks it was agreed that Soviet Foreign Minister Gromyko would visit Yugoslavia at a later date."[114]

Timing and motives of the Soviet decision to increase the pressure on China

The systematic, well-organized character of the Soviet moves adversely affecting Sino–Soviet relations in mid-summer 1961 provides prima facie evidence of a definite policy decision. The fact that both Khrushchev and the leading internal oppositionists, Suslov and Kozlov, took part in the campaign to woo the Asian communist parties indicates that the heightened pressure on the Chinese was the result of an agreed decision within the Presidium. Available evidence makes it possible to specify within fairly narrow limits the time when the Presidium reached this decision. On the assumption that the effort to win over the Asian communist parties was an integral part of the strategy, the decision must have been taken shortly before the signature, on June 19, of the Soviet–CPR agreement on economic, scientific, and technical cooperation. It was also at about this time that the Soviets decided to divulge existence of the Chinese trade debt to the USSR. (The issue of *Vneshniaia Torgovlia* which included the report on the debt unfortunately failed to specify the exact date on which the text was sent to the press.)

A significant clue to the date of the Presidium decision on China was the announcement in the Soviet press, on June 16, of the forthcoming visit to the Soviet Union of North Vietnam Premier Pham Van Dong, since this was the

---

[112]Griffith, *Albania*, p. 83.
[113]Ibid. For the communiqué, see *Pravda*, July 14, 1961, p. 5; *CDSP*, XIII/28, p. 22.
[114]*CDSP*, XIII/28, p. 22.

first in the series of visits between Soviet and Asian communist leaders. Announcement of the North Korean visit followed on June 24.[115]

In this context it can be recognized as significant that Khrushchev's speech at Alma Ata, on June 24, emphasized the importance of Russian–Kazakh ties (Kazakhstan is the Union Republic with the longest common border with China), and dwelt in particular on the economic progress of Kazakhstan in comparison with its neighbors Turkey, Pakistan, and India, but with the conspicuous omission of any reference to China. As Harrison Salisbury has pointed out, it is also noteworthy that no representative of the Chinese People's Republic was present at the celebration.[116]

Assuming therefore that a Presidium decision on a harder line toward China was taken shortly before June 16, it must be regarded as a striking coincidence (if it is no more than a coincidence) that on that date, June 16, a feature article in the Uzbek republic newspaper, *Pravda Vostoka*, dealt with the seldom-discussed question of debates and decisionmaking within the Presidium. "The Central Committee Presidium," the article stated,

> is a model of Leninist collegiality; it meets, as a rule, at least once a week. Characterizing the style of these meetings, N. S. Khrushchev says: "Most often various viewpoints are expressed in the examination of questions at meetings of the Central Committee Presidium, since Presidium members try to study the question under discussion as deeply as possible. During the discussion, Presidium members usually arrive at a single viewpoint. If a single viewpoint cannot be arrived at on some question, then this question is resolved by a simple majority vote. There are, of course, questions over which very heated arguments arise; this is natural in democratic discussion."[117]

To say that the decision was a collective one, however, is not necessarily to imply that all members of the Presidium were equally enthusiastic in support of it. (As Khrushchev had noted, some Presidium decisions were reached on the basis of a simple majority vote, when complete unanimity proved to be unattainable.) There can be little doubt that Khrushchev personally was a leading proponent of the anti-Chinese campaign. The emphasis in the CPSU draft program approved on June 19 on Soviet priority in the building of communism and on the obligatory character of the Soviet experience for other communist parties, a serious irritant to Chinese sensibilities, expressed Khrushchev's personal views. And it was Khrushchev who hogged the limelight during the visits to Moscow of the Asian communist party and government delegations.

---

[115]*Pravda*, June 24, 1961, p. 1.

[116]*NYT*, July 7, 1961, p. 2.

[117]A. V. Bakhabov in *Pravda Vostoka*, June 16, 1961. The quote is from an interview with Khrushchev by Turner Catledge, editor-in-chief of the *NYT*, May 10, 1957, published in *Pravda*, May 14, 1957. Ploss, p. 226, links the *Pravda Vostoka* report with the debate in the party leadership on economic priorities.

Suslov's speech to the Mongolian party congress, on July 4, enables us to identify him as another firm supporter of the decision to increase pressure on the Chinese. Carefully avoiding any reference to China, Suslov stressed the close ties linking the Soviet Union with the Mongolian People's Republic and even went so far as to assure his listeners of the "firm security" of the Mongolian borders, a pledge which could only have been aimed against China.[118]

Suslov also flouted Chinese sensitivity by staunchly defending the Vienna meeting between Khrushchev and Kennedy:

> As everyone knows, the Vienna meeting was useful. It made it possible through frank talk to bring to light the position of the United States and at the same time to present the position of the Soviet government on a number of major international questions. In championing and defending the interests of the Soviet people, Comrade N. S. Khrushchev, the untiring fighter for peace, at the same time was championing and defending the interests of all the peoples of the socialist countries, the great cause of socialism and lasting peace on earth.[119]

By contrast, Kozlov's speech at the Mongolian embassy, on July 11, as we have seen above, was much more menacing in its treatment of the United States. Kozlov, it would seem, had gone along with the Presidium decision on China only with great reluctance.

* * *

To sum up: the evidence points to a decision within the Presidium, on or shortly before June 16, to increase pressure on the Chinese. Khrushchev was the prime mover, but he had the strong support of Suslov and at least the tacit acquiescence of Kozlov (if the decision was, as is likely, a split one, Kozlov may well have cast a negative vote).

As to the motives for the decision, a primary factor was undoubtedly the calculation that the economic setbacks which the Chinese had been undergoing offered a favorable opportunity for weakening their position in the international communist movement, both in the ideological struggle for primacy and in the organizational struggle for the allegiance of the Asian communist parties—both of which factors, significantly, were of special concern to Suslov.

The fact that the Presidium decided to intensify the struggle with the Chinese just as the Soviet campaign against the West over Berlin was getting under way is an indication of the confidence felt within the Soviet leadership with regard to the Berlin venture. At the same time, the fact that they were mounting a major campaign against the West may well have helped convince the Soviet leadership that the time was particularly well suited for stepping up their bid for supremacy in the international communist movement.

[118]Radio Moscow, July 4, 1961, cited in Zagoria, p. 380.
[119]*Izv.*, July 5, 1961, p. 2; *CDSP*, XIII/27, p. 19.

Initial Western recognition and evaluation of the Sino-Soviet dispute

The first general recognition on the part of a number of Western observers of the reality of the Sino–Soviet dispute and its companion, the Soviet–Albanian dispute, can be dated to the summer of 1961. Among the harbingers of this recognition were *New York Times* articles, on July 5, by Harry Schwartz on Soviet–Chinese economic difficulties and Wallace Carroll on indications of the shift of Albania's loyalty from Moscow to Peking. Harrison Salisbury followed, on July 7, with a full-dress analysis of recent evidence pointing to the exacerbation of Sino–Soviet relations, with special reference to the Soviet wooing of the Asian communist parties.

Isaac Deutscher, an influential British analyst (and former Polish communist), attempted to link the Sino–Soviet dispute with the Berlin campaign in an article published on July 5. "The need to compete with Mao for leadership in the communist camp," Deutscher argued,

> has been an important factor in Khrushchev's decision to take action over Berlin. He has to refute Mao's charges. He has to show himself tough and determined. He has to demonstrate that he is not "appeasing Western imperialism." He has to calculate his diplomatic moves with an eye on their effect on the intense Russo-Chinese contest for the allegiance of so many Communist parties in Asia, Africa, Europe, and Latin America. This makes it difficult for Khrushchev to engage in genuine bargaining with the West, and imposes on him that diplomatic rigidity which so surprised President Kennedy in Vienna. On the other hand, Khrushchev is anxious to avoid the risk of war, because by courting it, he would not only endanger Russia's interests, but virtually surrender to Mao. Khrushchev is thus facing the prospect of a difficult and complicated operation over the German peace treaty and Berlin, an operation ostensibly directed only against the West but actually aimed at China as well. To hold his ground against Mao, Khrushchev must be able to produce results and to flaunt a success, however small, and to follow it up by another, imaginary or real. But he has also to beware of pressing too hard and over-reaching himself.[120]

Deutscher thus accounted for Khrushchev's "diplomatic rigidity" at Vienna (i.e., his presentation of sharply defined position papers at the end of the meeting) by invoking the Sino–Soviet dispute. Deutscher was on the right track in recognizing that Khrushchev's "diplomatic rigidity" was a striking phenomenon which demanded explanation, but, lacking an insight into the internal Soviet political pressures on Khrushchev which had produced that rigidity, he was forced to seek for an explanation in an external cause—the Sino–Soviet conflict.

As we have seen, however, the increase of tension in Sino–Soviet relations in mid-summer 1961 resulted from a Soviet decision taken at a time of Chinese economic difficulties. It is therefore impossible to explain Khrushchev's oddly circumscribed behavior at Vienna on the grounds of Chinese pressure. Deutscher's analysis, nevertheless, contains a valuable indication of Khrush-

---

[120] *Washington Post*, July 5, 1961, p. A–1.

chev's wish to give the appearance of militancy vis-à-vis the West, to impress the Chinese, while taking care to avoid measures which might result in war.

While informed observers and analysts were increasingly aware, by early July 1961, of the deepening split between Soviet Russia and China, official U.S. policy continued to be predicated on the obsolete concept of Soviet–Chinese solidarity. In a speech at the National Press Club, on July 10, Secretary of State Dean Rusk defined the "central issue" of the contemporary world crisis as "the announced [communist] determination to impose a world of coercion on those not already subjected to it."[121] The issue, Rusk continued, "is posed between the Sino–Soviet empire and all the rest, whether allied or neutral; and it is posed in every continent."[122]

In the question period following his speech Rusk modified somewhat his picture of a monolithic "Sino-Soviet empire," but indicated considerable skepticism as to the evidence of a split between the two communist powers.

According to an academic specialist who served in the State Department at this time: "Despite much earlier predictions and reports by outside analysts, policy makers [in the U.S. government] did not begin to accept the reality and possible finality of the Sino–Soviet split until the early weeks of 1962."[123]

The fullest treatment of the problem, Donald Zagoria's book, *The Sino–Soviet Conflict*, was ready for the press only at the end of 1961,[124] and did not appear until mid-1962, although its conclusions and the evidence they were based on were available earlier.[125] William E. Griffith's indispensable study, *Albania and the Sino–Soviet Rift*, was not completed until November 1962.

---

[121]*DSB*, 45 (1961): 177.

[122]Ibid.

[123]James C. Thomson, Jr., "How Could Vietnam Happen? An Autopsy," *Atlantic*, vol. 221, no. 4 (April 1968): 48.

[124]Zagoria, p. x.

[125]As an analyst for the U.S. government, Zagoria wrote a series of unpublished papers analyzing the evidence of the growing estrangement between the Soviet Union and communist China in the period from late 1958 through 1961. His was at that time, however, a minority view. Several chapters from an advance draft of *The Sino–Soviet Conflict* were published in *The China Quarterly* (July–Sept. 1961): 17–34, and (Oct.–Dec. 1961): 1–15.

4 The Western Riposte, June 29–July 25

For President Kennedy the first half of July was a period of intense absorption in the Berlin problem, as the search for a viable policy was pursued in a series of conferences and consultations, both formally in Washington, where the National Security Council met on July 13 and 19, and informally but no less intensively at the President's summer home at Hyannis Port, Massachusetts, where a group of advisers met with him on July 8 to weigh the alternatives.

The reply to the Vienna note on Berlin

Highly frustrating to the President was what he considered the slow pace of the Berlin Task Force and the State Department in drafting a reply to the Soviet note of June 4 on Berlin.[1] When a month had gone by with no visible evidence of progress, he called for the text of the latest draft to review. The results were discouraging. In Sorensen's words: "He found, to his dismay, not a clear, concise response which all Americans, Germans and Russians could understand, but a compilation of stale, tedious and negative phrases, none of them new. The whole document could have been drafted in one-quarter as much time and with one-tenth as many words."[2]

Hoping to speed up the process of preparing a reply, at the same time sharpening and strengthening the draft, Kennedy asked Sorensen to produce "a shorter, simpler version." But he had not reckoned with the need to clear the draft within the bureaucratic complexities of the U.S. government and with the nation's principal allies. The shorter version prepared by Sorensen, he learned,

---

[1] For the assertion that the Berlin Task Force was charged with drafting the reply to the Soviet note, see Schlesinger, p. 383. Sorensen, *Kennedy*, p. 587, attributes the drafting to the Department of State.

[2] Sorensen, p. 587.

"could not be substituted for the formal note without starting all over again with inter-Allied and interdepartmental clearances."[3]

It took another two weeks—until July 17—before the Western replies to the Soviet note on Berlin were finally ready. Each of the three Western allies sent a separate note, though the British and French notes were so similar in structure and content that they indicate a high degree of consultation during the drafting process.[4]

Common to all three notes was the denial of the Soviet charge that the status of West Berlin and the policies of West Germany constituted a threat to peace, coupled with the assertion that it was in fact the announced Soviet intention to end Western rights in Berlin by signing a separate peace treaty with the communist regime in East Germany which constituted the real threat to peace. All three notes maintained that West Berlin was not, as asserted by the Soviets and their East German followers, situated on or a part of East German territory, citing in support the war-time and postwar agreements on the status of Berlin to which the Soviet Union was a signatory. All three asserted that no unilateral Soviet action could terminate Western rights in Berlin.

The final paragraph of all three notes (as originally drafted—the U.S. note was subsequently "improved" by the somewhat incongruous addition of several paragraphs from Sorensen's alternate draft) stated the Western powers' willingness to negotiate with the Soviets over Berlin and the German question, but insisted that this could only be done on the basis of self-determination for the Germans and respect for the rights of all nations concerned (the French note substituted "the interests of peace in Europe"). The notes concluded with a warning to the Soviets not to present the West with a fait accompli, which could have "unforeseeable consequences," and expressed the hope that the Soviets would join the West in the search for conditions "in which a genuine and peaceful settlement of outstanding problems can be pursued."

Since most of the weight of defending the Western position in Berlin fell on the United States, it was appropriate that the American note should be more detailed and circumstantial than the other two. It not only summarized the postwar historical record of negotiations between the Soviets and the Western powers on Germany but also cited recent developments, for example, Ulbricht's veiled threats against West Berlin's life line to the West in his June 15 news conference. In the strongest single passage in any of the three notes the United States charged that the Soviet government was threatening to "try to obtain what it wants by unilateral action" unless the Western powers accepted its proposals, and then continued:

---

[3]Ibid.

[4]The texts of all three Western notes are given in United Kingdom, *Documents About the Future of Germany (Including Berlin), June to July 1961* (London: H.M.S.O., 1961, Cmnd. 1451) (hereinafter cited as Cmnd. 1451). Text of the U.S. note in *DSB*, 45 (1961): 224–30.

The Soviet government thus threatens to violate its solemn international obligations, to determine unilaterally the fate of millions of Germans without
their consent, and to use force against its World War II Allies if they do not
voluntarily surrender their rights and vital positions. The Soviet Government must understand that such a course of action is not only unacceptable,
but is a more [most?] serious menace to world peace, for which it bears full
responsibility before all mankind.[5]

Considering the complexities of the issues involved, the grave threat to
peace inherent in the Soviet challenge and the need to coordinate the far from
uniform views of the three allied powers, completion of the Western replies
within just over a month (the French were not officially informed of the Soviet
position until June 16) must be regarded as a noteworthy achievement. By
contrast the West German government, which was much more immediately
concerned, took nearly six months to prepare its reply to the Soviet note of
February 17. Nor can the U.S. note properly be described as "a compilation of
stale, tedious, and negative phrases, none of them new"[6] or "a tired and turgid
rehash of documents left over from the Berlin crisis of 1958–59."[7] The substitute text which Sorensen drafted and which Kennedy read at his news conference on July 19 was, by contrast, a public relations text aimed at influencing
the reader's emotions but fearful of boring him with the specific facts and dates
needed to build a case in international law. And the Sorensen/Kennedy statement of July 19 fell far short of the State Department note in its failure to
identify clearly the underlying issue in the conflict—the Soviet threat "to use
force against its World War II Allies if they do not voluntarily surrender their
rights and vital positions."

Kennedy addresses the nation, July 25

As matters turned out, however, neither the official Western replies nor
the shorter, more rhetorical statement drafted by Sorensen constituted the
really operative Western response to the Soviet challenge. As the *Survey of
International Affairs* correctly observes: "The notes made no notable impact
in Moscow or in the DDR [East Germany]."[8] The real and effective Western
response took the form of a radio and television address to the nation by the
President on the evening of July 25, in which he outlined the specific
measures—military, diplomatic, and financial—which his administration proposed to take to meet the Soviet challenge not only on Berlin but throughout
the world.[9] The decisions announced in Kennedy's July 25 speech had been

[5]*DSB*, 45 (1961):227.
[6]Sorensen, p. 587.
[7]Schlesinger, p. 384.
[8]*SIA, 1961*, p. 238.
[9]Text in *DSB*, 45 (1961):267–73.

reached at a conference on the afternoon of July 19, and reflected the final resolution of the heated debates which had been going on within the administration ever since the President returned from Vienna. (There were actually two high-level conferences on the afternoon of July 19: the first, at which the President announced to a small group of top advisers the decisions he had reached the preceding day on strategy in the Berlin crisis, followed by the second, a formal session of the National Security Council at which the decisions already reached were "decided" for the record.)[10]

After prolonged wrestling with the alternative courses of action proposed to him by his advisers, ranging from Acheson's clearcut recommendation for a hard line backed up by the proclamation of a national state of emergency to Rusk's preference for some form of negotiation, the President had reached a decision which incorporated elements from both opposing schools of thought but which, in his view, offered a sounder basis than either for a workable long-term strategy of confrontation with the Soviets. U.S. military power would be strengthened, but in ways which would not be directly provocative to the Soviets; the Western military presence in Germany and West Berlin would be built up to a point where it could more effectively discourage a rash Soviet gamble on a quick local triumph; the door to the negotiating chamber would be invitingly left ajar; and the American people would be warned, firmly rather than in an alarmist tone, that they faced a long and difficult haul for the future.

Basing himself on the decisions of the July 19 conference, Kennedy, in his July 25 speech, called for an additional $3.5 billion in military appropriations, bringing to $6 billion the increase in the military budget for the current fiscal year since his administration took office in January. The new increases fell entirely in the non-nuclear, "conventional" area of the budget. They included $3,247,000,000 for the armed forces, to provide for an increase in army strength from 875,000 to 1 million, and increases of 29,000 and 63,000 in the navy and air force respectively; doubling and trebling the draft; calling reserve units to active duty; increasing the airlift capacity of the air force; strengthening the air force and navy by retaining or reactivating ships and planes; and adding nearly $2 billion for procurement of weapons, ammunition and equipment. As a separate category the President called for $207,600,000 to organize civil defense, thus carrying out the recommendation of his speech of May 25.

Although at first glance it might appear that the military increase called for by Kennedy on July 25 was the counterpart and response to Khrushchev's announcement of a one-third increase in the Soviet military budget on July 8, and thus represented a calculated but short-term move in the strategic game being played over Berlin, in actuality the U.S. military build-up of the summer of 1961 was an integral part of the long-range strategic plan which had been in process of development since the very outset of the Kennedy administration. The President himself made this point explicit in his July 25 speech: "The new

[10]Sorensen, pp. 586–90.

preparations that we shall make to defend the peace are part of the long-term buildup in our strength which has been under way since January."[11]

While there was indeed an element of direct response to Soviet challenge in the underlying concepts of U.S. strategy, the challenge was one which, in U.S. eyes, had been hurled by Khrushchev at the very outset of the new phase in U.S.–Soviet relations marked by the advent of the Kennedy administration, most specifically in Khrushchev's January 6 speech, with its pledge of Soviet support for wars of "national liberation." The challenge had been explicitly renewed, Kennedy and his advisers felt, at the "somber" confrontation between him and Khrushchev at Vienna in early June. Thus Khrushchev's July 8 announcement merely served to harden and confirm an already well-advanced U.S. strategic plan in which the Berlin crisis was seen as the most immediately threatening aspect of a worldwide Soviet–U.S. confrontation.

Since the U.S. response to the Soviet challenge was primarily military rather than diplomatic, it was appropriate that the principal architect of most of the specific measures adopted by the United States in the Berlin crisis of 1961 was not the man officially charged with directing the nation's foreign policy, the secretary of state, but its director of military policy, the secretary of defense, Robert McNamara. Working in close association with the President, McNamara from the outset of the new administration had been striving to achieve a more flexible overall military capability, in which in any given international crisis involving U.S. interests the President would not be limited to the stark choice between "holocaust or humiliation."[12] Or, as McNamara explained to the Senate Armed Services Committee two days after the President's July 25 speech: "We feel very strongly that the U.S. defense establishment must have a greater degree of flexibility in responding to particular situations. We need to expand the range of military alternatives available to the President in meeting the kind of situation which may confront us in maintaining our position in Berlin."[13]

The shrewd and well-informed Washington correspondent of the *New Yorker*, Richard H. Rovere, recognized at the time the real significance of the relationship between Khrushchev's challenge and the U.S. response. Kennedy, Rovere wrote two days after the July 25 speech,

> has used Khrushchev's plan for a 1961 peace treaty with the East Germans not simply to generate support for an adequate response to that specific challenge but to advance the whole of his foreign policy and, in particular, to gain for the United States and its allies military capabilities that will permit "a wider choice than humiliation or all-out nuclear action." Of the re-

[11]*DSB*, 45 (1961):268. For the view that the U.S. military build-up announced by Kennedy on July 25 was a direct response to Khrushchev's July 8 speech, see Horelick and Rush, p. 124.

[12]Kennedy's term, cited by Sorensen, p. 587.

[13]William W. Kaufmann, *The McNamara Strategy*, (New York: Harper & Row, 1964), p. 67 (hereinafter cited as Kaufmann).

quests he made to the Congress yesterday and of the Presidential decisions he announced in his speech of two nights ago, only the plan to call up reservists as needed was not among those he had been intending to make at the beginning of next year, Berlin or no Berlin. The objective is to achieve the freedom and flexibility of maneuver for which General Maxwell Taylor, now Mr. Kennedy's closest military adviser, has been calling ever since the days of Charles E. Wilson, George M. Humphrey, and "massive retaliation." *Behind the military purpose lies a diplomatic one—the restoration of American and Western initiative.* Khrushchev gave the President a chance to ask for these measures now—to make his budget requests for fiscal 1963 in fiscal 1962—and he has done so, and Congress is not likely to deny him, as it very well might have done in the absence of what it regarded as a clear and present danger.[14]

* * *

If McNamara helped more than any other single figure to shape the military-strategic policy outlined in Kennedy's July 25 speech, the speech itself and the policies it set forth reflected Kennedy's own deepest convictions.[15] In it he succeeded in making clear, in a way which neither the July 17 note nor his July 19 press conference statement had done, the real issues at stake in the crisis as he saw them:

> The immediate threat to free men is in West Berlin. But that isolated outpost is not an isolated problem. The threat is worldwide. Our effort must be equally wide and strong and not obsessed by any single manufactured crisis. We face a challenge in Berlin, but there is also a challenge in southeast Asia, where the borders are less guarded, the enemy harder to find, and the danger of communism less apparent to those who have so little. We face a challenge in our own hemisphere and indeed wherever else the freedom of human beings is at stake.[16]

Briefly, but effectively, he summarized the historical and legal situation of West Berlin and defined his government's policy on the question: "We cannot and will not permit the Communists to drive us out of Berlin, either gradually or by force."[17]

It was not enough to assert Western rights and pledge their defense, however: at stake was the real possibility that war might break out over Berlin. Kennedy, no less than Khrushchev earlier, felt it essential to absolve his nation in advance from any responsibility for this dread calamity, if it should follow upon the actions he proposed to take. Khrushchev had argued, for example, in his July 8 speech, that if war came it would be because the West insisted on

---

[14]Richard H. Rovere, "Letter from Washington," *New Yorker*, vol. 37, no. 25, Aug. 5, 1961, p. 32; emphasis supplied.

[15]For a list of passages added to the speech at the suggestion of various advisers, not always to its improvement, see Sorensen, p. 591.

[16]*DSB*, 45 (1961):267.

[17]Ibid., p. 268.

using force to challenge the allegedly peaceful measures taken by the Soviet Union and its allies. In a key passage in his July 25 speech, Kennedy tackled the same problem, but reached a diametrically opposed conclusion:

> There is peace in Berlin today. The source of world trouble and tension is Moscow, not Berlin. And if war begins, it will have begun in Moscow and not Berlin.
>
> For the choice of peace or war is largely theirs, not ours. It is the Soviets who have stirred up this crisis. It is they who are trying to force a change. It is they who have opposed free elections. It is they who have rejected an all-German peace treaty and the rulings of international law. And as Americans know from our history on our own old frontier, gun battles are caused by outlaws and not by officers of the peace.[18]

But the President immediately balanced this show of firmness by an appeal for peaceful negotiation: "In short, while we are ready to defend our interests, we shall also be ready to search for peace—in quiet exploratory talks, in formal or informal meetings. *We do not want military considerations to dominate the thinking of either East or West.*"[19]

Reluctant to close without a last appeal to his countrymen for their sympathetic understanding and support, and an implied appeal to the Soviets to avoid misjudging the West, the President just before delivery of the speech added a final section in which he spoke with unusual directness of the burden of responsibility resting on him and—one of his principal concerns—the danger of war by miscalculation:

> I would like to close with a personal word. When I ran for the Presidency of the United States, I knew that this country faced serious challenges, but I could not realize—nor could any man realize who does not bear the burdens of this office—how heavy and constant would be those burdens.
>
> Three times in my lifetime our country and Europe have been involved in major wars. In each case serious misjudgments were made on both sides of the intention of others, which brought about great devastation. Now, in the thermonuclear age, any misjudgment on either side about the intentions of the other could rain more devastation in several hours than has been wrought in all the wars of human history.
>
> Therefore I, as President and Commander in Chief, and all of us Americans are moving through serious days. . . . In meeting my responsibilities in these coming months as President, I need your good will and your support —and above all, your prayers.[20]

Khrushchev's July 8 speech, though it did not trigger the U.S. military build-up announced by the President on July 25, had not been without its

---

[18]Ibid., p. 272.

[19]Ibid.; emphasis supplied. According to Sorensen, p. 591, the second sentence had been used by the President at the July 19 meeting, and was added to the July 25 speech on his (Sorensen's) suggestion. It represents a key and abiding element in Kennedy's thinking about Soviet–American relations.

[20]*DSB*, 45 (1961):273. For the drafting of this passage, see Sorensen, pp. 591–92.

effect, however. At a meeting with his top military and diplomatic aides on July 8, following receipt of an advance text of Khrushchev's speech, the President ordered a review of U.S. military strength, the preliminary results of which were announced by McNamara two days later: "Currently we are [as] strong—if not stronger—than any potential aggressor. But in the face of the inescapable realities that confront us, such as threats to dispossess us of our rightful presence in Berlin, we can do no less than re-examine our needs."[21]

On the following day Deputy Secretary of Defense Gilpatric disclosed that the Joint Chiefs of Staff were considering "sizable" increases in the armed forces over the course of the next six months, at the request of the President.[22]

Though the July 25 speech was not deliberately planned as a direct response to Khrushchev's announcement of an increase in the Soviet military budget, however, by its timing and content it could hardly fail to appear in that guise to the Soviet leadership, and, as we shall see presently, there is strong evidence that Khrushchev himself so interpreted it.

Cross-currents in U.S. policy toward the Soviets

At the very time when the United States and Soviet Russia appeared to be heading for a violent clash over Berlin, business-as-usual negotiations between the two powers were proceeding in three separate fields—air communications, cultural exchange, and disarmament. In part, these "untimely" contacts were the result of a simple bureaucratic lack of coordination—the diplomatic right hand not knowing what the military-strategic left hand was doing. The air communications and cultural exchange talks, for example, can be explained on this basis. In regard to the bilateral disarmament talks, however, the apparent lack of coordination reflected the deliberately broad and complex policies of Kennedy himself, who never forgot his own maxim: "We do not want military considerations to dominate the thinking of either East or West." A glance at the relevant data will help clarify the situation.

The air communications talks

The Soviet–U.S. negotiations on a Moscow–New York air link, held in Washington from July 18 to August 7, 1961, represented the realization of plans going back to the first U.S.–Soviet cultural exchange agreement of January 27, 1958.[23] Section XIV of that agreement had provided that: "Both parties agree in principle to establish on the basis of reciprocity direct air flights between the United States and the Soviet Union. Negotiations on terms and con-

---

[21]*Keesing's Contemporary Archives*, 1961, p. 18223.

[22]*NYT*, July 12, 1961, p. 1.

[23]For a summary of the historical background of the negotiations, see *NYT*, Aug. 8, 1961, p. 1.

ditions satisfactory to both parties will be conducted by appropriate representatives of each Government at a mutually convenient date to be determined
later."[24]

Nothing having been done to implement this provision during the term of
validity of the 1958 agreement, it was repeated verbatim in the 1960–61 agreement signed on November 21, 1959.[25]

At their meeting in 1959 Khrushchev and Eisenhower agreed that formal
talks on the subject should be opened, but after the collapse of the Paris summit meeting in May 1960 and the shooting down by the Soviets of an RB–47
reconnaissance plane on July 1, 1960, the United States requested that the
talks be postponed.

Following the release of the surviving RB–47 crewmen, the Kennedy administration in February 1961 inquired whether the Soviets still wished to initiate
talks and received an affirmative response in June. On July 7 the State Department announced that the United States and the Soviet Union had agreed to
conduct talks "on the establishment of reciprocal commercial air services between New York and Moscow."[26] The talks, it was announced, would get
under way in Washington on July 18, with James M. Landis, special assistant
to the President, as chairman of the U.S. delegation, and Col. Gen. Yevgenii F.
Loginov, chief of the Main Administration of the Civil Air Fleet under the
USSR Council of Ministers, as head of the Soviet delegation. Pan-American
World Airways, which had been certified by the Civil Aeronautics Board to
operate a U.S.–Moscow route, was to be represented at the talks in an observer
status. Confirmation and additional details were provided by a second State
Department announcement on July 15.[27]

The talks, held in Washington from July 18 to August 7, resulted in the
initialing of an agreement which the State Department announced on August
7, with the comment, "The Department issued the announcement, even though
the formal agreement has not been completed, because the Soviet Government
chose to inform the Soviet press of it in Moscow."[28]

The tentative agreement, pushed through despite the mounting tension over
Berlin, fell victim to the international crisis, when the State Department announced on August 21 that the agreement would not be signed "in the light of
the overall world situation."[29]

---

[24]*DSB*, 38 (1958):246.

[25]*DSB*, 41 (1959):957.

[26]Text of announcement, *DSB*, 45 (1961):163.

[27]Ibid., p. 197.

[28]*NYT*, Aug. 8, 1961, p. 1.

[29]Smith, *Defense of Berlin*, p. 299; *NYT*, Aug. 22, 1961, p. 1; Radio Moscow, Aug. 22,
1961. Neither the announcements of Aug. 7 and 21 nor the text of the agreement itself were
published in the *DSB*.

The cultural exchange negotiations

When the Kennedy administration took office in 1961 the two-year exchange agreement with the Soviet Union, signed on November 21, 1959, was still in effect. Preliminary negotiations for a renewal of the agreement for 1962–63 were held in Washington from July 27 to 31, 1961. In announcing the talks the State Department referred to "a frank discussion of the problems involved in carrying out specific exchanges," an indication that the talks had not gone smoothly. The announcement noted, nevertheless, that: "It was agreed that proposals for a new exchange agreement would be discussed during the next several months, with negotiations tentatively scheduled to begin in November."[30]

Like the air communications talks, however, the negotiations on cultural and other exchanges fell victim to international tension. It was not until the end of January 1962 that talks were finally resumed in Washington for renewal of the exchange agreement for the years 1962–63.[31]

The bilateral disarmament talks

The first phase of the Soviet–U.S. bilateral talks on disarmament, which had been announced on March 30, 1961, took place in Washington on June 19–30. There appeared to be little promise for an eventual meeting of minds, since the two sides could not even agree on the purpose of the talks. The U.S. approach was to press for agreement on a basic statement of principles for future disarmament negotiations, while the Soviets insisted that the first and indispensable step was to reach accord on the basic provisions of a specific disarmament plan.[32] Both sides accepted the idea that a primary goal should be agreement on the composition of a negotiating body for disarmament talks, but while they had no difficulty in finding a mutually acceptable list of ten nations, five from each bloc, to serve as members of a disarmament conference, they were far apart in their recommendations for "neutral" nations to be invited to participate.[33]

In an effort to break the deadlock which appeared to be developing at the very outset of the talks, President Kennedy, on June 30, held a half-hour discussion in the White House with Soviet Ambassador Menshikov and V. A. Zorin, the Soviet negotiator.[34] Following the White House meeting it was announced that the talks would resume in Moscow after a two-week recess.[35]

[30] *AFP, 1961*, p. 612, citing Department of State press release, Aug. 1, 1961.

[31] *DSB*, 46 (1962): 652–53.

[32] See McCloy's summary of the negotiations in his report to the President dated Oct. 6, 1961, in *Documents on Disarmament, 1961*, pp. 520–21.

[33] *SIA, 1961*, p. 241.

[34] *NYT*, July 1, 1961, p. 1.

[35] *DSB*, 45 (1961): 106.

The second phase of the talks got under way in Moscow on July 17 and continued until July 29. At first the prospects seemed no more favorable than they had in Washington, but a break occurred on July 27, when the Soviet side for the first time agreed to discuss a statement of basic principles.[36] At this point McCloy was in Sochi, where he had flown on July 25 at Khrushchev's invitation. There on July 27 he was made the recipient of something far more weighty than a Soviet concession in the bilateral disarmament talks, however: nothing less than Khrushchev's emotional reaction to Kennedy's speech of July 25, an event which signaled the opening of the next phase in the Soviet campaign on Berlin.

[36]*Documents on Disarmament, 1961*, p. 521.

5 The Soviets Decide on the Minimum Objective

The Western notes to the Soviet Union of July 17 and the Kennedy/Sorensen statement of July 19, however one might judge their relative merits as exercises in swaying men's minds, left completely unchanged the basic power balance between the Soviets and the West, and for that reason evoked only verbal response from the Soviets. Kennedy's speech of July 25, on the other hand, and the administrative steps which were promptly taken to translate its recommendations into reality, clearly and unmistakably marked the end of the period in which Khrushchev and his associates had been able to base Soviet foreign policy on inflated claims of military superiority over, or even parity with, the West. The July 25 speech therefore elicited an immediate and sharply worded response from Khrushchev, which was followed by a linked series of Soviet moves, extending from late July to mid-September, constituting an implicit recognition of the new power balance.

McCloy and Pham Van Dong at Sochi, July 25-27

On the evening of July 25, John J. McCloy, the chief U.S. negotiator in the bilateral talks on disarmament, flew to Sochi at Khrushchev's invitation to confer with the Soviet leader at his dacha.[1]

A TASS bulletin from Sochi, on July 26, prominently featured in *Pravda* the following day, described McCloy's visit in strikingly cordial terms: "In the conversation, which took place in a friendly atmosphere, questions of the Soviet–American exchange of opinions now being carried on in Moscow on the subject of disarmament were touched on, as well as other questions of Soviet–American relations."[2]

[1] *NYT*, Aug. 1, 1961, p. 1.
[2] *Pravda*, July 27, 1961, p. 1.

The TASS bulletin noted that in addition to V. A. Zorin, McCloy's counterpart in the bilateral disarmament talks, those present at a dinner given by Khrushchev included family members of both host and guest—McCloy's wife, daughter, and son-in-law, together with Mrs. Khrushchev and Khrushchev's daughter and son-in-law, Mr. and Mrs. Adzhubei.

The immediate purpose behind Khrushchev's hospitable gesture, it would appear, was to lend his personal support to the bilateral talks (as Kennedy had done in his White House conference with Menshikov and Zorin on June 30) and to inform McCloy of the Soviet concession in agreeing to discuss the basic principles for disarmament negotiations. That this was no sudden impulse on the part of Khrushchev was indicated by the fact that a carefully worked out draft document, "Basic Principles of a Treaty on General and Complete Disarmament," had been prepared by the Soviets.[3]

Of particular interest in the Soviet draft was its final paragraph, which read: "Both sides reaffirm their resolve, until a treaty on general and complete disarmament is concluded, to refrain from acts which may increase international tension and to strive to the end that all international disputes may be solved by peaceful means alone, through negotiation."[4]

Considering that this draft was prepared and submitted only a few weeks before the Soviet Union was to make some of its most provocative and risky foreign policy moves since Stalin's death, it is tempting to speculate on the reason for the inclusion of this paragraph at this particular time. Was it an instance of unusually crass hypocrisy? Was it an attempt to lull the West into a false sense of security in order to maximize the effect of surprise? Should it be regarded as a rather pathetic effort at achieving international respectability on the part of a habitual offender? Or was it a sincerely meant statement of intention at the time of drafting which acquired its ironic overtones only in the light of subsequent events? Whatever the explanation, the fact remains that not since Stalin's heyday had Soviet words so glaringly failed to match Soviet actions.

In retrospect, the last hypothesis seems the most likely. At the time the draft was being prepared the general assumption in the Soviet leadership was that while the West might protest against Soviet actions in Germany and Berlin, it would not run the risk of war by taking any decisive action to oppose them. Ambassador Menshikov's reports on the U.S. mood could be cited in support of that reading of the probable course of events.

Schlesinger's account of McCloy's conference with Khrushchev also appears to confirm this analysis. (Schlesinger was evidently privileged to read the lengthy cable which McCloy sent to the President on July 29,[5] reporting on his meeting with the Soviet Premier.) According to Schlesinger, on the first day of the meeting (July 26), "He [Khrushchev] was in a jolly mood, compar-

[3]*Documents on Disarmament, 1961*, pp. 267–69.
[4]Ibid., p. 269.
[5]*NYT*, Aug. 1, 1961.

ing the exchange of diplomatic notes to kicking a football back and forth and adding that this would probably continue until a treaty was signed and the Soviet Union kicked a different kind of ball."[6]

Khrushchev's mood changed abruptly, however, after he had read the text of the President's speech of July 25, a Russian translation of which was in his hands by the evening of the 26th or the early hours of the 27th.[7] According to Schlesinger:

> . . . he [Khrushchev] told McCloy emotionally that the United States had declared preliminary war on the Soviet Union. It had presented an ultimatum and clearly intended hostilities. This confirmed, Khrushchev said, the thesis of his January [6] speech that the capitalist world had lost confidence in its capacity to triumph by peaceful means. The President, he added, seemed a reasonable young man, filled with energy and doubtless wishing to display that energy; but, if war occurred, he would be the last President. However, Khrushchev concluded, he still believed in the President's good sense. After thunderstorms, people cooled off, thought problems over and resumed human shape.[8]

The basic pattern of Khrushchev's reaction as reported by Schlesinger—an initial violent outburst, followed by threats and then simmering down to a more temperate conclusion—is confirmed by a *New York Times* story of August 1, which was evidently based on information derived from McCloy's cable to Kennedy of July 29. According to this source:

> The Wednesday [July 26] discussions . . . were cordial. By Thursday, however, Mr. Khrushchev had read the address [of July 25] and he opened the discussions of that day with what one official described as "a fair-sized explosion."
>
> Mr. Khrushchev repeated many of the things he had said privately to other Western diplomats—that the Soviet Union intended to sign a separate peace treaty with East Germany and that if the Western powers wanted to shoot their way through to West Berlin they should remember that the Soviet Union had superiority in arms and divisions and was nearer to the field of battle. All during this outburst, it was said, Mr. Zorin, who was also present, was completely relaxed.
>
> Mr. Khrushchev went on to say what nonsense this all was; that war, if it came, would be decided by the biggest rockets, and that the Soviet Union had them.
>
> He then softened his tone, it was related, and observed that the Soviets and Americans were both great peoples and should be friends. The prestige of both countries had become involved, he was reported to have said, but there was nothing to go to war about if there was reasonableness on both sides. Therefore, he said, let us be reasonable . . . .

[6]Schlesinger, p. 392. Schlesinger's dates need minor adjustments.

[7]The Voice of America beamed a Russian translation of Kennedy's speech to Russia, which was not jammed: *U.S. News and World Report*, vol. 51, no. 6, Aug. 7, 1961, p. 8. A summary of the speech was published in *Pravda*, July 26, 1961, p. 3.

[8]Schlesinger, p. 392.

Repeatedly, it was stated, Mr. Khrushchev came back to the refrain: Why could not the United States and the Soviet Union work this out between themselves. It was said that he was obviously reverting to a theme he has often used before that the Soviet Union and the United States were the only powers that counted. He was said to have referred to Britain's economic problems and to President de Gaulle's troubles in Algeria.

But always, it was said, Mr. Khrushchev assumed that the settlement between "friends" would have to be on his terms.[9]

In line with his emphasis on the decisive role of the United States and the Soviet Union, Khrushchev told McCloy that he was convinced that the U.S. allies would not fight to defend Western occupation rights in Berlin.[10]

It was McCloy himself who publicly revealed, in a speech to the National Press Club in Washington on August 22, that during their meeting on July 27, ". . . the Soviet Premier boasted of Soviet ability to build and deliver by rocket on U.S. territory a hundred-megaton bomb, and spoke of his scientists' eagerness to test such a weapon. Mr. Khrushchev also linked any agreement on disarmament with a satisfactory solution of the Berlin question."[11]

Schlesinger provides a fuller context in which Khrushchev's reference to the 100-megaton bomb occurred:

At the end of July, Khrushchev himself told McCloy that he was under strong pressure to test, especially from his scientists, and that the Berlin crisis had increased the pressure. He had been successful thus far, he said, in holding off the decision, but, the more the United States intensified its threats of war, the more arguments it gave those in the Soviet Union who wanted to resume. His scientists favored a one-hundred-megaton bomb as the most economical, and, though they had the rockets to lift it, the bomb itself needed to be tested. He had cheered his scientists, he said, by telling them that the United States would resume testing and thus release them to try out their own bomb: "Don't piss in your pants—you'll have your chance soon enough."[12]

Khrushchev's threatening allusion to a Soviet superweapon is of cardinal importance in evaluating his response to Kennedy's speech and its meaning for Soviet strategy: "the first hint to the outside world of the momentous intimidation offense then being planned in the Kremlin"[13] appeared in immediate reaction to the strong Western response to the Soviet challenge.

In evaluating the significance of Khrushchev's "superbomb" threat, one should take into account the fact that at almost the same moment the chief Soviet negotiator at the nuclear test ban talks, Semyon Tsarapkin, was

[9]NYT, Aug. 1, 1961, pp. 1, 4.

[10]See the report of McCloy's statement to the Republican Policy Committee, NYT, Aug. 11, 1961, p. 7.

[11]SIA, 1961, p. 242, citing the Manchester Guardian, Aug. 23, 1961. See also Jacobson and Stein, p. 279.

[12]Schlesinger, p. 454.

[13]Earl H. Voss, Nuclear Ambush. The Test-ban Trap (Chicago: Regnery, 1963), p. 467.

strongly disavowing any Soviet intention of clandestinely violating the de facto test ban. "We have officially notified the whole world," Tsarapkin stated on July 28, "that we are not carrying out nuclear weapon tests, and we have not undertaken, we are not undertaking, nor do we intend to undertake, any clandestine activities of that kind."[14]

Accusing the United States of preparing to carry out nuclear tests, Tsarapkin said, that this "revolts the conscience of the peoples of the world. The peoples of the world demand cessation of tests."[15]

The conclusion to be drawn is not that Tsarapkin was being deliberately hypocritical but that no decision had yet been taken by the Soviet leadership to authorize the resumption of nuclear tests. Khrushchev's outburst to McCloy enables us to establish a link between the Soviet campaign in Berlin, Soviet possession of a 100-megaton bomb, and the resumption of nuclear testing by the Soviets. At the same time it shows that as of late July 1961, Khrushchev was still counting on the United States to resume nuclear testing before the Soviets did so.

* * *

McCloy was not the only foreign visitor at Sochi on July 27. North Vietnamese Premier Pham Van Dong was also received by Khrushchev on that day, despite the fact that the DRV governmental delegation had long since left the Soviet Union. The possibility must therefore be reckoned with that the two diplomatic items in Khrushchev's July 27 guestbook were connected in some way. A plausible hypothesis would be that the North Vietnamese delegation's primary purpose in coming to Moscow had been to solicit Soviet support for their campaign of subversion against the South Vietnamese government of Ngo Dinh Diem; that the Soviet leadership had at first avoided giving them a direct answer, pending the outcome of the current phase of the struggle with the Western powers over Berlin, meanwhile keeping the North Vietnamese handy in case a decision was reached (instead of returning directly to Hanoi the Vietnamese delegation flew to Prague after leaving Moscow, and later visited Poland); and that Khrushchev decided to increase Soviet support to North Vietnam only after he had learned of the U.S. military build-up announced by Kennedy on July 25. Appropriately, *Izvestiia* on July 28 published an article attacking Diem's government.[16] It will be recalled that Adzhubei, the editor of *Izvestiia* (and son-in-law of Khrushchev), was at Sochi on July 26 and was thus in an excellent position to learn at first hand of any new decision in Soviet–North Vietnamese relations.

Confirmation of this line of analysis is provided by a study of the purpose and results of the North Vietnamese mission to the Soviet Union in the sum-

[14]Quoted by Dean at the Nov. 29, 1961, session: *Documents on Disarmament, 1961*, p. 685. Note that Tsarapkin's statement referred only to *clandestine* testing, and thus did not rule out the possibility that the Soviet Union might be preparing *open* tests.

[15]Quoted by Stelle at the Sept. 4, 1961 session: ibid., p. 352.

[16]*Izv.*, July 28, 1961, p. 5.

mer of 1961 made by P. J. Honey, a specialist in Southeast Asian affairs.[17] After noting the change in the mission's itinerary which took Pham Van Dong to Sochi to confer with Khrushchev, Honey sums up the achievements of the mission as follows:

> Pham Van Dong's mission did achieve a great measure of success. It secured military aid to the value of 220,000,000 new roubles for the DRV's struggle to reunify Vietnam. The principal donor was Russia, but some of this aid was also given by Czechoslovakia, Poland, and China. Now under the terms of the Geneva agreements of 1954, the DRV is not allowed to import new armaments or military equipment, and, furthermore, Poland is one of the three countries with the task of ensuring that she does not do so. The DRV's acceptance of this military aid suggests that she may be contemplating tearing up these agreements, refusing to admit the International Truce Supervisory Commission, and increasing the military attacks on South Vietnam.
>
> The mission also secured the cancellation of the DRV's outstanding debts which were incurred under her earlier three-year plan. These debts were enormous and had been causing very considerable embarrassment to the North Vietnamese authorities. At the beginning of 1961, they amounted to 430,000,000 new roubles, so that Pham Van Dong's success in negotiating their cancellation was of very great importance for the DRV. Thus, Pham Van Dong's mission received a grand total of 650,000,000 new roubles in aid, and possibly promises of more aid in the future. It won approval for the DRV's objective of reunifying Vietnam, possibly at the risk of a major war, and Ho Chi Minh appears to have been given the green light to step up his attacks on the South. From the point of view of the Vietnamese Communists, the mission must be considered most successful, but the implications of the military aid and the approval of DRV plans for reunification are extremely ominous.[18]

The decision to seal off West Berlin

Kennedy's speech of July 25 confronted Khrushchev with the necessity of making a fundamental choice. Either he would have to raise his bid in striving for the maximum objective of Soviet policy—inflicting a major diplomatic defeat on the Western powers by forcing them to accept the fait accompli of a Soviet–East German peace treaty, bringing with it the end of Western occupation rights in West Berlin—or settle for the minimum objective—shoring up the East German regime by shutting off the escape route via West Berlin.

Khrushchev's meeting with McCloy on July 27 can be identified as the point at which he decided to settle for the minimum objective. The primary reason for the decision, obviously, was his recognition that the United States, in Kennedy's July 25 speech, had raised the stakes to a level which the Soviet Union could not afford to match. A potent secondary reason was the intense

[17]P. J. Honey, "Pham Van Dong's Tour," *China Quarterly* 8 (Oct.–Dec. 1961): 42–44.
[18]Ibid., p. 44.

pressure being exerted on the communist regime in East Germany by the rising tide of refugees fleeing to the West. By mid-July the tide was flowing at the rate of 1,000 or more refugees a day, stimulated by rumors that the East German regime was preparing to cut off West Berlin.[19]

Though aware of the rumors, U.S. officials in Washington generally tended to discount them. Asked in a television interview on July 23 whether he expected "any move by the Soviets to seal off the [East German] frontiers to keep their people from fleeing," Rusk replied: "There have been some reports in recent days of efforts being made to interrupt traffic of passengers who come into East Berlin and catch the U-Bahn [subway] to cross over to West Berlin, but nevertheless the numbers who actually arrive are still very large."[20]

In his speech of July 25 the President called West Berlin "a beacon of hope behind the Iron Curtain, an escape hatch for refugees,"[21] but gave no indication of awareness that the escape hatch might be closed.

Complacency in Washington was not matched in East Germany, however, where Ulbricht, on July 26, demanded that "all means" be used to stop the drain of refugees to the West.[22] That some form of border-sealing was the obvious solution to the East German regime's refugee problem had meanwhile occurred to a number of perspicacious Western observers, among them Senator Fulbright, who candidly remarked in a television interview on July 30, "I don't understand why the East Germans don't close their border because I think they have a right to close it."[23] Richard Rovere, in an analysis of the Berlin situation, observed that Khrushchev had "the means at hand for ending the largest of his problems with West Berlin; the flow of refugees could be sealed off at any time—at a heavy but almost certainly not unbearable cost to economic and political stability in East Germany—and he could keep the viruses of West Berlin political attitudes out of his zone by tougher methods of political sanitation."[24]

The *New York Times* agreed: "There has never been any East–West agreement that would prevent the Communists from closing the border between East Germany and East Berlin. Why they have not done so in the past is something of a mystery."[25]

Common to all these attempts to pierce the veil shrouding Soviet intentions were two erroneous assumptions: (1) that Soviet action with regard to Berlin, if it came, would be limited to some form of border-sealing between East Germany and the Soviet sector of Berlin, and (2) that the action would follow, not precede or replace, the signing of the Soviet–GDR peace treaty, which for so

---

[19]*NYT*, July 23, 1961, sect. 4, p. 1.

[20]*DSB*, 45 (1961): 286.

[21]*JFK, 1961*, p. 534.

[22]*Washington Post*, July 27, 1961, p. A–5.

[23]Schlesinger, p. 394.

[24]*New Yorker*, vol. 37, no. 25, Aug. 5, 1961, p. 34.

[25]*NYT*, Aug. 6, 1961, sect. 4, p. 4.

long had been made to appear the central pillar of Soviet policy in Germany. That the Soviets would deliberately violate the postwar international agreements providing for four-power occupation of Berlin and that they would do so suddenly, without any warning, and without even bothering to provide an attempt at legal justification by signing a so-called German peace treaty were possibilities which occurred to no one in the West.

The Western powers, therefore, continued to ignore the obvious danger of a border-sealing operation and focused their attention instead on what they regarded as the major threat to their position, Soviet–East German interference with Western occupation rights in West Berlin. The fact that the Western alliance's strategy was aimed exclusively at meeting the Soviets' maximum objective made it considerably easier for Khrushchev and the Soviet leadership to execute the risky and delicate maneuver of shifting from maximum to minimum objective in the midst of a major international crisis and to achieve complete tactical surprise in doing so.

The Presidium ratifies Khrushchev's decision

As soon as he learned of the U.S. military build-up, announced in Kennedy's speech of July 25, Khrushchev decided that the Soviet Union would not try to top the American bid and that it would therefore be necessary to shift from the Soviets' maximum objective in the Berlin crisis. Because he was operating in accordance with a strategic plan already decided on by the Presidium, Khrushchev had the power to reach this decision immediately and without consulting his colleagues in the Presidium.

In order to translate the basic decision into action, however, consultations would be required, first within the Soviet leadership, to discuss and ratify the decision and to lay plans for the sequence of moves which it would entail, and then to communicate the decision and its attendant plan of action to the East European ally-satellites of the Soviet Union.

Late July found the Soviet leaders scattered. Some, like Khrushchev, were on vacation: Kosygin, for example, was in Bulgaria, where he ended his vacation on August 1 to return to Moscow.[26]

While it was urgent, however, to convene an early meeting of the Presidium, it was desirable from the standpoint of concealment to avoid any overt sign of precipitancy. Above all, no direct indication must be allowed to appear of a causal link between the American action (Kennedy's July 25 speech) and the Soviet counteraction which was in preparation.

Khrushchev therefore did not hurry back to Moscow immediately after leaving Sochi, but conducted a well-publicized and apparently leisurely return to the capital, his attention far away, it would seem, from foreign policy problems. On July 28 he visited the Kuban Scientific Research Institute for Testing Tractors and Agricultural Machinery, accompanied by two full mem-

[26]Radio Sofia, Aug. 1 and 2, 1961.

bers of the Presidium—D. S. Polyansky, chairman of the Council of Ministers of the RSFSR, and N. V. Podgorny, first secretary of the Communist party of the Ukraine—and two candidate members—G. I. Voronov, deputy chairman of the Central Committee's Bureau for the RSFSR, and V. P. Mzhavanadze, first secretary of the Communist party of Georgia, as well as a number of agricultural officials.[27] July 29 found Khrushchev at a kolkhoz in Kharkov oblast, along with most of the same officials and some new ones.[28] Khrushchev's whereabouts on July 30 were not reported by the Soviet press, but by July 31 he was back in the Kremlin, where he welcomed a party-government delegation from Rumania and received a group of African diplomats.[29]

As a supporter of Khrushchev on several important aspects of foreign and internal policy—including Germany—Kosygin's presence at a Presidium meeting on Germany would be of cardinal importance from Khrushchev's point of view. We can be fairly certain, therefore, that the Presidium meeting to debate Khrushchev's basic decision of July 27 was not held before Kosygin's return to Moscow on August 1; probably it was held on the following day. It had definitely taken place by the 3rd, since on that date a hurriedly improvised meeting of the East European communist leaders was convened in Moscow, obviously in accordance with a decision by the Soviet leadership.

Blandishments and threats, August 1–5

Having decided on the course of action to be followed in Berlin—a course which involved the danger of Western counteraction—Khrushchev devoted the first days of August to creating the proper international atmosphere for the successful carrying out of Soviet plans. The means used for this purpose were a shrewd mixture of threats and blandishments—warnings to the West not to risk war, combined with professions of willingness to negotiate disputed issues.

The campaign was launched on August 1 at a reception in the Kremlin for the visiting Rumanian delegation. In a short speech of welcome Khrushchev confidently affirmed the unity of the socialist bloc against "imperialist" attempts to reduce the communist nations to "capitalist slavery." A U.S. presidential proclamation of July 14 announcing "Captive Nations Week" provided a convenient pretext for bluster: "We have already said, and announce once again, that no kind of 'weeks,' no provocations can change the course of history or have the power to divert the free peoples of the socialist countries from the path they have chosen."[30]

[27] *Pravda*, July 29, 1961, p. 1, with a prominently displayed photograph showing Khrushchev grinning broadly; similarly *Izv.*, July 29, 1961, p. 1.

[28] *Pravda, Izv.*, July 30, 1961, p. 10.

[29] Khrushchev, *Kommunizm*, 2:354.

[30] Ibid., 1:287; partial translation, *NYT*, Aug. 2, 1961, p. 3.

Communists, Khrushchev affirmed, are "the most consistent and determined defenders of the cause of peace in the world," but "we decisively warn all lovers of military adventures: behave sensibly and remember that we have all the necessary means to cool off your hot heads."[31]

More valuable for Soviet purposes than the Rumanian visit, however, was the visit to Moscow of Italian Premier Fanfani, accompanied by his foreign minister, Signor Segni, since Italy, as a member of NATO, might be expected to play a significant role in modifying Western policies if it could be cajoled or threatened into weakening its allegiance to the Western alliance. During the brief visit by the Italian delegation (August 2–5), Khrushchev employed his usual mixture of promises and threats in order to dramatize the Soviet demand for a German peace treaty. Since genuine negotiations on Germany and Berlin were not a Soviet objective, however, Khrushchev was careful to rule out specifically the known Western conditions for negotiation, particularly the demand for all-German elections as a prerequisite toward reunification: "[Khrushchev] stated that Soviet officials would leave the negotiating table if the Western powers were to press the subject of German reunification through elections."[32]

During the discussion Khrushchev raised the subject of NATO bases in Italy and was told by Fanfani that they were located in orange groves—a piece of information which Khrushchev was to put to effective use in a speech on August 11. The question about the bases was intended to convey a menace, direct or indirect, and from available evidence it appears that Khrushchev used the opportunity to threaten the Italians with missile attacks in case of war between the Soviet Union and the West, just as he had done with the British Ambassador in early July.

The Italian delegation was able to convince itself, however, that the real meaning of what Khrushchev said lay not in his threats, open or implied, but in his professed readiness to negotiate over Berlin and Germany: "They seem to have believed that in what they had extracted from the Soviet leader two new elements could be found, namely, a willingness to discuss a demilitarized zone in the middle of Europe, and, much more important, new and more solidly formulated guarantees for the independence of West Berlin and for western access to the city."[33]

The Italian visit could be considered a positive achievement for Khrushchev, however, only if the Soviets really wished to negotiate, or if the Italians succeeded in modifying the policy of their NATO partners by convincing them that this was true. Since neither condition obtained, as quickly became apparent, the Italian visit must be rated as no more than a diversion.

[31]Khrushchev, *Kommunizm*, 1:287–88.

[32]Seymour Topping, *NYT*, Aug. 5, 1961, p. 1. For a summary of the talks based on the Italian press, see *SIA, 1961*, p. 243.

[33]*SIA, 1961*, p. 244.

The Soviet replies of August 3

While the Italian delegation was winding up its discussions with Khrushchev, on August 3 the Soviet Foreign Ministry dispatched answers to the three Western notes of July 17 and to the West German note of July 12.[34]

The basic pattern of the three notes to the Western allies was identical: a historical summary of postwar exchanges on Germany, designed to prove that the Soviet Union, not the West, had been the only sincere and consistent advocate of the conclusion of a German peace treaty; a portrayal of West German policy as militarist, aggressive, and revanchist; the insistence that German reunification could be achieved only by the Germans themselves, by means of direct negotiations between the two German governments rather than on the basis of free elections and self-determination; a description of the benefits a peace treaty would bring to Germany and to the cause of world peace; a defense of Soviet proposals for converting West Berlin into a "free city"; expressions of willingness to negotiate, combined with doubts as to the sincerity of the West in this regard; and, in conclusion, warnings that Western threats would be powerless to affect Soviet policy.

Embedded in the texts were individual touches designed to make the notes more directly appropriate to their recipients. Thus: "The note to Britain attacked the British grant of training facilities to West German troops in Britain. That to France sought to play on old French fears of Western Germany, while attacking French policy in Algeria. That to the United States sought to find logical contradictions in the American position, and expressed 'serious doubts' as to the American readiness to enter into talks on Berlin."[35]

A major aim of all three notes was to drive a wedge between the three Western allies and the West German government by convincing them that they might be dragged into war unless they curbed West German policies toward the Soviet Union. "The population of West Germany," the notes asserted, "lives amid the rampaging of revanchist passions. The Government of the Federal Republic of Germany continually brings forward demands to alter the existing frontiers."[36]

The West German government was portrayed as a potential lunatic who might precipitate a war no one wanted: "It would be dangerous to lose sight of the fact that the Federal Republic of Germany even now has more than enough armed forces and arms at its disposal to bring about a general military conflict. After all it is not necessary to be the commandant of a powder-

---

[34] *Pravda* and *Izv.*, Aug. 6, 1961; texts in *Vneshniaia Politika Sovetskogo Soiuza i Mezhdunarodnye Otnosheniia, Sbornik Dokumentov. 1961 god*, pp. 205–20 (note to the U.S.), 220–33 (note to Britain), 233–47 (note to France), and 247–58 (note to West Germany). Translation of the note to the U.S., *NYT*, Aug. 5, 1961, p. 2. Hereinafter cited as *VPSS 1961*.

[35] *SIA, 1961*, p. 244.

[36] United Kingdom, *Selected Documents on Germany and the Question of Berlin 1944–1961* (London: H.M.S.O., 1961, Command 1552), p. 457 (hereinafter cited as Cmnd. 1552).

magazine in order to blow it up. It is enough that there should be a madman among those in attendance on the commandant to strike a match."[37]

In identical language all three notes stated that the German peace treaty would secure [*zakrepit*] the boundaries of Germany which, it was asserted, had been "established" [*ustanovlennye*] after World War II. In the TASS translation of the note to the United States this passage was rendered in a stronger, more provocative way: "This treaty will juridically *seal* the frontiers of Germany established after World War II,"[38] thereby providing one of the few indications in the notes of any explicit anticipation of the plan to seal off West Berlin.

More obviously and unmistakably related to this plan was a paragraph suggesting that the problem of West Berlin's status could be settled by negotiation *after* conclusion of a German peace treaty (again, the texts of the three notes were identical at this point): "The proposal to turn West Berlin into a demilitarized free city signifies nothing other than the readiness of the Soviet Union to settle, jointly with all interested parties, the question of the status of West Berlin *after* the signing of a German peace treaty."[39]

The implication was that the Western allies could safely take part in the proposed negotiations for a German peace treaty without thereby prejudicing their occupation rights in West Berlin, since these would be the subject of later negotiations.

The view that this passage was intended to be read in this way in the West is strengthened by the fact that all three notes maintained a studied silence on the most controversial aspect of the Soviet proposal, the threat to turn over control of the access routes to West Berlin to East German authorities after conclusion of a peace treaty. At least one prominent Western official, Adlai Stevenson, appears to have so interpreted the passage, since he made a personal trip to see Kennedy at Hyannis Port at this time to argue in favor of negotiations with the Soviets.[40]

The concentration in the notes of August 3 on the proposal to conclude a German peace treaty and the enticing implication that the status of West Berlin could be the subject of separate negotiations after a peace treaty had been concluded were by no means accidental, but formed part of the Soviet cover plan to mask the preparations for sealing off West Berlin. By focusing the West's attention on the peace treaty proposal, the Soviets could hope to improve their chances for achieving surprise in their plans for West Berlin. To make the prospect more enticing, the notes omitted any reference to the 1961 deadline for conclusion of a German peace treaty.

The note to the West German government, which was drafted separately from the other three notes of August 3, attempted to answer point by point the arguments set forth in the West German note of July 12. Its most significant

[37]Ibid., p. 459.
[38]*Documents on Germany, 1944–1961*, p. 710.
[39]Cmnd. 1552, p. 462; emphasis supplied.
[40]*NYT*, Aug. 6, 1961, p. 3.

passage occurred toward the close, with the flat assertion that "the F.R.G. [West Germany] did not and does not have rights of any kind in West Berlin."[41]

Otherwise the note to West Germany was distinguished chiefly by the fact that it alone among the four notes of August 3 included a reference to the 1961 deadline for conclusion of the German peace treaty, apparently reflecting a desire to maintain maximum pressure on West Germany while dangling the prospect of unforced negotiations before the Western allies.

The Soviets brief the East European leaders, August 3–5

On August 3 the first secretaries of the East European communist parties— except Enver Hoxha, the Albanian first secretary[42]—met in Moscow for what was officially described as a conference of the Warsaw Pact powers on the German question. The circumstances surrounding the conference indicate not only that it was held in secrecy but that it had been convened on extremely short notice. For example, East German party boss Walter Ulbricht flew to Moscow on the day the conference opened (amid rumors that he was going "to seek Russian agreement to a complete closure of the frontier between East and West Berlin").[43] Similarly, Czechoslovak party First Secretary Antonín Novotný flew to Moscow on August 3, to "spend his vacation" in the Soviet Union.[44] As we have seen, Rumanian First Secretary Gheorghiu-Dej was already in the Soviet Union, where he was leading an official delegation.[45] The Bulgarian party leader, Todor Zhivkov, may also have been in the Soviet Union; on July 23 he had visited Khrushchev at Sochi, along with the general secretary of the French communist party, Maurice Thorez.[46] Except for voluminous reports on the Rumanian visit, however, the Soviet press maintained a strict silence on the presence in Moscow of the East European leaders until the end of the conference.

The task which the conference was called on to perform was twofold: first, to take cognizance of the Soviet plan to seal off West Berlin, and second, to devise a cover story designed to achieve tactical surprise and to conceal the fact that the Soviets were preparing to scuttle their demand for a German peace treaty in 1961. The actual measures to seal the border were the direct responsibility of the Soviet forces in East Germany and the East German authorities; so far as the conference was concerned, all that was required was that the other East European regimes should receive advance notice of what was being planned, so that they could prepare the necessary statements approving and justifying the action.

[41] *VPSS, 1961*, p. 257.

[42] Griffith, *Albania*, pp. 83–84.

[43] *SIA, 1961*, citing the *Frankfurter Allgemeine Zeitung* and the *NYHT*, Aug. 4, 1961.

[44] Radio Prague, Aug. 3, 1961.

[45] The Rumanian visit had been announced by *Pravda* on July 23, long before the August 3–5 conference was thought of.

[46] Khrushchev, *Kommunizm*, 2:353.

The second aspect was a little more difficult. Banking on the calculation that the Western powers were by now thoroughly hypnotized by the blare of the Soviet demand for a peace treaty, the conference solved this problem in a simple but effective way: they continued to insist publicly that the demand retained its full validity, while doing nothing in actual fact to achieve it. Thus the communiqué issued at the end of the meeting gave only the most indirect hint of the decision to seal off West Berlin, while reaffirming in ringing tones the determination of the Soviet Union and its allies to conclude a peace treaty with East Germany by the end of 1961:

> The meeting expressed the *inflexible determination* of all its participants to achieve a peace settlement with Germany *before the end of this year*. At the same time it was unanimously resolved that, should the Western powers continue to evade the conclusion of a German peace treaty, the states concerned will be impelled to conclude a peace treaty with the German Democratic Republic which will draw a line beneath the last war *and safeguard conditions for stabilization of the situation in that part of Europe*.[47]

A command change evidently decided on (or announced by the Soviets) at the August 3–5 conference was the appointment of Marshal Ivan S. Konev, a senior Soviet commander from World War II, as commander of Soviet troops in East Germany.[48] According to East German Foreign Minister Lothar Bolz, on August 11, the appointment of Konev was one of the measures which had been decided on by the Soviet bloc to prepare for a Soviet–GDR peace treaty. Khrushchev, said Bolz, had given his "solemn assurance" to the Warsaw Pact countries that a German peace treaty would be signed during the year.[49] Since the GDR Foreign Minister would certainly be informed of Soviet intentions in Berlin, we can rule out the possibility that Bolz was ignorant of the plan to seal off West Berlin (two days before the operation was to take place). His statement was clearly intended as a contribution to the Soviet cover story.

* * *

In the well-drilled ranks of the East European communist regimes, it was the Albanians, as usual, who were out of step. As we have seen, they alone among the East European parties failed to send their first secretary to the Warsaw Pact conference. Following the conference they again demonstrated their divergent tendencies by publishing a statement of their own, rather than the communiqué adopted at the conference.[50]

[47]*Pravda*, Aug. 6, 1961; *Documents on International Affairs, 1961*, pp. 339–41; *NYT*, Aug. 6, 1961. Emphasis supplied.

[48]*NYT*, Aug. 11, 1961, p. 1.

[49]*Washington Post*, Aug. 12, 1961, p. A–7.

[50]Griffith, *Albania*, p. 83, citing *Zëri i Popullit* (Tirana), Aug. 1, 1961—evidently a misprint for Aug. 7 or 8, since the same issue carried a report on the space flight of Major Titov, which took place on Aug. 6–7. The Albanian statement was broadcast by Radio Tirana on Aug. 8, 1961.

This deviant behavior has led the historian of the Soviet–Albanian dispute, William E. Griffith, to conclude that by the late summer of 1961 the Albanians had accepted and were themselves contributing to the continuing deterioration of Soviet–Albanian relations. For example, Griffith calls the Albanian statement on the August 3–5 conference an "implicitly anti-Soviet declaration."[51] Since the question of who was the instigator in the continuing deterioration of Soviet–Albanian relations at this time has considerable significance for an understanding of Soviet policy in general, it will be useful to look at the Albanian statement in some detail.

The first point to be noted is that, according to the Albanians themselves, the statement was prepared *in advance* of the conference for distribution to the other participants.[52] The statement opens with an expression of pleasure at having been included in the conference: "Comrades! The Central Committee of the Albanian Workers' Party happily received the proposal for this important meeting to deal with the conclusion of a peace treaty with Germany."[53] The statement denounced Kennedy for "furiously fomenting the war psychosis and taking new steps for war," but this can hardly be regarded as an especially pro-Chinese, anti-Soviet attitude in the context of the time; after all, *Pravda*, in its summary of Kennedy's July 25 speech, had commented bitterly, "By his bellicose speech the President of the U.S.A. has put an end to the belief in the peaceful aspirations of the United States."[54]

Far from attacking Khrushchev or the Soviet Union, the Albanian statement came out strongly and explicitly in their support:

> We agree completely with the 20 June statement of Comrade Khrushchev maintaining that we, together with the other peace-loving states, will sign the peace treaty with the G.D.R. at the end of 1961. On the other hand we cannot fail to consider nor underrate our opponents. The attitude and recent activities of the United States, especially as regards the West Berlin question, seriously threaten peace. Facts prove, and as Comrade Khrushchev stated on 8 July, it should not be thought that the possibility of war has now been completely excluded as long as the imperialist powers exist.[55]

The statement strongly emphasized both the solidarity of the communist bloc and the close ties between Albania and the Soviet Union:

> . . . under any situation and at any dangerous moment, we will fight to the end alongside the U.S.S.R. and the other fraternal countries, regardless of any sacrifices. We will, as always and on any occasion, remain inseparable to the end and will honestly discharge our duties. The point of view of the Albanian Workers' Party is that, under the present situation, the main task of all our parties and countries is to strengthen the socialist camp around

[51]Griffith, *Albania*, p. 83.
[52]Radio Tirana, Aug. 8, 1961.
[53]Ibid.
[54]*Pravda*, July 26, 1961, p. 3.
[55]Radio Tirana, Aug. 8, 1961.

the U.S.S.R. The Albanian Workers' Party will, as always, spare no efforts in this direction.[56]

It would appear difficult to interpret these protestations of loyalty to the Soviet Union as devious manifestations of the Chinese line, nor do they make the impression of patent hypocrisy. Griffith argues that the Albanian statement "publicly opposed a Soviet policy position" by its "strong emphasis on signing a German peace treaty in 1961."[57] In the context of early August 1961, however, it would seem clearly impossible to criticize the Albanians for stressing a demand which Khrushchev himself had repeatedly voiced and which was included in the communiqué issued at the end of the August 3–5 conference.

These considerations make it necessary to reconsider the part played by that conference in the development of the Soviet–Albanian dispute. Taking the Albanian statement as the primary evidence (the Soviets maintained silence on the subject until early in 1962), the sequence of events can be reconstructed along the following lines:

1) On August 2 the Albanian party, like those of the other East European regimes, received an invitation to a hurriedly convened conference of the Warsaw Pact powers. The Albanian reaction was mixed: on the one hand they were genuinely pleased at being treated like an equal member of the Soviet bloc; on the other, they distrusted Khrushchev and suspected some ruse. Knowing that personal relations between the Soviet leader and their own first secretary, Enver Hoxha, were bad, they decided not to send Hoxha as chief of their delegation. To compensate for this lack of strict compliance with the terms of the Soviet invitation, however, they prepared a statement affirming in strong terms their undying loyalty to the Soviet Union and supporting what they believed to be Soviet policies, buttressing their declaration by quotations from Khrushchev himself.

2) On arrival in Moscow, the Albanians circulated their statement but learned to their astonishment that the primary purpose of the conference was not to build up pressure for the signing of a German peace treaty but to coordinate actions in the light of a Soviet decision which entailed the abandonment of that goal.

3) Realizing that the Soviet leadership was preparing another of its sudden foreign policy shifts, the Albanians, on their return home, decided not to publish the conference communiqué, but to substitute for it their own militantly anti-Western, pro-Soviet statement of August 3. The statement's strong emphasis on the demand for a German peace treaty in 1961 had now acquired an ironic aspect, however; knowing that the Soviets had already secretly abandoned this objective, the Albanians were in the strong position of supporting an announced Soviet policy. If the Soviets subsequently dropped the policy, no one could accuse the Albanians of disloyalty.

[56]Ibid.
[57]Griffith, *Albania*, p. 83.

By this course of action the Albanians may well have believed that they had ensured themselves against charges and recriminations from the Soviet side. They had shown their good faith by cooperating with the Soviets and supporting their avowed policies. The next move would be up to the Soviets; if Soviet–Albanian relations continued to deteriorate, it would not be the fault of the Albanians.

This reading of the evidence is strengthened by the fact that it places Soviet–Albanian relations at this time in the same perspective as Soviet–Chinese relations, with which they were closely linked. In both cases it seems clear that in the summer of 1961, the initiative for better or worse relations lay with the Soviets. We shall see presently the use to which Khrushchev put this opportunity.

Putting pressure on France: Soviet support for Tunisia

The Bizerte crisis which broke out in mid-July provided the Soviets with a welcome opportunity to embarrass the Western alliance.[58] Confronted with a French refusal to evacuate the strategic naval base, the Tunisian government took its case not only to the United Nations but also to the two superpowers. At the end of July it was announced in Tunisia that Dr. Saddok Mokkadam, Tunisian foreign minister, was to fly to Moscow on August 1.[59] At the same moment Tunisian Defense Minister Bahi Ladgham was on his way to Washington, where he had a long but unproductive discussion with President Kennedy on August 2.[60] Caught between its desire to help the emerging ex-colonial nations and its urgent need for French support in the Berlin crisis, the Kennedy administration felt incapable of offering any tangible aid to the Tunisians.[61]

Very different was the reception accorded the Tunisian mission to Moscow. Dr. Mokkadam, meeting with Soviet Foreign Minister Gromyko on August 3–5, found ready, even enthusiastic willingness to support the Tunisian side in the Bizerte dispute. "The Soviet people and the Soviet government," it was stated in the communiqué issued at the conclusion of the Gromyko–Mokkadam talks,

> support the just demands of Tunisia for the immediate cessation by France of all actions in violation of the sovereignty and independence of the Tunisian Republic and the withdrawal from Tunisia of French troops. The Soviet people are deeply indignant at the bloodthirsty crimes of the French colonialists in the area of Bizerte. They resolutely condemn them and express their sincere sympathy and condolences for the government

[58] *SIA, 1961*, pp. 240–41, 564–65.
[59] *NYT*, July 31, 1961, p. 9.
[60] *NYHT*, Aug. 3, 1961, p. 1.
[61] Schlesinger, p. 561.

and people of Tunisia in connection with the casualties that the Tunisian people sustained as a result of the French aggression.[62]

Gleefully the Soviets seized on the Bizerte dispute as an example of the evils of colonialism:

> The bloody events in Bizerte once more confirm that the military bases of Western powers on the soil of other states serve aggressive and imperialistic purposes, undermine the sovereignty and independence of the countries on whose territory they are situated, and are dangerous hotbeds of international conflict. These bases are necessary to the imperialists in order to keep in harness those peoples who have recently thrown off the colonial yoke. The military adventure of the French colonialists against the Tunisian people is one more attempt by the NATO partners to prolong their colonial domination by force of arms and to retain their military posts on the African continent.[63]

Soviet willingness to support Tunisia, moreover, was not limited to anti-colonialist rhetoric; midway through the Gromyko–Mokkadam talks the official Tunisian news agency jubilantly announced a Soviet credit of 25 million rubles ($27.7 million) for building dams and other construction—the first economic aid granted to Tunisia by any nation in the communist bloc. Contrasted with the unsuccessful results of the mission to Washington, the Soviet action made a deep impression in Tunisia: "The impact of the announcement [of the Soviet credit] on Tunisians was tremendous. . . . In the view of the Tunisians, the Soviet offer was an outstretched hand when the West had turned its back on Bizerte."[64]

Dr. Mokkadam's mission to Moscow ended triumphantly with an hour-and-a-half meeting with Khrushchev, on August 5, at which Khrushchev was reported to have pledged "all possible help" to Tunisia in ousting French troops from Bizerte and to have accepted an invitation to visit Tunisia at a later date.[65]

As matters turned out, however, the Soviet diplomatic success in Tunisia played no lasting role either in the Franco-Tunisian dispute over Bizerte or in the overshadowing Berlin crisis. Aware no doubt of the danger of Soviet intervention in the dispute, the French government, on August 11, announced the recall of one of three parachute regiments which it had sent to defend Bizerte in July, a move which was widely interpreted as a conciliatory gesture.[66] A special session of the U.N. General Assembly, convened on August 22–26 to consider the dispute, was boycotted by France

---

[62]*Pravda*, Aug. 6, 1961, p. 6; *CDSP*, XIII/31, p. 16.

[63]*CDSP*, XIII/31, p. 16.

[64]*NYT*, Aug. 7, 1961, p. 2.

[65]Theodore Shabad, *NYT*, Aug. 6, 1961, pp. 1, 16.

[66]*NYT*, Aug. 12, 1961, p. 1.

and limited itself to passing a resolution expressing regret at French behavior and characterizing the continuing presence of French troops in
Tunisia as "a violation of Tunisian sovereignty" and "a permanent source
of international friction [which] endangers international peace and security."[67]

Early in September, following a conciliatory statement by de Gaulle,
France and Tunisia reached a compromise agreement under which French
occupation of Bizerte was continued on an interim basis. A personal letter
from Kennedy to Tunisian President Habib Bourguiba helped repair the
damage to U.S.–Tunisian relations.[68] The base was finally evacuated by
French forces in October 1963.[69]

For the purposes of the present study, the significance of Soviet intervention in the Bizerte dispute lies not so much in the effect of Soviet action,
which was ephemeral, as in the light it casts on Soviet tactics and objectives. In the broad-scaled Soviet offensive centered around Berlin, Khrushchev was willing to seize on any opportunity to put the opposing coalition
on the defensive and sow discord in its ranks. If his purpose had really been,
as many in the West believed at the time, to force the West into negotiations on Berlin, it would have been stupid in the extreme to choose this
particular moment to strong-arm the French, who were the most intransigent opponents in the Western alliance of negotiations with the Soviets
over Berlin. It would have made little sense to win over the Italians, whose
role in the Berlin crisis was strictly peripheral, to the idea of negotiations
while driving the French into an even more unyielding stance. The conclusion to be drawn is that the Soviets' real purpose in the Berlin crisis was to
inflict a major diplomatic defeat on the Western alliance, not to negotiate
a compromise settlement of the Berlin problem.

The flight of Vostok 2, August 6–7

An important contribution to the Soviet campaign of pressure on Berlin was
the demonstration of Soviet heavy rocket capability provided by the twenty-
five-hour, seventeen-orbit space flight on August 6–7 of the Soviets' second
manned earth satellite, Vostok 2, piloted by Major Gherman S. Titov. In a
special edition of *Pravda* the flight was called "unprecedented in human history," while a joint party-government appeal hailed it as proof of "the great
advantage of the most advanced social system in the world, the socialist
[system]."[70]

[67]*SIA, 1961*, pp. 568–69.
[68]Schlesinger, p. 562.
[69]*SIA, 1961*, p. 572.
[70]*VPSS, 1961*, pp. 261–62.

"There is no power on earth," the appeal proclaimed, "which can hinder the indomitable progress of mankind to its bright future," and then continued: "The enemies of peace are fanning military hysteria. To this hysteria we counterpose our grandiose plans of communist construction, our firm confidence in our powers, in the justice of the path marked out by Marxist–Leninist science."[71]

The implications which the Soviets wanted the West to draw from this exploit were duly noted by *New York Times* military analyst Hanson W. Baldwin:

> As far as man in single orbit is concerned, it [Titov's flight] demonstrates what was already clear. That is, *the Russians are at least eight months ahead of us*, and we shall probably not be able to match Major Titov's twenty-five-hour orbit for eighteen months or two years.
>
> *We lag, too, in the power of our booster rockets.* How much is anyone's guess, but *it will certainly be many months before we can equal or exceed the present Soviet capability.*[72]

Yet Khrushchev's propaganda exploitation of Vostok 2, unlike that which he had accorded its predecessor in April, was to prove curiously muted. One has the impression that the flight of Vostok 2 had been planned as a climactic contribution to the Soviet campaign of pressure on Berlin, at a time when the maximum objective was still on the agenda, and that it no longer dovetailed so neatly into the tactical plan after the shift in objectives had been decided on.

Khrushchev sums up the Soviet position, August 7

The official Soviet reply to Kennedy's speech of July 25 took the form of a radio and television address by Khrushchev on August 7.[73] The principal purpose of the speech, it can be seen in retrospect, was to warn the West against using force to prevent the Soviets and their East German allies from carrying out their plan to seal off West Berlin and to incorporate the remainder of the divided city into the East German state.

In order to portray the Soviet position as one of unchallengeable strength, Khrushchev opened with a highly optimistic survey of the current state and future prospects of the Soviet economy. "Industry," he claimed, "is functioning well, and as a whole it is overfulfilling the [seven-year] plan assignments."[74] As for agriculture: "In the current year the harvest and purchase of farm products will apparently be such as we have not had in all the years of

---

[71] Ibid., p. 262.

[72] *NYT*, Aug. 8, 1961; emphasis supplied.

[73] *Pravda*, Aug. 8, 1961, pp. 1–2; *Izv.*, Aug. 9, 1961, pp. 1–3; *CDSP*, XIII/32, pp. 3–8, 20.

[74] *CDSP*, XIII/32, p. 3.

the Soviet regime's existence."[75] Still brighter were the prospects for the future: "The long-range prospects for the development of our entire national economy are stupendous. They are set forth in the draft of the new program of the Communist Party of the Soviet Union."[76]

The continuing growth of the Soviet economy, Khrushchev maintained, indicated clearly what the eventual outcome of "peaceful economic competition" would be: "The superiority of the socialist economy over the capitalist economy is no longer being proved by theoretical arguments alone. Today the material evidence of this is clearly visible. The countries of the socialist community have year after year been demonstrating their superiority in rates of economic growth, in the progress of scientific and technological thought, in raising the working people's living standard and in many other areas."[77]

The communist system would therefore eventually triumph, Khrushchev continued, not by force of arms but by the free choice of the peoples of the world:

> Those who are confident of the economic victory of their social system have no need to impose that system on other people by force of arms. This is why we say to the leaders of the capitalist states: Let us leave it to the peoples, to history, to settle the argument over which system, the socialist or the capitalist, is the more viable and progressive. The peoples will make a free choice, and the system that does a better job of satisfying men's material and spiritual requirements will triumph.[78]

From this point the transition to an exposition of current Soviet foreign policy was easy. The cornerstone of that policy, in Khrushchev's portrayal, was the quest for peace: "The Soviet Union, like the other socialist countries, not only has no interest in war but is doing everything it can to erect insurmountable barriers to the unleashing of wars by the imperialists. The Communists have always considered the struggle for peace to be their paramount task."[79]

In proof Khrushchev pointed to Soviet proposals for "universal and total disarmament," and asked why these well-meant offers had been rejected by the West. The answer, he maintained, was: "Because the imperialists have not renounced the idea of armed struggle against socialism and against the peace-loving peoples."[80]

Using a standard communist argument first developed by Lenin, Khrushchev asserted that the capitalist states were inherently aggressive: "Since the second world war the capitalist monopolies have made preparation for war, the arms race, an integral part of their countries' economic development."[81]

[75] Ibid.
[76] Ibid.
[77] Ibid.
[78] Ibid., pp. 4–5.
[79] Ibid., p. 5.
[80] Ibid.
[81] Ibid.

Fearful of an economic competition with socialism, in which they were doomed to failure: "It is apparently the case that the most aggressive imperialist circles want to wreck the plans for the peaceful construction of a communist society."[82]

President Kennedy, Khrushchev continued, had shown some signs of sense, but had failed to draw the proper conclusions from his insights:

> U.S. President Kennedy said during my talks with him in Vienna that a balance of forces had now been established between the two world camps and that a direct clash between the U.S.S.R. and the U.S.A. must be prevented, because such a clash would have the most disastrous consequences. In this instance Mr. Kennedy took a sober view of things and displayed definite realism. He must be given his due on this score. Life demands, however, that statesmen not only express sensible judgments but that in their policy, too, they not venture to overstep the line beyond which the arguments of reason fall silent and blind and dangerous gambling with the destinies of peoples and states begins.[83]

There followed a long exposition of the standard Soviet position on Germany: the alleged aggressiveness of the West German government and its leader, Chancellor Adenauer; the urgent need for a German peace treaty and an end to the occupation regime in West Berlin; the unalterable opposition of the Soviets to negotiations on Germany, based on the principle of self-determination through free elections; and the desirability of direct talks on reunification between the East and West German governments.

The Soviet proposals, Khrushchev complained, had not been fairly presented by the West: "What have they not been thinking up in the West in order to distort our position on the question of a peace treaty with Germany!"[84] Particularly offensive in this respect had been Kennedy's July 25 speech:

> In his recent speech the President of the United States said that the U.S. faces a challenge of some kind from the Soviet Union, that the freedom of the people of West Berlin is threatened, that the Soviet Union is all but ready to employ armed force. At the same time he never even mentioned the main point, which is that the Soviet Union is proposing that a peace treaty be concluded with Germany and is eager to draw up the terms of that treaty jointly with all the states that took part in the war against Germany. After listening to their President's speech, the American people may indeed think that our intention is not to do away with the vestiges of the last war but to start a third world war.[85]

It was not the Soviet Union, Khrushchev charged, that was resorting to threats, but the United States: "The person who really has ventured to resort to threats is the President of the United States. He went to the length of pre-

[82]Ibid.
[83]Ibid.
[84]Ibid., p. 6.
[85]Ibid.

senting us with a kind of ultimatum in response to the proposal on concluding a peace treaty with Germany. To back up his threats, as it were, the President announced a 217,000-man increase in the numerical strength of the armed forces, and American senators began loudly proclaiming the necessity of mobilizing several categories of the reserves."[86]

Khrushchev himself, of course, was no slouch when it came to threats, as he proceeded to demonstrate:

> . . . it would be criminal frivolity on the part of the American leaders if they were seriously expecting that once they had unleashed a war against the socialist states it could be kept within certain bounds. If there is a clash between the two giants—the Soviet Union and the United States—that possess powerful economies and big stocks of nuclear weapons, neither side, of course, will want to concede defeat before resorting to the use of all weapons, including the most devastating ones. Is this what the American people want? Does the American government really desire it? But if the U.S. leaders appreciate the nature of modern war involving the use of thermonuclear weapons, then why do they inflame the atmosphere, as President Kennedy did in his speech?[87]

Khrushchev was at pains to make it clear that his threats were not directed merely against the United States:

> Clearly, a third world war, should it break out, would not be confined to a duel between the two great powers—the Soviet Union and the United States. For a great many states have become enmeshed in the military alliances established by the U.S. and would, of course, find themselves in the orbit of war. We are taking all this into consideration, and we have at our command the weapons necessary, should the imperialists start a war, not only to deal a shattering blow to the territory of the United States but also to render the aggressor's allies harmless and to crush the American military bases scattered all over the world. Any state that is used as a springboard for an attack on the socialist camp will feel the full devastating force of our mighty blow.[88]

Modulating abruptly to a more reasonable tone, Khrushchev added innocently: "We have no wish to threaten anyone. We merely want to prompt some sensible thoughts in the minds of those upon whom the policy of the NATO member states depends."[89]

Thus far Khrushchev had been using the lurid prospect of a major nuclear war as a means to intimidate the West. The inescapable consequence of such a gambit, however, was that he might also alarm Soviet citizens and perhaps cause them to wonder what their government was doing to avert the threat of war. He accordingly devoted a passage of his speech to calming the Soviet population: "I want to assure you [the Soviet citizens] that the Party Central

[86] Ibid.
[87] Ibid., p. 7.
[88] Ibid.
[89] Ibid.

Committee and the Soviet government are doing and will do everything in their power to prevent the unleashing of war. But not everything depends on us. If the moment does come when imperialism decides on an insane step and launches a military adventure, a situation of extreme peril for the entire world may develop. We must be on the alert."[90] As to the Western leaders, Khrushchev found grounds for hope: "We are convinced that if the question of whether or not there is to be war depends on sober-minded people in the Western countries, they will not allow a war to be unleashed."[91] The danger Khrushchev saw was that "if persons obsessed with a suicidal mania gain the upper hand, there is no vouching for them."[92]

To help guard against this danger, Khrushchev proceeded to relate a cautionary tale from his own experience during World War II when a fellow-member of the Military Council of the Southwest Front, General Vashugin, panicked as the result of Nazi military successes at the outset of the war and shot himself in Khrushchev's presence.

The moral of the tale, Khrushchev maintained, was directly applicable to the present situation: "In the story I have related it was only one man who perished, but should some one of the Western leaders act rashly under present-day conditions and push the world into a new war, this suicidal act would entail the death of millions upon millions of people."[93]

After this direct appeal for Western sobriety, Khrushchev returned obsessively and repetitively to the Soviet arguments in favor of a German peace treaty. This time, however, the stale rhetoric was enlivened by several novelties. The first of these was a nearly explicit advance notice of the Soviet intention to seal off West Berlin:

> The imperialists feel that the present situation gives them a convenient loophole, with the aid of which they can place obstacles in the way of the G.D.R.'s development as a socialist state. They are using West Berlin as a jumping-off point for subversive activities against the G.D.R. and the other socialist countries; they have been infiltrating their agents to keep constantly fanning the military situation there. The imperialists' sole concern is to enlarge that loophole, to weaken the German Democratic Republic, but they are being told: "Stop, gentlemen. We know very well what you want, what you're after; we are going to sign a peace treaty *and close your loophole into the G.D.R.*"[94]

In his second innovation Khrushchev raised the basic question of national prestige as the fundamental factor in the struggle over Berlin:

[90] Ibid.
[91] Ibid.
[92] Ibid.
[93] Ibid.
[94] Ibid.; emphasis supplied. Cf. the passage in Kennedy's speech of July 25 in which he called West Berlin an "escape hatch" from East Germany.

The question of access to West Berlin and the whole question of the peace treaty is for them [the Western Powers] only a pretext. If we abandoned our intention of concluding a peace treaty, they would take this as a strategic breakthrough and would in no time broaden the range of their demands. They would demand the abolition of the socialist system in the German Democratic Republic. If they achieved this too, they would, of course, undertake to wrest from Poland and Czechoslovakia the lands that were restored [sic] to them under the Potsdam Agreement—and these are Polish and Czechoslovak lands. And if the Western powers achieved all this, they would come forward with their principal demand—that the socialist system be abolished in all the countries of the socialist camp. They would like this even now.[95]

"That is why," Khrushchev added, "we cannot put off settling the question of a peace treaty." (But since it would be plain to his more perceptive listeners that it was he who had raised the question of a German peace treaty in the first place, it must have occurred to some of them that it was also he who had risked the stability of the socialist system in order to win a round in the game of national prestige.)

Khrushchev thus publicly acknowledged that the basic issue in the Berlin crisis was the question of national prestige. His nightmare vision of what would happen if the Soviets lost the contest was intended to rally support for his risky policy not only in the Soviet Union itself but also in the communist-ruled states adjoining Germany, whose population would be most directly exposed to the devastation of nuclear attack if war broke out.

Topping even these two candid revelations in importance, however, was a third disclosure: the Soviet Union was dropping out of the bidding on the game being waged over Berlin, and would not attempt to meet or raise the U.S. bid of July 25. "Soviet citizens may wish to know whether we shall need to allocate even greater funds for strengthening our armed forces. I can answer that the tentative view of the Central Committee and the government is that this should not be done. *The funds that have already been appropriated for strengthening the country's defenses and the arms that have already been and are being forged by industry are sufficient for us.*"[96]

This passage indicates that a meeting of the Presidium had ratified the decision to shift to the minimum objective rather than raise the stakes to a still higher level. Had the opposite decision been taken, this would have been the point to cite the flight of Vostok-2, with its brilliant demonstration of Soviet rocket prowess. Instead, Khrushchev contented himself with generalities: "Carrying out defensive measures and strengthening the might of our socialist homeland, we have been developing a diversity of rockets: intercontinental ballistic missiles and also rockets of various ranges, designed for strategic and tactical use and bearing atomic and hydrogen warheads. Our rocketry is moving along well, as they say, and hence *there is no necessity for us to ear-*

[95]Ibid.
[96]Ibid.; emphasis supplied.

mark additional funds. We are giving the necessary attention to other types of military equipment as well."[97]

Making a virtue of necessity, Khrushchev explained the decision to stand pat on the Berlin bidding as one dictated by regard for the people's well-being: "In our socialist country the interests of the people and the interests of the government are one and indivisible. We are not willing to saddle the people with *unnecessary hardships that are not warranted by the needs of the situation.*"[98]

The peroration of the speech was an appeal for international reasonableness: ". . . we once again appeal to the governments of the United States, Britain, and France: Let us sit down as honest men around the conference table, let us not create a war psychosis, let us clear the atmosphere, let us rely on reason and not on the power of thermonuclear weapons."[99]

The Soviet leadership, Khrushchev pledged, would do its part to avoid war: "Our party's Central Committee and the Soviet government have been doing and will continue to do everything possible so that the Soviet people and the peoples of all countries may emerge from this tense moment, too, without war. We do not want war, but our peoples will not falter in the face of trials: They will meet force with force, and will rout any aggressor."[100]

Like Kennedy in his July 25 speech, Khrushchev closed with a personal appeal for support from his countrymen: "On behalf of the Party Central Committee and the Soviet government, let me address an appeal to all Soviet citizens, whatever their occupations and wherever they may be at this time: Let us fortify the might of our beloved socialist motherland."[101]

More perhaps than any other of Khrushchev's major statements during the Berlin crisis of 1961, the August 7 speech came close to disclosing the real aims and intentions of Soviet policy. Its transparent references to "closing the loophole" constituted by West Berlin, had they been read with attentive insight by Western leaders, might have given them a vital five-day interval in which to prepare their reactions to what lay in store for them. Those who had most at stake—the ordinary disenchanted citizens of East Germany—*did* read Khrushchev's speech with sufficiently intense scrutiny to make out the looming outlines of Soviet intentions, though many of them still failed to appreciate the urgency of the situation. According to a *New York Times* report from the crowded reception centers in West Berlin: "Refugees fleeing into West Berlin on August 8 disclosed that Khrushchev's speech had made them fear that the escape route would be closed before the end of 1961."[102]

[97] Ibid.; emphasis supplied.
[98] Ibid.; emphasis supplied.
[99] Ibid., p. 20.
[100] Ibid.
[101] Ibid.
[102] *NYT*, Aug. 10, 1961, p. 3.

Khrushchev's August 7 speech was also noteworthy for the candor with which he identified national prestige as the underlying factor in Soviet strategy. Most noteworthy of all was the speech's public announcement that the Soviet leadership had decided not to reply to the U.S. military build-up with still another round of arms budget increases.

Why, then, was the August 7 speech not recognized at the time as a turning point in Soviet policy? Primarily because it was followed almost immediately by Soviet actions which precipitated the very danger of an armed clash which the speech had been designed to avert. The real purpose of the speech, as Jean Edward Smith, historian of the Berlin crisis, has observed, was to warn the West "against intervention in Berlin to halt the impending border closure."[103] It was for the same reason that Khrushchev chose to indicate so plainly what was being prepared in Berlin: he hoped in this way to condition the West psychologically to accept the fait accompli of the sealing off of West Berlin. Besides, with Khrushchev the truth could never be completely suppressed for long.

[103]Smith, *Defense of Berlin*, p. 254.

6 The West Looks for an Opening

Although the decisions announced by Kennedy on July 25 directly affected only the United States, he hoped that they would be supported and reinforced by similar measures on the part of the British and French. It was at just this point, however, that strains within the Western alliance, which had been present from the onset of the Berlin crisis, began to manifest themselves.

Britain and France under pressure

On July 21 Rusk had given the Western ambassadors an outline of proposed U.S. measures to strengthen the Western alliance economically and politically, as well as an advance text of the President's July 25 speech.[1] Their response, according to an unofficial source, was favorable.[2] The U.S. administration, however, was hoping for more than mere approval; it wanted definite actions to bolster the Western military position in Berlin and West Germany in order to present a strengthened common front to the Soviets. For a number of reasons the British and French were unable or unwilling to meet American wishes in this regard.

The climax of the Berlin crisis found the British cabinet sharply divided as to how best to deal with the problem. Immediately following Kennedy's July 25 speech the British government issued a press release fully endorsing the American stand,[3] but it was forced to confess almost simultaneously that Britain was in no position to match U.S. policy in actions. Faced by a serious financial crisis which had come to a head at just this time, the British government was even considering *reducing* the size of its forces in Germany.

[1] *SIA, 1961*, p. 240.
[2] James Reston, *NYT*, July 25, 1961, p. 1.
[3] *SIA, 1961*, p. 240.

Far from having reserves which could be sent to Germany, Britain had already committed her strategic reserve to a holding operation in the oil-rich sheikdom of Kuwait, which had been granted its independence in June and which was experiencing difficulties in adjusting to its new status.[4]

Added to the financial and military weaknesses which prevented Britain from throwing her full weight behind Kennedy's Berlin strategy were serious differences of opinion among the British leaders.[5] Speaking in the House of Commons on July 31, Edward Heath, Lord Privy Seal, offered guarded support to the U.S. position. The Berlin crisis, Heath said, "is a test of will between the Communist world and the Western world in which we are not the challengers but the defenders. Mr. Khrushchev . . . is the challenger and we must stand up for ourselves."[6]

While praising Kennedy's July 25 speech, however, Heath placed the emphasis on Western reasonableness and the desire to avoid war: "The West would . . . be failing in its duty if it did not take precautionary measures, but they should be unprovocative and designed to convince Mr. Khrushchev that it is too dangerous for him to put his threats into effect. Unilateral action cannot lead to conditions in which a just and peaceful settlement can be reached. As I have already said, we are prepared to go into negotiations and to discuss these problems."[7]

Prime Minister Macmillan, in a television talk on August 4, laid even greater stress on the conciliatory aspect of Western policy. Omitting any reference to military measures, Macmillan sought to flatter Khrushchev and soothe his ruffled feelings of national prestige. "Everyone knows," Macmillan said, "that Russia is a great and powerful country. Everyone knows that Mr. Khrushchev is a strong leader. What we're wondering is whether he can prove to be a statesman too."[8]

A discordant note was struck by British Foreign Secretary Lord Home a few days later when he sharply criticized the prevalent British attitude of "looking on the word negotiate as if it were a magic incantation . . . that will solve everything."[9] Khrushchev, in Lord Home's view, was "playing a game of political poker" with regard to Berlin. Discrediting the idea, then widely popular in Britain, that the West should make definite proposals for a change in the status of West Berlin as a means of luring the Soviets into negotiations, Lord Home observed that in a poker game the players do not disclose in advance the cards they are holding.[10]

[4]On the British financial crisis, see ibid., pp. 89–90; on the Kuwait incident, ibid., pp. 519–45.

[5]On the split in the British cabinet, see a well-informed report in the *Washington Post*, July 23, 1961, p. A–11.

[6]Cmnd. 1552, p. 453.

[7]Ibid., pp. 454–55.

[8]*Washington Post*, Aug. 5, 1961, p. B–4.

[9]*SIA, 1961*, p. 245, citing the British daily press, Aug. 10, 1961.

[10]See the TASS commentary on Lord Home's statement, Radio Moscow, Aug. 9, 1961.

The French government, though it suffered from none of the internal divisions which plagued the British, was hardly any better placed to offer tangible support to the American strategy in Berlin. The dispute with Tunis over Bizerte was tying up a large number of French troops. To offset this, the French had just concluded an agreement on atomic cooperation with the United States, designed to "make possible effective cooperation . . . in NATO mutual defense planning and in the training of French NATO forces."[11]

The chief difference between the French position in the Berlin crisis and that of the British and Americans lay in de Gaulle's steadfast refusal to consider the possibility of negotiations in the face of what he regarded as Khrushchev's exorbitant and inflexible demands. As for the West German government, having more at stake than any of the other Western powers, it strongly endorsed the French resistance to negotiations.

Washington hopes for negotiations

It was within the American government itself that some of the principal proponents of negotiation were to be found. Anxious not to let U.S. policy be dominated by military considerations, Kennedy had been careful to include a passage on American willingness to negotiate in his July 25 speech:

> As signers of the U.N. Charter, we shall always be prepared to discuss international problems with any and all nations that are willing to talk—and listen—with reason. If they have proposals—not demands—we shall hear them. If they seek genuine understanding—not concessions of our rights— we shall meet with them. We have previously indicated our readiness to remove any actual irritants in West Berlin, but the freedom of that city is not negotiable. We cannot negotiate with those who say "What's mine is mine and what's yours is negotiable." But we are willing to consider any arrangement or treaty in Germany consistent with the maintenance of peace and freedom, and with the legitimate security interests of all nations.[12]

At a press conference on July 27 Rusk sounded sanguine. "We expect," he said, "that negotiations [on Berlin] will in fact at some stage take place."[13] Leaving Washington for a conference of Western foreign ministers, on August 3, Rusk again stressed Western willingness to negotiate: "There is no reason why this problem [Berlin] cannot be solved by peaceful means if those others beyond the Iron Curtain are willing to approach it in the same spirit. President Kennedy has indicated to the entire world this combination of firmness and readiness to discuss, which must be characteristic of a responsible, great nation."[14]

[11]See Kennedy's special message to Congress transmitting the agreement, *JFK, 1961*, pp. 594–95. For a Soviet commentary, see *Pravda*, Sept. 11, 1961; *CDSP*, XIII/37, pp. 23–24.

[12]*JFK, 1961*, pp. 537–38.

[13]*DSB*, 45 (1961):276.

[14]Ibid., p. 361.

In order to underline the U.S. wish not to exacerbate the crisis, the Department of State on August 4 issued a statement rejecting the idea of using economic measures to put pressure on the Soviets in Berlin.[15]

The meeting of the Western foreign ministers, which was held in Paris on August 4–5, failed to bridge the gap between the French–West German refusal to consider negotiations in the existing situation and the Anglo–American disposition to sound out Soviet responsiveness. According to Schlesinger, de Gaulle wrote to Kennedy after the conference "that the opening of negotiations would be considered immediately as a prelude to the abandonment, at least gradually, of Berlin and as a sort of notice of our surrender."[16]

A few days later (August 7–8), a meeting of the NATO Council was held in Paris, at which Rusk outlined proposed U.S. measures to reinforce NATO troop strength and asked for similar action by the allies. The response was disappointing: "Mr. Macmillan revealed later that he had at this time considered whether to call up reserves so as to put B.A.O.R. [the British command in West Germany] on a war footing, but had decided against it as it 'would have created a thoroughly undesirable atmosphere of panic.' "[17]

In words, however, the NATO meeting was adamant. The communiqué issued at the end of the meeting contained not a single reference to negotiations but reiterated the demand for German reunification on the basis of self-determination, a demand which Khrushchev had just told the Italians would lead to an immediate Soviet walkout from the negotiating table.

Kennedy keeps the door open

The flickering hopes for negotiations were carefully nursed back to life by Kennedy at his news conference on August 10. Asked to comment on Khrushchev's August 7 speech, the President studiously avoided an emotional or inflammatory response and made the most he could of the meager indications Khrushchev had given of a willingness to negotiate.

> He [Khrushchev] did state his desire, as I have done before, to have negotiations on these matters which are in dispute, and I can say that it is the strong conviction of the United States Government that every means should be employed, every diplomatic means, to see if a peaceful solution to this difficult matter can be achieved.
>
> I think that we will, in the coming months, . . . use every device available to us to see if we can get a more precise definition of the phrases and words and thoughts which the Soviet Union has expressed in the matter of Berlin, Germany, and Central Europe.[18]

---

[15]Ibid., p. 334.

[16]Schlesinger, pp. 393–94.

[17]*SIA, 1961*, p. 246, citing a speech by Macmillan in the House of Commons on Oct. 18, 1961.

[18]*JFK, 1961*, p. 555.

That the President's emphasis on negotiations was a deliberate part of his general policy of ensuring that "military considerations should not dominate . . ." was indicated later on during the press conference, when he turned aside a question on the possibility of nuclear war resulting from a clash over Berlin by replying: "Well, we are hopeful that we would be able to reach peaceful solutions to these problems."[19]

The August 10 press conference also provided an opportunity for Kennedy to comment on the possibility of a Soviet–East German action to seal off West Berlin. His reply to a question on this subject indicated no concern over the possibility and no plans to meet it if it occurred: ". . . the United States Government does not attempt to encourage or discourage the movement of refugees and I know of no plans to do so."[20]

On the eve of the building of the Berlin Wall, the United States was thus looking forward to eventual negotiations rather than to an immediate crisis. Leaving Paris after the NATO meeting, Rusk summed up the American view by saying: "I think there will be negotiations. It is only a question of how and where that remains to be worked out."[21]

*   *   *

The subjects on which the United States hoped to negotiate with the Soviets included not only Berlin but also a nuclear test ban. At his August 10 news conference the President disclosed that he had received the report from the special panel on nuclear testing which he had ordered established at the end of June. The panel had reported, according to Schlesinger, ". . . that it was feasible for the Soviet Union to have conducted secret tests, that there was no evidence it had done so (or had not done so), and that there was no urgent technical need for immediate resumption by the United States."[22] At his press conference the President said that the report had made him feel "more urgently than ever that without an inspection system of the kind proposed by the United States and the United Kingdom at Geneva no country in the world can ever be sure that a nation with a closed society is not conducting secret nuclear tests."[23]

Despite strong pressure from the Joint Chiefs of Staff to resume nuclear testing,[24] Kennedy had decided against resumption of testing, and no preparations for that purpose were being made.[25] Instead, responding to the views of some of his civilian advisers (including Schlesinger), Kennedy had decided to make another effort to find out how serious the Soviets were in their insist-

[19]Ibid., p. 558.
[20]Ibid., p. 557.
[21]*Washington Post*, Aug. 11, 1961, p. A–1.
[22]Schlesinger, p. 456.
[23]*JFK, 1961*, p. 554.
[24]Schlesinger, p. 456.
[25]Jacobson and Stein, p. 278.

ence on a three-man executive (*troika*) in the test ban control agency and in linking a test ban treaty with an agreement on general and complete disarmament. Despite the receipt of a more than ordinarily sterile and unpromising Soviet note on disarmament, on August 9,[26] the President at his news conference on the following day announced that he was

> asking Ambassador Dean to return to Geneva on August 24 in an effort to ascertain whether the Soviet Union is now prepared to bring a safeguarded test ban agreement into being. It is my hope that he will succeed in convincing the Soviet representatives that the test ban treaty which we have proposed and stand ready to use as a basis for serious negotiations is a necessary and rational means of reducing the likelihood of nuclear war, and if we were successful, would be an admirable beginning in the long road towards general disarmament. His return to Geneva is with our hopes and prayers, and I believe with the hopes and prayers of all mankind who are most concerned about further developments of this deadly weapon. This meeting is most important, most critical, and I am hopeful that we will find a favorable response by those who will participate in this negotiation.[27]

Asked whether he intended to set a specific date for the resumption of nuclear testing "in the event that Mr. Dean fails in his mission in Geneva," the President replied,

> I think we will be able to tell almost immediately whether the Soviet Union has made any change in its insistence upon the Troika, and therefore a unilateral veto on any inspection system. That of course is the fundamental issue which has up till now made it impossible to secure the acceptance of a treaty. . . . We'll be able, therefore, to tell quite quickly whether there is any prospect for success, and if there is not, Mr. Dean will come home and I will make the appropriate decisions.[28]

But the President rejected the suggestion that Dean's mission represented in any sense a "last try":

> We will try always if there's any genuine hope of success. But as I have indicated, this is probably a decisive meeting, because we will now find out whether there's any prospect of bringing an end to nuclear testing. And if we cannot agree on a system for [an] effective inspection system on nuclear testing, which is really the easiest kind because of the various mechanisms that are available to determine testing—which is the easiest kind of disarmament in a sense, or at least limitations on arms, to police—how possibly can any country which will refuse to accept an effective inspection system on nuclear testing, how can they possibly say and argue in the General Assembly or any place else, that they're really for disarmament?[29]

[26]Text in *Documents on Disarmament, 1961*, pp. 273–74.
[27]*JFK, 1961*, p. 554.
[28]Ibid., p. 556.
[29]Ibid.

Kennedy's hopes and fears in the field of space exploration also found expression at the August 10 press conference. The nation, he said, was making "what I consider to be a maximum effort": ". . . we are spending as much money and devoting as large a percentage of scientific personnel, engineering and all the rest, as we possibly can to the space program. We are constantly concerned with speeding it up."[30]

The fundamental reason for this tremendous national effort, he disclosed at a later point in the conference, was his belief that the Soviets were well ahead in the race to explore space:

> . . . we have a good many very talented scientists, but we did not make a major effort in this area for many years, and we are now behind and paying the price of having the Soviet Union exploit a great propaganda advantage now on three separate occasions, with the flight of the Sputnik, the flight of Mr. Gagarin, and the most recent one. They are still, as I've said before, many months ahead of us. And therefore, we can look for other evidences of their superiority in this area. We are making a major effort which will cost billions of dollars. *But we cannot possibly permit any country whose intentions toward us may be hostile to dominate space.*[31]

But Kennedy immediately expressed the hope that space exploration could be separated from its potential military aspects: "What I would like to see at the United Nations and elsewhere is an effort made to have space insured for peaceful purposes. And the United States delegation to the General Assembly is going to make a major effort in that regard this year."[32]

Toward the end of the press conference a reporter raised the subject of the "neutron bomb," a project under discussion which had recently received an enthusiastic endorsement from Senator Thomas Dodd (D., Conn.).[33] The reporter asked the President, "Can you give us your estimate of the feasibility of developing a weapon which would destroy human beings without destroying real estate values?" to which Kennedy answered briefly and noncommittally, "No."[34] But this seemingly insignificant passage, overshadowed though it was by Kennedy's detailed and patient exposition of the U.S. position on the test ban talks and disarmament, was to be singled out by Khrushchev in a speech on the following day and blown up into a symbol of the crass attitudes and values of the "capitalist world."

Kennedy's August 10 press conference, held just two and a half days before Soviet action in Berlin, informed the Soviet leadership that the United States

[30]Ibid., p. 558.

[31]Ibid., pp. 559–60; emphasis supplied.

[32]Ibid., p. 560.

[33]See his article, "N-bomb: ideal weapon for defense," *U.S. News and World Report*, vol. 51, no. 3, July 17, 1961, pp. 48–50.

[34]*JFK, 1961*, p. 560. For evidence that the neutron bomb was taken seriously by some scientists and had been discussed by the President and his advisers, see Schlesinger, pp. 457–58.

hoped for and expected negotiations on Germany; that it was still trying to breathe new life into the stalemated test ban talks; and that it was not thinking of opposing a possible Soviet move to block the flow of refugees to West Berlin. If there had been any genuine Soviet desire for negotiations on Berlin or on a test ban treaty, Kennedy's statements would have provided a suitable opening. Soviet policy, however, was geared to a rigid timetable which permitted no leeway or delays. The President's cautious and promising words therefore were powerless to avert the impending Soviet actions; rather, by offering convincing evidence that the United States would do everything possible to avoid war, they provided the last incentive needed for Soviet action in Berlin. The final formal step in preparation for that action was taken on August 11, when the East German legislature "unanimously approved" certain unspecified measures which the regime proposed to take to curb the flight of refugees to the West.[35]

[35]Harry Gilroy, *NYT*, Aug. 12, 1961, p. 4.

7 Climax: The Soviets Act

On the eve: Khrushchev takes last minute precautions, August 9 and 11

Khrushchev's August 7 speech was not his final effort to prepare a favorable psychological climate for Soviet action with regard to West Berlin. As the deadline approached, with all its nagging uncertainties as to possible Western reactions, Khrushchev grew more and more emotional. His public utterances became increasingly inflammatory and menacing as he redoubled his efforts to frighten the Western powers out of any thought of reacting to Soviet deeds by force.

A Kremlin reception on August 9 for cosmonaut Titov provided a ready-made opportunity for Khrushchev to boast of Soviet prowess in rocket development. As we have seen, in his speech of August 7 Khrushchev had deliberately bypassed the opportunity to make capital of this event. The Titov flight, however, could still be effectively used as an instrument of intimidation. The Soviet Union, Khrushchev now claimed, had the capacity to develop a rocket with an explosive warhead of 100 megatons. "Our rocket forces," he bragged, "have said they could send it aloft." If war broke out over Berlin, he warned, the Soviet Union, despite its wish for peace and disarmament, would use all available weapons. And he claimed decisive superiority in rocket power over the West: "The Americans," he taunted, "do not launch any sputniks. They hop up and fall down in the ocean."[1]

This was Khrushchev's first public reference to the superbomb with which he had tried to intimidate McCloy on July 27. Noteworthy again was the close link in Khrushchev's mind between the bomb (and Soviet plans to test it) and the Berlin crisis, for he proceeded to reaffirm Soviet determination to sign a peace treaty with Germany: "No threats will intimidate us and we will sign a peace treaty with Germany." His underlying anxiety became apparent, however, when he added, "We, the Soviet government, consider that after this [the peace treaty] there will

[1]Seymour Topping, *NYT*, Aug. 11, 1961, p. 3.

be no war because only lunatics would counter with war . . . [but] you cannot exclude the possibility that such lunatics exist."[2]

The meaning of Khrushchev's allusion to "lunatics" can be understood when it is compared with the passage in the Soviet notes of August 3 (above, p. 98) characterizing the West German government as a potential madman. The implication again was that while the leaders of the three Western allies could be relied on not to risk war, the reaction of the West German government was unpredictable and it was therefore the responsibility of the Western allies to curb West Germany.

Continuing the policy of intimidation which he had begun in early July, Khrushchev now threatened West Germany with nuclear annihilation. If Adenauer, he said, ". . . with his Bundeswehr [West German army] thinks he can achieve reunification of the German nation by war and we are attacked, there will be no German nation left after that, all Germany will be reduced to dust."[3]

The policy of intimidation reached its climax two days later in a speech by Khrushchev to a Soviet–Rumanian friendship meeting in the Kremlin. On August 9 West Germany had been threatened with nuclear annihilation; now the same tactics were applied to two other members of NATO, Italy and Greece, and by extension to all the NATO powers.

After perfunctory praise of the Rumanian communist regime and affirmations of Soviet–Rumanian solidarity, Khrushchev got down to his real subject, the Berlin crisis.

"The Soviet people," said Khrushchev, "have no hostile feelings for the Italian people. On the contrary, we want to live in peace and friendship with the people of Italy. But that country has been drawn into the aggressive Atlantic bloc, which threatens us with war if a peace treaty is concluded with Germany."[4]

"The laws of war are cruel," Khrushchev continued,

I repeat, we have nothing against the Italian people and we sincerely wish them good fortune and happiness. But if the aggressive circles of the U.S.A. and Adenauer cause a conflict between our peoples, then, defending our security, we will have to strike at the NATO military bases wherever they are situated, even if they are in the orange groves. . . . Then not only the orange groves of Italy but also the people who created them and who have exalted Italy's culture and arts, people in whose good feelings we believe, may perish.[5]

The threat against Italy was followed by an identical menace to Greece. "I have twice had occasion," Khrushchev said,

to talk with the Greek ambassador at receptions. . . . In talking with the ambassador, I said that our peoples had always been brothers and that we

[2]Ibid.
[3]Ibid.
[4]*Pravda*, Aug. 12, 1961; *CDSP*, XIII/32, p. 10.
[5]*CDSP*, XIII/32, p. 10.

had always wished the same happiness for the Greeks as for ourselves. Yet now the government of Greece has allied itself with NATO, the aggressive North Atlantic bloc. We know that there are military bases in Greece directed against the Soviet Union. And now, when the ruling circles of the U.S.A. and Adenauer are increasing tension and threatening to unleash a war if a peace treaty is signed with Germany, we are being threatened in the name of the entire bloc, in the name of all the NATO countries. Consequently we are threatened with war even by such countries as Greece, Italy, Norway, Denmark, Belgium and Holland, not to mention such countries of Europe as France, Britain and West Germany.

We, of course, will sign a peace treaty with the German Democratic Republic. If the imperialist states unleash a war, they will force us, in self-defense, to deal crushing blows not only against the territories of the principal countries but also against the military bases situated in other countries of the North Atlantic bloc. It is well-known that military bases are not located in deserts. In Italy they are reportedly located among orange groves, and in Greece among olive groves. Perhaps there are some who expect that certain cities will be proclaimed open cities, as it was possible to do during the last world war. But one should not allow oneself to indulge in illusions. In a future thermonuclear war, if it is touched off, there will be no difference between the front and the rear.[6]

In his August 7 speech Khrushchev had portrayed the Western powers as eager to disrupt the Soviet bloc. The dismantling of NATO, he now revealed, was one of the goals toward which his policy of intimidation was directed:

I told the Greek ambassador that the most sensible policy for Greece would be to withdraw from NATO. Then, if war broke out, Greece would not suffer. The ambassador told me: I trust the Chairman of the Council of Ministers of the Soviet Union never to give the order to drop atomic bombs on the Acropolis and other historical monuments of Greece. Mr. Ambassador, I would not want to disappoint you, but you are deeply mistaken.

Of course, as Chairman of the Council of Ministers of the Soviet Union, I will not issue orders that bombs be dropped specifically on the Acropolis. But we will not hesitate to strike a blow at the military bases of the North Atlantic bloc, which are also located in Greece. In such cases the responsibility will fall on those who have placed cities, peoples and historical monuments in jeopardy.[7]

Continuing his campaign of intimidation, Khrushchev ridiculed the idea that the West would risk nuclear war for the sake of defending West Berlin:

. . . they [the Western powers] allege that they will fight for the freedom of the Germans in West Berlin. But this is a fairy tale. There are 2,200,000

[6]Ibid., pp. 10–11. Khrushchev's interviews with the Greek ambassador were not reported in the Western press.

[7]CDSP, XIII/32, p. 11. The text as actually delivered was somewhat more brutal: "But I should without wavering give my military men the order to come down on the military bases of the North Atlantic bloc located in Greece, and naturally they will not spare the olive groves nor the Acropolis because bombs do not differentiate." *Documents on Germany*, p. 717.

people living in West Berlin. But if a war is unleashed, hundreds of millions might perish. What sensible person would find such arguments of the imperialists convincing? Under the pretext of defending freedom, which no one is threatening, the imperialists want to test our firmness; they want to do away with our socialist achievements. Your arms are too short, Messrs. Imperialists![8]

By this time, according to a Western observer, Khrushchev had worked himself into a frenzy, waving his arms and shouting.[9] It was in this state of excitement that he launched into the touchy subject of national prestige, revealing a sharp sense of grievance at real or imagined Western slights:

Our country has become a great and mighty power. We have created a powerful industry and a highly developed agriculture and have raised science and culture. Yet the imperialists look at us as they did at the Russia of 100 or 50 years ago. . . .

This shows that the imperialists have lost a sense of reality and are now going through an agonizing reappraisal of many things. When President Kennedy talked with me in Vienna, he stressed, "We are a great country." And I replied: "True, but, Mr. President, the Soviet Union is also a great country." . . .

Incidentally, in 1960 in Paris Mr. Macmillan kept urging me to sit down at a table with Eisenhower, when the latter had committed an unworthy act with regard to our country. He said: "You must understand, Mr. Khrushchev, that this is a great country; it cannot apologize." I replied: "Pardon me, we also are a great country. We demand an apology, and without such an apology we cannot sit down at the same table with those who insulted our country."

May those who are threatening us know that his majesty the working class of the Soviet Union, of all the socialist countries, has assumed power and has created states with which the imperialists and colonialists must reckon, and they must treat the peoples of the socialist countries and their interests with respect![10]

After this outburst, Khrushchev calmed down and returned more or less to his prepared text (". . . after all," he said, "there is still the speech by Comrade [Gheorghiu-] Dej to come"). American discussion of the possibility of creating a neutron bomb, a subject which had figured briefly in Kennedy's press conference of the preceding day, served as a convenient pretext for an attack on Western moral standards:

More and more frequently now we hear talk from statesmen and military leaders, especially in the U.S.A., to the effect that they are developing [sic] a neutron bomb. The neutron bomb, as conceived by its creators, would kill everything living but leave material assets intact.

[8]*Pravda*, Aug. 12, 1961; *CDSP*, XIII/32, p. 11.
[9]Seymour Topping, *NYT*, Aug. 12, 1961, pp. 1, 3.
[10]*CDSP*, XIII/32, p. 11.

Yes, comrades, this is what these people are thinking. They are acting according to the principle of robbers; they want to murder a man without staining his suit with blood so that they can use the suit. This is in effect what the neutron bomb means. It is talked about in the U.S. Congress and in the press. Even at a press conference, the President was openly asked what his attitude was toward development of such a bomb. But the President declined to give an answer.

To build a bomb with which it is possible to kill people but preserve all wealth—here is the bestial ethics of the most aggressive representatives of imperialism. Is this the law of man? Man is nothing to them. To them the main thing is plunder, the quest for profit, which prods the imperialists to the most horrible crimes.[11]

Obsessively, however, Khrushchev kept coming back to his principal theme, the threat of atomic destruction against the Western powers, a theme he linked with an attack on the allegedly aggressive policies of West German Chancellor Adenauer: "We appeal to the Greek people, to the peoples of other nations forming part of NATO; realize what a dangerous path it is on which you are being led by Chancellor Adenauer, the revanchists and all those who share his policies. For if the imperialists unleash war, the logic and laws of war will force the Soviet Union and the other socialist states, even against their will, to deal crushing blows against the aggressors, no matter where their military bases are located."[12]

Khrushchev's acute concern about the policies of Adenauer was understandable. Knowing that the Soviets were about to destroy the last vestiges of four-power control in Berlin, Khrushchev feared more than anything else the unpredictable reaction of the West German government and people to this act of international lawlessness. He could not, of course, openly admit Soviet intentions, but the real intent of his words is clear enough when read in the light of subsequent events. "Adenauer states that he wants to serve his people," Khrushchev charged. "But if he unleashes war, the very existence of the population of West Germany will be placed in question, and not only its existence but also that of the population of many other nations, because a thermonuclear war could scarcely be restricted within the boundaries of a single country."[13]

In order to avoid a general nuclear war, Khrushchev was in effect saying, the West must accept Soviet actions without opposition, since the Soviet Union was now too powerful to be coerced.

Come to your senses, gentlemen! I appeal to those who have not lost the ability to think calmly and soberly and on whom the development of the international situation depends. There was a time when American Secretary of State Dulles brandished thermonuclear bombs and pursued a "position

[11]Ibid.
[12]Khrushchev, *Kommunizm*, 1:306–7.
[13]Ibid., p. 307.

of strength" policy with respect to all the states that disagreed with the imperialist claims of the United States. This was barefaced atomic blackmail, and it had to be reckoned with at the time because we did not have sufficient means of retaliation, or if we did, ours were fewer and less powerful than those of our opponents. But now the situation has radically changed. And specific conclusions must be drawn from recognition of the fact that the capitalist countries are unable to impose their outlook and way of life by force, they cannot force the socialist countries to turn back. It is necessary to follow a sensible policy on our essentially small planet, which man can now circle 17 times in the course of a day.[14]

Khrushchev paid lip service to the desirability of negotiation on disputed issues, including Berlin, but showed absolutely no willingness to modify the basic Soviet demands which were the crux of the dispute:

West Berlin is situated on the territory of the German Democratic Republic. The government of this state has displayed a profound understanding of the interests of peace. In the interest of reducing tension and establishing normal relations in postwar Europe, it has agreed to recognize West Berlin, on the conclusion of a peace treaty, as a free city, respect its sovereignty, and guarantee to it free communications with the outside world *in accordance with agreements with the government of the German Democratic Republic.*[15]

And to the end, Khrushchev staunchly maintained the fiction that the real goal of Soviet policy was the conclusion of a peace treaty with Germany:

Today I read a report about President Kennedy's press conference. In reply to a question about the threat of a military conflict in connection with the conclusion of a German peace treaty, the President stated: "We hope that we will be able to achieve a peaceful solution of the problems." Such a statement is to be welcomed. It is precisely for a peaceful solution that the Soviet government is striving. But in order to ensure a peaceful solution, it is necessary to conclude a peace treaty with Germany. Only in this way can the remnants of the second world war be removed.[16]

The main points having been made, all that remained to be done now was to reassure the Soviet people that their leaders were doing everything possible to avoid war. A number of Soviet factory workers (or more probably, overzealous local party leaders) had apparently interpreted Khrushchev's August 7 speech to mean that the Soviet Union faced a real threat of attack from the West and had volunteered to increase their hours of work in order to strengthen Soviet power.[17] Khrushchev gently restrained their eagerness: "Permit me to express the gratitude of the Party Central Committee and the Council of Ministers to all workers, technicians, engineers, scientists and

[14]*CDSP*, XIII/32, pp. 11–12.

[15]Khrushchev, *Kommunizm*, 1:309; emphasis supplied.

[16]*CDSP*, XIII/32, p. 12.

[17]*Pravda*, Aug. 9, 1961, p. 2; Radio Moscow, Aug. 9, 1961; *NYT*, Aug. 9, 1961, p. 6.

employees for their correct understanding and support of the government. As for the working people's proposal to shift certain defense enterprises to an eight-hour working day, permit us to avail ourselves of it depending on the situation. Leave this to your government and the party central committee."[18]

After the emotional tensions and histrionic display of the speech—the most provocative and risky he was to deliver during the entire Berlin crisis of 1961— Khrushchev was able to relax and display the lighter side of his complex temperament. According to a Western press report: "After his speech, Mr. Khrushchev went out of his way to make amicable approaches to Moscow Ambassadors of the Western powers. . . . During a Kremlin reception for the visiting Rumanian President, Mr. Khrushchev sought out the Canadian, British, French, and Italian ambassadors and chatted good-humoredly with them for some 20 minutes. Without referring to his earlier speech, he flatly said there would be no war."[19]

His confident mood was the result not only of the satisfaction felt by a man who has carried out a difficult and dangerous task but of the reassurances he had received from the West—most notably in Kennedy's August 10 press conference— that war would not result from the Soviet actions scheduled to follow in the next forty-eight hours.

The Berlin Wall

The erection of a physical barrier (it was not at first a wall, merely a barbed-wire obstacle) cutting off the beleaguered western sectors of Berlin from the Soviet-occupied eastern sector and the surrounding territory of the East German regime was carried out shortly after midnight on Sunday, August 13. (The date and time were obviously chosen to give the operation the maximum degree of surprise and to minimize the possibility of prompt and effective counteraction from the West.)

To lend the action a semblance of legality two documents (neither, in form, emanating from the Soviet Union) were issued in quick succession just before the sealing of the border was initiated: a joint declaration of the governments of the Warsaw Treaty members and a statement by the Council of Ministers of the GDR.[20]

The Warsaw Pact statement (which must have been drafted or at least approved in principle at the August 3–5 conference, since no subsequent meeting of the Warsaw Pact powers before August 12 is known to have taken place) opened with the affirmation that the problem of a peace treaty with Germany "is ripe for decision and can tolerate no further delay." Instead of proceeding in logical fashion to announce preparations for the signing of a treaty, however, the declaration dropped the subject and turned to its real theme, the al-

[18]*CDSP*, XIII/32, p. 12.
[19]*NYT*, Aug. 12, 1961, p. 1.
[20]Texts in *DIA 1961*, pp. 343–45 (Warsaw Pact declaration) and 341–42 (GDR statement).

leged militarist and revanchist policies of the West German government and, more immediately, the threat which West Berlin allegedly presented to the security, economy, and stability of the GDR and the other Warsaw Pact nations. To meet this threat, the declaration appealed to ". . . the People's Chamber [GDR legislative body] and the government of the GDR and to all workers of the German Democratic Republic with the proposal that such measures be taken as will insure that the diversionist activities against the socialist countries are stopped, and that around the entire area of West Berlin including its border with democratic Berlin [i.e., East Berlin] reliable guards and effective controls are established."[21]

Or, in plainer terms: "The present abnormal situation must be ended by a strengthened guard and control along the West Berlin border."[22]

In conclusion the declaration defined the measures to be taken as temporary in nature, ". . . [to be] removed as soon as a peace settlement with Germany is reached and, on that basis, the solution to current problems is found."[23]

The statement by the GDR Council of Ministers, supposedly adopted in response to the Warsaw Pact declaration, followed it in general outline but drew an even sharper picture of the allegedly aggressive policies of the West German government, which it claimed was preparing nothing less than an attack on the Soviet Union itself: ". . . it is the aim of this aggressive policy and disruptive activity to incorporate the whole of Germany into the western military bloc of NATO, and to extend the militarists' rule of the Federal Republic to the German Democratic Republic. By all kinds of fraudulent maneuvers, such as so-called 'free elections,' the West German militarists first aim at extending their military bases as far as the Oder River [eastern frontier of the GDR] in order then to start another big war."[24]

Basing itself on "the decision of the political advisory commission of the Warsaw Treaty states" and "in the interests of ensuring peace in Europe, protecting the German Democratic Republic, and in the interest of the socialist camp states," the statement then proceeded to announce the establishment of "the forms of control which are customary on the frontier of every sovereign state" along the borders of the GDR, "including the borders of the Western sectors of Greater Berlin." As to East Berlin, which the statement characterized as "the capital of the German Democratic Republic (democratic Berlin)," entry was to be permitted to all but "revanchist politicians and agents of West German militarism." The statement's description of the actual border control measures to be instituted made it clear that their real purpose had nothing to do with the alleged danger of subversion from the West, but was to prevent inhabitants of East Germany from entering West Berlin.

[21] Ibid., p. 344.

[22] Ibid., p. 345.

[23] Ibid.

[24] Ibid., pp. 341–42. Slight revisions have been made in the translation.

Whereas West Berliners, under the new regulations, could enter the eastern sector of the city merely by showing their identity card, citizens of the GDR would henceforth need "special permission" and a "special pass" to cross over into West Berlin.

The statement was careful to note that the new regulations made no change in existing procedures for "citizens of West Berlin traveling abroad using the lines of communication through the German Democratic Republic" or in "previous regulations governing transit traffic between West Berlin and West Germany through the German Democratic Republic"—the two points on which the Western powers had insisted most strongly in their resistance to Soviet demands for conclusion of a Soviet–GDR peace treaty. Thus the sole immediate effect of the new regulations was to seal off West Berlin from the eastern sector of the city and from East Germany and to prevent the inhabitants of East Germany from entering West Berlin. Like the Warsaw Pact declaration, the GDR statement concluded with the assurance that the measures being taken would remain in force only until the conclusion of a German peace treaty.

The units which carried out the actual sealing of the border belonged to the East German militarized police, but they were backed up by formations of the Soviet command in Germany, estimated at two infantry divisions and one armored division[25]—a force fully adequate both to quell any attempts at outbreaks by the East German population and to discourage any possible Western ideas of counteraction.

The Soviet leaders disperse

From a tactical point of view, the operation of sealing off West Berlin was a model of concealment, deception, and surprise. In the wisdom of hindsight, some Western analysts ruefully confessed that the action was logical and should have been foreseen,[26] but this verdict seems not only unduly harsh on Western observers (some of whom, as we have seen, did recognize the likelihood that the Soviets would institute some kind of border control) but insufficiently appreciative of Soviet tactical skill in preparing and carrying through the action.

It took some time after the erection of the Wall before perceptive Western analysts recognized this action as the real turning point in the Berlin crisis. Sorensen, for example, writing of events which took place in 1962, observes that the "tides of crisis" over Berlin had receded by that time, "in part because the ending of East German emigration [i.e., flight to the West] eased the pressure on him [Khrushchev] for immediate action."[27] Similarly Geoffrey

[25]Department of State, *Background Berlin—1961* (Washington, D.C., G.P.O., 1961), p. 26.

[26]E.g., *SIA, 1961*, pp. 246–47.

[27]Sorensen, p. 596.

McDermott, who served as British Minister in Berlin during the 1961 crisis, writes: "One result of the Wall, unsavoury object though it is, has been to allow the Communists to relax over Berlin and not to insist on their ultimata being met. The Wall has in fact served to stabilise a situation which was getting dangerously fluid."[28]

The delay in comprehension was due primarily to the fact that for more than a month after August 13 the Soviets maintained or even increased their pressure on the West and continued to insist that they intended to sign a peace treaty with the GDR. A *Pravda* editorial on August 28, for example, said that nothing would prevent the Soviet Union from signing a peace treaty with East Germany before the end of the year. "A postponement in the conclusion of the German peace treaty for an indefinite period," the editorial maintained, "would be tantamount to a deliberate contribution toward increasing the threat of a new war."[29]

Recognition in the West that the building of the Wall was a turning point was also hindered by the fact that the sharpest tactical confrontations in Berlin between the Western powers and the Soviets and their East German allies still lay ahead. It would have been instructive, however, if Western observers had paid due attention to the apparent nonchalance with which Soviet leaders left Moscow just before or immediately after the building of the Wall.

Khrushchev, for example, returned to his vacation retreat in Sochi, stopping en route in Kiev on August 14 to attend a political meeting at which he delivered a speech on agriculture.[30] According to plans which he made known at the reception following his August 11 speech, he expected to remain on the Black Sea coast until the first week in September, when he was due back in the Kremlin to play host to India's Premier Nehru.[31] Khrushchev's friend and political ally, Presidium member Anastas Mikoyan, left Moscow on August 12 to open a Soviet trade and industrial fair in Tokyo[32] and remained in Japan until August 21.

This departure from Moscow of two of the most important members of the Presidium provides strong evidence that the Soviet leadership was confident that there was no real risk of international conflict growing out of the Berlin crisis and that the moment of maximum danger was safely past.

Mikoyan in Tokyo

Although it was little more than a side-show during the Berlin Crisis, Mikoyan's mission to Tokyo is of interest because of what it reveals about Soviet intentions and expectations. In his well-advertised capacity as the lead-

---

[28]Geoffrey McDermott, *Berlin: Success of a Mission?* (New York and Evanston, Harper & Row, 1963), p. 42.

[29]*NYT*, Aug. 28, 1961, p. 11; *Pravda*, Aug. 28, 1961.

[30]*Pravda*, Aug. 15, 1961.

[31]Seymour Topping, *NYT*, Aug. 12, 1961, p. 3.

[32]Radio Moscow, Aug. 12, 1961.

ing Soviet commercial traveler, Mikoyan was a flop in Japan, primarily because the wares he had to offer were too skimpy to be attractive to his hosts. His proposal of a Soviet trade credit of $200 million, spread over a number of years, could make little impression on an industrial nation whose trade with the United States amounted to twenty times that figure.[33]

Mikoyan's visit was not merely a failure from the economic point of view, however; diplomatically it represented a Soviet setback, as the result of Mikoyan's clumsy attempts to contribute to the Soviet campaign of intimidation which Khrushchev had initiated in early July. In a conversation with Japanese Premier Ikeda on August 16, Mikoyan warned that the presence of U.S. military bases in Japan would make that nation vulnerable to Soviet military attack in case of war—a sally which earned him a sharp semiofficial rebuke from the ruling Liberal–Democratic party on the following day for interference in Japanese internal affairs.[34] Undeterred and unrepentant, Mikoyan warned the West in a speech on August 21: "You may not like the German Democratic Republic. But you will have to ask them for a pass if you want to enter Berlin. Without it you will not get through. No one can fight over this. Only a lunatic would fight over this."[35]

It would seem that Mikoyan had only partly grasped the rather complicated Soviet tactical plan for the Berlin campaign and, failing to pay attention to current developments, was laboring under the mistaken impression that the maximum goal was still in effect and would in due course be attained. No such confusion existed in East Berlin, however, where Ulbricht told a rally on August 25 that his regime would not seek to control allied communications with West Berlin until a peace treaty had been signed.[36]

All in all, Mikoyan's trip to Japan has to be recognized as a serious diplomatic blunder, one which had the effect of still further strengthening an already lively Japanese antipathy to the Soviet Union. The Soviet resumption of nuclear testing, which lay just ahead, would still further reinforce that antipathy.

The pattern of Soviet and Western policy, August 13–30

During the period between the first measures to seal off West Berlin on August 13 and the Soviet announcement of the resumption of nuclear testing on August 30, Soviet policy was directed toward three separate but related goals: (1) to ensure that the West would not react by force to the building of the Wall; (2) to hold out the continuing hope to the West that the Soviets were sincerely interested in achieving a mutually satisfactory solution of the Berlin problem and would eventually consent to negotiations; (3) meanwhile to

---

[33]A. M. Rosenthal, *NYT*, Aug. 27, 1961, sect. 4, p. 4.

[34]*NYT*, Aug. 17, 1961, p. 3, and Aug. 18, 1961, p. 1.

[35]A. M. Rosenthal, *NYT*, Aug. 22, 1961, p. 5.

[36]*NYT*, Aug. 26, 1961, p. 1.

strengthen the wall, under cover of continuing threats to the Western position in Berlin, and after carefully testing Western reactions step by step.

In addition, a number of subsidiary issues occupied the attention of Soviet policymakers at this time, all related in one way or another to the basic question of Soviet–American relations. First, the Soviet secret police mounted a diversionary action in the Middle East with the publication of allegedly top secret Western military plans for the area; second, the Soviets moved closer towards a full-scale diplomatic break with Albania; and third, Soviet economists and party spokesmen carried on a lively but in part esoteric debate on questions of investment priorities, in a new phase of the controversy which had flared up in the spring and early summer.

Behind the scenes, moreover, there was a sharp clash at the highest levels with regard to the aims and methods of Soviet foreign policy.

During this period the policies of the Western powers in the Berlin crisis were essentially reactive, though a determined effort was made in Washington to recapture the initiative. Caught off guard by the establishment of the Berlin Wall, the West thereafter shifted uneasily between two pairs of balanced but mutually incompatible alternatives: first, a fixed determination not to risk war over Berlin, countered by the desire to stand firm in the defense of Western rights and Western prestige; second, a strong urge to negotiate and to believe in Soviet protestations of willingness to negotiate, countered by the realization that the Soviets had already secured much of what they sought in Berlin and the fear that they might achieve still more if the West agreed to bargain.

The task of framing a common Western position, as usual, was made more difficult by the existence of divergent views in Washington, London, Paris, Bonn, and West Berlin and by the presence of sharp internal disagreements in several of the Western nations on how best to respond to the Soviet challenge.

The complications resulting from the interaction of these two complex processes of policy formulation and action—the Soviet and the Western—make this period one of the most confused and intricate in the history of Soviet–Western relations.

Protest and counterprotest, August 13–18

The Soviets did not have long to wait for an authoritative definition of the line the West would take in response to the establishment of the Wall. At midday on August 13, shortly after receipt of the first reports of the action, Secretary of State Rusk issued a "Statement concerning travel restrictions in Berlin," the very title of which showed a tendency to underplay the gravity of the Soviet move.[37] In his statement Rusk charged, correctly, that the prin-

---

[37]*DSB*, 45 (1961):362. Rusk's statement had the approval of the President: see the TV interview with Rusk on Aug. 20, *Document on Germany*, p. 746.

cipal purpose of the measures taken by "the authorities in East Berlin and East Germany" (Rusk carefully avoided naming the Soviets as responsible for the action) was "to deny to their own people access to West Berlin." Initiating a line which was to receive heavy emphasis in coming weeks, Rusk maintained that the erection of the Wall had exposed "the pretense that communism desires only peaceful competition," and then proceeded, with an almost audible sigh of relief, to note that: "Available information indicates that measures taken thus far are aimed at residents of East Berlin and East Germany and not at the Allied position in West Berlin or access thereto."[38] Thus no drastic response was called for. To keep the legal record straight, however, Rusk noted that ". . . limitation on travel within Berlin is a violation of the four-power status of Berlin and a flagrant violation of the rights of free circulation throughout the city. Restrictions on travel between East Germany and Berlin are in direct contravention of the four-power agreement reached at Paris on June 20, 1949."[39] And what did the United States propose to do about these "flagrant violations"? Rusk provided the answer in his final sentence, the only passage in the statement which would be of operative interest to the Soviets: "These violations of existing agreements will be the subject of vigorous protest through appropriate channels."[40]

Rusk's statement was intended to serve as a stop-gap measure while Kennedy and his advisers worked out a course of action, and as a palliative aimed not only at calming public opinion in the West but also at reassuring the Soviets as to the West's intentions. Kennedy, whom the crisis found at his weekend retreat at Hyannis Port, questioned his principal advisers by phone[41] and called the Berlin Task Force, which he had set up after the Vienna meeting, into emergency session.[42] No one, it seemed, had any useful advice, beyond the obvious recommendation of strengthening Western military forces in Berlin.

The caution displayed in the initial U.S. response to the Wall reflected a very real political and military dilemma; the Soviet action was being carried out on territory which they occupied legally, under postwar international agreements, and which they had already incorporated de facto, with tacit Western acquiescence, into the East German regime.[43] For the Western powers to use military force at this stage to attempt to prevent the erection of the Wall would have been to risk a crushing response from the overwhelmingly superior Soviet forces in and around East Berlin, not to mention the possibility of an even more devastating general military counteraction.

[38]*DSB*, 45 (1961):362.

[39]Ibid.

[40]Ibid.

[41]Sidey, p. 234.

[42]Schlesinger, p. 395.

[43]The basic action whereby the Soviets annexed East Berlin to their East German satellite was a Soviet–GDR agreement of Sept. 20, 1955.

(Khrushchev's threats of nuclear destruction, it could now be seen, had been aimed at producing precisely this situation.)

While a formal protest at governmental level was being hurriedly drafted, the three Western commandants in Berlin, on August 16, sent their own note to their Soviet counterpart protesting what they described as "the illegal measures introduced on August 13." The protest, however, petered out on a note of resigned futility: ". . . [we] hold you [the Soviet commandant] responsible for the carrying out of the relevant agreements."[44]

Assured that the three Western allies planned no forcible counteraction to the Wall, the Soviets took precautionary measures with respect to the most unpredictable and most directly involved member of the Western alliance, West Germany. On August 16 the Soviet ambassador to the Federal Republic, Andrei A. Smirnov, paid a well-publicized call on FRG Chancellor Adenauer, at which he was reported to have conveyed orally a message from Khrushchev to the effect that the Soviets did not intend to intensify the crisis in Berlin.[45] In response, Adenauer was reported to have ruled out any action by the Federal Republic which would impair good relations with the Soviet Union or endanger international peace.[46]

Adenauer's political position at this time was complicated by the fact that the Federal Republic was scheduled to hold national elections in September, in which the continuation of the coalition government which he headed would be at stake. Moreover, his most challenging rival, Willy Brandt, mayor of West Berlin and a leading member of the opposition SPD (Socialist party), could be expected to react vigorously to the Soviet action isolating his domain and to make political capital out of the crisis.

Of all the Western leaders, it was Brandt, in fact, who reacted most strongly and directly to the building of the Wall. Stung by the evident Western readiness to accept the Wall as a fait accompli and even, in some sense, an easing of a dangerous and risky situation, Brandt on August 16 sent a personal letter to Kennedy in which he called the Soviet action "a serious turning point in the city's postwar history such as there has not been since the [1948] blockade," and proposed that the three Western occupying powers formally proclaim a new three-power status for West Berlin.[47]

Brandt's letter, reinforced by alarming reports from U.S. diplomatic advisers as to the harmful effect of the Wall on West Berlin morale, acted as a catalyst in Washington, where it helped produce a presidential decision to

[44]*DSB*, 45 (1961):396. For an explanation of the military reasons against attempting to block construction of the Wall by force, see a statement by the then U.S. Army Commander in Europe, General Bruce C. Clarke, in Sidey, p. 234.

[45]*NYT*, Aug. 17, 1961, p. 3; Schlesinger, p. 396.

[46]The Soviet government on or about Aug. 18 "began a direct exchange of messages with Dr. Adenauer designed to seduce the West Germans again into direct talks with them on the recognition of East Germany." *SIA, 1961*, p. 250.

[47]Brandt's letter was published in the *Frankfurter Allgemeine Zeitung* on Aug. 19 and, in translation, in the *NYT*, Aug. 20, 1961, p. 6. See also Schlesinger, pp. 395–96.

demonstrate U.S. concern for the continued security and vitality of West Berlin by two symbolic but significant gestures: to send the Vice President, Lyndon Johnson, to West Berlin as the President's personal representative, carrying a personal reply from Kennedy to Brandt in which the U.S. commitment was reaffirmed in the most solemn terms, and to dispatch a battle group of 1,500 U.S. soldiers from West Germany across GDR territory to the encircled city. To lend a touch of color to the Vice President's mission, Kennedy asked retired General Lucius Clay, a hero to West Berliners because of the key role he had played in defeating the 1948 Berlin blockade, to accompany Johnson.[48]

These actions, as Sorensen explains, had as their basic objective "to rekindle hope in West Berlin."[49] They were not intended to intimidate the Soviets or East Germans or to prevent them from carrying out the policies on which they had embarked. The actions ordered by Kennedy were therefore consistent with the basic Western decision not to try to block the sealing off of West Berlin.

It was nevertheless recognized in the White House that the dispatch of the battle group would raise the tension in Berlin and might lead to an overt clash. According to Sorensen, the period between the departure of the battle group from West Germany and its safe arrival in West Berlin after an uneventful journey was Kennedy's "most anxious moment during the prolonged Berlin crisis."[50]

Soviet acquiescence in the movement of the U.S. battle group through East German territory served as a valuable confirmation of the conclusion derived from a reading of the GDR statement of August 13, that the border control measures being taken were not aimed at cutting or interfering with allied communications between West Germany and West Berlin. From this point on, Western policy in Berlin was thus directed not toward preventing the Soviets and the East Germans from splitting Berlin and sealing off its Western sectors, but toward defending Western rights in West Berlin and maintaining the city's morale and economic viability. A program directed toward the latter goal was initiated, at Kennedy's direction, under White House aide Walt Rostow, and, in Sorensen's words: "That effort succeeded, and in the years that followed West Berlin not only survived but flourished."[51]

Four days after the start of work on the Wall—a strikingly short interval for the preparation of a major three-power diplomatic paper—the Western allies were ready with their formal protest.[52] In the stiffest terms yet used by the West, the notes called the border-sealing action of August 13 "a flagrant, and particularly serious, violation of the quadripartite status of Berlin." They

[48]Sorensen, p. 594.
[49]Ibid., p. 595.
[50]Ibid., p. 594. See also Sidey, pp. 236–41.
[51]Sorensen, p. 595.
[52]Text, *DSB*, 45 (1961):397.

denied that the boundary between the Soviet sector and the Western sectors of Berlin was, as the Soviets claimed, a state frontier, and rejected the claim that the Soviet sector of Berlin "forms a part of the so-called 'German Democratic Republic'" and that Berlin was situated on GDR territory. They challenged "the right of the East German authorities to authorize their armed forces to enter the Soviet sector of Berlin" and charged the Warsaw Pact states with "intervening in a domain in which they have no competence."

After these stalwart affirmations of the Western position, the notes ended on the customary tone of futility: "The United States Government [Great Britain, France] solemnly protests against the measures referred to above, for which it holds the Soviet Government responsible. The United States Government expects the Soviet Government to put an end to these illegal measures. This unilateral infringement of the quadripartite status of Berlin can only increase existing tension and dangers."[53]

To lend some muscle to the Western protest, France and Britain on the same day, August 17, announced reinforcements of their troop strength in Germany.[54] Thus belatedly the U.S. pleas to its allies to strengthen the Western military position in Germany received some response.

On August 18 Soviet authorities sent two replies to the West: an answer to the note from the Western commandants of August 15 and a reply to the governmental notes of August 17. The reply to the commandants' note was brief and straightforward, limiting itself to the claim that "the matter which you referred to me lies entirely within the competence of the Government of the German Democratic Republic in the fulfillment of the normal rights of each sovereign nation to protect its legal interests."[55] On this basis the note rejected the Western protest "as devoid of any basis whatsoever."[56]

The reply to the Western governmental notes, sent on the same day, was a longer and more imposing document.[57] Its principal theme, developed in great detail and with an almost passionate intensity, was the alleged existence of activities in West Berlin which were harmful to the GDR, the Soviet Union, and "other socialist countries." The note rejected Western appeals to postwar quadripartite agreements on Germany and Berlin on the ground that it was the Western powers themselves who had abrogated these agreements by their policies in Germany. The Western protest was therefore declared to be "without foundation and is categorically rejected by the Soviet Government."

This uncompromising rejection was not, however, the final word: in its final paragraph the Soviet note declared the "measures taken by the Government of the GDR" to be "temporary," and again held out the prospect of East–West negotiations on a German peace treaty: "The Soviet Government re-

[53] Ibid.
[54] *NYT*, Aug. 18, 1961, p. 1.
[55] *DSB*, 45 (1961):396.
[56] Ibid.
[57] Ibid., pp. 397–400.

peatedly has emphasized that the conclusion of a peace treaty with Germany and normalization on such a basis of the situation in West Berlin will not infringe the interests of any of the parties and will contribute to the cause of peace and security of all peoples. To this end it appeals to the Government of the U.S.A. [, Britain, and France]."[58]

Emboldened by the indications that the West would not try to interfere with the sealing off of West Berlin, the East German authorities, on August 18, began the second stage of their operation, "the erection of a five-foot wall of concrete blocks topped with barbed wire."[59] Eventually the Wall would run like an ugly scar across the face of the divided city and form an effective component in the tight border control system which had been established earlier along East Germany's frontiers facing West Germany.

Diversion in the Middle East

For some time Khrushchev and other Soviet leaders had been attempting to intimidate the nations of the Western alliance by threatening them with nuclear annihilation if war broke out between the Soviets and the NATO powers. The presence of NATO military bases on the territory of Italy and Greece had served as the basis for attempts of this kind.

On August 18 a more elaborate form of this technique was initiated with the announcement by TASS that the Soviets had obtained and were publishing certain top secret military plans emanating from the Central Treaty Organization (CENTO, the successor to the Baghdad Pact), dating from February 1958, in accordance with which it was planned, in the event of war between the CENTO powers and the Soviet Union, to create "nuclear shields" in the territories of some of the CENTO states themselves—Iran, Pakistan, and Turkey—by means of atomic devastation of border areas in order to deny them to the Soviets and prevent them from using these areas as bases for rocket attacks on the West.[60] The TASS announcement strongly implied that similar plans were in existence for NATO and SEATO (the South–East Asia Treaty Organization).

The purpose behind the disclosure of the "documents," as the TASS announcement made clear, was twofold: to put pressure on the states concerned to withdraw from their alliances with the Western powers and to add another element of pressure behind the Soviet campaign on Berlin.

Although the "documents" were immediately denounced as forgeries by Iranian officials[61] (U.S. and British spokesmen treated the disclosure as unworthy of rebuttal), the Soviets continued to use them as a weapon of intimida-

---

[58]Ibid., p. 400.

[59]*SIA, 1961*, p. 250.

[60]*Pravda*, Aug. 19, 1961, p. 2; *VPSS, 1961*, pp. 291–97. The alleged documents were published in *Krasnaia Zvezda*, Aug. 19, 1961, pp. 5–6.

[61]*NYT*, Aug. 20, 1961, p. 17.

tion for some time. On August 23 it was reported that Soviet Ambassador Mikhail S. Kapitsa had delivered an official note to Pakistan Foreign Minister Manzur Quadir, requesting an explanation of the "documents."[62] The principal focus of the attack, however, was Iran, as indicated by a virulent *Pravda* article on September 6.[63]

Shortly thereafter, however, the Soviets toned down the campaign. On September 9 it was reported from Istanbul that the Soviet consulate there had dropped plans to exhibit the "documents" in Turkey in response to a "stiff Turkish protest."[64]

An echo of the campaign followed a week later when *Izvestiia* published a statement by a U.S.–educated Iranian army officer who had asked for political asylum in the Soviet Union and who said that the "secret CENTO documents published by the Soviet government" had been influential in his decision to defect.[65] On the following day *Pravda* published an interview with the officer in which he described his training in the United States and accused the United States of having used bacteriological warfare.[66] After this final flurry the campaign was quietly dropped.

The CENTO "documents" look very much like a fabrication prepared by the Soviet secret police. Rabidly anti-American in its outlook, the KGB was no doubt delighted to have an opportunity to give vent to its hostility to the Western alliance while at the same time contributing to an officially approved policy.

Shikin leaves Tirana

On August 21 Radio Tirana, in reporting the opening of a Soviet film festival, mentioned a certain Pavel Krekoten as Soviet *chargé d'affaires ad interim*—the first reference to the presence of this minor Soviet diplomatic official in this capacity in Albania.[67] The implication was that an important change had taken place in the personnel of the Soviet embassy in Tirana. Radio Liberty, in its analysis of the report, suggested that it might indicate the recall to Moscow of K. I. Novikov, chief counselor of the Soviet embassy.[68]

The real meaning of Krekoten's appearance, however, was much more sensational: early in December, at a time when the Soviet Union and Albania had finally reached the stage of an open break in diplomatic relations, the Albanians disclosed that the Soviet ambassador to Albania, Iosif Shikin, had

---

[62]*NYT*, Aug. 25, 1961, p. 9.
[63]O. Orestov, "Criminal playing with fire," *Pravda*, Sept. 6, 1961, p. 5; *CDSP*, XIII/36, pp. 21–22.
[64]*NYT*, Sept. 10, 1961, p. 16.
[65]*Izv.*, Sept. 16, 1961, p. 2; *CDSP*, XIII/37, p. 24.
[66]*Pravda*, Sept. 17, 1961, p. 6; *CDSP*, XIII/37, pp. 24–25.
[67]Radio Liberty dispatch, Sept. 1, 1961.
[68]Ibid.

been recalled on August 19.[69] It was to fill the vacancy created by his departure, obviously, that Krekoten had been named *chargé d'affaires ad interim*.

The reasons for Moscow's drastic decision were spelled out, according to a later Albanian report (which the Soviets neither confirmed nor denied), in a violent diatribe from the CPSU Central Committee to its Albanian counterpart on August 24, ". . . which culminated in the assertion that the Albanian leadership had become 'agents of foreign intelligence services' [and which] reiterated all its charges against Hoxha and his associates which Khrushchev made public the following October."[70]

Accompanying this blast were a number of actions whereby the Soviets moved to cut their few remaining ties with the intransigent Albanians.

"According to the Albanians, on August 26 all scholarships for Albanian students were withdrawn by Moscow; 'shortly after' the Albanian students were all expelled."[71]

More damaging to the Albanian economy was the recall of Soviet technicians: "By the end of August, in spite of Albanian requests for postponement, all Soviet and East European technicians in Albania had left."[72]

The bitter Soviet charges against the Albanians which were lodged in the August 24 CPSU note were to form one of the most sensational aspects of Khrushchev's oratory at the Twenty-second CPSU Congress in October. The events surrounding the recall of Shikin indicate that these charges were not brought up by Khrushchev in October on the spur of the moment, nor solely on his own responsibility. They had their immediate origin in the events of August 1961. Again, as in the case of the escalation of the Soviet–Albanian and Soviet–Chinese disputes in late June and early July, one has the strong impression that the initiative for the sharpening of the quarrel came from the Soviet side.

The recall of an ambassador is a serious step in international relations, inasmuch as it is generally regarded as an action stopping just short of a total diplomatic break. At the same time, it is an action which does not require extensive preparation, involving as it does only a single individual. We are justified therefore in assuming that a meeting of the Presidium took place, shortly before August 19, at which this decision was taken. It would be reasonable to suppose that at the same meeting the main lines were laid down concerning the charges to be lodged in the CPSU note of August 24 and that the subsidiary decisions on cutting remaining ties with Albania were also adopted.

At the reception for the Rumanians on August 11, Khrushchev had let Western newsmen know of his plans for a long vacation at Sochi, following a stopover in the Ukraine. In accordance with this schedule, as we have seen, he duly attended a party meeting at Kiev on August 14. If he had proceeded from

[69]Griffith, *Albania*, p. 85, citing an Albanian note of Dec. 6, 1961.

[70]Griffith, *Albania*, p. 85.

[71]Ibid.

[72]Ibid., p. 84.

Kiev directly to Sochi, there would appear to have been no possibility of a Presidium meeting in the period immediately preceding Shikin's recall.

On August 17, however, *Pravda* featured prominently on its front page a telegram from Khrushchev and Brezhnev to Indonesian President Sukarno. The content of the telegram in itself would not have merited such attention— it was a routine message of congratulation on the anniversary of Indonesian independence. Its interest, and the reason for the prominence given it by *Pravda*, lay in the fact that it was dated August 16 *from the Kremlin*. It would seem therefore that instead of continuing on south to Sochi after the Kiev meeting on August 14 Khrushchev turned back to Moscow for a brief period. Assuredly, the purpose of his return to the Kremlin was not to co-sign a tele-gram of congratulation to Sukarno; rather, the prominently displayed publi-cation of the telegram was a device to inform party officials that Khrushchev was back in the Kremlin on August 16.

This fact enables us to fit the decision on the recall of Shikin into its proper place in the sequence of events. We can postulate a meeting of the Presidium on August 15 or 16 at which Khrushchev pressed successfully for a sharp escalation in the Soviet quarrel with Albania.

Could not the decision have been taken by Khrushchev personally, or, alternatively, by someone in the Kremlin in his absence? No, a meeting of the Presidium is indicated because of the gravity of the step taken, and the fact that it was accompanied by a message to the Albanian Central Committee, sent in the name of the Central Committee of the CPSU.

(Incidentally, the disclosure that Khrushchev had returned to the Kremlin by August 16 helps to explain the impulse behind Smirnov's call on Adenauer on that date: evidently Smirnov's mission was the result of a directive from Khrushchev personally, designed to reassure the West German leader that Soviet aims in the Berlin crisis were limited.)

The result of this analysis is to identify Khrushchev once again as the prime mover behind major Soviet steps deepening the conflict with Albania (as he had been earlier, in February, April, and June 1961, and as he was to be once again in October). A striking consistency thus runs through Khrush-chev's attitude toward the Albanians (and, looming behind them, the Chinese).

What were Khrushchev's motives in pushing Soviet relations with Albania closer to an open break at just this time, in the period immediately following the building of the Berlin Wall? The answer to this question lies in the inter-action of Soviet foreign and domestic policy. In acceding to the demands of the internal opposition for a solution of the Berlin question on their terms Khrushchev had made a concession under pressure. He was determined, how-ever, not to permit the opposition to parlay this concession into further gains at his expense. He therefore interrupted his journey to Sochi and returned briefly to Moscow to take actions designed to set a limit to Soviet aims in the Berlin crisis and to deliver a stinging new affront to the external opposi-tion, the Albanians and the Chinese.

Intensifying the pressure on West Berlin

The original border security measures announced by the GDR on August 13 had made only minimal provision for controlling the entrance to East Berlin of inhabitants of West Berlin and West Germany or foreigners. On August 22 the GDR Ministry of Internal Affairs promulgated new regulations "to protect the republic," designed to close these loopholes in its border security system.

Three new measures were announced: (1) an instruction "advising" all citizens of East and West Berlin, "in the interests of their own security," to keep at least 100 meters away from either side of the boundary; (2) an order requiring that West Berlin citizens wishing to enter East Berlin must obtain a permit from the GDR travel office; and (3) an order establishing a "special crossing point" for foreigners, members of the diplomatic corps, and representatives of the Western occupation forces.[73]

As in the case of the August 13 regulations, the new measures were described as temporary: "The [GDR] Minister of Internal Affairs points out that these measures will remain in force until the conclusion of a peace treaty."[74]

The three Western commandants in Berlin responded promptly with a note on August 23 protesting what they described as "another step in the unfolding of the brutal and callous policy of the East German regime" (the note contained no reference to Soviet responsibility for the new measures).[75] The commandants denounced the new measures as "contrary to existing four-power agreements" and called them "further evidence that the East German Government cannot tolerate the maintenance of even the simplest human contacts between friends and families." As to the East German regime's "advice" to stay away from the border, the note was forthright: "The three Western commandants take a most serious view of the effrontery of the East German authorities in warning the citizens of West Berlin to keep at a distance of 100 meters from the sector border, a border which the Communists themselves have violated on numerous occasions in the last few days. The commandants are taking the necessary action to insure the security and integrity of the sector borders."[76]

Thus far the actions taken to seal off West Berlin had been, at least ostensibly, the work of the East German authorities. The Soviets had remained in the background, and their statements and diplomatic notes, e.g., those of August 18, had been limited to support and defense of the East German

[73]*Pravda*, Aug. 24, 1961, p. 5; *CDSP*, XIII/34, p. 18.

[74]*CDSP*, XIII/34, p. 18. For a Soviet article attempting to justify the new measures, see V. Kuznetsov, "New blow at provocateurs," *Pravda*, Aug. 24, 1961, p. 5; *CDSP*, XIII/34, pp. 18–19. For details of the closing of border-crossing points on Aug. 22 and 23, see *SIA, 1961*, pp. 250–51.

[75]Text in *Documents on Germany*, p. 753.

[76]Ibid.

actions. On August 23 the Soviets for the first time advanced claims and made demands which went beyond this limited involvement in the growing turmoil over Berlin. In notes to the three Western occupying powers the Soviet government charged that the air lanes from West Germany to West Berlin were being used to move "revanchists, extremists, saboteurs, and spies" into the city, and demanded that the Western allies "immediately take measures to end the unlawful and provocative activities" of the Federal Republic.[77]

Legally the Soviet claim was without any foundation whatsoever, since the postwar four-power agreements on air communications with Berlin had been signed long before the separation of Germany into two states and contained neither any limitation on the use to which the air corridors might be put nor any authorization for the Soviets to inspect or control their use.[78]

The fact that the claims put forward in the August 23 note were not based on existing international agreements was acknowledged in the note itself: ". . . the United States, Britain, and France are plainly abusing their positions in West Berlin, *taking advantage of the absence of control over air communications*."[79] The Soviet claim therefore represented an attempt to force the Western allies to accept a revision of existing agreements and to replace them by four-power control over air communications between the Federal Republic and West Berlin.

Recognizing that the new Soviet move threatened a vital aspect of their position in West Berlin, the Western allies reacted with unusual promptness and sharpness. A White House statement, issued on August 24, called the Soviet charges "false, as the Soviet Government well knows," and issued a "solemn warning": ". . . any interference by the Soviet Government or its East German regime with free access to West Berlin would be an aggressive act for the consequences of which the Soviet Government would bear the full responsibility."[80] The British and French governments expressed similar views.[81]

The formal Western replies to the Soviet note of August 23, delivered to the Soviets on August 26, restated the President's warning, except for toning down his characterization of possible Soviet interference with air communications as "an aggressive act": "The whole world will be concerned at the scarcely veiled threat of aggression against the Allied air routes to and from Berlin. The United States [, Britain, and France] must serve a solemn warning to the Soviet Union that interference by the Soviet Government or its East German regime with free access to Berlin would have the most serious consequences for which it would bear full responsibility."[82]

[77]Text of the Soviet note, *NYT*, Aug. 25, 1961; *VPSS, 1961*, pp. 197–99; *Documents on Germany*, pp. 753–55.

[78]For an analysis of the legal aspects, see *SIA, 1961*, p. 252.

[79]*Documents on Germany*, p. 754; emphasis supplied.

[80]*JFK, 1961*, pp. 568–69.

[81]*SIA, 1961*, p. 252.

[82]*Documents on Germany*, p. 757.

On the same day the three Western ambassadors in Bonn sent notes to their Soviet counterpart protesting the GDR border control measures announced on August 22 and warning that "any attempt to enforce this illegal prohibition [the 100-meter zone 'advice'] could only have the most serious consequences."[83] In their explicit recognition that the Soviets were responsible for the actions taken in the name of the GDR authorities, the ambassadors' notes indicated a new sense of realism in Western response to the Soviet moves.

Khrushchev stresses the desirability of negotiations

Just as the tension over Berlin seemed to be entering the phase of "threatening danger of war" (to use the historic term employed by Germany in the period immediately preceding the outbreak of World War I), Khrushchev took a number of actions designed to guide Soviet–Western relations back onto the path of negotiation.

Pursuing the views they had brought back from their visit to Moscow in early August, the Italians, on August 20, ". . . proposed that confidential preparations should begin 'promptly' for negotiations on Berlin with the Soviet Union 'within two or three weeks'."[84]

Seizing on the opening thus provided, Khrushchev, on August 24 sent a letter to Italian Premier Fanfani ". . . affirming his willingness to negotiate with the Western Allies on Berlin and other European problems."[85]

Khrushchev's message, sent via Soviet Ambassador in Rome Semyon P. Kozyrev, was not delivered until August 27.[86] Meanwhile Khrushchev had taken another means to stress the desirability of Soviet–Western negotiations. On August 25, *Pravda* and *Izvestiia* carried a laconic TASS announcement to the effect that Khrushchev had "received the American journalist Drew Pearson and had a visit [*beseda*] with him." Although TASS failed to specify the exact date on which the visit had taken place, the announcement itself was dated August 24, 1961, from Sochi.[87]

The text of Khrushchev's interview with Pearson was released by both Soviet and Western news media four days later, August 28.[88] Thus Khrushchev

[83]Text, ibid., pp. 757–58.

[84]*SIA, 1961*, p. 254, citing *NYHT*, Aug. 21, 1961, and providing an analysis of the internal tensions in the Italian government which in part motivated Italian eagerness to explore the possibility of negotiations with the Soviets.

[85]*SIA, 1961*, p. 254, citing *NYT*, Aug. 28, 1961. For the date of Khrushchev's letter, see *NYT*, Sept. 4, 1961, p. 1.

[86]*SIA, 1961*, p. 254, citing *NYT*, Aug. 28, 1961.

[87]In Khrushchev, *Kommunizm*, 2, the date of the Pearson interview is listed simply as "August."

[88]It was broadcast by Radio Moscow on that date; text in *Documents on Germany*, pp. 548–63. *Pravda* and *Izv.* carried it on Aug. 29, 1961; translation (excerpts), *CDSP*, XIII/35, p. 16. In the United States it was carried in newspapers of the Bell Syndicate, including the *Washington Post* and the *New York Mirror*; excerpts were published in the *NYT* and *NYHT* on Aug. 28, 1961.

once again made use of an American journalist to put his views before world public opinion, including the citizens of his own country.

This time, however, most of what Khrushchev had to say was in no sense novel or newsworthy. The bulk of the interview, as published, consisted of a restatement of the standard Soviet position on the need for a German peace treaty and the Soviet determination to sign one with the GDR, if the Western powers refused to agree to an all-German peace treaty. Even the few showy features designed to make it appear that something new was being proposed proved on closer inspection to be old hat: thus Khrushchev's suggestion that after conclusion of the peace treaty West Berlin should be given the status of a neutral, free city under four-power guarantee, with "symbolic" contingents of troops supplied by the United States, Britain, France, and the Soviet Union, had already been included in his speech to the North Vietnamese on June 28 (above, p. 42).

It would be difficult to believe that Khrushchev was naïve enough to expect that a proposal for negotiations couched in these terms stood any chance of acceptance in the West; clearly, he was either unwilling or unable to make any meaningful modification in the standard Soviet position on Germany and Berlin.

Why, then, had he called in Pearson for the interview? His purpose was made clear in its concluding paragraphs, in which he came forward as an ardent proponent of negotiations, with a direct appeal to President Kennedy:

> You [i.e., Pearson] ask when it would be desirable to hold negotiations. The answer is that *a solution of the question permits no delay*. We are therefore ready at any moment to meet with leaders of the Western powers on this matter if they have a sincere desire to achieve a realistic settlement of the German problem on a mutually acceptable base. To this I should like to add that they no less than we—and perhaps even more so—should be interested in having this problem peacefully solved. And if leaders of the Western powers, notably President Kennedy, want such a settlement, we declared long ago that we are always ready to come to a round table for peaceful negotiations.[89]

The choice of Drew Pearson as Khrushchev's mouthpiece is not difficult to explain. An article on the Berlin crisis which Pearson had written earlier in August had attracted Soviet attention. On August 15, Radio Moscow broadcast a TASS report which summarized the article as follows: "Declaring that Berlin is not worth starting a world war over, Pearson says Kennedy nevertheless is allowing himself to be pushed nearer to the brink because he fears rightwing Republican attacks."[90] On the same day, *Pravda* gave prominent

[89]*Documents on Germany*, pp. 762–63; emphasis supplied.
[90]Radio Moscow, Aug. 15, 1961.

attention to the Pearson article,[91] while *Izvestiia* followed two days later with a similar article.[92]

Pearson was therefore a logical choice as an American journalist who could be expected to serve as a sympathetic listener to a plea for cool heads and a "reasonable" approach to the Berlin question. But why was Khrushchev interested at this particular time in stressing his willingness to negotiate? As we have seen, it was on August 24, the day on which TASS reported the Pearson interview (and on which, in all probability, it actually took place), that Khrushchev wrote to Fanfani, taking up the Italian proposal for negotiations. Thus it is clear that on that date Khrushchev initiated a flurry of activity designed to move the Berlin crisis toward negotiation.

It will be remembered that the Soviet government on August 23 entered the Berlin crisis directly, with a note to the Western allies which for the first time threatened their basic position in West Berlin. Kennedy was quick to recognize that this move introduced a totally new element into the situation, and to characterize it as a possible *casus belli*. Khrushchev, at Sochi, evidently reacted to the Soviet note of August 23 in a similar way. Drafted and dispatched from Moscow during his absence from the Soviet capital, the August 23 note represented a deliberate attempt to use the Berlin crisis as the basis for a direct confrontation between the Soviet Union and the Western powers.

The conclusion to be drawn is that the August 23 note was the work of authorities in Moscow who were willing to push the Soviet offensive to the limit in the belief that the West would give in before risking war. Learning of the note and recognizing its explosive implications, Khrushchev took immediate action to stress Soviet willingness to negotiate with the West over the Berlin crisis. But because he was still bound by the conditions imposed by the basic Presidium decision in the Berlin campaign, he was unable to offer anything new to the West and was reduced to stressing negotiations as an end in themselves, strengthened by a personal appeal to Kennedy.

Despite the absence of any sign of Soviet flexibility in the bargaining position he proposed, however, Khrushchev had achieved his immediate goal: the sharp tension engendered by the Soviet note of August 23 was partially dissipated by publication of the Pearson interview on August 28. The Western alliance meanwhile, under internal pressures which were now being manifested most strongly in Washington, seemed to be moving ponderously but unmistakably toward negotiation.

The dialectical interplay between Khrushchev at Sochi and the opposition, temporarily the masters of the Kremlin, continued, however, to affect Soviet

[91]"Myths and Reality. Drew Pearson on the German question," *Pravda*, Aug. 15, 1961, p. 6.

[92]"Is Gettysburg [home of former President Eisenhower] dictating to the White House?", *Izv.*, Aug. 17, 1961, p. 2.

policy. By his appeals for negotiations on August 24 Khrushchev had succeeded in blunting somewhat the edge of the Soviet offensive launched with
the August 23 note. The opposition still had a trump card to play, however—
the resumption of nuclear testing.

To understand how this final action in the climactic phase of the Berlin
crisis came about, it must be understood that Khrushchev's diplomatic initiatives on August 24 were aimed not merely at guiding Soviet–Western relations back onto the path of negotiations, but at heading off, almost literally
at the last moment, the by now well-advanced Soviet preparations for the
resumption of testing, which needed only the final authorization of the Presidium. If Khrushchev's appeals to the West, and specifically to Kennedy, had
been published promptly and had found an affirmative response, Khrushchev
would have been able to cite this response as proof of the success of his approach to the West and therefore a justification for postponing the decision to
resume testing. It was a long shot, but it was the kind of move which would
have an irresistible appeal to a gambler like Khrushchev.

Faced with the imminent danger that Khrushchev might succeed, at the
last moment, in achieving Western assent to negotiations on Berlin, the opposition in the Kremlin took prompt and effective countermeasures. Release
of the text of Khrushchev's interview with Pearson was delayed until August
28, on which date a *Pravda* editorial did its best to scotch the possibility of
Soviet participation in negotiations on Berlin by reaffirming the standard
Soviet position in uncompromising terms: "A postponement in the conclusion
of the German peace treaty for an indefinite period would be tantamount to a
deliberate contribution toward increasing the threat of a new war."[93]

It was during the four-day interval between Khrushchev's interview with
Pearson and its release on August 28 that the final authorization was given for
the resumption of Soviet nuclear testing. The approximate time of this action
can be established by the fact that on August 24 the head of the Soviet delegation at the Geneva test ban talks, Semyon Tsarapkin, was suddenly recalled
"for consultation"—not to Sochi, but to Moscow.[94] The directive for his recall
was evidently issued in Moscow immediately after word was received there of
Khrushchev's attempts to obtain Western agreement to negotiations. When
Tsarapkin returned to Geneva on August 27 it was with the knowledge that
final preparations for the resumption of testing were in full swing.

During Khrushchev's temporary absence from the Kremlin a more accom-
modating Soviet attitude toward the Chinese made possible the signature
in Peking on August 26 of an agreement providing for an increase in trade
during the remainder of 1961.[95] According to the communiqué on the agreement published in the Soviet press: "The talks between the two delegations

---

[93]"The will of the peace-loving peoples is unflinching," *Pravda*, Aug. 28, 1961, p. 1. For
a commentary, see *NYT*, Aug. 28, 1961, p. 11.

[94]*NYT*, Aug. 25, 1961, p. 8; *SIA, 1961*, p. 255.

[95]The agreement was announced in Peking: *NYT*, Aug. 27, 1961, p. 29, citing a
Reuters dispatch from Hong Kong, based on a Hsinhua release from Peking.

proceeded in a spirit of sincere fraternal friendship and complete mutual understanding."[96] A noteworthy feature of the trade talks was the high-level reception accorded the chief Soviet delegate by the Chinese. According to the communiqué: "During the talks P. N. Kumykin, the head of the Soviet delegation, was received by Chou En-lai, premier of the State Council of the Chinese People's Republic, and by Li Hsien-nien, vice premier. The meeting proceeded in an atmosphere of sincerity and fraternal friendship."[97]

In addition to signing the supplementary trade pact the two sides agreed that "preliminary talks on the expert level to discuss problems of trade in 1962 would begin in Moscow in October 1961."[98] By that date, however, Soviet–Chinese relations had cooled off again, with the return of Khrushchev to the Kremlin, and the preliminary talks did not in fact get under way until December.[99]

The West moves toward negotiations

Khrushchev's turn toward negotiation on August 24 coincided with a drive in Washington toward the same goal. Within the President's staff a strong urge to propose negotiation to the Soviets made itself felt immediately after the erection of the Berlin Wall. According to Schlesinger: "On August 14, the day after the first crossing-points were closed, [Presidential adviser McGeorge] Bundy reported to the President unanimity in his immediate staff for the view that we should take a clear initiative for negotiation within the next week or ten days."[100] Not all U.S. policymakers took this point of view, however: "The State Department . . . was more cautious about American action, preferring to keep things within the four-power process."[101] In line with this approach, Rusk proposed that the four Western foreign ministers, due shortly in New York for the September session of the U.N. General Assembly, could prepare a Western proposal for negotiations, an idea of which Kennedy approved.[102] In a television interview on August 20, Rusk expressed full confidence that negotiation over Berlin would eventually take place: "We do expect that negotiations will take place on this matter. Just when and where will be determined by consultation among governments, including the government of the Soviet Union. But negotiations will occur."[103]

[96]*Pravda*, Aug. 27, 1961, p. 5; *CDSP*, XIII/34, p. 20.

[97]Ibid. See also Harry Schwartz, *NYT*, Sept. 5, 1961, p. 10, for an analysis emphasizing the difficulties encountered by the Chinese in meeting their trade obligations to the Soviets and suggesting that it was this question which explained the attention given the Soviet delegation by the Chinese.

[98]*CDSP*, XIII/34, p. 20.

[99]Oleg Hoeffding, "Sino-Soviet economic relations 1958–1962," (Santa Monica, RAND Corporation, 1963), p. 16.

[100]Schlesinger, p. 398.

[101]Ibid.

[102]Ibid.

[103]*Documents on Germany*, p. 746.

Impatient over the slow pace of interallied discussions, Kennedy, on August 21, wrote to Rusk, "I want to take a stronger lead on Berlin negotiations," adding that the United States must inform its allies that it intended to invite the Soviets to negotiations before September 1, leaving it up to them to decide whether to join the negotiations or not.[104] Meanwhile, the President worked at the task of preparing a Western position for eventual negotiations, using the Acheson report as his point of departure.[105]

Within the Western alliance it was the Italians who were most receptive to the idea of negotiation—it was they, after all, who had discussed this question directly with Khrushchev a few weeks earlier and who believed they had found him receptive to the idea. The other NATO partners took stands more or less in accordance with their earlier views. British Prime Minister Macmillan, interviewed on a golf course, on August 26, put the Berlin crisis in perspective by calling it "very worrying but nothing more. Nobody is going to fight about it." The chief concern, Macmillan added, was to see that "nobody does anything foolish." Paradoxically, he found a basis for hope in the very destructiveness of modern weapons: comparing the situation in August 1961 with that preceding the outbreak of World War I, he observed: "There would be much more danger of war if weapons were not so destructive. Fifty years ago we could have had a war. Now it is not much fun for anybody."[106] Aside from these comforting generalities, however, the British provided no positive leads for the Western alliance, leaving it to the United States to take the initiative.

The French, as usual, were strongly opposed to the idea of negotiations. French intransigence was greatly strengthened by the East German border control measures of August 22 and the Soviet note of August 23 threatening interference with the allies' air communications to West Berlin.[107] In an attempt to overcome French resistance, Kennedy wrote directly to de Gaulle, a move which was reported to have "reduced the French reluctance over the West's initiative in suggesting the talks."[108]

The West Germans had previously been no less adamant than the French in opposing negotiations; the crumbling of their resistance at about the same time as that of the French was authoritatively indicated by a statement by FRG Foreign Minister von Brentano to the effect that "the Western powers would soon propose negotiations to the Soviet Union on Berlin."[109]

In New York, on August 28, for consultation with Adlai Stevenson and other U.N. officials, Rusk said that the Western powers would hold talks with the Soviet Union on the Berlin crisis, noting however that "the exact timing,

[104]Schlesinger, p. 398.

[105]Ibid., pp. 398–400.

[106]SIA, 1961, p. 248, citing Observer, Aug. 27, 1961; NYT, Aug. 27, 1961, p. 1.

[107]SIA, 1961, p. 255.

[108]Tad Szulc, NYT, Aug. 29, 1961, p. 1; SIA, 1961, p. 255, citing the Washington correspondent of the (London) Times, Aug. 28, 1961.

[109]NYT, Aug. 29, 1961, p. 4. On the West German attitude, see SIA, 1961, p. 255.

place and circumstances" of the talks remained to be worked out.[110] On the following day the State Department announced that the four Western foreign ministers would meet in New York before the opening of the U.N. General Assembly and that meanwhile the Western ambassadors in Moscow might sound out the Soviet Foreign Ministry on the possibility of talks.[111]

Thus as the end of August approached, the Western alliance, urged on by Kennedy, was at last moving with determination and something approaching unanimity toward negotiation with the Soviets. It was at just this moment, however, that the Soviets announced the resumption of nuclear testing.

The Soviet debate over economic priorities

From the beginning of August to the opening of the Twenty-second CPSU Congress in October, Soviet economists, journalists, and party spokesmen engaged in a public discussion of the question of the priorities which should be observed by the party and government in the allocation of resources and investment funds. The immediate occasion for the discussion was the publication, on July 30, of the draft Party Program which had been adopted by the Central Committee plenum of June 19 and which was to be ratified in final form by the Twenty-second Congress.

In its pronouncements on economic priorities the draft program steered a middle course between the position of the extreme conservatives, who favored an unmodified continuation of the traditional emphasis on heavy industry, ferrous metallurgy, and armaments, and the position taken by Khrushchev and his supporters, who wanted a shift toward increased allocations for agriculture and consumer goods.[112]

In general the discussion of economic priorities was carried on without overt reference to the international crisis over Berlin which was reaching its climax at just this time. In two respects, however, the discussion had direct implications for Soviet foreign policy in the Berlin crisis. (1) Proponents of the conservative view on occasion alluded to the international tension as an argument in support of their position. For example, an article in *Party Life* misquoted the draft Party Program as follows: "The Communist Party considers that the chief aim of its foreign policy activity is to *foil the sanguinary designs of the imperialists*, provide peaceful conditions for building a communist society in the U.S.S.R. and developing the world socialist system, and together with all peace-loving peoples to deliver mankind from a world war of extermination."[113] The same issue of *Party Life* carried an article which defended ". . . 'preponderant' development of heavy industry and advised

---

[110]*Washington Post*, Aug. 29, 1961, p. A–8.

[111]*SIA, 1961*, p. 255, citing *Le Monde* and the (London) *Times*, Aug. 30, 1961.

[112]"James Biddleford" (pseudonym of Sidney I. Ploss), "Deadlock in the Party Presidium," *New Leader*, Vol. 44, No. 35, Oct. 16, 1961, pp. 19–22, and Ploss, pp. 231–34.

[113]*Partiinaia zhizn'*, no. 17, 1961, p. 19, cited by Ploss, pp. 232–33. The words in italics do not appear in the official text of the draft party program.

limitation of the production race with the U.S.A. to 'certain' consumer goods."[114] (2) The cost of the Soviet space program as a significant factor in the allocation of investment priorities was defended in a prominently featured article in *Pravda* on August 27.[115] The article gave foremost credit for the development of the Soviet space program to Khrushchev, explaining, however, that security considerations prevented the Soviet authorities from publicly identifying the many other individuals who had contributed to it. The timing of this defense of the expensive space program appears significant when viewed in relation to the debate over the resumption of nuclear testing, which was reaching its climax just at the time the article was published. Like the increase in the Soviet military budget, announced by Khrushchev in his speech of July 8, the resumption of testing would damage the prospects for Khrushchev's economic program at the same time that it would bring to a temporary halt the growing movement toward negotiation on the Berlin question.

The course of the debate on economic priorities, as reflected in articles and editorials in *Pravda*, clearly reflects the struggle between Khrushchev and the opposition. An editorial, on August 2, at a time when Khrushchev was in Moscow, stressed the goal of overtaking the United States in per capita output of consumer goods.[116] An editorial, on August 22, during a period of Khrushchev's absence from the Kremlin, took a staunchly conservative, anti-Khrushchev view: "Creation of the material technical base of communism demands first of all the further development of heavy industry. . . . And the party will in the future increasingly concern itself about the growth of heavy industry, which provides the development of productive forces and the defense capacity of the country."[117] At the end of the month, at a time when Khrushchev was beginning to reassert his influence, *Pravda* showed a greater willingness to give expression to his views, printing an article by V. Tiukov, an economic planner, which made the typically Khrushchevian prediction of an abundance of consumer goods by 1980.[118]

Collision at Geneva

At his news conference on August 10 Kennedy had announced the return of Ambassador Dean to the test ban talks at Geneva and had indicated that the Soviet response to the new proposals he would be bringing with him would be regarded in Washington as a significant clue to the Soviet attitude toward disarmament. Although the President denied that Dean's mission represented in any sense a "final effort" to achieve agreement with the Soviets on a test

---

[114]Ploss, p. 233.

[115]Vladimir Orlov, "Creators of the cosmic ships," *Pravda*, Aug. 27, 1961, p. 4. For commentary, see Nancy Nimitz, "Soviet expenditures on scientific research," (Santa Monica, RAND Corp., 1963), p. 27.

[116]Cited by Ploss, p. 231. The same editorial is cited by Zagoria, p. 373, in regard to the ideological dispute between the Chinese and the Soviets.

[117]"The main economic task of the Party and the people," *Pravda*, Aug. 22, 1961, p. 1.

[118]V. Tiukov, "For the benefit of the Soviet people," *Pravda*, Aug. 31, 1961, p. 3.

ban treaty, there is no doubt that he tended to regard it in that light. It was during the period while the new U.S. position was being prepared that the interrelated problems of the test ban talks, the resumption of testing, and proposals for general disarmament reached the stage of crystallization in Kennedy's mind.

In a letter to British Prime Minister Macmillan in early August, Kennedy stated that while his mind was not yet made up, he did not expect to be able to defer a decision on the resumption of testing beyond the start of 1962. Sharing the British leader's deep dislike for atmospheric testing, with its accompaniment of radioactive fallout, Kennedy added that if the United States did resume tests, they would be underground as long as the Soviets refrained from testing in the atmosphere.[119] Aside from these foreshadowings of future decisions, the letter to Macmillan was noteworthy for providing the first statement of what was later to emerge as the Test-Ban Treaty of August 1963. Acting on a suggestion made by Ambassador Thompson, Kennedy sounded Macmillan out on the idea of proposing a limited test ban agreement, covering only tests in the atmosphere and underwater.

The President's advisers split on the merits of proposing a partial test ban, Dean arguing that it might appear as a weakening of the West's interests in a comprehensive agreement covering all environments, Schlesinger and Bundy supporting it enthusiastically. The President's decision was a compromise: he directed ". . . that Dean should fight for the whole treaty in Geneva, but, if nothing happened, we could come out for the limited ban later."[120]

During the summer the United States, through its chief disarmament aides, Dean and McCloy, had made a number of efforts to secure Soviet agreement to an exchange of inspections of atomic facilities to demonstrate American good faith in observing the de facto test ban, but the Soviets, for reasons which became obvious on August 30, rejected these proposals as "impractical."[121]

Faced with an apparent impasse in the test ban negotiations and under strong pressure from his top military advisers to order an immediate resumption of tests, the President, during the first half of August, decided to authorize preparation for underground testing but meanwhile to defer giving the actual order for testing ". . . until it was absolutely clear—not only to him but to the world—that he had done everything possible to obtain a treaty, that the Soviets had not bargained in good faith or really wanted such a treaty, and that the security of the free world required this country to test."[122]

[119]Schlesinger, p. 459.

[120]Ibid. This statement summarizes Soviet–U.S. disarmament negotiations during the Kennedy administration.

[121]Jacobson and Stein, p. 279.

[122]Sorensen, p. 618. Sorensen dates this decision "early August." Schlesinger, however (p. 459), writes, "In mid-August the President concluded that, when Dean returned from Geneva and the Defense Department had completed its review of weapon requirements, the Atomic Energy Commission might announce contingency preparations for underground testing, though this would not mean that we had actually decided to resume tests."

The President's slow and reluctant steps toward the resumption of testing were counterbalanced by intensive efforts to prepare a comprehensive and realistic U.S. position on disarmament. To facilitate coordination of governmental work on this problem and to demonstrate the seriousness of purpose of his administration in seeking agreement with the Soviets, the President, on June 29, had sent a message to Congress proposing the establishment of a "U.S. Disarmament Agency for World Peace and Security."[123] In mid-August the Senate Committee on Foreign Relations held public hearings on the bill, with testimony from twenty-nine witnesses, including McCloy and Rusk, in support of the measure, which was enacted into law on September 26.

Since early May intensive work had been going on within U.S. government agencies and panels of civilian and military specialists for the purpose of drafting a new U.S. disarmament plan. By mid-August the draft, having been cleared with all interested U.S. government agencies and submitted for comments and suggestions to the allies, was ready for final approval, which it received from Kennedy on August 18. Without further substantial change, it formed the basis of the U.S. "Proposal for General and Complete Disarmament in a Peaceful World" which he submitted to the U.N. General Assembly on September 25 (below, p. 243).[124]

Although the comprehensive disarmament plan represented the Kennedy administration's most ambitious effort in this field, it was Dean's mission to Geneva which aroused its immediate interest. In his brief statement on the occasion of Dean's departure from Washington, on August 22, the President indicated the importance he attached to it:

> Mr. Dean is leaving to return to Geneva on a most vital mission. He will make a further effort to reach agreement on a treaty for an effective ban on nuclear testing. He goes with my full support and confidence. Our proposed treaty carries hope for our country and for the world, for relief from great dangers, and the United States continues to attach the highest importance to these negotiations. We must all hope that the Soviet Union will make some affirmative response to this renewed effort.[125]

The Geneva test ban talks, which had been briefly recessed during the temporary absence of the principal U.S. and Soviet delegates, resumed on August 28, when Dean for the United States and Tsarapkin for the Soviet Union returned with new instructions—Dean with concessions which he hoped would tempt the Soviets out of their recalcitrance, Tsarapkin with the knowledge that an announcement of Soviet resumption of testing was imminent.

[123]*Documents on Disarmament, 1961*, pp. 214–16; text of the accompanying draft bill, ibid., pp. 216–27.

[124]For an authoritative account of the drafting of the plan, see ibid., pp. 522–25. Commentary, Schlesinger, pp. 476–77. Sorensen, p. 518, maintains that Kennedy was originally skeptical about the possibilities of disarmament, but that he eventually "underwent a degree of redemption on this subject himself." This view appears to underestimate Kennedy's commitment to some form of disarmament as early as 1961.

[125]*JFK, 1961*, p. 567.

In accordance with the President's compromise ruling it had been decided that the West would not at this time put forward the suggestion of a partial test ban. The U.S. concessions which were announced by Dean and his aides were less sweeping, but under other circumstances might well have formed the basis for serious negotiation. In his opening speech, on August 28, Dean put forward a proposal for the "immediate lowering or even removal of the treaty threshold," i.e., the inclusion in an agreement on banning nuclear tests of low-yield explosions falling below the 4.75 measurement on the seismic scale, on condition that the Soviets indicated a readiness to study "those improvements or adjustments in the control system which could so increase its scientific capabilities from the outset as to warrant the lowering or removing of the threshold."[126] Linked with the proposal was an invitation to the Soviets to take part in "a large-scale seismic improvement research program underground" designed to enhance scientific capabilities for detecting low-yield tests.

Dean made it clear that he had not brought with him any shift in the Western position on the two most controversial Soviet demands: "At the same time, I must make it clear that I reiterate the complete unacceptability of the Soviet three-man administrative council proposal below the top eleven-man control commission, on which the West and the East have equal voices, and the Soviet theory of self-inspection."[127] Even on these disputed issues, however, the United States showed some flexibility by offering new concessions on August 30. As summarized later by Charles C. Stelle, a member of the U.S. delegation:

> The two amendments put forward on 30 August 1961 represented an attempt to give the Soviet Union assurance that States not associated with the original parties would have major responsibilities in the operation of the verification system. One amendment provided that the administrator could be recalled by a vote of 7 out of 11 of the control commission, which would in effect have given the deciding voice on the competence and impartiality of the administrator to the three non-associated States which we have proposed should be on the control commission. The second amendment put forward on that date provided that there should be a certain number of nationals of non-associated States on inspection teams sent out to investigate unidentified events.[128]

The new U.S. proposals of August 30, representing the high point to that date of Western efforts to meet the Soviets halfway in the test ban talks, evoked absolutely no interest from the Soviet delegation. In a statement on the same day, delivered only a few hours before the official Soviet announcement of the resumption of testing, Tsarapkin in effect ruled out any discussion of questions of detail as irrelevant. Commenting on Dean's lengthy analysis

[126]*Documents on Disarmament, 1961*, p. 300.
[127]Ibid., p. 302.
[128]Ibid., pp. 160–61. Jacobson and Stein, pp. 331–32, summarize the Aug. 30 proposals.

of the executive authority of the control system, Tsarapkin said: "I do not intend to plunge into a discussion of the details relating in particular to this question; we have already talked about that here at length and in the greatest detail, as you are well aware."[129] Nor had he any new proposals to offer on behalf of the Soviet Union: "I can only repeat again what we have already told you several times at this table that we are ready to accept any of your proposals on control—on its scope, its forms of organization, its administrative structure and the like—if you accept the Soviet proposals on general and complete disarmament."[130] Instead, Tsarapkin directed the attention of the conference to "what is now happening in the world as a result of the policy of the Western Powers, which continue to whip up the arms race, enlarge their military budgets, and intensify their military preparations."[131] The present situation, he continued,

> . . . shows beyond all doubt that the problem of cessation of nuclear weapon tests can be dealt with only in conjunction with that of disarmament. As we have already said more than once, the Soviet Union will be prepared to sign immediately a treaty on general and complete disarmament and to agree to any control of disarmament, and hence to any control of cessation of nuclear weapon tests. But it will not agree to any control so long as the armaments race continues and preparations are still being intensified; that is to say, it will not agree to control separated from disarmament.[132]

The implication was that Soviet response to Western proposals, policies, and actions would be given elsewhere than at the Geneva conference table. A few sharp-eyed and well-informed Western observers were already aware what form the Soviet action was likely to take: on the afternoon of August 28 two of Kennedy's scientific advisers, Jerome Wiesner and Carl Kaysen, had reported to him in some excitement that a Soviet broadcast had been picked up warning aircraft to stay out of a designated area over Siberia, and had suggested that this might mean that Soviet tests in the atmosphere were imminent.[133] It did not take long before the surmise was verified.

August 28 brought another indication that the Soviet leadership had moved into a phase of greatly increased hostility to the West and of willingness to risk a direct military confrontation. A TASS bulletin broadcast by Radio Moscow on that day charged that "foreign" submarines had recently committed "a number of violations of the state seacoast of the Soviet Union."

> The foreign submarines have been entering Soviet territorial waters while submerged, maneuvering there and making observations for intelligence purposes.

[129]*Documents on Disarmament, 1961*, p. 335.
[130]Ibid.
[131]Ibid., pp. 336–37.
[132]Ibid., p. 337.
[133]Schlesinger, p. 459.

The entry of submarines while submerged into the territorial waters of a foreign state without permission is a gross violation of the sovereignty of this state and is contrary to the generally recognized norms of international law.

In view of this, the U.S.S.R. government has instructed the U.S.S.R. Ministry of Defense, in case of discovery in Soviet territorial waters of foreign submarines that violate the state frontier of the U.S.S.R. and that are submerged, to take measures to destroy the violators.[134]

The Soviets announce the resumption of testing

In his speech of August 7 Khrushchev had indicated that the Soviet leadership had decided that the situation did not call for any further increase in allocations for the Soviet armed forces (above, p. 112). He had specifically linked that decision with an overall evaluation of the international situation, saying: "We are not willing to saddle the people with unnecessary hardships that are not warranted by the needs of the situation."

Despite provocative and threatening actions and statements by Soviet and East German authorities, the Western allies, during the remainder of the month of August, were careful to avoid anything which might appear to threaten the Soviet Union or indicate preparations for immediate hostilities. The only overt military step taken by the West during this period—the reinforcement of the West Berlin garrison by an American battle group on August 18—was clearly intended as a symbolic gesture aimed at shoring up popular morale in West Berlin, and its prompt acceptance by the Soviets indicates that they correctly gauged its real significance.

During the same period the Western allies, urged on by the Kennedy administration, gave a number of unmistakable indications of their wish to bring the Berlin question to the negotiating table, and as the end of the month approached it was clear that a Western proposal for talks on Berlin was imminent. At the same time the British and Americans were showing a strong desire to get the test ban talks at Geneva moving ahead once more.

There was thus nothing in the objective facts of the international situation toward the end of August which would have justified the Soviet leadership in reaching a conclusion as to the need for strengthening the Soviet armed forces, diametrically opposed to the one announced by Khrushchev on August 7. Nevertheless, that is exactly what happened. On August 29 the Soviet government announced its decision to defer temporarily the release of service men to the reserves, and on the following day it announced the resumption of the testing of nuclear weapons.

Because of its far greater significance the Soviet announcement on the resumption of testing had tended to overshadow the decision to retain service men (neither Schlesinger nor Sorensen mentions the August 29 announcement). The latter deserves consideration in its own right, however, as an indi-

[134]Radio Moscow, Aug. 28, 1961; *Pravda*, Aug. 29, 1961, p. 2; *CDSP*, XIII/35, p. 19.

cation of Soviet policy objectives and as a clue to the process of policy formulation in the Soviet leadership.

The most noteworthy aspect of the statement announcing the prolongation of military service was that it portrayed the international situation as one in which the Soviet Union and its allies were being threatened by a belligerent Western alliance, spurred on by rabidly revanchist West German political and military leaders, while ignoring completely both the Soviet contributions to international tension, particularly the Berlin Wall and the August 23 note, and Western efforts to end the crisis by moving it toward the negotiating table. "The Soviet Union," the announcement stated, "cannot but take this enforced measure under conditions in which the member countries of the NATO military bloc are in every way aggravating the international situation, addressing direct threats to the U.S.S.R. and the other socialist countries, stepping up the arms race, and fanning war hysteria."[135]

Flatly contradicting Khrushchev's judgment in his August 7 speech, the statement declared that: "The interests of the security of the Soviet Union demand that the best trained Soviet soldiers continue their service in the armed forces of the Soviet Union until a peace treaty with Germany is concluded."[136]

Briefly, for the record, the statement asserted Soviet willingness to discuss the terms of a German peace treaty with the Western allies, but only after it had made clear that the Soviet position on the question was fixed and non-negotiable: "It is clear that in solving the problem of a German peace treaty one must take into consideration the real state of affairs, and proceed from the recognition of the existence of two German states—the G.D.R. and the German Federal Republic. With the conclusion of a peace treaty, West Berlin will obtain the status of a demilitarized free city with guarantees of nonintervention in its internal affairs."[137]

At wearisome length the statement drew the usual stark contrast between the allegedly peace-loving policy of the Soviet Union and the rabidly militarist and aggressive policy of the Western alliance, citing particularly the military build-up announced by Kennedy on July 25 and the allegedly revanchist plans of the West German government, which it asserted were identical with those of Hitler and the Nazis:

The conclusion of a German peace treaty is opposed, above all, by the militarists and revanchists in West Germany who are hatching plans for new war gambles. Those who in their time nurtured Hitler, placed arms at his disposal. Those who engineered World War II today have seized again commanding positions in the economy and policy of the German Federal Republic. The West German revanchists and militarists took over from fascist Germany the program for enslaving other peoples and conquering alien territories. Chancellor of the German Federal Republic Adenauer and

[135]*Documents on Disarmament, 1961*, p. 309, citing Radio Moscow, Aug. 29, 1961.
[136]Ibid.
[137]Ibid., p. 312.

the forces backing him made revanchism the foundation of their official political course. . . . The program of the West German revanchists is a program of war.[138]

Soviet determination to sign a peace treaty with the GDR in 1961 was defiantly reasserted:

> The Central Committee of the CPSU and the Soviet Government believe that a firm barrier must be erected blocking the road to the engineering of another war in Europe. It is impermissible that West German militarism, taking advantage of the maintenance of the postwar unsettled state and of the lack of a peace treaty, should gradually lead the world to an armed clash. It is the duty of the peace-loving states to prevent the drift toward war. That is precisely why the Soviet Union insists on the immediate conclusion of a German peace treaty, and *we will conclude it jointly with other peace-loving states by the end of this year.* If the Western powers and the German Federal Republic reject a peaceful settlement, the Soviet Union will be compelled, together with other states that wish to do so, to sign a peace treaty with the G.D.R. alone.[139]

As to the danger that war might result from a clash over Berlin, the statement affirmed Soviet ability to defeat and destroy the Western alliance in almost hysterical tones:

> If the imperialists, with regard to the signing of a peace treaty with Germany, again seek to draw us into the abyss of war, we are fully resolved to put an end once and for all to the forces threatening aggression, and to strangle the trouble-makers who seek to creep out and to inflict innumerable losses and suffering on the peoples. The lovers of gambles must know that, taking into consideration the new balance of power now existing in the world arena, the aggressors will be crushed if they unleash war.[140]

In direct contradiction to the decision announced in Khrushchev's August 7 speech, though without having cited any specific evidence to justify a policy change of such magnitude, the statement set forth its central position as follows:

> Guided by the interests of safeguarding the security of the country, taking into consideration the existing situation and the ceaseless threats on the part of the United States and its NATO allies, the Central Committee of the CPSU and the U.S.S.R. Council of Ministers instruct the Minister of Defense to issue orders on the temporary deferment, until the conclusion of a peace treaty with Germany, of the transfer to the reserve of the necessary number of soldiers, sailors, sergeants, sergeant majors, and noncommissioned officers, whose term of service expires in 1961.[141]

---

[138]Ibid., p. 314.
[139]Ibid., pp. 314–15; emphasis supplied.
[140]Ibid., p. 315.
[141]Ibid., p. 316.

The brief concluding passages of the statement were noteworthy for the assertion that the Soviet armed forces already possessed the world's most powerful weapons: "The Soviet homeland has entrusted its soldiers with powerful, the most perfect, and the world's best combat weapons and techniques. Nowhere in the world are there such intercontinental and other types of rockets as those which are now in the arsenal of the Soviet army."[142]

Just a day later, however, the Soviet government would issue a statement asserting that it was forced to resume the testing of atomic weapons in order not to be outdistanced in military power by the West.

The statement emphasized the exclusively defensive character of Soviet armament: "The Soviet Union will never be the first to use arms, will never take the road to unleashing war. But our armed forces are always in constant and full combat readiness to give a crushing rebuff to any aggressor."[143] It concluded on a note of peace: "We need peace. We extend a hand of friendship to the peoples of the United States, Britain, France, and to the peoples of all other countries and say: Let us live in peace; strengthen the peace. It can be upheld by joint efforts."[144]

Internal evidence points to the conclusion that the August 29 statement represents the views of members of the Soviet leadership who differed profoundly from Khrushchev in their analysis of the international situation, the nature of the Western alliance and the policy which would best serve Soviet interests. Reinforcing this conclusion is the fact that the decision to delay the release of servicemen represented a victory for the conservative economic-military bloc and a defeat for Khrushchev and his adherents in the struggle over resource allocations. Appearing as it did just after a major effort by Khrushchev to stress the urgency and desirability of negotiations on Berlin, the August 29 statement clearly stands in direct opposition to Khrushchev's policies, interests, and intentions.

The form in which the August 29 announcement was presented by *Pravda* to its readers suggests a deliberate effort to provide a coded message identifying the factional allegiance of the announcement's sponsors. The first page of *Pravda* on August 30, 1961, contained only three items: the announcement itself, occupying most of the page; a TASS bulletin from Yalta, dated August 29, in the lower left-hand corner, reporting that Khrushchev had visited Kwame Nkrumah, chief of state of Ghana, at the latter's residence on the southern shore of the Crimea; and a photograph of workers in a Moscow machine-construction factory. Deciphered, the message conveyed by this rebus was plain: the decision on the deferment of the release of troops to the reserves had been taken in the Kremlin while Khrushchev was vacationing on the Black Sea; the men responsible for the decision were those members of

---

[142]Ibid., p. 317.

[143]Ibid.

[144]Ibid. Note the implication that it was the "peoples" of the Western nations— not their governments—who should cooperate in the search for peace.

the collective leadership who gave top priority to the policy of strengthening Soviet military-industrial power.

Similar conclusions follow from an analysis of the Soviet announcement on the resumption of testing issued on August 30. Here too the Soviet statement pointedly ignored both Soviet aggressive actions and threats and the strong indications of Western desire for negotiation, portraying matters instead in terms of a peace-loving Soviet Union menaced by a rabidly militarist Western alliance.

> The peoples are currently witnessing the ever-growing aggressiveness of the policy of the NATO military bloc. The United States of America and its allies are spinning the flywheel of their war machine harder and harder, are pushing the arms race to unprecedented proportions, are increasing the numerical strength of their armies and are bringing international tension to a white heat. Things have reached a point where the leaders of the U.S.A. and the countries allied with it are resorting to threats of taking up arms and unleashing a war in retaliation for the conclusion of a peace treaty with the German Democratic Republic.[145]

Under these conditions, the statement continued,

> . . . the Soviet government considers itself duty bound to take all necessary measures so that the Soviet Union will be in a state of complete readiness to render harmless any aggressor should he attempt to make an attack. The tragedy of the earliest months of the Great Patriotic War [i.e., the Soviet phase of World War II], when Hitler attacked the U.S.S.R. after making sure of his superiority in military equipment, is too fresh in people's minds to allow this to happen today. This is why the Soviet government has already taken a number of serious measures to strengthen the security of the U.S.S.R. For the same reason, after profound and thorough reflection on the matter, it has come to a decision to carry out experimental explosions of nuclear weapons.[146]

The remaining passages of the lengthy statement constituted a labored attempt to justify the decision taken and to cast responsibility for it onto the Western powers. As a revealing exposition of the fears and hopes of the opposition in the Soviet leadership, the statement merits close study.

The attempted justification of the Soviet decision led off with the assertion that any war among the great powers would inevitably involve the use of nuclear weapons:

> Those who are preparing a new world slaughter are today sowing illusions that a new world war, should one be unleashed, could be fought without the use of thermonuclear weapons. But this is an attempt to delude the peoples. The experience of history teaches that it has never been possible to contain the flames of war within predetermined bounds. Wars have their own cruel and inexorable laws. An aggressor unleashes a war with the purpose of

---

[145]*Pravda*, Aug. 31, 1961, p. 1; *CDSP*, XIII/35, p. 3.
[146]Ibid.

bringing his victim to his knees, of imposing his will upon that victim. But even the aggressor realizes that in the event of defeat he himself will be overtaken by the fate he had in store for his victim. Hence any state engaged in a war, regardless of whether it is the attacker or is defending itself, will stop at nothing to gain the victory and will not concede defeat without having used and exhausted every means of warfare at its command. Such being the case, any armed conflict, however minor at first, would inevitably develop into a general nuclear-missile war should the nuclear powers be drawn into it.[147]

"The Soviet government," the statement maintained, "was the first to speak out for universal and total disarmament and the cessation of nuclear weapons tests."[148] Responsibility for the failure to achieve these goals, it asserted, lay with the Western powers: "It is no exaggeration to suppose that had only the governments of the U.S.A., Britain, France, and several other states in the Western military bloc reciprocated in showing an eagerness for this, mankind could this very day be living in a world without arms and without armies."[149]

Following the line adopted in the Vienna memorandum on disarmament, the statement argued that the cessation of nuclear weapons tests could best be achieved not as a separate goal in itself but within the framework of an overall comprehensive disarmament agreement: "The main thing in our day is disarmament, universal and total, and an agreement on this kind of disarmament would also dispose of the problem of nuclear tests."[150]

Going beyond the position set forth in the Vienna memorandum, however, the statement expressed skepticism about the value of a test ban agreement: ". . . a mere agreement on the cessation of nuclear weapons tests cannot in and of itself put an end to the arms race. The states already in possession of atomic weapons will inevitably be tempted to circumvent the agreement and seek more and more ways and loopholes for improving the weapons, to say nothing of the fact that the tests that have been conducted by the three or four powers are quite sufficient for the unlimited stockpiling of the most dangerous thermonuclear weapons of existing types."[151]

In a passage which could be read as providing advance justification for the development of atomic weapons by communist China, the statement continued:

States that do not yet have thermonuclear weapons will in turn be trying to develop them, in spite of the existence of an agreement banning atomic tests. Incidentally, they may in so doing advance arguments that the pro-

[147]Ibid.
[148]Ibid.
[149]Ibid.
[150]Ibid.
[151]Ibid.

ponents of nuclear disarmament will not find it easy to parry. Indeed, is it realistic to believe that a situation can long endure where some states which have forged ahead in harnessing atomic energy for military purposes continue to build up mountains of atomic and hydrogen bombs on the basis of experiments they have already conducted, while others stand idly by and see themselves falling farther and farther behind the nuclear powers in their military might, and therefore in their capability of safeguarding their security?

Experience argues otherwise.[152]

At considerable length the statement summarized the Soviet position on nuclear tests in terms of repeated Soviet efforts on behalf of disarmament, rendered fruitless by Western refusal to agree to reasonable Soviet proposals. With scant regard either for the truth or for the complexities of the technical problems involved, the statement portrayed the Western powers as totally committed to the continuation of underground tests:

The governments of the Western powers have insisted and continue to insist that a treaty on the cessation of nuclear testing contain no ban on underground nuclear explosions. And yet it is obvious to any well-informed person that such explosions, even if it is claimed that they are being conducted for peaceful purposes, are purely and simply a clandestine method of improving already existing nuclear weapons and perfecting new types. . . . Thus while paying lip service to the necessity of stopping nuclear tests, the U.S. and Britain have in fact been showing concern for something quite different— for somehow building into the treaty loopholes for the further perfection of thermonuclear weapons by means of underground explosions or explosions for so-called peaceful purposes.[153]

The position set forth in the Vienna memorandum on disarmament calling for subordinating the test ban talks to negotiations on general and complete disarmament—a position clearly aimed at bringing the test ban talks to a complete halt—was portrayed instead as a promising and potentially valuable contribution to the talks' success:

To break the deadlock in the talks, the Soviet government proposed that settlement of the question of nuclear-test cessation be coupled with the problem of universal and total disarmament. This important proposal was advanced in the Memorandum delivered at the meeting in Vienna between N. S. Khrushchev, Chairman of the U.S.S.R. Council of Ministers, and U.S. President J. Kennedy. This initiative on the part of the Soviet government opened up additional possibilities for the achievement of mutually acceptable solutions on the whole range of disarmament problems and—what is particularly important—removed the obstacles to the establishment of the

[152]Ibid., pp. 3, 6. For the suggestion of a link with China, see Harry Schwartz, *NYT*, Sept. 3, 1961, p. 2.

[153]*CDSP*, XIII/35, p. 6.

broadest and most comprehensive international control, including control over the cessation of nuclear tests.[154]

Alleged U.S. plans for construction of a neutron bomb rated a paragraph of virulent denunciation: "The plans for developing a neutron bomb lay bare the whole misanthropic nature of present-day imperialism, which is no longer willing to content itself with merciless exploitation of working people and is prepared for the sake of gain to engage in crimes whose enormity would blot out memories of the gas chambers and execution vans of the Hitlerite butchers."[155]

The United States, in any case, was said to be already on the point of resuming underground testing: "It is no secret that the U.S. is on the verge of conducting underground nuclear explosions and is simply looking for the first suitable pretext for starting them. Is there anyone, however, who cannot clearly see that once the U.S. government has decided to resume nuclear weapons tests it is only a matter of time?"[156]

At no point in the lengthy statement, however, was an attempt made to answer the obvious question why, if in fact the United States was about to resume testing, the Soviet government did not delay its own test series in order to demonstrate the purity of its intentions before world public opinion, at the same time allowing the United States to incur the odium of breaking the de facto test ban. In general, the weakest aspect of the August 30 statement was its failure to explain why the resumption of Soviet testing was obligatory at this particular moment, a weakness it shared with the August 29 statement on the armed forces. The real explanation for the timing of the two measures, however, could not very well be set forth in official statements, since it had nothing to do with the alleged reasons for the actions.

The August 30 statement dwelt at great length upon the French atomic tests, citing them as an additional justification for the Soviet decision.

Acknowledging the harmful effects of nuclear testing, the statement called the decision to resume testing "not an easy one": "It [the Soviet Government] has been forced to do this reluctantly, with regret and *only after having given the matter the most careful and thorough study*."[157]

This statement was patently false, however, since, as we have seen, the decision to resume testing was made before the U.S. delegation had had an opportunity to present the new U.S. proposals to the Geneva test ban conference.

The argument now shifted to the alleged militarist and revanchist policies of West Germany:

The Soviet people and the Soviet government cannot ignore the fact that once again, as was the case 20 years ago, ominous war clouds are swirling

[154]Ibid.
[155]Ibid.
[156]Ibid.
[157]Ibid., p. 7; emphasis supplied.

at the approaches to our homeland's frontiers, and that West Germany and the present allies of the German militarists are seized with a fever of war preparations. . . .

Adenauer and the forces behind him are pursuing a course aimed at turning West Germany into a militarist state armed to the teeth. The principal aim of that state's foreign policy is revenge and the revision of the borders established in Europe as a result of the second world war. The government of the F.R.G. is currently seeking to make up for the time lost in the years just after the unconditional surrender of Hitlerite Germany, when the U.S., Britain and France had not yet entirely abandoned the allied agreements calling for the demilitarization of Germany.[158]

When it came to producing specific examples of Western actions which might justify the Soviet decision, however, the statement could find nothing more imposing than the token military build-up in West Berlin: "The U.S. and Britain have made a new show of force in response to the Soviet proposals on the conclusion of a German peace treaty by bringing additional armed forces and armaments into West Berlin. This does not count for much in the reinforcement of the Western powers' military garrisons in West Berlin, and it has plainly been undertaken for provocation and for that alone, a fact that is best known to those who took the decision in ordering this contingent of troops to West Berlin."[159] In other words, the reinforcement of the West Berlin garrison, even to the authors of this violently anti-Western statement, could not be made to appear as convincing evidence of Western preparations for an aggressive war against the Soviet Union.

Having exhausted its arsenal of arguments in defense of the Soviet decision, the statement finally came out with a summary of the proposed actions: "The Soviet Union has worked out plans for developing a series of nuclear bombs of higher yield—20, 30, 50 and 100 megatons; powerful rockets, similar to those with the help of which Major Yu. A. Gagarin and Major G. S. Titov orbited the earth in their unparalleled space flights, are capable of lifting these nuclear bombs and delivering them to any point on the globe from which an attack might be made on the Soviet Union or the other socialist countries."[160]

Betraying an uneasy awareness that the arguments it had advanced did not really provide adequate justification for the decision to resume testing, the statement asked for special indulgence on the part of

> those people in foreign lands who might be inclined to judge harshly the testing of new types of thermonuclear weapons by the Soviet Union. The Soviet Union is undertaking this step in the firm belief that the peoples will understand that this measure has been forced upon us and is unavoidable in the circumstances that have arisen. To discourage an aggressor from

[158]Ibid.

[159]Ibid., pp. 7–8.

[160]Ibid., p. 8. Note the close link between the Soviet space program and its armament program.

criminally playing with fire we must let him know and see that there is in the world a force armed at all points and ready to repulse any challenge to the independence and security of peace-loving states and that the weapon of retribution will smite the aggressor in his own lair.[161]

But the Soviet government, the statement continued, was concerned with more than merely justifying the decision to resume testing:

The Soviet government's reasons for speaking of all this are not limited to the desire to make perfectly clear its motives in conducting nuclear tests at this moment. It is calling all this to mind in the first place so that the peoples of the whole world may know whence the growing danger comes, so that they have their eyes open to the intrigues of the enemies of peace and so that they may make common cause to combat this danger. Let all who hold dear the preservation of peace know that they can confidently rely on the Soviet Union, on the titanic efforts it is making to bring the inciters of war hysteria to their senses and halt the accelerating rush to a new war.[162]

After a solemn pledge that ". . . the armed forces of the U.S.S.R. will never be the first to resort to arms,"[163] the statement concluded with an affirmation that ". . . the Soviet people's efforts in the struggle to strengthen international security will not have been in vain but will merge with the efforts of all other peoples aimed at the achievement of lasting, inviolable peace on earth and the triumph of the ideas of peace and progress."[164]

Unlike the August 29 statement on the armed forces, the August 30 statement on tests contained not a single line concerning the desirability of negotiations on Berlin and Germany. It was left to Khrushchev, still on vacation, to remedy this glaring omission by the characteristic device of calling in two foreign guests who could serve as mouthpieces for his views.

This time Khrushchev's choice fell on two left-wing British MP's, Sir Leslie Plummer and Konni Zilliacus. The reason for the choice was clear: Zilliacus had achieved a well-founded reputation as a consistent fellow-traveler of communism, while Plummer only a few days earlier had attracted favorable Soviet attention as an outspoken critic of British support for U.S. policy in the Berlin crisis.[165]

Khrushchev's purpose in arranging the interview was made clear by Western press reports of the event:

. . . Khrushchev said in a three-hour interview at Yalta that he resumed nuclear testing in order to shock the Western powers into negotiations over Germany and disarmament. . . . When the British MP's suggested to

---

[161]Ibid.

[162]Ibid.

[163]Ibid.

[164]Ibid.

[165]V. Silant'ev, "Englishmen do not wish to fight," based on an interview with Plummer, *Izv*, Aug. 26, 1961, p. 2. The date of Khrushchev's interview with the two MP's, August 31, is given in Khrushchev, *Kommunizm*, 2:354.

Khrushchev that his decision would cause alarm, he replied: "I knew it would, but I have had enough. I am going to do something about it. We are not going to go on with the present situation." In summing up his impressions of Khrushchev's feeling, Sir Leslie said: "He is in deadly earnest. He obviously intends to shock the world and this was no flash in the pan."[166]

By means of the hastily arranged interview with Plummer and Zilliacus, Khrushchev was attempting to convince the world that the decision of the resumption of testing was his and his alone. (The fact that the decision was made while he was at Sochi and that there is no evidence of the presence there at the time of any other members of the Presidium rules out a formal decision by the collective leadership.)

In a confidential diplomatic message sent just after the announcement on the resumption of testing, however, Khrushchev told a very different story. On August 31 he sent a cable to Prince Norodom Sihanouk, chief of state of Cambodia, offering what purported to be the real reasons behind the decision to resume testing:

I have the honor to inform Your Royal Highness confidentially that *the Soviet Government has been forced to take some measures*—such as the testing of nuclear weapons—to safeguard the security of the U.S.S.R. and the world. Because of the sincere relations and friendship between our two countries I have decided to inform Your Royal Highness of this very important decision before the other countries. . . .

I beg at this point to draw your attention to the following: *My comrades in the Soviet Government and myself have taken the above decision regretfully.* We are aware that our decision will provoke great emotion in the group of countries—to which we also belong—that sincerely desire a cessation of nuclear explosions. However, we have been forced to take the decision because, though we are an energetic defender of peace and progress, our views are not shared by the other party.[167]

Two deductions can be drawn: first, that Khrushchev, in order to reassert his personal authority for the conduct of Soviet foreign policy and to maintain thereby the fiction of a unified process of policy formulation, was laying claim to a decision which had in fact been taken by his opponents in the Soviet leadership, and second, that he was striving desperately to make it appear that the decision on the resumption of testing was directly linked with his advocacy of negotiations, whereas in fact it had as one of its main purposes precisely the disruption of the growing movement on both sides toward negotiation.

Such was the hold of the prevailing concept in the West of the monolithic character of Soviet foreign policy formulation, however, that this bold exercise

[166]*NYT*, Sept. 2, 1961, p. 1.

[167]The message, originally sent to Prince Norodom in Belgrade, where he was preparing to attend an international conference of neutralist nations, was broadcast over Radio Phnom Penh on Sept. 22, 1961. Emphasis supplied.

in barefaced deception achieved complete success. Sorensen, for example, accepted the Khrushchev position at face value: "His hope, Khrushchev told two British visitors, was to shock the West into concessions on Berlin and disarmament."[168] Kennedy himself accepted without question the rationale of the Soviet decision on testing offered by Khrushchev. On September 5, at a time when the Soviets had already carried out a number of nuclear tests in the atmosphere, Kennedy told Rusk that the reason the Soviets appeared to be showing little interest in negotiation was because, "It isn't time yet. It's too early. They are bent on scaring the world to death before they begin negotiating, and they haven't quite brought the pot to boil. Not enough people are frightened."[169]

It was only gradually, in retrospect and with a knowledge of the full course of the Berlin crisis of 1961, that some perspicacious observers came to realize that the Soviet announcement on the resumption of testing did not represent, as was widely believed at the time and as Khrushchev stoutly protested, an additional effort on the part of the Soviets to apply pressure to force the West to negotiate, but instead marked the tacit abandonment of any Soviet desire for negotiation.

A shrewd analysis of the point is provided by the *Survey of International Affairs*: "The motive behind the choice of this moment to resume testing was taken by opinion generally all over the world as the desire further to increase the pressure on the western alliance. . . . Yet seen in retrospect, the Soviet test-programme was to serve less as a means of pressure on the west than as a smoke-screen to distract attention from the Soviet abandonment of its much-heralded plan to sign a treaty of peace with East Germany before the end of the year."[170]

Even this analysis, however, falls short of identifying the real reason behind the Soviet decision to resume testing. Not only did the announcement of Soviet resumption mark the temporary abandonment of the impulse toward negotiation from the Soviet side, just at a time when Khrushchev was doing his best to give it additional impetus, it also cut off and decisively blocked the similar impulse on the Western side.

As we have seen, the most favorable response Khrushchev had as yet been able to elicit from the Western alliance had come from the Italians. The Soviet resumption of testing brought this promising lead to a sudden and abrupt end. On September 1 Khrushchev wrote again to Fanfani proposing negotiation, but this time his appeal found no answering response, for reasons which the *Survey of International Affairs* makes clear:

The invitation found the Italian government more and more divided between pleasure at the leading role forced on them, anger that Italy should

[168]Sorensen, p. 619.
[169]Schlesinger, p. 398.
[170]*SIA, 1961*, p. 256.

be selected as the "weak link" in the NATO chain, and fear lest Mr. Khrushchev was trying to force Italy out of NATO. . . .

The sentiments of the Republican and Social Democrat elements in the [Italian government] coalition in favour of negotiating over Berlin could nevertheless have succeeded in dividing the cabinet and in forcing its resignation in favour of one definitely tilted either to left or right, had not they been bitterly offended by the Soviet resumption of testing and therefore totally disinclined to do anything at that moment from which the Soviet leadership would benefit. As a result, despite a second letter from Mr. Khrushchev on 12 September, the Italian Government did nothing and the Soviets abandoned further attempts to use them as a mediator.[171]

The Soviet decision to resume testing and the closely associated decision to retain servicemen in the armed forces thus stand revealed as measures decided on in Moscow during a period of Khrushchev's absence from the Kremlin, representing the policies of his political opponents and aimed both at securing gains for the conservative economic-military bloc and preventing Khrushchev from entering into negotiation with the West over Berlin.

* * *

Striking evidence of the split personality which afflicted the Soviet leadership in its relations with the United States was provided on August 31, when an Institute of Soviet–American Relations was established in Moscow.[172] The main report at the inaugural session, delivered by N. N. Blokhin, president of the USSR Academy of Medical Sciences, stressed the "enormous historic responsibility placed upon the peoples of our countries for maintaining and strengthening general peace." "In the opinion of the Soviet people," Blokhin said, ". . . there is a reliable basis for building, through joint efforts, a bridge of friendship and cooperation that will cross the ocean and link our peoples for their common good. This basis is peaceful coexistence between states with different social systems, which has been the basis of the foreign policy of the Soviet state since the very first days of its existence."[173]

Blokhin called for "persistent new efforts by each and every one of us— Soviet people and Americans alike—" to "break a path toward mutual trust and peaceful cooperation between the U.S.S.R. and the U.S.A. . . . Friendly joint efforts by the broad public in our two countries will help to eliminate completely all distrust and suspicion in relations between the U.S.S.R. and the U.S.A. and to replace them with relations of good will, mutual understanding and peaceful and friendly cooperation."[174]

---

[171]Ibid., pp. 260–61.

[172]*Pravda*, Sept. 1, 1961, p. 6; *CDSP*, XIII/35, pp. 21–22; Theodore Shabad, *NYT*, Sept. 1, 1961, p. 6.

[173]*CDSP*, XIII/35, p. 21.

[174]Ibid.

Coming as they did just on the heels of the Soviet announcement of the resumption of nuclear testing, Blokhin's words sounded like deliberate hypocrisy. When one takes into account the time needed to coordinate the activities of the various prominent people who attended the opening meeting of the Institute, however, it seems clear that its timing in relation to the announcement on the resumption of testing was purely coincidental. Rather, the establishment of the Institute should be recognized as a manifestation primarily of Khrushchev's concept of the form relations between the Soviet Union and the United States should take. There is no need to engage in elaborate analysis to prove this point, since among the sixteen vice presidents of the Institute, elected at the first session of its board immediately following the general meeting, was N. P. Khrushcheva—Khrushchev's wife, who was making one of her rare appearances as a public figure in her own right.

The initial reaction: Washington

As we have seen (above, p. 156), Kennedy had been alerted on August 28 to the possibility that the Soviets might be preparing to resume nuclear testing. He had thus had several days in which to consider his reaction and that of the United States to the Soviet decision. At his regular press conference, on the afternoon of August 30, however, the President made no direct allusion to the possibility of a resumption of testing by the Soviets, stressing instead his hope that the Berlin problem could be solved by negotiation. While he declined to specify the exact terms on which the United States and its allies would be willing to negotiate, he strongly endorsed the concept of negotiation in general:

> We have indicated—and I've said before that we are prepared to participate in any exchange of views, to use all available channels which are open to us to see if a peaceful solution can be reached on the problems in Europe and in Germany—any solution which can provide greater guarantees to the people of West Berlin that they will have the right to live out their lives in a way of their own choosing and that we will be glad to participate in any conversations which we have hopes will advance that prospect.[175]

In an implied appeal to the Soviet leadership's sense of responsibility he continued, "I'm hopeful that all people involved will realize that in these days of massive forces available on every side that—for the future of the countries involved and for the human race—we should attempt to work out a peaceful solution and that neither side should attempt to impose its will by brute force, because in that case it would be unsuccessful and disaster would be the common result."[176]

[175]*JFK, 1961*, pp. 573–74.
[176]Ibid., p. 574.

In answer to a question on the test ban negotiations in Geneva, the President replied that the talks were continuing and that "by the end of next week . . . we'll have an answer as to whether it's going to be possible to reach an agreement."[177]

Ambassador Thompson, he told another reporter, would soon be returning to Moscow, and it should then be possible to see "whether a satisfactory solution [of the Berlin problem] can be reached."[178] Asked whether he thought the United States might have been at fault in not conveying to Khrushchev with sufficient urgency a sense of his responsibility for involving the world in the threat of a nuclear war over Berlin, Kennedy replied in terms which indicated his own intense concern over this very question and his hope that Khrushchev did in fact share "this grave responsibility":

> Well, every country operates under different systems and—Mr. Khrushchev — there has been a good deal of brandishing of nuclear weapons, but I am hopeful, as I've said, that anyone—and I'm sure Mr. Khrushchev knows very well what the effect would be on the people of this world of ours if nuclear weapons were exchanged in a massive way between the countries which possess them—and I'm conscious of this and I'm sure Mr. Khrushchev is— and we will have to wait and see now whether from the consciousness on both sides peace can be achieved, which is our objective.[179]

A reporter having questioned the President with regard to a charge by former Vice President Richard Nixon that the reinforcement of the West Berlin garrison by a token force of U.S. troops was, in the reporter's paraphrase, "a useless gesture which Mr. Khrushchev might interpret as weakness rather than strength," Kennedy replied,

> I'm quite aware that Berlin is, from a military point of view, untenable, if it were subjected to a direct attack by the Soviet Union. What we hope will prevent that direct attack is the awareness of the Soviet Union that we mean to defend our position in West Berlin, and that American troops, who are not numerous there, are our hostage to that intent.
>
> It would seem to me, and I think at the time, that the West Berliners would benefit from a reminder of that commitment, and it was for that reason that those troops were added to the garrison of West Berlin. I don't see really how that weakens our commitment. If troops were withdrawn, would that strengthen it?[180]

In the same reply he delivered an indirect rebuke to the Republican National Chairman who, in the words of the reporter, "has said that your administration's attitude in general is one of appeasement toward Communism

[177]Ibid., p. 577.
[178]Ibid., p. 576.
[179]Ibid., pp. 577–78.
[180]Ibid., p. 576.

throughout the world": "We are in a situation in Germany which is fraught with peril, and I think that anyone who is aware of the nature of the destructive power that's available to both sides should, I would think, be careful in attempting to take any political advantage out of our present difficulties."[181]

Earlier in the conference Kennedy had announced the appointment of General Lucius Clay as his "personal representative" in Berlin. "The situation in Berlin is a serious one," he said, "and I wish to have the advantage of having on the scene a person of General Clay's outstanding capacity and experience."[182]

Several of the President's replies dealt with the complex and touchy problem of relations between the United States and its allies in the face of the Berlin crisis. A meeting of the foreign ministers of the United States, Britain, France, and West Germany would be held in Washington on September 14, he stated, as part of the continuing interallied consultation "with respect to Germany and Berlin in light of the Soviet challenge to our position there."[183] But when he was asked whether he was "satisfied with what our NATO allies are doing to increase their strength," the President implied rather strongly that he was not:

> We have in the meeting of the foreign ministers in early August urged very strongly that the NATO countries commit larger forces to the defense of Europe. It involves their security and it involves peace in this area, and I'm hopeful that all the countries that are involved will make the kind of effort which is required.
>
> And I think if they do not, then, Europe has diminished to that degree. I am hopeful that we're going to meet our responsibilities and we're asking them to meet theirs. And by the end of September we'll know whether that's going to be done.[184]

Beneath the carefully chosen formulations and the dogged emphasis on hope for a negotiated settlement of the Berlin crisis could be sensed the President's feeling of foreboding, a feeling which found guarded expression toward the end of the conference: "I . . . do not have information today which would make me wholly sanguine about present prospects."[185]

Back in his office in the White House, after the press conference, the President was handed an intelligence report confirming the August 28 warning: a Soviet message had been intercepted indicating that the resumption of nuclear testing would be announced that evening at 7 P.M. Washington time.[186] Sorensen gives a vivid picture of the President's immediate response:

---

[181]Ibid.
[182]Ibid., p. 573.
[183]Ibid., pp. 572–73.
[184]Ibid., p. 578.
[185]Ibid., p. 579.
[186]Sorensen, p. 619; Sidey, p. 242; *NYT*, Sept. 1, 1961, p. 2.

"His first reaction is unprintable. It was one of personal anger at the Soviets for deceiving him and at himself for believing them. For their tests had obviously been under secret preparation even before Vienna and throughout the Geneva negotiations. His second reaction was one of deep disappointment—deeper, I believe, than that caused by any other Soviet action during his tenure."[187]

Three hours after the Soviet announcement the White House was ready with a soberly worded "Statement on Soviet Resumption of Nuclear Weapons Tests."[188] Neither Sorensen nor Schlesinger provides any information on the drafting of this important document, but its careful phrasing and skillful handling of complex policy questions indicate that it must have been in preparation for a longer period than the short time available on the afternoon and evening of August 30. Probably it had occupied the President's attention ever since the August 28 advance warning.

The opening paragraph of the statement, with rhetorical emphasis, hammered home the dread implications of the Soviet action:

The Soviet government's decision to resume nuclear weapons testing will be met with deepest concern and resentment throughout the world. The Soviet government's decision to resume nuclear weapons testing presents a hazard to every human being throughout the world by increasing the dangers of nuclear fallout. The Soviet government's decision to resume nuclear weapons testing is in utter disregard of the desire of mankind for a decrease in the arms race. The Soviet government's decision to resume nuclear weapons testing presents a threat to the entire world by increasing the dangers of a thermo-nuclear holocaust. The Soviet government's decision to resume nuclear weapons testing indicates the complete hypocrisy of its professions about general and complete disarmament.[189]

The statement then drew a connection between the Soviet decision, the behavior of their delegation at the test ban negotiations in Geneva, and the Berlin crisis:

The pretext offered by the announcement for Soviet resumption of [nuclear] weapons testing is the very crisis which they themselves have created by threatening to disturb the peace which has existed in Germany and Berlin. It is not the first time they have made such charges against those who have dared to stand in the way of Soviet aggression. In addition, the announcement links the Soviet resumption of testing with threats of massive weapons which it must know cannot intimidate the rest of the world.

The purpose and motivation of this Soviet behavior now seems apparent: The Soviet Government wished to abandon serious negotiations in order to free its hand to resume nuclear weapons testing.[190]

[187]Sorensen, p. 619.
[188]Text, *JFK, 1961*, pp. 580–81.
[189]Ibid.
[190]Ibid.

Continuing U.S. interest in the conclusion of a test ban agreement was strongly affirmed: "The United States continues to share the view of the people of the world as to the importance of an agreement to end nuclear weapons tests under effective safeguards. Such an agreement would represent a major breakthrough in the search for an end to the arms race. It would stop the accumulation of stock piles of even more powerful weapons. It would inhibit the spread of nuclear weapons to other countries with its increased risks of nuclear war."[191]

In solemn words the statement charged the Soviets with responsibility for blocking these bright prospects: "The Soviet Union bears a heavy responsibility before all humanity for this decision, a decision which was made in complete disregard of the United Nations."[192] As to the U.S. response, the statement was noncommittal but somber: "The termination of the moratorium on nuclear testing by the Soviet unilateral decision leaves the United States under the necessity of deciding what its own national interests require. . . . Under these circumstances, Ambassador Arthur Dean is being recalled immediately from Geneva."[193]

On the morning of August 31, amid a rising tide of clamor in the American press and the Congress for an immediate and drastic response to the Soviet announcement, the President held two high-level conferences in the White House: a meeting of the National Security Council at 10 A.M. and a briefing of congressional leaders three quarters of an hour later.[194]

The views presented to the National Security Council represented a wide spectrum of choices, ranging from Rusk's proposal, embodied in a draft presidential announcement, for the immediate resumption of testing by the United States, to the more moderate counsel of Edward R. Murrow, director of the United States Information Agency, to the effect that the United States would be well-advised to defer its decision, meanwhile allowing the Soviets to reap the worldwide harvest of condemnation which their action could be expected to produce.

The President's own views, it soon became clear, were closer to those of Murrow than of Rusk. He toned down the Rusk statement "to make it announce, not a decision to resume, but a decision to begin preparations for resumption,"[195] and then, swayed by Murrow's forceful advocacy of a cautious approach, dropped the statement entirely.

A consideration which could not fail to weigh heavily in the President's mind as he contemplated the various alternatives open to him was the need to reassure members of the government, as well as the nation in general and its allies, of the adequacy of U.S. military strength in the face of the challenge

---

[191]Ibid.
[192]Ibid.
[193]Ibid.
[194]Schlesinger, pp. 448–50, has the fullest available account of these meetings.
[195]Schlesinger, p. 449.

posed by the impending Soviet test series. Under attack by the Republicans as being insufficiently tough with the communists, and vividly aware of the shaky political base on which his administration rested (the House of Representatives had just defeated the administration's school construction bill by the unexpectedly wide margin of 242 to 169), Kennedy was forced to include considerations of domestic politics in his calculations.

To his credit, however, the President's final decision was made primarily in the light of his responsibilities to the nation and to mankind in general, rather than on narrow domestic political grounds. The formal outcome of the August 31 mid-morning conferences was a brief statement which condemned the Soviet announcement as "primarily a form of atomic blackmail, designed to substitute terror for reason in the present international scene," and then went on to reassure the nation and its allies as to the continuing adequacy of U.S. strength: "The President is entirely confident that the size of the U.S. nuclear weapons stockpile and the capabilities of individual weapons and delivery systems are wholly adequate for the defense needs of the United States and of the free world."[196]

In line with Murrow's advice, the statement said nothing about forthcoming U.S. tests. Nor was this restraint a mere tactical maneuver designed to yield a temporary propaganda advantage over the Soviets. There was more than mere rhetoric in the concluding words of the statement: "The President shares the disappointment registered throughout the world that serious and sustained attempts to ban nuclear testing have come to this abrupt end."[197]

Determined to give the Soviets every opportunity to reconsider their decision, the President in the next few days sought for and obtained British Prime Minister Harold Macmillan's assent to a joint U.S.-British appeal to Khrushchev to halt the new Soviet test series. Before considering that appeal and the reply it received from the Soviets, however, we must take account of the Chinese reactions to the Soviet announcement.

The initial reaction: Peking

In Peking no less than in Washington, the Soviet decision to resume the testing of nuclear weapons was recognized as a policy move of major importance. In their evaluation of the move, however, the two capitals took diametrically opposed stands. Whereas Washington deplored and regretted the Soviet decision, Peking greeted it with unfeigned jubilance. Only in one respect did the reactions in the two capitals coincide: in both there was evidence that the Soviet decision had been known in advance.

Kennedy, as we have seen, was forewarned of the Soviet decision as early as August 28 and received final confirmation a few hours before the actual announcement on the evening of the 30th. The evidence for foreknowledge in

[196] *JFK, 1961*, pp. 584–85.
[197] Ibid.

the case of Peking is indirect—there have been no Chinese counterparts to the historical memoirs of Sorensen or Schlesinger, nor has the Chinese press disclosed the details of how the news was conveyed to the Chinese communist leadership. Though the evidence is indirect, however, its import is unmistakable.

It will be recalled that the CPR leadership manifested an unusual interest in the Soviet–Chinese trade talks which ended with the signing of a supplementary trade agreement at Peking on August 26 (above, p. 149). The Soviet decision to resume testing, it will be recalled, had been made in the Kremlin two days earlier (above, p. 148).

On August 29, the day before the Soviet test announcement, the CPR news agency issued a statement accusing the United States of being on the verge of resuming nuclear testing: "In the atmosphere of war psychosis in the United States, reactionary U.S. politicians one after another have urged the Kennedy administration to resume nuclear weapon tests, according to reports from New York."[198]

The statement went on to cite articles by prominent U.S. political figures in a number of periodicals urging the administration to resume testing. The significance of the timing of the statement was recognized by *New York Times* Soviet affairs specialist Harry Schwartz: ". . . it appears clear that Peiping [Peking] knew in advance of the Soviet plans. This is indicated from an article transmitted by Hsinhua [NCNA], the Chinese Communist press agency, the day before the Moscow announcement. In the present perspective the article appears to be an advance attempt to justify the decision. It was a comprehensive review of statements by various Americans urging the United States to resume nuclear tests."[199]

Further evidence pointing to Soviet–Chinese consultation in the period immediately preceding the publication of the August 30 announcement can be found in the announcement itself. We have already noted the occurrence in the announcement of a passage which could be read as authorization for the development of nuclear weapons by communist China (above, p. 162). This fact, too, was duly noted by Schwartz, who wrote that the passage in question "appears to read like an advance Soviet justification for Chinese tests" and "sounds like advance Soviet capitulation to Chinese communist arguments on why Peiping should be permitted to test nuclear weapons."[200]

The next piece of evidence pointing to interaction between Moscow and Peking came from the Chinese. About twelve hours after the Soviet announcement the Chinese government was ready with an official endorsement which stated:

> The Chinese government and people resolutely support this important step taken by the Soviet government. The Chinese government considers that this decision of the Soviet government is a cooling dose for the hotheaded

[198]Radio Peking, Aug. 29, 1961.
[199]*NYT*, Sept. 3, 1961, p. 2.
[200]Ibid.

war plotters but a powerful inspiration to all the peoples striving for world peace. . . .

The Soviet decision to conduct experimental explosions of nuclear weapons and the unanimous support by the other socialist countries of this action not only show the solid unity of the socialist camp and its determination to defend world peace, but also demonstrate that the socialist camp possesses the powerful might capable of halting imperialist military adventures. The imperialists should know that if they persist in imposing a nuclear war on the people of the world, the final result for the imperialist countries will not be victory, nor simply defeat, but the sweeping of the entire imperialist system from the face of the earth. It can be seen from the current situation that the danger of a new war prepared by imperialism is increasing. However, the contemporary forces of peace, with the socialist camp as their nucleus, far surpass the forces of war. So long as the people of the whole world unite and persevere in their struggle, the imperialist plan for war adventure can be frustrated.[201]

Here, too, Schwartz recognized the significance of the event: "The speed with which Peiping issued an official endorsement of the Soviet decision points in the same direction."[202]

There is thus strong evidence for some kind of policy consultation between Moscow and Peking in the period immediately preceding the Soviet announcement of August 30. In the absence of direct evidence, however, the problem of identifying who initiated the communication, and for what purposes, has resisted solution. The essential clue which has hitherto been missing lies in the consideration of relations within the Soviet leadership.

The Soviet decision to resume testing, as we have seen, was made in the Kremlin during Khrushchev's temporary absence on vacation on the Black Sea, and must therefore be recognized as a decision made by his political adversaries in the pursuit of policies diametrically opposed to his own. Once that point is grasped, the details fall into place.

We can reconstruct the course of events as follows: The decision to resume testing was made on August 24. No later than the 26th, under cover of the Soviet–Chinese trade negotiations which were already under way, the Chinese were informed of the decision. The significance of Chou En-lai's cordial reception for the chief of the Soviet trade delegation can now be recognized: conclusion of the supplementary trade agreement for 1961, beneficial as it was to the Chinese, was only a part, and not the most important part, of what they obtained from the Soviets at this point.

Forewarned, the Chinese played their part by publishing, on August 29, the article on U.S. preparations for test resumption, thus helping to provide a suitable background for the Soviet announcement on the 30th. Within a minimum time after the Soviet announcement, the Chinese followed with their enthusiastic endorsement of the Soviet decision.

[201]Radio Peking, Aug. 31, 1961.
[202]*NYT*, Sept. 3, 1961, p. 2.

That the Soviet announcement represented a sudden shift in Soviet policy toward a more pro-Chinese position was apparent at the time to Harry Schwartz: "The rulers of Communist China," he wrote, "appear to be the indisputable beneficiaries of the Soviet decision to resume nuclear weapons tests."[203] Without hazarding a guess as to the reasons for the shift, Schwartz added cautiously: "The Chinese gain has inevitably encouraged suspicion that pressure from Peiping was one of the factors behind Moscow's decision."[204] Available evidence points to the conclusion, however, that it was not Chinese pressure on the Soviet leadership—pressure which the Chinese at this point were incapable of exerting—that lay behind the Soviet decision to resume testing, but the temporary ascendancy of a faction in the Soviet leadership which believed wholeheartedly in the paramount need for close Soviet–Chinese collaboration, just as it believed equally wholeheartedly in the need for irreconcilable opposition to the United States. The action to provide the Chinese leadership with advance notice of the decision to resume testing was thus a logical corollary of the basic decision itself, and in full conformity with the policy views of those who were responsible for it.

[203]Ibid.
[204]Ibid.

8 The Collective Leadership Reviews the Situation

During the first week of September 1961 a major shift took place in the Soviet power structure. For the historian this period is of exceptional interest, for it provides in concentrated form and in close succession a number of the possible variants in the configuration of power at the Soviet summit: dominance of the policy-formulating process by an internal opposition faction; collective leadership wielded by a group of nominally equal figures; temporarily reasserted predominance by the man who holds the major power positions; and an uneasy balance between conflicting and unreconciled factions.

At the outset of the period, Frol Kozlov and his supporters appeared to be firmly in control of the levers of power in the Kremlin; their actions and decisions during the final week of August had sharply altered the course of Soviet foreign policy and by a series of risky and provocative moves had brought the Soviet Union dangerously close to a direct military confrontation with the West. A week later Kozlov was on his way to the remote capital of a Soviet ally-satellite on the Pacific coast of Asia, his bid for power sharply curtailed and his immediate task the announcement of what was, in effect, the abandonment for the present of the policies he had sponsored.

At the outset of the same period Khrushchev had just returned to the Kremlin after a two-week sojourn on the Black Sea, where he had been isolated from the seat of power and forced to watch his most threatening rival put through a series of measures directly opposed to his own on internal and foreign policy. At the end of the period Khrushchev had successfully reasserted his primacy within the collective leadership and had agreed with the majority of his colleagues on a new orientation for Soviet foreign policy.

The intense and concentrated power struggle in the collective leadership, effectively masked from the outside world, took place within the framework of the Soviet–Western conflict over Berlin, with disarmament and the problem

179

of nuclear testing as closely related issues. As the result of urgent consultation within the Western alliance, a bold new attempt was made during this period to persuade the Soviet leadership to modify or abandon its announced policy of nuclear testing. In the background, meanwhile, a number of subsidiary but related processes and events were taking place, the most important of which was a conference of neutralist and nonaligned states in Belgrade, at the conclusion of which delegations from the conference carried urgent messages to Moscow and Washington. All of these interrelated events and processes, to a greater or lesser extent, affected the internal Soviet struggle for power and the course of Soviet–U.S. relations.

Because the period under discussion was one in which a major power shift in the collective leadership was taking place, its pattern of events presents what seems at first sight a confusing mixture of inconsistent policy moves by the Soviet Union. Actions which reflect a continuation of the Kozlov-dominated line of late August were interspersed with others representing the reassertion of Khrushchev's influence. To some extent, this confusing medley was the result of a bureaucratic lag at lower levels in recognizing and responding to the power shift at the top; from another aspect, however, the patchwork policy pattern of early September 1961 was the result of the operation of one of the Kremlin's basic policy rules, which calls for the maintenance of an appearance of continuity in Soviet policy even when—especially when—the shifts at the summit are most abrupt and precipitous. Since a major aim of the Soviet political system as a whole is to maintain security against the outside world—in other words, to conceal or disguise the real nature of its internal power arrangements—it is one of the rules of the political game on which all factions and individuals agree, that actual shifts in the power balance shall not be immediately and unmistakably reflected in sharp changes in the policy line. Rather, the line pursued by a previously dominant but now defeated faction will often be continued briefly, though without emphasis or conviction, while at the same time new measures, new initiatives, express the policy of the victorious faction or coalition.

Khrushchev's resurgence

The principal stages in Khrushchev's recovery of power can be demonstrated by tracing the changes in the treatment accorded him in the central Soviet press during the first week of September. On September 1 his renewed presence in the Kremlin was briefly signified by his signature, along with that of Brezhnev, to a message to North Vietnam President Ho Chi Minh and Premier Pham Van Dong. Three days later, when *Izvestiia* reported Khrushchev's visit to a French national exhibition in Moscow, a photograph accompanying the article showed him in a white suit occupying the center of attention, while his more soberly garbed colleagues were pushed into the background, but the caption, in strict accordance with the principle of collective leadership, read, "Soviet leaders at one of the pavilions of the French national exhibition."[1]

By September 6 *Izvestiia* was once again giving Khrushchev top billing. Its first page on that date included three items singling out Khrushchev for special attention. A report on a visit by French communist leader Maurice Thorez, on September 4, pointedly identified Khrushchev as "First Secretary of the CPSU"; the story on Nehru's arrival in Moscow provided an opportunity for further stress on Khrushchev, who was given credit for having extended the invitation to Nehru and who headed the party of welcome for him at the airport; and an announcement, in which the Komsomol promised to support the Soviet government's "wise actions" to strengthen Soviet defense, was so worded as to give enhanced prominence to Khrushchev. "In answer to the call of N. S. Khrushchev," the announcement stated, "the young citizens of our country . . . will increase tenfold their efforts in the struggle for the establishment of a stable peace."[2]

Khrushchev's enthusiastic sponsorship of a program of growing corn (maize) in Soviet agriculture provides a convenient index to the degree and timing of his influence. *Izvestiia* on September 6 carried a story on the harvesting of seed corn in a Ukrainian collective farm, and *Pravda* published an article on September 7, "One hundred dishes from corn," in which the First Secretary was credited with recommending increased sowings of corn after the January plenum of the Central Committee. *Izvestiia* followed with a similar article, "Menu of 100 dishes—corn at the dinner table," on September 8.

High point and decline of the hard line

During Khrushchev's absence from the Kremlin the initiative in Soviet foreign policy had been seized by his adversaries. The direction in which events were moving was indicated by a brief announcement from the United Nations on the evening of September 1. "Frol R. Kozlov, secretary of the Soviet Communist Party Central Committee," the announcement stated, ". . . will head the Soviet delegation to this year's United Nations General Assembly session, informed diplomats said tonight.

"Mr. Kozlov, sometimes called Premier Khrushchev's No. 2 man, is expected to be here for the opening days of the assembly's sixteenth session starting September 19."[3]

The announcement made it clear that Kozlov was preparing to appear before the world as a spokesman for Soviet foreign policy in his own right. Had he done so, the deep split in the Soviet leadership could hardly have been concealed, for Kozlov was assuredly not planning the trip to the United Nations

[1] *Izv.*, Sept. 4, 1961, p. 1.
[2] *Izv.*, Sept. 6, 1961, p. 1.
[3] *NYT*, Sept. 2, 1961, p. 6.

simply to echo Khrushchev's line. But Kozlov was fated never to head a Soviet delegation to the United Nations; when the General Assembly met in New York on September 19 he was on the opposite side of the world, and his plan to attend the United Nations had been quietly shelved.

The bellicose direction given Soviet foreign policy during the brief period of Kozlov's ascendancy in the Kremlin was vigorously maintained in a Soviet note to the Western powers on September 2, continuing the attack on the unrestricted use of the air corridors from West Germany to West Berlin, which had been started with the Soviet note of August 23.[4]

The Soviet government, said the note, ". . . insists that the Government of the United States, which together with the Governments of Britain and France is exercising at present occupation functions in West Berlin, should put an end to the unlawful and provocative actions of the FRG [West Germany] in that city. The Soviet Government deems it necessary to warn the United States Government that it bears full responsibility for the possible consequences of the continuation of such provocative activities."[5]

The Western powers replied on September 8, in notes which repeated "in the most solemn terms" earlier warnings "against any action to interfere with flights in the air corridors to West Berlin."[6]

The Soviet armed forces newspaper carried forward the campaign with an article on September 9 which charged that ". . . the Western powers have created an artificial question about access to West Berlin. Instead of putting an end to the provocative actions of the FRG [West Germany] in this question, they are arousing a military psychosis, they are trying to create a pretext for unleashing war against the socialist countries."[7]

For a brief time the Soviets resorted to direct action: "There followed a certain amount of Soviet harassment of the commercial air lines flying at night into Berlin, and on 14 September two Soviet MIG fighters 'buzzed' two American commercial air-liners in broad daylight."[8]

The Soviet government made no official reply, however, to the Western notes of September 8; after the incident of September 14 its campaign against unrestricted Western use of the air corridors to West Berlin was simply dropped.

The September 2 note thus marked the last major Soviet attempt in 1961 to force the Western powers to accept a restriction on their access by air to West Berlin. Together with the September 1 announcement concerning Kozlov's

---

[4]Text of the Sept. 2 note in *Documents on Germany*, pp. 776–79, citing a Soviet Embassy press release of Sept. 5. Analysis and commentary, *SIA, 1961*, p. 260; Seymour Topping, *NYT*, Sept. 4, 1961, p. 1.

[5]*Documents on Germany*, p. 779.

[6]Ibid., p. 787; full text, pp. 784–87. The Western notes of Sept. 8 were accompanied by a dossier of "quadripartite agreements regarding the Berlin air corridors": ibid., pp. 787–91.

[7]Col. I. Alekseev, "The air corridors are not for revanchists!", *Krasnaia Zvezda*, Sept. 9, 1961, p. 5.

[8]*SIA, 1961*, p. 262.

plan to head the Soviet delegation to the U.N. General Assembly, it marks the high point in the drive by Kozlov and the faction he headed to seize control of the direction of Soviet foreign policy. Thereafter, as Khrushchev reasserted his power, Kozlov's hard line gave place to more moderate policies—not immediately, not obviously, but nonetheless effectively.

Kennedy and Macmillan propose a partial test ban

The first Soviet nuclear explosion in the new test series, a medium-range blast, took place on September 1. Two days later, following hurried consultations between Kennedy and Macmillan, the two leaders issued a joint appeal directly to Khrushchev ". . . that their three governments agree, effective immediately, not to conduct nuclear tests which take place in the atmosphere and produce radioactive fallout."[9]

The Western leaders urged Khrushchev to cable his immediate acceptance of this offer, and then went on to propose that representatives of the three powers at Geneva ". . . meet not later than September 9 to record this agreement and report it to the United Nations."[10] The offer, they continued, would remain open until that date.

As we have seen, one of the major points at issue in the long East–West negotiations on a test ban agreement had been the failure of the parties to agree on control measures. In an obvious effort to overcome Soviet hesitations on this score, the September 3 proposal broke sharply with earlier Western negotiating positions and dropped all demands for international control of nuclear tests in the atmosphere. "With regard to atmospheric testing," the statement said, ". . . the United States and the United Kingdom are prepared to rely upon existing means of detection, which they believe to be adequate, and are not suggesting additional controls."[11]

To guard against misinterpretation, however, the proposal expressed continuing Western support for a comprehensive test ban agreement: ". . . they reaffirm their serious desire to conclude a nuclear test ban treaty, applicable to other forms of testing as well, and regret that the Soviet Government has blocked such an agreement."[12]

Disregarding for the moment the gratuitous and ill-advised propaganda shot in the concluding passage, the September 3 proposal, taken as a whole, must be recognized as one of the major contributions by the Western powers to the eventual success of the test ban negotiations. The origin and underlying purpose of the proposal therefore deserve careful attention.

Available evidence points to the conclusion that the proposal originated in Washington and that the British assented to what was basically an American

[9]*JFK, 1961*, p. 587.
[10]Ibid.
[11]Ibid.
[12]Ibid.

initiative. The British-based *Survey of International Affairs* stresses the desire in Washington "to maintain a united Anglo-American front" as a contributing factor in the genesis of the proposal, but does not in any way suggest that the initiative for it came from the British.[13] According to Sidey, "Kennedy had wanted to make a final plea to halt the tests. He had sought and received British Prime Minister Harold Macmillan's endorsement."[14]

Neither Sorensen nor Schlesinger casts any light on the specific circumstances in which the proposal originated. Schlesinger traces its germ to a suggestion made by U.S. Ambassador to Moscow Llewellyn Thompson during the debate in August as to whether or not the United States should resume testing. According to Schlesinger, Thompson had recommended ". . . that we try once again for a limited ban, outlawing tests in the atmosphere and under water."[15] For the United States, it was pointed out, such a ban would have a number of advantages: "These [tests in the atmosphere and under water] were the ones that caused fallout; they did not require inspection; and they were presumably the tests which would help the Russians the most."[16]

A circumstantial but unsupported account of the genesis of the September 3 proposal is offered by Jacobson and Stein:

> The Kennedy–Macmillan proposal was formulated in Secretary of State Rusk's office by a small group of British and American policy-makers and advisers. Their prime objective was to embarrass the USSR. The proposal was a serious offer, which the participants in the sessions were willing to implement. . . . On the other hand, none of those who formulated the September 3 proposal seriously expected the USSR to accept it. Nor did any among them see much prospect for fruitful negotiation in the future. Although the effects of the proposal on past and possible future Western positions were discussed, because of the immediate objective and the expectations about the future, such effects were accorded little weight in the final decision.[17]

This account fails, however, to make due allowance for the motives and intentions of Kennedy himself, the prime mover in the September 3 proposal. The entire record of his administration's ultimately successful struggle to achieve an international agreement banning nuclear tests causing radioactive fallout provides convincing testimony to the genuineness of the concern which underlay the September 3 proposal.

This conclusion is reinforced when one takes into account the strong pressures which were being brought to bear on Kennedy at this time to resume

[13]*SIA, 1961*, p. 259.

[14]Sidey, p. 244.

[15]Schlesinger, p. 459.

[16]Ibid.

[17]Jacobson and Stein, pp. 282–83, citing Schlesinger, p. 459. Schlesinger does not, however, provide the details of the drafting of the agreement and the evaluation of its intent given in Jacobson and Stein.

testing without the slightest delay.[18] With the beginning of the new Soviet test series on September 1 the demand in Congress and the press for a resumption of testing by the United States became almost irresistible, yet Kennedy still held out, hoping against hope that a direct appeal to Khrushchev might still avert a new phase in the nuclear arms race.

The Anglo–American proposal was transmitted to the Soviets on Sunday, September 3, while Kennedy was relaxing at Hyannis Port. There was no Soviet response on the following day, unless the second blast in the Soviet test series could be so regarded, but on Tuesday, September 5, TASS issued a bulletin from Geneva deriding the proposal as "deceitful, unrealistic, and propagandistic." Only the Soviet program for general and complete disarmament, TASS maintained, could solve the problem of nuclear tests.[19] A further clue to Soviet intentions was provided by the fact that the Soviet press refrained from publishing the Kennedy–Macmillan proposal.[20] This was in line with general Soviet policy on the resumption of testing: the first acknowledgement by Soviet news media that the new test series was under way came in a roundabout form on September 5, when a Soviet radio broadcast in Urdu and English to south and southeast Asia commented on an article in the *Times of India* which mentioned the Soviet tests.

For Kennedy, the decisive action was the third Soviet test, word of which was received in Washington on September 5. Sidey reports the President's reaction in his own words: "I had no choice. I had waited two days for an answer to the message that Macmillan and I sent to Khrushchev. That was plenty of time. All they did was shoot off two more bombs."[21] Schlesinger quotes Kennedy as saying, "The third test was a contemptuous response to our note."[22]

Without further delay Kennedy issued a statement announcing the immediate resumption of underground testing by the United States:

> In view of the continued testing by the Soviet Government, I have today ordered the resumption of nuclear tests, in the laboratory and underground, with no fallout. In our efforts to achieve an end to nuclear testing, we have taken every step that reasonable men could justify. In view of the acts of the Soviet Government, we must now take those steps which prudent men find essential. We have no other choice in fulfillment of the responsibilities of the United States Government to its own citizens and to the security of other free nations. Our offer to make an agreement to end all fallout tests remains open until September 9.[23]

[18]For analysis of the mounting pressures on Kennedy to authorize the resumption of testing by the United States, see *SIA, 1961*, pp. 257–58; Sorensen, pp. 618–19; Schlesinger, pp. 454–58.

[19]*Izv.*, Sept. 6, 1961, p. 2; Seymour Topping, *NYT*, Sept. 6, 1961, p. 1.

[20]Note, *CDSP*, XIII/36, p. 3.

[21]Sidey, p. 245.

[22]Schlesinger, p. 483.

[23]*JFK, 1961*, pp. 589–90.

Because of the lack of preparation for nuclear testing in the United States—in part a legacy from the previous administration, in part a consequence of Kennedy's own strong desire to avoid ordering the resumption of testing until forced to do so—the September 5 announcement was not followed by an immediate series of test explosions. The first U.S. test took place on September 15, and, in the words of Jacobson and Stein, "The test series which followed was minor. The United States was not prepared to conduct major experiments!"[24] Contrast the brief interval between the Soviet announcement of the resumption of testing on August 30 and the first Soviet test shot on September 1, as well as the tight chronological pattern of the Soviet test series: during September alone the Soviets conducted tests on the 1st, 4th, 5th, 6th, 10th, 12th, 13th, 16th, 17th, 18th, 20th, and 22nd.[25]

*   *   *

Viewed as a contribution to the test ban negotiations, the September 3 proposal represented a striking shift in the Western position, a fact which is effectively brought out by Jacobson and Stein.

> . . . This proposal was almost revolutionary in terms of past Western positions. For the first time, the West announced its willingness to accept a ban on testing in some environments, without the establishment of any international control machinery. Never before had the Western powers admitted that national detection systems would be sufficient. Whenever the Western powers discussed a partial ban previously, they always maintained that at least some international control machinery would be necessary.[26]

Later, as the test ban talks at Geneva continued, both sides would cite the September 3 proposal in support of their positions—the Soviets to claim that in making the proposal the Western powers had admitted that existing control mechanisms were adequate to monitor certain kinds of nuclear tests, the Western powers to maintain that by rejecting the proposal the Soviets had negated the Western concession, which by its stated terms was a temporary one. In any case, the proposal was rejected by the Soviets, in a message from Khrushchev on September 9 which we shall consider below.

Among the President's counsellors there were some who advocated taking the question of nuclear testing to the United Nations. Harlan Cleveland, assistant secretary of state for international organization matters, for example, urged him to bring the question before the Security Council.[27] Having alre. 'y made up his mind, however, that sooner or later the United States would be forced to resume testing in response to the Soviet action, Kennedy rejected this advice when it was relayed to him by Schlesinger, who quotes him as say-

[24]Jacobson and Stein, p. 283.

[25]*Facts on File*, 1961, pp. 326, 350, 379. For later tests in the Soviet series, totaling thirty-one in all, see ibid., pp. 385, 393, 405.

[26]Jacobson and Stein, p. 282.

[27]Schlesinger, p. 481.

ing: "I don't see how we can do it. It would look hypocritical for us to take the question to the Security Council if we have already decided to resume testing. The two things seem to me incompatible."[28]

But Cleveland's suggestion of an appeal to the United Nations evoked a sympathetic response from Kennedy, coming as it did during an extended and continuing debate within his administration as to the nature of political power and the weight to be assigned to imponderables, particularly that intangible and elusive factor—world public opinion. Schlesinger quotes John J. McCloy, a supporter of the hard-headed "realist" position, as expostulating: "World opinion? I don't believe in world opinion. The only thing that matters is power. What we have to do now is to show that we are a powerful nation and not spend our time trailing after the phantom of world opinion."[29]

To Kennedy, however, public opinion at home and abroad was a reality no less significant than the material instruments of power—a fact which may help to explain the worldwide response he evoked during his lifetime and the enduring legend which has grown up around him after his death.

It was thus entirely characteristic of the man that on September 5, the day he ordered resumption of underground nuclear testing by the United States, he also took a tentative decision to address the forthcoming General Assembly of the United Nations and directed several of his aides to begin work on a suitable speech.[30]

The Belgrade conference of neutralist and nonaligned nations and its sequel—Nehru's mission to Moscow

It is likely that the timing and character of Kennedy's reaction to the Soviet resumption of nuclear testing were significantly affected by the proceedings of a conference of neutralist and nonaligned nations which was held in Belgrade on September 1–5.

Preparations for the conference date back to the spring and summer of 1961 when Yugoslav President Tito, the originator of the idea, was joined by Egyptian President Nasser, Ghana President Nkrumah, and Indonesian President Sukarno in sponsoring a bid for the conference.[31]

When the idea for the conference was first broached it was the general expectation among its sponsors that the major topic to be discussed would be colonialism, with condemnation of the Western powers for their alleged imperialism as its foreordained outcome. As the time for the conference ap-

---

[28]Ibid., p. 482.

[29]Ibid., p. 481.

[30]Ibid., p. 482. Sorensen, p. 520, dates Kennedy's tentative decision to address the United Nations Sept. 15—the day of the first U.S. nuclear nest in the new series. Schlesinger dates the original decision Sept. 5, placing it in the context of the debate over the resumption of testing. The final decision was taken on Sept. 18, under the impact of the news of Dag Hammarskjöld's death: Schlesinger, p. 484, and Sidey, p. 250.

[31]*SIA, 1961*, pp. 365–78, gives the background and preparation of the conference.

proached, however, the great power conflict over Berlin tended to overshadow the neutralist leaders' concern with colonialism and to give them a feeling that they could exert little influence over the great issue of war or peace in the world. The Soviet government's announcement that it had decided to resume nuclear testing, coming as it did on the very eve of the Belgrade conference, served to reinforce this feeling of impotence. It also led some of the neutralists, who had hitherto tended to view with sympathy the Soviet side in the controversies over disarmament and Berlin, to reassess their evaluation of the great powers.

The Soviet resumption of testing thus produced some rather sharp criticism from individual leaders attending the Belgrade conference. Nasser, for example, said that the Soviet decision "shocked me, just as it shocked world opinion," and Nkrumah concurred: "This was a shock to me as it must have been to all of you."[32]

Nehru, too, expressed grave concern over the Soviet decision, which he said had brought the danger of war nearer. To reduce this danger, Nehru strongly advocated the resumption of negotiations between Washington and Moscow, thereby providing a lead for the one significant action which emerged from the conference.[33]

At its session on September 4 the conference approved a proposal for a joint appeal to Kennedy and Khrushchev urging them to meet without delay, and appointed a commission to draft a suitable message.[34] The message, ready by the following day, stressed the "deep concern" felt by the conference "at the deterioration in the international situation and the prospect of war which now threatens humanity," and then presented its appeal:

> Having regard, however, to the gravity of the crisis that menaces the world and the urgent need to avert the developments that may precipitate it, we take the liberty of urging on the Great Powers concerned that negotiations should be resumed and pursued so that the danger of war might be removed from the world and mankind adopt ways of peace. In particular, we earnestly request for [sic] direct negotiations between Your Excellency [i.e., Kennedy] and the President of the Council of Ministers of the U.S.S.R. [Khrushchev], who represent the two most powerful nations today and in whose hands lies the key to peace or war.[35]

Bearing this message, Nehru flew from Belgrade to Moscow on September 6, with Nkrumah arriving in the Soviet capital on a separate plane. Indonesian President Sukarno, meanwhile, accompanied by President Modibo Keita of the Republic of Mali, was journeying toward Washington in order to deliver a copy of the message to Kennedy, who had agreed to meet the two emissaries on September 12.

[32]Quoted, ibid., p. 380.
[33]Nehru's Sept. 2 speech is in *DIA, 1961,* pp. 612–21; his plea for renewed Soviet–U.S. negotiations is on page 616. See also M. S. Handler, *NYT,* Sept. 3, 1961, p. 1.
[34]*NYT,* Sept. 5, 1961, p. 1.
[35]*DSB,* 45 (1961): 543; *Pravda,* Sept. 12, 1961, pp. 1–2; *CDSP,* XIII/37, pp. 8–9.

In Washington, the prevailing view was that the Belgrade conference had failed to display true neutralism by refusing to censure the Soviets for resuming nuclear testing. "We all knew," Schlesinger writes, ". . . how they would have blackened the skies with resolutions if we had been the first to resume; and the contrast drove Kennedy to great and profane acrimony."[36] Sorensen concurs: Kennedy, he writes, ". . . was particularly angry when the 1961 conference of neutrals at Belgrade, asserting [its right] to speak for 'the conscience of mankind,' passed the usual resolution against Western colonialism but timidly failed to condemn the Soviets for suddenly resuming nuclear testing."[37]

Sorensen goes on to provide documentary evidence of Kennedy's indignant reaction: "His anger was reflected in a statement issued at that time upon the signing of the foreign aid bill. The administration of the bill, said Kennedy coldly, 'should give great attention and consideration to those nations who have *our* view of the world crisis'."[38]

Taking into account the fact that the President's anger with the Belgrade conference was expressed on September 4, it appears probable that this reaction was one of the factors which led him on the following day, when news of the third Soviet test shot had been received, to decide that there was nothing more to be gained by extending the period of restraint and to issue the order for the resumption of underground testing by the United States.

*   *   *

Leaving to a later point in the narrative an analysis of the significance of the exchange between Nehru and Khrushchev, it will be useful at this point to establish the basic chronology of Nehru's visit.

The party to greet Nehru on his arrival in Moscow on September 6 was headed by Khrushchev and included N. G. Ignatov, A. N. Kosygin, and D. S. Poliansky. (Khrushchev was also among those who met Nkrumah, but without the accompaniment of any other members of the Presidium.)[39] A state dinner for Nehru was held in the Kremlin on the night of his arrival.[40] The message from the Belgrade conference was presented to Khrushchev on the same evening.[41]

The next day Nehru held a two-and-one-half-hour talk with Khrushchev from which he emerged gloomy;[42] publicly, he and Khrushchev exchanged short speeches at a luncheon given by the Indian leader in honor of Khrushchev.[43] The rest of Nehru's day was taken up with a ceremonial visit to Brezh-

---

[36]Schlesinger, p. 520.

[37]Sorensen, p. 538.

[38]Ibid.; emphasis in the original. Text of the Sept. 4, statement, *JFK, 1961*, p. 588.

[39]*Izv.*, Sept. 7, 1961, p. 1.

[40]*Pravda*, Sept. 7, 1961, p. 2; *CDSP*, XIII/36, pp. 5–6.

[41]*NYT*, Sept. 8, 1961, p. 1.

[42]Ibid.

[43]*Pravda*, Sept. 8, 1961, p. 1; *CDSP*, XIII/36, p. 6.

nev as head of state, a talk with Soviet scientists, a visit to museums, and a performance of *Romeo and Juliet* at the Bolshoi Theater.

On September 8 a Soviet–Indian friendship rally was held in the Kremlin at which both Nehru and Khrushchev spoke. Nehru left the Soviet capital the next day for Tashkent, where he spent the following day talking with Uzbek officials. He returned to India on September 11, on which date a joint Soviet–Indian communiqué summing up the results of his visit was issued.

Khrushchev grants an interview to Sulzberger

On August 26 C. L. Sulzberger, the roving *New York Times* senior diplomatic correspondent, who was vacationing on the isolated Greek island of Spetsai, was surprised to receive a cable from Yuri Zhukov, a Soviet journalist and state official, urgently asking Sulzberger to contact him.[44] "After unsuccessful attempts to reach him [Zhukov] on the island's single telephone," Sulzberger writes, ". . . I took the boat to Athens and called him Monday morning, August 28. He asked me if I would interrupt my holiday September 3 or 4, indicating that Mr. Khrushchev would see me but making no guarantee. I agreed, arrived September 3 and was received two days later."[45]

The resulting interview, which took place on September 5, constitutes the most extensive and intensive, as well as the most significant use by Khrushchev of this mode of communication during 1961, overshadowing in importance his earlier interviews with Walter Lippmann and Drew Pearson. Both with regard to the international crisis over Berlin and the internal Soviet political struggle the Sulzberger interview occupies a central position, and it is therefore necessary to study its setting and substance with some care.

The messenger—Yuri Zhukov

The first point to be noted is the closeness of the ties linking Zhukov, the messenger, with Khrushchev. Georgi Aleksandrovich Zhukov (to give him his full and formal name) was a prominent Soviet journalist who since 1957 had held the position of chairman of the State Committee for Cultural Ties with Foreign Countries.[46] He had accompanied Khrushchev to the United States in 1959, sharing in the Lenin Prize awarded in 1960 to the collective authors of the volume *Face to Face with America*, which described Khrushchev's tour.[47] To clinch the evidence linking him with Khrushchev, his name appeared, along with that of Khrushchev's wife, in the list of sixteen vice presidents of the newly established Institute of Soviet–American Relations, on August 31, 1961 (above, p. 170).

[44]C. L. Sulzberger, "On interviewing Mr. Khrushchev," *NYT,* Sept. 13, 1961, p. 44.

[45]Ibid.

[46]See his biography in *Yezhegodnik Bol'shoi Sovetskoi Entsiklopedii 1961* (Moscow, "Sovetskaia Entsiklopediia," 1961), p. 597 (hereinafter cited as *BSE, 1961*) and the note in Tatu, p. 221.

[47]*BSE, 1961*, p. 561.

For Sulzberger, Zhukov was an old and trusted acquaintance, one whose role as a confidential emissary of the highest spheres in Soviet politics was well known. It was at a small dinner party given by Sulzberger at the end of December 1950, for example, that Zhukov had provided the first indications of a Russian desire to bring about a cease-fire in the Korean war.[48]

The timing of the invitation

What could Khrushchev have learned on or shortly before August 26 which impelled him to extend an urgent invitation to a prominent American journalist? On August 24, as we have seen, he had tried to counter the threat to Western air communications with West Berlin by a renewed call for Soviet–U.S. negotiations, making use of the services of Drew Pearson for the purpose. Something dramatic must have occurred between the 24th and the 26th to make Khrushchev feel the need for an even more extended interview with another American journalist.

The new development on August 26 may well have been the information, conveyed to Khrushchev by some trustworthy informant (Adzhubei is a likely candidate), that his adversaries in the Kremlin had not only authorized the resumption of nuclear testing but were informing the Chinese in advance of the decision and were thus launching a full-scale challenge both to Khrushchev's predominance in the formulation of Soviet foreign policy and to the character and direction of that policy.

If this analysis is correct, we are faced with the question, why did Khrushchev not simply hasten back to Moscow, assert his power by disciplining Kozlov, and reverse or modify the course of Soviet foreign policy? Two possible answers to this at first sight puzzling question may be suggested, one tactical, the other operational.

First, for Khrushchev to return precipitously to the Kremlin in order to put through a drastic, undisguised change of direction in Soviet foreign policy, accompanied by high-level personnel changes, would have been to admit openly, before all the world, that there was a deep conflict within the Soviet leadership over foreign policy. From the standpoint of Khrushchev's own power, furthermore, such an action would have been to confess publicly that he was not fully in control of Soviet policy; in fact, that his policies and wishes could be at least temporarily defied by opposition leaders in the Kremlin. Considerations of Soviet security against the outside world, as well as of Khrushchev's own power position, therefore argued against hasty action to discipline Kozlov and change the line he was implementing.

Second, the possibility must be considered that Khrushchev *did not have the right* to return to the Kremlin before the date set for the end of his "vacation"—in other words, that the length of his stay at Sochi had been *fixed in advance* by agreement within the Presidium. This possibility at first glance conflicts so flagrantly with commonly held notions of power in the Kremlin

[48]C. L. Sulzberger, "Peace-making à la Russe," *NYT*, June 26, 1970, p. 38.

that it scarcely seems worthy of consideration. But a little reflection will show that if the basic power structure in the Soviet political system at the time with which we are concerned was that of a collective leadership operating under certain fixed rules designed to preserve the power of the collective and prevent the re-emergence of a dictator similar to Stalin, then some form of collective control over the travels and sojourns away from Moscow of the members of the collective leadership, particularly the man best able by reason of his position to try to emulate Stalin, would be an inescapable necessity.

We have seen (above, p. 132) that Khrushchev told foreign journalists on August 11 of the timetable for his vacation. Later, however, he interrupted his journey from Moscow to Sochi in order to launch a new attack on the Albanians (above, p. 142). If that unscheduled return to the Kremlin represented an action on the part of Khrushchev not sanctioned in advance by the Presidium, we would have an additional motive for Kozlov's action in brusquely shifting the course of Soviet foreign policy away from Khrushchev's line as soon as the latter had resumed his journey to Sochi. Outraged by Khrushchev's sudden assault on the Albanians, which led to the recall of Shikin from Tirana on August 19, Kozlov responded by moving sharply in the direction of embroilment with the West and rapprochement with Peking.

Under these circumstances, Khrushchev would have an additional and very compelling reason to remain at Sochi until the allotted end of his "vacation." To rush back prematurely would entail the risk that the choleric and impetuous Kozlov, while he still controlled the levers of power, might take some further foolhardy action designed to test to the limit the Western powers' forbearance in the Berlin crisis. Acutely aware of that looming danger, conscious also of the shakiness of his own power base, Khrushchev may well have preferred to wait out the crisis with as much patience as he could muster, meanwhile laying his plans for the recovery of a larger share of power and a new shift in the foreign policy line. Part of those plans, the evidence indicates, was to be an interview with a prominent American journalist who could serve to give Khrushchev's views the widest and most resounding hearing in the Western press—and who might also be willing to serve as a confidential messenger from Khrushchev to Kennedy.

The structure of the interview

In preparation for his meeting with Khrushchev, Sulzberger had written out a list of questions. "I gave Zhukov," he reports,

> . . . twenty-one questions I had prepared—reduced from an earlier list of sixty on the grounds such an agenda "would take three days." The selection was made by me. These questions were translated and sent to Mr. Khrushchev only an hour before he received me. I doubt if he had had time to read them carefully. In any case, I posed the questions directly and added to them as we went along. His answers were spontaneous.
>
> I had been advised Mr. Khrushchev could spare me only an hour and a half. After I had finished the twenty-one questions he told me to continue

"because you have come a long way." We conversed almost four and a half hours until he was visibly fatigued. So was I: I took sixty-two long pages of notes and the Soviet transcript ran to about 25,000 words. This will never be published or translated, I was told.[49]

More precise details are provided by Sulzberger elsewhere: "Our talk lasted from 4 P.M. until about 8:30 P.M. I was conducted to the Premier's office by Georgi A. Zhukov . . . , and we were joined by Mikhail A. Kharlamov . . . , and by Viktor M. Sukhodrev, Mr. Khrushchev's young interpreter, who takes shorthand notes in his own strange mixture of English and Russian. . . . Throughout the interview a battery of women stenographers quietly moved in and out of the room to keep a running account."[50]

After the interview, later on the same evening, Sulzberger wrote up a lengthy and wide-ranging dispatch covering those points he considered most important and then, on the following day, September 6,

> . . . went over it painstakingly together with Yuri Zhukov . . . , Mikhail Kharlamov . . . , and the interpreter present at my interview. The dispatch was translated into Russian and the Russian shorthand transcription was translated into English, so both sides had all the material in extenso.
>
> There was no attempt to censor what I had written, although it was suggested that a few adjectives which apparently had a pejorative connotation in Russian be amended. But there was a meticulous comparison of all quotations with the stenographic record. I had had no English stenographer with me but compiled sixty-two pages of notes in a large note-book, as against a 25,000-word Russian text of everything said *on the record*.
>
> Once the text of my dispatch had been agreed upon in terms of accuracy, it was sent to the Kremlin together with the stenographic account plus a separate text of eleven questions and answers I planned to publish verbatim.[51]

Thus on the evening of September 6—the same evening on which Khrushchev entertained Nehru at a Kremlin dinner—three documents relating to the interview were forwarded to Khrushchev: the agreed text of Sulzberger's dispatch; a separate, more formal set of questions and answers taken from the interview; and the full stenographic record of the interview.

On the morning of September 7 Sulzberger was surprised to learn from Zhukov that Khrushchev had indicated a desire for several substantive changes in the record. In addition, Khrushchev sent Sulzberger ". . . a special statement dictated that morning and saying 'he would always be glad to meet with the United States President to resolve pressing international problems'."[52] Recognizing the importance of the shift and sensing that he had the makings

[49]*NYT*, Sept. 13, 1961, p. 44.

[50]*NYT*, Sept. 8, 1961, p. 10.

[51]C. L. Sulzberger, "How Khrushchev changed his mind," *NYT*, Sept. 11, 1961, p. 26; emphasis in the original.

[52]Ibid.

of a journalistic scoop, Sulzberger incorporated the changes in his dispatch, giving special prominence to the message concerning a meeting with Kennedy.

It was therefore in a somewhat modified form that the two accounts of the interview—the dispatch and the questions-and-answer text—were published in the *New York Times* on September 8. *Izvestiia* followed a day later with a meticulously accurate Russian translation of Sulzberger's dispatch, and on September 10 *Pravda* published a Russian text of the questions-and-answers— accurately reproducing the *New York Times* version except for an additional final paragraph which significantly altered the tone and import of the document.

Khrushchev, according to Sulzberger, showed a keen personal interest in the careful preparation of the interview for publication: "In my presence, the rewritten first page of my account of the interview was read over the telephone to Mr. Khrushchev Thursday [September 7]. He expressed satisfaction to me personally in the Kremlin when I saw him again there Friday [September 8]."[53]

Over the next week or so, Sulzberger published several columns amplifying the record, describing the conditions under which the interview had taken place, and giving his overall impression of Khrushchev as a human being. On October 4 he had a long discussion with Kennedy in the White House at which the significance of the interview was analyzed.

Five years later, with Kennedy dead and Khrushchev toppled from power, Sulzberger added a vital element to the record by revealing that Khrushchev at the interview had given him a confidential message for Kennedy—thereby emphasizing the great importance which the interview had in Khrushchev's eyes and providing for the first time an adequate basis for understanding his motive in arranging it.

For purposes of analysis it will be useful to consider first the question-and-answer text published in the *New York Times* and *Pravda*, then the Sulzberger dispatch published in the *New York Times* and *Izvestiia*, together with the supplementary notes provided by Sulzberger subsequently, and, finally, the confidential message given Sulzberger by Khrushchev for transmittal to Kennedy.

The eleven questions and answers

Sulzberger's **first question** concerned Khrushchev's attitude toward a renewal of the test ban negotiations and the moratorium on nuclear tests. Under what conditions, Sulzberger asked, would Khrushchev agree to resumption of the talks? What was his opinion of the Kennedy–Macmillan proposal to bar atomic tests in the atmosphere?

Bypassing the query about the negotiations, Khrushchev addressed himself solely to the Kennedy–Macmillan proposal, stating that "We are preparing an answer and will send it in several days," but meanwhile offering his own opinion "in a preliminary way." That the Soviet government would formally

---

[53] Ibid.

reject the proposal was clearly foreshadowed by Khrushchev's reply, which made three points: first, that the proposal was unsatisfactory because it said nothing about atomic testing by France; second, that overall disarmament, not the mere cessation of nuclear tests, must be the goal; and finally, that the Soviet Union was behind the Western powers in the number of tests it had conducted and therefore had a "moral right" to test.

In any case, the Soviet test series would continue, Khrushchev asserted:

> We shall continue the tests that we have started because we cannot ignore the danger which is now being created for our country and the countries of the socialist camp by the Western countries of the NATO military bloc. We cannot remain inactive while the United States, France, Britain, and West Germany are mobilizing their forces, while West Germany is demanding that the Bundeswehr be armed with atomic weapons, while Adenauer and Brandt are doing their utmost to heat up the atmosphere by seeking revanchist goals, demanding the restoration of the borders of Hitlerite Germany and openly threatening the socialist countries.[54]

Khrushchev went on to express skepticism as to the Western leaders' concern over the dangers of radioactive fallout:

> The leaders of the Western powers are now hypocritically complaining that these tests contaminate the atmosphere. But we Russians have a proverb which says that once you have lost your head, you do not cry over your hair. Who will believe that these statesmen are seriously concerned over the health of man, when they refuse to sign a disarmament treaty, indulge in an all-out buildup of thermonuclear weapons, and mobilize their forces for war? But war spells death for human beings and not just damage to their health.[55]

Sulzberger's **second question** concerned the 100-megaton bomb whose existence Khrushchev had mentioned on several occasions. "I would like to ask," Sulzberger said, ". . . what sense you see in creating such a superbomb. It seems to me that that bomb is too big to be used for military purposes."[56]

In reply Khrushchev maintained that possession of "several such superpowerful bombs" by the Soviet Union ". . . will considerably increase the defense capability of our country. Then the aggressors will think twice before attacking us. They will understand that a decision to launch aggression against us is tantamount to a decision to commit suicide."[57]

The bombs, like all Soviet armaments, were exclusively for defense, Khrushchev assured Sulzberger: "We, for our part, have repeatedly declared that we have no intention of attacking anyone and will never do so. We are only creating means to defend our socialist camp and secure peace."[58]

[54]*NYT*, Sept. 8, 1961, p. 11.
[55]Ibid.
[56]Ibid.
[57]Ibid.
[58]Ibid.

Khrushchev portrayed the West German government as ruled by madmen desirous of repeating Hitler's attack on the Soviet Union; it was to restrain such "new Hitlers with other names—for example, with the names Adenauer, Brandt, or Strauss—" that the Soviet Union needed these weapons, he said.

As originally delivered, according to Sulzberger's later account, Khrushchev's reply at this point included the categorical assertion that the Soviet Union already possessed the 100-megaton bomb and intended to test it.[59] This was one of the substantive points in the record of the interview, however, on which Khrushchev requested a change on the morning of September 7, so that in its revised, published version, his reply at this point reads: "Let those who dream of new aggression know that we will have a bomb with a power equivalent to 100 million tons of TNT—and we already have this bomb, and *shall test the exploding device for it*—and that if they attack us, it will mean complete ruin for them."[60]

In his **third question** Sulzberger asked whether the Soviet Union would agree never to be the first to use atomic weapons in warfare. The Soviet Union, Khrushchev replied, will ". . . never be the first to start a war against any country. We want to live in peace with all nations and do not want to attack anyone."[61]

But he was careful to avoid a categorical commitment not to initiate the use of atomic weapons if war broke out:

> . . . it would be untimely at present to say that in the event of war, atomic weapons would not be employed. Anyone who made such a statement would turn out to be untruthful, even though when making such a pledge he is sincere and does not lie. Let us assume both sides were to promise not to employ nuclear weapons, but retained their stockpiles. What would happen if the imperialists unleashed war? In such a war if any side should feel it was losing, would it not use nuclear weapons to avoid defeat? It would undoubtedly use its nuclear bombs.[62]

Blandly disregarding the standard Soviet assertion that the defeat of Japan in World War II was caused not by the U.S. use of the atomic bomb but by the entry of the Soviet Union into the war against Japan, Khrushchev cited this example in support of his position: "At the close of World War II the United States was considerably stronger than Japan and was waging successful offensive action against it. Yet, to bring victory closer, the United States dropped atomic bombs on Japanese cities. All this goes to show that if atomic weapons are preserved and if war is unleashed it will be a thermonuclear war."[63]

[59]*NYT*, Sept. 11, 1961, p. 26.
[60]*NYT*, Sept. 8, 1961, p. 11; emphasis supplied.
[61]Ibid.
[62]Ibid.
[63]Ibid.

The sovereign remedy, as usual, was general and complete disarmament: ". . . world peace must be assured not by pledges to refrain from the use of nuclear weapons, but by a radical solution of the cardinal issues. The best guarantee of peace is the destruction of armaments and the elimination of armies—in other words, disarmament."[64]

Sulzberger's **fourth question** probed into a sensitive and significant area: the relation between Soviet policy in the Berlin crisis and Soviet internal development: "I would like to ask whether you consider that your long-range plans set forth in the party's draft program might be endangered as a result of the situation that is taking shape through the West's interpretation of your policy over Berlin and on nuclear tests."[65]

Khrushchev's reply provides a revealing example of his technique of sidestepping or ignoring awkward or dangerous questions. He disposed of the internal aspects of the question in a single uninformative sentence: "I think the present crisis, as you call it, will not hinder the fulfillment of our program."[66] He then went on to explain at length why he felt the Western powers would eventually accept the Soviet demand for a peace treaty with Germany and the replacement of the occupation regime in West Berlin by the status of a free city. All the well-worn Soviet arguments in favor of this solution of the Berlin and German questions were advanced, together with the usual threats against those nations containing U.S. military bases. The Soviet strategy of attempting to split the Western alliance by nuclear threats was displayed with brutal candor:

I think neither France, Britain nor Italy will ever go to war over the signing of a peace treaty. Even if reckless heads in the United States try to force the President into war over the signing of a peace treaty, I am sure the statesmen of those countries will display sufficient statesmanship and political responsibility to prevent matters from going that far. After all, they know that if war broke out their countries would be destroyed because they have American military bases that we would be compelled to hit. And they cannot but know that if the United States pushed their countries into war it would be tantamount to pushing them into an abyss, to death and destruction. I think they appreciate this and will oppose attempts to unleash war in reply to the signing of a German peace treaty.[67]

In his **fifth question** Sulzberger took up the problem of Soviet support for so-called "wars of liberation." Did not the Soviet position provide a justification, he asked, for other nations to make war against communist states under the guise of "wars of liberation"? The Soviet position on this question, Khrushchev replied, was different from the one depicted by Sulzberger: "We do not recognize the right of any nation to wage war for the liberation of

[64]Ibid.
[65]Ibid.
[66]Ibid.
[67]Ibid.

another country."[68] The Soviets, he continued, ". . . recognize the right of a people for its own liberation—this is a completely different matter."[69] Such wars—that in Algeria, for example— "are sacred popular wars against enslavement, against a colonial regime. And we are in favor of such wars. We sympathize with peoples who are fighting for their freedom and consider that they have the right to count on the aid of all freedom-loving peoples."[70] Adroitly but inaccurately associating this position with that of Abraham Lincoln in the American Civil War, Khrushchev reaffirmed the Soviet intention of coming to the aid of "peoples who are fighting for their liberation."[71]

Sulzberger's **sixth question** dealt with the Soviet proposal for a three-man secretariat in the United Nations and in the administrative machinery to supervise a nuclear test ban agreement. The Soviet position on these questions, Khrushchev explained, was that

> . . . in setting up disarmament controls there should be no veto and no "troika." There should be the strictest control and no one should limit it. If an agreement on disarmament is reached, and if disarmament is carried out in practice, there will be no need for state secrets, which are necessary only to protect one's country from the danger of war. If an agreement on disarmament is reached, and disarmament is effected, then far from there being any need for secrets, it will be necessary to know in the greatest detail what is going on in another country, so that it would not be able to threaten the peace. The "troika" principle will be necessary only in the event that international forces are set up. The command of these forces should be based on this principle. This would be necessary to guarantee that no state or group of states could use the international U.N. forces to the detriment of any other state or group of states.[72]

The United States would be wise, Khrushchev added, to recognize the trend in international affairs which was inevitably leading toward acceptance of the troika principle in all operational posts at the United Nations.

The possibility of U.S.–Soviet agreement on the regulation of questions concerning the use of outer space was taken up in Sulzberger's **seventh question**. The U.S. proposal for an international organ to deal with such questions was sensible, Khrushchev replied, but it could not be acted upon until general disarmament had been carried out because it was impossible to separate the exploration of space from the military development of intercontinental ballistic missiles. (In Soviet administrative practice there was—and is—a direct link between the space exploration program and the armed forces.)

What is the difference, Sulzberger asked in his **eighth question**, between "peace" and "peaceful coexistence" in Soviet usage?, thereby giving Khrush-

[68]Ibid.
[69]Ibid.
[70]Ibid.
[71]Ibid.
[72]Ibid.

chev an opportunity to set forth in broad terms his concept of the principles on which relations between the capitalist and socialist states should be based: "Noninterference in each other's internal affairs, the recognition of sovereignty, refraining from war and ensuring peace—these are what constitute the coexistence of states with different social systems."[73]

With the possible exception of the question on the 100-megaton bomb, Sulzberger's questions thus far had elicited from Khrushchev few new insights into Soviet policy. His **ninth question**, however, broke new ground by raising the possibility of Soviet military aid to Yugoslavia in the event of an attack on that country. Khrushchev began his reply by saying: "We would like that there should be no military attack and no need for retaliatory blows."[74] He then went on to remind Sulzberger that Yugoslavia was not a signatory of the Warsaw Pact and was therefore not eligible for Soviet aid under the guarantee given to members of that alliance by Marshal Malinovsky in 1960. With deceptive nonchalance Khrushchev then executed a sharp turn in the Soviet foreign policy line: "But we, of course, consider Yugoslavia a socialist country, and should she be attacked by an imperialist state and appeal to us for help I think we would not turn down the request and would come to her help."[75]

Since one of the most hotly contested doctrinal issues in the Soviet–Chinese and Soviet–Albanian disputes concerned the precise nature of the Yugoslav regime, with the Chinese and Albanians stoutly denying the claim on the part of the Yugoslavs to be practicing a form of socialism in their country, Khrushchev's assertion, as William E. Griffith has pointed out, amounted to a direct affront to the Chinese and Albanians.[76] Of greater immediate relevance, however, was the fact that Khrushchev's statement was a sign that he was making a clean break with the policies of the opposition faction which had pursued the pro-Peking line of late August.

What about Cuba?, Sulzberger asked in his **tenth question**—"Castro considers that he is socialist." "As far as I know," Khrushchev replied, ". . . Castro is not a member of the Communist Party. He is a revolutionary, a patriot of his motherland. If he were to join the Communist Party I would welcome him. . . . But this depends on him alone."[77] Again raising the possibility of Soviet military aid to Cuba, Khrushchev continued: "We have no treaties with Cuba but if it appeals to us for aid in case of aggression against it, we of course will not leave this request without an answer."[78]

The pledge of July 1960, as reinterpreted in October of that year, was thus implicitly renewed. But Khrushchev shied away from the idea of an actual military confrontation with the United States: "What is needed in interna-

---

[73]Ibid.
[74]Ibid.
[75]Ibid.
[76]Griffith, *Albania*, p. 86.
[77]*NYT*, Sept. 8, 1961, p. 11. For further details, see ibid., Oct. 27, 1972, p. 39.
[78]Ibid., Sept. 8, 1961, p. 11.

tional relations is restraint and patience."[79] Look at the Soviet Union in its relations with Iran, he continued: although the latter country is dominated by the United States, the Soviet Union is exercising patience and restraint in its policies toward Iran. The sensible thing for the United States to do, Khrushchev recommended, would be to liquidate its overseas bases, since they have lost their significance as the result of the development of space vehicles by the Soviets.

In his **eleventh question** Sulzberger asked Khrushchev whether communists, as atheists, fear war more than people with a religious belief in an afterlife. Khrushchev's reasons for selecting this question to conclude the question-and-answer text become obvious from the character of his reply, which stressed the positive side of his policies and voiced a renewed plea for peaceful coexistence. The version of the text published in the *New York Times* ended on a note of international reconciliation and harmony: "So let us live reasonably and work so that no one should start a war. Let us employ our strength to ensure world peace. Let us compete in developing our economies and creating the good things of life for our peoples. That system will triumph which provides more material and spiritual benefits for its people. So let history pass its judgment without war."[80]

When the Russian-language text was published in *Pravda* two days later, however, someone had added a bellicose final paragraph which significantly altered the tone of Khrushchev's reply, and with it of the document as a whole: "Thus we communists, not believing in a life beyond the grave, want to live and develop in peace, but if we are attacked, we will fight like lions against imperialism, against aggression."[81]

Sulzberger's dispatch

Far more than the rather stiff and formal question-and-answer record of the interview, Sulzberger's dispatch of September 7 gives a direct and vivid impression of Khrushchev the man. His characteristic mannerisms, his facial expressions, even the clothes he was wearing, are described with the observant eye of a trained journalist. Moreover, the dispatch contains material of the greatest value for analyzing Khrushchev's real position on certain key issues, as opposed to the official position which he sometimes voiced or sponsored. Both with regard to foreign policy, especially the central issues of Soviet relations with the United States and China, and with regard to the internal processes of Soviet policy formulation, the statements attributed to Khrushchev in the dispatch are highly revealing. What gives the dispatch its special importance, of course, is the fact that it was published in full in *Izvestiia* after being translated with the textual care usually reserved for treaties or other state documents.[82]

[79]Ibid.
[80]Ibid.
[81]*Pravda*, Sept. 10, 1961, p. 3.
[82]The Russian text of the dispatch was also broadcast over Radio Moscow on Sept. 9.

In form the dispatch as published is an amalgam, with Khrushchev's message of September 7 affirming his willingness to meet again with Kennedy tacked on at the beginning. The main body of the dispatch as prepared by Sulzberger on the night of September 5 then follows, with the change requested by Khrushchev in his reply to the question on the 100-megaton bomb. This section in turn is divided into two approximately equal parts, of which the first deals with the twenty-one questions approved in advance and the second with the discussion carried on after completion of the approved questions. Since there is a significant difference in tone and content between the three parts of the dispatch, it will be useful to take them up in that order.

In his original dispatch, Sulzberger later wrote, he had said ". . . that Mr. Khrushchev saw 'no use' in another meeting at this time with President Kennedy unless the President is ready to agree at least to the essentials of a settlement along such lines—meaning Soviet concepts for a German and West Berlin formula."[83] On the morning of September 7, however, just as Sulzberger was getting ready to send off the dispatch, Khrushchev sent him ". . . a special statement dictated that morning and saying 'he would always be glad to meet with the U.S. President to resolve pressing international problems'."[84] For this, Khrushchev said, he "would spare neither strength nor time. But the main thing is that such a meeting must be fruitful."[85]

The statement continued:

> The first meeting has already taken place in Vienna. In the course of that meeting the two sides compared their viewpoints. The task now is to find solutions for the major international issues now causing concern. And if President Kennedy agrees to a meeting with Premier Khrushchev it will be important that both sides display understanding of the need to resolve such important matters as the signing of a German peace treaty and the solution on this basis of the question of West Berlin as well as the problem of disarmament under strict international control.[86]

Khrushchev's concept of a new meeting with Kennedy was developed more fully in the main part of Sulzberger's dispatch (unfortunately, it is not clear from the dispatch as published just which portions of Khrushchev's statements on this subject are based on his September 7 message and which were made at the September 5 interview). In a new meeting, Khrushchev indicated, there should be genuine discussion, not merely the exchange of fixed positions known in advance:

> "I met the President in Vienna and had comprehensive talks. It was our introduction, in which we, so to say, felt each other out. We parted after the meeting, each sticking to his position."
>
> "That is natural for a first contact," the Premier went on. "But if at a second meeting we were to limit ourselves to an exposition of each other's

[83]*NYT*, Sept. 11, 1961, p. 26.
[84]Ibid.
[85]*NYT*, Sept. 8, 1961, p. 1.
[86]Ibid.

position, which both of us know, the situation will of course not improve but, on the contrary might even deteriorate."

"It would be another thing if both sides were to come to the meeting prepared to relieve tension and reach agreement on the conclusion of a German peace treaty, on giving West Berlin the status of a free city, and especially on the more important problem of disarmament."

"In that case we could achieve important positive solutions and that would be a great happiness for our peoples. I consider that we must spare neither our strength nor time for achievement of this goal."[87]

There are several puzzling aspects to these remarks. First, at Vienna it had been Khrushchev, not Kennedy, who had limited himself to an exposition of his position; it had been Khrushchev's "oddly circumscribed behavior" which had struck Isaac Deutscher and other observers. Khrushchev, therefore, seemed to be hinting that at a new meeting he would have greater freedom of action. But at the same time he appeared to be dictating not only the agenda for any new meeting but also the foreordained basis for eventual agreement— Berlin, the German peace treaty, disarmament on Soviet terms.

A possible explanation of the apparent discrepancies in Khrushchev's remarks may be suggested along the following lines: Khrushchev was urging Kennedy to agree to a new meeting at which he, Khrushchev, would have greater freedom to negotiate and introduce modifications into the Soviet position than he had enjoyed at Vienna. He was unable, however, because of the pressures on him from the other members of the collective leadership, to say this openly and was even forced to blunt the apparent meaning of his words by reiterating the standard Soviet position as the basis for agreement. No wonder Kennedy was cautious in picking up this olive branch!

Since the remainder of the dispatch dealt with a number of points already covered in the question-and-answer report, without substantially modifying or adding to them, our analysis can be limited to the new topics introduced in the dispatch and to significant modifications or elaborations of points made in the other document.

At the outset of the interview Khrushchev made an odd statement concerning vacations for Soviet officials: "Mr. Khrushchev commented that he had ordered all Soviet officials to take at least a month's holiday each year, but he added ruefully: 'As so often happens, the man who makes the rules is the first to break them'."[88] By calendar count, Khrushchev had already, as it happens, spent more than a month on vacation in 1961. Was he alluding obliquely to his action in "breaking the rules" by returning to the Kremlin in mid-August?

Sulzberger opened the serious discussion with the first of his twenty-one questions (one not, however, included in the question-and-answer text): "Mr. Khrushchev," I inquired, "do you believe war is still neither inevitable nor

[87]Ibid.
[88]Ibid.

desirable?"[89] Khrushchev's reply embodies a good deal of his general concept of international relations:

> "Yes, and very profoundly, too," he replied. "In spite of the acute crisis which, as you say, has now taken shape, I believe in the common sense of statesmen who bear the responsibility for the destiny of their countries. They cannot but understand that in our day wars must not be a means of settling any issue and I hope they come to the conclusion that it is necessary to resolve urgent international problems peacefully—first and foremost the German problem. This can and must be settled by conclusion of a peace treaty with the two German states actually in existence."[90]

Nowhere in the question-and-answer text was China directly mentioned, and there was no reference, direct or indirect, to Soviet–Chinese relations as reported therein. In the dispatch also Khrushchev was portrayed as saying nothing about China directly. Sulzberger, however, inserted a comment of his own on China which assumed the significance of an explicit policy statement approved by Khrushchev because of its appearance in the text of the dispatch as published in *Izvestiia*. Following his comments on possible Soviet military aid to Yugoslavia and Cuba, Khrushchev ". . . said that all Soviet nuclear warheads and long-range missiles were under Soviet military control and stationed on Soviet territory. However, he made this exception: 'Possibly there is something in [East] Germany. If not, there might eventually be. But these are dangerous weapons and we are very careful'."[91] To this Sulzberger added the comment: "It would follow specifically that there are no such weapons in Communist China."[92] Even more than Khrushchev's identification of Yugoslavia as a "socialist" nation, this passage, the only place in the published records of the interview which directly names China, must be read as a deliberate action by Khrushchev to signal the shift in Soviet policy away from the pro-Peking line pursued by the Soviet government in late August.

This passage is also interesting for what it reveals with regard to Soviet policy in Germany. Evidently as early as September 1961 the Soviet leadership was considering the possibility of stationing nuclear weapons and long-range missiles in East Germany. The obvious purpose would have been to threaten the nations of western and southern Europe in order to weaken or split the Western alliance and facilitate the settlement of the Berlin and German questions on Soviet terms. Elsewhere in the dispatch Sulzberger quoted Khrushchev as describing France, Britain, and Italy as "hostages" to the Soviets against war—a stronger term than that used in the corresponding passage in the question-and-answer text (above, p. 197).

A considerable part of the dispatch was taken up with Khrushchev's comments on possible ways to improve Soviet–American relations. He indicated,

[89] Ibid.
[90] Ibid.
[91] Ibid.
[92] Ibid.

for example, that the Soviet government was considering the possibility of freeing Francis Gary Powers, the pilot of the U–2 spy plane shot down on May 1, 1960: "Mr. Khrushchev said, furthermore, that there was provision in Soviet law for the early release of prisoners but that he was not sure whether this could technically apply to Francis Powers, the U–2 pilot. Nevertheless, he hinted that Mr. Powers, who is serving a ten-year sentence, might be released if and when relations between Moscow and Washington should improve."[93]

Current U.S. policies, however, said Khrushchev, made such an action impossible at present:

> "His sentence could be appealed to the Supreme Soviet, but such a step would be misunderstood right now by both Americans and our own people. . . . The time has not come for such a move," the Premier declared. "After all, when Mr. Kennedy was elected, we freed the two RB–47 fliers. . . . We had hoped this display of goodwill would be correctly understood and relations would improve."
>
> "That would have led to the release of Powers, too. But to our regret, our relations at present are in such a state that it prevents any possibility of releasing Powers."[94]

Khrushchev made it clear that he did not hold Kennedy personally responsible for the obstacles to better Soviet–U.S. understanding: "It is difficult for me to indulge in speculation," Mr. Khrushchev went on. "Nevertheless my impression after our Vienna meeting was that Mr. Kennedy understands the need to improve relations between our countries. But evidently he is meeting with many difficulties. . . . If you want to know what these are, I suggest you ask him."[95]

The direction being projected for the Soviet space program and the difficulties it was facing were indicated by Khrushchev's comment, in Sulzberger's paraphrase, that "there was not yet any fixed schedule for the landing of a Soviet citizen on the moon." (Kennedy, by contrast, had already committed the United States to landing a man on the moon by 1970.) Khrushchev gave this explanation: "It is not a question of mooning him [the lunar explorer] but of demooning him. Our national emblem is already on the moon, but we don't want to place a coffin beside it. We are now studying the possibility of such a flight, but I cannot yet say when it could be scheduled. We can fly a man to the moon, but the difficulty is getting him away from there."[96]

Khrushchev went on to contrast U.S. and Soviet prowess in space exploration in a rather garbled Darwinian metaphor: "You remember Darwin's theory on the maturation of species—from those which crawled, like reptiles, to those which jumped and those which flew. Well, you are still in the jumping stage, while we have already learned how to fly, and to land again. . . . But that is

[93] Ibid.
[94] Ibid.
[95] Ibid.
[96] Ibid.

still insufficient. We still have to learn how to land on other planets and then to take off from them back to this earth."[97] As the history of the next ten years would show, it was to be the United States, not the Soviet Union, which solved this problem.

Khrushchev's comments on space exploration concluded the part of the interview covered by the twenty-one questions selected in advance. When Sulzberger complimented Khrushchev on the "frankness" with which he had answered, Khrushchev responded: "We want to be strong in politics, but to do that you must be frank. . . . I do not remember who it was who said that a diplomat is given a tongue in order to conceal his thoughts," he said. "He who does that is no diplomat, but a cheap politician. His policy is bound to end in failure. I do not belong to that sort."[98] And with this preface to the second, less formal half of the interview, Khrushchev proceeded to talk, if not with entire openness, at least more frankly than he had done earlier. His most significant revelations about Soviet policy come from this portion of Sulzberger's dispatch.

The dominant motif throughout this portion of the interview was Khrushchev's desire for better relations with the United States:

> After some reminiscing, Mr. Khrushchev expressed hope that the United States and the Soviet Union would never fight each other and said he had told this to former President Dwight D. Eisenhower.
>
> "We would consider it a great happiness if the soldiers of these two countries should never stand face to face but always shoulder to shoulder," he declared. "We are the strongest countries in the world and if we unite for peace there can be no war. Then if any madman wanted war we would but have to shake our fingers to warn him off."[99]

Khrushchev then proceeded to dissociate himself from the Soviet decision on the resumption of nuclear testing: "Now the United States is arming and we are, too. We are spending money and energy in preparations to destroy people. We are making nuclear tests. . . . But what the hell do we want with tests? You cannot put a bomb in soup or make an overcoat out of it. Nevertheless, we are compelled to test."[100]

Thus Khrushchev in effect answered Sulzberger's earlier question about the effect of Soviet policy in the international crisis on his internal economic goals—and answered it this time frankly and honestly, not evasively.

Continuing with a consideration of various ways to reduce international tension, Khrushchev ". . . expressed the hope that 'we should agree to revoke our orders we both have given to strengthen our military forces'."[101] Thus in short order Khrushchev made it plain that he regretted the decision to resume

[97] Ibid.
[98] Ibid.
[99] Ibid.
[100] Ibid.
[101] Ibid.

nuclear testing and that he would like to rescind the decision on the strengthening of the Soviet armed forces—the two decisions announced by the Soviet government at the end of August.

Sulzberger commented that ". . . the United States was a strong nation and did not like to be threatened or bullied. I said that I thought his methods of seeking a German settlement were of that nature, that the United States felt he was threatening."[102] Khrushchev conceded the point: "That is true. I understand it and take it into account."[103]

But since he could not openly admit to Sulzberger that the real reason for the threatening character of Soviet policy lay in the internal split in the Soviet leadership, Khrushchev was reduced to making a plea for mutual comprehension and forbearance: "We must reciprocally spare each other's feelings. The West wants to threaten us with force and deny us the right to sign a peace treaty. But nothing will come of that. We will sign it just the same, because we also have strength."[104]

The last substantive matter taken up in the discussion was the situation in Laos, where a three-way squabble between the Laotian leaders was providing a tumultuous background to the stalemated Geneva negotiations. Sulzberger ". . . ventured the opinion that the United States was disappointed by Soviet failure to appreciate its change of policy in the civil war in Laos."[105] Khrushchev "implied acceptance of this complaint," and then went on to lay the blame on the Laotian leaders themselves:

> "We reached agreement on this in Vienna, Kennedy and myself. We reached agreement speedily. But it is difficult for us to apply this agreement quickly. But we are both evidently facing difficulties. It is not us, Russia, which is negotiating in Laos. What can I do with those three Princes? or Kennedy? They decide, the three Princes. We can only advise."
>
> "But I feel the ice is beginning to melt on this question. I feel we are approaching a solution. We are seeking no goals of our own there. I told this to President Kennedy. We want nothing in Laos. Far from impeding matters, we are trying to help."[106]

By now it was almost dark in the Kremlin office where the interview was being conducted. Both Khrushchev and his guest were tired. After calling for lights, Khrushchev concluded the interview with what amounted to a personal invitation to Kennedy to visit the Soviet Union: "We hope that we shall be able to resolve reasonably all the questions at issue between our two countries. Thereby the possibility would present itself for me to invite President Kennedy to this country as our guest. We will give him a warm reception and all the honors that are due to him as a President and a guest."[107] It was on

[102]Ibid.
[103]Ibid.
[104]Ibid.
[105]Ibid.
[106]Ibid.
[107]Ibid.

that note, deliberately chosen by Khrushchev as his parting message, that the interview ended.

The confidential message to Kennedy

In 1966 Kennedy's press secretary, Pierre Salinger, published his memoir, *With Kennedy*, in which he described how Mikhail Kharlamov, Soviet Foreign Ministry press chief, got in touch with him in September 1961 in order to deliver an urgent personal message for Kennedy from Khrushchev. After surprising Salinger by his opening words—"The storm in Berlin is over"—Kharlamov ". . . came straight to the point of his visit. Earlier that month in Moscow, Khrushchev had given an exclusive interview to Cyrus L. Sulzberger, Paris correspondent of the *New York Times*. But he had also given a most urgent message for JFK. Had Sulzberger delivered it yet? I said I didn't know. 'Then I will repeat the message to you,' said Kharlamov, 'and you will deliver it to the President'."[108]

Shortly after the publication of Salinger's book, Sulzberger gave his own account of how Khrushchev had made use of his services to convey a confidential message to Kennedy. "The story was hitherto confidential," Sulzberger wrote,

> . . . but since Salinger has some of it wrong, and since I served as the messenger, I feel qualified to straighten out the record. On September 5, in Moscow, Khrushchev asked me to tell Kennedy: "I would not be loath to establishing some sort of contact with him to find a means, without damaging the prestige of the United States, to reach a [German] settlement—but on the basis of a peace treaty and a free Berlin. And through such informal contacts the President might say what is on his mind in ways of solving the problem."
>
> "If he does wish to make such contact he can express his opinions on the various forms and stages of a settlement and how to prepare public opinion so as not to endanger Kennedy's prestige and that of the United States."[109]

Feeling that a message of this importance could best be dealt with through the regular diplomatic channels, Sulzberger ". . . urged Khrushchev to send his message through Ambassador Llewellyn Thompson, but he asked me to take it personally, saying, 'Thompson is very able but he is an Ambassador. He would have to send such a message to Secretary Rusk. Rusk would tell Kennedy what was wrong with it before he told him what the message was and Kennedy would end up wearing Rusk's corset. Kennedy could not get a fair initial reaction and Rusk is just a tool of the Rockefellers'."[110]

Khrushchev then went on to explain more fully what he had in mind: "I believe if we can settle the Laos question it will improve the atmosphere for Berlin and Germany. That appeals to Kennedy; it doesn't affect my position.

---

[108]Salinger, p. 191.
[109]C. L. Sulzberger, "The Two K's and Germany," *NYT*, Nov. 6, 1966, sect. 4, p. 10.
[110]Ibid.

I want to help Kennedy. I am hopeful that I shall be the one to welcome him in this country as a guest."[111]

Khrushchev's confidential message, it will be seen, fits neatly into the final portion of the Sulzberger interview, parallelling the last two subjects taken up there—a negotiated settlement in Laos and a visit by Kennedy to the Soviet Union. The tactical plan behind the message can be deciphered fairly readily: by using Soviet influence to help reach a settlement in Laos—an area in which the Soviet Union was "seeking no goals of [its] own"—Khrushchev hoped to prepare the way for U.S. agreement to a settlement in Berlin and Germany on Soviet terms. This triumph for Soviet foreign policy in turn would strengthen Khrushchev's internal position sufficiently to enable him to invite Kennedy to the Soviet Union, thereby setting in place the keystone in the arch of Soviet–American rapprochement of which Khrushchev aspired to be the builder.

Thus analyzed, however, the defects of the scheme become all too apparent. It amounted to trading Soviet influence in Laos—for the Soviets, an area of minor significance, for the United States a troublesome but far from vital area—for a Western pull-back from Berlin, which Kennedy had defined as a vital element in the Western political and diplomatic position. Furthermore, the neutralization of Laos would be meaningless without a settlement at the same time of the deepening conflict in Vietnam. By his support to the North Vietnamese communists in their aim of reunifying the country by force, however, Khrushchev had effectively nullified the value of any concession he might make with regard to Laos. Moreover, the unsatisfactory sequel to the agreement on Laos, which he and Kennedy had reached at Vienna, greatly diminished the attractiveness of a new offer of the same shopworn goods.

The inherent weaknesses of Khrushchev's hare-brained scheme were thus sufficient to weaken it seriously once it was available for Kennedy's scrutiny. In addition, the unorthodox means Khrushchev chose for conveying the offer contributed nothing to its success. Anxious perhaps not to risk his standing with the diplomatic hierarchy and mindful of the responsibilities placed on him by Khrushchev's commission, Sulzberger promptly told Ambassador Thompson about Khrushchev's overture: "On September 6 I saw Thompson and, strolling in his garden to reduce the risk of eavesdropping, said the Soviet leader had asked me to take a message to the President, bypassing him. Thompson told me not to feel embarrassed."[112]

Wary of any kind of back-stairs deal, the administration in Washington was determined to negotiate with the Soviets only through the standard diplomatic channels. Its reaction to the published text of the Sulzberger interview was one of guarded and watchful anticipation: "Llewellyn E. Thompson, Jr., United States Ambassador to Moscow . . ., has been waiting in the wings during the Moscow festivities honoring Prime Minister Jawaharlal Nehru of India. He has instructions to get from the Soviet leaders any indication of their

[111]Ibid.
[112]Ibid.

willingness to 'negotiate' settlements for Berlin, Germany, and Central Europe on terms broader than they have so far suggested. But he has got nowhere so far, officials said."[113]

Thompson, we may reasonably assume, had lost no time in cabling a report to Washington on the confidential message about which Sulzberger had told him on September 6. In any case, on September 9 Sulzberger himself sent a letter from Paris "by a special diplomatic courier to the President's adviser, McGeorge Bundy,"[114] so that the message was available for Kennedy's consideration by the 10th at the latest. "The President studied this," Sulzberger reports, ". . . with Bundy, Charles Bohlen, then his Soviet expert, Rusk, and Attorney General Robert Kennedy."[115]

Their evaluation of Khrushchev's proposal can be deduced from their action, or lack of action: the proposal lacked any official sanction; it might be a trap to trick the Americans into making an overly generous offer on Berlin; it took no account of America's responsibilities to its allies; it made no sense in terms of the prevailing U.S. interpretation of power relationships in the Soviet leadership. Obviously, the best thing to do was to wait for some more formal, more concrete overture from the Soviets through the regular diplomatic channels. It was the lack of response from Washington, of course, which led Khrushchev to surmise that the message had not been delivered by Sulzberger, with the result that he followed it up with the second out-of-channels message sent via Kharlamov and Salinger.

On October 4 Sulzberger, back once more in the United States, had a long discussion with Kennedy in which the possible significance of Khrushchev's message was explored. Sulzberger recalled later that Kennedy had said "it was hard to figure precisely what Khrushchev meant." Knowing something of the deviousness of the Russian mind, Sulzberger suggested an ingenious interpretation: "I said that to me the only way of interpreting this was in terms of Aesopian language and that one must stress the point of *prestige*. But wherever the word 'Kennedy' was used the word 'Khrushchev' must be substituted and where the word 'Rusk' was used the word 'Gromyko' must be substituted. I felt Khrushchev wanted to ease pressures and do a deal but to make the arrangements outside normal official channels and thus avoid embarrassment to himself."[116]

It was not merely, however, the officials of the Soviet Foreign Ministry whom Khrushchev's unorthodox maneuver was designed to circumvent, but his own colleagues in the collective leadership. The principal motive behind the gesture was evidently Khrushchev's desire to achieve a personal triumph in foreign policy through a direct man-to-man deal with Kennedy, which he could then present to his colleagues as proof of the success of his methods.

[113]*NYT*, Sept. 9, 1961.
[114]*NYT*, Nov. 6, 1966, sec. 4, p. 10.
[115]Ibid.
[116]Ibid.; emphasis in the original.

Sulzberger's October 6 talk with Kennedy concluded on a somber note: tension in Berlin seemed to be easing—Khrushchev, said Kennedy, "had been 'much softer' in his approach to the Berlin problem"—but the gain in Berlin was offset by trouble in Vietnam: "The President thought the situation in Southeast Asia was getting rapidly worse, above all in South Vietnam. He said that at least in Europe over the Berlin Crisis it was perfectly plain how we would have to fight a war if war broke out, but it is far more difficult to face the problem of fighting a war in Southeast Asia."[117]

The Khrushchev–Sulzberger interview provides an unusual opportunity to observe at close range the Soviet collective leadership engaged in the decision-making process during a period of rapid change. It is clear that some high-level discussions must have been held and some basic decisions reached in the interval between Sulzberger's arrival in the Soviet capital on September 3 and the moment four days later when he cabled the revised text of his dispatch to New York. Before we attempt, however, to analyze the problem, it will be necessary to consider concurrent developments in a number of related areas.

The Soviet reply to the Kennedy–Macmillan proposal

In his September 5 interview with Sulzberger, Khrushchev, as we have seen, offered his preliminary evaluation of the Kennedy–Macmillan proposal to ban nuclear tests in the atmosphere. In so doing, he provided unambiguous evidence that this was a subject which the collective leadership already had under consideration, by saying: "*We are preparing a reply* and will send it in several days, but I am ready in a preliminary way to voice my opinion."[118]

Khrushchev had then presented three arguments against accepting the Western leaders' proposal: that it did not extend to France; that a test ban agreement would be useless without general and complete disarmament; and that the Soviet Union had a "moral right" to test as long as the total number of tests it had conducted fell short of the total number carried out by the Western powers.

These arguments, and the rejection of the proposal to which they pointed, were duly repeated in the formal reply by the Soviet government issued on the day the Western offer expired, September 9, over Khrushchev's signature as chairman of the USSR Council of Ministers.[119] For good measure, some additional arguments were adduced, for example, that in their proposal Kennedy and Macmillan ". . . make no mention whatever of the critical nature of the time we are living through, of the tension in the international situation, although one would think it would be clear to them that the state of affairs with regard to nuclear testing cannot possibly be considered in isolation from the international situation."[120]

[117]Ibid.
[118]*NYT*, Sept. 8, 1961, p. 11; emphasis supplied.
[119]Text, *Izv.*, Sept. 9, 1961, pp. 1–2; *CDSP*, XIII/36, pp. 3–5.
[120]*CDSP*, XIII/36, p. 3.

Proof of Western hypocrisy was found in the fact that Kennedy had ordered the resumption of U.S. underground testing on September 5, "the day after their [Kennedy's and Macmillan's] approach to the Soviet Union" (calculating no doubt from the official date of delivery and ignoring the fact that the offer was broadcast from the United States and therefore received in Moscow on September 3). Ignoring also the fact that Kennedy in his September 5 statement had explicitly reaffirmed the validity of the Western offer until September 9, as well as the fact that no U.S. tests had yet been conducted (and of course ignoring completely the Soviet test shots of September 4 and 5), the statement accused the United States of unbecoming haste: "The U.S. government was seized with such impatience that evidently it never even crossed its mind to wait, if only for propriety's sake, for the Soviet government's reply to the Anglo–American statement. Is it not clear from this that from the very beginning it had no intention of suiting its actions to the Soviet Union's forth-coming reply to this statement?"[121]

Unfortunately for Soviet credibility, there was available by this time the of-ficial report of Khrushchev's September 5 interview with Sulzberger in which he had authoritatively forecast the Soviet rejection of the Western offer, and even the specific arguments to be employed in the Soviet reply. Thus the ref-erence to Kennedy's September 5 statement was mere camouflage designed to conceal the fact that the Soviet leadership from the beginning had had no in-tention of responding favorably to the Western appeal, or even of considering it on its merits. Once the decision to resume testing had been taken, the Soviet leadership—including Khrushchev—treated it as an irreversible action which must proceed to its foreordained conclusion.

The real reason for the Western proposal, the Soviet statement declared, was to secure a unilateral advantage for the Western powers in continuing to perfect their nuclear arsenal by testing underground and in outer space. "Needless to say," it needlessly said, ". . . the Soviet government cannot and will not accede to such a deal, which is desired by those whose policy is built on deception of the peoples, on playing at negotiations."[122]

As for the Soviet decision to resume testing, it had not been undertaken lightly:

> In deciding to resume tests, the Soviet government was, of course, aware that there might at first be people who would be unable to appreciate just how complicated the international situation is and would show a certain amount of misunderstanding of this move of the Soviet Union's. It was clear to us in advance that some people in the West would be sure to seize upon this to try to make propaganda capital. And yet the Soviet Union could not act otherwise. Having weighed all the pros and cons, the Soviet government was forced, *with a feeling of anguish, with an aching heart*, to undertake the resumption of experimental explosions.[123]

[121]Ibid.
[122]Ibid.
[123]Ibid.; emphasis supplied.

Western concern with the dangers of radioactive fallout, the statement charged, ". . . turns out on closer inspection to be feigned, specious."[124] The only solution to the problem of nuclear testing was the one championed by the Soviet Union—universal and total disarmament: "Once this problem has been solved, no one would be tempted to test nuclear weapons on the ground, underground, in the atmosphere or in outer space, and in fact there would be nothing to test, since all weapons, and nuclear missiles first of all, would have been scrapped. Life itself has linked these two questions in one indissoluble whole."[125]

The Soviet government, however, saw no signs of Western recognition of these principles: "Unfortunately, as the bilateral Soviet–American talks show, the U.S. government does not even want to approach universal and total disarmament with the establishment of the strictest international control over the actions of states in this sphere."[126]

The statement concluded with a recapitulation of Soviet demands: "Universal and total disarmament with the elimination of the entire war machinery of states, conclusion of a German peace treaty without delay and the writing of finis to the second world war—this, in the present circumstances, is the straight road to deliverance of the peoples from war and from the miseries and affliction it brings people. We call upon the governments of the United States and Great Britain to set foot on that road."[127]

In a document which charged the Western leaders with manipulating the issue of nuclear testing for propaganda purposes, it is noteworthy that no reference whatever was made to the actual terms of the Western proposal. (As we have seen, the text of the Kennedy–Macmillan proposal was not published in the Soviet press.) The Soviet statement showed not the slightest recognition of the fact that the Western powers had made a significant concession in dropping their demand for some form of international inspection over nuclear tests in the atmosphere. Neither did the statement mention the fact that the proposal explicitly reaffirmed the Western leaders' "serious desire to conclude a nuclear test ban treaty applicable to other forms of testing as well." As distorted in the Soviet statement, the Western proposal for a ban on atmospheric testing was made to appear as an end in itself rather than as an emergency measure aimed at heading off an immediate threat to world health. The conclusion to be drawn is that the statement issued by the Soviet government on September 9 was nothing but an exercise in propaganda designed to conceal the fact that the Soviet leadership had no intention of halting the test series which it had been preparing for so long and on which it had embarked.

On receipt of the Soviet statement rejecting their proposal Kennedy and Macmillan issued a brief statement expressing their "deepest regret" at the

[124]Ibid.
[125]Ibid.
[126]Ibid.
[127]Ibid.

Soviet action, which, they said, "contrasts vividly with the Soviet Union's own repeated expressions of concern as to the health hazards of such testing," and then reaffirmed their nations' readiness ". . . to negotiate a controlled nuclear test ban agreement of the widest possible scope."[128]

On the same day the three-power test ban negotiations in Geneva adjourned for an indefinite recess after Tsarapkin, head of the Soviet delegation, had read into the record the Soviet reply to the Kennedy–Macmillan proposal and had then refused to accept a proposal by the Western delegations that the recess should be a temporary one and that negotiations should be resumed after conclusion of the forthcoming debate on nuclear testing in the U.N. General Assembly.[129]

Kozlov at Pyongyang

After September 1 nothing more was heard of the plan to have Frol Kozlov head the Soviet delegation to the sixteenth session of the U.N. General Assembly (above, p. 181). During the first week in September the Soviet press observed a total blackout on all mention of Kozlov. He seemed to have disappeared from view completely—he took no part in any of the official or public ceremonies performed by the Soviet leadership as reported by the Soviet press and radio during this period, for example, the visit of the collective leadership to the French industrial exhibition on September 4, the funeral of U.S. communist leader William Z. Foster on September 5, the receptions for Nehru and Nkrumah on September 6, or the entertainment and festivities for Nehru on September 7.

The temporary eclipse of Kozlov ended on September 8 when *Pravda* reported a luncheon, held evidently on the preceding day, at the North Korean embassy in honor of a delegation from the CPSU which was to attend the forthcoming IV Congress of the Workers' Party (Communist party) of North Korea. Kozlov, it was disclosed, was to head the delegation, the other members of which were figures of secondary importance.[130]

The departure of the delegation from Moscow was reported on September 9,[131] and its arrival in Pyongyang on the evening of the same day.[132]

It was in Pyongyang on September 12 that Kozlov delivered a speech which marked the real end of the Soviet campaign to force Western acceptance of its demands on Berlin and Germany by the end of 1961. The core of the message Kozlov had been sent to Pyongyang to deliver, almost buried in a

[128]*Documents on Disarmament, 1961*, p. 404.

[129]*NYT*, Sept. 10, 1961, p. 18.

[130]*Pravda*, Sept. 8, 1961, p. 4. The other two members of the delegation were Raisa Fedorovna Dement'eva, secretary of the Moscow City Committee of the CPSU, and Lev Nikolaevich Tolkunov, deputy chief of the Central Committee department for liaison with ruling communist parties.

[131]*Pravda*, Sept. 9, 1961, p. 1.

[132]*Izv.*, Sept. 9, 1961, p. 2.

heavy shroud of rhetoric, was a brief statement with regard to Berlin: "Our proposals are not an ultimatum."[133] "The Soviet Union," Kozlov continued, ". . . is ready, together with interested countries, *to discuss and consider any reasonable amendments to our draft treaty.*"[134]

Thus Kozlov announced the lifting of the Soviet Union's self-proclaimed deadline for the signing of a German peace treaty by the end of 1961. Only gradually, however, did the West come to realize that an important shift had taken place in Soviet policy.

Before we take up the wider significance of Kozlov's statement, the reasons why it was made, and the reception it was accorded in the West, it will be convenient to consider several other noteworthy passages in his speech.

Homage to Khrushchev as the party leader was duly rendered by Kozlov at the outset of his speech. Addressing his hosts, the delegates to the North Korean party congress, Kozlov said: "We are grateful to you for the high evaluation of the successes of our people in the building of a communist society, achieved under the leadership of the Leninist Central Committee of the Communist Party of the Soviet Union headed by Comrade N. S. Khrushchev [*stormy applause*]."[135]

Kozlov pledged Soviet support for North Korean efforts to reunify the country: "If the American troops left the southern part of the country, providing the Korean people with the opportunity to decide their own fate, Korea would long since have been unified by the hands of the Koreans themselves. The Soviet Union firmly supports the demand of the Korean people for the immediate withdrawal of American troops from South Korea [*stormy applause*]."[136]

He evoked laughter by ridiculing U.S. space efforts: ". . . look at what is taking place in America, in that citadel of imperialism. They are unable to fly around the earth and only hop in one place and fall back in another [*laughter in the hall*]."[137]

Turning to more serious matters, Kozlov took up the question of relations among socialist nations, with particular reference to the touchy matter of Soviet preeminence in economic and social development. The new draft Party Program called for the transition to full communism in the Soviet Union by 1980, and there were many critics of Khrushchev's policies—including the Chinese communists—who regarded the draft program as the expression of a self-centered, complacent nationalism on the part of the Soviet Union. On this point Kozlov expressed a point of view which distinguished him clearly from Khrushchev and brought him close to the position of the Chinese communists:

The building of communism in the U.S.S.R. is viewed by our party as an integral part of the establishment of a communist community of nations of

[133]*Pravda*, Sept. 13, 1961, p. 2.
[134]Ibid.; emphasis supplied.
[135]Ibid.
[136]Ibid.
[137]Ibid.

the entire world socialist system. The Soviet Union is moving forward, to communism, not in isolation but in close cooperation with the other socialist nations. The comradely cooperation and fraternal mutual aid will assist our countries to utilize better all the wealth of their lands, to accelerate the tempos of construction, to improve the life of our peoples. The Soviet Union sees its duty in aiding by its experience, its example, its support, the fraternal peoples to shorten the time for the construction of socialism, in every way to bring about *a more or less simultaneous transition of these nations into the communist society [prolonged applause]*.[138]

On the subject of the Soviet decision to resume nuclear testing Kozlov was brief and concise, but managed to convey an entirely different rationale for the decision and an entirely different attitude toward it from those of Khrushchev:

> With regard to the peoples of the socialist countries *it would be unforgivable to do nothing in such a responsible moment of history*, to sit with folded hands, *relying on the mercy of god and the "good sense" of military maniacs*. The strengthening of the defense power of the socialist camp corresponds not only to the interest of the toilers of our countries, but to those of all the peoples of the earth. Our love of peace does not mean, as some people mistakenly believe, that we are weak. Our defence strength is growing from day to day, and *for every one who tries by force to test the fortress of our boundaries there waits inevitably full and final destruction [stormy applause]*.[139]

Apparently the only Western newspaper which showed an awareness of the importance of Kozlov's speech was *Le Monde* in Paris. Citing a Reuters dispatch based on a Radio Moscow broadcast of the speech, *Le Monde* singled out for emphasis the key passage in which Kozlov announced the lifting of the deadline for signature of a German peace treaty.[140] The brief account of the speech given in the *New York Times* was also based on a Reuters dispatch, but had been cut down to the point of inanity: "Frol R. Kozlov, a Soviet Communist Party secretary, said today the Soviet Union was ready to hold talks on a peace treaty with Germany."[141]

Beyond this, Kozlov's speech apparently stirred no interest in the West. No one in Washington paid any attention to it; neither Sorensen nor Schlesinger mentions it, nor shows any awareness that a major shift in Soviet policy in the Berlin crisis occurred as early as September 12. It was only with the advantage of retrospect that the authoritative *Survey of International Affairs* was able to recognize the speech as a turning point in Soviet policy on Berlin.[142]

Despite the West's failure to spot the significance of Kozlov's speech, however, the fact that a softening of the Soviet position had set in soon became ap-

[138]Ibid.; emphasis supplied.
[139]Ibid.; emphasis supplied.
[140]*Le Monde*, Sept. 14, 1961, p. 6.
[141]*NYT*, Sept. 13, 1961, p. 6.
[142]*SIA, 1961*, p. 263, citing *Le Monde*, Sept. 14, 1961.

parent. The evidence came first in the form of a favorable Soviet response to Kennedy's patient reiteration of Western willingness to enter into negotiations on Berlin. On September 13, at the end of the two-day White House visit of Sukarno and Keita (the emissaries of the Belgrade conference), Kennedy issued a statement reaffirming his willingness to negotiate: ". . . we are ready to discuss these matters with other governments, including the Government of the Soviet Union, and to search for the means to preserve an honorable peace. If that is the purpose on all sides, there is no need for resort to force."[143]

Going beyond familiar generalities, Kennedy made a concrete proposal for Soviet–U.S. talks:

> The Foreign Ministers of the Western powers are meeting in Washington tomorrow. Next week the Secretary of State will head the United States Delegation to the General Assembly of the United Nations. We understand that Foreign Minister Gromyko will be present. This will provide an opportunity for serious talks about Germany and other problems if the Soviet side proves willing. The channels of diplomacy are open for the exploration of constructive steps toward a reduction of tension. Other means are available when they can serve a useful purpose. Meanwhile, it is clearly of the utmost importance that there be no unilateral acts which make peaceful progress impossible.[144]

The British Foreign Office quickly gave its approval to the proposal, a fact noted in a statement by the Soviet Foreign Ministry issued by TASS on September 14:

> In view of the aforesaid desire of the Government of the United States and President Kennedy personally, and taking into consideration the positive attitude to this proposal of the United Kingdom, the Ministry of Foreign Affairs of the U.S.S.R. is authorized to state that Andrei Gromyko, the Minister of Foreign Affairs of the U.S.S.R. . . . is ready to enter into a relevant exchange of opinions with Dean Rusk, the Secretary of State of the United States.
>
> The Soviet Government proceeds from the assumption, as its head Nikita Khrushchev emphasized more than once, that the sides will display a serious attitude to the talks and will jointly search for a solution of the problem of the conclusion of a German peace treaty and a settlement on its basis of the situation in West Berlin.
>
> Such is the Soviet Government's reply to the statement by the President of the United States and the British Foreign Office.[145]

The significance of the Rusk–Gromyko talks, which duly got under way on September 21, lay not in their substance—they led to no real Soviet–Western agreement on Berlin—but in the fact that they were held at all. While the talks were in progress the tension over Berlin gradually subsided and the great powers drew back from the brink of nuclear catastrophe.

---

[143]*JFK, 1961*, p. 601.
[144]Ibid., pp. 601–2.
[145]*Documents on Germany*, p. 796.

Kozlov had flown from Moscow to Pyongyang, making the journey in a few hours, but he seemed to be in no hurry to return to Moscow. On September 20, the day after the conclusion of the North Korean party congress, TASS reported his arrival in Vladivostok, where he attended a party conference of personnel of the Pacific Ocean fleet,[146] and on the following day noted his arrival in Khabarovsk.[147] (On the same day Gromyko was appearing at the U.N. General Assembly as head of the Soviet delegation, the position Kozlov had aspired to at the beginning of the month.) Kozlov and the members of his delegation returned to Moscow on September 22.[148]

Soviet military leaders provide camouflage

Western failure to recognize that the Soviets had lifted the deadline in their demand for a German peace treaty can be understood and condoned in the light of an extensive and concerted campaign mounted by Soviet military leaders at this time to stress Soviet armed power and readiness to fight if war broke out over Berlin. "If Frol Kozlov's speech of 13 September was intended as the first tentative display of the olive branch by the Soviet leadership," the *Survey of International Affairs* comments, ". . . its effect was quickly countered by senior officers of the Soviet armed forces in a very different vein."[149]

The campaign was launched on September 13—the date of publication of Kozlov's speech—with an article in the Soviet army newspaper by Marshal K. S. Moskalenko, commander-in-chief of Soviet rocket troops.[150] The series of articles of which this was the first was characterized by a common pattern: first, warnings of the imminence of war, as the result of the aggressive policy of the Western powers, followed by praise of a particular branch or service of the armed forces, and concluding with staunch affirmations of the readiness of Soviet military men to fight and die, if need be, in the defense of the Soviet Union. Moskalenko, for example, began by portraying "the ominous clouds of war [which] are gathering on the approaches to our motherland's borders, as they did 20 years ago," a situation he attributed to the aggressive policy of the West: "The constant threats of war from U.S. imperialist circles and their allies in the military blocs, the rebirth of militarism and revanchism in West Germany, the unceasing arms race and the creation of military bases around the Soviet Union and the socialist camp countries have obliged us constantly to strengthen the country's armed might and to give a great deal of attention to developing the armed forces."[151]

[146]*Krasnaia Zvezda*, Sept. 21, 1961, p. 2.

[147]*Izv.*, Sept. 22, 1961, p. 1.

[148]*Pravda*, Sept. 23, 1961, p. 1.

[149]*SIA, 1961*, p. 263.

[150]K. S. Moskalenko, "Rocket troops on guard over the security of the Motherland," *Krasnaia Zvezda*, Sept. 13, 1961, p. 3; condensed translation, *CDSP*, XIII/37, pp. 12–13; summary, *NYT*, Sept. 14, 1961, p. 7.

[151]*Krasnaia Zvezda*, Sept. 13, 1961; *CDSP*, XIII/37, p. 12.

Moskalenko went on to praise the power of the Soviet rocket troops in superlative terms:

> The world knows no intercontinental missiles or other types of missiles to compare with those now in use by the Soviet Army.
>
> Our long-range ballistic missiles are capable of delivering nuclear warheads to any point on the globe at any time of the day or year and under any weather conditions. They make it possible to strike powerful blows at a considerable number of targets simultaneously, and at the same time they are invulnerable to modern countermeasures. The great ranges and speed of these missiles make it possible to alter the direction of fire rapidly and to move the main effort from one set of fronts or theaters of war to another and to exert decisive influence in order to change the situation in our favor.[152]

To make sure that the target of his observations was clearly understood, Moskalenko cited an American general's testimony in support of his claims: "The power of our missile weapons is also recognized abroad. General Thomas Power, head of the U.S. Strategic Air Command, openly stated that at the present time any target, even ones at a range of 8000 to 10,000 km., could be destroyed with an accuracy of 95%. Powers concluded: 'For all practical purposes the Soviets need only 300 missiles to put all of our atomic armament out of commission. All of this can be done in about 30 minutes'."[153]

The development of Soviet missiles, Moskalenko claimed, had destroyed the value of U.S. military bases abroad: "Now that there are nuclear weapons and missiles, U.S. military circles can no longer attach any importance to their bases in NATO countries. Operational-tactical missiles would suffice to destroy them; long-range ballistic missiles would not even be necessary."[154]

To drive the point home, Moskalenko referred to the testing of "still more powerful and improved versions of multistage carrier rockets, which are to be launched between September 13 and October 15 in the central Pacific."[155]

Moskalenko concluded with praise for the Soviet rocket troops: "The motherland has entrusted Soviet missile troops with the most powerful and highly developed weapons we have. Missiles are collective weapons. Success in their use depends on the knowledge and mastery of every man in the unit. This is why increased demands are being made of missile troops in their combat and technical training."[156]

On the day following the publication of Moskalenko's article Soviet Marshal R. Ya. Malinovsky, minister of defense, in a *Pravda* article ostensibly devoted to a discussion of the draft Party Program, mounted a vigorous attack on the Western position, portraying the United States in particular as incorrigibly aggressive and imperialistic:

[152]Ibid.

[153]Ibid., p. 13.

[154]Ibid.

[155]Ibid. The TASS announcement of the forthcoming Pacific range rocket tests was published in *Pravda* on Sept. 11; *CDSP*, XIII/37, p. 31.

[156]Ibid., p. 13.

In our times the role of chief savior of capitalism has been assumed by U.S. imperialists. Hiding behind the false banner of freedom and democracy, the American imperialists are actually playing the role of a world gendarmerie. The recklessness and aggressiveness of the U.S. ruling circles' policy appears in especially bold relief in Europe.

The U.S.A. and its partners in the aggressive NATO bloc are attempting to use the vestiges of World War II and the absence of a German peace treaty for adventuristic purposes—the establishment of their own world domination. To this end they wish to make the occupation regime in West Germany and West Berlin permanent and to transform the Federal German Republic into the chief striking force in order to swallow the German Democratic Republic at a convenient moment, then to seize from Poland and Czechoslovakia lands that were returned to these countries under the terms of the Potsdam agreement, and finally, to enter their chief claim: the liquidation of the socialist camp.*

The imperialists' answer to the peaceful proposals of the Soviet government—to eliminate the vestiges of World War II, to conclude a peace treaty with Germany and to normalize the situation in West Berlin—has been to threaten the unleashing of a new world war.[157]

A new world war, Malinovsky warned,

... if the imperialists unleash it, will be in political essence a decisive armed clash between two opposing social systems. It must be completely clear to us that the distinct class nature of such a war will foreordain the extremely decisive nature of the military and political goals of the combatant sides. On the other hand, the use of weapons of mass annihilation and demolition will impart to the war an unprecedentedly destructive aspect. It is for such an intense, difficult and exceptionally violent war that we must prepare our armed forces.[158]

Malinovsky concluded by praising the party's concern for building up the Soviet armed forces: "The Leninist Party Central Committee and N. S. Khrushchev personally give daily attention to the problems of building and further strengthening our armed forces, to their technical equipment, to improving the quality of the military training of fighting men and to intensifying Party political work in army units and in the navy."[159]

Moskalenko and Malinovsky were followed on September 16 by Marshal K. A. Vershinin, commander-in-chief of the Soviet air force. Like his colleagues, Vershinin portrayed the Western powers as bent on driving the world to war:

The events of the most recent times give evidence of the constantly increasing aggressiveness of the policy of the NATO military bloc, the

---

*Note the similarity between this portrayal of Western aims and that given by Khrushchev in his military speech of June 21, 1961 (above, p. 15).

[157]R. Ya. Malinovsky, "The defense of the socialist Fatherland is our sacred duty," *Pravda*, Sept. 14, 1961, pp. 3-4; condensed translation, *CDSP*, XIII/37, p. 11.

[158]Ibid., p. 12.

[159]Ibid.

strengthening of military preparations by the United States of America and its allies in answer to the proposal of the Soviet Union concerning conclusion of a German peace treaty. The imperialists, especially the Americans, have been seized by an unrestrained military psychosis. . . .

Today it is clear to every citizen, and even more to us military men: the aggressors have set their course towards the unleashing of a third world war. A real threat has been created to the Soviet Union, to the socialist camp, to the cause of peace in the entire world.[160]

Vershinin gave details of technical improvements in the Soviet air force, saying, "We have not sat with hands folded for 16 years since the war."[161]

A representative of the land forces, General of the Army A. S. Zhadov, made his contribution to the campaign on September 20. "Leading figures in the U.S.A. and other nations forming part of the NATO military bloc" Zhadov charged, ". . . have literally lost their head and have reached the point of openly threatening the Soviet Union with war if it concludes a peace treaty with the German Democratic Republic."[162]

Zhadov admitted that "the main role" in a new world war "will be played by the strategic rocket troops as the basic force for the employment of atomic weapons," but consoled himself with the thought that ". . . the successful defeat of the adversary in war can be achieved only by the combined efforts of all the branches of the armed forces. A very important role in the attainment of the complete defeat of the enemy will belong to the infantry troops."[163]

Soviet Marshal S. S. Biriuzov, commander-in-chief of the anti-aircraft forces, weighed in with an article on September 22, in which he charged that: "Matters have reached the point where leading figures in the U.S.A. and other nations of the aggressive NATO bloc have resorted to direct threats to take up arms and unleash war against the Soviet Union and the entire camp of socialism."[164] "Under such circumstances," he continued, ". . . there is demanded from our Armed Forces, including the anti-aircraft defense of the country, as never before, high watchfulness and complete combat readiness."[165]

A spokesman for the marines, Admiral A. G. Golovko, added his voice to the chorus on September 29, charging that: "The American military complex, having been given by the government almost unlimited freedom of action, has set its course towards the unleashing of a third world war. The proposals of

[160]K. Vershinin, "The Military Air Force is able to stand up for the Motherland," *Krasnaia Zvezda*, Sept. 16, 1961, p. 2.

[161]Ibid. For Western summaries of Vershinin's article, see *NYT*, Sept. 17, 1961, p. 20; *Washington Post*, Sept. 17, 1961, p. A–18.

[162]A. S. Zhadov, "The land forces are in readiness," *Krasnaia Zvezda*, Sept. 20, 1961, p. 2.

[163]Ibid.

[164]S. S. Biriuzov, "Vigilant guards of the Soviet sky," *Krasnaia Zvezda*, Sept. 22, 1961, p. 2.

[165]Ibid.

the U.S.S.R. to conclude a peace treaty with Germany have evoked from the West a new fit of military hysteria."[166]

In its later stages the series of "preparedness" articles by Soviet military leaders was modified by a significant revision of U.S. intelligence estimates of Soviet military capabilities. As we have seen, Moskalenko, in his September 13 article which opened the series, cited General Power's statement concerning the annihilating power which the possession of 300 long-range missiles would give the Soviet Union, thereby tacitly implying that the Soviet armed forces actually had this number of missiles. Some Western military analysts still accepted inflated claims of this kind, e.g., the influential British military writer B. H. Liddell Hart, who at about this time asserted flatly that "The Soviet Union has surpassed the U.S. in rocket production."[167] More and more frequently, however, challenges to such views were being voiced. The West Germans, it appeared, took a much more modest view of Soviet capabilities than did some Western analysts. According to *New York Times* military specialist Hanson W. Baldwin: "Despite the sometimes inflated estimates of Washington intelligence sources, relatively low capability is attributed in West Germany to Soviet missile strength and tactical nuclear weapons."[168]

The West German estimate, Baldwin reported, was not only lower than that of the United States in tactical weapons but also in overall strategic power: "In the larger missile field the Russians appear to have a far more limited capability than has been estimated in the past in Washington. . . . Soviet intercontinental ballistic missiles are believed to be numbered in two figures."[169]

Discounting the importance of the current Soviet test series, General Curtis LeMay, U.S. air force chief of staff, told the 15th annual convention of the Air Force Association that the Soviet Union was behind rather than ahead of the United States in "superbombs." If the United States had wanted to build a 100-megaton bomb, said LeMay, it could have done so "a long time ago."[170]

The most precise and influential published report on the revised Western evaluation of Soviet strategic power was an article by Joseph Alsop. "Prior to the recent recalculation," Alsop wrote,

> . . . the maximum number of ICBMs that the Soviets were thought to have at this time was on the order of 200—just about enough to permit the Soviets to consider a surprise attack on the United States. The maximum has now been drastically reduced, however, to less than a quarter of the former figure—well under 50 ICBMs and therefore, not nearly enough to allow the Soviets to consider a surprise attack on this country. The number of Soviet

[166]A. G. Golovko, "The Marines are always ready for the defense of the Fatherland," *Krasnaia Zvezda*, Sept. 29, 1961, p. 2.

[167]German translation of an article by B. H. Liddell Hart, "Why we cannot defend West Berlin," broadcast by Radio Moscow to West Germany, Sept. 15, 1961.

[168]*NYT*, Sept. 19, 1961, p. 11.

[169]Ibid.

[170]Jack Raymond, *NYT*, Sept. 22, 1961, p. 2.

heavy bombers of intercontinental range meanwhile remains unchanged, at about 150.[171]

An awareness that Soviet policy could no longer be based on claims for Soviet missile superiority was reflected in the formulation adopted in a second article by Marshal Biriuzov which appeared on October 3: "If the U.S. imperialists who are threatening the Soviet people with thermonuclear war should dare to unleash one they will have to pay for it. Neither the oceans surrounding the shores of North America nor the deepest atomic shelters now so strenuously advertised by the monopolistic press will save them from *just and inevitable retribution.*"[172]

In place of earlier claims, actual or implied, for a specific number of long-range missiles, Soviet military spokesmen and political leaders in the autumn of 1961 began to employ the formulation that such weapons were available in "sufficient" or "necessary" numbers.[173]

In the minds of Soviet military leaders, the fact that the Soviet Union was known by U.S. planners to lack the means for launching a successful surprise attack on the United States carried with it the corollary that the reverse possibility—a surprise attack on the Soviet Union by the United States—might become a reality. It is not mere coincidence, therefore, that the latter theme was also stressed at this time in statements by Soviet military leaders. In the series of "preparedness" articles which we have cited, this note was sounded for example by Malinovsky: "We cannot sit with folded hands and look on with indifference at the way in which the ruling circles of the Western powers are pushing the world toward war. We do not want to find ourselves in the position in which we were in 1941. This time we shall not allow the imperialists to catch us unawares."[174]

"We must constantly sharpen [our vigilance] in order to frustrate the plans of the imperialists for a surprise attack on our country and to prevent a repetition of the sorry lessons of the initial period of the last war."[175]

Stoking the fires

Military spokesmen and political leaders on both sides contributed to the crisis atmosphere of early September 1961 by inflammatory statements and provocative actions. On September 3, for example, the USSR Ministry of Defense announced that "training exercises" by the northern fleet, jointly with rocket troops and air force units, would be held in the Barents and Kara Seas from September 10 to November 15, 1961.[176]

[171]Joseph Alsop, *Washington Post*, Sept. 25, 1961, cited by Horelick and Rush, p. 89. For the evidence on which the reassessment was based, see Philip J. Klass, "Keeping the nuclear peace: spies in the sky," *NYT Magazine*, Sept. 3, 1972, p. 7.

[172]S. Biriuzov, *Sovetskaia Rossiia*, Oct. 3, 1961, cited by Horelick and Rush, p. 89; emphasis supplied.

[173]Ibid., p. 99.

[174]*Pravda*, Sept. 14, 1961; Horelick and Rush, p. 92.

[175]*Krasnaia Zvezda*, Sept. 20, 1961; Horelick and Rush, p. 92.

[176]"In the interests of security," *Izv.*, Sept. 3, 1961, p. 4; *CDSP*, XIII/35, p. 28.

At a press conference on September 5, French President de Gaulle called on the West to resist by force if necessary the menace of what he called the Soviet "totalitarian empire." He attributed the Berlin crisis, which he called "arbitrary and artificial," to the Soviet desire to divert attention from unrest in the Soviet Union and in the communist bloc.[177]

An *Izvestiia* article on September 6 described the factory in the Urals which produced rockets of the kind which, the article claimed, brought down the U–2 plane in May 1960. "If the dreaded hour strikes," the author of the article warned, ". . . all the means of defense created by the labor and talent of the workers, engineers and technicians at this remote plant in the Urals will be thrown against the foul enemy, will wipe him from the face of the earth and will reduce him to ashes."[178]

On September 7 Paul H. Nitze, U.S. assistant secretary of defense for international security affairs, in an address to the Association of the U.S. Army on the Berlin situation, summarized U.S. military planning and expressed confidence in the capacity of the United States and its allies to meet successfully the Soviet challenge:

> In summary, first, we have great nuclear capabilities. We are not particularly impressed with the Soviet threat to develop nuclear weapons in the 100-megaton range. We are not interested in arms of a terroristic nature, but rather our nuclear capability is tailored to specific tasks.
>
> We have a tremendous variety of warheads which gives us the flexibility we require to conduct nuclear actions from the level of large-scale destruction down to mere demolition work. I could not, of course, give specific numbers, but I can say that the number of nuclear delivery vehicles of all types which the United States possesses provides the flexibility for virtually all modes and levels of warfare. Second, at the same time, we have a growing nonnuclear capability with a large growth potential. The economic base represented by the United States and our Western European Allies far outdistances that of the Communist bloc.[179]

Nitze warned that "determination, will and sacrifice" would be required "to offset fully the Communist conventional power," but expressed confidence "that the American people will respond as they always have when their leaders lay great issues before them, and that our Allies will do their share."[180] Reflecting the apocalyptic view of the situation taken by some officials in Washington, Nitze said that the events of the next ninety days might decide the future of the world for the next century.[181]

The defense ministers of the Warsaw Pact nations held their first publicly announced meeting on September 8–9 in Warsaw, with the participation of

[177]*NYT*, Sept. 6, 1961, p. 1; *SIA, 1961*, p. 262.

[178]P. Visimov, "Urals arsenal," *Izv.*, Sept. 6, 1961, p. 1; *CDSP*, XIII/36, p. 31.

[179]*NYT*, Sept. 8, 1961; *Documents on Germany*, pp. 783–84.

[180]Ibid.

[181]Cited by Rusk in a speech to the Association of the United States Army in Washington: *NYT*, Sept. 9, 1961, p. 2.

the chiefs of staff of the nations' armed forces. Soviet Marshal A. A. Grechko, commander-in-chief of the combined armed forces of the Warsaw Pact countries, served as chairman of the meeting. The communiqué issued after the meeting stressed the military build-up being undertaken by the Warsaw Pact nations to meet the threat of war:

> The conference noted that the countries of the aggressive North Atlantic military bloc (NATO) have greatly stepped up their military preparations recently, are fanning the arms race and increasing the size of their armies, and in reply to the proposals of the socialist countries on concluding a German peace treaty are even threatening to unleash a new war.
>
> In view of the present situation, and guided by the directives of their governments, the Defense Ministers and chiefs of staff reviewed specific questions of strengthening the combat readiness of the troops that make up the combined armed forces of the Warsaw Pact countries.[182]

British Defense Minister Harold Watkinson, in a speech on September 9, announced the formation of an army division to be maintained at "a high state of readiness" for assignment to West Germany if the Berlin crisis grew more acute. British officials were quoted as saying that this was Britain's response to Khrushchev's assertion (in the Sulzberger interview) that Britain, France, and Italy were "hostages" to the Soviet Union and would not support the United States if war broke out over Berlin. Khrushchev, said Watkinson, had ". . . completely miscalculated the resolution of the British Government and of the British people to fulfill in concert with our allies, our international obligations."[183] Also on September 9, the United States announced the despatch of 40,000 troops as reinforcements to its garrison in West Germany.[184]

Khrushchev, in a speech dedicating a new electric power station at Volzhsky on September 10, reacted sharply to the challenge launched in de Gaulle's September 5 press conference:

> . . . the President of France should be asked about something he neglected to mention: Just what would be left of his country should the imperialists plunge the world into war? President de Gaulle is after all a military man and is well aware that so huge a country as the Soviet Union cannot be destroyed, whereas for France, as well as West Germany, Britain and other countries with a dense population and great cities and industrial centers concentrated in a small territory, there will be no surviving a thermonuclear war.[185]

Khrushchev used the occasion to demonstrate his close links with the military; as described in *Pravda*: "(. . . *N. S. Khrushchev heartily embraces* [Marshals] *A. I. Yeremenko and V. I. Chuikov and kisses them affectionately. Shouts: Hurrah!)*"[186]

[182]*Izv.*, Sept. 12, 1961, p. 3; *CDSP*, XIII/37, p. 13.
[183]*NYT*, Sept. 10, 1961, p. 4; *SIA, 1961*, p. 262.
[184]Ibid.
[185]*Pravda*, Sept. 11, 1961, p. 3; *CDSP*, XIII/37, p. 6.
[186]Ibid., p. 3.

Despite its bluster and bragging, however, the dominant note of Khrush-chev's September 10 speech was the attainment of peace through negotia-tion:

> . . . to judge from pronouncements by leading Western statesmen, encour-aging signs have now appeared. United States President Kennedy and Bri-tish Prime Minister Macmillan, it is known, are in favor of negotiations. General de Gaulle and Chancellor Adenauer, who have often been described in the press as opposing negotiations, are also declaring for peace nego-tiations.
> We have right along proposed peace negotiations. And had the Western statesmen listened to the voice of reason, the present particularly acute in-ternational tension would not exist, there would not be the war psychosis that currently reigns in the West. The most compelling problems causing that tension would long since have been solved, and the way would have been cleared for cooperation among states. But it is never too late to do a good deed. We therefore hail those who are advocating peaceful coexistence and the settlement of issues by peaceful means, through negotiations and not with weapons.[187]

It was on September 10, however, that TASS announced that Soviet rocket tests would be held in the central Pacific in the period September 13–October 15, and warned foreign planes and ships to stay out of a designated area.[188]

Meanwhile the explosions of Soviet nuclear tests were following one another at brief intervals—two on September 13, which the U.S. Atomic Energy Commission estimated in the low-to-intermediate range.[189] The threat of a direct Soviet–Western air clash over Germany was added on the following day when two Soviet MIG fighters buzzed two American commercial airliners en route to Berlin,[190] and when two West German jet fighters strayed briefly over the air space of East Germany before landing at a West Berlin airport. The latter incident was made to be the subject of a stiff protest on September 17 by the Soviet government, which, the note said, ". . . gives warning that in the future in such cases intruder war planes which fail to comply with the demand to land at an indicated spot will be destroyed with every means, including missiles."[191]

To help prepare the American people for the grim possibility of a nuclear-missile war with the Soviet Union, the President wrote an article for the September 15 issue of *Life* magazine, urging the large-scale construction of fallout shelters.[192] It was on the same day that the first U.S. nuclear explosion in the new series was carried out at the underground proving grounds in Nevada. The Soviets, also on the 15th, announced that their rockets in the new

[187]Ibid., p. 6.

[188]Radio Moscow, Sept. 10, 1961; *Pravda* and *Izv.*, Sept. 11, 1961; *CDSP*, XIII/37, p. 31; Seymour Topping, *NYT*, Sept. 11, 1961, p. 2.

[189]*NYT*, Sept. 14, 1961, p. 1.

[190]*SIA, 1961*, p. 262.

[191]*Documents on Germany*, p. 803.

[192]*Life*, vol. 51, no. 11, Sept. 15, 1961, p. 95.

Pacific test series, which had begun on September 13, had landed "less than one kilometer from the target, which confirms the high accuracy of the rocket's guidance system."[193]

Breakthrough in the McCloy–Zorin talks

In the crisis atmosphere of mid-September 1961 few Americans would have ventured to predict that the Soviet Union and the United States would shortly reach agreement on the basic principles of disarmament. Yet to the surprise of many—including Kennedy himself[194]—this is exactly what happened.

The bilateral Soviet–U.S. talks on disarmament, it should be noted, had been broken off on July 29, following Khrushchev's stormy reaction to Kennedy's speech of July 25 (above, p. 90). When the talks resumed in New York on September 6, the United States submitted a draft statement on principles stressing two points which McCloy, the chief American negotiator, ". . . had made the center of his argument—that the process [of disarmament] should take place in stages 'under such strict and effective international control as would provide firm assurance that all parties are honoring their obligations,' and that it should go hand in hand with the development of international peace-keeping institutions."[195]

A crucial point in the U.S. draft was the proposal that verification of disarmament measures should cover not only weapons destroyed but those retained: "Such verification should ensure that not only agreed limitations or reductions take place but also that retained armed forces and armaments do not exceed agreed levels at any stage."[196]

Both the TASS bulletin and the Soviet–American communiqué announcing resumption of the talks were strictly factual and noncommittal, but there was a cautious note of optimism in *Izvestiia's* heading to its story on the event, "Dialogue has been resumed."[197]

Evidence that some high-level Soviet rethinking on the talks might be under way came when the meeting scheduled for September 12 was cancelled at Soviet request.[198] On the resumption of the talks on September 14, McCloy was ready with a carefully worked out summary of the whole course of the discussion, from its onset in March down to the break-off at the end of July.[199] In addition, the September 14 memorandum recapitulated and amplified the principles set forth in the U.S. draft of September 6. As a statement of the U.S. position on disarmament which had Kennedy's full endorsement, the September 14 memorandum repays careful study.

[193]*Pravda*, Sept. 15, 1961, p. 1; *CDSP*, XIII/37, p. 31.

[194]Sorensen, p. 519.

[195]Schlesinger, p. 475. Text of the U.S. draft of Sept. 6 in *Documents on Disarmament, 1961*, pp. 360–61.

[196]Ibid., p. 361.

[197]*Izv.*, Sept. 8, 1961, p. 1.

[198]*NYT*, Sept. 12, 1961, p. 2.

[199]*Documents on Disarmament, 1961*, pp. 431–48.

Its first point was the importance of working out a "total over-all program for complete disarmament." This, of course, sounded very much like the ceaselessly reiterated Soviet proposal for "general and complete disarmament." The difference between the two positions was made clear in McCloy's memorandum: ". . . the United States cannot accept a situation where nothing concrete can be done until the very last word has been agreed for the total program. Consequently, it urges acceptance of the proposition that without prejudice to eventual development of the total program an attempt must be made to find the widest possible area of agreement—including any individual measures or groups of measures—and to implement such measures just as soon as they are agreed."[200]

Second, the memorandum continued, ". . . the United States stresses the inseparable relationship between the drastic scaling down of national armaments and the building up of international peace-keeping machinery and institutions."[201] Such measures, in the U.S. view,

> . . . would be within the framework of the United Nations as part of the program for general and complete disarmament in a peaceful world. These procedures and institutions would not permit nations to invoke doctrines of sacred or just wars in behalf of unilateral military action since they would ensure that no one really seeking justice or the fulfillment of legitimate aspirations will need to have recourse to their own force. They would not permit arbitrary revisions of established international agreements and infringements of other nations' rights. The United States believes firmly that nations must be prepared to moderate gradually the exercise of unrestricted sovereignty and to abide by the decisions and judgments of tribunals and other bodies, even if such decisions at times may not meet with a particular nation's approval.[202]

Most vital, in the U.S. view, was its third principle:

> . . . the United States insists upon effective verification of disarmament measures from beginning to end. The fundamental precept guiding the United States is that the implementation of every obligation entered into must be subject to effective verification in order to provide each participating State with confidence that every other State is fulfilling its commitments. Verification only of the process of reducing or destroying particular elements of military strength, as proposed by the Soviet Union, does not meet the criterion of effective verification of all obligations entered into. What must be certain is not only that nations are removing certain numbers of forces and armaments from their military establishments, but also that they are not maintaining forces and armaments or engaging in activities in excess of those permitted at a given step or stage in the disarmament program.[203]

Taking up the frequently voiced Soviet assertion that the Soviet Union would be willing to accept any control procedures demanded by the Western

[200]Ibid., p. 433.
[201]Ibid., p. 434.
[202]Ibid.
[203]Ibid., pp. 434–35.

powers, if the latter would first accept the Soviet demand for general and complete disarmament, the U.S. memorandum pointed out the difficulties which would nullify in practice the effectiveness of any agreement concluded on this basis:

> The phrase frequently used in Soviet statements that "under conditions of general and complete disarmament the most thorough control must be implemented" is ambiguous and does not adequately reflect the necessity for effective verification at every step and stage of the disarmament process. Indeed, it must be pointed out that if, as the Soviet Union suggests, control can be "most thorough" only "under conditions" of general and complete disarmament, but not during the process of implementing the measures leading to general and complete disarmament, it may never be possible to determine whether the "conditions" of general and complete disarmament have in fact arrived or to protect a complying party against the consequences of violation or evasion of a disarmament agreement by others.[204]

McCloy's memorandum proceeded to spell out in detail the kind of "inspection machinery" which, in the U.S. view, would ensure "effective verification." The Soviet demand for a three-headed executive for the central body was rejected as administratively unworkable: "Sound administrative practice the world over and the requirement of effective verification demand efficient administration of the disarmament verification machinery. For this reason the United States rejects firmly the concept of some sort of multi-headed administrative machinery."[205] The memorandum concluded with a consideration of the vexed and disputed questions of the stages of disarmament and the composition of an international forum in which general disarmament negotiations could be resumed.

There was no immediate response from Zorin to McCloy's temperate and closely reasoned memorandum of September 14, but there were renewed indications that the Soviets were giving serious consideration to the U.S. initiatives. On September 15 it was reported that the Soviets had again requested a postponement of a scheduled session of the bilateral talks.[206]

Then, suddenly and unexpectedly, came the breakthrough. At the session of September 18, Zorin on behalf of the Soviet government accepted the American draft Statement of Principles of September 6, with the exception of the clause concerning verification of retained armed forces during disarmament. Rather than let the lack of agreement on this single—though vital—point stand in the way of at least a limited degree of Soviet–U.S. understanding, McCloy on September 19 agreed to delete the clause to which the Soviet Union objected, thus enabling the two nations to reach agreement on a broad statement of principles just in time for presentation to the sixteenth session of the U.N. General Assembly. Both sides, in letters exchanged on September

[204]Ibid., p. 435.
[205]Ibid.
[206]*NYT*, Sept. 16, 1961, p. 2.

20, reiterated their stands on the disputed clause—McCloy describing it as ". . . a key element in the United States position which we believe is implicit in the entire joint statement of agreed principles that whenever an agreement stipulates that at a certain point certain levels of forces and armaments may be retained, the verification machinery must have all the rights and powers necessary to ensure that those levels are not exceeded, . . ."[207] while Zorin charged that in defending this position ". . . the United States is trying to establish control over the armed forces and armaments retained by States at any given stage of disarmament, . . ."[208] and that such control ". . . which in fact means control over armaments, would turn into an international system of legalized espionage, which would naturally be unacceptable to any State concerned for its security and the interests of preserving peace throughout the world."[209]

Both sides recognized that a basic question of principle was involved and that failure to agree on this question would inevitably be reflected in the form of complications at any future disarmament negotiations. Nevertheless, the achievement of the negotiators in the bilateral talks was an impressive one. At a time when the two most powerful nations in the world seemed to be teetering on the brink of an atomic war, their ability to reach a broad though limited agreement on the principles of disarmament came as a welcome indication of the fundamental sanity and commitment to peace of their leaders.

The Belgian diversion

Up until the beginning of September it had been the Italians who had seemed to offer Khrushchev the most promising opening for bringing at least one of the Western powers to the negotiating table, but Italian indignation over the Soviet resumption of nuclear testing had closed off that avenue of approach (above, p. 168). Never an easy man to rebuff, however, Khrushchev as late as September 12 was still courting the Italians, with yet another letter in what by that time had become a one-sided correspondence.[210]

It was at just this point, however, that another possible Western negotiating partner for the Soviets appeared on the horizon. On September 12, Belgian Premier Paul-Henri Spaak ". . . publicly appealed to the West to make a greater effort of unity without delay to clarify their objectives and reach a positive policy of negotiations with the Soviet Union."[211] The Soviets lost no time in exploiting this promising opening. On September 13 Radio Moscow announced that Spaak would visit the Soviet Union for a meeting with Khrushchev on the 19th, a report which was promptly confirmed from Brussels.[212]

---

[207] *Documents on Disarmament, 1961*, p. 442.
[208] Ibid., p. 443.
[209] Ibid.
[210] *SIA, 1961*, p. 261.
[211] Ibid., p. 264.
[212] Radio Moscow, Sept. 13, 1961; *NYT*, Sept. 14, 1961, p. 4.

Summarizing Western press comment, the *Survey of International Affairs* provides a useful insight into the purpose behind the Belgian statesman's trip:

> M. Spaak's motives, it emerged, were a combination of resentment at the way the smaller N.A.T.O. powers had been excluded from the most important inter-allied consultation and a conviction common to the non-Communist left in Europe that to fight a war over Berlin would be criminal. He seemed also to be convinced that time was running short and that unless something was done, Mr. Khrushchev would be forced to make some gesture at the 22nd Party Congress due to meet in Moscow in the third week of October.[213]

A favorable augury for the Belgian visit was provided on September 15 when former French Premier Paul Reynaud emerged from a three-hour visit with Khrushchev to say: "I arrived in Khrushchev's study very pessimistic and I left confident of the future. . . . The impression I have is there is no impasse and there is a hope of getting out of what was considered an impasse."[214]

In reporting Reynaud's visit, the *New York Times* added: "Western diplomats here [Moscow] also reported that Soviet officials in private conversation had expressed optimism about the possibility of a settlement that would arrest the danger of war."[215]

After this build-up, the actual discussion between Khrushchev and Spaak came as something of an anticlimax. Spaak was later reported to have told a NATO council meeting in Paris, on September 24, that Khrushchev denied ever having placed a deadline on Western acceptance of Soviet demands for a German peace treaty and free-city status for West Berlin, but that aside from that concession he showed no willingness to budge from previously announced Soviet positions.[216]

The only clear outcome of the Belgian Premier's initiative thus seemed to be the demonstration that the Soviets had no real desire to negotiate seriously with the West on Berlin at this time, and had used the Belgian visit simply in order to gain time and to give the appearance of reasonableness. For those who had missed the significance of Kozlov's Pyongyang speech, however, Spaak's September 24 report to the NATO Council came as the first indication that the Soviets might be relaxing their demands on Berlin.

"The Storm in Berlin is over"

Aside from Soviet acceptance of the U.S. proposal for talks on Berlin between Secretary of State Rusk and Foreign Minister Gromyko, Kozlov's dis-

---

[213]*SIA, 1961*, p. 264, citing *Le Monde, Le Soir*, the *Times* (London), Sept. 19, 1961, and the *Christian Science Monitor*, Sept. 25, 1961.

[214]*NYT*, Sept. 16, 1961, p. 2; Sept. 29, 1961, p. 4.

[215]*NYT*, Sept. 16, 1961, p. 2.

[216]*Washington Post*, Sept. 25, 1961, p. A–1.

closure in his Pyongyang speech that the Soviet deadline on Berlin had been lifted was not followed by any dramatic Soviet action indicating a real willingness to end the Berlin crisis. The two- or three-week period which followed the speech was characterized rather by a confused medley of Soviet statements on Berlin, the German peace treaty, nuclear testing, and disarmament, from which the prevailing impression emerges of a continuing high-level struggle for the control of Soviet policy, in which conflicting and even contradictory statements could be made by Soviet spokesmen with little or no regard to consistency. Any attempt to impose unity on the expression of Soviet policy during this period can be successful only at the cost of ignoring the tangled welter of policy statements and selecting only those which support a simplistic, rationalized interpretation.

Certain consistent lines, nevertheless, run through the period, and provide a basis for sorting out the various forces which were at work. Khrushchev's policy goals, for example, were defined with relative clarity in a series of statements. In his reply to the message brought to him by Nehru and Nkrumah from the Belgrade conference, which was dated September 16, though for some reason the Soviet press did not publish it until the 22nd, two passages stand out for their note of personal involvement amid much that is routine and stereotyped. With regard to the measures recently taken by the Soviet government to strengthen its military power, Khrushchev expressed unfeigned regret: "I should like to tell you directly and frankly, although it will be no news to you, that the Soviet Union does not wish to follow the rut of military rivalry with the Western powers. This is not our policy, it is not our path and *we should prefer not to follow this path if we were not forced to do so.*"[217]

And in answer to the central theme of the Nehru–Nkrumah message, the plea for direct U.S.–Soviet negotiations, Khrushchev expressed full assent: "You know, of course, that the Soviet Union has always favored settling outstanding issues by negotiation. Naturally, now too we believe that talks between states, especially between the U.S.S.R. and the U.S.A., the mightiest and most influential states, can and should play an important role in clearing the international atmosphere. In the name of ensuring peace, *we are ready for negotiations at any time, in any place, and at any level.*"[218]

True, the force of this hearty assent was seriously weakened when Khrushchev went on to make it clear that the Soviet Union would enter negotiations only when the agenda and conclusions were to its liking:

> . . . I want you to understand me correctly. The Soviet government is ready to take part in negotiations that are really aimed at the speediest solution of pressing international problems—in the first place, in a peace conference on the question of *concluding a German peace treaty and normalizing the situation in West Berlin on this basis.* It is convinced that the sooner such serious negotiations begin, the better. It would be an expression of great states-

---

[217]*Pravda*, Sept. 22, 1961, pp. 1–2; *CDSP*, XIII/37, pp. 9–10; emphasis supplied.
[218]Ibid., p. 10; emphasis supplied.

manship if such a treaty were concluded on an agreed basis in the shortest time.[219]

On September 21 *Pravda* and *Izvestiia* published a short interview with Khrushchev by two of their correspondents in which he seized on an opening provided by Pope John XXIII, in a recent speech in which he had voiced his concern over the danger of war, to reiterate his (Khrushchev's) belief in the responsibility of statesmen to avoid actions which might lead to war:

> In our times, when the most destructive means of annihilation have been created, it is especially inadmissible to play with the fate of the peoples. Here of course it is not a matter of fear of "God's judgment," about which the Roman Pope speaks. As a communist and an atheist, I do not believe in "divine providence," but I can say one thing firmly: the great responsibility of governments to their peoples, to humanity, demands that they make every possible effort and undertake joint efforts for the path leading to the liquidation of the remnants of the second world war, to the elimination of hotbeds of tension, to the curbing of the torchbearers of a new world conflagration.[220]

Khrushchev went on to make a direct allusion to two prominent Western statesmen who were Catholics: ". . . Do such adherents of the Catholic faith as J. Kennedy, K. Adenauer and others listen to the 'sacred warnings' of the Pope of Rome?"[221]

*   *   *

The news of U.N. Secretary-General Dag Hammarskjöld's death in a plane crash in the Congo was brought to Kennedy on September 18. For months the Soviet Union and its allies had been waging a propaganda war against Hammarskjöld of such unrestrained bitterness and violence that the term "character assassination" would be none too strong a designation for it. In addition, the Soviet Union had been attacking the office of secretary-general itself, in its existing form, and demanding that it be replaced by a three-man secretariat to include representatives of the West, the Soviet bloc, and the nonaligned states. The Soviet attack on the office, of course, was directly linked with its attack on the character and policies of the man who held it, for it had been Hammarskjöld's unwearying labors to make the secretary-generalship the center of U.N. efforts at maintaining peace in the Congo and elsewhere that had earned him the unrelenting hostility of the Soviet bloc.

Although he had already given several of his aides instructions to prepare a speech for him to deliver at the forthcoming U.N. General Assembly (above, p. 187), Kennedy had not yet made a final irrevocable decision to attend the

[219]Ibid.; emphasis in the original.

[220]*Pravda* and *Izv.*, Sept. 21, 1961, p. 1. In a speech on Sept. 10 the Pope had called on leaders on both sides to negotiate their differences over Berlin in order to remove the threat of war. He urged them to "face squarely the tremendous responsibilities they have before the tribunal of history and, what is more, before the judgment seat of God." *NYT*, Sept. 21, 1961, pp. 1, 11.

[221]*Pravda* and *Izv.*, Sept. 21, 1961, p. 1.

session. Asked on September 17 to comment on reports that the President would attend, White House press secretary Pierre Salinger replied, "I found those reports a little hard to understand in view of the fact he has made no such decision."[222]

A number of well-informed observers agree that it was the news of Hammarskjöld's death, with the ominous implications it carried for the future of the United Nations itself, which provided the final stimulus for Kennedy's decision to address the General Assembly.[223] The decision was announced by the White House immediately after the President had issued a brief statement paying tribute to Hammarskjöld, James Reston reported, with the additional comment:

> Originally, President Kennedy had withheld an announcement about going to the United Nations personally pending the outcome of the forthcoming conversations between Secretary of State Dean Rusk and the Soviet Foreign Minister, Andrei A. Gromyko, on the German problem. This afternoon, however, after talking on the telephone to Secretary Rusk and Adlai E. Stevenson, United States delegate to the United Nations, he decided to redraft his speech and attend the General Assembly in order to pay his respects to Mr. Hammarskjöld and to reassure the delegates that the United States would support all efforts to uphold the authority of the Secretary General's office.[224]

The decision was not taken lightly, however, or without strenuous debate. Ambassador Arthur H. Dean reports that: "Theodore Sorensen telephoned me on September 18, 1961, to say that the President was being counseled not to make his disarmament speech, on which Mr. McCloy and I had worked, to the UN General Assembly on September 25. Distressed by this information, I sent a telegram to Mr. Kennedy at Hyannisport, urging him to view disarmament in the long-term perspective."[225]

It was to be expected that the Soviets would take advantage of the opportunity provided by Hammarskjöld's death to push with renewed vigor their demand for a three-man secretariat, and Soviet news media were not slow in producing evidence to support this expectation. Just as word of the Secretary General's death was received in the Soviet capital, in fact, a broadcast over Radio Moscow was declaring that "the time is ripe for structural changes" in the United Nations.[226] An article in *Izvestiia* on September 21 claimed that:

[222]*NYT*, Sept. 18, 1961, p. 12.

[223]Schlesinger, p. 484; Sidey, p. 250.

[224]James Reston, *NYT*, Sept. 19, 1961, pp. 1, 16. For Kennedy's statement on the death of Hammarskjöld, see *JFK, 1961*, pp. 605–6.

[225]Arthur H. Dean, *Test Ban and Disarmament. The Path of the Negotiations* (New York and Evanston, Harper & Row, 1966), p. 26 (hereinafter cited as Dean). Dean's dates are frequently garbled. Sorensen, p. 520, also implies a conflict over the question of whether or not the President should address the United Nations.

[226]Seymour Topping, *NYT*, Sept. 19, 1961, p. 5, comments that the broadcast was "probably written before word reached here [Moscow] of Mr. Hammarskjöld's death."

The U.N. circles recognize that it may be difficult to concentrate the executive power of the U.N. once again in the hands of one man, not only for political reasons but also because the U.N. Secretary General's death in the line of duty left the organization without a leader and without a successor.

The U.N. circles admit that the most *important* task will be to decide on what form the new U.N. leadership is to take. They express the view that Hammarskjöld's sudden and tragic death may lend weight to the Soviet proposal for a "troika," replacing the U.N. Secretary General with a committee of three, i.e., representatives of the East [sic], the West and the neutral countries.[227]

By September 21 Kennedy's decision to address the General Assembly was firm, but debate still continued among his advisers as to the substance of what he should say, in particular, whether he should make a plea for general disarmament as a major part of his speech. According to Dean: "Throughout the day there was much discussion, which he [Kennedy] finally resolved by deciding to make the speech putting the United States on record for general and complete disarmament in a peaceful world. President Kennedy was a man firmly anchored in reality, but he had the rare quality of not allowing the reality of a particular moment to paralyze his capacity to take bold, imaginative, and courageous steps."[228]

On the evening of Friday, September 22, Kennedy flew from Washington to Hyannis Port for the weekend. According to Sorensen:

> . . . the speech [for the United Nations] was written and rewritten over an intensive weekend at Hyannis Port. I worked with the President at his cottage, on the phone and, finally, on his plane as it flew in heavy fog from Cape Cod to New York. Because both the Presidential and passenger cabins were crowded and noisy, we squatted on the floor in the bare passageway between the two, comparing and sorting pages. He suggested that we each write a peroration and then take the best of both. In New York he read the latest draft aloud to Rusk and his UN team—an unusual practice for him—and then made his final revisions that night [i.e., Sunday, September 24].[229]

*   *   *

A recurring worry to Kennedy was the fear that the policies and goals of the United States under his administration were not being fairly and fully presented to the Soviet people. This worry was by no means groundless. We have

[227]"Possible successors to Hammarskjöld," *Izv.*, Sept. 21, 1961, p. 4; *CDSP*, XIII/38, p. 17; emphasis in the original.

[228]Dean, p. 26. Dean's testimony is confused as to location (he puts Kennedy in New York on Sept. 21) but appears to be correct in substance.

[229]Sorensen, p. 521. For reports on Kennedy's whereabouts and actions during the period from his arrival at Hyannis Port on the evening of Friday, Sept. 22, to his departure for New York on the evening of Sunday, Sept. 24, see the *NYT*, Sept. 24, 1961, p. 46 (Tom Wicker), and Sept. 25, 1961, pp. 1, 5. Care in the dating of this period is essential because Pierre Salinger, as we shall see presently, has quite a different version of how Kennedy was occupied at this time.

noted for example, that the Soviet press failed to publish the actual text of the Kennedy–Macmillan test ban proposal of September 3, substituting for it a distorted and mutilated paraphrase.

On the afternoon of September 19 or 20, Kennedy held a long discussion with James Wechsler, editor of the *New York Post*, in the course of which he frankly expressed his hopes and fears about the prospects for world peace.[230]

It was Wechsler, according to Schlesinger, who came up with the proposal ". . . that he write a column about Kennedy's thoughts on war and peace and challenge the Soviet press to republish it. Pierre Salinger thought this a good idea, and *the President personally approved the Wechsler text.*"[231] Surprisingly enough, Kennedy, usually a fast learner, had not yet fully grasped the potentialities of the controlled and directed newspaper interview as a vehicle for the expression of his policy views, despite Khrushchev's repeated demonstrations of the flexibility and value of this form.

Wechsler's report appeared in two parts, the first of which was concerned primarily with the strong internal pressures being brought to bear on the President, in particular a slashing attack delivered a few days earlier by former President Dwight D. Eisenhower on Kennedy's conduct of foreign affairs.[232]

For his second article Wechsler turned to the field of foreign affairs, in particular Soviet–U.S. relations. The proposal for Soviet reprinting was voiced at the very outset: ". . . it is my hope that *Pravda* and *Izvestiia* will reprint this portrait of the President of the United States, or some reasonable facsimile thereof. This may seem both a wistful and immodest suggestion, but it is made in all solemnity at a time when all our lives may hinge on the capacity of these two men [Kennedy and Khrushchev] to keep open the lines of communication."[233] Wechsler then offered a portrait of Kennedy after eight months in office:

> The first and perhaps crucial thing to be said about John F. Kennedy is that he has no illusions about the nature of victory in nuclear war. If the worst happens, he does not propose to lose, but he has no relish for the role of presiding over an atomic wasteland. He has set modest sights for his place in history. He has no simple-minded view that the deep discords of our time can be deftly and finally resolved by diplomatic gamesmanship. He is aware that any honorable settlements he may negotiate will subject him to know-nothing cries of "appeasement" in many local places. He is genuinely disturbed by the frustrated fury of many of his countrymen who believe our national manhood can be affirmed only by some act of bloody bluster, in Cuba or Laos or almost anywhere on earth.

[230]Schlesinger, p. 400. The approximate date of the interview can be fixed by Wechsler's reference to a state dinner for President Manuel Prado y Ugarteche of Peru which occurred on the same day. For Prado's visit to the White House on Sept. 19–21, see *JFK, 1961*, pp. 607–13.

[231]Schlesinger, p. 400; emphasis supplied.

[232]James Wechsler, "As JFK sees it," *N.Y. Post*, Sept. 21, 1961, p. 28.

[233]James Wechsler, "JFK (Contd.)," *N.Y. Post*, Sept. 22, 1961, p. 46.

He is prepared to risk the storm of domestic political strife that agreements short of victory will invite. This is one of the changes I detect in the man: occupancy of this terrible, lonely office for less than a year has made him far more conscious of the awesome burdens he bears, of the limited goals he can seek, and the transient quality of public applause.[234]

The President, Wechsler continued, recognized and accepted the fact that ". . . any narrow accommodation he may—and must—achieve will subject him to lower-depth assault from those who believe we can whip the world with a smaller budget."[235] What he was not prepared to accept, however, was ". . . to be the target of a campaign of humiliation. If that is Mr. Khrushchev's design, we are all in trouble. Mr. Kennedy is not disposed to play the role of a stooge and he has, I believe, achieved a certain composure about the brutal nature of the choice he may have to face in the solitude of some ghastly night."[236]

In words directed specifically at Khrushchev, Wechsler portrayed Kennedy's broad views on negotiations: "Nothing in his view is non-negotiable except the dignity of free men; to put it another way, there can be full negotiations about the future of Germany and of China and almost any explosive area if Mr. Khrushchev is ready to negotiate rather than to dictate."[237]

Wechsler concluded his portrait of Kennedy on a "personal note" which unconsciously echoed the words with which Sulzberger had ended his report on his interview with Khrushchev: "In the twilight of a gray afternoon I sat with a man one year younger than myself whose decisions may be the final ones of our century."[238]

Since Khrushchev's evaluation of Kennedy was, in Wechsler's (and in Kennedy's own) view a crucial element in Soviet–U.S. relations, Wechsler devoted his final efforts to ensuring that an accurate image of Kennedy the man, stripped of all ideological camouflage, should be presented to the reader, including, he hoped, that of the Soviet press.

He [Kennedy] is the son of a very wealthy man, and therefore the perfect caricature for the Communist propagandists who like to equate all our deeds with the mischievous plots of "Wall Street imperialists." If that doctrinaire rubbish is what Mr. Khrushchev believes, he is mad and we are all doomed.

John F. Kennedy may be utterly wrong in some matters and fallible on others, but what he seeks is an honorable peace. Caught in the crossfire of Russian intransigence and domestic Know-nothingism, he is both keeping his head and sustaining his nerve.

There are things I wish he would say to the country that he has not said. He may be unduly sensitive to domestic pressures—as I believe he was in his

[234]Ibid.
[235]Ibid.
[236]Ibid.
[237]Ibid.
[238]Ibid.

decision to resume nuclear tests so soon after the unilateral Russian move. He may be too modest about the capacity of his own voice to rise above the clamor and frenzy. But I have no doubt about the authenticity and depth of his desire for rational settlements in a world that has trembled on the brink so long. Russian papers, please copy.[239]

Four days later, "considerably to our surprise,"[240] the Russian papers did just that. (For an attentive reader of the Soviet press, it would have come as no surprise to find the Soviet press selectively reprinting important U.S. newspaper or magazine articles on U.S. policy. On September 21, for example, *Pravda* published a translation of a recent Drew Pearson column analyzing differences of opinion within the U.S. government on policy toward Germany under the title, "Time and events are against the U.S.A.")

Schlesinger notes that the Russian translation of Wechsler's article included ". . . even the suggestion that Khrushchev was a madman if he considered Kennedy a Wall Street imperialist, . . ."[241] thereby implying that the Russian translation was complete and accurate. Except for some minor omissions of no great importance it *was* in fact, complete, but it was not accurate. By a single tendentious and obviously deliberate mistranslation the Russian text altered the tone and significance of the entire article. Where Wechsler had described Kennedy as a man "whose decisions may be the final ones of our century," the Russian version of this passage read: ". . . a man . . . whose decisions may be the final ones *for our country* [*chelovekom . . . ch'i resheniia mogut stat' reshaiushchimi dlia nashei strany*]."[242]

Thus altered, the import of Wechsler's portrait of Kennedy was that of a man who was prepared to face internal criticism as the price he must pay for making concessions to the Soviets in order to reach agreements in the absence of which his own country—not the entire world—would face destruction.

*   *   *

On the same day that the second part of the Wechsler interview appeared, the U.S. Embassy in Moscow sent a note to the Soviet Ministry of Foreign Affairs in which it pointed out that

> . . . the full texts of the major communications of the Government of the Soviet Union on the question of Berlin have been carried by major daily newspapers in the United States. Furthermore, Crosscurrents Press, which is a firm chartered in the United States, but registered with the Department of Justice as an agent of the Soviet state export monopoly for publications and thus a channel for the views of the Soviet Government, has recently published in the United States, as one of a series of pamphlets containing Soviet materials, a mass edition of a pamphlet entitled "The Soviet stand on

[239]Ibid.
[240]Schlesinger, p. 400.
[241]Ibid.
[242]*Pravda*, Sept. 26, 1961, p. 5; *Izv.*, Sept. 27, 1961, p. 2; emphasis supplied.

Germany." This contains a collection of documents presenting Soviet views on the Berlin question, with an introduction by the Chairman of the Council of Ministers of the U.S.S.R., Nikita S. Khrushchev.[243]

The note complained that, although the Soviet press had published some official statements of the U.S. government on the Berlin problem, ". . . the Soviet people have had no opportunity to study the American viewpoint on the Berlin problem in a fashion similar to the opportunity given the American people to study the Soviet viewpoint as presented in the pamphlet published by Crosscurrents Press."[244] To remedy this situation the U.S. note proposed ". . . that the Government of the Soviet Union make available to the United States Government facilities for the distribution at this time of comparable material presenting American views on the Berlin question. In this way, the Soviet people will have an opportunity, as the American people have had, to study in some depth both sides of this question, which is of such great importance."[245] The note concluded with an expression of the hope ". . . that the Government of the Soviet Union will give its immediate attention to making the requested facilities available."[246]

One can hardly fail to be struck by the air of futility and naïveté which pervades the U.S. note of September 22. Particularly striking was its failure to base its case on specific factual evidence, as it could easily have done by citing, for example, the failure of the Soviet press to publish the Kennedy–Macmillan limited test ban proposal of September 3. Equally striking was the note's failure to recognize that tight state control of the press, as well as other information media, has always been a fundamental principle of the Soviet system of government. To expect that the state-controlled Soviet press would readily make available its pages for the presentation of policy statements which might undermine the Soviet government's own position was equivalent to expecting the Communist party voluntarily to abdicate and make way for some more liberal form of rule.

Publication in the Soviet press of Wechsler's interview with Kennedy four days after the U.S. note of September 22 might be regarded as an implicit admission by the Soviets of the justice of the U.S. case, but in view of the tendentious distortion in the Russian-language version of the Wechsler article, it seems more likely that the two events were not causally related. Furthermore, as we shall see presently (below, p. 254), September 26 was a day which fell in a period of Khrushchev's absence from Moscow and the resurgence of his most intransigent adversary, Frol Kozlov. In republishing the Wechsler interview, with its (by Soviet standards) shockingly disrespectful references to the Soviet premier, Khrushchev's internal opponents were thus able to score a point in the factional struggle.

[243]*DSB*, 45 (1961): 718.
[244]Ibid.
[245]Ibid.
[246]Ibid.

When the Soviets did reply directly to the U.S. note, on October 12, their response took the form of a bland refutation of the complaint lodged in the American note and an outright refusal to take any steps to change the situation in the direction requested by the U.S. government.[247]

*   *   *

Pierre Salinger, Kennedy's press secretary, states that he accompanied the President to New York on September 22 (a Friday).[248] There, on the night of their arrival, Salinger reports, he received a call from Georgi Bolshakov, a Soviet official whom Salinger describes as "a one-man troika in himself . . . interpreter, editor, and spy."[249] It was most urgent, Bolshakov said, that Salinger ". . . have dinner with Kharlamov, who was in town as press spokesman for Andrei Gromyko, chief Soviet delegate to the UN."[250] Already tied up for that evening, Salinger arranged to see Kharlamov privately at his hotel room on the following night (i.e., Saturday, September 23). The Russian's opening words, which we have already quoted (above, p. 207), were, "The storm in Berlin is over." Kharlamov then inquired whether Kennedy had received the confidential message sent him by Khrushchev via Sulzberger, and on Salinger's reply that he "didn't know," Kharlamov said, "Then I will repeat the message to you, and you will deliver it to the President."[251]

"The message," Salinger continues, ". . . was urgent. Khrushchev saw the increase in our military forces in Germany as an imminent danger to peace. He was now willing, for the first time, to consider American proposals for a rapprochement on Berlin. He was eager for an early summit but would leave the timing up to JFK because of the President's 'obvious political difficulties'."[252]

Salinger provides his own gloss on Khrushchev's reference to "difficulties": "What he meant, in effect, was that I, Khrushchev, have total freedom of action in negotiating with you, Mr. President. I don't have to concern myself with political opposition or public opinion. But you do. You must prepare your country for the compromises a settlement of the Berlin question will require, and I am willing to give you time to do that."[253]

Salinger thus took at face value the term employed in Khrushchev's message, a straightforward approach which contrasts sharply with the more subtle suggestion by Sulzberger that Khrushchev's references to "difficulties" could best be understood as Aesopian language referring to his own position. Perhaps it would be fair to say that both interpretations contained some truth:

[247]Ibid., pp. 718-19.

[248]Salinger, p. 190.

[249]Ibid., p. 191. Bolshakov at this time was editor-in-chief of *USSR* and was later named a director of radio and television for the Novosti news agency. Ibid., p. xv.

[250]Ibid., p. 191.

[251]Ibid.

[252]Ibid.

[253]Ibid., p. 192.

Khrushchev knew that both he and Kennedy faced internal "difficulties" which stood in the way of agreement between them.

Kharlamov stressed the need for speedy action: "There was *intense pressure on Khrushchev* from within the Communist bloc to recognize East Germany. But apart from that, the danger of a major military incident in Berlin was too great to delay a settlement very much longer."[254] To conclude his message, Kharlamov ". . . had one final word from Khrushchev. 'He hopes your President's speech to the UN won't be another warlike ultimatum like the one on July 25. He didn't like that at all'."[255]

After Kharlamov had delivered his message he and Salinger settled down to a friendly discussion over scotch-and-sodas. Salinger complained of the Russians' failure to follow through on their promise to' rebroadcast the Soviet–American television debate on freedom of the press (above, p. 34), to which Kharlamov somewhat lamely replied that the tapes sent for rebroadcast had proved to be incompatible with Soviet equipment. He promised, however, that "When you come to the Soviet Union with your family to visit Adzhubei next summer, I will put you on live television and you can say whatever you want."[256] Kharlamov added that there was "great interest" in Moscow with regard to Salinger's proposal that Kennedy and Khrushchev engage in a series of TV "debates," and that "he would have an answer for me soon."[257]

Salinger then brought up the question of interviews in the foreign press as a vehicle for the expression of policy views:

All the Russian Premier had to do to command a direct audience of millions in this country was to invite an American correspondent to his office. In addition to Sulzberger, Walter Lippmann and Drew Pearson had been given recent interviews and all received tremendous circulation in the American press. But until now the Kremlin had never permitted a Soviet journalist to interview President Kennedy. I told Kharlamov the time had come for a little reciprocity. JFK was entirely willing to receive a prominent Russian reporter. When could he expect one?[258]

Kharlamov demurred: "It would be most difficult. You have chosen a very bad time to ask."[259] The immediate difficulty, it appeared, lay in the State Department's alleged refusal to grant visas to fifteen Soviet correspondents who had been scheduled to cover the U.N. General Assembly.[260]

[254]Ibid.; emphasis supplied. Salinger's reference to Soviet "recognition" of East Germany is a slip for "conclusion of a peace treaty" with the GDR.

[255]Ibid.

[256]Ibid.

[257]Ibid., p. 193.

[258]Ibid.

[259]Ibid.

[260]For Soviet comment on this incident, see *Pravda*, Sept. 28, 1961, p. 6; *CDSP*, XIII/39, p. 21.

In return for Salinger's promise to try to clear up the problem of the correspondents, Kharlamov agreed to work on the possibility of a Soviet interview with President Kennedy. An ideal interviewer, he suggested, would be Khrushchev's son-in-law, Adzhubei, editor of *Izvestiia*.

On the night of Salinger's talk with Kharlamov, Kennedy, according to Salinger, ". . . had gone to a Broadway play, was having a late supper with friends, and wouldn't return to the hotel until after midnight."[261]

On his return to his hotel Kennedy called Salinger at 1 A.M. and then listened to the message from Khrushchev. Salinger asserts flatly that: "He [Kennedy] hadn't heard from Sulzberger. This was his first knowledge of Khrushchev's message and he had me repeat the key points a number of times."[262] Salinger quotes Kennedy as saying: "There's only one way you can read it [Khrushchev's message]. If Khrushchev is ready to listen to our views on Germany, he's not going to recognize the Ulbricht regime—not this year, at least—and that's good news."[263] Kennedy then talked by telephone with Rusk before dictating ". . . a memorandum that I [Salinger] was to read to Kharlamov the next morning."[264]

Knowing from the Khrushchev–Sulzberger message that what Khrushchev had in mind was a new U.S.–Soviet agreement on Laos as a prelude to an accord on Berlin (a fact of which Salinger was ignorant), Kennedy made this the central point in his reply: "The President was cautiously receptive to Khrushchev's proposal for an early summit on Berlin. But first, he said, there should be a demonstration of Soviet good faith in Laos. . . . [He] told Khrushchev that if the Kremlin was now willing to honor its commitments in Laos, a summit on the much more difficult question of Germany would be more likely to produce significant agreement. We would be watching and waiting."[265]

Before turning in for the night, Kennedy, according to Salinger, ". . . took a long look at his UN speech. He didn't change a word. It was already moderate in tone—not at all the 'ultimatum' Khrushchev was afraid it might be."[266]

Shortly before he left for the United Nations on the morning of Monday, September 25, Kennedy ". . . gave his approval to the typescript of his memorandum to the Russian leader. A half hour later, I [Salinger] read it to Kharlamov and Bolshakov in my room."[267]

Salinger meanwhile had been able to clear up the matter of the visas for the fifteen Soviet correspondents: "I informed Kharlamov of this fact and said I would now expect him to follow through with Adzhubei on the interview with

[261]Salinger, p. 191.

[262]Ibid., p. 193.

[263]Ibid.

[264]Ibid., pp. 193–94.

[265]Ibid., p. 194.

[266]Ibid.

[267]Ibid., p. 195.

President Kennedy. He said he would but couldn't resist a final swipe at State [Department] for its 'stupidity' in not admitting the correspondents in the first place."[268]

Thus the groundwork was laid for Kennedy's first venture into the novel realm of policy exposition by means of the journalists and press of a foreign nation.

Salinger's account of his confidential meetings with the Russians is inaccurate as to dates and requires emendation before it can be fitted into the sequence of events. Kennedy, as we saw earlier (above, p. 234), flew from Washington to Hyannis Port on Friday, September 22, and spent the next two days there, and therefore could not have arrived in New York with Salinger on the 22nd.

Salinger's testimony, however, is too important to be discarded simply because of its inaccuracies. It can be salvaged if we assume that his first discussion with Kharlamov took place on the night of Sunday, September 24, i.e., the night before Kennedy was to deliver his speech to the United Nations. Kennedy, as we know, *was* in New York that evening, having just flown in from Hyannis Port. Salinger, we must assume, is in error not only as to the date but also in stating that he came to New York with the President. If in fact he came a day earlier, he could have received the call from Bolshakov on Saturday, September 23, and set up the appointment with Kharlamov for the following evening. It will be noticed, incidentally, that Salinger does not provide in any way for the events of Sunday the 24th, portraying Kennedy as going directly to the United Nations on the morning after he, Salinger, had delivered the message from Khrushchev.

Indications that the Soviet position on Berlin was softening had meanwhile reached the alert ears of Max Frankel, Washington reporter of the *New York Times*. The Soviets, Frankel wrote, had indicated ". . . in a number of quiet ways that their threat and deadline on Germany might be subject to another temporary delay. Communist diplomats were reported as saying that the West did not have to feel itself under an artificial 'deadline' if serious negotiations were undertaken. Khrushchev was also reported as saying that Western access might be guaranteed in a separate treaty between the two Germanys, and that the treaty could be registered with the UN."[269]

*   *   *

In his address to the U.N. General Assembly on September 25, Kennedy brought together all the major foreign policy issues and concerns of his administration in an organized, logical manner. In direct and forthright language, largely devoid of propaganda or rhetoric, the speech was one of Kennedy's most effective and helped establish his reputation as a world leader.

---

[268]Ibid., pp. 195–96. The difficulty lay in a bureaucratic technicality: the Soviet journalists, it seems, had neglected to apply for accreditation at U.N. headquarters. *NYT*, Sept. 26, 1961, p. 5. For a report on the belated granting of the visas, see *NYT*, Sept. 29, 1961, p. 9.

[269]*NYT*, Sept. 24, 1961, p. 1.

The President opened with simple words of grief for Dag Hammarskjöld, coupled with an affirmation of his abiding faith in the cause for which the Secretary-General had lived and died—strengthening of the United Nations as an instrument for world peace and security. The alternative, Kennedy warned, was war, and in the modern age, war could no longer be limited to the great powers: "For a nuclear disaster, spread by wind and water and fear, could well engulf the great and the small, the rich and the poor, the committed and the uncommitted alike. Mankind must put an end to war—or war will put an end to mankind."[270]

The chief immediate threat to the United Nations, Kennedy maintained, lay in the proposal (he did not specifically identify it as a Soviet proposal) for a three-man executive to replace the single general secretary. Shrewdly, Kennedy built his case not on the interests of the United States as a great power but on the need for a strong, effective executive to provide security for the smaller nations: "Whatever advantages such a plan [the troika proposal] may hold out to my own country, as one of the great powers, we reject it. For we far prefer world law, in the age of self-determination, to world war, in the age of mass extermination."[271]

Kennedy then summarized the new U.S. program for "general and complete disarmament under effective international control," prefaced by a warning of the dire situation in which humanity found itself: "Today, every inhabitant of this planet must contemplate the day when this planet may no longer be habitable. Every man, woman and child lives under a nuclear sword of Damocles, hanging by the slenderest of threads, capable of being cut at any moment by accident or miscalculation or by madness. The weapons of war must be abolished before they abolish us."[272]

Noting the newly signed Soviet–U.S. accord on disarmament principles as an encouraging augury, Kennedy nevertheless warned that ". . . we are well aware that all issues of principle are not settled, and that principles alone are not enough."[273]

The new U.S. disarmament program, he continued, represented a challenge to the Soviet Union ". . . to go beyond agreement in principle to reach agreement on actual plans."[274] The U.S. plan, he said,

> . . . moves to bridge the gap between those who insist on a gradual approach and those who talk only of the final and total achievement. It would create machinery to keep the peace as it destroys the machinery of war. It would proceed through balanced and safeguarded stages designed to give no state a military advantage over another. It would place the final responsibility for verification and control where it belongs, not with one's adversary

[270]*JFK, 1961*, p. 619.
[271]Ibid., pp. 619–20.
[272]Ibid., p. 620.
[273]Ibid.
[274]Ibid.

or one's self, but in an international organization within the framework of the United Nations. It would assure that indispensable condition of disarmament—true inspection—and apply it in stages proportionate to the stage of disarmament. It would cover delivery systems as well as weapons. It would ultimately halt their production as well as their testing, their transfer as well as their possession. It would achieve, under the eyes of an international disarmament organization, a steady reduction in force, both nuclear and conventional, until it had abolished all armies and all weapons except those needed for internal order and a new United Nations Peace Force. And it starts that process now, today, even as the talks begin.[275]

"The logical place to begin," Kennedy urged, would be a nuclear test ban. In addition, the new U.S. disarmament plan provided a number of proposals "to halt the spread of these terrible weapons, to halt the contamination of the air, to halt the spiralling nuclear arms race . . .":

—First, signing the test-ban treaty by all nations. This can be done now. Test ban negotiations need not and should not await general disarmament.
—Second, stopping the production of fissionable materials for use in weapons, and preventing their transfer to any nation now lacking in nuclear weapons.
—Third, prohibiting the transfer of control over nuclear weapons to states that do not own them.
—Fourth, keeping nuclear weapons from seeding new battlegrounds in outer space.
—Fifth, gradually destroying existing nuclear weapons and converting their materials to peaceful uses; and
—Finally, halting the unlimited testing and production of strategic nuclear delivery vehicles, and gradually destroying them as well.[276]

To provide security in a disarmed world, Kennedy called on all member nations of the United Nations to strengthen the U.N. Emergency Force, and pledged that for its part the United States would ". . . suggest a series of steps to improve the United Nations' machinery for the peaceful settlement of disputes—for on-the-spot fact-finding, mediation and adjudication—for extending the rule of international law."[277]

The rule of law, Kennedy urged, must be extended to outer space. Hailing the "brave cosmonauts of the Soviet Union" (significantly, one of the few passages in the entire speech in which he referred directly to the Soviets), Kennedy called for an extension

. . . of the United Nations Charter to the limits of man's exploration in the universe, reserving outer space for peaceful use, prohibiting weapons of mass destruction in space or on celestial bodies, and opening the mysteries

[275]Ibid., pp. 620–21.
[276]Ibid., p. 622.
[277]Ibid.

and benefits of space to every nation. We shall propose further cooperative efforts between all nations in weather prediction and eventually in weather control. We shall propose, finally, a global system of communications satellites linking the whole world in telegraph and telephone and radio and television.[278]

Turning his attention from outer space to the earth itself, Kennedy advocated cooperative efforts within the framework of the United Nations to develop the earth's resources, ". . . to enable all nations, however diverse in their systems and beliefs, to become in fact as well as in law free and equal nations."[279]

In the most polemical section of his speech Kennedy took up the challenging issue of colonialism, an issue to which Soviet spokesmen had given great emphasis in their foreign policy. "We agree," said Kennedy, ". . . with those who say that colonialism is a key issue in this Assembly."[280] But he immediately went on to call for "full discussion . . . of that issue." First, he said, the record showed that great progress had already been made in this area: ". . . since the close of World War II, a worldwide declaration of independence has transformed nearly 1 billion people and 9 million square miles into 42 free and independent states. Less than 2 percent of the world's population now lives in 'dependent' territories."[281]

As to the "remaining problems of traditional colonialism which still confront this body," Kennedy predicted that they "will be solved with patience, good will and determination," and he pledged that the "sympathy and support" of the United States would be extended to "that continuing tide of self-determination which runs so strong."[282] But the United States, once itself a colony, knows from experience what colonialism means, the President continued: ". . . the exploitation and subjugation of the weak by the powerful, of the many by the few, of the governed who have given no consent to be governed, whatever their continent, their class, or their color."[283] And colonialism in this broad sense, he charged, still exists in ". . . the Communist empire where a population far larger than that officially termed 'dependent' lives under governments installed by foreign troops instead of free institutions—under a system which knows only one party and one belief—which suppresses free debate, and free elections, and free newspapers, and free books and free trade unions—and which builds a wall to keep truth a stranger and its own citizens prisoners."[284] Let the debate on colonialism include these areas too,

[278]Ibid., pp. 622–23.
[279]Ibid., p. 623.
[280]Ibid.
[281]Ibid., p. 623.
[282]Ibid.
[283]Ibid.
[284]Ibid.

he urged: "Let us debate colonialism in full—and apply the principle of free choice and the practice of free plebiscites in every corner of the globe."[285]

Kennedy concluded his speech with a brief analysis of "two threats to peace." First, "The smoldering coals of war in Southeast Asia": "South Viet-Nam is already under attack—sometimes by a single assassin, sometimes by a band of guerrillas, recently by full battalions. The peaceful borders of Burma, Cambodia, and India have been repeatedly violated. And the peaceful people of Laos are in danger of losing the independence they gained not so long ago."[286]

Explicitly rejecting the argument on which the Soviets based their military aid to North Vietnam, Kennedy declared that: "No one can call these 'wars of liberation.' For these are free countries living under their own goverments. Nor are these aggressions any less real because men are knifed in their homes and not shot in the fields of battle."[287] The problem, he maintained, concerned all the United Nations: "The very simple question confronting the world community is whether measures can be devised to protect the small and the weak from such tactics. For if they are successful in Laos and South Viet-Nam, the gates will be opened wide."[288]

Disclaiming any special U.S. interests in Southeast Asia—"The United States seeks for itself no base, no territory, no special position in this area of any kind"—Kennedy reaffirmed his support for the concept of a neutral Laos on which he and Khrushchev had agreed at Vienna. But peace in Southeast Asia was not yet in sight: ". . . the negotiations over Laos are reaching a crucial stage. The cease-fire is at best precarious. The rainy season is coming to an end. Laotian territory is being used to infiltrate South Viet-Nam. The world community must recognize—and all those who are involved—that this potent threat to Laotian peace and freedom is indivisible from all other threats to their own."[289]

The Berlin crisis formed the final substantive subject dealt with in Kennedy's speech. Without naming the Soviet Union, he made it clear that in his view the crisis had its real origin in Soviet actions and policies: "If there is a crisis it is because an existing peace is under threat, because an existing island of free people is under pressure, because solemn agreements are being treated with indifference. Established international rights are being threatened with unilateral usurpation. Peaceful circulation has been interrupted by barbed wire and concrete blocks."[290]

Kennedy made it clear that the basic issue was not (as Soviet spokesmen had been repeating ad nauseam) the Soviet proposal to sign a peace treaty

[285]Ibid., pp. 623–24.
[286]Ibid., p. 624.
[287]Ibid.
[288]Ibid.
[289]Ibid.
[290]Ibid.

with East Germany: "It is absurd to allege that we are threatening a war merely to prevent the Soviet Union and East Germany from signing a so-called 'treaty' of peace. The Western Allies are not concerned with any paper arrangements the Soviets may wish to make with a regime of their own creation, on territory occupied by their own troops and governed by their own agents. No such action can affect either our rights or our responsibilities."[291]

"If there is a dangerous crisis in Berlin," he continued, "—and there is—it is because of threats against the vital interests and the deep commitments of the Western Powers, and the freedom of West Berlin."[292] But there was no real need for the Berlin crisis, Kennedy maintained:

> The elementary fact about this crisis is that it is unnecessary. The elementary tools for a peaceful settlement are to be found in the charter. Under its law, agreements are to be kept, unless changed by all those who made them. Established rights are to be respected. The political disposition of peoples should rest upon their own wishes, freely expressed in plebiscites or free elections. If there are legal problems, they can be solved by legal means. If there is a threat of force, it must be rejected. If there is desire for change, it must be a subject for negotiation and if there is negotiation, it must be rooted in mutual respect and concern for the rights of others.[293]

In words which strongly implied flexibility and a willingness to reach new international arrangements for Germany and Berlin, Kennedy continued: "We are committed to no rigid formula. We seek no perfect solution. We recognize that troops and tanks can, for a time, keep a nation divided against its will, however unwise that policy may seem to us. But we believe a peaceful agreement is possible which protects the freedom of West Berlin and allied presence and access, while recognizing the historic and legitimate interests of others in assuring European security."[294]

For all its somberness, Kennedy's speech to this point had been straightforward and matter-of-fact. In its concluding passages, however, he resorted to apocalyptic terms which make plain the intense strain which the international crisis through which he had been living had imposed on him: "The events and decisions of the next ten months may well decide the fate of man for the next ten thousand years. There will be no avoiding those events. There will be no appeal from these decisions. And we in this hall shall be remembered either as part of the generation that turned this planet into a flaming funeral pyre or the generation that met its vow 'to save succeeding generations from the scourge of war'."[295] To help avoid disaster, Kennedy pledged "every effort this Nation possesses": ". . . I pledge you that we shall neither commit nor provoke aggression, that we shall neither flee nor invoke the threat of force,

---

[291] Ibid.
[292] Ibid., pp. 624–25.
[293] Ibid., p. 625.
[294] Ibid.
[295] Ibid.

that we shall never negotiate out of fear, [but that] we shall never fear to negotiate."[296] He closed with an eloquent appeal to the members of the United Nations to save mankind: "Ladies and gentlemen of this Assembly, the decision is ours. Never have the nations of the world had so much to lose, or so much to gain. Together we shall save our planet, or together we shall perish in its flames. Save it we can—and save it we must—and then shall we earn the eternal thanks of mankind and, as peacemakers, the eternal blessing of God."[297]

In linking the problems of Laos and Berlin in the final section of his speech, was Kennedy hinting at a connection between them, knowing that Khrushchev had already done so in his confidential message sent via Sulzberger? At least one of the President's listeners thought it likely. In a commentary on the speech, Sulzberger wrote: "By inference, the President connected the troubles in Laos with the Berlin crisis when he spoke of the 'smoldering coals of war in Southeast Asia.' This implies to Mr. Khrushchev that the atmosphere would be far more favorable for a German settlement were it preceded by a Laotian settlement. And Mr. Khrushchev seems to recognize this fact. He recently implied readiness to arrange a peace in that tormented kingdom."[298]

Thus without actually disclosing that Khrushchev had made a confidential approach to Kennedy, Sulzberger managed to put on the record the substance of Khrushchev's proposal and thus do his part in furthering Soviet–American understanding.

*   *   *

Among those who appeared to be totally unmoved by the President's words was Soviet Foreign Minister Andrei Gromyko. When he in his turn addressed the General Assembly on the day following Kennedy's speech, Gromyko showed no sign whatever of recognizing Soviet responsibility for the Berlin crisis. "The true reasons for the heightening of international tensions," he maintained, ". . . must be sought in the aggressive nature of the policies of the powers of the NATO bloc."[299]

Gromyko offered a lengthy but one-sided analysis of the situation in the two Germanys, winding up with an uncompromising presentation of the Soviet formula for a German settlement—just as though Kozlov had never signaled the relaxation of the Soviet deadline on signature of a German peace treaty: "Where then is the way out of the existing situation and how can the threat of war in connection with the present situation in Germany and in West Berlin, where there still exists the occupation regime which has long since outlived itself, be staved off? There is a way out. The way out is to sign *already in 1961* a German peace treaty and to normalize the situation in West Berlin on

[296]Ibid.
[297]Ibid., p. 626.
[298]*NYT*, Sept. 27, 1961, p. 40.
[299]*Documents on Germany*, p. 813.

its basis by turning it into a demilitarized free city and promptly to call a peace conference for this purpose."[300]

"These," Gromyko added redundantly, "are the well-known proposals of the Soviet Government."

Heartened perhaps by Gromyko's intransigent stand, the official East German newspaper, *Neues Deutschland*, on September 27 warned the Western powers that: "Whoever wants something from the G.D.R., including agreements on access routes to West Berlin, must negotiate with us."[301]

In its report on the President's speech to the United Nations, *Pravda* limited itself in the main to a factual summary, with frequent quotations from Kennedy's actual words.[302] An article in the Soviet army newspaper, however, was highly critical of Kennedy's speech; his statement that war must no longer be a way of settling international disputes and his challenge to the Soviet Union to enter into a "peace race," the article charged, ". . . do not tally at all with what actually goes on in the country [the United States]. At every turn, an objective observer here will encounter a feverish arms race, troop maneuvers and deafening militarist propaganda."[303]

The article portrayed the Pentagon, not President Kennedy, as the actual master of U.S. policy: "The 'ultras' of the Pentagon, disregarding the new winds in international relations, *as well as the new correlation of forces in the international arena*, tirelessly shout about a supposed threat to the Western powers in connection with the proposal to conclude a peace treaty with Germany. Everything indicates that the Pentagon, methodically and in a planned manner, is preparing for a rocket and nuclear war."[304]

The article devoted particular attention to Kennedy's portrayal of South Vietnam as threatened by external aggression, a charge which it dismissed as "an old myth that the reactionary U.S. press has been spreading for many years," and which had "not a grain of truth in it."[305] The true situation in Vietnam, the writers maintained, was that: "The American imperialists in effect have transformed South Vietnam into their own colony. With American help, the butchers are exterminating fighters for the independence and national unity of the country."[306]

*   *   *

On September 29 Pierre Salinger returned from a round of golf in Newport to find a message waiting for him from Georgi Bolshakov in New York. Bol-

---

[300]Ibid., p. 817; emphasis supplied.

[301]*NYT*, Sept. 28, 1961, p. 1.

[302]*Pravda*, Sept. 27, 1961, p. 5; *CDSP*, XIII/39, p. 20.

[303]Lt. Colonel A. Kascheev and Major S. Vladimirov, "What the U.S. President did not mention.—Colonialists 'pacify' South Vietnam," *Krasnaia Zvezda*, Sept. 29, 1961, p. 4; *CDSP*, XIII/43, p. 27.

[304]Ibid.; emphasis supplied.

[305]Ibid., p. 28.

[306]Ibid.

shakov, contacted by phone, ". . . said it was urgent that he see me immediately and he was willing to charter a plane and fly up that evening."[307]

To avoid the complications that the sudden appearance in Newport of a Russian editor might cause, Salinger put off the meeting until his return to New York the following day. There, on the afternoon of the 30th, Bolshakov brought Salinger a twenty-six-page personal letter to Kennedy which Khrushchev had sent from his Black Sea vacation retreat on September 29.[308] While the text of the letter is not available, two of the men who were privileged to read it, Sorensen and Salinger, have provided summaries of it which serve to characterize its content and general tone. According to Salinger, ". . . Khrushchev's first letter was a direct response [to Kennedy] on Laos but sections of it also dealt with the high[ly] volatile situation in Berlin. Khrushchev was now ready to back off from the unconciliatory positions he had taken at Vienna. He saw no reason why negotiations in good faith could not produce settlements in both Southeast Asia and Germany. He was willing, if JFK was, to take another look at positions that had been frozen hard through fifteen years of cold war."[309]

As to the tone of the letter, Salinger reports:

> . . . it was remarkable not only for its contents but for its candor. In contrast to the sterile gobbledegook that passes for high-level diplomatic correspondence, Khrushchev wrote with almost peasant simplicity and directness. He said, in effect, that you and I, Mr. President, are the leaders of two nations that are on a collision course. But because we are reasonable men, we agree that war between us is unthinkable. We have no choice but to put our heads together and find ways to live in peace.[310]

Sorensen's account in general confirms that of Salinger and provides some additional details:

> Khrushchev had planned to write, his first letter said, earlier in the summer after Kennedy's meeting in Washington with his son-in-law and a Soviet press officer. But Kennedy's July [25] speech to the nation on Berlin had been so belligerent in its nature that it led to an exchange of militant actions taken, he said, *under pressure in both countries which must be restrained.* He emphasized almost pridefully the special burdens resting on their shoulders as the leaders of the two most influential and mighty states. It might be useful to have a purely informal, personal correspondence, he wrote, which would *by-pass the foreign office bureaucracies in both countries,* omit the usual propaganda for public consumption and state positions without a backward glance at the press. If Kennedy did not agree, he could consider that this first letter did not exist. The Chairman [Khrushchev] in any event would not refer to the correspondence publicly. The letter, which

[307]Salinger, pp. 197–98.
[308]Sorensen, p. 552.
[309]Salinger, pp. 198–99.
[310]Ibid., p. 199.

had opened "Dear Mr. President," was signed: "Accept my respects, N. Khrushchev, Chairman of the Council of Ministers of the U.S.S.R."[311]

Acutely aware of the opportunities as well as the dangers which this overture presented (Sorensen quotes Bohlen as saying, "The answer to this letter may be the most important letter the President will ever write."[312]), Kennedy took two weeks to draft a reply. In it he adopted the same familiar tone used by Khrushchev. According to Sorensen,

> . . . he opened with a chatty note about his retreat, the children and their cousins, and the opportunity to get a clearer and quieter perspective away from the din of Washington. He welcomed the idea of a private correspondence, though making clear that the Secretary of State and a few others would be privy to it. A personal, informal but meaningful exchange of views in frank, realistic and fundamental terms, he wrote, could usefully supplement the more formal and official channels. Inasmuch as the letters would be private, and could never convert the other, they could also, he added, be free from the polemics of the "Cold War" debate. That debate would, of course, proceed, but their messages would be directed only to each other.[313]

The president "kept his letter cordial and hopeful," Sorensen notes, ". . . with a highly personal tone and repeated first-person references (which were rare in his speeches). He agreed with the Chairman's emphasis on their special obligation to the world to prevent another war. They were not personally responsible for the events at the conclusion of World War II which led to the present situation in Berlin, he added, but they would be held responsible if they were unable to deal peacefully with that situation."[314]

The tone of Kennedy's reply, like that of Khrushchev's letter, was easy and informal: "Having opened with 'Dear Mr. Chairman,' he closed with best wishes from his family to Khrushchev's and the expression of his deep hope that, through this exchange of letters and otherwise, relations between the two nations might be improved, making concrete progress toward the realization of a just and enduring peace. That, he said, was their greatest joint responsibility and their greatest opportunity."[315]

Thus was inaugurated a unique private correspondence between the world's two most powerful political leaders. Normal diplomatic channels were bypassed, Salinger or another trusted aid of Kennedy and Bolshakov continuing to serve as intermediaries. Khrushchev, Salinger writes, ". . . would always initiate the exchange of letters. If I was in Washington, I would have a call from Bolshakov, who would tell me simply that 'there is a matter of

[311]Sorensen, p. 552; emphasis supplied.
[312]Ibid., p. 553.
[313]Ibid.
[314]Ibid.
[315]Ibid.

urgency.' We would agree on a rendezvous, either on a Washington street corner or in a bar. If I wasn't available, the Russian would contact the President's brother, Bob, Ted Sorensen, or another White House staffer. When I was the courier and JFK's answer was ready, I would call Bolshakov and arrange to deliver it to him."[316]

At his meeting with Salinger in New York on September 30, Bolshakov also reported that Khrushchev had approved the proposal for an interview of Kennedy by a prominent Soviet journalist: ". . . either Aleksei Adzhubei or Pavel Satyukov of *Pravda* would fly over for that purpose within the next two months."[317]

Salinger was cautious: "I told Bolshakov we would expect the interview to run in full in the Soviet Union, and after agreement on our part that the Russian translation was accurate. He saw no difficulties."[318]

Taken in conjunction with the first letter to Kennedy from Khrushchev, the latter's approval of the interview plan did indeed mark a turning point in Soviet-American relations. While it was still too early for anyone in a position of responsibility in Washington to breathe easily—there was to be an acute flare-up of the Berlin crisis in mid-October—it was apparent that a definite shift in the Soviet attitude had occurred and that in this sense, Kharlamov's words, "The storm in Berlin is over," had some validity.

In addition to its great substantive value, Khrushchev's confidential letter of September 29 to Kennedy is useful for the clue it provides as to its author's whereabouts at this time, since Soviet communications media provided strikingly spare indications on the subject. The last date in September 1961 recorded in the contemporary Soviet press for Khrushchev's public appearance in Moscow is the 21st, when he accompanied a group of his colleagues to the airport to see off Cuban President Dr. Osvaldo Dorticos.[319] A few days later two new ambassadors arrived in Moscow, but were unable to see Khrushchev: the ambassador from Pakistan on September 24 and the ambassador from Mexico on the 25th.[320]

While Khrushchev's location and activities during the last nine days of September are obscure, those of Kozlov were extensively reported in the Soviet press. On the 22nd he and the other members of the delegation to the North Korean Party Congress returned to Moscow from the Far East and were met at the airport by a group which included two candidate members of the Presidium—Mzhavanadze and Voronov.[321] The next press reference to Kozlov

[316]Salinger, p. 200.

[317]Ibid., p. 199.

[318]Ibid.

[319]*Pravda*, Sept. 22, 1961, p. 1. Other members of the group at the airport were Ignatov, Kosygin, Suslov, and Shelepin. On the same day Brezhnev left Moscow for a state visit to Finland. Ibid.

[320]*Izv.*, Sept. 25 and 26, 1961.

[321]*Pravda*, Sept. 23, 1961, p. 1.

came on the 27th, when he took part in a conference of the Moscow city party committee, along with Kosygin, Kuusinen, Poliansky, Suslov, Mme. Furtseva, Shvernik, and Voronov.[322] On September 29 Kozlov was unusually active: he participated in a conference of the Moscow oblast party committee, along with Ignatov, Kosygin, Kuusinen, Poliansky, Suslov, Mme. Furtseva, Shvernik, Pospelov, and Grishin[323] and on the same day delivered an important speech at a reception at the Chinese People's Republic embassy in honor of the twelfth anniversary of the establishment of the CPR. (We shall consider presently the substance of his speech.)[324] When Brezhnev returned to Moscow on September 30 at the conclusion of his state visit to Finland, Kozlov was on hand to meet him at the airport, along with Ignatov, Kosygin, Kuusinen, Poliansky, Suslov, Mme. Furtseva, Shvernik, Pospelov, and Grishin.[325]

During this same period the only indications provided by the Soviet press of Khrushchev's presence in Moscow were two telegrams: one to Tunisian President Habib Bourguiba, dated "Moscow, the Kremlin, September 25," which was not, however, published until October 5;[326] the other, dated "Moscow, the Kremlin, September 30, 1961," signed by Khrushchev and Brezhnev, conveying congratulations to the Chinese People's Republic on its twelfth anniversary.[327] (On the 25th Khrushchev also sent a long message to Japanese Premier Ikeda, replying to one dated August 26.)[328]

Unlike Khrushchev's telegram of August 16 to Sukarno which we have cited as evidence for his presence in the Kremlin on that date (above, p. 142), the telegrams of September 25 and 30 do not carry the same conviction, primarily because there is no evidence from the sphere of Soviet policy formulation which would serve to confirm that Khrushchev actually was in the Kremlin on those dates. The long delay in publication of the September 25 telegram looks suspicious. Even stranger are the circumstances surrounding the telegram of September 30. If Khrushchev and Brezhnev both signed a telegram of congratulation to the Chinese on that date, why was Khrushchev the only member of the Presidium who failed to go to the airport to meet Brezhnev on his return from Finland, and—more important—why did he boycott the reception at the CPR embassy?

Khrushchev's confidential letter to Kennedy, as we have seen, puts the Soviet Premier at Sochi on September 29. It is reasonable to suppose that the earlier confidential message to the President, sent orally via Kharlamov on the 22nd or 23rd, originated at the same spot. If we throw out the two suspect

[322]*Izv.*, Sept. 28, 1961, p. 1.
[323]*Pravda*, Sept. 30, 1961, p. 1.
[324]Ibid.
[325]*Izv.*, Sept. 30, 1961, p. 1.
[326]*Izv.*, Oct. 5, 1961, p. 1.
[327]*Izv.*, Sept. 30 and Oct. 1, 1961.
[328]*International Affairs* (Moscow: Nov. 1961), pp. 6–8; place of origin not indicated.

telegrams of September 25 and 30 we are left with no evidence for Khrushchev's presence in Moscow between September 21 and October 6, when a message from Khrushchev was sent to Souvanna Phouma, signed and dated from the Kremlin.[329] By October 9, Khrushchev's full operational presence back in the Kremlin was indicated by his reception of three ambassadors, those of Afghanistan and Mexico (who had been waiting since September 25) and the United Arab Republic.[330]

It is noteworthy that in early October Khrushchev wrote a series of short letters to various kolkhoz members, congratulating them on their agricultural achievements.[331] Taken as a group, these letters indicate that Khrushchev's mind in early October was taken up with questions of internal policy.

To sum up, it seems highly probable that Khrushchev was absent from the Kremlin from September 22 to October 6. We know that Kozlov was active during at least part of this period, both in the fields of internal and foreign policy. There is no recorded occasion during this period in which Khrushchev and Kozlov were seen in public together. Was this the result of an agreed division of labor, or did it reflect the operation of some kind of exclusion principle, some mutual antipathy, which led Khrushchev voluntarily to absent himself from the Kremlin during Kozlov's presence there?

The scarcity of any kind of hard evidence for Khrushchev's whereabouts during this period points to the conclusion that his "vacation" this time, unlike that in August, was not one decreed in advance by the Presidium, but resulted from his own decision not to take part in the proceedings of the collective leadership at this time. Yet at the same time he made no important statements and took no actions in the field of foreign policy. The result was a virtual paralysis of decision-making in the collective leadership during a crucial phase of the Berlin crisis. It was clear that Khrushchev was lying low, perhaps preparing himself for some dramatic move at the now imminent Twenty-second Party Congress.

In his speech at the CPR embassy reception on September 29 Kozlov began by paying fulsome tribute to Khrushchev: "Closely united around their own native Communist Party and its Leninist Central Committee headed by the tireless fighter for the happiness of the peoples, the true Leninist N. S. Khrushchev, the Soviet people are performing noteworthy deeds, are accomplishing an upsurge of work in the name of the victory of communism."[332]

In the main body of his speech, however, Kozlov expressed views on Soviet foreign policy and international relations sharply at variance with those known to be held by Khrushchev. "In the settlement of questions of contemporary international relations," said Kozlov, ". . . the role of the Chinese People's

---

[329]*Izv.*, Oct. 7, 1961, p. 1.

[330]Khrushchev, *Kommunizm*, 1: 355.

[331]Khrushchev, *Stroitel'stvo*, 5: 446–47 (letter of Oct. 2), 448–49 (letter of Oct. 5), 450–51 (letter of Oct. 6), 452–57 (letter of Oct. 7), and 458–59 (letter of Oct. 12). Place of origin not indicated.

[332]*Pravda*, Sept. 30, 1961, p. 2.

Republic is great. Its authority has grown immeasurably in the entire world. After all, it is clear that *without the participation of the C.P.R. it is impossible to settle important international problems today.*"[333]

To Khrushchev, by contrast, it was only the United States and the Soviet Union which really counted in world politics; "We are the strongest countries in the world," he had told Sulzberger (above, p. 205), "and if we unite for peace there can be no war." The same thought, which was basic to Khrushchev's world outlook, evidently found expression in his confidential letter to Kennedy on September 29, the same day on which Kozlov affirmed that the CPR's participation in the settlement of "important international problems" was indispensable.

Gromyko's talks with Rusk and Kennedy

On September 14 TASS announced that Soviet Foreign Minister Gromyko, who was to leave shortly for New York to attend the fifteenth session of the U.N. General Assembly, was "ready to enter into a relevant exchange of opinions" with his American counterpart, Secretary of State Dean Rusk (above, p. 216). The idea of a series of exploratory talks at the foreign minister level had been suggested by Kennedy in his reply to the message from the Belgrade conference of nonaligned nations; the TASS announcement of September 14 was made in direct response to this suggestion.

While the British showed alacrity in endorsing the American bid for exploratory talks, the other principal nations in the Western alliance, France and West Germany, greeted the idea with a notable lack of enthusiasm.[334] At a meeting of the four Western foreign ministers in Washington on September 15 16, an agreement was nevertheless reached "that an effort should be made to ascertain if there exists a reasonable basis for negotiations with the Soviet Union."[335]

It was as the authorized representative of the Western alliance, therefore, rather than merely that of the United States alone, that Rusk held his three meetings with Gromyko on September 21, 27, and 30.[336] This fact was explicitly acknowledged by British authorities when Gromyko held a separate discussion with British Foreign Secretary Lord Home on September 28. According to a report in the *New York Times*: "British sources emphasized that Lord Home's talks with Mr. Gromyko were quite separate from those between

[333]Ibid.; emphasis supplied.

[334]On French coolness, see *SIA, 1961*, p. 263, citing a speech by French Foreign Minister Couve de Murville, *Le Monde*, Sept. 19, 1961. The West German position on negotiations throughout the Berlin crisis was close to that of the French.

[335]*Documents on Germany*, p. 801.

[336]For contemporary press reports of these meetings, see (1) *NYT*, Sept. 22, 1961, pp. 1, 3 (Thomas Hamilton); (2) ibid., Sept. 28, 1961, pp. 1, 9 (unsigned); (3) ibid., Oct. 1, 1971, pp. 1, 4 (Thomas Hamilton); and (4) ibid., Oct. 6, 1961, p. 4 (Robert Doty). *SIA, 1961*, p. 266, misdates the third meeting Oct. 3.

Mr. Gromyko and Mr. Rusk, and that the latter constituted the principal Western effort to ascertain Soviet intentions."[337]

Neither Soviet nor U.S. sources have published any official records of the Rusk–Gromyko talks, nor were joint comminiqués issued during the talks or at their conclusion, a fact which in itself testifies to their barrenness. The resulting unsatisfactory situation with respect to historical analysis has been characterized by the *Survey of International Affairs* in words which still (1972) remain true: "The conversations were to be so surrounded by rumours, so bedevilled by *ballons d'essai* and leakages, so confused by reports put out by non-participants in the hope of seeing them denied, that it is almost impossible to give an accurate account of them at this stage."[338]

Despite the paucity of solid information on the talks, however, their general outline is tolerably clear. At a news conference on October 18 Rusk provided some light on the substance, if not the details, of the talks. Noting that in his opening speech to the Twenty-second CPSU Congress Khrushchev had indicated that the Soviets would not insist on the conclusion of a peace treaty with Germany in 1961, Rusk commented, "This confirms publicly what has been said in private talks, including our talks with Mr. Gromyko."[339] In answer to a question at the conference, Rusk said: "I think that we have indicated publicly, as well as privately, that the framework of negotiation to which the Soviets most frequently refer is too narrow, that a discussion about a peace treaty with Germany and a solution of the problem of West Berlin on that basis is too restrictive an agenda for serious discussions of the problems of Germany and Berlin."[340] The *New York Times* had already identified this issue as one of the basic causes of Soviet–U.S. disagreement in its report on the first Rusk–Gromyko meeting.[341]

Sorensen adds a useful detail when he notes that in his talks with Gromyko, Rusk stressed that ". . . the West would not sign an agreement giving concessions [on Berlin] in exchange for nothing more than its present ill-defined rights. 'That,' he said, 'would be buying the same horse twice'."[342]

While the three talks between Rusk and Gromyko produced absolutely no evidence of promising areas for negotiation, they were judged by the Americans to have been sufficiently worth while to warrant a meeting between Gromyko and President Kennedy before the Soviet Foreign Minister returned to Moscow on October 9. The substance of the discussion between Gromyko and Kennedy, which took place in the White House on October 6, is somewhat better known than is the case with regard to the Rusk–Gromyko talks, thanks to the fact that administration spokesmen, including the President himself,

[337]*NYT*, Sept. 29, 1961, p. 4.
[338]*SIA, 1961*, p. 264.
[339]*DSB*, 45 (1961): 746.
[340]Ibid., p. 748.
[341]*NYT*, Sept. 24, 1961, section 4, p. 1.
[342]Sorensen, p. 599.

provided the press with reliable data on it.[343] (That the press reports on the whole range of talks with Gromyko were substantially accurate was testified to by Kennedy in his press conference on October 11, when he stated that "a good deal of information on the talks has already been printed in the press," and characterized the available information on them as "quite lucid and only slightly inaccurate.")[344]

Improving on the technique employed by Khrushchev at the Vienna meeting, Gromyko not only came to the White House prepared with a lengthy and dogmatic position paper but took up an entire hour—half of the time available for the meeting—to read it and have it translated.[345] This left little scope for any genuine exchange of opinions on even an exploratory basis, and the meeting was no less barren than its predecessors. Kennedy summed up the situation in a homely simile predestined for inclusion in most historical accounts of the meeting: "You've offered to trade us an apple for an orchard," he said. "We don't do that in this country." The remark evidently pleased him, for he later repeated it to ". . . close associates . . . and said it seemed to him to summarize the present state of diplomacy over Berlin and Germany."[346]

Bearing in mind the confidential message from Khrushchev for which Sulzberger had served as courier, Kennedy linked a Soviet–U.S. agreement on Laos with the chances for a settlement in Berlin:

> There was considerable discussion, too, of Laos and again the President conveyed to Premier Khrushchev his anxiety over developments there.
> Mr. Kennedy made it quite plain that he considered the attempt to pacify and neutralize the Southeast Asian kingdom to be very important. . . .
> It would be extremely helpful, Mr. Kennedy is reported to have declared, if the Soviet Union and the United States reach an equitable solution of the Laotian problem and in this way demonstrate their ability to negotiate in good faith. As in his United Nations speech two weeks ago, the President implied that a settlement in Southeast Asia was a kind of "test" of the two sides' good faith that had an important bearing on the German problem as well.[347]

To this Gromyko replied as graciously as his dour nature permitted, that "Moscow, too, was in favor of solving the Laos problem."

On the crucial problem of Germany and Berlin, however, Gromyko showed absolutely no willingness to budge. Faced with the blank wall of Gromyko's unresponsiveness, Kennedy strove to convey two points in particular: first, that the Western powers would not agree to negotiate on Berlin under the

---

[343]See especially two reports by Max Frankel, *NYT*, Oct. 7, 1961, pp. 1, 2, and Oct. 8, 1961, pp. 1, 3.

[344]*JFK, 1961*, pp. 659–60.

[345]*NYT*, Oct. 8, 1961, p. 1.

[346]Max Frankel, *NYT*, Oct. 7, 1961, p. 3. Both Sorensen, p. 599, and Sidey, p. 261, quote Kennedy's remark.

[347]Max Frankel, *NYT*, Oct. 7, 1961, p. 1.

threat of a Soviet deadline for conclusion of a German peace treaty, and second, that Khrushchev "had embarked on a collision course in Berlin and would have to reverse engines to avoid disaster."[348]

The absence of reliable documentary evidence on Gromyko's talks with Rusk and Kennedy is made less critical for the historian by the simple and obvious fact that the talks *did* serve their primary purpose: to ascertain whether in fact any realistic basis existed for Soviet–Western negotiations on Berlin and Germany. The West, despite French foot-dragging, West German nervousness, and differences of opinion in the U.S. administration, was ready for serious negotiations; the Soviet Union was not. This fact, which stands out as the principal result of the talks, throws a revealing light on Soviet policy throughout the Berlin crisis of 1961. The will to negotiate had never been present on the Soviet side. There was only one Soviet position on Berlin, and it never varied, from the onset of the crisis to its muffled conclusion. Not negotiations but Western capitulation was the goal of the Soviet campaign in Berlin, and when it became clear to the Soviet leadership that the West could not be bluffed or intimidated, they simply called the campaign off, keeping their demands in readiness for revival at some later time.

On his way home from Washington, Gromyko stopped off in England, where he had a brief conversation with Prime Minister Macmillan. The result was simply to underline the result of Gromyko's talks in the United States: according to the *New York Times'* London correspondent, Gromyko "reiterated the standard Soviet position on Berlin" in a way which led Macmillan, following the talk, to remark that he did not believe that "any firm basis" for negotiations had emerged from the discussions between Gromyko and Western leaders.[349] From London, Gromyko flew on to Moscow to report to the Soviet leadership, accompanied by his deputy, Vladimir S. Semyonov, a specialist on German affairs who had been present at the talks with Rusk and Kennedy.[350]

Timed to coincide with Gromyko's return to the Soviet capital were a number of other significant arrivals: from East Germany there came Marshal Ivan S. Konev, commander-in-chief of Soviet troops in East Germany, and Mikhail G. Pervukhin, Soviet ambassador to the GDR. Concerning these events, *New York Times* Moscow correspondent Seymour Topping reported that observers there believed that ". . . Premier Khrushchev had undertaken a major review of the Berlin crisis and recent efforts to find a basis for negotiations with the Western powers."[351] Strengthening this belief, Topping reported, was the fact that ". . . the Soviet press and radio displayed reluctance to comment on the exchanges between the Soviet Union and the Western powers on Berlin and

[348]Ibid.

[349]Drew Middleton, *NYT*, Oct. 11, 1961, p. 1.

[350]For Semyonov's presence, see *NYT*, Sept. 22, 1961, p. 3, and Oct. 7, 1961, p. 2. Soviet Ambassador Mikhail Menshikov was also present at the Kennedy–Gromyko talk, as were Rusk and State Department Soviet specialist Foy Koyler (ibid.).

[351]*NYT*, Oct. 13, 1961, p. 9.

Germany. This is the usual indication here that a policy review is under way."[352]

The Soviets drop their demand for a three-man secretary-generalship in the United Nations

In sharp contrast to the Soviets' intransigence on Berlin was their unexpected reasonableness in another area of acute international tension—the search for a successor to Dag Hammarskjöld as secretary-general of the United Nations. Ever since Khrushchev in September 1960 had introduced the Soviet proposal for a *troika* to replace the single secretary-general, the Soviets had trumpeted this demand with all the fanfare appropriate to a major policy objective.

The Kennedy administration from the outset had promptly and vigorously taken up the cudgels in defense of the office of the secretary-general as defined in the U.N. Charter and as it was currently being exercised by Hammarskjöld. When Khrushchev, at a luncheon honoring Kwame Nkrumah on July 11, bellicosely backed up his demand for a *troika* with a blunt assertion of Soviet power, Rusk issued a prompt rejoinder warning that the United States would use its veto in the Security Council to block any attempt to carry out the Soviet demand.

During the summer and early autumn of 1961, Soviet scholars and journalists kept up a steady fire of criticism, both of Hammarskjöld himself and of the existing structure of the office he held.[353]

The Soviet campaign for a restructuring of the office of secretary-general was being furthered in the Soviet press at the very moment when word of Hammarskjöld's death reached Moscow (above, p. 233). At the United Nations itself, the report set off an impromptu Soviet proposal for ". . . rotating the Secretaryship among three under-secretaries representing the major blocs (Ralph J. Bunche, Georgi Arkadiev, and Chakravarthi Naramsimhan). Jointly the three would form a 'coordinating committee,' which would constitute a step in the direction of the *troika*. The proposal could presumably be carried out immediately—a clear advantage over the full Soviet reorganization proposals, which required Charter amendment."[354] But this attempt to achieve a coup while the delegates at the United Nations were still stunned and bewildered by the news of Hammarskjöld's death was unsuccessful; before the Soviet proposal could be debated, an informal conference of medium-sized and small noncommunist states had reached agreement that a single successor to Hammarskjöld should be elected and that there should be no deviation from

[352]Ibid.

[353]See, for example, E. Korovin, "Time for reform," *New Times*, no. 39, Sept. 27, 1961, pp. 7–8, and A. Alexeyev, "Once more about the structure of the U.N. executive agencies," *International Affairs* 8 (Moscow, 1961): 35–40.

[354]Alexander Dallin, *The Soviet Union at the United Nations* (New York: Praeger, 1962), p. 174 (hereinafter cited as Dallin).

the established procedure of having the Security Council recommend the appointment of a new secretary-general to the General Assembly.[355]

In Washington, the news of Hammarskjöld's death clinched Kennedy's decision to address the General Assembly and reaffirm U.S. support for the integrity of the United Nations against the Soviet challenge (above, p. 233). It was entirely appropriate, therefore, that in his September 25 speech to the General Assembly Kennedy included a passage uncompromisingly rejecting the *troika* proposal: "However difficult it may be to fill Mr. Hammarskjöld's place, it can better be filled by one man rather than by three. Even the three horses of the Troika did not have three drivers, all going in different directions. They had only one—and so must the United Nations executive. To install a triumvirate, or any panel, or any rotating authority, in the United Nations administrative offices would replace order with anarchy, action with paralysis, confidence with confusion."[356]

What made the President's stand on this issue appealing to the great majority of the members of the body he was addressing was that it was based not merely on arguments of administrative convenience or efficiency, or that it represented the views of one of the great powers. Kennedy skillfully and effectively portrayed preservation of the integrity of the office of secretary-general as a matter of vital concern to *all* members of the United Nations, particularly the small and weak: "The Secretary General, in a very real sense, is the servant of the General Assembly. Diminish his authority and you diminish the authority of the only body where all nations, regardless of power, are equal and sovereign. Until all the powerful are just, the weak will be secure only in the strength of this Assembly."[357]

Kennedy's stand was strengthened, moreover, by the fact that it was not motivated simply by the blind desire to oppose anything the Soviets proposed. Taking implicit account of the Soviet demand for larger representation in the staffing of U.N. agencies, and recognizing "the enormous change in membership" which had taken place in the United Nations since its founding, Kennedy pledged U.S. support for "any effort for the prompt review and revision of the composition of United Nations bodies."[358]

To break up the top executive position of the United Nations, he warned, however: "—to give this organization three drivers—to permit each great power to decide its own case, would entrench the Cold War in the headquarters of peace. Whatever advantages such a plan may hold out to my own country, as one of the great powers, we reject it. For we far prefer world law, in the age of self-determination, to world war, in the age of mass extermination."[359]

When Gromyko followed the President to the speaker's stand on the following day, he proved to be unexpectedly conciliatory on the *troika* issue.

[355]Ibid.
[356]*JFK, 1961*, p. 619.
[357]Ibid.
[358]Ibid.
[359]Ibid., pp. 619–20.

Without specifically identifying the Soviet proposal he reaffirmed it in general terms: "We stand for the immediate solution of the administration of the United Nations Secretariat on a basis corresponding to the actual situation in the world."[360] When he came down to specific details, however, Gromyko dropped the *troika* demand: "We call upon the States, Members of the United Nations, to solve this problem by agreement. *Let it be a provisional solution for the beginning* but one which, instead of deepening the rift between the States, will provide a still firmer basis for their cooperation within the framework of the United Nations."[361]

There followed a complex and unpublicized series of negotiations at U.N. headquarters in which U.S. Ambassador to the United Nations Adlai Stevenson played a major role, along with his Soviet counterpart, V. A. Zorin.[362]

A major factor in leading the Soviets to abandon, at least temporarily, their campaign for a three-man secretaryship was the clear evidence that the overwhelming majority of the members of the United Nations was firmly opposed to any attempt to do away with the office of secretary-general in its existing form. (According to the *Survey of International Affairs*, the Soviets carried out a "private 'opinion poll' of all 90 non-communist delegations at the U.N." on the *troika* proposal toward the end of September, which convinced them that the idea enjoyed no popularity in the General Assembly.)[363]

By the beginning of October the Soviets were preparing formally to abandon the *troika* campaign. A statement submitted by the Soviet delegation in the General Assembly on October 1 accepted the principle of a provisional one-man appointment to the office of secretary-general, and called only for the appointment of three deputies who would serve in an advisory capacity and who would be expected to "strive for mutual agreement on the basic questions" and "to act in the spirit of concord."[364]

Despite the accumulating evidence that the Soviets were by now in full retreat on their *troika* demand, the President considered it to be one of the issues likely to be taken up by Gromyko in their talk scheduled for October 6, and prepared himself appropriately. According to a circumstantial and probably accurate account of the talk by *Time* correspondent Hugh Sidey, the *troika* proposal was in fact taken up toward the end of the two-hour meeting. When Gromyko raised the issue, ". . . the President casually picked up a book from a nearby table, thumbed through it until he found the place he wanted. Then he silently handed it to Gromyko to read."[365]

The passage to which Kennedy directed Gromyko's attention was a fable by the Russian poet Ivan Krylov, "The Swan, the Pike, and the Crayfish,"

---

[360]*Documents on Germany*, p. 823.

[361]Ibid., pp. 822–23; emphasis supplied.

[362]The course of the negotiations from the Soviet standpoint is explored in Dallin, pp. 174–75. For an analysis setting developments in a broader context, see *SIA, 1961*, pp. 285–95.

[363]Ibid., p. 293.

[364]Ibid.; Dallin, p. 175; text of Soviet statement, *DIA, 1961*, pp. 510–11.

[365]Sidey, p. 262.

which drew the obvious moral from the unsuccessful efforts of the ill-assorted trio to draw a cart. Kennedy's use of the fable was an effective move, all the more so since the text chosen was that of a Russian classic. But there is no reason to believe that it served to sway either Gromyko or Soviet policy in general; the direction of Soviet policy toward a compromise solution of the question was already set before the October 6 meeting. (By contrast, a *New York Times* dispatch from U.N. headquarters, published on October 8, quoted a "reliable source" as stating that Gromyko had not brought up the *troika* proposal at his meeting with Kennedy, to the President's surprise, and that "When he did not do so, the President did not mention it either.")

The way in which the President came to use Krylov's fable to make his point was disclosed some nine years later.[366] The fable was called to his attention by Walter Bestermann, a legislative staff assistant to the House Judiciary Committee, a few days after Kennedy's address to the United Nations (above, p. 243), in which he had made plain his opposition to the *troika* proposal. Recognizing the fable's aptness to the controversy, and delighted to be able to use a Russian classic to prove his point, Kennedy had several deluxe reproductions of the volume of Krylov's fables which Bestermann had sent him printed on parchment for use in his talk with Gromyko. A few days after the talk he sent Bestermann one of the copies inscribed, "For Walter Bestermann—this won the argument—with thanks and best wishes—John F. Kennedy. October 12, 1961."

According to Norman Cousins, the decisive shift in the Soviet attitude came after this incident: "Several days later, the President received a reply [from the Soviets]. The Soviet Union would withdraw its opposition to the election of a single successor to Dag Hammarskjöld."[367]

As we have seen, however, the Soviet decision to abandon, at least temporarily, the campaign for a three-man secretary generalship had already been formed before October 6 (Gromyko's September 26 speech and the agreement on a single secretary-general on October 1 are clear evidence to that effect). The major value of the incident for the historian, therefore, is the light it casts on Kennedy's own perception of the Soviet position.

*   *   *

Step by step the difficult and delicate negotiations at the United Nations proceeded, centering around such issues as whether or not the newly appointed acting secretary-general should be required to make a declaration of intent (proposed by Zorin on October 13),[368] or the exact relationship between the secretary-general and his three assistants. Zorin, also on the 13th, acknowledged the right of the secretary-general to act on his own responsibility, even in cases where he disagreed with one or more of his assistants.[369]

[366]N. C. (Norman Cousins), "President Kennedy and the Russian Fable," *Saturday Review*, Jan. 9, 1971, pp. 20–21.

[367]Ibid., p. 20.

[368]*SIA, 1961*, p. 294.

[369]Ibid.; Sam Brewer, *NYT*, Oct. 14, 1961, p. 1.

October 13, the day which saw this important concession by the Soviets, was also marked, however, by a sudden flurry of irritation on their part directed against Dr. Andrew Cordier, principal adviser to Dag Hammarskjöld in the Secretariat and a particular *bête noire* of the Soviets ever since his role in the events surrounding the fall of Lumumba in September 1960. Cordier, the Soviet delegate now charged, had carried out a "seizure of power" in the Secretariat which made him its real though illegitimate master.[370] The Secretariat promptly countered Zorin's charge with a strong statement by the under-secretaries, ". . . indicating that 'there has been no change whatsoever in the responsibilities of each of the under-secretaries,' and that even their meetings had been held without a chairman."[371]

Aside from this brief flare-up, progress toward a resolution of the crisis proceeded steadily. Khrushchev himself, the originator of the *troika* proposal, mentioned it in only the most muted form in his opening speech to the Twenty-second Party Congress on October 17, calling merely for "an essential improvement in the mechanism of the United Nations." The final hurdles were cleared on October 23 when compromise agreements were reached on the problem of the relationship between the acting secretary-general and his deputies and on the timing of a declaration of intent by the nominee. By this time, Burma's principal U.N. delegate, Dr. U Thant, had emerged as the man on whom all interested parties could most easily agree.[372]

The final formalities ending the crisis took place on November 3. In the morning the Security Council formally nominated U Thant for the post of acting secretary-general, and in the afternoon he was elected by a unanimous vote in the General Assembly. Showing a sound political instinct, U Thant promptly named as his principal advisers representatives of the two superpowers—Ralph Bunche of the United States and Georgi Arkadiev of the USSR.[373]

In a statement congratulating the new Acting Secretary-General, Ambassador Zorin maintained the line which had characterized Soviet policy on this issue ever since Gromyko's speech to the General Assembly on September 26: insistence on the basic correctness of the Soviet demand for an eventual restructuring of the office of secretary-general, combined with a willingness to accept "a temporary solution to this problem in view . . . of the necessity of taking speedier action here and now to ensure that the work of the Secretariat is effectively directed. . . ."[374]

How is Soviet policy in the U.N. crisis of the autumn of 1961 to be evaluated? Alexander Dallin provides a balanced judgment which emphasizes both the immediate losses and the long-term gains of the Soviets: "The ap-

[370]*SIA, 1961*, p. 294.

[371]Dallin, p. 177.

[372]*SIA, 1961*, p. 294.

[373]Ibid.

[374]Text of Zorin's statement in *AFP, 1961*, pp. 85–86, citing U.N. Document A/PV 1046, pp. 552–53. For a Soviet comment on U Thant's election, which amplifies Zorin's statement, see Ye. Litoshkov and B. Strelnikov, "Good Luck," *Pravda*, Nov. 5, 1961, p. 4; *CDSP* XIII/44, p. 24.

pointment [of U Thant] marked a triple Soviet failure: Instead of a *troika*, a single individual was named; he was not required to make any prior commitments to the states sponsoring him; his authority was not circumscribed either by agreement or by the impinging prerogatives of political deputies."[375]

Viewed in long-term perspective, however, the Soviet attack on Hammarskjöld and on the office of secretary-general has paid handsome dividends:

> In agreeing to the election of U Thant, the Soviet Union acknowledged its failure to achieve its expressed aim—the tripartite reorganization of the Secretariat. Yet it had accomplished several things. The U.N.'s new official was bound to have less authority than his predecessor had built up over the course of years. The temporary tenure of U Thant added to the precariousness of his position in office. After the object lessons of Trygve Lie and Dag Hammarskjöld, any Secretary-General was bound to give more weight to the attitudes of the Great Powers—especially the U.S.S.R.—or else invite dismissal. Under the new dispensation there was likely to be a strong temptation for the Secretariat to equate neutrality with passivity—all of which was perfectly all right with the U.S.S.R.[376]

The *Survey of International Affairs* puts matters in a broader context, while essentially agreeing with Dallin's evaluation:

> The end of the year thus saw the main Soviet effort to capture the U.N. Secretariat and prevent any future independent action on its part formally and directly defeated. The battle had, however, left its scars on the Secretariat, and it cannot be said that the "neutral" members of the U.N. had either accepted or necessarily understood the development of the Secretariat as its architect, Mr. Hammarskjöld, had envisaged it. His death represented a major set-back to the cause of the development of the United Nations.[377]

Finally, how is Soviet policy in the U.N. crisis of autumn 1961 to be explained in terms of the dynamics of the Soviet political process? Why, after making the *troika* proposal a major issue for an entire year, did the Soviets tamely drop it just when the opportunity to press it most vigorously presented itself? Why, at a time (October 13) when they were already well launched on the course of compromise and concessions, did the Soviets show a sudden hardening which, however, was not permitted seriously to impede progress toward an agreed solution of the crisis?

We must not expect, of course, to find explicit answers to these or similar questions on the pages of Soviet publications or in the public statements of Soviet leaders. But we can assemble some indirect evidence from which reasonable answers can be deduced.

A major clue is the fact that the Soviet demand for a three-man secretary-generalship was an improvisation devised by Khrushchev to cover up an em-

[375]Dallin, p. 176.
[376]Ibid., pp. 178–79.
[377]*SIA, 1961*, p. 295.

barrassing setback in Soviet foreign policy, the September 1960 fiasco in the Congo. The decision to launch the demand for a *troika* was taken by Khrushchev while on the high seas en route to New York, and it therefore did not have the sanction of the collective leadership as a whole. Khrushchev thus retained control of the issue in a way which was not true of those questions on which the Presidium reached an agreed position after debate.

This circumstance helps to explain why the Soviet delegation at the United Nations was in a position to offer an impromptu "solution" to the problem created by the death of Dag Hammarskjöld as early as September 18 (above, p. 259); in the absence of any standing instructions from the Presidium on this issue, the Soviet delegation enjoyed a certain latitude for maneuvering within the general parameters of Soviet policy—with which it was, of course, adequately acquainted.

We have already presented evidence for the conclusion that no meeting of the Presidium could have taken place between September 21 (the last day of Khrushchev's proven presence in Moscow) and October 6 (the first certain day of his return). This was precisely the period, however, when the main lines of Soviet policy on the U.N. structural crisis were being worked out. The inescapable conclusion is that the policy of back-tracking on the *troika* demand represented a personal decision on the part of Khrushchev rather than one agreed to by the collective leadership. This conclusion is strengthened by our earlier conclusion that the demand for a *troika* in its inception represented a personal initiative on the part of Khrushchev. Having begun it himself he was in an excellent position to call it off when it suited him to do so.

What were the reasons which led Khrushchev to decide to call off the *troika* demand in the autumn of 1961? The answer lies in the field of Soviet internal politics as much as in the field of international relations.[378] In September–October 1961, Khrushchev was embroiled in a sharp conflict with the hardliners in the collective leadership, who had shown that they were willing to exacerbate Soviet relations with the West up to the brink of war, if need be, in the hope of forcing a showdown over Berlin. Convinced that this line carried the very real danger of an all-out war between the great powers, Khrushchev had already begun to search for a way out of the crisis. To press the *troika* demand at this point, however, and thereby to keep international tension at fever pitch, would have been to play into the hands of his internal opponents.

If the general trend in Soviet policy toward a compromise settlement of the U.N. structural problem can be explained in these terms, how are we to account for the brief flare-up of Soviet intransigence on October 13? For an answer to that question we must turn to a consideration of Soviet internal politics during this period. Khrushchev's domestic foes, it will be seen, had achieved a significant advantage over him just at the moment when the Soviet stance at the United Nations manifested its sudden stiffening.

---

[378]For an analysis of the considerations which made continuation of the *troika* campaign appear unadvisable to the Soviets, see Dallin, p. 176.

The pattern of Soviet politics from late August
to early October 1961

We are now in a position to undertake an analysis of the pattern of Soviet politics during the period of the first climax in the Berlin crisis of 1961. One thing is clear at the outset: what was involved was not a single meeting of the Presidium at which a sudden, dramatic shift in policy was decided on, but at the very least several meetings at which a new policy was hammered out by a process of successive modifications. It is likewise clear that the final outcome of the process was not a clearcut policy line on which all members of the collective leadership agreed, but a stand-off in which conflicting views were temporarily suspended rather than being reconciled or settled by the unambiguous victory of one policy over another.

September 4 is the first date for which we can postulate with some confidence a meeting of the Presidium. At that point two important questions required the attention of the collective leadership: first, the Kennedy–Macmillan proposal of September 3 for a limited test ban agreement, and second, Khrushchev's plan to grant an interview to the American journalist, C. L. Sulzberger. (Sulzberger had arrived in Moscow on the 3rd.)

In his interview with Sulzberger on September 5, Khrushchev said, "We are preparing an answer [to the Kennedy–Macmillan proposal] and will send it in several days" (above, p. 194), thereby providing a solid indication that the Presidium had already met to consider the proposal. Moreover, Khrushchev in effect divulged the actual decision taken—to reject the proposal—and even provided an advance indication of the arguments which would be employed to justify the rejection (above, p. 195).

That the Presidium concerned itself in advance with the Sulzberger interview and reached certain decisions concerning its form and content is indicated by the interview itself. The careful choice of a limited number of questions out of the sixty originally submitted by Sulzberger is evidence of a preceding high-level policy decision, as is the obviously deliberate exclusion of any questions concerning China—an exclusion which Khrushchev adroitly evaded and in effect nullified by conveying to Sulzberger the important information that no Soviet nuclear weapons or long-range missiles were stationed in the CPR (above, p. 203).

The meticulous care displayed in the preparation of the Russian versions of the question-and-answer text and Sulzberger's dispatch likewise points to the concern of the Presidium with the interview. Recalling the three-part division of the interview (above, p. 201), we can recognize the skill with which Khrushchev maneuvered within the restrictions imposed on him by the Presidium in order to state some of the personal views for which he would have been unable to obtain the sanction of his colleagues. The question-and-answer text can be recognized as that part of the interview which had the explicit advance sanction of the Presidium and which formed the center of its attention. The tendentious paragraph added to its conclusion in the *Pravda* version, which shifted its emphasis from the prospect of peace to the threat of war (above, p. 200), represented the views of those members of the Presidium who disagreed with and distrusted Khrushchev's desire for better relations with the United States.

In the question-and-answer text Khrushchev was operating under tight restrictions, and even in the more relaxed first portion of Sulzberger's dispatch he was still bound to some extent by the agreed twenty-one questions. Only in the second, more personal, "franker" part of the interview did he feel free to state his own personal views—on Soviet nuclear testing, on the build-up of the Soviet armed forces, on Laos, and on the prospects for a visit by Kennedy to the Soviet Union.

Close study of the question-and-answer text enables us to postulate one of the specific points decided on by the Presidium at its September 4 meeting. It will be recalled that in one of his replies to Sulzberger Khrushchev defined Yugoslavia as a "socialist" country and indicated that the Soviet Union would come to its defense if it were attacked by the West, if Yugoslavia requested it to do so (above, p. 199). Immediately after making this pledge to Yugoslavia, Khrushchev extended a similar pledge to Cuba, even though he stopped short of characterizing Cuba as a "socialist" nation. The symmetrical, complementary nature of these two pledges strongly suggests that they reflect a bargain struck in the Presidium: in return for the inclusion of Yugoslavia in the "socialist camp" and the indirect pledge of Soviet military aid to it (a score for Khrushchev), a similar pledge was extended to Cuba (a point for Kozlov). The background and implications of the pledge to Cuba merit further consideration in their own right.

On the morning of September 5, shortly before the interview with Sulzberger, Khrushchev held a "cordial" conversation with Blas Roca, first secretary of the Cuban Communist party, in which the two ". . . exchanged opinions on international problems, and also on other questions of interest to the Soviet Union and the Republic of Cuba."[379]

In his interview with Sulzberger, Khrushchev hinted at the possibility that Soviet long-range missiles with nuclear warheads might be stationed now or at some future time in East Germany (above, p. 203), and we have suggested that the purpose of such a move could only have been to put pressure on nations within the Western alliance in order to facilitate a settlement of the Berlin problem on Soviet terms.

On September 8 it was reported from Havana that the Castro regime had executed five members of the invasion force which had been defeated at the

[379]Radio Moscow, Sept. 5, 1961; *Pravda*, Sept. 6, 1961, p. 1. Technically speaking, Blas Roca at this point was simply "one of the Cuban revolutionary leaders," the Cuban communist party having been officially absorbed into the Integrated Revolutionary Organization (ORI) which was set up in July 1961. Also present at the discussion on Sept. 5 were Kosygin, Suslov, and Boris Ponomarev.

Bay of Pigs in April 1961.[380] In March 1962 the Castro regime put on trial the remaining survivors of the invasion force.[381] President Kennedy, who felt a personal sense of responsibility for the fate of the men who had fought against Castro at the Bay of Pigs, at some point not far from Havana's announcement of the March 1962 trial, let Castro know through diplomatic channels that if the death penalty were imposed on the prisoners "it would touch off such a storm of protest in the United States that the President would be forced to take drastic new action against Cuba."[382]

This veiled but unmistakable threat of possible U.S. military action against Cuba came at just about the point when the Soviet leadership is believed to have been considering the fateful decision to move long-range missiles into Cuba.[383]

Thus the general outlines of Soviet strategy in the Cuban missile adventure of 1962 were dimly visible as early as September 1961, and some of the principal elements which would enter into that drama had already manifested themselves.

*   *   *

The September 4 meeting of the Presidium led to no significant modifications of Soviet policy toward Berlin and in its decision to reject the Kennedy–Macmillan test ban proposal represented a continuation of the hard line toward the West. A few days later, however, Khrushchev was able to win a major victory in the Presidium which led to the most substantial modifications in the Soviet foreign policy line since mid-February 1961. There are a number of converging lines of evidence which indicate that a major decision on foreign policy was taken by the Presidium at some time on September 6—probably during the evening.

The most obvious indication of the shift comes from Sulzberger's report of the message he received from Khrushchev on the morning of September 7, just as he was preparing to send off his report of the interview. Khrushchev, it will be recalled, requested two changes in the report: first, that a statement be added expressing his willingness to meet with Kennedy and second, that his comment on the scheduled explosion of a 100-megaton bomb be amended to refer only to the testing of the explosive device for the bomb, not to the bomb itself (above, p. 196). These changes, it is clear, represented concessions which Khrushchev had won from his colleagues. What clinches the case for a victory by Khrushchev, however, is the unambiguous evidence that Kozlov suffered a defeat. In his Pyongyang speech on September 12 Kozlov was forced to announce the lifting of the 1961 deadline on conclusion of a peace treaty with

---

[380]Richard Eder, *NYT*, Sept. 9, 1961, p. 7.

[381]Haynes Johnson et al., *The Bay of Pigs: The Leaders' Story of Brigade 2506* (New York: Norton, 1964), p. 265.

[382]Ibid., p. 275.

[383]Tatu, p. 233, dates the decision "probably in April 1962."

Germany, thereby signaling the end of the Soviet campaign on Berlin for 1961. In doing so, Kozlov was being required to play the classic role of a member of the collective leadership whose policy has been voted down by his colleagues—to preserve at least the appearance, if not the substance, of unity by himself announcing the policy measure which he had unsuccessfully opposed.

The first sign that Kozlov was slated to go to North Korea was his presence at the luncheon given by the North Korean Embassy on September 7 (above, p. 213). Since some advance coordination with the North Korean communists must have preceded this affair, we can be fairly certain that the decision to send Kozlov to Pyongyang must have been reached at the latest by the evening of the 6th.

What part did the message brought to Khrushchev by Nehru from the Belgrade conference play in the Presidium decision to lift the deadline on signing a peace treaty with Germany? Nehru had dinner at the Kremlin on the evening of September 6 and delivered his message to Khrushchev on that occasion, and Sulzberger was inclined to attribute the shift in Soviet policy (which he assumed to be a shift in Khrushchev's personal views) to Nehru's influence.[384]

At most, however, Nehru's message could only have played the role of a catalyst in the process of change in Soviet policy which was already under way. Khrushchev may well have used the prestige of Nehru and his recognized high standing in world public opinion as an additional argument with his colleagues for a policy change which they already had under debate, but it is highly unlikely that Nehru, alone, or the message he brought from Belgrade, really caused the change. The reasons for this conclusion are, first, that the decisions reached went far beyond the policy modification requested by the Belgrade conference—an indication of willingness on the part of the Soviets to negotiate the Berlin problem with the United States—and second, that in his personal appeal to Khrushchev for a halt in the Soviet nuclear test series, Nehru got nowhere.[385]

The core of the Presidium decisions of September 6 was the lifting of the 1961 deadline for signing a peace treaty with Germany. Working backward, we can reconstruct to some extent the context within which this decision was taken and suggest some of the reasons which lay behind it.

The basic prerequisite for the decision was the fact that the conditions imposed on Khrushchev at the February session of the Presidium had been

[384]*NYT*, Sept. 11, 1961, p. 26: "The Thursday changes were changes in Mr. Khrushchev's own attitude . . . I assume Mr. Nehru's arguments induced Mr. Khrushchev to soften his stand."

[385]See the report of Nehru's speech on arriving in Moscow, in which he criticized the Soviet tests as a peril to world health (*SIA, 1961*, p. 385) and his later characterization of the tests as "very harmful–a disastrous thing" (ibid., p. 441). See also the report of his conference with Khrushchev on Sept. 7 from which he emerged gloomy, saying, "Once again the foul winds of war are blowing. There are atomic tests and the world grows fearful." *NYT*, Sept. 8, 1961, p. 1.

fulfilled. While the West had not been forced to yield its position in West Berlin (the maximum objective of the Berlin campaign), the immediate threat to the stability of the East German regime had been removed by the construction of the Berlin Wall (the minimum objective). Furthermore, the optional corollary to this adoption of the minimum objective—Soviet resumption of nuclear testing—had been implemented. Clearly the majority in the Presidium had no desire to go back on this decision, either in answer to the Kennedy–Macmillan test ban proposal or in response to Nehru's anguished plea. The most Khrushchev was able to obtain from his colleagues was the concession that the 100-megaton bomb would not actually be exploded as the climax of the series.

Another necessary condition for the decision on lifting the deadline on a German peace treaty was the evidence that the West clearly was not preparing for an aggressive war against the Soviet Union, but on the contrary, particularly in the statements and policies of President Kennedy, was steadfastly showing its readiness to solve the Berlin crisis by negotiation.

The conditions imposed on Kozlov, the loser in the September 6 Presidium debate, carried unmistakably punitive implications. Not merely was he required to announce the shift of Soviet policy on Berlin, but he was instructed to do so in a way and at a place which removed him completely from Moscow for two weeks—from his departure on September 8 to his return on the 22nd. His colleagues thus saw to it that his stridently anti-Western and pro-Chinese voice would be temporarily muted just as the Berlin Crisis seemed to be approaching its climax.

Kozlov's September 12 announcement of the shift in Soviet policy was not, however, intended to be recognized by the West as an "olive branch" (to use the expression of the *Survey of International Affairs*); its real function was to serve as a coded indication of a Soviet policy decision designed primarily for the instruction of communists in the Soviet party and abroad. Proof of this assertion lies in the well-coordinated and carefully planned series of "preparedness" articles by service chiefs, the first of which (Biriuzov's) was published in the Soviet press on the same day as Kozlov's Pyongyang speech. Thanks to the general failure of Western observers to understand the nature of the Soviet political process at this point, this piece of camouflage served its purpose nearly perfectly: Kozlov's statement on a German peace treaty was almost totally ignored in the West, while the "preparedness" series of articles received wide attention. The "preparedness" articles, together with various bellicose Soviet actions in the period immediately following Kozlov's Pyongyang speech, were thus intended to mask what might otherwise have been recognized in the West as a sign that the Soviets had decided to beat a retreat in their Berlin campaign.

The evident animus against Kozlov which the implementation of the September 6 decision indicated provides a basis for hazarding a guess as to another aspect of the motivation behind the decision, as well as some indication of the actual line-up of votes in the Presidium. The most interesting figure in this connection is Mikhail Suslov, who shared some policy views with Kozlov—notably in regard to internal resource allocation—but who is known to have differed with him on the question of the policy to be adopted toward the Chinese communists.

By informing the Chinese in advance of the Soviet intention to resume nuclear testing and by shaping the announcement of the decision in such a way as to provide justification for eventual Chinese development of the bomb (above, p. 162), Kozlov had caused Soviet foreign policy to lurch sharply in the direction of Peking. If, as seems probable, Suslov was unwilling to support him in this risky venture, the emergence of an anti-Kozlov majority at the September 6 Presidium meeting would be readily explainable.

In this connection it is suggestive that Soviet press reports of early September 1961 portray Suslov as frequently appearing in public in company with Khrushchev (Kozlov, as we have noted, was conspicuous by his absence from the Soviet press during the first week of September). Examples are the visit of the collective leadership to the French national exhibition on September 5;[386] Khrushchev's discussion with Blas Roca on September 5;[387] the ceremony honoring the late William Z. Foster, also on the 5th;[388] and the state dinner for Nehru on the 6th.[389]

As a consequence of the shift in Soviet foreign policy decided on at the September 6 Presidium meeting, the secret police were instructed to drop the case of the "CENTO documents," as we know from the fact that on September 9 the Soviet government quietly yielded to Turkish pressure and abandoned its announced plan to exhibit the "documents" in Turkey (above, p. 140).

The next indication, or series of indications, of high-level Soviet decisions on foreign policy comes from the area of the U.S.–Soviet bilateral negotiations on disarmament. After a long interval, these talks resumed on September 6— providentially, just as the Presidium was about to reassess its policies in the Berlin crisis and, by extension, toward the West in general. It was this favorable conjunction, evidently, which serves to explain the success achieved in this phase of the talks, a success which came as a surprise to the President and his advisers (above, p. 226).

No decision in favor of reaching an agreement with the United States in the talks was taken at the September 6 meeting of the Presidium, however, as we know from the fact that in the Soviet government statement of September 9, rejecting the Kennedy–Macmillan limited test ban proposal, the failure thus far to reach an accord in the talks was cited as proof that "the U.S. government does not even want to approach universal and total disarmament with the establishment of the strictest international control over the actions of states in

[386] *Pravda* and *Izv.*, Sept. 5, 1961, p. 1.
[387] *Pravda*, Sept. 6, 1961, p. 1.
[388] Ibid.
[389] *Pravda*, Sept. 7, 1961, p. 2.

this sphere" (above, p. 212). If the Presidium had decided in favor of a limited agreement with the United States at its September 6 session, reference to the bilateral talks would either have been omitted entirely from the September 9 statement or couched in a less negative form.

That the policy to be adopted toward the talks was under high-level review, however, was indicated by the Soviet requests on September 12 and 15 for cancellation of scheduled sessions (above, p. 226). Comparison between developments in the talks in late July and those in September serves to identify Khrushchev as the principal advocate of agreement with the United States in the talks; as we have seen, he had been on the point of putting through an agreement at Sochi just as Kennedy's July 25 speech rendered his plan abortive. This time, however, nothing intervened to block the attainment of a limited agreement on the principles of disarmament.

Was the decision to reach agreement with the United States in the bilateral talks one taken by the collective leadership as a whole, or did it represent a one-man initiative on the part of Khrushchev? The fact that Kozlov, the number two man in the party hierarchy, was absent from Moscow from September 8 to 22, the period during which the decision was taken, strongly militates against the view that it was a collective one. More likely, the Presidium was not consulted directly on what we have identified as a personal policy goal of Khrushchev. The two delays requested by the Soviets in scheduled sessions of the talks would then correspond to consultations between Khrushchev and specialist advisers as to how much of the U.S. draft proposal of September 6 could be accepted without endangering Soviet interests. No session of the Presidium would have been needed to spot the danger to Soviet security in McCloy's "key" proposal for international inspection of retained weapons, and even with this provision eliminated, it seems doubtful that Khrushchev could have won a majority in the Presidium at this time for agreement on the U.S. draft.

The Presidium session of September 6, thus, was probably the last meeting of that body (at least on foreign policy) until the second week in October at the earliest, for not only is there reason, as we have seen, to believe that Khrushchev was away from Moscow during the period September 22–October 6 (above, p. 254), but there are no clear indications during this period of the continuing functioning of any coherent machinery of Soviet foreign policy formulation. The most striking manifestation of the lack of direction of Soviet foreign policy during this period comes from the actions and statements of Foreign Minister Gromyko, who operated at this time as a virtually autonomous agent, under no fixed instructions and on occasion (as in his wilfull attempt at resurrection of the moribund 1961 deadline on conclusion of a peace treaty with Germany in his September 26 speech to the United Nations), virtually making policy in his own right. Incidentally, Gromyko's behavior during this period serves to identify him as a proponent of the hard line in Soviet policy on Germany, and thus enables us to specify one of the elements of "pressure" on Khrushchev which created "difficulties" for him in his efforts to reach agreement on Berlin with Kennedy.

Why was Khrushchev willing to leave Moscow, for the second time in less than a month, just as Kozlov was returning from Pyongyang? Should he not have feared a renewal of the kind of provocative actions and risky policies which Kozlov had carried through during his period of brief dominance in the Kremlin in late August?

For several reasons, this danger could be regarded as remote. First and most important, Kozlov had just sustained a defeat at the hands of his colleagues which in effect constituted a reprimand for his pro-Peking policies of late August. Then, too, U.S.–Soviet negotiations on Berlin had actually been initiated, in the form of the Rusk–Gromyko talks, a fact which provided a certain degree of insurance against the outbreak of hostilities in Berlin through accident, even though Gromyko himself was a hard-liner and could be expected to reduce the talks to futility by his unyielding posture.

Probably Khrushchev's major reason for absenting himself from the Kremlin after September 21, however, was the realization that if the Presidium continued to concern itself with the Berlin question—especially now that Kozlov had returned—it might well swing back to a tougher position vis-à-vis the West. Better to permit matters to drift, Khrushchev may have reasoned, than risk a return to Kozlov's hard-line position. Meanwhile Khrushchev devoted his attention to the always congenial field of Soviet agriculture and made his last-minute preparations for the Twenty-second Party Congress.

How close did contemporary observers in the West come to understanding the power struggle in the Soviet leadership which caused and explains the confusing surface pattern of Soviet foreign policy in the period from late August to mid-October 1961? The answer is, surprisingly close in places— some key pieces of the puzzle were recognized and correctly identified and the general outlines of the conflict were glimpsed by a few observers, though fleetingly and in somewhat distorted guise. There was no attempt, however, at an overall synthesis of the evidence; some major pieces of the puzzle were inaccessible to contemporary observers, or were overlooked; and the basic theoretical postulate on which virtually all Western analysis was based—that Soviet foreign policy formulation, whether it proceeded from the mind of a single dominant leader or was the result of a process of discussion and debate within the collective leadership, was a rational, coherent process—effectively blocked insight into the real nature of Soviet politics at this period.

For official Washington the most baffling aspect of the problem was the Soviet decision to break the nuclear test ban. "The motives that prompted the Soviet decision to resume nuclear testing," Max Frankel reported from Washington immediately after the announcement of the decision,

> . . . preoccupied and in some measure puzzled Washington today. The basic questions were: Why did Moscow feel compelled to resume testing? Why was it willing to accept the onus for resuming testing before the United

States? Why, in any case, did it time the announcement to coincide with a meeting of neutralist leaders in Belgrade and precede the gathering of delegates to the United Nations General Assembly?

Officials felt the Soviet decision was especially puzzling because of the obvious pressure building up here for the United States to take the initiative in a resumption of testing. . . . Why, it was asked, did Moscow feel it could not wait a few weeks or even months more?[390]

Attempts in Washington to solve the riddle, Frankel reported, took one of several lines:

The wide[ly] accepted but by no means unanimous view was that the military necessity of catching up with the United States in nuclear development coincides with an opportunity to terrorize the world at the height of the Berlin crisis. This view, apparently shared for the time being by the White House, held that Moscow's main purpose was to impress the world with its might, to lend credence to Soviet contentions that the balance of power had shifted to the Communist world, and thus to bring pressure on the West to yield to Soviet formulas for stabilizing Central Europe.[391]

Some observers in Washington took a different view, however. According to Frankel, ". . . there were officials here today who dissented sharply. . . . They saw the Soviet decision as the culmination of an extensive shift in Moscow's military thinking essentially unrelated to events in Berlin. They felt that *the decision really was made six months ago* [N.B.!] and that *its announcement now betrayed Moscow's realization that the United States could not be goaded into making the first nuclear tests.*"[392]

Very striking in this report is the pinpointing of the decision to begin active preparations for the current Soviet test series six months earlier—i.e., late February 1961. That an estimate in this general range enjoyed quasi-official standing in the Kennedy administration is indicated by the phrasing of an official note sent by the United States to Japan on September 13, in reply to a Japanese protest of September 6 on Kennedy's decision to resume nuclear testing. "The Soviet Union's program of testing," said the U.S. note, ". . . is progressing rapidly, suggesting that extensive secret preparations for test resumption were undertaken *during a major portion of this year's session of the Geneva conference.*"[393]

In reporting this note, the *New York Times* added: "This formal accusation of bad faith followed earlier statements by various administration officials that Moscow must have decided on a new test program several months ago, *probably as long ago as last March.*"[394]

---

[390] *NYT*, Sept. 1, 1961, pp. 1–2.

[391] Ibid.

[392] Ibid.; emphasis supplied.

[393] *DSB*, Oct. 2, 1961, vol. 45, no. 1162, p. 544; emphasis supplied. The 1961 meetings of the Geneva three-power disarmament conference opened on March 21.

[394] *NYT*, Sept. 14, 1961, p. 7; emphasis supplied.

Apparently no one in Washington, however, made any sustained effort to work out the implications for Soviet politics which this insight carried; official Washington rested content with the observation that the Soviet decision to resume testing proved the hypocrisy of their behavior at the Geneva test-ban talks.

Another *New York Times* reporter, Harry Schwartz, came within hailing distance of working out the Chinese aspect of the problem, but failed to bring all the elements into focus. In an article of September 3, from which we have quoted extensively (above, p. 176), Schwartz cited evidence pointing to some kind of interaction between Peking and Moscow just prior to the Soviet announcement on test resumption. All that was lacking was an insight into the mechanism whereby the influence was transmitted and recognition that the impulse came from Moscow rather than from Peking. Two days later, in reporting on the August 26 Soviet–Chinese supplementary trade agreement (above, p. 149), Schwartz had in his grasp the key piece to the puzzle, but missed its significance because he interpreted it in the light of the Sino–Soviet controversy, the Chinese trade deficit vis-à-vis the Soviet Union—and most damagingly—the implicit belief, shared by even the most intrepid Western analysts, in the existence of a unitary, rational modus of Soviet foreign policy formulation.

A direct challenge to this belief, as it happened, had been launched in a *New York Times* dispatch from Belgrade on September 4. "One of the best-informed East European sources on the inner workings of the Soviet Communist Party and Government," M. S. Handler reported from the Yugoslav capital, ". . . said today that certain dangerous developments in the Soviet system had a direct bearing on the events that produced the Berlin crisis and the Soviet decision to resume nuclear testing."[395]

The identity of his source, Handler stated, could not be revealed "because of the position he occupies," but he made clear the source's serious concern with conveying the urgency of the situation to policymakers in the West:

> Carefully weighing his words in response to questions on the situation in the Soviet Union, the East European source said: "There is a process going on in the Soviet Union today that could create the conditions for the emergence of a military clique." He reiterated this several times so that there would be no possible conclusion that a military clique already existed.
>
> Asked if there were any clearly identifiable military figures who might form the clique, the official said it was premature to say. But he added that it was urgently necessary to pay attention to this power development in the Soviet system because it constituted a process which, if it ran its normal course, could produce the conditions from which a military power group might emerge.[396]

[395] *NYT*, Sept. 5, 1961, p. 5.
[396] Ibid.

The conclusion which the unidentified "East European" source obviously wished to convey was that Khrushchev's power position was shaky and that his overthrow or the serious weakening of his position might lead to a dangerous shift in Soviet politics: "The situation in the Soviet political system is such that any weakening of Premier Khrushchev's control could accelerate the emergence of a military group, he [the source] declared."[397]

Having thus gone to the very brink of revealing the true facts about the power struggle in the Kremlin, Handler's unidentified but well-informed source took out protective insurance to safeguard his own position (which might be seriously threatened if Khrushchev's internal opponents won their battle for control of Soviet policy) by throwing in several false leads: "The official said that it would be a serious mistake to identify this or that member of the Soviet Communist Party's Presidium or Central Committee as Mr. Khrushchev's personal rivals and therefore his critics. The criticism, he continued, is in the nature of a general climate of party opinion that Mr. Khrushchev has been weak in dealing with the issues of Berlin, Germany, and disarmament."[398]

Furthermore: "The source cautioned against any assumption that the power process in the Soviet Union had any relationship to purely domestic affairs. The process, he said, was set in motion solely by external issues, in which Mr. Khrushchev's policies and methods had failed to satisfy the Communist Party."[399]

Thus disguised, the valuable information provided in Handler's report could make little significant contribution to Western enlightenment on the structure of Soviet politics. The "East European" source's partly false clue pointing to a "military clique," and his outright denial that any single member of the collective leadership might be Khrushchev's rival and critic, as well as his assertion that only questions of foreign policy were involved in the power struggle, seriously impaired the usefulness of the report, which could all too easily be read as an attempt to weaken the West's resistance to Soviet pressure on the grounds that Khrushchev's internal position was insecure and that if he fell, in consequence of Western refusal to yield to his demands, Soviet policy would become even more belligerent.[400]

These negative considerations do not apply to a report which the *New York Times* published almost exactly a month after Handler's dispatch. "An informed Italian Communist . . . who is in a position to know the topics under discussion in the inner councils of the Italian Communist party," Paul Hoffman reported from Rome on October 3,

[397]Ibid.

[398]Ibid.

[399]Ibid.

[400]For a warning to U.S. leaders against ruses of this kind, based on the prevailing assumption in the West that Khrushchev's power was not under serious internal challenge, see Philip E. Mosely, "Soviet myths and realities," *Foreign Affairs*, vol. 39, no. 3 (April 1961): 341–54.

. . . predicted today that the Communist parties of Western Europe would support Premier Khrushchev against "Maximalists."

The source said many Communists have believed that Mr. Khrushchev would need such backing at the forthcoming twenty-second congress of the Soviet Communist Party and at the conferences of international communist leaders which will be held simultaneously in Moscow. The opposition to Mr. Khrushchev was said to be made up of Stalinists in the Soviet Union, radicals in Communist China and their admirers elsewhere in international communism.[401]

The conflict was said to be directly related to Soviet policy in the Berlin crisis, Hoffman reported: "The source said [the] opposition to Premier Khrushchev tended to broaden the East–West conflict over Berlin into a world-wide showdown, regardless of the risks of nuclear war."[402]

The report from the "East European" source who had talked to Handler could be suspected of being a deliberate ruse to weaken the West's firmness, but it was impossible to discount the report by Hoffman's unidentified Italian communist source on this basis: not the influencing of Western policy but the desire to provide an authoritative inside explanation of the motives guiding the Italian Communist party's policies vis-à-vis the Kremlin was clearly his dominant motive. The accuracy of his information, furthermore, was vouched for by the fact that the PCI (Italian Communist party) was acting in accordance with precisely the analysis of Soviet politics which he provided: the PCI delegation to the Twenty-second CPSU Congress, it had just been announced, would include as its ranking member, after PCI Secretary-General Palmiro Togliatti, a right-wing communist named Umberto Terracini, whom Hoffman described as ". . . a Communist who got into trouble with his party in Stalin's time when he advocated peaceful coexistence between the Communist and capitalist camps. . . . Signor Terracini has recently been kept in the background by his party. His inclusion in the official delegation to Moscow caused surprise and was seen as indicative of the Italian communists' aversion to Maximalist currents in international communism."[403]

The explanation of Terracini's appointment to the PCI delegation, it should be noted, was not to be found in any internal conflict or rivalry between him, or a faction he represented, and the party's strong man, Togliatti, for the latter had already publicly revealed his disapproval of the Soviet atomic tests by saying, "We are against all nuclear tests, of any nature."[404]

The report by the well-placed but unidentified Italian communist source, taken together with Togliatti's statement on nuclear testing (a statement he

---

[401]*NYT*, Oct. 4, 1961, p. 6. In the dispatch Hoffman explained that the term "Maximalism" had "entered Italian political parlance, where it stands for Left-wing extremists."

[402]Ibid.

[403]Ibid.

[404]*NYT*, Sept. 11, 1961, p. 11 (a Reuters dispatch from Rome citing a speech by Togliatti in Siena as reported by an Italian news agency).

would hardly have made if he had not been aware that there were differences of opinion in the Soviet leadership on the subject), as well as the appointment of an advocate of "peaceful coexistence" as second in charge of the PCI delegation to the Twenty-second CPSU Congress, provides reliable evidence that the inner circle of the Italian Communist party believed that it was essential to come to Khrushchev's aid because his position, both in the Soviet party hierarchy and in the international communist movement, was threatened by "Maximalist" communists who "tended to broaden the East–West conflict over Berlin into a world-wide showdown, regardless of the risks of nuclear war." It would be hard to find a more concise characterization of the views and policies of the hard-line faction in the Soviet Communist party, whose most highly placed representative was Frol Kozlov.

Disregarding the unorthodox and challenging insights into Soviet politics provided by its reporters, the editorial staff of the *New York Times* meanwhile was vigorously propagating the view that Khrushchev, enjoying unchallenged dominance over Soviet foreign policy formulation, was deliberately pushing the world to the brink of atomic warfare. Typical of the *Times's* approach was an editorial on September 1 denouncing the Soviet decision to resume nuclear testing: "In an action that shocks the world and edges it closer to the brink of atomic holocaust, Premier Khrushchev announces that the Soviets are resuming nuclear testing to produce monstrous super-bombs capable of being dropped at any point on the globe from space. This marks another climax in the Soviet ruler's campaign to terrorize the world and cow it into submission in his plans for world domination."[405]

The *Times's* continuing torrent of editorial denunciation of Khrushchev, liberally sprinkled with epithets like "Caesar" and "Hitler," moved C. L. Sulzberger (who after all had just seen Khrushchev at close quarters) to enter a demurral. In a dispatch from London on September 15, Sulzberger warned that ". . . we should not lose sight of the fact that he [Khrushchev] is a very human man with a liking for distinctly normal things."[406]

Taking direct issue with his newspaper's editorial staff, Sulzberger continued: ". . . he [Khrushchev] is not a 'Hitler.' Hitler was an abnormal man; Mr. Khrushchev is normal, even if both are associated with abnormally ambitious policies."[407]

Sulzberger then offered his own evaluation of the complex figure who held the most powerful political position in Soviet Russia: "I believe Mr. Khrushchev is tough, relentlessly ruthless, coldly scheming and controlled, convinced by what I personally consider his miscalculation that the tide of

---

[405]"Soviet Policy of Terror," *NYT*, Sept. 1, 1961, p. 16. In his column, "In the Nation," on the same page, Arthur Krock treated the Soviet decision on testing as exclusively Khrushchev's.

[406]C. L. Sulzberger, "The Need to Choose Words Precisely," *NYT*, Sept. 16, 1961, p. 18.

[407]Ibid.

history is immutably with him. But, unlike Hitler, I consider him entirely normal and human."[408]

Useful though it was as a corrective to emotion-laden rhetoric, Sulzberger's portrait of Khrushchev was deficient in one crucial respect: it made no effort to evaluate Khrushchev's power position *within* the Soviet leadership or the strength of any possible opposition to him. Lacking an insight into that aspect of the problem, Sulzberger was in effect reduced to saying, Khrushchev the man is eminently human, even though the policies he is pursuing are undeniably dangerous for the world.

For help in solving this baffling enigma, the *Times* turned to the world of scholarship. In an article addressed to the problem of the degrees and kinds of ignorance about Soviet politics which beset Western observers, Leon Goure, an analyst for the RAND Corporation, observed that: "The exact extent of Khrushchev's power and the factors affecting his [sic] policy decisions have been much debated. The public image of Khrushchev in the West has undergone many startling changes in recent years."[409]

After recapitulating some of the analyses, theories, and guesses which had been propounded to define the nature and extent of Khrushchev's power, Goure came out in favor of the position held by the majority of Western scholars: "A more sober analysis, supported by events [sic], indicates that Khrushchev has a firm grip on power and that, far from being threatened by any Stalinist faction, he has succeeded in consolidating and expanding his position."[410]

The most Goure was willing to concede was that Khrushchev had not yet achieved a position equivalent to that of his most prominent predecessor: "Nevertheless, it is generally agreed that Khrushchev does not wield the same degree of power as Stalin did."[411]

A few American journalists, as we have seen, gave serious thought to the motives behind the Soviet decision to resume nuclear testing; they came close to recognizing the nature of the link between Moscow and Peking, and they provided searching, though flickering, light on the Soviet struggle for power. The impetus which their valuable and challenging reports could have provided for a fundamental reevaluation of the nature of Soviet power under Khrushchev was lost, however, primarily because of the prevailing belief in the West that in the Soviet political system, one-man rule is the norm—established by Lenin, perfected by Stalin, and currently exemplified, though not perhaps in its full extent, by Nikita Khrushchev. Blinded by this belief, Western observers failed to give adequate attention to the role played by other actors in the Soviet drama. In particular, Kozlov's key role escaped their no-

---

[408]Ibid.

[409]Leon Goure, "Russia: What We Don't Know," *New York Times Magazine*, Oct. 1, 1961, p. 84.

[410]Ibid.

[411]Ibid.

tice entirely, even when he publicly proclaimed the major turning point in Soviet policy on Berlin on September 12.

Contemporary observers are always at a disadvantage in attempting to analyze current Soviet politics. What of the scholars—the historians, the political scientists, the specialists in international affairs—who later made an intensive study of Soviet foreign policy during this period? This is not the place to undertake a full-scale review of everything that has been written by scholars in the West on Soviet foreign policy in the early 1960's. Fortunately the relevant point can be established by a selective survey of a few writers. It can safely be assumed that the majority of Western scholars, in discussing Soviet foreign policy in this period, followed the well-worn path of attributing all major foreign policy initiatives to the generally recognized "leader," i.e., Khrushchev, and that they explained the sharp turns and twists in Soviet foreign policy by reference either to shifts in his own views, to ambiguities and inconsistencies in his foreign policy objectives, or—at most—to various forms of institutionalized pressure brought to bear on him.

What is surprising, nevertheless, is to discover that even scholars who consciously challenged to a greater or lesser extent the orthodox concept of Soviet politics, nevertheless implicitly accepted it as the basis for their analysis. Three examples will establish the point.

In his pioneering and still standard study of the origins and early development of the Sino–Soviet conflict, Donald S. Zagoria traces the course of events down to the summer of 1961, when tension between the two powerful communist states had reached a new peak, and then jumps directly to a consideration of the conflict as it affected the Twenty-second Congress of the CPSU, in October 1961, ignoring almost completely the intervening period, with its puzzling but unmistakable evidence of some kind of interaction between Moscow and Peking. A major reason for Zagoria's failure to grasp the significance of the Soviet swing toward Peking in late August 1961 is his unquestioning assumption that the decision to resume nuclear testing was taken by Khrushchev personally. Quoting the Soviet announcement of August 30, Zagoria describes it as a statement made *by Khrushchev, "after* the USSR resumed testing."[412] Strangely, Zagoria recognized that the Soviet announcement expressed "*Chinese* opposition to a test-ban agreement between the USSR and the United States," but in the light of his unsupported assumption that the decision was Khrushchev's personally, this recognition was not followed by a deeper insight into the conflicts within the Soviet leadership over policy toward Peking.

Carl Linden, in his book, *Khrushchev and the Soviet Leadership, 1957–1964*, takes issue with the orthodox view of Soviet power in order to show that ". . . despite his primacy, Khrushchev in the years after 1957 continually engaged in an intensive and complex battle behind the scenes to sustain and extend his power within the leading group."[413]

---

[412]Zagoria, p. 439; emphasis supplied.
[413]Linden, p. 1.

In his analysis of the events of the late summer of 1961, however, Linden falls back on the traditional view of Soviet power, attributing to Khrushchev alone the initiative for the major twists and turns of Soviet foreign policy. He recognizes that there was a fundamental contradiction between Khrushchev's internal economic goals and the power imperatives of Soviet foreign policy in the Berlin crisis, but attempts to combine the two by a reference to "the inherent dilemma of *Khrushchev's* policy."[414] Recognizing that a number of Soviet actions in the field of foreign policy at this time "were in conflict with the goals of Khrushchev's political program at home," Linden seeks for an explanation of the discrepancy in the direction of "pressure" on Khrushchev, primarily from the military but also "from within the leadership."[415] In the final analysis, however, according to Linden, it was still Khrushchev who was the real architect of Soviet foreign policy: "In sum, Khrushchev's erratic behavior during the summer of 1961, stoking the Cold War one day and dampening it down the next, was more a sign of weakness than of strength. He was not in so secure a position that he could pursue a single and consistent course; he could not ignore the powerful pressures and cross pressures of the internal politics of the Soviet ruling group."[416]

Even more directly than Linden, the French journalist and scholar Michel Tatu, in his book, *Power in the Kremlin*, set out to challenge the orthodox concept of Soviet politics and to replace it by a more realistic one in which the tensions and conflicts in the Soviet leadership would find adequate expression. Surprisingly, however, Tatu also unquestioningly accepts the view that in the period of the Berlin crisis of 1961, Khrushchev personally and unilaterally was responsible for the direction of Soviet foreign policy, with all its glaring inconsistencies and sudden shifts of direction.

In a paragraph summarizing the course of the crisis, Tatu gives Khrushchev sole credit for "launching" it, "brandishing *his* rockets with unprecedented fierceness," and "topp[ing] it all off during the [Twenty-second] Congress with the blast of the super-bomb of over 60 megatons, the most powerful ever tested."[417]

Assuming that foreign policy was Khrushchev's "personal area,"[418] Tatu feels justified in skipping lightly over the international conflict of the summer and early autumn of 1961: "We need not pursue the diplomatic intricacies of the crisis, which subsided in the same way as it had broken out, i.e., *when its instigator* [i.e., Khrushchev] *so willed.*"[419]

In sum, then, neither well-informed contemporary observers nor scholars studying the evidence at a later date have hitherto succeeded in penetrating the heavy shroud composed in approximately equal parts of Soviet secrecy,

[414]Ibid., p. 114; emphasis supplied.
[415]Ibid., p. 115.
[416]Ibid., p. 116.
[417]Tatu, p. 170; emphasis supplied.
[418]Ibid., p. 171.
[419]Ibid., pp. 170–71; emphasis supplied.

faulty or fragmentary information, and Western preconceptions which obscured the true nature of the Soviet political process.

The explanation of this problem offered here gains additional strength from a comparison with events in Soviet internal and foreign policy which took place almost exactly twenty-five years earlier.

Stalin and the internal opposition in 1936: the twenty-five-year parallel

In the summer of 1961 the Soviet Union confronted a nation possessing a stronger economic base, greater military power, and a socioeconomic system regarded by many staunch communists as the antithesis of that which had been established in Soviet Russia. In his evaluation of this situation, the dominant figure in the Soviet political system, whose real power lay in his position as first secretary of the Communist party of the Soviet Union (although he also held, for good measure, the post of premier), was motivated primarily by the desire to safeguard his nation against what he regarded as the threat of disaster should war with the stronger power break out. The avoidance of such a war was thus the primary foreign policy goal of the most powerful Soviet political figure. His attempts to achieve this goal, however, were characterized not only by a willingness to make concessions to the stronger power but also by a clearly marked personal affinity, combining admiration, a rudimentary kind of trust, and even a certain personal affection, for the dominant political figure of the stronger nation.

Sharply differing from the party First Secretary in their view of the situation were the members of a faction united above all by their passionately held conviction that any kind of compromise with or conciliation of the stronger power was not merely morally wrong—a betrayal of the ideological essence of the communist faith—but also shortsighted and, ultimately, suicidal for the Soviet Union since, in the view of this faction, underlying the ideological differences between Soviet communism and the socioeconomic system of the stronger power lay an irreconcilable, total conflict which would ultimately lead to an armed clash which, from the Soviet standpoint, might better come sooner than later, since the adversary was meanwhile straining every sinew to prepare for what he, too, believed would be an inevitable and decisive showdown.

During the temporary absence from the Kremlin of the First Secretary, the opposition faction seized the opportunity to put into effect measures which reflected its view of the world situation, thereby breaking sharply with the policy of restraint and prudence which the First Secretary had hitherto pursued and greatly increasing the likelihood of that very armed confrontation with the stronger power which the opposition faction considered unavoidable.

The scenario we have outlined, which describes the struggle over foreign policy in the Soviet leadership during the Berlin crisis in the summer of 1961, could be applied with only minor changes to the struggle over foreign policy which took place in the Soviet leadership in the summer of 1936, exactly twenty-five years earlier. Some details, of course, would have to be altered, but in their essential structure the two situations are strikingly similar. For the United States in 1961, read Nazi Germany in 1936; for Khrushchev, read Stalin; for a hard-line opposition faction headed by Frol Kozlov, substitute an unorganized but strongly motivated group in the party which had its intellectual spokesman in Nikolai Bukharin and its most highly placed representative in Sergo Ordzhonikidze.

The actions taken by the hard-line faction during its temporary dominance in the Kremlin during the late summer of 1961 included: (1) launching a direct challenge to the Western powers' right of unrestricted access to West Berlin by air (the Soviet note of August 23); (2) reversing Khrushchev's policy of making no further build-up of Soviet armed strength (the announcement on retention of service men in the armed forces of August 29); (3) the decision to violate the de facto nuclear test ban by resuming nuclear testing (announcement of August 30); (4) the preceding clandestine report of this decision to the Chinese Communist leadership (August 26); and (5) the decision to name the principal figure in the opposition faction, Frol Kozlov, to head the Soviet delegation to the sixteenth U.N. General Assembly (announcement of September 1).

The principal actions taken by the unorganized oppositionists in the summer of 1936 were to intervene clandestinely on the side of the Loyalists in the Spanish Civil War, in defiance of Stalin's publicly announced policy of nonintervention, and to quash a criminal investigation against Bukharin and several of his associates which had been undertaken at Stalin's insistence.

The evidence for the internal party struggle over foreign policy in the summer of 1936 has been set forth in an essay by the author, and need not be repeated here. Heretical in the eyes of most scholars at the time the essay was first published, the thesis it advances is still too unorthodox to have won general acceptance. It has, however, recently been incorporated into a textbook, without specific identification, as part of the established interpretation of Soviet foreign policy. In Robert G. Wesson's book, *Soviet Foreign Policy in Perspective* (1969), the Soviet decision to intervene in the Spanish Civil War is explained as follows: "Fighting [in Spain] began in late July [1936], but not until September [more probably, some time in August] was the decision taken to send military aid—*a decision taken in Stalin's absence from Moscow and perhaps contrary to his wishes, by those whose internationalist idealism was stronger than his.*"[420]

In 1936–37, open defiance of the General Secretary's wishes was followed by a major purge, in which not only were those who had ventured to challenge him systematically routed out and destroyed, but hundreds of thousands of

---

[420]Robert G. Wesson, *Soviet Foreign Policy in Perspective* (Homewood, Ill., Dorsey Press, 1969), p. 123.

party and government officials as well, together with uncounted multitudes of ordinary Soviet citizens—everyone, in fact, who could be remotely suspected of still harboring any lingering tendency to doubt the wisdom of the policies decided on by the First Secretary.

Would the defiance of the First Secretary's wishes in the summer of 1961 lead to a similar holocaust as the means to destroy the opposition, actual or potential, and establish his power on the basis of unrestrained terror? This was the question which would be answered at the Twenty-second Congress of the Communist party of the Soviet Union, an event to which we must now turn our attention.

9 Second Climax: The Twenty-second Party Congress

Behind these starts, stops and postponements lies a power struggle that comes to light from time to time in flashes of disclosures such as the Kremlin showdown in 1957 and the Albanian schism of 1961.

It is at such times that policy differences become embodied in names—Molotov, Malenkov, Zhukov, Khrushchev—and the pretense of complete unity is temporarily dropped. Even when the disclosures cast light on the nature of the men and policies involved in the struggle, there is always the nagging puzzle of what really happened and what the defeated men stood for, since in Soviet politics the victor writes the record without challenge or contradiction, and this record is often obscure.

In this continuing power struggle every clue is of value to the analyst and observer; and the Congress documents and Congress proceedings are among the most valuable of our clues.*

One might logically have expected the crisis in Berlin to fade away after Khrushchev's private assurance to Kennedy that "the storm in Berlin is over." Yet a full month after that message had been relayed to the President, Soviet and American tanks were being drawn up in hostile confrontation in the beleaguered city, ready for a military showdown. At the same time, the shattering roar of the most mammoth nuclear explosions yet unleashed on earth was providing sobering evidence of the power of the Soviet armed forces and of the willingness of the Soviet leadership to use that power in defiance of a nearly unanimous world public opinion.

These events formed the background of the Twenty-second Congress of the Communist Party of the Soviet Union and significantly influenced the context within which that event took place. Khrushchev's original plans and hopes for

*Leo Gruliow, "Introduction," *Current Soviet Policies IV: The Documentary Record of the Twenty-second Congress of the Communist Party of the Soviet Union* (New York: Columbia University Press, 1962), p. vii (hereinafter cited as *CSP IV*).

the congress were clear: in his eyes, its major purpose was to adopt the new Party Program on which he and others had labored, a program designed to chart the course for the building of full-scale communism in the Soviet Union within a mere twenty years. The attainment of this goal—something of which Marx, Engels, and Lenin had dreamed, but which they had considered a task for the remote future—would entitle Khrushchev to recognition as their worthy successor, one of the principal architects of the new communist society.

In a manner which baffled and fascinated contemporary observers, the congress turned out quite differently. True, it did register its unanimous approval of Khrushchev's new Party Program, but its prevailing tone was not one of enthusiasm for the bright gleam of the future but rather of rancor and indignation at the sordid past and the intractable present. The congress's most notable speeches were not those hailing the vision of a communist society but those directed in anger against the dead Stalin and his still surviving adherents and against the stubbornly defiant Albanian communist leaders and their patrons in Peking.

As to the events in Berlin, despite the threat they carried of an immediate outbreak of all-out nuclear war, the congress simply ignored them; not a single speaker at the congress mentioned the military confrontation in Berlin, and the Soviet press preserved an uncanny silence on a subject which was making headlines elsewhere in the world. A few speakers, notably Khrushchev himself, did refer to the continuing series of Soviet nuclear tests, but only, it seemed, to serve notice that the series would continue to completion.

What, if anything, was the connection which linked these events? Why did the congress turn its attention from its allotted task, the adoption of a new Party Program and new Party Statutes, and once again drag up the unedifying subject of the crimes of Stalin and his associates? Why did Khrushchev use the occasion to launch his first public attack on the Albanian leaders, thereby bringing out into the open his smoldering feud not only with them but with their powerful Chinese patrons? Why did the Berlin crisis reach a new climax at just this point, and why did the congress pretend that the crisis did not exist? For an answer to these questions we must study the record of the congress, taking into consideration not only what went on inside the walls of the new Palace of Congresses in the Kremlin, where the congress was held, but also those aspects of international relations which helped shape the general context within which it met. Before we consider the congress itself, however, it will be useful to take note of certain developments which occurred just as the delegates were assembling.

On the eve: Khrushchev in trouble

We have suggested (above, p. 273) that one reason why Khrushchev chose to absent himself from Moscow after Kozlov's return from Pyongyang was the desire to avoid having to submit the Berlin problem to the Presidium at a time when he realized that he could not command a majority for his policies in that body. That Khrushchev had good reason to fear the power of his internal opponents is indicated by a series of setbacks which he encountered in the final days before the convening of the Twenty-second CPSU Congress on October 17.

As we have seen, a fundamental aim of Khrushchev's economic policies was to bring about a reallocation of investment priorities away from heavy industry, ferrous metallurgy, and armaments, for the benefit of agriculture, the chemical industry, and consumer goods. It was therefore a sharp setback for him when a joint party-government decree on October 13 maintained that an "*acute shortage of ferrous and nonferrous metals,* pipes, various kinds of equipment and machinery, synthetic and other types of materials" existed in the Soviet economy, and called for measures to remedy the situation.[1]

Further evidence that Khrushchev was encountering difficulties appeared the following day, when an unscheduled one-day plenum of the Party Central Committee met to hear reports on the draft Party Program (by Khrushchev) and the draft Party Statutes (by Kozlov), and then adopted both, with certain changes and additions.[2] The significance of this event has been analyzed by Sidney Ploss, who points out that in the entire history of the CPSU there was only one earlier instance (December 15, 1925) of a Central Committee plenum being held immediately before a party congress. The effect in 1961, Ploss points out, was to usurp the proper functions of the congress: "Originally, the Congress was supposed to examine and *approve* the Draft [Program]. The improvised procedure tended to subordinate the nominally supreme Congress to the Central Committee, whose formal mandate was about to expire."[3] As to the motivation behind the move, Ploss suggests that ". . . the neo-Stalinists Kozlov and Suslov desired to keep Khrushchev from bringing their disputes into the private meetings of delegation leaders which are sometimes held at party Congresses."[4]

Pravda's brief report on the plenum referred only to the discussion of the draft program and statutes, but it was revealed at the congress that the plenum had also considered questions of Soviet foreign policy. In the congress speeches of P. A. Satiukov, editor-in-chief of *Pravda*, and P. N. Pospelov, director of the Institute of Marxism–Leninism, former Soviet Foreign Minister V. M. Molotov was reported to have sent a letter to the plenum in which the draft Party Program was stigmatized as "anti-revolutionary, pacifist, and revisionist," and condemned for failing to "link the building of communism in the U.S.S.R. with the prospects for the revolutionary struggle of the working class in the capitalist countries and for socialist revolution on the international scale."[5]

---

[1]Text in *Spravochnik partiinogo rabotnika. Vypusk chetvertyi* (Moscow: Gospolitizdat, 1963), pp. 277–91 (quote at p. 277); emphasis supplied. See also Ploss, p. 234.

[2]*Pravda*, Oct. 15, 1961, p. 1.

[3]Ploss, p. 234; emphasis in the original.

[4]Ibid. Ploss presents no evidence directly linking Kozlov and Suslov with the Oct. 14 plenum.

[5]Cited in Tatu, p. 146.

Considering the quasi-religious reverence attached to Lenin's name in the Soviet Communist party, however, Molotov's gravest charge was that "Lenin nowhere said anything about peaceful coexistence among states with different social regimes."[6] There was perhaps nothing surprising in the fact that Molotov, a leading member of the so-called "Antiparty Group" which had almost succeeded in its conspiratorial efforts to oust Khrushchev as first secretary in June 1957, still harbored a grudge against him and was sharply critical of his policies. What was startling was that four years after his defeat, Molotov's views should be given a hearing in the party just on the eve of a congress which Khrushchev had expected to dominate and at which he had confidently looked forward to hearing his name extolled as that of a theorist worthy to rank with Marx, Engels, and Lenin.

Michel Tatu, the well-informed and alert Moscow correspondent of *Le Monde*, reports that: "According to information obtained at the time, Molotov's letter to the Central Committee meeting of October 1961 was distributed to all the delegates as a 'congress document.' "[7] This action (for which there is additional evidence) could only have been taken by someone very high up in the party hierarchy, someone who harbored deep-seated differences with Khrushchev in regard to foreign policy, someone whose views came close to those enunciated by Molotov and espoused by the Chinese communists; someone, in short, whose objective characteristics fitted only one man in the party leadership, Frol R. Kozlov.

The series of rebuffs administered to the First Secretary continued on October 16 when *Pravda* and *Izvestiia* published the approved list of slogans for the forty-fourth anniversary of the Bolshevik Revolution on November 7.[8] Generally regarded as a reliable index to the views of the party's ideological specialists, the anniversary slogans on this occasion manifested a sharp break with the known views of Khrushchev. The slogan for the Chinese People's Republic (No. 15), invoked the "eternal, indestructible friendship" between the "great peoples of the U.S.S.R. and China." Placed first in the list because of the paramount importance assigned to relations with China, it was followed by the list of Soviet allies and satellites in alphabetical order, leading off with the slogan for Albania (No. 16), which applied to that nation the ritualistic phrases certifying to the recipient's good standing in the world communist movement: "Fraternal greetings to the working people of the People's Republic of Albania, *who are building socialism*! Hail to *the eternal, indestructible friendship and cooperation* between the Soviet and Albanian peoples!"[9]

By contrast, the slogan for Yugoslavia (No. 26) was dropped below Czechoslovakia (i.e., the end of the alphabetical listing of Soviet satellites and

---

[6] Ibid.

[7] Ibid.

[8] *Pravda* and *Izvestiia*, Oct. 16, 1961; *CDSP*, XIII/40, p. 16.

[9] *CDSP*, XIII/40, p. 16; emphasis supplied.

allies) and, more important, omitted the magic phrases "who are building socialism" and "eternal, indestructible friendship," thus excluding the Yugoslav communists from the approved list of socialist nations and assigning them a place below that of their bitter rivals, the Albanians. Clearly, Khrushchev's statement to Sulzberger on September 5—"Of course, we consider Yugoslavia a socialist nation"—had been rudely ignored by the party ideologues responsible for drawing up the anniversary slogans.

Accompanying the series of pre-congress rebuffs to Khrushchev were a number of Soviet foreign policy actions characterized by a sharply intensified anti-Western coloration. To be noted here, first of all, is Zorin's attack on Cordier's policies in the U.N. Secretariat on October 13 (above, p. 263). Also relevant is the dusty Soviet reply of October 12 to the U.S. request for an opportunity to present its position on the Berlin crisis to Soviet readers (above, p. 239).

On the 14th *Izvestiia* reported that the Soviet government had sent a note to the United States charging it with harboring a "war criminal," and requesting that the individual in question, a certain Karl Linnas, be handed over for trial. The timing of the note is revealing: Soviet authorities, according to *Izvestiia*, had known for over a year that Linnas was living in the United States. The decision to raise the issue at just this time can therefore be legitimately viewed as evidence of a desire to defame the United States—and obstruct any tendency towards Soviet–U.S. rapprochement—on the eve of the congress.

We would probably be justified in adding to this list of anti-Western actions the break in diplomatic relations between the Soviet Union and The Netherlands which occurred on October 13 with the recall to Moscow of the Soviet ambassador to The Hague, an old-line Stalinist named Pantaleimon K. Ponomarenko. The immediate cause of Ponomarenko's sudden withdrawal was an incident which occurred at Amsterdam airport on October 9 in which the Soviet ambassador had attempted to intervene forcibly to prevent the defection of a Soviet biochemist seeking asylum. While the precipitating incident was local and accidental in nature, however, the weighty decision to make it the occasion for an open diplomatic break points to action at the Presidium level.[10]

Khrushchev's strategy for the congress

While Khrushchev's opponents in the party leadership were flaunting their strength in the days before the congress, the First Secretary was mapping out a strategy designed to weaken their position. The problems Khrushchev faced in internal and foreign politics were extremely serious, and the strategy he devised to deal with them was correspondingly bold and risky, carrying with it

---

[10]*NYT*, Oct. 10, 1961, p. 1, and Oct. 14, 1961, p. 1. Text of the Soviet protest, *Pravda*, Oct. 14, 1961, p. 4; *CDSP*, XIII/41, p. 26.

as it did the danger of reopening old wounds in the party and inflicting new ones in the international communist movement.

In internal politics, Khrushchev was confronted with a challenger in the party leadership—Kozlov—who held a key position in the Secretariat, from which he could carry out damaging raids on Khrushchev's political-territorial base (e.g., the purges in Armenia and Tadzhikistan). If Khrushchev had in reality wielded the dictatorial powers ascribed to him by many Western observers, there would of course have been no problem; at the first sign of insubordination from Kozlov his head would have rolled, figuratively if not literally. But Khrushchev could take action in a matter affecting membership in the party's policymaking bodies only with the approval of the Presidium, and this he was unable to obtain in the face of the stubborn defense of collegiality adopted by the Presidium majority as a bar to the re-establishment of a personal dictatorship a la Stalin. As long as enough Presidium members resisted Khrushchev's demand for stronger disciplinary powers, Kozlov's position was secure.

It was because Kozlov enjoyed a virtually impregnable position that he was able to defy Khrushchev, not only in internal politics by his party purges but also in the field of foreign policy, where he had been taking actions directly at variance with Khrushchev's line in order to force a showdown with the Western powers over Berlin. Unable to discipline or oust Kozlov, acutely aware of the danger of nuclear devastation which Kozlov's actions in the field of foreign policy were incurring, Khrushchev was forced to make the best of a bad situation by mounting an attack on secondary targets, in the hope that the sheer impetus of his assault would somehow carry him through to a stronger and more solid position.

To deal with the internal problem, he would revive the anti-Stalin issue which had proved so potent a weapon in 1956 and later, joining to it a renewed attack on the Antiparty Group in order to win congress approval for more severe punitive measures directed against the group's leaders, with the hope of creating conditions in which the disciplining of Kozlov and others of his ilk would become feasible.

To deal with the foreign policy problem, Khrushchev would attack the Albanian party leaders, who were known to hold views on international relations nearly indistinguishable from those of Kozlov. In taking this course of action, it is true, Khrushchev would be admitting publicly the existence of the estrangement between Moscow and Tirana which both sides had hitherto agreed on concealing in order to maintain the fiction of international communist unity. The risk was heightened by the strong probability that the Chinese communists would come to the support of their Albanian allies in the face of Khrushchev's onslaught. But precipitating an open break in the international communist movement was less distasteful than the prospect of an all-out fight for power in the Communist party of the Soviet Union itself. Not since the late twenties had such an open struggle occurred, and by now the cumulative weight of a tradition which prized party unanimity, however artificial, as the highest of political goods was too strong to be defied. Nor could Khrushchev be absolutely certain of victory in a head-on clash with Kozlov. There were many in the party who shared or were at least sympathetic with Kozlov's views, and the congress itself could not be counted on to support Khrushchev in view of Kozlov's pre-congress factional purges. Better to accept the situation for the time being, Khrushchev must have reasoned, meanwhile seeking to improve his position by indirect means.

For his opening moves, therefore, Khrushchev would seek the Presidium's approval for a renewal of the attack on Stalin and the Antiparty Group and for an open admission of the break with Albania. On these issues he could muster a larger show of support than on a direct confrontation with Kozlov.

That this was to be Khrushchev's strategy at the congress could be deduced from a number of pre-congress events whose significance, it must be admitted, is easier to recognize with the advantages of hindsight than was possible for observers at the time. There were, for example, a number of signs pointing to a renewal of the attack on Stalin. Tatu notes that the Soviet television network made available its state-monopoly facilities just before the congress for a showing of a new and strongly anti-Stalinist film, "Clear Skies," by a young Soviet director named G. N. Chukhrai.[11] The anti-Stalin theme was also recognizable in an article published in the issue of the party theoretical journal, *Kommunist*, which was sent to the press on October 12.[12] Using a historical survey of the party's Twelfth Congress in 1923 as a convenient peg on which to hang some currently relevant comments, the article, as Ploss has pointed out, ". . . recalls that Lenin addressed to the 12th party Congress a letter which included criticism of Stalin's 'personal shortcomings',"[13] an allusion which Ploss characterizes as a "degrading" of the Stalin symbol on the eve of the party congress. Also relevant was the fact that the article emphasized the priority which a party congress enjoys over a plenum of the Central Committee, a theme which Ploss finds "all the more fascinating" in view of the directly contrary implications of the October 14 plenum of the party Central Committee.

To clinch the evidence for the immediate relevance of the *Kommunist* article, Grey Hodnett has pointed out that it

> . . . noted that the expansion of the Central Committee at the Twelfth Congress in 1923 had promoted "collegiality" and party "unity," and linked Lenin's sanction of disciplinary measures against Shliapnikov and the Workers' Opposition faction with the steps taken more recently against the Antiparty Group. At the Twenty-second Congress a week later, the Central Committee *was* increased by almost one hundred full and candidate mem-

[11]Tatu, p. 148.

[12]A. Sidorov and G. Shitarev, "Lenin and Party Congresses," *Kommunist* 15 (1961): 92–101.

[13]Ploss, p. 234.

bers, leaving little doubt as to the contemporary relevance of this "historical" article.[14]

Also dimly visible in the days before the congress were the outlines of Khrushchev's battle plan in the field of foreign policy and international communist relations. By October 12 the Albanian communist leaders knew that they would not be invited to send a delegation to Moscow to attend the congress,[15] so that the designation of their country as "building socialism" in the anniversary slogans issued four days later came too late to prevent them from drafting a sizzling letter to Moscow calling on the Central Committee which the congress would elect to "examine the situation" which had been created as the result of "the brutal anti-Marxist actions of N. Khrushchev and his group," and "to take the necessary measures for its normalization."[16]

As we shall see when we come to the congress itself, there is ample evidence that Khrushchev and his supporters in the party apparatus were able to maintain a tight grip on its operating arrangements. The exclusion of the Albanian Party of Labor from the list of visiting delegations thus serves as a reliable clue to Khrushchev's intentions, for it indicates that his decision to launch a direct attack on them—something he would hardly have done if he had expected them to be present at the congress—had been taken by October 12 at the latest. (We have already seen that Khrushchev's charges against the Albanians had figured in a Central Committee letter of August 24—above, p. 141).

The pre-congress deliberations of the Presidium

The crowded events of the week before the opening of the party congress, as well as the gravity of the issues facing the Soviet leadership, leave little doubt that the Presidium must have met, perhaps several times, to determine policy in a number of fields. It is also clear that top-level consultation was indispensable for the purpose of reviewing the text of the report which the First Secretary would deliver on behalf of the Central Committee on the opening day of the congress.

With the approach of the congress, party leaders from all over the Soviet Union—including, of course, the members of the Presidium—began flocking to Moscow. On October 8, for example, Moscow Radio reported a visit to the new congress building in the Kremlin by a group of Soviet leaders which included all the full members of the Presidium except Aristov (who was in Warsaw as ambassador to Poland, and who may already have been dropped from the Presidium), Podgorny (party chief in the Ukraine, who had evidently not

---

[14]Grey Hodnett, "Khrushchev and Party-State Control," in Alexander Dallin and Alan F. Westin, eds., *Politics in the Soviet Union: 7 Cases* (New York: Harcourt, Brace & World, 1966), p. 134.

[15]Griffith, *Albania*, p. 88.

[16]Ibid., p. 343, citing *Zëri i Popullit*, March 25, 1962.

yet left for Moscow), and Mikoyan (who was in East Germany heading a delegation to attend ceremonies marking the anniversary of the establishment of the GDR).[17]

Mikoyan returned to the Soviet capital on October 11,[18] accompanied (as we noted earlier, above, p. 258) by Marshal Konev, commander-in-chief of Soviet troops in Germany, and M. G. Pervukhin, Soviet ambassador to the GDR. Since the Berlin crisis was the most important foreign policy issue confronting the party leadership, it seems probable that the arrival in Moscow of this group of high party, government, and military officials with special knowledge of conditions in Germany was related to a Presidium discussion of Soviet foreign policy in preparation for the report Khrushchev was to deliver to the congress.

A meeting of the full Presidium may have taken place, therefore, as early as October 11; probably there were several sessions, which may well have continued through October 12. The convergence on that date of a number of lines (e.g., the *Kommunist* article degrading the Stalin image, the refusal of an invitation to the Albanians, the decision to recall Ponomarenko) points to the 12th as the date on which the Presidium wrapped up its deliberations with a series of decisions setting the main lines of Soviet policy for the opening phase of the congress.

On the whole, the balance at this stage was unfavorable to Khrushchev, and the opposition made good use of the difficulties in which he found himself to press its advantage. But Khrushchev was a past master at the game of party politics, and he managed to score a number of points in the battle with his opponents, points which he would later be able to parlay into more substantial gains.

Our primary source for the decisions of the pre-congress meetings of the Presidium is Khrushchev's Central Committee report itself, since the positions it contained, as we shall see, provide indications of being the result of an agreed compromise. On this basis we can identify a number of the basic decisions reached by the Presidium at the session or sessions which centered around October 12: (1) There would be renewed reference at the congress to Stalin's crimes, but the image of him presented to the delegates would be balanced by reference to his positive services to the cause of communism. No decision was reached as to the punishment to be meted out to the leaders of the Antiparty Group, but it was agreed that they would be the object of renewed attack. (2) The hostile attitude of the Albanian party leaders vis-à-vis the CPSU would be openly admitted, but in a way which emphasized the desire on the Soviet side for eventual reconciliation (on Soviet terms, of course). To maintain a balance, the reproof to the Albanians for their "dogmatism" would be accompanied by criticism of the Yugoslavs for their "revisionism." (3) The hard-liners' demand for a military confrontation with the Western

[17]Radio Moscow, Oct. 8, 1961.
[18]Radio Moscow, Oct. 11, 1961.

powers in Berlin was voted down, in the interests of prudence in the face of Western military power; in addition, the decision reached on September 6 to call off the campaign for the signing of a German peace treaty by the end of the year (a decision which had remained secret, thanks to the failure of the West to recognize the significance of Kozlov's September 12 speech at Pyongyang) would now be publicly proclaimed. (4) Balancing this concession to proponents of the "soft" line on Germany (including Khrushchev), the series of Soviet nuclear tests would not only be continued throughout the duration of the congress but would culminate in the detonation of a number of superbombs in the 25- to 50-megaton range, thus partially erasing the concession Khrushchev had won on September 6 when it had been decided not to carry out the explosion of a 100-megaton superbomb but merely to test the detonating device for such a monstrosity.

The structure of the congress

A great deal can be learned about the purposes the congress was intended to serve—and the way in which those purposes came to be modified as events unfolded—by studying the structure of the congress itself.

The first point to be noted is the exceptional size of the congress: nearly five thousand delegates were present, three and a half times as many as in the preceding three congresses (see Table 1). In part this expansion reflected growth in the size of the party, which was now approaching the ten million mark, having added nearly 1.5 million members since the Twenty-first Congress in 1959. The principal reason for the increase, however, was the change in ratio between the size of a given party organization and the number of delegates it was entitled to send to the congress. The effect was to make the Twenty-second Congress, far more than its predecessors, a mass phenomenon in which the struggle for power between the contending factions in the party leadership was fought out in terms of the fight for control of blocs of delegates. To a large extent, of course, the fight had already been waged in the months preceding the congress, in the form of factional purges aimed at capturing individual party organizations. In its most highly developed form this struggle was directed toward capture of the Union Republic party organizations. Despite the inroads which Kozlov had been able to make into Khrushchev's areas of strength, however, neither of the principal opposing factions could be sure just how the balance in the party stood until the final vote for the Central Committee and other central party bodies was taken toward the end of the congress. This continuing uncertainty is the reason why the congress developed into a stubborn struggle for the support and votes of the delegates.

For just over two weeks (October 17–31) the congress delegates met in the newly built Palace of Congresses in the Kremlin. On its working days the congress held sessions in the mornings, starting usually at 10 A. M., and in the late afternoon and early evening, starting usually at 4 P. M. but on occasion as late as 5:30 P. M. The delegates put in a solid six-day week, taking a respite

Table 1.

Congress	Number of delegates			Number of party members			Source of figures
	Voting	Non-voting	Total	Full	Candidate	Total	
XIX (1952)			1,359	6,013,259	868,886	6,882,145	Report by Aristov, Sten. ot., 1956, I, p. 233
XX (1956)	1,355	81	1,436	6,795,896	419,609	7,215,505 (up 333,360)	Ibid.
XXI (1959)	1,269	106	1,375	7,622,356	616,775	8,239,131 (up 1,023,626)	Report by Churaev, Sten. ot., 1959, I, pp. 258-59
XXII (1961)	4,408	405	4,813 (4,799 actually present)	8,872,516	843,489	9,716,005 (up 1,476,874)	Report by Titov, Sten. ot., 1961, I, pp. 422-24
XXIII (1966)	4,620	323	4,943	11,673,676	797,403	12,471,079 (up 2,755,074)	Report by Kapitonov, Sten. ot., 1966, I, pp. 279-80

from the grueling and often boring round of speeches only on Sunday (October 22 and 29).

This schedule, it will be seen, provided ample opportunities for meetings of the top party leaders while the congress was in session. In addition to the two full-day Sunday intervals, meetings of the Presidium could be held, if desired, during the early morning hours or in the mid-day interval between the morning and evening sessions. It would have been possible, therefore, for the party leadership to schedule its policymaking meetings during the congress in such a way that their timing would not find reflection in the congress protocols. Interestingly enough, this was not done. The protocols provide evidence— negative, it is true, but unmistakable—of the times during which the party leadership could have met while the congress was in session. The clue is the presence or absence of Khrushchev from a given session.

We may take it as a basic principle that no meeting of the Presidium could be held without the presence of the First Secretary. When Khrushchev's presence is indicated at a session of the congress, therefore, a meeting of the Presidium could not be taking place. Conversely, when Khrushchev's presence at a given session is either not recorded in the protocols or—more strongly— *when his absence is explicitly noted*, a meeting of the Presidium *could* have been under way. Obviously not every indicated or inferred absence of Khrushchev must necessarily be equated with a Presidium meeting: he may have been indisposed at times, or bored, or forced to deal with other urgent business, leaving the congress to carry on its work without him. Nevertheless, the list of recorded and possible absences of Khrushchev will serve as a convenient index to the *most probable* times for meetings of the Presidium during the congress. Evidence from other areas must then be studied to identify specifically those times at which we can confidently postulate a meeting of the Presidium.

In what way do the protocols provide evidence of Khrushchev's presence or absence? There is no difficulty, first of all, in identifying the sessions at which he was present. The most direct indication, of course, is provided by his appearance as speaker. Then there are the numerous occasions on which he made his presence known through interjections during the speech of another delegate (see Table 2). In addition the protocols provide still a third way of identifying Khrushchev's presence or absence at a given session (or part of a session—on a number of occasions a session was divided by a thirty-minute break, and Khrushchev's presence or absence was indicated separately for each half session). The clue is a recurrent regularity in the congress ritual.

In addition to the nearly five thousand delegates from the CPSU itself, the Twenty-second Congress was attended by a number of delegations representing foreign communist parties or (in a few cases) sympathetic foreign governmental or other political organizations. In all, sixty-six foreign visitors spoke at the congress, grouped into fifteen sessions.[19] For each of these guest speakers there was a set, formalized ritual which was performed at the end of

[19]For a list of foreign speakers at the congress, see *CSP IV*, pp. 122–23.

Table 2.   Interruptions by Khrushchev

Speaker	Date and time of interruption
P. N. Demichev	Oct. 19, morning
K. T. Mazurov	Oct. 19, morning
M. V. Keldysh	Oct. 20, morning
A. V. Gitalov	Oct. 21, morning
Blas Roca	Oct. 21, evening
V. M. Kavun	Oct. 23, evening
N. G. Ignatov	Oct. 23, evening
M. A. Sholokhov	Oct. 24, morning (second half)
V. V. Grachev	Oct. 24, evening
D. A. Lazurkina	Oct. 30, morning (first half)

his speech. In the words of the protocols, this ritual usually took the following form: "[*Stormy, prolonged applause. All rise.*] Comrade Chou En-lai [or one of the other guest speakers] exchanges warm greetings with comrade Khrushchev and other members of the Presidium of the congress."[20]

(One must distinguish, incidentally, between the Presidium of the Central Committee—the party policymaking body—and the Presidium of the congress, a temporary body elected at the congress's opening session, consisting of forty-one carefully chosen individuals representing the party, government, public bodies (such as the trade unions and the Academy of Sciences), and—for purposes of presenting a democratic image—a sprinkling of factory and collective farm workers. All the full members of the party Presidium were included in the congress Presidium, but their absence would not prevent the latter body from carrying out its largely formal functions.)[21]

The same ritualistic formula is repeated verbatim in the protocols for the first seven sessions at which foreign guests addressed the congress. Beginning with the eighth session, however, on the morning of October 24, the protocols introduce a significant variation by *omitting any reference to Khrushchev*, so that the formula reads: "[*Stormy, prolonged applause. All rise.*] Comrade Codovilla [or one of the other guest speakers] exchanges warm greetings with members of the Presidium of the congress."[22]

For the evening session of October 24 the protocols revert to the full ritualistic formula, i.e., they indicate Khrushchev's presence. The abbreviated formula is then employed for the sessions of the morning of October 25, both

[20]*XXII S"ezd Kommunisticheskoi Partii Sovetskogo Soiuza 17–31 oktiabria 1961 goda. Stenograficheskii otchet*, 3 vols. (Moscow Gospolitizdat, 1962), 1:328 (hereinafter cited as *Sten. ot.*).

[21]For the list of members of the Congress Presidium, see ibid., 1:9.

[22]Ibid., 2: 126.

sessions on October 26, the second half of the morning session of October 28, and the evening session of the same day. (No foreign guests spoke on October 27.)

Making use of this indicator, we obtain the following table of possible times for meetings of the party Presidium, corresponding to Khrushchev's absences, explicit or implied, from the congress:

> first half of morning session, October 24 (Tuesday)
> morning session, October 25 (Wednesday)
> morning and evening sessions, October 26 (Thursday)
> morning session, October 27 (Friday)
> second half of morning session and evening session,
>   October 28 (Saturday).

In addition, of course, the entire day of Sunday, October 29 (as well as the preceding Sunday) was available for Presidium consultations. This may look at first glance like a rather extensive list of possible meeting times, but there were some urgent and weighty problems to be discussed and, as we shall see, there is good reason to believe that the Presidium did in fact make use of a number of these possible meeting times.

The first two days of the congress—four sessions—were taken up by two marathon speeches by Khrushchev. On October 17 he presented the Report for the Central Committee and on the following day he introduced the new Party Program. This portion of the congress was followed by eleven sessions (morning October 19 through morning October 25) in which the top party regional officials—primarily the first secretaries of the Union Republics—mounted the rostrum (see Table 3).

Table 3.   Speeches by Union Republic party chiefs

Name	Position	Day and time of meeting
V. Yu. Akhundov	First secretary, CP Azerbaidzhan	Oct. 20, morning
I. I. Bodiul	First secretary, CP Moldavia	Oct. 25, morning
I. P. Kazanets	Second secretary, CP Ukraine	Oct. 28, morning
I. G. Kebin	First secretary, CP Estonia	Oct. 20, evening
D. A. Kunaev	First secretary, CP Kazakhstan	Oct. 19, morning
K. T. Mazurov	First secretary, CP Belorussia	Oct. 19, evening
M. P. Mzhavanadze	First secretary, CP Georgia	Oct. 19, evening
B. Ovezov	First secretary, CP Turkmenistan	Oct. 20, morning
A. Ya. Pel'she	First secretary, CP Latvia	Oct. 24, morning
N. V. Podgorny	First secretary, CP Ukraine	(1)Oct. 19, morning
		(2)Oct. 30, morning
Sh. R. Rashidov	First secretary, CP Uzbekistan	Oct. 19, morning
D. Rasulov	First secretary, CP Tadzhikistan	Oct. 20, morning
N. N. Rodionov	Second secretary, CP Kazakhstan	Oct. 30, morning
A. Yu. Snechkus	First secretary, CP Lithuania	Oct. 23, morning
T. Usubaliev	First secretary, CP Kirghiziia	Oct. 23, morning
Ya. N. Zarobian	First secretary, CP Armenia	Oct. 21, evening

Beginning with the evening session of October 25 and continuing through the evening session of the 28th, seven governmental officials of ministerial rank addressed the congress, beginning with Foreign Minister Andrei Gromyko and concluding with Marshal F. I. Golikov, head of the Central Committee's and Ministry of Defense's Main Political Administration, the body charged with political indoctrination of the Soviet armed forces (see Table 4).

Table 4.　Speeches by USSR ministers and officials of equivalent rank

Name	Position	Day and time of speech
B. T. Beshchev	Minister of transportation	Oct. 27, morning
V. E. Dymshits	First deputy chairman, Gosplan	Oct. 26, morning
Ye. A. Furtseva	Minister of culture	Oct. 20, morning
F. I. Golikov	Chief, Main Political Administration	Oct. 28, evening
A. A. Gromyko	Minister of foreign affairs	Oct. 25, evening
R. Ya. Malinovsky	Minister of armed forces	Oct. 23, evening
I. T. Novikov	Minister of power plant construction	Oct. 27, morning
M. A. Ol'shansky	Minister of agriculture	Oct. 27, morning
A. N. Shelepin	Chairman, Committee of State Security	Oct. 26, morning

Clearly, a coherent organizational plan must have underlain these symmetrical arrangements, and we are entitled to attach special significance to any violations of the symmetry. There were two exceptions: first, Mme. Furtseva, Soviet minister of culture, spoke at one of the earlier sessions (morning, October 20). In addition to being a high government official, however, Mme. Furtseva was a member of the Presidium who was reputed to enjoy a specially cordial relationship with the First Secretary. Second, Soviet defense minister Marshal Malinovsky delivered a major address during the evening session of October 23, interrupting the sequence of speeches by party regional officials, none of whom spoke at this session. There was good reason, however, as we shall see, for moving Malinovsky's speech up to this place in the congress.

At its twentieth session on the evening of October 27, the congress listened to some "Concluding Remarks" by Khrushchev, on the discussion of the two major reports he had presented earlier, and then elected a commission to prepare a draft resolution on the Report for the Central Committee and to review changes and additions to the draft Party Program.

The second major item of internal political business on the congress agenda, the Report on the draft Party Statutes, was delivered during the first half of the morning session of October 28 by Kozlov—the first time he had addressed the congress (he had, however, presided briefly at the opening session on the morning of October 17).

With the delivery of Kozlov's report and the completion of the discussion of the draft statutes which followed it, the congress had finished its allotted tasks and would normally have proceeded to the election of the new Central Committee and the other top party bodies. Instead, following the day-long break of Sunday, October 28, there occurred a stormy, melodramatic session on the morning of October 29 which is clearly recognizable, on purely formal grounds, as an improvisation which was hurriedly inserted into the congress schedule. Three of the speakers on this occasion (Spiridonov, Demichev, and Podgorny) had already delivered major speeches to the congress, making this the only occasion during the entire congress in which anyone except Khrushchev addressed it twice.

With this interruption out of the way, the congress returned to its regular schedule, electing the new Central Committee and Central Auditing Commission on the evening of October 30. The two concluding sessions of the congress, on October 31, were devoted to the adoption of a series of resolutions, following which Khrushchev announced the membership of the new central bodies and then delivered a brief statement bringing the congress to a close.

Each session was presided over by a temporary chairman, the list of chairmen forming a pattern which points to an underlying organizational plan (see Table 5). The pattern is defective, however, suggesting that a plan was sketched out, but then modified and finally abandoned completely.

The three top party leaders—Khrushchev, Kozlov, and Suslov—were assigned the chairmanship on the first two days, followed during the next four sessions by junior members of the Presidium. After the evening session of October 20, no full member of the Presidium chaired a session until near the close of the congress, when Shvernik presided over the first half of the morning session on October 30.

The top party leaders were thus relieved of the honorary but routine job of chairmanship early in the congress. On the other hand it is undoubtedly significant that four of the Presidium members who were not asked to preside—Aristov, Mme. Furtseva, Ignatov, and Mukhitdinov—were to lose their seats on the Presidium at the end of the congress. Evidently their impending fate was known in advance to those charged with drawing up the organizational plans for the congress. The other two full Presidium members who did not chair sessions of the Congress, Kuusinen and Mikoyan, were "senior statesmen" (Kuusinen was eighty, Mikoyan sixty-six), who might well claim exemption from this onerous task.

The assignments to Demichev and Spiridonov on October 21 represent the first break in the pattern, and may be viewed as a reward for their sterling performance as speakers on October 19. Beginning with the eleventh session on the morning of October 23 a new pattern was instituted, the assignment of presidial functions to first secretaries of Union Republics. (The first two party officials who served in this capacity, Mazurov and Mzhavanadze, were also candidate members of the Presidium.) This pattern was maintained for seven sessions and then abandoned, leaving six Union Republic first secre-

Table 5.   Presiding officers at congress sessions

Session	Chairman	Date
One	N. S. Khrushchev[a]	Oct. 17, morning
Two	F. R. Kozlov[a]	Oct. 17, evening
Three and Four	M. A. Suslov[a]	Oct. 18, morning and evening
Five	L. I. Brezhnev[a]	Oct. 19, morning
Six	A. N. Kosygin[a]	Oct. 19, evening
Seven	N. V. Podgorny[a]	Oct. 20, morning
Eight	D. S. Poliansky[a]	Oct. 20, evening
Nine	P. N. Demichev	Oct. 21, morning
Ten	I. V. Spiridonov	Oct. 21, evening
Eleven	V. P. Mzhavanadze[b,c]	Oct. 23, morning
Twelve	K. T. Mazurov[b,c]	Oct. 23, evening
Thirteen	Sh. R. Rashidov[c]	Oct. 24, morning
Fourteen	V. I. Gaganova	Oct. 24, evening
Fifteen	A. Yu. Snechkus[c]	Oct. 25, morning
Sixteen	A. Ya. Pel'she[c]	Oct. 25, evening
Seventeen	V. Yu. Akhundov[c]	Oct. 26, morning
Eighteen	D. A. Kunaev[c]	Oct. 26, evening
Nineteen	G. G. Abramov	Oct. 27, morning
Twenty	V. V. Grishin	Oct. 27, evening
Twenty-one	G. I. Voronov	Oct. 28, morning
Twenty-two	V. V. Shcherbitsky	Oct. 28, evening
Twenty-three	N. M. Shvernik[a]	Oct. 30, morning (first half)
	L. N. Yefremov	Oct. 30, morning (second half)
Twenty-four	—	Oct. 30, evening
Twenty-five	M. T. Yefremov	Oct. 31, morning
Twenty-six	N. S. Khrushchev[a]	Oct. 31, evening

[a] Member of the Presidium
[b] Candidate member of the Presidium
[c] First secretary of a Union Republic Communist party

taries still unrepresented in the list of session chairmen (Kebin, Bodiul, Zarobian, Rasulov, Ovezov, and Usubaliev).

Toward the end of the congress there emerged the faint outlines of still another pattern, with three men, Voronov, Grishin and Shcherbitsky, who were slated to join the Presidium as full or candidate members, assigned as chairmen. Evidently it was intended in this way to introduce them to the party and give them a taste of ceremonial administrative responsibility.

*   *   *

In a political organization as acutely conscious of rank and protocol as the CPSU, significant omissions from the list of speakers at a congress can be just as revealing as inclusions. Two striking omissions characterize the list of speakers at the Twenty-second Congress.

Ranking on a level with or slightly above the fourteen Union Republic first secretaries in the party hierarchy are the first secretaries of the two most important Soviet cities and their adjoining oblasts: the city and oblast of Moscow, the capital, and those of Leningrad, the Soviet Union's second city in size and importance. If we add the second secretaries of each of these party organizations, we obtain a list of eight of the most influential and powerful officials in the party. Six of the officials on this list duly addressed the Twenty-second Congress, the first secretaries in each case being allocated choice time spots testifying to their importance (see Table 6).

Table 6.   Speeches by party officials of Moscow and Leningrad

Name	Position	Date and time of speech
1a. P. N. Demichev	First secretary, Moscow city	(1)Oct. 19, morning (2)Oct. 30, morning
b. N. G. Yegorychev	Second secretary, Moscow city	Oct. 28, morning
2a. G. G. Abramov	First secretary, Moscow oblast	Oct. 24, evening
b. O. P. Kol'china	Second secretary, Moscow oblast	Oct. 28, evening
3a. I. V. Spiridonov	First secretary, Leningrad oblast	(1)Oct. 19, morning (2)Oct. 30, morning
b. V. S. Tolstikov	Second secretary, Leningrad oblast	Oct. 28, evening

Neither the first nor second secretary of the Leningrad City party committee (Leningrad gorkom), however, spoke at the congress, notwithstanding the fact that both of them—G. I. Popov, first secretary, and A. P. Boikova, second secretary—were present at the congress as delegates. Why were these important party officials passed over as speakers, at a time when the congress was given the opportunity to hear from such an obscure individual as V. I. Gaganova, a worker from Kalinin, who addressed the morning session on October 23? The answer to that question may lie in the fact that the Leningrad city party organization had been Frol Kozlov's chief political base since the time when he was sent there by the Central Committee as a party organizer at the Kirov factory in 1949. The pointed omission of the Leningrad city party chiefs could then be interpreted as evidence of an intention to deny the floor to Kozlov's closest party associates.

Confirmation that this hypothesis has validity is provided by a second glaring omission from the list of congress speakers. In a congress whose principal function was to adopt a blueprint for building communism in the Soviet Union within the next twenty years, it must have struck many delegates as odd that the rostrum was never given to the chief of the State Planning Commission, V. N. Novikov, on whose shoulders would fall much of the detailed work involved in translating the blueprint into reality, whereas his deputy, V. Ye. Dymshits, delivered a speech in which, among other things, he heaped praise on Khrushchev for services allegedly rendered in the large-scale construction industry. Like the Leningrad city party chiefs, Novikov was a delegate to the congress; like them, however, he was a long-time close associate of Kozlov and shared with him the view that heavy industry, ferrous metallurgy, and armaments (industries in which Leningrad was a leader, incidentally) should retain their position at the head of the list of investment priorities for the Soviet economy.[23]

In its choice of speakers, then, the Twenty-second Congress manifested a clear factional bias against Kozlov and his supporters. As we shall see, the congress speakers' schedule was heavily weighted on the side of Khrushchev and those who followed his lead. The two biases were aspects of a single tendency.

Khrushchev's opening speeches (October 17 and 18)

For a man who had fueled his rise to power in large part by attacking the "cult of personality" under Stalin, N. S. Khrushchev showed a marked tendency to reproduce in his own actions the pattern established by the late unlamented tyrant. Few congresses in the Stalin era were so completely dominated by one man as the Twenty-second Congress appeared to be by Khrushchev. His determination to control the congress was manifested at the very outset by his appropriation of nearly the entire first two days for the delivery of two lengthy reports.

The Report for the Central Committee (October 17)

In a speech requiring six hours for delivery, a man of Khrushchev's restless temperament and voracious mind can cover a lot of territory. It is obviously impossible to note here all the points touched on in Khrushchev's opening speeches to the congress; we shall limit ourselves, therefore, to those matters directly or indirectly relating to U.S.-Soviet relations and the struggle for power in the CPSU. At the same time, it is essential to understand what Khrushchev said with regard to these matters in the overall framework of his speeches rather than as unrelated fragments taken out of context. To maintain general continuity, therefore, we shall cite the "chapter headings" of the major divisions and subdivisions of the speeches, getting down to particulars only when Khrushchev makes a statement relevant to our immediate concerns.[24]

The preamble to Khrushchev's Report for the Central Committee stressed the unity of the CPSU, its close links with the Soviet people, and its sense of responsibility to the international communist movement. The first major sec-

[23]Tatu, p. 175, notes the "strange" omission of Novikov's name from the list of congress speakers.

[24]Text of Khrushchev's Oct. 17 speech in *Pravda* and *Izv.*, Oct. 18, 1961; *Sten. ot.*, 1: 15–132; translation, *CSP IV*, pp. 42–77.

tion of the speech was devoted to "The Present World Situation and the International Position of the Soviet Union." Here Khrushchev reaffirmed the validity of the innovations in Soviet foreign policy which he had introduced at the Twentieth Party Congress in 1956:

> Events have shown that our party's course worked out at the 20th Congress was correct and true: The congress noted that the chief feature of our epoch is the emergence of socialism beyond the framework of a single country and its conversion into a world system. A new and important advance has occurred since the congress: *the world socialist system is becoming the decisive factor in the development of society.*
>
> The party drew the conclusion that *the collapse of colonialism is inevitable.* Under the powerful blows of the national-liberation movement the colonial system has in effect caved in.
>
> The party propounded the important thesis that *wars among states are not inevitable in the present epoch,* that they can be prevented. The events of the past years have confirmed this conclusion also. They have shown that the mighty forces standing guard over peace possess great means in our times for preventing the imperialists from unleashing a world war. *The superiority of the forces of peace and socialism over the forces of imperialism and war has become even more sharply delineated.*[25]

For his first subsection, Khrushchev took up:

1. *Further Growth of the Might of the Socialist System. Its Conversion Into the Decisive Factor of World Development; Strengthening of the International Brotherhood of Socialist Countries.*

After describing the growth of the economies of the socialist nations and their increasing interdependence, Khrushchev turned to the "subversive activities" being carried out by "the ruling circles of some imperialist powers." Even though their sphere of domination was steadily contracting, Khrushchev said, the "imperialists" still presented a threat: "As long as the imperialist aggressors exist, we must be on guard, keep our powder dry, improve the defense of the socialist countries, their armed forces and the state security agencies. If, in the face of common sense, the imperialists dare attack the socialist countries and plunge mankind into the abyss of a world war of annihilation, this mad act of theirs would be their last act, *it would be the end of the whole system of capitalism.*"[26]

Khrushchev thus reasserted the controversial view that in a new world war only capitalism, not socialism, would perish. But he immediately shifted the emphasis to "peaceful competition": "We believe that in the competition with capitalism socialism will win [*prolonged applause*]. *We believe that this victory will be won in peaceful competition and not by way of unleashing a war.* We have stood, we stand and we will stand by the positions of peaceful competition of states with different social systems; we will do everything to strengthen world peace [*prolonged applause*]".[27]

[25]*CSP IV*, p. 43; emphasis supplied.
[26]Ibid., p. 45; emphasis supplied.
[27]Ibid.; emphasis supplied.

Having dealt with the "socialist camp," Khrushchev next turned his attention to its competitor:

2. *Sharpening of Contradictions in the Countries of Capitalism. Growth of Revolutionary Struggle and Upsurge of the National Liberation Movement.* The inexorable tendency in the capitalist world, Khrushchev asserted, was "further decay." The economy of the United States of America, he said, was characterized by feverish upswings and debilitating depressions. Automation was throwing millions of workers out of their jobs. Noting that the United States alone had spent over $220 billion in armaments over the last five years, Khrushchev asserted that militarization of the American economy, while it enriched the "branches of industry connected with arms production," had unbalanced the economy as a whole and added to the burden of chronic unemployment.

If the U.S. economy was in serious trouble, the situation was even worse in its relations with its capitalist allies, according to Khrushchev: "First, the United States of America has lost its absolute supremacy in world capitalist production and commerce. . . . The result is that the United States of America today occupies approximately the same position among the capitalist countries as it did before the war."[28]

Britain and France, meanwhile, had grown weaker: they were in the process of losing their colonies and had proved "unable to recover their prewar position in world industrial production."[29] The spectacular economic recovery of defeated Japan and West Germany, in Khrushchev's view, was not a factor strengthening the capitalist world or a proof of its unimpaired vitality but rather one which threatened to undermine it by arousing "contradictions"— rivalries—among the capitalist nations. Alarmed by their darkening prospects, Khrushchev said, the capitalist powers were tempted to seek a way out in aggression: "Today the United States of America, which has become the center of world reaction, takes the role of the chief aggressive nucleus. The U.S. imperialists are acting in alliance with the West German militarists and revanchists and threatening the peace and security of peoples."[30] The temptation to seek a militaristic solution, however, was rendered risky not only by the defensive might of the socialist states but also by the rising tide of the movement of anticolonialism and national liberation. Once again Khrushchev pledged Soviet support for these movements: ". . . from the bottom of our heart we wish success to all who are now fighting for their freedom and happiness against imperialism. We believe that it is the inalienable right of people to put an end to foreign oppression, and *we shall support their just fight.*"[31]

The reactionary program of the imperialists, Khrushchev continued, was being sharply challenged by the workers in the capitalist countries. Support for their struggle, he asserted, was the duty of the international communist

28 Ibid.
29 Ibid.
30 Ibid., p. 46.
31 Ibid.; emphasis supplied.

movement, and to carry out this task successfully it was essential that the unity of that movement be maintained. Here Khrushchev came to grips with the first of the thorny issues which encumbered his path, Yugoslav "revisionism":

> To Marxist–Leninists it is indisputable that the vital interests of the international communist movement demand consistent and undeviating unity of action, and the Communist and Workers' Parties observe it faithfully. *Only the leaders of the League of Communists of Yugoslavia*, who plainly suffer from national narrow-mindedness, *have turned from the straight Marxist–Leninist road* onto a winding path that has landed them in the bog of revisionism. . . .
>
> *Revisionist ideas pervade not only the theory but also the practice of the leadership of the Yugoslav League of Communists.* The line they have adopted—that of development in isolation, apart from the world socialist community—is harmful and dangerous. It plays into the hands of imperialist reaction, foments nationalist tendencies and may in the long run lead to the loss of socialist gains in the country, which has broken away from the friendly and united family of builders of a new world. Our party has criticized and will continue to criticize the Yugoslav leaders' revisionist conceptions. As internationalists, we cannot but feel concern for the destiny of the fraternal peoples of Yugoslavia, who fought selflessly against fascism and after victory chose the path of socialist construction.[32]

Nothing here recalled Khrushchev's words to Sulzberger on September 5 affirming Yugoslavia's right to be regarded as a "socialist" nation. Like most of the rest of the October 17 speech, this passage has the ring of an agreed committee product, representing the consensus in the Presidium rather than the views of Khrushchev personally. It is entirely consistent with the November 7 slogan for Yugoslavia issued on the eve of the congress (above, p. 288), and with the fact that the Yugoslav party, like that of Albania, had been omitted from the list of invited guests to the congress.

Knowing that later in the same speech Khrushchev was to make some sharp criticisms of the Albanians, one might consider that this would have been the logical place to introduce the Albanian issue, which could then have been represented as part of a balanced condemnation of both Albanian "dogmatism" and Yugoslav "revisionism." Instead, as we shall see, Khrushchev linked the Albanian affair with Soviet internal politics and played down its connections with the international communist movement. This would indicate that Khrushchev had won approval in the Presidium for an attack on the Albanians, but only in connection with his proposal to reopen the assault on Stalin's "cult of personality" and the Antiparty Group.

In the third subsection of Part I of his report Khrushchev offered a reasoned defense of the policy of peaceful coexistence between the socialist and capitalist states. At the very outset he claimed that a decisive shift in the world balance of power had occurred: ". . . the fact that *the preponderance of strength is on the side of the socialist commonwealth of peoples* is extremely

[32]Ibid., p. 48; emphasis supplied.

fortunate for all mankind."[33] This shift, he went on to explain, resulted not only from the growing military power of the socialist states but also from the emergence of the countries of Asia, Africa, and Latin America which, despite their "neutralist" label, "as a rule . . . take their stand for peace and against war."[34] Khrushchev thus confidently included the new nations on the side of the socialist states in the "struggle of the countries of socialism and all peace-loving forces against the preparations for new aggression and war" which, he said, "constitutes the main substance of world politics today."[35]

But the stubborn imperialists, despite a series of setbacks, were still bent on stirring up trouble, their most recent effort in this regard being "the dangerous situation in Central Europe" resulting from their refusal to accept the Soviet proposals on Germany and West Berlin. To counter this threat, Khrushchev said,

> . . . *we were forced to take steps* necessary to render our country secure against encroachments by aggressors and to save mankind from the danger of a new world war. The Soviet government was *forced* to suspend the reduction of its armed forces planned for 1961, to increase its defense expenditures, to postpone the transfer of servicemen into the reserves and to resume tests of more powerful new weapons. *These are measures that we were forced to take*; they were unanimously backed by our people and were correctly understood by the peoples of other countries, who know that the Soviet Union will never be the first to take the road of war.[36]

Note how Khrushchev repeatedly stresses the forced nature of the measures taken by the Soviet government; note, also, his avoidance of a plain statement that the Soviet government had resumed nuclear weapons tests.

Obviously aware that there was a serious discrepancy between the measures he had just defended and the principles of peaceful coexistence, Khrushchev continued: "Some people in the West are now claiming that the measures taken by the Soviet government to strengthen our homeland's defenses represent a renunciation of the policy of peaceful coexistence. This, of course, is plain nonsense. The policy of peaceful coexistence derives from the very nature of our system."[37] The reason for this happy circumstance, he explained, was that the basic principles of peaceful coexistence had been included in the foundation plans of the Soviet state by its architect, Lenin: "The principles of peaceful coexistence worked out by V. I. Lenin and developed in our party's documents remain unalterably the general course of Soviet foreign policy. The entire foreign policy of the Soviet government attests convincingly to the fidelity of the Party and of all the Soviet people to this peaceful Leninist course."[38]

[33] Ibid.; emphasis supplied.
[34] Ibid., pp. 47–48.
[35] Ibid., p. 49.
[36] Ibid.; emphasis supplied.
[37] Ibid.
[38] Ibid.

Khrushchev thus asserted in strong terms the Leninist origins of the policy of peaceful coexistence. He was aware, of course, that there were those in the party who denied this and who asserted that Lenin had in fact said nothing about peaceful coexistence; a spokesman for party members holding these opposite views had been found in Molotov, who had expounded them in his letter to the Central Committee on the eve of the congress (above, p. 287).

Explaining why he believed that war could now be averted (a view for which he neither claimed nor could have found sanction in Lenin's writings), Khrushchev envisioned a coordinated action in defense of peace by all the peoples of the world, including those of the capitalist states: "It must be realized that whether there is to be peace on earth or whether mankind is to be plunged into the catastrophe of a new world war depends above all on the peoples themselves, on their determination and vigorous action."[39]

In the fourth subsection of Part I of his speech, Khrushchev turned from the general principles of Soviet foreign policy to specifics. At the head of his list of measures, following a precedent which he had done more than anyone else to establish, Khrushchev placed *"the struggle for general and complete disarmament,"* which he portrayed as an exclusively Soviet initiative, opposed by the Western powers on various flimsy pretexts. With the compulsive behavior of a man probing an open wound, however, Khrushchev came back again to the subject of the Soviet resumption of nuclear testing:

> As a blind, the imperialists are now hypocritically making a great to-do over the fact that *we have been forced* to conduct experimental explosions of nuclear weapons. But this has not kept the peoples from realizing that we have done this only because the Western powers, having deadlocked solution of the disarmament problem and the nuclear-test talks, have pulled the throttle of their war machine all the way out in an effort to achieve a preponderance of strength over the socialist countries. *We got the jump on them and thereby kept the advantage with the socialist camp*, which is standing guard over the peace [*stormy applause*]. *Our measures were forced on us.* It was known that the United States had been preparing for a long time to resume tests, while France had been conducting them recently.[40]

Again, there is the emphasis on the forced character of the Soviet military measures; now, however, Khrushchev ventures to take a further step toward candor by identifying one of the measures as the resumption of nuclear tests. Noteworthy too is the implication that by resuming nuclear testing the Soviet Union was maintaining a lead over the United States which might otherwise have been endangered, whereas in actual fact the Soviet Union's arsenal of nuclear weapons lagged behind that of the United States.

After disarmament, the German problem and West Berlin. Khrushchev led off this section of his speech with a brief repetition of the stereotyped Soviet arguments in favor of the signature of a peace treaty with Germany, but then

[39]Ibid., p. 50.
[40]Ibid.; emphasis supplied.

veered off in a way which must have made his more perceptive listeners realize that they were witnessing the unveiling of a major shift in Soviet policy:

> Recently, while attending the United Nations General Assembly, Comrade Gromyko, U.S.S.R. Minister of Foreign Affairs, had talks with the Secretary of State and the President of the United States. He also had talks with the Minister of Foreign Affairs and the Prime Minister of England. These talks left us with the impression that the Western powers were showing a certain understanding of the German problem and that they were disposed to seek a settlement of the German problem and the question of West Berlin on a mutually acceptable basis.[41]

What followed was Khrushchev's contribution to an indirect dialogue between himself and Kennedy, his reply to the President's statement of the Western position on Berlin during his talk with Gromyko: "The Western press has been presenting the question of a German peace treaty in unreasonable and unrealistic terms. The reproach is heard, for example, that someone is trying to give an apple in return for an orchard in settling the German question. This figure of speech may perhaps please its authors, but it fails to reflect the true picture in this case."[42] The crux of the matter, Khrushchev made clear, was the contest of strength and will power between the Soviets and the Western powers which was being waged over Berlin: "*We believe that the forces of socialism, all the forces that stand for peace, are today more powerful than the aggressive imperialist forces.* But even if one agreed with the President of the United States that our forces are equal—he said this quite recently—it would plainly be unwise to threaten war. The fact that equality is conceded should lead to the drawing of appropriate conclusions. Nowadays it is dangerous to pursue a 'position of strength' policy."[43] And he added flatly: "A German peace treaty must and will be signed, with or without the Western powers."[44] Soon, however, Khrushchev was off again on the new trail of reasonable compromise at which he had hinted earlier:

> Some Western spokesmen say that our proposals that a German peace treaty be concluded this year are an ultimatum. But this is an erroneous contention. After all, the Soviet Union's proposals on concluding a peace treaty and on that basis settling the question of West Berlin, turning it into a free city, were put forward as early as 1958. A good deal of time has passed since then. We have not rushed settlement of the question, hoping for the achievement of mutual understanding with the Western countries. Where, may I ask, is the ultimatum? *In proposing conclusion of a German peace treaty, the Soviet government has been presenting no ultimatum but has been moved by the necessity of finally settling this compelling question.*[45]

---

[41] Ibid. The translation in *CSP IV* is defective in this passage. See *Sten. ot.*, 1: 43.

[42] *CSP IV*, p. 50.

[43] Ibid., p. 51; emphasis supplied.

[44] Ibid.

[45] Ibid.; emphasis supplied.

Here at last was the word for which Western statesmen had been straining their ears: an authoritative statement, from the highest Soviet source, that the 1961 deadline on Berlin which Khrushchev himself had laid down in June (despite his disclaimer) had been lifted. To make matters crystal clear (and, incidentally, providing instant refutation of the assertion he had just made that there had been no Soviet deadline), Khrushchev added: "The question of a time limit for the signing of a German peace treaty will not be so important if the Western powers show a readiness to settle the German problem; *we shall not in that case absolutely insist on signing the peace treaty before December 31, 1961*. The main thing is to settle the question, to do away with the vestiges of the second world war, to sign a German peace treaty. This is basic, that is the heart of the matter."[46]

What about the Soviet demand for a three-man secretaryship in the United Nations, a demand which had aroused the most serious concern in the West over the fate of the United Nations itself? Matching the soft line currently being pursued by Zorin in his confidential negotiations with Adlai Stevenson at U.N. headquarters, Khrushchev touched on this controversial issue only briefly and with no suggestion of urgency: "The time has come to establish genuine equality in all U.N. agencies for the three groups of states that have formed in the world—the socialist, the neutralist and the imperialist. It is time to put a stop to the attempts to use this organization in the interests of the military alignment of the Western powers."[47]

In the same relaxed spirit Khrushchev called for the admission of communist China to the United Nations, but deflated the importance of this mildly voiced aspiration by following it immediately with a proposal for settlement of "the German people's representation in the United Nations," thus placing China on the same level as defeated Germany.

The problem of "finally eliminating colonial oppression in all its forms and manifestations" rated a brief paragraph, following which Khrushchev turned to various proposals for solving "pressing regional political problems." A single brief sentence expressing Soviet support for "setting up atom-free zones in Europe and the Far East first of all" served to imply in veiled form the highly controversial proposal, a major offense to Peking, for keeping communist China from developing its own nuclear weapons.

After a rapid *tour d'horizon* of Soviet relations with the newly liberated and developing nations, Khrushchev turned to Soviet–U.S. relations. "We attach great importance," he said, ". . . to relations with the principal countries of the capitalist world, above all the United States of America."[48] In striking contrast to the earlier passage of his speech which had characterized the United States as "the center of world reaction [which] takes the role of the chief aggressive nucleus," Khrushchev now portrayed the United States as

[46]Ibid.; emphasis supplied.
[47]Ibid.
[48]Ibid., p. 52.

susceptible to reasonable guidance in its foreign policy: "If realism wins out in U.S. policy, one of the serious obstacles to normalization of the entire international situation will have been removed. Not only the peoples of our countries but other peoples as well, and the cause of peace the world over, stand to gain from this kind of approach."[49]

Soviet relations with the other major capitalist nations and with the Soviet Union's neighbors rated a brief mention, after which Khrushchev summarized Soviet economic and cultural ties with foreign nations. His own wide and extensive travels were deprecatingly mentioned: "I too have had occasion to do quite a bit of traveling the wide world over. It can't be helped—my position requires it, it is called for in the interest of our cause."[50] But here, as elsewhere in his speech, Khrushchev strove to link his own policies and actions with those of Lenin: "As we know, V. I. Lenin, who was directly engaged in guiding the foreign policy of the Soviet state, for all his busy schedule used to meet with figures from the United States, Britain, Finland, Afghanistan, and other countries, conducted negotiations with them and was intending to participate in person in the Genoa Conference of 1922. The Central Committee has made a point of steadfastly observing this tradition established by Lenin."[51]

Concluding his exposition and defense of Soviet foreign policy, Khrushchev reiterated his conviction that communism could achieve world victory without war: "*Present conditions have opened up the prospect of achieving peaceful coexistence over the entire period within which the social and political problems now dividing the world must be resolved.* Matters are reaching a point where even before the total victory of socialism on earth, while capitalism holds on in part of the world, there will be a real chance of eliminating war from the life of society."[52]

The second major portion of Khrushchev's report dealt with internal developments under the general heading: *The Soviet Union Enters the Period of Full-scale Construction of Communism.* In the preamble to this section Khrushchev set the tone for the congress as a whole: "Our great goal is drawing nearer and nearer, and the bright peak on which the Soviet people in the near future will raise the banner of communism is already distinctly visible."[53] First to be taken up were the party's goals for the next planning period. Figures for the basic sectors of production were cited, ranging from ferrous metallurgy to consumer goods (Khrushchev devoted approximately equal time to both). From his statistical presentation of economic data, however, Khrushchev (perhaps sensing a growing restlessness on the part of his audience) switched to a portrayal of Soviet military prowess, particularly in the field of rocket development. Recent Soviet tests, he said, had shown the high degree of

[49]Ibid.
[50]Ibid.
[51]Ibid.
[52]Ibid.; emphasis in the original.
[53]Ibid., p. 53.

accuracy characterizing Soviet long-range rockets. Apparently yielding to a sudden impulse, Khrushchev at this point departed from the prepared text of his report and gleefully cited U.S. confirmation of Soviet press reports: "It should be pointed out that there are also American ships in this [testing] area, and they too are tracing the Soviet rockets in flight. The Americans have been publishing their respective data on these flights, and we have been comparing their figures with our own. Naturally, we have confidence in the comrades aboard our ships. But what we're getting in this case is something of a double check—ours and our adversary's."[54]

One might have thought "adversaries" (*protivniki*) a surprisingly mild term for Khrushchev to apply to the Americans (his restraint strikingly echoes that shown by Kennedy in his inaugural address), but Khrushchev proceeded to water down still further the lingering trace of hostility the term contained: "Our adversaries—true, we wish we did not have to call them our adversaries, but the nature of imperialism must be reckoned with—confirm the fact that the Soviet rockets have been hitting the mark accurately. That's fine! We never doubted they would."[55]

And then, well launched on the detour from the high road of his prepared text, Khrushchev jolted his listeners with a startling revelation:

> Since I have already wandered from my written text, I want to say that our tests of new nuclear weapons are also coming along very well. We shall shortly complete these tests—presumably at the end of October. We shall probably wind them up by detonating a hydrogen bomb with a yield of 50,000,000 tons of TNT [*applause*]. We have said that we have a 100-megaton bomb. This is true. But we are not going to explode it, because even if we did so at the most remote site, we might knock out all our windows [*stormy applause*]. We are therefore going to hold off for the time being and not set the bomb off. However, in exploding the 50-megaton bomb we are testing the device for triggering a 100-megaton bomb.[56]

Khrushchev's tone in making this impromptu revelation was jaunty, almost jocular, but he quickly added the fervent hope that the 100-megaton super-bomb would never be needed: "But may God grant, as they used to say, that we are never called upon to explode these bombs over anybody's territory. This is the greatest wish of our lives! [*stormy applause.*]"[57]

In the West, where Khrushchev's words caused a sensation, it was universally assumed that his purpose in revealing Soviet plans for testing a 50-megaton H-bomb was to intimidate the Western powers in order to force them to accept Soviet demands on Germany and Berlin. This explanation does not fit the facts, however: first of all, because Khrushchev himself had just lifted the deadline on signing a peace treaty with Germany, thereby taking the pressure off the West; and second, because the statement concerning the super-

[54]Ibid., p. 54.
[55]Ibid.
[56]Ibid.
[57]Ibid.

bomb was introduced almost apologetically, in a context strongly suggesting an affectionate comradeship between the Soviets and the Americans. Significant too is the fact that Khrushchev's revelation occurred in a portion of his speech which he explicitly identified as a departure from the prepared text, i.e., one which had not been sanctioned in advance by the collective leadership. (This is not to say that the plan to detonate a 50-megaton bomb did not have Presidium sanction, but that the revelation of this plan had not been included in the agreed text of the Report of the Central Committee.) Note, finally, that Khrushchev linked the preparations to test a 50-megaton bomb with the compromise plan, of which he had informed Sulzberger on September 7, to substitute the testing of the detonating device for the 100-megaton superbomb for the testing of the bomb itself. No one, of course, could accept the contention that testing a 50-megaton superbomb was the equivalent of merely testing a detonating device.

The disclosure of Soviet plans to test a 50-megaton bomb, as we shall see presently, set off a powerful reaction in the West, which found its most concentrated expression in the adoption of a series of resolutions in the U.N. General Assembly calling on the Soviet Union to desist from its plan. The reaction also included the dispatch of personal letters to Khrushchev from a number of heads of state and prominent individuals.

In the light of these considerations it must be regarded as a strong probability that Khrushchev's real motive in disclosing plans for the 50-megaton bomb test was precisely to evoke that worldwide revulsion which did, in fact, promptly follow, *in order to force the Presidium to reconsider its decision to include the 50-megaton superbomb in the current test series.* As we shall see, there is evidence indicating that this is exactly what happened, with Khrushchev pleading the case for cancellation of the superbomb test.

Now well launched on a digression concerning Soviet military development, Khrushchev continued with an account of the Soviet submarine fleet, which he said had the task of defending the Soviet Union against missile attacks from submarines (i.e., the Polaris missiles of the United States). In a heavily stressed statement Khrushchev assured his listeners that "... *the rearming of the Soviet Army with nuclear and rocket weapons has been fully completed.* Our armed forces are now in possession of weapons powerful enough to enable us to crush any aggressor."[58] The implication was that extensive additional appropriations for the armed forces would not be needed.

Khrushchev brought this militaristic intrusion into his speech to an adroit end by modulating abruptly back from war to peace: "The Soviet people have no need of war. Their thinking is directed toward the development of an economy of peace, the accomplishment of the great plans for communist construction, the creation of an abundance of material and spiritual benefits for all working people."[59]

[58]Ibid.; emphasis in the original.
[59]Ibid.

Back to his prepared text, Khrushchev provided his listeners with a rapid survey of the development of the Soviet economy, which we can leave to specialists in that field, with the exception of a few details bearing on the internal struggle over investment allocation priorities. For example, in giving figures for Soviet steel production, Khrushchev revealed that there existed a difference of opinion on this subject within the leadership: "There are some who suggested that steel output be boosted to 100,000,000 tons a year. But *we restrained them.* We said that *all branches of the economy had to be developed proportionately*, that along with metal output we had to remember housing construction, children's institutions, the manufacture of footwear and clothing, etc. In this matter we must rigorously abide by the directives which were adopted by the 21st Party Congress."[60]

Also of interest for our purposes were Khrushchev's claims that the Soviet economy was rapidly overtaking that of the United States: "You recall, comrades, that even during the first five-year plans we outdid the United States in the rate of growth of industrial output, but we were considerably overshadowed with respect to its absolute increase, to say nothing of the substantial disparity in levels of production. *In recent years our country, while continuing to outstrip the United States substantially in rate of growth, has also begun to leave it behind in absolute increase in the output of many major products.*"[61] After citing production figures from a wide range of branches of industry, Khrushchev offered the triumphant conclusion: "Completion of the seven-year plan will bring our nation to a stage where it will take little time to outdistance the United States economically. *By accomplishing its basic economic task, the Soviet Union will win a world-historic victory in the peaceful competition with the United States of America.*"[62]

Primarily of limited internal interest was the following section of Khrushchev's report, which dealt with the administration of the Soviet economy. The emphasis here was on the need to renovate the industrial plant, eliminate inefficiency, and maximize production. Khrushchev's criticism of hide-bound reactionaries included a swipe at L. M. Kaganovich, commissar of transportation under Stalin and a member of the Antiparty Group which had tried to oust Khrushchev in 1957—the first intimation in the report that a renewed attack on this group was imminent.

Following industry, Khrushchev took up the problems facing Soviet agriculture, offering a review of achievements since 1956 and a preview of the tasks which lay ahead. The achievements, as Khrushchev presented them, were so many milestones marking the course of his stewardship, including strengthening of the material base of the collective and state farms; reorganization of the machine-tractor stations; and assimilation of the Virgin Lands. On the latter subject, Khrushchev dwelt at length and with pardonable pride (the lean, dry years on the risky Virgin Lands program still lay in the future).

[60] Ibid., p. 55; emphasis supplied.
[61] Ibid., emphasis in the original.
[62] Ibid.; emphasis in the original.

But with all its achievements, for which he took full credit, Khrushchev was forced to admit that agriculture was still the most backward sector of the Soviet economy: "Comrades! The successes in agriculture are indisputable and substantial. But the question arises: Why do we still not have enough of some products, particularly meat? Why, despite the general substantial achievements, do we still encounter considerable difficulty in supplying the public with livestock products?"[63]

Inescapably, the answer lay in the root problem of Soviet economic planning, the question of investment priorities: "This is explained, above all, by the fact that *the rate of growth of agricultural output still lags behind the rate of growth of industry* and the increasing requirements of the public."[64] Unobtrusively but firmly, Khrushchev stated the principle which he wished to see embodied in the party's approach to agriculture—a principle which by no means enjoyed the unanimous support of the party leadership: ". . . we must always keep agricultural problems in the center of attention and *ensure such a rate of agricultural growth that output of farm products is always ahead of demand.*"[65]

The remainder of this section of the report was devoted to a characteristically Khrushchevian survey of the state of Soviet agriculture, with praise (e.g., to the Ukrainians) or blame (e.g., to errant officials in Voronezh oblast) being passed out with a lavish hand.

Treatment of the problems of Soviet agriculture was continued in the following section of the report, in which Khrushchev-the-farm-expert (probably his own favorite among the many roles he assumed) took the floor. Inevitably the Khrushchevian *idée fixe* came in for its share of attention:

It must be understood, comrades, that without corn the collective and state farms will not achieve the required level of grain production. Corn has shown its possibilities in all parts of the Soviet Union. If in certain areas of the country corn is introduced for form's sake only and the collective and state farms harvest small crops, it is not the climate that is to blame but the people in charge. Where corn does not thrive, there is an "ingredient" that is not conducive to its growth. This "ingredient" is to be sought in the leadership. On what level? First and foremost, on the collective and state farms, and also at the district, province, territory, and even the republic level. Officials who have themselves withered and are letting a crop like corn wither, giving it no chance to develop for all it's worth, must be replaced.[66]

After this scarcely veiled threat to purge party officials who stubbornly persisted in underrating the potential of corn, Khrushchev went on to call for increased cotton production and to extol the merits of a wide range of other crops. And he implied united support in the party leadership for his agricul-

[63]Ibid., p. 59.
[64]Ibid.; emphasis supplied.
[65]Ibid.; emphasis supplied.
[66]Ibid., p. 61.

tural program: "We all proceed from the premise that progress in agriculture is one of the chief requirements for the steady improvement of the people's well-being."[67]

Culture was the subject of the next section of Khrushchev's report. Of interest here was a new form of Soviet–Western competition: "*The Soviet Union leads the world in the volume and rate of housing construction. In the past few years our country has been building twice as many apartments per 1000 people as the United States and France and more than twice as many as Britain and Italy*."[68] What Khrushchev neglected to point out, of course, was that the Soviet Union, having suffered from an acute housing shortage for decades, had to overcome the tremendous lag in housing construction which was one of the most harmful social legacies of the Stalin era.

Noteworthy also was the slogan Khrushchev provided to characterize party policy: "Our party's policy is pervaded with the great communist idea: *Everything in the name of man, for the benefit of man!*"[69]

In the field of education Khrushchev was able to draw still another contrast between the Soviet Union and the West: "The Soviet Union is training three times as many engineers as the United States, while the total number of persons engaged in mental work in our country is more than 20,000,000!"[70] Chester Bowles, a prominent State Department official in the Kennedy administration, was cited for his observation that with the launching of the first sputnik America was faced with a serious challenge to its "industrial, military and scientific superiority."[71]

This part of Khrushchev's report was brought to a conclusion with a section devoted to the problem of developing new social relationships as the basis for building communism in the USSR. Once again, Khrushchev cited the canonic authority of Lenin as the precedent for his recommendations. And once again, the dominant theme was competition between the Soviet system and that of the capitalist West, with socialism's eventual triumph a foreordained conclusion: "We have long proposed to the capitalist world that we compete not in an arms race but in improving the working people's lives. We are confident that capitalism cannot stand up under that kind of competition! We are confident that in the end all peoples will make the correct choice, will give their preference to the truly free world of communism and turn their backs on the so-called 'free world' of capitalism."[72]

Thus far, Khrushchev had managed to avoid any really controversial subjects in the fields of internal party politics or the international communist movement, although his passing slur on Kaganovich and his strictures on

[67]Ibid., p. 62.
[68]Ibid., p. 63; emphasis in the original.
[69]Ibid.; emphasis in the original.
[70]Ibid., p. 64.
[71]Ibid., pp. 64–65.
[72]Ibid., p. 67.

Yugoslav "revisionism" gave a foretaste of what was to come. In the third major subdivision of his report, however, delivered at the evening session of October 17, Khrushchev more than made up for the blandness of its first two sections, giving his audience their first good look at some of the tensions which were wracking both the party and the movement. The heading was noncommittal: *III. The Leninist Party Is the Organizer of the Struggle for the Victory of Communism.*

In his preamble to this section of his report Khrushchev again stressed the Leninist bases of party policy, seeking to associate the measures carried out on his initiative with the principles laid down by Lenin. He asserted that the party had already fulfilled its first two programs (those adopted at the Second Congress in 1903 and at the Eighth Congress in 1919) by carrying through the Bolshevik Revolution and achieving "the complete and final victory of socialism in the Land of Soviets."[73] It was for the present congress, then, to adopt a new, third, program which would chart the building of communism in the USSR.

The first subsection of this part of the report, however, was focused on the past, with the heading:

1. *Overcoming the Consequences of the Cult of the Individual. Developing Leninist Norms of Party Life and Principles of Leadership. Increasing the Party's Combat Readiness.*

In earlier sections of his report Khrushchev had affirmed the essential correctness of the line adopted by the Twentieth Party Congress in foreign policy and relations with the international communist movement. Now he turned to the most controversial of the innovations introduced by the Twentieth Congress, its condemnation of the Stalinist "cult of personality." The situation which had confronted the party on the eve of the 1956 congress, he asserted, was a serious one:

Either the party would openly and in a Leninist manner condemn the errors and distortions committed during the period of the cult of J. V. Stalin and reject those methods of party and state leadership that had become an impediment to progress, or the forces that had chained themselves to the old and were resisting everything new and creative would gain the upper hand in the party. This is exactly how serious the problem was. Was it necessary to make such sharp and frank criticism of the major errors and the serious consequences of the cult of the individual?[74]

Answering his own rhetorical question, Khrushchev categorically affirmed that it "was necessary," because investigations carried out after the arrest of "the inveterate enemy and adventurer Beriya" had disclosed ". . . instances of the grossest violations of socialist legality, abuses of power, instances of arbitrary action and repression against many honest people, including outstanding

---

[73]Ibid.
[74]Ibid.

figures in the party and the Soviet state."[75] The exposure of these "abuses of power during the period of the cult of the individual" became an "inner moral requirement and obligation of the party and its leadership."[76]

As usual, Khrushchev called on Lenin for validation and support, and this time was able to produce a highly apposite quotation from the founder of the party affirming in ringing tones the overriding necessity for the party to face up frankly to its mistakes: "To admit a mistake openly, to ascertain its causes, to analyze the situation that gave rise to it and to discuss attentively the means for correcting it—this is the sign of a serious party, this is the fulfillment of its obligations, this is the rearing and training of the *class*, and later of the *masses*."[77]

Out of respect, perhaps, for the sensibilities of the party functionaries who made up the greater part of his audience, Khrushchev approached his target with circumspection. Stalin was even accorded some praise at the outset: "Of course, J. V. Stalin did make great contributions to the party and the communist movement, and we give him his due."[78] But the praise was limited to this single sentence, and was followed immediately by renewed criticism: "However, it was incorrect to associate all the victories of the party and the people with the name of one man. This was a gross distortion of the true state of affairs."[79]

Calling on Lenin for support once again, Khrushchev adroitly shifted the responsibility for launching the criticism of Stalin from his own shoulders to those of Lenin. Lenin, he said, had "perceived Stalin's shortcomings, even vices," and in support he quoted Lenin's "Testament" in which he had warned the party of the danger it faced as the result of Stalin's character and the power he had accumulated. For nearly half a century this document, which Lenin had dictated in the winter of 1922–23 as he lay paralyzed from a stroke, had been kept secret in the Soviet Union (although it was published and known in the West since 1926). Khrushchev had quoted from it in his secret speech to the Twentieth Congress in 1956, but it had never previously been read in an open session of a party congress, and it must have come as a shock to many of the delegates, members of a generation which had been reared in the spirit of unlimited devotion to Stalin.

At the Twentieth Congress the primary target of Khrushchev's revelations had been Stalin himself. Now, however, his main object was to describe the conflict in the party leadership which had broken out after the 1956 congress over the question of whether or not to admit Stalin's crimes and make a clean break with the past. A powerful group in the party leadership, Khrushchev

[75]Ibid.

[76]Ibid.

[77]Ibid., citing V. I. Lenin, *Polnoe Sobranie Sochinenii*, vol. 31, p. 39; emphasis in the original.

[78]*CSP IV*, p. 67.

[79]Ibid.

said, had bitterly opposed the attack on Stalin, and he startled his listeners by adding a new name, that of Voroshilov, to the list of members of what he called the "antiparty group." But Voroshilov, the respected veteran of wars and revolution, was not merely a delegate to the present congress but had been elected a member of the congress Presidium at its outset!

Clearly, Khrushchev had some vital political aim in view. To indicate that the addition of Voroshilov's name had been no slip, Khrushchev proceeded to identify him as one of the first who had opposed "the party's line on condemning the cult of the individual," along with Molotov, Kaganovich, and Malenkov, all four being motivated by the fact that: "They bear personal responsibility for many mass repressions against party, Soviet, economic, military, and Komsomol cadres and for other similar manifestations that took place during the period of the cult of the individual."[80] At first only an "insignificant minority" in the Presidium, this group had picked up strength as the party undertook such innovating measures as ". . . developing the Virgin Lands, reorganizing the management of industry and construction, enlarging the rights of the Union Republics, improving the well-being of Soviet people, and restoring revolutionary legality."[81] With four additional recruits—"Bulganin, Pervukhin and Saburov, and Shepilov who joined them"—the group "succeeded in throwing together an arithmetical majority in the Presidium" and "went into open attack, . . . seeking to change the policy in the party and the country—the policy set forth by the Twentieth Party Congress."[82]

The showdown came in June 1957: "Members of the Central Committee who were then in Moscow, learning of the factional actions of the antiparty group within the Presidium, demanded the immediate calling of a Central Committee plenum. . . . The Central Committee plenum, held in June 1957, resolutely exposed the antiparty group and routed it ideologically."[83]

Faced with "unanimous condemnation" by the plenum, the members of the Antiparty Group confessed that they had conspired and admitted "the harmfulness of their antiparty activity." Voroshilov, Khrushchev disclosed (according him the honorary appelation, "comrade"), ". . . came forward at the plenum with an admission of his mistakes, saying that 'the factionalists misled' him and that he fully recognized his errors and firmly condemned them, together with the whole subversive work of the antiparty group."[84] Only Molotov had stubbornly held out, violating the sacred principle of unanimity by refusing to vote in favor of the resolution condemning the Antiparty Group; later, however, he too "declared that he considered the plenum's decision correct and accepted it."[85]

[80]Ibid.
[81]Ibid.
[82]Ibid.
[83]Ibid.
[84]Ibid.
[85]Ibid.

For an explanation as to how such an event could occur in a supposedly monolithic party, Khrushchev could only offer the lame and un-Marxist proposition that personal factors are often decisive in such matters:

> Such phenomena happen for various reasons: One person's powers deteriorate; another loses touch with life, becomes conceited, does not work; a third proves an unprincipled, spineless turncoat without stanchness in the struggle for the cause of the party. . . . What happens is something like the phenomenon that astronomers call light from extinct stars. Some very distant stars seem to continue to shine even though they have actually been extinct for a long time. The trouble with some people who have found themselves in the position of stars on the public horizon is that they think they are continuing to radiate light although they have long since turned into dying embers. This is what happened to some political figures who fell into the path of factional antiparty struggle.[86]

To wrap up this section of his report, Khrushchev added a brief account of the October 1957 Central Committee plenum at which Marshal Zhukov had been ousted from his position as candidate member of the Presidium.

Just as the Antiparty Group had resisted exposure of the crimes of Stalin, Khrushchev continued, so too in the international communist movement there were those who wanted to defend the "cult of personality." "Now the Albanian leaders do not conceal the fact that they do not like the course, taken by our party, of firmly overcoming the harmful consequences of the Stalin cult, of sharply condemning the abuse of power, of restoring Leninist norms of party and state life."[87] Khrushchev had a ready answer to the question as to why the Albanians had taken this course: "This stand of the Albanian leaders is explained by the fact that they themselves, to our regret and distress, are repeating the methods that occurred in our country in the period of the cult of the individual."[88]

Thus Khrushchev moved from the relatively mild charge that the Albanian leaders disapproved of the way the CPSU was handling its own affairs to the far graver charge that in their own country they were currently carrying out policies identical with those which he had just condemned.

Khrushchev expressed grave concern over the rift which had arisen in Soviet-Albanian relations—"We are deeply troubled by this situation . . ."— but ruled out any concessions on the Soviet side involving the sacrifice of principle:

> The course drawn up by the Twentieth Congress of our party is a Leninist course, and we cannot concede on this fundamental question to either the Albanian leaders or anyone else. To depart from the Twentieth Congress line would mean not heeding the wise instructions of Lenin, who discerned the danger of the appearance of the Stalin cult even when it was in embryo.

[86] Ibid.
[87] Ibid., p. 70.
[88] Ibid.

It would mean disregarding the costly lessons of history, forgetting the price that our party paid for not having heeded in time the instructions of its great leader.[89]

By portraying Lenin rather than himself as the real originator of the condemnation of Stalin's cult of personality, Khrushchev was in effect charging the Albanians with an attack on Lenin—one of the gravest charges one communist can lodge against another.

Khrushchev closed this section of his report with expressions of hope for reconciliation—of course, through concessions on the part of the Albanian leaders: "If the Albanian leaders hold dear the interests of their people and the cause of building socialism in Albania, if they really want friendship with the CPSU, with all the fraternal parties, they should renounce their mistaken views and return to the path of unity and close cooperation in the fraternal family of the socialist commonwealth, the path of unity with the whole international communist movement."[90]

Showing an awareness that he himself was sometimes accused of fostering his own cult of personality, Khrushchev devoted the next section of his report to extolling the principle of collective leadership. "There is not one major question of either domestic or foreign policy," he assured his listeners, ". . . that is not discussed collectively in our party, and the decisions adopted are the expression of the party's collective experience."[91] Not only at the top level but throughout the party, Khrushchev asserted, these Leninist principles were being observed: "It has become the practice to hold broad party-wide and nation-wide discussion of the questions that are introduced for consideration at Central Committee plenums and U.S.S.R. Supreme Soviet sessions."[92] The regular convening of party congresses and Central Committee plenums, Khrushchev continued, a custom which had been "grossly violated" in the period of the cult of personality, now characterized party life from top to bottom. All of this placed high demands on the individual party member, a theme Khrushchev developed at some length.

Having unveiled two of the controversial themes which were to dominate the Twenty-second Congress—the renewed attack on Stalin and the Antiparty Group and the dispute with the Albanian party leadership—Khrushchev, in the remainder of his October 17 report, turned to less sensitive topics. The next section of the report dealt with internal party policy, under the heading:

2. *Organizational Work of the Party and the Rearing of Cadres. The Active Participation of the Masses in Public Activities is the Key to New Successes.*

At the outset of this section Khrushchev called attention to a shift in the emphasis of party work which is highly characteristic of his conception of the

[89] Ibid.
[90] Ibid.
[91] Ibid.
[92] Ibid.

party and its role: "Comrades! In recent years the party has abruptly shifted toward questions of the concrete guidance of the national economy. The Central Committee has turned the attention of party organizations and executive cadres to the careful study and extensive dissemination of progressive experience in industry and agriculture; it has taught through specific positive examples how to conduct our great communist construction correctly."[93]

While he stressed the high requirements set for each individual party functionary, however, the dominant note was again the collective nature of party decisions. "*The strength of party leadership*," he said, "*. . . lies in its collective character, which is what helps to knit the talents, knowledge and experience of many people into a single talent, as it were, capable of doing great things.*"[94]

For the future, Khrushchev envisaged a gradual merging of the party with Soviet society in general. "We are moving toward communism," he asserted, ". . . under which the people themselves will manage the affairs of society without special apparatus."[95] And he proceeded to spell out the implications of this development:

> In our country the socialist system of government is in process of evolving into public self-government. As the vanguard of a people engaged in building a communist society, the party must also take the lead in organizing its own inner-party life; it must set an example, be a model in developing the very best forms of communist public self-government. In practice this may mean, for instance, that the apparatus of the party agencies will steadily shrink while the ranks of party activists will grow. The party agencies should have more and more commissions, departments, instructors and secretaries of raikoms and gorkoms who work on a public [unpaid] basis.[96]

The remainder of this section of the report dealt with shortcomings in party leadership, the choice of cadres, supervision of the execution of decisions, and the problems and responsibilities of the soviets, the trade unions, and the Komsomol.

For the final section of his speech Khrushchev took the high ground of theory and prophecy, under the heading:

3. *The Ideological Activity of the Party and the Strengthening of Ties with the Life of the People. The Building of Communism and the Development of Revolutionary Theory.*

As was to be expected, the new Party Program was placed in the center of attention here, and equally predictably it was linked closely with Lenin's teachings. "Our new Program," said Khrushchev, ". . . is the foundation for educating the masses in the spirit of communism. Vladimir Il'ich Lenin pointed out that the party program is the strongest material for propaganda and agitation.

[93]Ibid., p. 71.
[94]Ibid.; emphasis in the original.
[95]Ibid.
[96]Ibid., pp. 71–72.

'In our program,' he said, 'every paragraph is something that each worker must know, learn, and understand'."[97]

Highly significant though it was as an indication of Khrushchev's concept of communism, this section of his report contained little of direct relevance to our present concern. One point worth noting was Khrushchev's rejection of a Stalinist thesis in the sphere of economic theory:

> In our economic literature, for example, and not only economic literature, one thesis that persisted for a long time was that under socialism public demand backed by purchasing power supposedly must always keep ahead of production; it was even alleged that this represented some kind of special superiority of socialism over capitalism and was one of the moving forces of our society. This clearly erroneous assertion, which contradicts Marxist–Leninist teaching on the relation between production and consumption, arose on the basis of an uncritical, dogmatic acceptance of J. V. Stalin's mistaken thesis that in the U.S.S.R. "the growth of mass demand (purchasing power) exceeds the growth of production at all times."[98]

The implication was that the correct policy was to work for an economy of abundance, and this Khrushchevian proposition was, as usual, given the stamp of canonical authority by attributing it to Lenin: "V. I. Lenin pointed out that socialism means 'the planned organization of the public production process to ensure the welfare and comprehensive development of all members of society.' He repeatedly emphasized the need to ensure rates of development of production that would permit the creation of an abundance of goods for the people. We must be guided by this Leninist directive. Our party fights for the full satisfaction of the people's material and spiritual requirements."[99]

To bring his report to a close, Khrushchev restated the principal themes of Soviet foreign policy as he viewed them: disarmament, conclusion of a German peace treaty, and the need for the great powers to avoid war and to solve "pressing international problems by peaceful means."[100] He closed with a rousing affirmation of his faith in the inevitable world victory of communism.

*   *   *

The evening session of October 17 concluded with a report by ALEKSANDER F. GORKIN (born 1897, party member since 1916), head of the Central Auditing Commission of the party (since late 1960). Gorkin, who had had a long and varied career in the party and government, and who had served as chairman of the USSR Supreme Court since 1957, had emerged as one of the principal spokesmen for the group of liberal-minded reformers in the Soviet legal profession.

[97] Ibid., citing Lenin, *Polnoe Sobranie Sochinenii*, vol. 29, p. 168.
[98] *CSP IV*, p. 75.
[99] Ibid.
[100] Ibid., p. 76.

His October 17 speech contained no novelties or surprises, however, being in the main a workmanlike summary of the activities of the Central Auditing Commission since the Twentieth Party Congress. At the outset he paid tribute to Khrushchev for his personal role in exposing the "subversive, schismatic activity of the antiparty group" (in which he included Voroshilov), but he avoided any direct reference to Stalin or his cult of personality. Gorkin's report thus added nothing to what Khrushchev had already said on these sensitive subjects.

The report on the new Party Program (October 18)

Khrushchev's speech on the opening day of the congress had been in large part a composite product reflecting the agreed decisions of the Presidium as a whole. Only in his departures from the prepared text did he show a purely personal initiative.

The report on the new Party Program which he delivered at the morning and evening sessions of the second day was a much more personal document, reflecting as it did Khrushchev's intense absorption in the drafting of the program and his close personal identification with it. Whoever wants to understand Khrushchev's concept of communism will find this document a richly rewarding source. For our purposes, however, it contains less of note than the report for the Central Committee, since its general approach is in terms of party theory and an idealized party history in which the constructive contributions of Lenin are emphasized far more strongly than the negative actions of Stalin and the Antiparty Group. On these subjects, the speech adds nothing to what Khrushchev said on the preceding day.

In his vision of the future, Khrushchev took a global rather than a national view, and his confident prediction of the eventual world triumph of communism was based on a concrete concept of the relative strength of the socialist nations and those of the nonsocialist world. Since the U.S.–Soviet relationship lay at the core of this concept, the October 18 speech contains abundant material on this theme.

The first major section of the report was a retrospective summary covering "The historic victories of socialism." We can conveniently follow the course of Khrushchev's argument by citing some of the stressed statements in his speech:

> *The primary result of the activities of the party and the people has been the complete and final victory of socialism in the U.S.S.R.*[101]

> *The principal result of the forward movement of society in our time has been the formation of the world socialist system.*[102]

[101] Ibid., p. 84; emphasis in the original.
[102] Ibid., p. 85; emphasis in the original.

The second most important result of world development, from the historical standpoint, is the collapse of the colonial system.[103]

.   .   .

The third result of world development has been an acute all-around weakening of capitalism and a fresh sharpening of its general crisis.[104]

Finally: *"The political instability of world capitalism has increased, . . ."*[105] Here Khrushchev turned his attention specifically to the United States, and what he found bolstered his confidence in the future victory of socialism: "There is no denying that the United States is the richest and strongest power in the capitalist world. But more and more it is coming to be the epicenter of capitalism's economic troubles. And another fact deserves mention: For a whole decade now the U.S. share in world capitalist production and trade has been declining steadily. *American capitalism has passed its zenith, and its sun is setting."*[106]

If the United States was faced with serious troubles internally, Khrushchev maintained, its chances of achieving any kind of unification of the capitalist nations as a whole were even less promising. "There are two trends objectively at work and objectively intertwined in the camp of imperialism," Khrushchev asserted: ". . . One is toward the rallying of all its forces against socialism, and the other is toward mounting contradictions between the imperialist powers themselves and also between them and the other states in the capitalist world. The United States has been unable, and will be unable, to overcome this latter trend. The U.S. financial oligarchy lacks the power and means to make good its claim to the role of savior of capitalism, much less its claim to world domination."[107]

Concluding this section of his speech Khrushchev summed up his views succinctly: "The doom of imperialism and the triumph of socialism on a world scale are inevitable."[108]

Having dealt in summary form with the past and present, Khrushchev devoted the remainder of his report to drawing a glowing picture of the future, the construction of communism in the USSR. First he offered a vision of the beckoning ideal, which he declared to be within man's grasp.

Without explicitly referring to them, Khrushchev indirectly acknowledged that the Soviet government's recent decisions on a military build-up would have the effect of slowing down internal economic development. "Of course," he said rather apologetically, ". . . the imperialists are making every effort to impede the economic and social progress of the Soviet land by *compelling*

---

[103]Ibid., p. 86; emphasis in the original.
[104]Ibid.; emphasis in the original.
[105]Ibid.; emphasis in the original.
[106]Ibid., p. 87; emphasis supplied.
[107]Ibid., p. 87.
[108]Ibid.

*it to make expenditures for defense. If this were not so, the rate of our develop-
ment would be still higher."*[109]

Also of interest was a conspicuous omission from this section of the report.
Kozlov at Pyongyang had called for the more or less simultaneous transition
of *all* the socialist states to the higher level of communism, but Khrushchev
limited his perspective to the Soviet Union, portraying the building of communism there as the fulfillment of the party's obligation to the international
communist movement. "The party," he asserted, ". . . sees as *its chief international obligation* the building of communism in a historically short period of
time."[110]

In the third section of his report Khrushchev offered a detailed exposition
of just how the new communist society would emerge from the present system.
Of major interest, in the context of the Soviet debate over resource allocation,
was his definition of the role of heavy industry in the building of communism:

> The role of heavy industry in the growth of the people's well-being, as well
> as in solving the problem of accumulations, *now presents itself in a new
> way*. It is known that heavy industry is made up of two types of enter-
> prises: First, there are those that produce means of production for enter-
> prises that in their turn also produce means of production and second, there
> are the enterprises that produce means of production for the enterprises of
> light industry and the food industry, for agriculture, for housing construc-
> tion and for cultural and everyday services for the population. When our
> heavy industry had just been created we were obliged to direct accumula-
> tions primarily toward the development of enterprises of the first type and
> to limit investments in those of the second type. *We are now able to increase
> capital investments considerably in the second type of enterprise as well,
> and this will raise the growth rate of the consumer goods industry.* . . . In
> developing heavy industry, we proceed from the Leninist principle that
> "means of production are manufactured not for the sake of the means of
> production themselves but only because more and more means of produc-
> tion are required by those branches of industry making articles of consump-
> tion."[111]

Khrushchev thus cited Lenin as the authority for an eminently Khrushchevian proposition, which adroitly combined recognition of the continued
basic importance of heavy industry with an emphasis on the need for an increase in the consumer goods sector of the economy. He summed up his views
on this subject as follows:

> Heavy industry has always played and will continue to play a leading role
> in expanded reproduction. The party will continue to show concern for its
> growth, for it sees this growth as the decisive factor in the creation of the
> material and technical base and in rapid technical progress and as the basis
> for strengthening the defense capability of the socialist state. *At the same*

---

[109]Ibid., pp. 87–88; emphasis supplied.
[110]Ibid., p. 88; emphasis supplied.
[111]Ibid., p. 89; emphasis supplied.

time, the party will see to it that heavy industry makes an ever greater contribution to increasing the production of consumer goods.[112]

Thus for Khrushchev the continuing emphasis on heavy industry was justified by the contribution it could make to other sectors of the economy and was not an end in itself, and he did not assign armaments production a leading role in the economy, as did Kozlov and the "metal-eaters."

Citing an impressive list of statistics for the Soviet Union's estimated future economic development, Khrushchev proceeded to sketch a series of what he termed "magnificent, truly thrilling plans." Inevitably, comparisons with the U.S. economy were introduced to highlight the significance of the figures:

By 1980 oil extraction will have risen to between 690,000,000 and 710,000,000 tons. For comparison I will point out that in 1960 the U.S.S.R. extracted 148,000,000 tons and the U.S.A. 348,000,000 tons. The ferrous metallurgy industry will be in a position to pour 250,000,000 tons of steel annually. In 1960 the U.S.S.R. produced 65,000,000 tons of steel and the U.S.A. 90,000,000 tons. In only nine years, the Soviet Union will be producing some 55,000,000 tons more steel than the present U.S. output.[113]

Plans for the geographical redistribution of productive forces within the USSR were described, with Central Asia slated to emerge as a "major power-producing region"; here as elsewhere, however, Khrushchev's total silence on the effect these changes would have on neighboring China was striking.

In the section of his speech devoted to agriculture Khrushchev showed the same high-keyed optimism which characterized his views of the future of Soviet industry, and little or no awareness that the chronic problems which had long beset the Soviet peasant still remained unsolved, despite the innovations which Khrushchev had sponsored. He called for nearly doubling the output of grains and more than doubling the output of meat, milk, eggs, wool, and cotton by 1970.[114] "In the near future," he confidently predicted, ". . . the Soviet Union will occupy a position in the international grain market that will make the Messrs. Imperialists feel how our agriculture is growing!"[115]

A particularly bright spot in the Khrushchev vision of the future, as usual, was provided by corn, and this time Khrushchev added the incentive of outstripping the Americans at one of their acknowledged specialties, the development of hybrid corn varieties. Adopting a confidential, folksy tone, he said:

I must tell you that while I was preparing for this report I received a letter from a selection expert in Azerbaidzhan. He announced that he had succeeded in creating a variety of corn with a vegetation period of approximately 60 days. If this is really the case, then simply colossal opportunities open up for expanding and extending corn sowings for grain to the North.

[112]Ibid., p. 90; emphasis supplied.
[113]Ibid., p. 91.
[114]Ibid., p. 92.
[115]Ibid., p. 93.

Mr. Rusk told me in Vienna that in America there is supposedly a similar variety of corn. But his statement has not been confirmed, although Mr. Rusk promised to prove that this was so. Americans who know corn—Mr. Garst, for example—say that there is no such corn variety in America. But if there is none in America, it would be good to create such a variety of corn in the Soviet Union.[116]

Quickly and cautiously, however, Khrushchev got back to more solid terrain: "But it must be realistically understood that this is a very difficult task. And we are not making the development of agriculture dependent on the solution of this problem. If such a variety of corn is not developed, then even with the varieties that do exist we will not only fulfill but overfulfill our plans."[117]

And in fact, as he proceeded to explain, Khrushchev pinned his hopes for the future of Soviet agriculture on such standard measures as electrification of the countryside, expansion of chemical fertilizer production, large-scale irrigation, and an increase in labor productivity.

Perhaps the most immediately interesting portion of Khrushchev's report for our present purposes was the following section, headed:

3. *Improving the People's Well-being and Achieving the Highest Standard of Living.*

The achievement of material abundance in regard to diet, housing, and consumer goods was the prospect held out by Khrushchev, along with a steady upgrading of public services in the fields of medicine and education. Outstripping the United States was, as usual, an important part of the lure:

In 1980 real income per capita in the U.S.S.R. will exceed the present income level of U.S. working people by approximately 75%. But when average per capita consumption standards are discussed, it should be borne in mind that the U.S. figures conceal millions of fully and partially unemployed and of low-paid semi-skilled and unskilled workers, who live in slums and lack the most basic necessities. In our country every family will be assured a sufficiency, and later on an abundance, of material and cultural benefits.[118]

In this connection Khrushchev responded to unnamed Western critics of the draft program by issuing a "challenge to a competition in providing the best living conditions for the people," a competition he was confident socialism would win, since ". . . as we know, capitalism's motto is 'Squeeze a man dry.' And when a man can no longer work, capitalist society leaves him to the mercy of his fate; if he has no place to live, let him spend the night under a bridge. This is what the 'free world' means, what bourgeois 'freedom' means."[119]

From an exposition of the ways in which the material bases for communism would be built, Khrushchev turned in the next major section of his report to the corresponding changes in society and the individual. Most noteworthy

[116]Ibid.
[117]Ibid.
[118]Ibid., p. 99.
[119]Ibid.

here was his concept of the evolution of the structure and role of the government in the USSR, which was summed up in the subsection heading:

2. *From a State of the Dictatorship of the Proletariat to a State of the Entire People.*

Although this theme has only a peripheral relation to our present concerns, it is central to Khrushchev's concept of communism and must be taken into account in any attempt to understand his vision of the future.

In the course of his exposition Khrushchev found new opportunities to draw invidious contrasts between the Soviet system and that of the Western nations, with regard to such matters as the form of government, the system of elections, the role of the press, and the use of the police and armed forces to curb internal dissent.

A serious and intractable internal Soviet problem—the nationality question—was dealt with briefly and firmly. Khrushchev recognized that "even after communism has in the main been built, it will be premature to pronounce the fusion of nations,"[120] but he was completely unyielding on the ultimate goal: "With uncompromising Bolshevist implacability we must eradicate even the slightest manifestation of nationalist survivals."[121]

A section on "The Communist Education and All-Round Development of the Individual" provided Khrushchev with the opportunity to proclaim his staunch hostility to "peaceful coexistence" in the sphere of ideology. "We are revolutionaries and internationalists," he proclaimed, ". . . and therefore we cannot remain indifferent to the propagation of reactionary views; we cannot be reconciled to the befuddling and corrupting of people's minds, the stirring up of chauvinistic passions, by the bourgeoisie. The party will continue to expose imperialist ideology."[122]

The concept of Soviet–U.S. competition which underlay much of the draft program and which was basic to Khrushchev's world outlook was developed as a principal theme in the next major section of his report, entitled, "Communism and the Progress of Mankind."

The keynote was struck immediately: "Carrying out our Party Program will have the most profound effect on the course of world history."[123] And Khrushchev had a ready answer as to why this was the case: "Peaceful economic competition is the chief arena of the contest between the socialist and capitalist systems. *The outcome of this competition will be decided in tremendous measure by the competition between the Soviet Union and the United States of America.*"[124]

To win this competition Khrushchev set high and explicit goals:

The Party sets the task of making our country the world's leading industrial power within the next decade and within that time achieving preponderance over the U.S.A. both in absolute and in per capita volume of industrial out-

[120]Ibid., p. 104.
[121]Ibid.
[122]Ibid.
[123]Ibid.
[124]Ibid.; emphasis supplied.

put. Within approximately the same period the U.S.S.R. will surpass by 50% the present U.S. level of per capita output of farm products and will exceed the U.S. level of national income.

This is but the first objective. We shall not stop there. *In the course of the second decade—by 1980—our country will leave the United States of America far behind in per capita output of industrial and agricultural goods.*[125]

Belatedly, Khrushchev attempted to combine his vision of the building of communism in the USSR with that of the more or less simultaneous advance of all the socialist nations: "The building of communism in our country is an integral part of the building of communist society in the whole socialist commonwealth. The successful development of the world system of socialism opens up a prospect of a more or less simultaneous transition of the socialist countries to communism within a single historical epoch."[126]

By an act of faith for which nothing in the historical experience of the Soviet state provided any justification, Khrushchev flatly asserted that evenness of economic development was characteristic of the socialist states but not of the capitalist states:

The law of uneven economic and political development, leading to the deepening of contradictions and the intensification of the competitive struggle among states, is characteristic of the world system of capitalism. The world system of socialism develops by diametrically opposite laws. It is characterized by the steady and planned economic growth of each country, faster development of those states that lagged economically under capitalism, and the evening up of the general level of development of all the countries.[127]

There was one factor—nationalism—which Khrushchev reluctantly recognized as a possible threat to the unity of the socialist commonwealth: "Nationalism, in whatever guise it wraps itself, represents the most dangerous political and ideological weapon employed by international reaction against the unity of the socialist countries."[128]

Though he might well have been thinking of China, the example Khrushchev cited to illustrate this danger was Yugoslavia. In his report for the Central Committee, Khrushchev had already proclaimed Soviet opposition to what he termed Yugoslav "revisionism"; now he restated the CPSU's ideological position on this question in a modified form which considerably softened the force of the condemnation: "As for Yugoslavia, . . . we have fought and will fight against the revisionist positions of the leadership of the League of Communists of Yugoslavia; at the same time, we have stood and we stand for the utmost development and strengthening of relations with Yugoslavia along state

[125]Ibid.; emphasis in the original.
[126]Ibid.
[127]Ibid.
[128]Ibid.

lines. *On questions of the struggle for peace, our position and that of Yugoslavia coincide in many ways.*"[129]

This led Khrushchev to one of his favorite themes, the alleged underlying unity existing between the various forms of revolution currently present throughout the world. "The tasks of people's democratic, national-liberation and socialist revolutions," he said, ". . . are drawing closer together and becoming more intertwined in the present epoch. The logic of social development has caused all these revolutions to be directed primarily against one chief enemy—imperialism, the monopoly bourgeoisie."[130]

In order to be able to claim the national-liberation movement as an ally of socialism, Khrushchev unhesitatingly stripped the latter concept of virtually any specific content: "The seething, underdeveloped states of Asia, Africa and Latin America, upon carrying the anti-imperialist national-liberation revolution to the end, will be able to make the transition to socialism. *In the present epoch almost any country, regardless of the level of its development, can embark on the path that leads to socialism.*"[131]

In a passage more noteworthy for its flamboyant rhetoric than for its clear thinking, Khrushchev cited Cuba as an outstanding example of this progression:

> The freedom-loving Cuban people, having raised the banner of the people's anti-imperialist revolution, have cleansed their land of the foreign plunderers and their henchmen. The workers, peasants, intelligentsia and middle strata of the urban population have closed ranks under the banner of the revolution. Here is one of the chief sources of the strength of the Cuban revolution and a guarantee of its further development along the path of social progress. The small island, lost in the seas, has now become an undying beacon lighting the way to progress for all the peoples of Latin America.[132]

Although the CPSU had not yet formally applied the honorary designation, "socialist," to the Cuban revolution, Khrushchev took a further step toward that action by saying: "Our hearts are with you, heroes of Cuba, who are defending your independence and freedom from American imperialism, and *who have inscribed socialist goals on your battle standards!*"[133] And he implied, though he did not explicitly make, a renewal of the pledge of Soviet missile aid to Cuba: "Our people have extended *and will extend* help to the fraternal Cuban people in their sacred struggle for their just cause."[134]

For the remainder of this section of his report Khrushchev covered familiar ground in his analysis of the international situation and it is not necessary to

[129]Ibid.; emphasis supplied.
[130]Ibid.
[131]Ibid.; emphasis supplied.
[132]Ibid.
[133]Ibid.; emphasis supplied.
[134]Ibid.; emphasis supplied.

cite the specific formulations in which he clothed his clichés. Suffice it to note that the basic concept here was the claim that ". . . the balance of world political, economic, and military forces has already changed in favor of the peace-loving camp."[135]

Noteworthy also was Khrushchev's definition of the principal goal of Soviet foreign policy: "*In adopting our new Program, our great party solemnly proclaims before all mankind that it sees as the principal goal of its foreign policy not only the prevention of world war but its exclusion, within the lifetime of our generation, from the life of society for all time.*"[136]

Thus the internal goal of building communism in the Soviet Union within twenty years was matched by the foreign policy goal of eliminating world war "within the lifetime of our generation" (at the time of his speech, Khrushchev was sixty-seven years old). Obviously the two goals were thought of as complementary; the underlying assumption was that the building of communism in the USSR would so strengthen the socialist commonwealth that the remaining states of the world would have no choice but to submit to Soviet demands. And the foremost demand, Khrushchev made it clear, would be for "general and complete disarmament." "We have declared more than once and we declare again that we are prepared fully to disband the army, to sink atomic bombs and rockets in the sea, but of course only on the condition of general and complete disarmament under strict international control."[137] And in this context, Khrushchev forgot temporarily his emphasis on peaceful coexistence and on a reallocation of Soviet economic priorities and sounded virtually indistinguishable from Kozlov and the "metal-eaters": "Until the imperialist powers accept that [disarmament], we shall see to it that our armed forces possess the most modern means of defending the motherland—atomic and thermonuclear weapons and rockets of all ranges, so that all types of war materiel are maintained at the necessary level. Strengthening the defense of the U.S.S.R., the might of the Soviet Armed Forces, is the task of tasks of the Soviet people."[138]

There is little that need detain us in the sixth section of Khrushchev's report, in which he took up the "Results of the Discussion of the Draft Program," domestic and foreign. A few scattered passages, however, merit attention.

Noteworthy was Khrushchev's admission that the concept of the replacement of the dictatorship of the proletariat by a "state of the entire people" had encountered opposition in the party on ideological grounds. "In the opinion of certain comrades," he stated, ". . . the dictatorship of the proletariat must be preserved right up to the complete victory of communism."[139]

---

[135] Ibid., p. 108.
[136] Ibid.; emphasis in the original.
[137] Ibid.
[138] Ibid.
[139] Ibid., p. 111.

Rejecting such criticism as based solely on "arbitrarily excerpted quotations" from Marx, Engels, and Lenin, Khrushchev asserted, in a fashion much favored by communist theorists who wish to change the party line, that "life itself" had decreed these changes. "The state of the entire people," he said, ". . . has been generated by life, and it expresses our policy in the political organization of society—the all-round development of democracy."[140]

In his discussion of foreign reactions to and comments on the draft program, Khrushchev portrayed the capitalist world as watching the Soviet Union's triumphant progress toward communism in impotent frustration, unable to offer its citizens anything capable of matching the vision incorporated in the program. Lacking any positive prospects of its own, capitalism, he asserted, could only resort to "slander, insinuation, and distortion," as weapons to combat the popular appeal of the program. Though he ranged widely in his quotations from Western commentaries on the draft, however, Khrushchev passed over in complete silence a notable defection from the ranks of the "socialist commonwealth" which would be stressed in later speeches at the congress: Albania, it would be disclosed by subsequent speakers, had failed to publish the draft program, whereas the *New York Times* (which Khrushchev characterized as "the leading newspaper of the capitalist world") had published it in full.

For the final section of his report Khrushchev turned to a portrayal of the role the party would play in the next period of development. The principal change which had already taken place, in Khrushchev's view, was one which corresponded to the supersession of the dictatorship of the proletariat as the state form of the USSR. *"Our Marxist Leninist party,"* he said, with heavy stress, *". . . which arose as a party of the working class, has become the party of the whole people."*[141]

Anticipating what Kozlov would later present in his congress report, Khrushchev stressed that the new Party Statutes called for the *"systematic renewal of the membership of leading party bodies."*[142] This innovation, Khrushchev asserted, reflected the great changes that had taken place in the party's composition. Originally led by a core of "professional revolutionaries, selflessly devoted to the cause of communism," the party had now grown so strong that "the possibilities for promoting new people to executive cadres are inexhaustible." The party's belief that it must provide for "the constant renewal of cadres," Khrushchev explained, was founded in part on "the lessons ensuing from the consequences of the J. V. Stalin cult." The drafts of the program and statutes therefore ". . . formulate propositions that would establish guarantees against relapses into a cult of the individual and erect reliable barriers against it."[143]

[140]Ibid.
[141]Ibid., p. 114; emphasis in the original.
[142]Ibid.; emphasis in the original.
[143]Ibid.

In a formal pledge which carried obvious implications for his own position, Khrushchev continued: "We declare from the rostrum of the congress: the party must take all necessary measures to close the way forever to a cult of the individual."[144] The force of this pledge, it is true, was somewhat weakened by the immediately succeeding passage in which Khrushchev extolled the merits of "a continuity of leadership, especially in the higher bodies." As usual, Lenin's authority was invoked for this concept, and a suitable quotation from the Leninist scriptures was provided even though, it must be admitted, it said nothing directly in support of "continuity of leadership." Without attempting to reconcile them, Khrushchev asserted both the principles of "rejecting the cult of the individual" and providing for "continuity of leadership."

He brought his exposition of the party's future role to a conclusion with an assertion of the importance of Marxist–Leninist ideology for its continued development and growth, making the claim that: "The new Program is an outstanding theoretical and political document in which are concentrated the major propositions of Marxist–Leninist theory on communism and new conclusions flowing from the experience of applying these propositions in the practice of socialist and communist construction."[145]

If history validated that claim, then the speaker, Khrushchev, whose central role in preparing the new Party Program was common knowledge, could confidently expect to rank as one of the major prophets of communism. Poor Khrushchev! He was mercifully spared the knowledge that almost exactly three years later he was to be unceremoniously ousted from power by his colleagues and disowned by the Central Committee elected at the very congress he was now addressing, and that in books published in the Soviet Union after his fall his name, far from being hailed as that of one of the great Marxist–Leninist theorists, would be systematically expunged on the direct orders of a regime headed by men he now regarded as among his closest supporters.

In an emotional peroration, Khrushchev assured the congress delegates that they would live to see the attainment of communism, "the cherished ultimate goal of the Leninist party": "Not only our descendants but you and I, comrades, our generation of Soviet people, will live under communism!"[146] Responding enthusiastically, the delegates, in the words of the protocols, greeted his words with "*Stormy, prolonged applause, turning into an ovation. All rise. Shouts: 'Hurrah!' 'Hail to the Communist Party!' 'Hail to Leninism!' 'Hail to the Leninist Central Committee!' 'Hail to communism!'.*"[147]

One must give Khrushchev his due: at a time when it would have been easy to find someone to shout, "Long live Khrushchev, the Lenin of today!", his name was not once invoked in the ovation which closed the fourth session of the congress.

[144]Ibid., pp. 114–15.
[145]Ibid., p. 115.
[146]Ibid., p. 116.
[147]Ibid.; emphasis in the original.

The launching of the attack on the Antiparty Group
(October 19, morning)

In order to understand the reasons behind Khrushchev's decision to reopen the attack on the Antiparty Group at the Twenty-second Party Congress it is necessary to know something of its historical background. Khrushchev's victory in June 1957 had been an incomplete one in that it had not been followed by any of the steps provided by party ritual for the disgrace of fallen party leaders, ranging in ascending order from confession of error, through expulsion from the party, up to public trial and condemnation. In Stalin's time the supreme penalty—death by shooting—was the all-too-common end of the road for defeated political leaders, and it was to prevent the reestablishment of a personal dictatorship in which such actions could become routine that a number of members of the collective leadership, who otherwise felt little sympathy for the Antiparty Group, nevertheless opposed Khrushchev's efforts to carry his victory over them to its logical conclusion. However much they might agree with Khrushchev on individual issues of Soviet internal and foreign policy, men like Kosygin and Mikoyan drew the line at placing in his hands the weapon of personal reprisal which formal condemnation of the Antiparty Group leaders would have given him. It was the resistance of the moderates on this issue which not only shielded the Antiparty Group but also gave scope to the militant hard-line faction in the party, led by Frol Kozlov, with the tacit support of a number of other high officials as well as many medium-level functionaries.

At the Twenty-first Party Congress, in 1959, Khrushchev and his supporters had labored mightily to secure formal condemnation of the Antiparty Group, but in vain. Following the congress, in reprisal, a number of party officials who had helped balk the drive lost their posts and were replaced by others who had shown a willingness to support Khrushchev on this issue.

Among the party officials who had moved upward in the 1959 post-congress purge was PYOTR N. DEMICHEV, a relatively young man (born 1918, party member since 1939), who had served for a number of years under Khrushchev in the Moscow obkom and had then demonstrated his talents in the post of business manager of the Council of Ministers of the USSR, just at the time (1958–59) when Khrushchev was taking over from Bulganin the position of premier of the USSR. Demichev had then returned to the Moscow party organization as first secretary of the Moscow obkom, replacing Ivan V. Kapitonov, a party official who had opposed the drive to oust the leaders of the Antiparty Group.[148] In July 1960 Demichev had been elevated to the position of first secretary of the Moscow gorkom, and it was in that capacity that he rated the signal honor of being the first speaker to address the congress in the discussion of Khrushchev's two reports.

[148]On Kapitonov's demotion, see Linden, p. 77; on Demichev's career to 1961, see Tatu, pp. 196–97.

Setting the tone for most of the speeches which were to follow, Demichev found numerous occasions to praise the First Secretary. Khrushchev, he said, was personally responsible for the housing construction program which was being carried out in Moscow, and he had provided wise, fatherly guidance to writers and artists. When Demichev brought up the subject of housing, Khrushchev himself intervened to supply some of the statistics missing from Demichev's account, and then added disingenuously: "It turns out that I am inviting myself in, Comrade Demichev, as, so to speak, a co-author of your speech,"[149] to which Demichev replied, with perhaps a touch of irony: "Thank you for your great help, Nikita Sergeevich."[150]

If Khrushchev had hoped that Demichev would take a strong line on the Antiparty Group, however, he was doomed to be disappointed; Demichev touched on the issue only toward the end of his speech, and then cautiously and prudently, with the implication that the issue was closed.

A member of the younger generation in the party, Demichev had never had personal experience of the full fury of the Stalinist purges, and perhaps for that reason did not feel strongly about the need to cleanse the party of those responsible for them. It fell to the lot of the speaker who followed him, NIKOLAI V. PODGORNY (born 1903, party member since 1930), to open the attack on the Antiparty Group. Podgorny held some of the highest posts in the party: he was not only first secretary of the Ukrainian CP (since December 1957) but also a full member of the Presidium (since May 1960). One of Khrushchev's closest and most reliable supporters on questions of internal policy, Podgorny was not, however, in Tatu's words, "a mere client of the First Secretary"; their relations, rather, "were those of allies rather than of patron and protégé."[151]

For his primary target Podgorny chose L. M. Kaganovich, who as secretary of the Ukrainian CP in 1947 had been guilty, Podgorny charged, of "provocational activities," as well as "the grossest violations of revolutionary legality, of abuses of power, of arbitrary action and unfounded repressions against honest officials devoted to the party and the Soviet regime."[152] Stigmatizing Kaganovich as "a degenerate, in whom there has been nothing communist for a long time," Podgorny charged that his actions "are incompatible with the title of member of the great party of communists,"[153] thus initiating the formal proposal for expulsion of one or another of the members of the Antiparty Group. In so doing he established a standard by which all subsequent party officials who spoke at the congress would be measured.

The attack on the Antiparty Group was broadened and deepened by the next speaker, IVAN V. SPIRIDONOV (born 1905, party member since 1928),

[149] *Pravda*, Oct. 20, 1961; *CDSP*, XIII/48, p. 13.
[150] *CDSP*, XIII/48, p. 13.
[151] Tatu, pp. 95–96.
[152] *Pravda*, Oct. 20, 1961; *CDSP*, XIII/48, p. 16.
[153] *CDSP*, XIII/48, p. 16.

first secretary of the Leningrad obkom (since 1957). The problem of identifying Spiridonov's organizational loyalties has proved to be a difficult one, and students of Soviet politics have come up with widely divergent answers to the question. On the one hand, Spiridonov was clearly in the forefront of those who mounted the attack on the Antiparty Group, and would thus appear to belong to the group of Khrushchev's close supporters.[154] On the other hand, Spiridonov's career had been in the Leningrad party organization, a fact which would indicate an affiliation with Kozlov, as would his views on the need for assigning top priority in resource allocations to heavy industry. Perhaps the most judicious evaluation of his position is that provided by Carl Linden, who writes: "His loyalty appears to have been divided between Khrushchev and Kozlov."[155]

What does not appear open to doubt, however, is that at the time of the Twenty-second Congress Khrushchev regarded Spiridonov as a dependable ally; otherwise the assignment to him of one of the choicest spots in the congress schedule would be inexplicable.

Viewed from the standpoint of his treatment of the Antiparty Group, Spiridonov's speech supports Linden's analysis of his political position as an ambiguous one. As befitted a Leningrader, Spiridonov took for his principal subject the "Leningrad Case" of 1949–50, a case which he called "fabricated from beginning to end," primarily by Beriya and Malenkov. Beriya, of course, was dead, but Malenkov was very much alive, and Spiridonov's failure to follow through with a demand for Malenkov's expulsion from the party therefore contrasted strikingly with Podgorny's stand on Kaganovich.

This omission was made good, however, by the following speaker, KIRILL T. MAZUROV (born 1914, party member since 1940), first secretary of the Belorussian CP (since 1957) and candidate member of the Presidium (since June 1957). Although he accused Malenkov, Molotov, and Kaganovich of being "personally guilty of mass slaughter of party cadres and the grossest violations of Soviet legality," Mazurov directed his principal attack against Malenkov, whom he accused of personal responsibility for purging "almost the entire leadership" of the Belorussian Republic. Speaking on behalf of the party organization of Belorussia, Mazurov called for the expulsion of Malenkov from the party.[156]

Of the four speakers who opened the discussion of Khrushchev's reports, only one, Podgorny, could be rated as a full supporter of the First Secretary. Demichev was an independent who had fostered his career by adroit services to Khrushchev; neither Spiridonov nor Mazurov, however, really belonged in the First Secretary's camp. Why, then, did they help launch the attack on the Antiparty Group? To understand their motives one must abandon the oversimplified view that zeal in the attack on Stalin's cult of personality and on

[154]See, for example, Tatu, p. 23.
[155]Linden, pp. 244–45.
[156]*Pravda*, Oct. 20, 1961; *CDSP*, XIII/48, p. 19.

the Antiparty Group was equivalent to personal support of Khrushchev. The real situation was more complicated.

Revulsion against Stalin and his terrorist methods of rule—methods in which the leaders of the Antiparty Group were deeply implicated—was widespread in the party. It had not been invented by Khrushchev; rather, he recognized its strength and sought to harness it for his own political purposes. At the same time, in justice to Khrushchev, one must recognize that he himself shared the revulsion against Stalin and his methods, so that his attack on Stalin was in part the expression of a genuine, heartfelt determination that the party should never again fall victim to the kind of lawlessness which had flourished under Stalin.

It was because Khrushchev took seriously his pledge that "the party must take all necessary measures to close the way forever to a cult of the individual" that he was able to enlist the services of men like Spiridonov and Mazurov, who were by no means his enthusiastic supporters on other issues and whose careers owed nothing to his support but who had strong personal reasons for wanting to see criminals like Malenkov and Kaganovich thrown out of the party and brought to justice.

With the next two speakers the tension abated. SHARAF R. RASHIDOV (born 1917, party member since 1939), first secretary of the Uzbek CP (since March 1959), spoke of the "exposure and rout" of the Antiparty Group as an accomplished fact and neither gave any details concerning the repressive actions of its leaders nor demanded their expulsion from the party. Since it was prudent, however, for a non-Russian party boss to cultivate good relations with all factions in the leadership, Rashidov followed his (for Khrushchev) disappointingly bland reference to the Antiparty Group with fulsome praise for the First Secretary. Rashidov's political astuteness was to be rewarded at the end of the congress by election to the position of candidate member of the Presidium. Thanks to his prudence in avoiding too direct a commitment to Khrushchev, moreover, his career continued to prosper after the latter's overthrow in 1964.

The final speaker at the morning session on October 19 was another non-Russian Central Asian party boss, DINMUKHMAMED A. KUNAEV (born 1912, party member since 1939), first secretary of the Kazakh CP (since January 19, 1960). Improving on Rashidov's example, Kunaev avoided mentioning the Antiparty Group altogether, though he did touch lightly on the "elimination of the consequences of the cult of the individual"; in compensation, he too heaped praise on Khrushchev.

Kunaev, as we have seen (above pp. 18–19), seems to have been a faithful friend of Khrushchev whose loyalty to him would still be manifested after his overthrow. Kunaev's restraint on the Antiparty Group issue, therefore, like that of Rashidov, can best be explained in terms of political prudence. The dangers to which a non-Russian party leader might expose himself if he got caught in the cross-fire of the Khrushchev–Kozlov feud had been vividly demonstrated by the recent fate of two party officials in this category, Tovmasian in Armenia and Ul'dzhabaev in Tadzhikistan. Both had been purged by Kozlov, despite (or because of) their loyalty to Khrushchev. For a non-Russian party official, therefore, the best course was to avoid open commitment to one side or the other on the issues which divided the party leadership and to take refuge in the kind of personal praise which gives the recipient pleasure and causes no offense to his opponents.

Chou dissents (October 19, evening)

The Chinese communist leadership, encouraged by the evidence that its foreign policy views were shared by some high CPSU functionaries, had responded to the Soviet invitation to attend the Twenty-second Congress by naming a delegation headed by one of its most distinguished and influential members, Premier CHOU EN-LAI. Accompanied by a small delegation carefully balanced between "conciliators" and "militants,"[157] Chou reached Moscow on October 15, where he was met at the airport by a group of CPSU officials headed by Khrushchev. A *New York Times* report from Hong Kong, reflecting the opinion of expert "China watchers" in that strategically located observation post, stated that: "There is a strong belief here that Premier Chou was sent to the Moscow meeting to promote friendlier relations between Peiping and Moscow and to smooth over their ideological differences. As one of the most sophisticated Peiping leaders, Mr. Chou was regarded as a natural choice for such a task."[158] The importance attached to the Chinese visit by the Soviets was shown by the fact that Chou was the only foreign visitor to the congress whom Khrushchev greeted personally.[159]

If Chou had hoped to find that Khrushchev had yielded to Kozlov's pressure and was ready to adopt a line in foreign and internal policy more palatable to the Chinese, however, Khrushchev's first speech to the congress showed him the extent of his miscalculation. At the evening session of October 17, when Khrushchev openly attacked the Albanian party leadership, Chou manifested his displeasure in a way which caught the attention of an alert Western newsman present at the session. According to Seymour Topping: "The Chinese leader [Chou] began withholding his applause last night [October 17] when Mr. Khrushchev disclosed that Albania had been exiled from the international communist movement."[160]

Chou's behavior at the evening session of October 18, following Khrushchev's report on the new Party Program, was even more demonstrative: "Finishing a six-hour speech that included an attack on communist countries following 'the path of isolation,' Khrushchev walked over to where Chou and other foreign communists were sitting to shake hands. . . . But Chou had

---

[157]On the composition of the Chinese delegation, see Zagoria, p. 371.
[158]*NYT*, Oct. 27, 1961, p. 2.
[159]Seymour Topping, *NYT*, Oct. 16, 1961, p. 1.
[160]*NYT*, Oct. 19, 1961, p. 14.

slipped away before the Soviet leader could get to the row of seats in the Kremlin's new congress hall. As Khrushchev shook hands with east European communist leaders, Chou sauntered out the opposite exit with his hands in his pockets."[161]

Chou's opportunity for a counterblast came on the evening of October 19, when he delivered the first speech to the congress by the head of a foreign delegation (the importance attached to the CPC by the CPSU was emphasized by the signal honor indicated by this priority).

Although he paid perfunctory tribute to Soviet internal economic advances, Chou's major emphasis was on international relations, particularly the conflict between the socialist nations and those of the capitalist world. Soviet technical advances, he asserted, showed that the socialist states were pulling ahead: "Twice this year the Soviet Union has successfully launched into space manned spaceships, which triumphantly orbited the earth and returned to it. This new exploit in man's conquest of space is still more conclusive evidence that the Soviet Union is leaving the U.S.A. farther and farther behind in major fields of science and technology. It demonstrates strikingly that the socialist system is incomparably superior to the capitalist system."[162]

On behalf of the Chinese people Chou voiced resolute support for the measures of military build-up undertaken by the Soviet government at the end of August:

A short while ago the Soviet Union advanced proposals that a German peace treaty be concluded and the situation in West Berlin normalized on that basis. In the face of the serious situation that had resulted from intensification of the arms race and military preparations, the breakdown of the conference on the cessation of nuclear testing and the rejection of disarmament by the U.S.A., the Soviet Union was forced to take very important steps such as the resumption of test explosions of nuclear weapons. These proposals and these steps represent important moves to uphold world peace and protect the security of the socialist camp, and to put a stop to imperialist military adventures; they are fully consistent with the interests of the peoples of the whole world. *The Chinese people fully support all of these important moves by the Soviet Union aimed at defending world peace.*[163]

With regard to the international situation as a whole, Chou portrayed the world as animated by popular movements which had as their chief foe "the fiendish grip of American imperialism." In words far sharper than those Khrushchev had used to characterize the United States, Chou asserted that: "The worst enemy of peace is American imperialism. It is the bulwark of present-day colonialism and international reaction, the prime force of aggression and war."[164] After cataloguing a roster of U.S. misdeeds in Cuba, Laos,

---

[161] *Washington Post*, Oct. 19, 1961, p. A–16 (a Reuters dispatch from Moscow).

[162] *CSP IV*, p. 127.

[163] Ibid.; emphasis supplied.

[164] Ibid., p. 128.

Berlin, and elsewhere, Chou summed up his indictment in an all-inclusive statement: "The face of American imperialism as the common enemy of the peoples of the whole world has been completely exposed."[165]

Although he avoided expressing outright disagreement with Khrushchev's forecast that war between the major powers was no longer inevitable, Chou's formula for attaining world peace was far more militant and his belief in the possibility of avoiding general war far less robust:

All the actions of American imperialism indicate that *we still face the danger of war* and that the peoples of all lands must redouble their vigilance. The struggle against imperialist aggression and the defense of world peace remain, as they have been, a task of extreme urgency for the peoples of all countries. If the socialist camp, the international working class, the national-liberation movement and all peace-loving peoples and states make common cause, form a united front to combat the policy of aggression and war being pursued by the imperialist circles headed by the U.S.A. and wage an unflagging struggle, world peace is certain to be preserved.[166]

Chou placed heavy stress on the need to preserve the unity of the socialist system, in which he explicitly included Albania—an unmistakable signal that he intended to take up Khrushchev's challenge. Foreign journalists present at the congress once again had an opportunity to observe a key turning point in the deepening Sino–Soviet rift. A graphic report comes from Stanley Johnson, an Associated Press reporter in Moscow: "At the mention of Albania, the audience began strong stormy applause. But not Khrushchev. . . . Khrushchev and members of the Presidium did not applaud, showing the audience it was out of place. The applause subsided like a wave."[167]

Chou went on to administer a personal reproof to Khrushchev:

We hold that if, unfortunately, disputes and disagreements have arisen among the fraternal parties and fraternal countries, we should resolve them patiently, being guided by the spirit of proletarian internationalism and by the principles of equality and the achievement of identity of views through consultations. Open unilateral condemnation of a fraternal party does not make for solidarity, does not help settle issues. *Openly exposing disputes between fraternal parties and fraternal countries for enemies to see cannot be regarded as a serious, Marxist–Leninist approach.* Such an approach can only pain friends and gladden foes.[168]

After a plea for "the solidarity and unity of the whole socialist camp and of the whole international communist movement," and an assurance of the "deep friendship of long standing" which joined the peoples of China and the Soviet Union, Chou ended his speech by reading a short message of greeting to the

[165]Ibid.

[166]Ibid.; emphasis supplied.

[167]*Washington Post*, Oct. 20, 1961, p. A–19. For a similar eye-witness report, see Seymour Topping, *NYT*, Oct. 20, 1961, p. 1.

[168]*CSP IV*, p. 128; emphasis supplied.

congress signed by Mao Tse-tung and dated October 14, 1961 (the date of Chou's departure for Moscow), which asserted that "the solidarity and friendship between our two parties have stood up under testing and are eternal and inviolable."[169]

There are conflicting reports of what happened next. According to the official protocols of the congress, Chou "exchanged warm greetings with comrade Khrushchev and other members of the Presidium of the Congress."[170] A Western journalist who was present at the congress confirms that Chou shook hands with Khrushchev after his speech.[171] Carl Linden, however, citing unidentified "Western news reports," states that at the end of his speech Chou "brushed past Khrushchev and demonstratively shook hands with Kozlov on the rostrum."[172]

Linden's version of events, if substantiated by contemporary eyewitness observers, would constitute striking confirmation of the link between Kozlov and the Chinese leadership. It seems doubtful, however, that events took this form. For Chou to have expressed a clear preference for one Soviet leader over another at an official congress attended by foreign observers would have been a flagrant breach not only of manners but also of security which an old hand like Chou would scarcely have committed.

*   *   *

It will be convenient at this point to follow through to its conclusion the episode involving the Chinese delegation.

On the afternoon of October 21, two days after his speech, Chou made a demonstrative public gesture of the views of the Chinese party leadership by laying a wreath on Stalin's tomb in the mausoleum on Red Square, inscribed, "To Josif Vissarionovich Stalin—the great Marxist-Leninist."[173]

Chou remained in Moscow for another two days, including Sunday, October 22, a day during which the congress was not in session. Both the Russians and the Chinese subsequently divulged that before his departure on the 23rd Chou held talks with Khrushchev and other top Soviet leaders. Since the congress protocols indicate Khrushchev's presence at both the morning and evening sessions of October 21 and 23, it is probable that the talks between Chou and the Soviet leaders took place on Sunday, October 22. The fact that Chou did not depart immediately after laying the wreath on Stalin's tomb points to a period of consultation to ascertain whether an open break between the CPSU and the CPC could be avoided.

---

[169]Ibid., p. 129.

[170]*Sten. ot.*, 1: 328.

[171]Seymour Topping, *NYT*, Oct. 20, 1961, p. 1.

[172]Linden, footnote, p. 133. I have not been able to find any contemporary published confirmation of this statement.

[173]*NYT*, Oct. 22, 1961, p. 3. Chou also laid a wreath on Lenin's tomb, inscribed, "To the great leader and father of the proletarian revolution."

As to the substance of the discussions between Chou and the Soviet leaders, the fullest available account is that contained in an Open Letter addressed by the Central Committee of the CPSU to the Central Committee of the CPC released on July 14, 1963. According to this source:

In October 1961 the CPSU CC undertook new attempts to normalize relations with the CPC. Comrades N. S. Khrushchev, F. R. Kozlov and A. I. Mikoyan talked to Comrades Chou En-lai, P'eng Chen, and other leading officials who attended the Twenty-Second CPSU Congress. Comrade N. S. Khrushchev set forth in detail for the Chinese delegation the position of the CPSU CC on questions of principle discussed at the Twenty-Second Congress and emphasized our unchanging desire to strengthen friendship and cooperation with the Chinese CP.[174]

The Chinese, in a counterblast dated September 6, 1963, gave their version of the discussion, adding some salient details:

The Communist Party of China resolutely opposed the errors of the Twenty-Second Congress of the CPSU. Comrade Chou En-lai, who headed the delegation of the CPC to the congress, stated our party's position in his speech there, and he also frankly criticized the errors of leadership of the CPSU in subsequent conversations with Khrushchev and other leaders of the CPSU. In his conversations with the delegation of the CPC, Khrushchev flatly turned down our criticisms and advice *and even expressed undisguised support for antiparty elements in the Chinese Communist Party.* He openly stated that after the Twentieth Congress of the CPSU, when the leaders of the CPSU were beginning to take a "road different from that of Stalin" (that is, when they were beginning to take the road of revisionism), they had still needed the support of the fraternal parties. He said, "The voice of the Chinese Communist Party was then of great significance to us," but "things are different now," and "we are doing well" and "we shall go our own way."[175]

Thus, according to the Chinese, Khrushchev had attempted to interfere in the internal politics of the Chinese Communist party; the fact that he had just publicly called for internal changes in the Albanian Party of Labor lends substance to the charge. For his part, Khrushchev could well retort that the Chinese were playing the same game in their clearly expressed preference for the views and policies of Kozlov, though it was to be some time yet before they reached the point of publicly advocating the ouster of Khrushchev.

In this respect the Albanians were well out in front of their Chinese allies. Radio Tirana on October 20 broadcast a statement by the Albanian party Central Committee promising to "unmask the anti-Marxist and anti-Albanian activities of N. Khrushchev and his group" and warning that "the unity of the socialist camp and the international communist and workers' movement is

[174]*Pravda*, July 14, 1963; *CDSP*, XV/28, p. 18.

[175]William E. Griffith, *The Sino–Soviet Rift* (Cambridge, Mass.: M.I.T. Press, 1964), p. 408; emphasis supplied.

being seriously endangered by the anti-Marxist activities of N. Khrushchev and his followers."[176]

Skimpy as they are, the two available accounts of the talks between Chou and the Soviet leaders form the basis for some useful conclusions. From the composition of the Soviet group at the talks, it is clear that the Soviets made an attempt to provide the appearance of a balanced group, with the leading advocates of two diametrically opposed policies toward China, Khrushchev and Kozlov, balanced by a third party leader, Mikoyan. (As we shall see presently, however, Mikoyan was far from neutral on the question of policy toward China.) From the Chinese version it appears that Khrushchev dominated the presentation of the Soviet case; if Kozlov attempted to influence the course of the talks in the direction of mollifying Chou and avoiding an open break, he was obviously unsuccessful. In view of Kozlov's characteristic preference for indirection and subterfuge, however, it seems more likely that he avoided a head-on clash with Khrushchev during the talks, giving him the opportunity to present the Soviet case, but meanwhile laying clandestine plans for a counterstroke. We shall see presently the form which that counterstroke took.

The 1963 disclosures that Chou had conducted talks with a group of Soviet leaders before his return to Peking put the affair in a somewhat different light from the one available to observers at the time. (Neither Griffith when he wrote his book on Albania, nor Zagoria when he wrote *The Sino-Soviet Conflict* knew of the top-level talks held before Chou's departure.) It becomes clear that Chou's departure from Moscow did not represent a sudden impetuous gesture of defiance, but was decided on only after he had sounded out the Soviet leaders in private talks and had become convinced that further discussion would be useless. The four-day interval between Chou's speech and his departure was also important for the opportunity it provided for Chou to consult with the CPC leaders in Peking by cable, so that the decision that he should return to Peking had their full approval.

Convinced that there was nothing to be gained by remaining any longer in Moscow, Chou left for home on Monday, October 23, turning over the leadership of the Chinese delegation to his deputy, P'eng Chen. This time not only Khrushchev but other members of the Presidium as well—Podgorny and Kozlov—accompanied Chou to the airport, along with a sizable group of lesser luminaries.[177]

En route back to Peking Chou sent a telegram of thanks to Khrushchev, the diplomatic phrasing of which, given the circumstances, must be recognized as bitterly ironic: "In leaving the borders of our great ally, I express to you and to the Central Committee of the Communist Party of the Soviet Union sincere gratitude for *the cordial welcome and warm concern* shown us. May the great

---

[176]*NYT*, Oct. 22, 1961, pp. 1, 3 (Paul Underwood from Belgrade); full text in Griffith, *Albania*, pp. 228–30, citing *Zërri i Popullit*, Oct. 21, 1961.

[177]The group included A. A. Gromyko, Yu. V. Andropov, N. R. Mironov, S. V. Chervonenko (Soviet ambassador to the C.P.R.), L. N. Tolkunov, et al. *Pravda*, Oct. 24, 1961, p. 1; *CSP IV*, p. 129.

eternal and indestructible friendship between the peoples of China and the Soviet Union flourish forever."[178]

To provide a plausible cover for the awkward incident, TASS reported that Chou's departure was "in connection with the forthcoming session of the National People's Congress,"[179] despite the fact that no session of that body had previously been announced. (The next NPC session was in fact not held until March 1962.)[180] As a studied gesture of contempt, *Pravda* placed its report on the departure of Chou immediately above a news item reporting the publication of a brochure with the text of Khrushchev's report on the new Party Program in an edition of five million copies.[181]

As to the Chinese, they made no effort to conceal the fact that Chou's departure constituted a walkout from the congress; the Chinese news agency simply reported his departure from Moscow without offering any explanation.[182] Even clearer in its implications was the demonstrative welcome given Chou by the CPC leadership on October 24: the top members of the Chinese Politburo, including Mao himself, were on hand at the airport to greet Chou, a gesture which foreign observers were quick to recognize as a sign that the break with the Soviets had the support of the entire Chinese leadership.[183]

Following Chou's departure the remaining members of the CPC delegation left Moscow for a sight-seeing trip to Leningrad, from which they returned only on the final day of the congress, October 31. They left for Peking immediately. This time only one member of the CPSU Presidium was present to see them off: F. R. Kozlov, a fact which provides eloquent testimony to the split in the CPSU leadership.[184]

With the delivery of Chou's report, on the evening of October 19, the battle-lines for the struggle for supremacy in the international communist movement had been clearly drawn, just as the lines in the internal struggle for power in the CPSU had been drawn earlier on the same day by the call for expulsion of the leaders of the Antiparty Group. These two actions, coming thus early in the congress, predetermined its character as one of the most tense and dramatic in the history of the CPSU and the international communist movement.

*   *   *

Two other foreign communist leaders—WLADYSLAW GOMULKA of Poland and MAURICE THOREZ of France—followed Chou En-lai to the rostrum at the evening session of October 19, and both expressed support for

[178]Ibid.; emphasis supplied.

[179]Ibid.

[180]Griffith, *Albania*, p. 94.

[181]*Pravda*, Oct. 24, 1961, p. 1.

[182]Zagoria, pp. 370–71.

[183]*NYT*, Oct. 25, 1961, p. 5.

[184]*Pravda*, Nov. 2, 1961, p. 10. In addition to Kozlov the group included P. F. Lomako, Yu. V. Andropov, S. V. Chervonenko, N. R. Mironov, et al.

Khrushchev in the now publicly disclosed dispute between the Soviets and Albania. On specific issues they diverged notably, however, Gomulka manifesting a strong tendency to give total support to Khrushchev's innovations in foreign and internal policy, Thorez taking a more traditionalist line. Of all the speakers at the congress, Gomulka went furthest in explicitly endorsing Khrushchev's action in lifting the deadline for signing a German peace treaty. Cautiously alluding to the internal tension over Berlin and the widespread fear that Khrushchev would announce the signing of a peace treaty with the GDR at the congress and thereby precipitate a crisis, Gomulka said that Khrushchev's statement on this question "will meet with full approval *and gratitude* from the peoples of Europe and of the whole world."[185] By contrast, Gomulka said not a word in support of the Soviet military build-up.

As the leader of a communist party in one of the leading Western Powers, Thorez's position was very different from that of Gomulka, and his speech reflected the difference. He expressed "understanding" and "full approval" of "all the measures [the Soviet Union] has taken to strengthen its defense capacity," but was silent on Khrushchev's policy in Berlin.[186]

Speeches by three high-ranking CPSU leaders—Brezhnev, Mzhavanadze, and Voronov—brought the evening session of October 19 to a close. Generally regarded at this time as one of Khrushchev's closest supporters, BREZHNEV in his speech failed to support this analysis, though he uttered unusually effusive praise for the First Secretary. Much more meaningful, however, was the fact that the speech included no specific details on the crimes of the Antiparty Group, and instead of supporting the call for the expulsion of the group's leaders, merely expressed the view that "they should bear responsibility to the party and the people [for] the mistakes and crimes that had been committed."[187]

On the Albanian issue Brezhnev took a somewhat stronger stand, not only backing Khrushchev's charge that the Albanian leaders were fostering their own cult of personality but crediting Khrushchev with attempts to improve Soviet–Albanian relations. There was still, however, no reference to any foreign policy implications in the split between the Soviet and Albanian parties.

If Brezhnev showed himself to be restrained in his support of Khrushchev, V. P. MZHAVANADZE (born 1902, party member since 1927) was downright cool. The First Secretary of the Georgian CP (since 1953) treated the problem of the Antiparty Group as a closed issue, avoided the word "crimes," and said nothing about expulsion from the party. Nor had he anything to say on the subject of Albania. A few passages of moderate praise for Khrushchev as an "inspiring" leader in the field of agricultural policy were more than counterbalanced by outspoken support for the Soviet military build-up: "the

---

[185] *Pravda*, Oct. 20, 1961; *CDSP*, XIII/49, p. 13; emphasis supplied.
[186] *Sten. ot.*, 1: 337.
[187] *Pravda*, Oct. 20, 1961; *CDSP*, XIII/49, p. 16.

toilers of Georgia, like the entire Soviet people, entirely approve the necessary measures undertaken by the [Soviet] government in the face of the direct threats by the imperialist powers."[188]

The most lukewarm of the three party speakers at the evening session on October 19 was GENNADY L. VORONOV (born 1910, party member since 1931), deputy chairman of the Bureau for the RSFSR and candidate member of the Presidium (both since January 1961). In his speech Voronov avoided any direct reference either to the Antiparty Group or to the Albanians, covering himself by vague threats against "all sorts of apostates from Marxism, revisionists and dogmatists, . . . who are trying to impede the socialist development of the peoples and to push the communist and workers' parties from the correct Leninist path."[189]

Much of Voronov's lengthy speech dealt with agriculture in the Russian Republic, a subject which provided numerous opportunities for favorable references to Khrushchev, opportunities which Voronov, however, ignored. His tone was businesslike and matter-of-fact, and he referred candidly to differences of opinion he had had with Khrushchev on several occasions. On the basis of his congress speech it would be difficult to prove that the Deputy Chairman of the Bureau for the RSFSR was a strong or loyal supporter of Khrushchev.

Pattern for disarray (October 20 and 21)

The morning session on October 20 opened with a speech by another of the non-Russian party bosses, VELI Yu. AKHUNDOV (born 1916, party member since 1939), first secretary of Azerbaidzhan (since July 1959). Akhundov followed the pattern established earlier by Rashidov and Kunaev: praise for Khrushchev but silence on the controversial issues of the Antiparty Group and Albania.[190] Not that Akhundov manifested any personal hostility toward Khrushchev; in words which fitted completely into the First Secretary's attempt to link his policies with those of Lenin, Akhundov said: ". . . if Lenin could see with what ability and wisdom our affairs are being run, if Lenin could see the course which the Central Committee of our party headed by N. S. Khrushchev has taken since the Twentieth Congress, he would say: The right course, straight ahead!"[191]

A novelty in Akhundov's speech was a passage extolling the CPSU for having improved the position of women in Soviet society, a passage which served as a graceful introduction to the following speaker, Mme. YEKATERINA FURTSEVA (born 1910, party member since 1930), USSR Minister of Culture (since May 1960), full member of the Presidium (since June 1957).

[188]*Sten. ot.*, 1: 354.
[189]*Pravda*, Oct. 21, 1961; *CDSP*, XIII/50, p. 12.
[190]*Sten. ot.*, 1: 375–83; condensed translation, *CDSP*, XIII/50, pp. 14–15.
[191]*Sten. ot.*, 1: 376.

The opening section of Mme. Furtseva's speech took the form of a standard report on work accomplished since the last party congress in the speaker's field of competence. Interlarded with the statistics on libraries, films, etc., were unusually warm encomiums to Khrushchev, which substantiated the generally held view that Mme. Furtseva was one of the First Secretary's closest and most dependable followers.

After the conclusion of her formal report, Mme. Furtseva turned to what was obviously a hastily assembled appendix dealing with recent party history, which she justified on the grounds that "It seems to me that after the Twentieth Congress, *the Twenty-second Congress is a congress for rendering accounts*, and that we must know and understand how difficult and complicated the situation was in the party leadership."[192]

Mme. Furtseva's principal revelations concerned the opposition by members of the Antiparty Group, particularly Molotov, to a series of reform measures—housing, the Virgin Lands, reorganization of the management of industry—which Khrushchev had sponsored in the period 1955–57. Her most telling disclosure, however, came toward the end of her speech when she described a meeting of the Presidium held shortly before the June 1957 CC plenum, at which Malenkov had taunted Khrushchev by saying, "Why are you trying to frighten us with a plenum? The plenum is our home territory, we'll go and tell everything to the plenum."[193]

Without directly identifying the Albanians, Mme. Furtseva made it clear that she condemned their refusal to support Khrushchev's attack on Stalin, but there was still nothing to suggest that issues of foreign policy were involved in the dispute between the CPSU and the Albanian party, or that the conflict had any immediate relevance to the current international situation.

Following Mme. Furtseva to the speaker's stand was one of the party's middle-rank functionaries—the first such to address the congress: LEONID N. YEFREMOV (born 1912, party member since 1941), first secretary of Gorky obkom (since 1958). Yefremov, a specialist in agriculture, had enjoyed Khrushchev's patronage throughout his career and came through with a solid hit for the First Secretary on this occasion. He opened with praise for Khrushchev's reports to the congress, for the "courageous, resolute and principled struggle" he had led against the cult of the individual and for the measures of "truly revolutionary internal transformation" carried through on his initiative.

When he came to the subject of the Antiparty Group, Yefremov directed the brunt of his attack against Malenkov, whom he charged with repressions which had seriously damaged the party organization in Gorky. Speaking on behalf of the Gorky party organization, Yefremov seconded the call for expulsion of Malenkov from the party.

The remainder of Yefremov's speech, which dealt with the economic problems and prospects of Gorky oblast, need not detain us, though it is worth

[192]*Pravda*, Oct. 22, 1961; *CDSP*, XIII/50, p. 18; emphasis supplied.

[193]*Sten. ot.*, 1: 396. This passage was omitted from the text of Mme. Furtseva's speech as published in *Pravda* and *Izv.*, Oct. 22, 1961.

noting that he included toward its close a passage of warm praise for the "inspiring example of the Leninist style of work" set by "the tireless, dedicated work" of Khrushchev.

Following Yefremov's speech the delegates took a thirty-minute break, and then reassembled to listen to a speech by MSTISLAV V. KELDYSH (born 1911, party member since 1949), president of the Soviet Academy of Sciences (since May 19, 1961). A brilliant scientist as well as a devoted party member, Keldysh was also a great admirer of Khrushchev, primarily because of the latter's consistent support of Soviet science. Early in his speech Keldysh cited the task set for Soviet science by the party—"*to take the leading position in world science* in all basic fields"[194]—the counterpart in science to the party's goals of world leadership in the political and economic fields. Khrushchev's close personal identification with the speaker was emphasized when he interrupted Keldysh approvingly following a call by the latter for the concentration of scientific resources.[195] As a scientist, remote from party politics and international policy, however, Keldysh had nothing to say on the controversial subjects of the cult of personality, the Antiparty Group, or the Albanian heresy.

The next speaker was another of the non-Russian Union Republic party bosses, DZHABAR R. RASULOV (born 1913, party member since 1939), first secretary of the Tadzhik CP (since April 12, 1961). It was thanks to Kozlov's direct intervention in the Tadzhik party organization's affairs that Rasulov had been brought back into the party apparatus after serving as ambassador to Togo. By the normal rules, therefore, his party loyalty should go to Kozlov, and on test questions such as the proposal for expulsion of the Antiparty Group leaders, one would have expected him to emulate the example of prudent silence set by his colleagues, Rashidov, Kunaev, and Akhundov.

Instead, Rasulov sharply criticized the group, especially Malenkov, whom he accused of harming the development of Soviet agriculture. Rasulov said nothing, however, of any crimes committed by Malenkov or the other members of the Antiparty Group, and he failed to support the proposal for expulsion, substituting an ambiguous call for "more severe punishment."[196]

Rasulov's political dexterity was manifested not only in warm personal praise for Khrushchev but also in his handling of the delicate subject of the Tadzhik CC plenum of April 1961 which had named him first secretary, and which Kozlov had supervised. Instead of giving Kozlov credit for the action, however, Rasulov attributed it to Khrushchev: "The communists and all the working people of Tadzhikistan express their deep appreciation to the Leninist Central Committee, to its Presidium and to comrade Nikita Sergeevich Khrushchev personally for their fatherly attention to the party organization of Tadzhikistan and to the Tadzhik people, for having helped to expose and put a stop to the mistakes that were being committed."[197]

[194]*Sten. ot.*, 1: 406; emphasis in the original.
[195]*Pravda*, Oct. 22, 1961; *CDSP*, XIII/50, p. 21.
[196]*Pravda*, Oct. 22, 1961; *CDSP*, XIII/50, p. 21.
[197]Ibid.

What was this—irony, naïveté, or insurance? All three motives may have played a part in determining Rasulov's apparent pro-Khrushchev position. One should not, however, rule out the possibility that Rasulov's praise for Khrushchev's alleged role in the Tadzhik party purge was a calculated piece of deception. After the fence-sitting speeches of Rashidov, Kunaev, and Akhundov, a similar display of ambiguity on Rasulov's part would have been insufficient; only a direct credit to Khrushchev as responsible for the Tadzhik purge could serve to conceal the link between that event and the factional activities of Kozlov.

The series of speeches discussing Khrushchev's two reports was interrupted by the next speaker, VITALII N. TITOV (born 1907, party member since 1938), head of the Central Committee Department of Party Organs for the Union Republics (since February 1961), who delivered the report for the Credentials Commission of the congress. Valuable for the statistical data it contained on party membership and the composition of the congress, Titov's speech offers little of relevance to our present concerns. He praised Khrushchev warmly for leading the fight against the Antiparty Group, but implied that the battle had already been won and that no further action was called for.

The final speaker at the morning session of October 20 was ANTONIN NOVOTNÝ, first secretary of the Czechoslovak Communist party. No friend of Khrushchev, and determined to run his own party in the good old Stalinist way, Novotný nevertheless swung into line on the major issue confronting the international communist movement by condemning the "schismatic actions of the present Albanian leadership, which are directed against our cause, against the unity of our international revolutionary movement, against Leninism."[198]

There were no surprises in the speech of BALYSH OVEZOV (born 1915, party member since 1939), first secretary of the Turkmenistan CP (since June 1960), who led off the evening session of the congress on October 20. Ovezov merely repeated the standard words of praise for Khrushchev ("experienced Leninist, tireless fighter for peace"), and touched only lightly on the controversial issues of the cult of personality and the Antiparty Group, citing no details and preserving silence on the proposal of expulsion. Only at the end of his speech, most of which dealt with the economic development of Turkmenistan, did he add a touch of color by assuring the party Central Committee "and you personally, dear Nikita Sergeevich," that the party and people of Turkmenistan would loyally fulfill the tasks set for them by the congress.[199]

The next speaker, ANASTAS I. MIKOYAN (born 1895, party member since 1915), was also a non-Russian, but unlike Ovezov he was one of the party's top leaders and a veteran of decades of bruising and dangerous life at the summit of the party, having joined the Politburo (later renamed the Presidium) as a candidate member as far back as 1926 and having served as a full member since 1935—a record of tenacity, skill, and sheer luck unmatched by any party leader, including Khrushchev.

---

[198]*Sten. ot.*, 1: 435.
[199]Ibid., p. 445.

Without wasting time on generalities, Mikoyan got down to business quickly. "The Twentieth Congress," he stated, "was a turning point in the life of our party and of the entire world communist movement."[200] But it was not to praise Khrushchev that Mikoyan had introduced this subject; he himself had delivered a speech criticizing Stalin at the Twentieth Party Congress, even before Khrushchev delivered his secret speech, and he was therefore in a unique position to give an accurate account of the background of that event. "The ideological orientation of the Twentieth Congress," he said, ". . . was not something that manifested itself in the space of a day before the congress or within the few days of its proceedings. *It evolved over a span of two years preceding the congress* in the process of critical re-examination of certain ideological principles, reorganization of the practical work of the party and the state, and the elimination of the harmful consequences of the cult of the individual."[201]

In opposition to the new party line, Mikoyan continued, a number of party leaders had formed what later came to be called the Antiparty Group. Referring only briefly to the group's concern with preventing the exposure of its members' past crimes and errors, Mikoyan devoted the major share of his attention to their position on questions of current party policy, especially foreign affairs. He depicted Molotov, who, he said, became the "chief ideologist" of the group, as fundamentally wrong both in his understanding of the situation in the USSR, where he asserted that only "the foundations of socialism," not socialism itself, had been built, and in his analysis of the existing world balance of forces.

The result of his underestimating the forces of socialism and, consequently, overestimating the forces of imperialism was that *Molotov made serious mistakes on questions of international development*—on peaceful coexistence and the possibility of preventing a world war, and on the multiplicity of the forms of transition to socialism in various countries.

In general, Molotov rejects the line of peaceful coexistence, reducing the concept to nothing more than a state of peace, or rather the absence of war at a given moment, and *denying the possibility of preventing a world war*. In its substance this view approximates that of the foreign adversaries of peaceful coexistence, who interpret it as a variant of the "cold war," as a state of "armed peace."

This conception is at odds with the Leninist understanding of relations between the two systems and would have led to repudiating the broad development of economic relations between them and to the curtailment of contacts and cultural ties. Finally, it would to all intents and purposes have meant *accepting the inevitability of war* and abandoning the active quest for agreements aimed at reducing international tension and at disarmament. It is no accident, therefore, that he should reject the historic thesis of the Twentieth Party Congress on the possibility of preventing world war in this age.[202]

---

[200] *Pravda*, Oct. 22, 1961; *CDSP*, XIII/51, p. 9.

[201] Ibid.; emphasis supplied.

[202] Ibid.; emphasis supplied.

At the Twentieth Congress Molotov and the other oppositionists had remained silent, Mikoyan said, a tactic which he admitted had deceived the party:

We assumed that unity had been established on the basic points of party policy. It turned out afterwards, however, that this was far from the case. The stand that Molotov and others had taken at the congress had been hypocritical. It is now clear that, knowing they would be isolated at the congress if they came out openly against the new congress theses advanced by the Central Committee, they chose different tactics for their struggle. *These were tactics calculated to keep them from suffering a defeat at the congress while enabling them at a later, more convenient time, to try, using other means, to bring about a revision of the party line.*[203]

A damaging admission, one would have thought, at a congress where the usual protestations of monolithic party unity were as much in evidence as ever, and where the opposition was being denied a voice by an efficient and smoothly running party machine. Inadvertently, perhaps, Mikoyan had disclosed the realities of factional struggle behind the façade of party unity.

In his review of developments down to the June 1957 plenum Mikoyan added nothing of interest, but his account of the post-plenum events broke new ground. "The group's members," he said, ". . . made appropriate statements at the plenum, and afterwards, a year to a year and a half later, wrote letters to the Central Committee in which they acknowledged and condemned their mistakes."[204] All except Molotov, that is: "Molotov was the only one who did not vote for the resolution of the Central Committee's plenum or anywhere in any form repudiate his antiparty activity or his views, which had inflicted great harm on the party. What he had said in the primary organization about agreeing with the decision of the plenum had been insincere, prompted by tactical considerations."[205] For the first time, Mikoyan revealed that Molotov's stubborn refusal to admit the error of his ways was not just a question of bygone days: *"To this day he clings bullheadedly to his conservative-dogmatic views."*[206]

Mikoyan explicitly ruled out a new party purge directed against the members of the Antiparty Group and their followers, while implying that matters would have turned out very differently if they had won the struggle for power:

The Central Committee consistently bases its activity on Leninist norms of party life. This has shown itself in the fact that the fight against the conservative-dogmatic group was waged by the methods of inner-party democracy, without resort to repressive state measures, as had been the case under the cult of the individual. But the victory of the antiparty group would

---

[203]Ibid., pp. 9–10; emphasis supplied.
[204]Ibid., p. 10.
[205]Ibid.
[206]Ibid.; emphasis supplied.

have led to reprisals against all the active supporters of the Twentieth Congress, by methods that the party can never forget.[207]

Here, however, Mikoyan drew the line; he had said nothing of any crimes of which the Antiparty Group members might have been guilty, and he failed to second the proposal for their expulsion from the party.

The central section of Mikoyan's speech dealt with the new Party Program, and while he abstained from personal praise of Khrushchev he did not hesitate to espouse controversial positions with which the First Secretary was directly associated, e.g., the supersession of the dictatorship of the proletariat by a "state of the entire people."[208]

Turning to the international communist movement, Mikoyan again went straight to the heart of the matter, the CPSU's quarrel with the Albanian Party of Labor, and he took a further long step along the path initiated earlier by Khrushchev of condemning the Albanian leadership for the internal situation which had arisen there. Albanian opposition to the line adopted at the Twentieth Congress, he said,

> . . . is also to be explained by the fact that Enver Hoxha and Mehmet Shehu have long been cultivating in their party practices and methods that are incompatible with Marxism–Leninism. How Mehmet Shehu, for example, interprets the norms of party life is plain from his statement at the recent congress of the Albanian Party of Labor that anyone who disagreed with the leadership on a question would be (and I quote) "spat in the face, punched in the mouth, and if need be, have a bullet put into his brain."[209]

Warming to his subject, Mikoyan gave some vivid personal details of Albanian party members who had been purged "merely because they did not wish to leave the tried and tested path of Albanian–Soviet friendship."[210]

Mikoyan showed that he was fully aware of the criticism Chou En-lai had voiced of Khrushchev's discussion of the internal affairs of the Albanian party at the congress, but that he rejected it: "It will be said that these are their [the Albanians'] internal affairs and must not be interfered in. But after all, the persecution and acts of repression are directed against Albanians who uphold the traditional friendship with the Soviet Union. And this is something that directly concerns us; *we cannot remain indifferent in the matter, and are obliged to state our opinion.*"[211] To remedy the situation, Mikoyan demanded a full-scale recantation by the Albanian leaders, though he stopped short of endorsing Khrushchev's call for their overthrow.

There is evidence that the actual terms used by Mikoyan in condemning the Albanian party leadership were even stronger than those included in the

---

[207]Ibid.
[208]Ibid., p. 12.
[209]Ibid., p. 13.
[210]Ibid.
[211]Ibid.; emphasis supplied.

official transcript of the congress. The Polish party newspaper *Trybuna Ludu* (Warsaw), in its issue of October 21, 1961, quoted Mikoyan as saying that: "Stalin—according to Mehmet Shehu [Albanian chief of state]—made only two mistakes: he died prematurely and before his death he should have liquidated the whole present leadership of the CPSU."[212]

It is not difficult to understand why the editors of the official congress record thought it advisable to cut out this passage—it called into question too directly the policies and character of the current party leadership.

For the remainder of Mikoyan's speech, which dealt with the international situation, we can limit ourselves to a few salient details. He portrayed U.S. policy toward Latin America, specifically including that of the Kennedy administration, as "neocolonialism" and said that its true face, "the face of the colonial robber," had been revealed by the attack on Cuba.

On the subject of a German peace treaty, Mikoyan showed a lingering fondness for the hard line:

> We have time and again spoken of *the urgent necessity of concluding a German peace treaty* and of our wish to settle questions by agreement with the Western powers, to guarantee the existing borders of the G.D.R. and the F.R.G. on that basis, to normalize the West Berlin situation and to eliminate the breeding ground of war in Europe. But if we become convinced that the Western powers do not want a peace treaty with the two German states, *we shall be compelled to conclude such a treaty with the G.D.R., and there is no force that could keep us from effecting this vitally essential peace settlement.*[213]

Dutifully, albeit reluctantly, Mikoyan signified his willingness to accept Khrushchev's lifting of the December 31 deadline by adding,

> We cannot today neglect to mention what a great effort Comrade Khrushchev, head of the Soviet government, has made in upholding peace and in making clear to the Western countries the urgency of concluding a German peace treaty and our stand regarding the purpose and substance of such a treaty. The fact that *certain encouraging shifts have become apparent in the position of the West*, and above all in public opinion in both the United States and the Western European countries, is in large measure attributable to this effort.[214]

The real sensation of Mikoyan's speech was not so much his detailed revelations about the purges in Albania as his disclosure that Molotov's opposition to the party line had centered around questions of Soviet foreign policy, *and that it still continued.* The way in which Molotov's views were presented,

---

[212]Cited in Harry Schwartz, ed., *Russia Enters the 1960s. A Documentary Report on the 22nd Congress of the Communist Party of the Soviet Union* (Philadelphia and New York: Lippincott, 1962), p. viii; hereinafter cited as Schwartz.

[213]*CDSP*, XIII/51, p. 14. The protocols at this point record "stormy, prolonged applause."

[214]Ibid.; emphasis supplied.

however, implied that they were still unknown to the congress delegates. Evidently, therefore, Molotov's letter to the pre-congress Central Committee plenum had not yet been distributed to the delegates.

Mikoyan's harsh condemnation of the Albanian leaders and his assertion of the party's right to raise the issue at the congress provided strong support for Khrushchev, and served to predetermine the outcome of Chou's talks with the Soviet leaders on October 22. Clearly a three-man team which included Khrushchev and Mikoyan would not be willing to make concessions to the Chinese on the Albanian issue.

Following Mikoyan to the speaker's rostrum was another of the non-Russian Union Republic party bosses, IVAN G. KEBIN (born 1905, party member since 1927), first secretary of the Estonian CP (since 1950). On the controversial internal issues confronting the congress Kebin showed himself even more restrained than the Central Asian party chiefs; his speech included only a bare mention of the cult of personality and nothing whatever on the Antiparty Group. Kebin's praise of Khrushchev was perfunctory; there was, in fact, no reason for him to contribute to the new cult of personality for his career owed nothing to Khrushchev.

The sense of boredom emanating from Kebin's speech was quickly dissipated by that of the following speaker, WALTER ULBRICHT, first secretary of the Socialist Unity party (SED), the Communist party of East Germany. Ulbricht stood close to the center of both the international crisis centering on Berlin and the internal political conflict in the CPSU. He was in the forefront of the hard-liners on the German question; the axis of the international conflict over Berlin ran squarely through his territory; it was to shore up his shaky regime that the Berlin Wall had been built; and it was to end the threat of collapse which still haunted his domain that the Soviets had demanded the neutralization of West Berlin and its full severance from West Germany.

As to the internal Soviet political conflict, Ulbricht, like Chou, by no stretch of the imagination could be considered a mere disinterested bystander; his ties to Kozlov were of long standing,[215] and his views of the world conflict coincided with those of the Soviet hard-liners in all important respects. Correspondingly, Ulbricht's regard for Khrushchev was low. Early in the congress his lack of enthusiasm for the First Secretary's Berlin policy was revealed in graphic body language which an alert Western journalist spotted. Describing the scene just after Khrushchev had announced the lifting of the deadline on signing a peace treaty with Germany, Seymour Topping reported:

> The first to reflect umbrage in his demeanor was Walter Ulbricht of East Germany, who sat with other foreign party chiefs on the rear bench of the stage. The bearded Ulbricht had been taking notes diligently and applauding vigorously. Then Mr. Khrushchev, dealing with the Berlin crisis, offered to delay the signing of a separate peace treaty with East Germany if the

[215]Kroll, pp. 366–67, provides evidence of the close link between Kozlov and Ulbricht.

Western powers displayed readiness to negotiate. Herr Ulbricht suddenly became less enthusiastic amid the general applause and limply padded one hand into the other in his lap.[216]

Ulbricht's opportunity to present *his* concept of what Soviet policy in the Berlin crisis should be came on the evening of October 20. Although he respected party discipline to the minimal extent of stopping short of a head-on clash with Khrushchev, in every other way his speech constituted a direct challenge to the Soviet Premier. The keynote was struck at the very outset, when he said that he brought to the congress "the most cordial, fraternal, *fighting* greeting" from the East German party.[217] Before getting down to his real subject—the Berlin crisis—Ulbricht fulfilled his party duty by praising the new CPSU Party Program and, in moderation, "Comrade Nikita Sergeevich Khrushchev" (for some reason—irony, perhaps—Ulbricht usually referred to Khrushchev by his full name).

On the Albanian issue Ulbricht lined up behind the CPSU, but whereas Khrushchev had emphasized questions of ideology and had centered his criticism of the Albanian leaders around their stand on the party line, Ulbricht stressed the harm which the Albanians' apostasy would do to the military power of the Soviet bloc.

These chores completed, Ulbricht turned to the German question. He portrayed the East German regime as standing on guard in the first line of defense of the entire socialist system "against West German militarism and imperialism, the deadly enemies of the German people and of mankind as a whole."[218] Conjuring up a vision of Armageddon, he warned that West Berlin might become "a second Sarajevo."[219] There was only one way to avoid the catastrophe of a new world war, he said: "Confronting the G.D.R., confronting the socialist camp and the peace-loving forces in the entire world stands the great historic task of cutting off the plans of the German militarists in good time so that they cannot unleash a third world war. Therefore the *conclusion of a peace treaty with Germany is the most urgent task*."[220]

While he thus brazenly ignored Khrushchev's conciliatory action in lifting the deadline on signing a German peace treaty, Ulbricht nevertheless showed that he was well acquainted with the substance of the Gromyko–Kennedy talk:

Political figures of the Western powers have stated that the Soviet Union and the German Democratic Republic allegedly want to receive an orchard from the Western powers and to give in return merely an apple. This is a strange assertion. After all these gentlemen know very well that it is not a question of an American but of a German orchard. Evidently they are con-

[216]*NYT*, Oct. 27, 1961, sect. 4, p. 3.

[217]*Sten. ot.*, 1: 472; emphasis supplied.

[218]Ibid., p. 474.

[219]Ibid.

[220]Ibid.; emphasis in the original.

fusing the expressions "mine" and "thine." But after all this is our German garden, notwithstanding the fact that the Bonn Chancellor, Herr Adenauer, in accordance with the Paris agreements, has given the finance capital of the U.S.A., Great Britain, and France permission to station their occupation troops at will in the West German zone right up to the year 2005.[221]

If any concessions were involved, Ulbricht asserted, they were on the side of the GDR: ". . . after all, it is *we* who are making a great concession in announcing readiness to permit West Berlin, which is situated in the center of the territory of the G.D.R., the status of a demilitarized free city."[222]

Ulbricht not only defended the Berlin Wall but unequivocally championed the use of military force to ensure the acceptance of the Soviet proposals in Berlin: "In connection with the aggressive actions of the Bonn revanchist circles, the German Democratic Republic was forced to erect around East Berlin a defensive wall against fascism and to secure the boundaries of the G.D.R. [*applause*]. *They say that we used tanks. But tanks also are needed for the defense of peace* [*applause*]. We carried out all of our measures in agreement and with the support of the member-states of the Warsaw Pact, in the first place the government of the U.S.S.R. [*applause*]."[223]

As a result of these measures, Ulbricht contended, the Western powers (with the exception of West Germany) now took a more realistic view of the situation: "In contrast to the ruling circles of West Germany, leading political figures of the Western powers after August 13 began to evaluate the situation more realistically. *They recognize the existence of two German states and the abnormality of the situation in West Berlin.*"[224]

If the Western powers were nevertheless delaying the signature of a German peace treaty, Ulbricht charged, this was because they wanted to gain time in which to arm the West German army with atomic weapons. On this assumption, he proceeded to offer his own formula for a settlement of the German problem, in which Khrushchev's search for a basis of negotiation with the Western powers had no part:

> The German Democratic Republic is striving for *the earliest conclusion of a peace treaty*, in order to strengthen the peace [*applause*]. We are prepared to agree that neither of the two German states should receive atomic weapons and should not have the right to produce them. We agree to the general and complete disarmament of both German states, all the more since the future democratic Germany can exist only in the form of a militarily neutral state. We are in favor of the conclusion of a nonaggression pact between NATO and the member-states of the Warsaw Pact. We are in favor of the admission of both German states as members of the U.N.[225]

[221]Ibid.
[222]Ibid., p. 476; emphasis in the original.
[223]Ibid.; emphasis supplied.
[224]Ibid., pp. 476–77; emphasis supplied.
[225]Ibid., p. 477; emphasis supplied.

Though he talked of peace, Ulbricht's emphasis was consistently on the need for military force. "We in the German Democratic Republic," he said, ". . . recognize that *peace must be secured also by military means*, and as participants in the organization of the Warsaw Pact, we are fulfilling our duties."[226]

After bringing his speech to a close with the usual slogans, Ulbricht presented to Khrushchev a message of greetings from the SED, which fully supported his militant stand on Berlin and added a few points of its own. It asserted, for example, that the "balance of power" in the world had irretrievably shifted in favor of the "world system of socialism."[227] It expressed the support of the East German population for the measures undertaken by the Soviet government for the strengthening of Soviet military power, including the resumption of the testing of hydrogen bombs—the first time that term had been employed publicly in the Soviet Union to describe the current test series; and it reiterated Ulbricht's demand for the signing of a German peace treaty: "[The friendship among the peoples of the socialist nations] strengthens us in our determination to sign *at last* a German peace treaty which will eliminate the danger of war which emanates from West Germany and West Berlin."[228]

Short of directly contradicting Khrushchev on the issue of the timing of a German peace treaty, there was little more that Ulbricht could have done. His speech constituted not only an act of deliberate and calculated defiance but also a blueprint for the military crisis which was shortly to erupt in Berlin. All that was required to translate the blueprint into reality was authorization by a ranking member of the CPSU leadership.

Ulbricht was followed to the rostrum by another grizzled veteran of the international communist movement, PALMIRO TOGLIATTI, general secretary of the Communist party of Italy. Reflecting his long years of service as a Comintern official in Moscow, Togliatti delivered his speech in Russian.

After a quick review of recent events in Italy, Togliatti concisely and unequivocally defined his party's position on some of the burning issues which confronted the congress. His praise for Khrushchev was moderate in tone but by no means perfunctory—Khrushchev's speech, he said, had been "great, profound, and pithy." On the Albanian issue Togliatti was forthright, adding a personal note to Khrushchev's condemnation of the Albanian leaders: "We fully approve of the criticism addressed to the leadership of the Albanian Party of Labor concerning its violation of the principles of democratic centralism reestablished by the Twentieth Congress of the CPSU and the principles of international proletarian solidarity [*stormy applause*]. We ourselves at the time of the last congress of the Albanian Party of Labor observed that an intolerable internal regime exists in that party, and we openly stated this."[229]

[226]Ibid.; emphasis supplied.
[227]Ibid., p. 479.
[228]Ibid., p. 480; emphasis supplied.
[229]Ibid., p. 483.

Equally clearcut was Togliatti's approval of the innovations introduced at the Twentieth Party Congress, including the criticism of Stalin's cult of personality. He told the delegates that these changes had helped the Italian CP carry on a successful drive for increased influence and power. Avoiding any direct reference to Germany, Berlin, or the proposal to conclude a German peace treaty, Togliatti nevertheless made clear his support for a moderate line in international affairs: ". . . *we manifest an understanding of and approve every step directed toward the lessening of international tension,* toward the solution of the most acute questions of the present moment by means of sensible negotiations, toward the elimination of the 'cold war' and the establishment of an atmosphere of peaceful coexistence between all governments and all peoples."[230]

The next speaker was GHEORGHE GHEORGHIU-DEJ, first secretary of the Rumanian Party of Labor, who showed on this occasion the political dexterity which had enabled him to hold on to power in one of the most turbulent political regimes in Eastern Europe. The Rumanian party boss's speech touched nearly all the bases: praise of Khrushchev ("ardent fighter for the course of Marxism–Leninism"), predictions of Soviet victory in the economic competition with the United States, condemnation of the Albanian party leadership, the need to conclude a German peace treaty (but at some unspecified time in the future), the value of negotiations to reduce international tension, but at the same time approval of "the measures taken for strengthening [Soviet] defense power."

In phrases so general as almost to qualify as a specimen of Orwellian New Speak, Gheorghiu-Dej *seemed* to be supporting Khrushchev's line in foreign policy: "With what power there resounded from this high tribunal in the speeches of Comrade Khrushchev the call for judicious, healthy thought! In the name of the Rumanian people we join our voice to this call. It is already high time to understand that the questions of the present era can be decided only by taking into account those irrevocable changes which have taken place in the life of humanity, the real relationship of forces!"[231] Whichever way the factional struggle in the CPSU leadership turned out, Gheorghiu-Dej could point to his congress speech as evidence that he had been on the side of the winner.

The final speaker at the evening session of October 20 was another East European party boss, JANOS KADAR, first secretary of the Hungarian Socialist Workers' party. Unlike Gheorghiu-Dej, Kadar made no bones about his stand on some of the outstanding issues dividing the international communist movement. He praised Khrushchev's "steadfast courage and sense of principle" in leading the struggle against "the cult of personality and all its harmful consequences," a struggle which he called "unavoidable and indis-

[230]Ibid., pp. 484–85; emphasis supplied.
[231]Ibid., pp. 491–92.

pensable."[232] Similarly he signified whole-hearted approval of the CPSU's struggle against the Antiparty Group and, by extension, against the "harmful actions of the Albanian leaders." In words directed toward Chinese ears he asserted that ". . . everyone to whom our unity is really precious, to whom the interests of socialism and peace are precious, can do only one thing—fight against depraved views [i.e., those of the Albanian leaders] with principled irreconcilability."[233]

The main tendency of Kadar's speech was thus clearly in the direction of support for Khrushchev's policies. It can only have been an example of crossed wires and the mistaken reading of esoteric signals, therefore, when toward the end of his speech Kadar came out in favor of the early signing of a German peace treaty, an event for which, as he informed the congress, the wheels of the Hungarian state machine had already been set in motion:

> The immediate common task of the peoples consists of urgently resolving questions which are poisoning international relations, and particularly the most urgent of them—drawing a line under the Second World War, localizing the revanchist hotbed, which has been created in West Germany. *On October 7 of this year* the National Assembly of the Hungarian People's Republic authorized our government to sign a German peace treaty. Our people are ready for the fulfillment of the task which confronts them in regard to the defense of peace.[234]

Kadar's gaffe provides useful confirmation of two conclusions reached earlier: first, that in the weeks preceding the Twenty-second Congress there was general expectation in the communist world (and not only there) that Khrushchev would make use of that forum to announce the long-anticipated signing of a peace treaty with East Germany, and second, that the decision to announce publicly the lifting of the deadline on signature of a German peace treaty was taken only very shortly before the congress met.

*   *   *

The big gun at the morning session of October 21 was Mikhail Suslov. Before he spoke, however, two other delegates addressed the congress, the first of whom was VIKTOR V. GRISHIN (born 1914, party member since 1938), boss of the Soviet trade unions as chairman of the All-Union Central Council of Trade Unions (since March 1956). An ex-worker who had risen in the party ranks with little or no help from Khrushchev, Grishin's speech showed him to be a hard-liner on most of the controversial questions on the congress agenda, even though he showered a string of laudatory epithets on Khrushchev at the outset of his speech, calling him "a true continuer of the cause of Lenin, a staunch fighter for communism, a talented political and government figure."[235]

[232]Ibid., p. 493.
[233]Ibid., p. 494.
[234]Ibid., p. 496; emphasis supplied.
[235]Ibid., p. 500; *CDSP*, XIII/51, p. 15.

In his treatment of the cult of personality and the Antiparty Group Grishin added nothing new, and he omitted any reference to the group's "crimes" or to the proposal for expulsion of its leaders (among whom he ranked Molotov as "their ideological inspirer").[236] On the subject of Albania he maintained complete silence, and when he turned to the international situation he spoke of the "firm determination of the toilers of all countries to fight for the signing of a German peace treaty and the securing of peace."[237]

If Khrushchev's power in the party had corresponded to the exaggerated estimate of it held by many Western observers at the time, Grishin's intransigence would have merited a sharp reproof and a setback in his party career. Instead, at the end of the congress he was raised to the high position of candidate member of the Presidium.

Grishin was followed by the first bona fide worker who had thus far addressed the congress, ALEKSANDR V. GITALOV, a tractor brigade leader from a collective farm in Kirovograd oblast, the Ukraine. Though Gitalov was formally billed as the speaker, his speech quickly developed into a dialogue, with Gitalov playing straight man to Khrushchev the expert on various aspects of agriculture. Gitalov, it was revealed, had worked for a year at an Iowa farm belonging to Mr. Garst, whom Khrushchev lauded as "on the whole, a man of common sense."[238] Matters soon reached the point where Khrushchev was handing around among the delegates "several large ears of corn" (to quote the protocols) and regaling them with music-hall patter:

I once read a newspaper article that correctly criticized the names of our farm machines. Try to pronounce "Ka-khe-dva" [KKh-2], "Ka-khe-ka" [KKhk] and the devil knows what else, or to get some idea what on earth they are! [*Laughter in the hall. Applause.*] What kind of dog's language are they imposing on us? [*Laughter in the hall. Applause.*] Name machines in human fashion, so that it is clear what kind of machines they are. The language shouldn't be cluttered with all these "Ka-khe-kas" and "ha-has!" [*Laughter in the hall, Prolonged applause.*][239]

On a more serious level, Gitalov's speech made the Khrushchevian point that Soviet agriculture could surpass U.S. yields if the collective farms adopted "integrated mechanization," i.e., the combined use of agricultural machinery for the production of such crops as sugar beets and—of course—corn.

There were no interruptions by the First Secretary during the speech of MIKHAIL A. SUSLOV (born 1902, party member since 1921), full member of the Presidium (since 1955) and of the Secretariat (since 1947), the party's top-ranking theorist in the fields of ideology and the international communist movement.

[236]*CDSP*, XIII/51, p. 15.
[237]*Sten. ot.*, 1: 506.
[238]*Pravda*, Oct. 23, 1961; *CDSP*, XIII/51, p. 17.
[239]*CDSP*, XIII/51, pp. 17–18.

Suslov took as his principal subject the new Party Program, but first he had a few words to say about the Antiparty Group. In carefully formulated terms, nearly every word of which was loaded with implications, Suslov picked his way through this mine-strewn field with the dour air of a man performing a chore for which he feels little enthusiasm. Suslov's list of the members of the group was oddly truncated, as Tatu has pointed out: "Suslov listed only 'Molotov, Kaganovich, Malenkov, Voroshilov, Bulganin, and others,' omitting Shepilov and especially Pervukhin and Saburov, two men who had also been members of the Presidium until 1957. He had done the same at the Twenty-First Congress and in all his speeches. This systematic omission may have been due to the fact that Pervukhin's and Saburov's reactions to Khrushchev's moves were scarcely cooler than his own."[240] On the subject of the group's "crimes" Suslov resorted to generalities, naming no specific individuals but referring vaguely to "many persons in this group" as being "directly guilty of mass repressions against honest communists in the period of the cult of the individual."[241]

Suslov followed Mikoyan and others in identifying Molotov as the group's principal spokesman in foreign affairs, and charged that the latter had done "everything possible to oppose the Central Committee's course of carrying out the principles of peaceful coexistence of states with different social systems and of ensuring a lasting peace."[242] But where Mikoyan had provided vivid details to portray Molotov's errors, Suslov was colorless and perfunctory. More important, he implied that the struggle against the Antiparty Group was a closed chapter in party history, requiring no further action, and even falsified the facts by asserting that the party had "ideologically routed *and cast out* the miserable clique of oppositionists."[243]

When he came to the new Party Program Suslov grew a little more enthusiastic. To sketch the historical background he linked the new program to its two predecessors, worked out with Lenin's participation in 1903 and 1919. A ghost from the past put in a brief appearance when Suslov cited Bukharin's proposal, in 1919, to include a description of communism in the program. The reason for this unexpected resurrection was quickly made clear, however: in 1919 Lenin had retorted to Bukharin that such a description would be premature at a time when the party had its hands full building the foundations of socialism. Since the new Party Program *did,* however, contain just the kind of detailed description of the future communist society for which Bukharin had called in 1919, Lenin's reproof to him might well have been construed by hostile critics as still valid. To spike this objection in advance, Suslov asserted that changed conditions now justified the inclusion of a definition of communism in the new program: "Now a socialist society has already been created in

---

[240]Tatu, footnote, p. 153.
[241]*Pravda*, Oct. 23, 1961; *CDSP*, XIII/51, p. 18.
[242]*CDSP*, XIII/51, p. 18.
[243]Ibid.; emphasis supplied.

our country, socialism has won fully and finally. Relying on the achievements of socialism, and creatively generalizing the experience of socialism in the Soviet Union, of the world socialist system and of the entire international workers' and national-liberation movement, our party now sets in its Program as an immediate practical task the building of the bright and majestic edifice of communist society."[244]

Not that the task of drafting the program had been simple; Suslov referred cryptically to "the chief theoretical difficulties" which had been encountered, with the implication that there had been some sharp conflicts in the committee preparing the draft, even though he went on to assert that the difficulties had been "brilliantly" overcome (perhaps out of modesty he failed to specify whose "brilliance" had been involved).[245]

In the warm reception accorded the draft program by foreign communist and workers' parties, Suslov complained, there had been one sour note, that contributed by the Albanian Party of Labor. (Suslov deliberately overlooked the unmistakable coolness toward the draft manifested by the Chinese communists.) The Albanians, he charged, had published the draft program only "in abridged and distorted form," and he asserted that "This unfriendly act of the Albanian leaders was no accident."[246] It was the result, he said, of the fact that the Albanian leaders were "inflating in every way the cult of the individual in their party and country and grossly violating Leninist norms of party life," as a result of which ". . . they do not wish to reconcile themselves to the course being carried out by our party of overcoming the harmful consequences of the cult of the individual and restoring revolutionary legality."[247]

Suslov had nothing to add to the details revealed by Mikoyan about the purge of pro-Soviet party members in Albania, but he did have a small sensation of his own for the delegates: "Now the leaders of the Albanian Party of Labor's Central Committee have sent a letter. This letter, comrades, is a mixture of hypocrisy and slanderous insinuations. Permit me to tell the leaders of the Albanian Party of Labor: We are well aware where friendship is, and where hypocrisy is."[248]

Suslov thus carried the dispute with the Albanians one step further by revealing the existence of interparty polemics currently under way. (The letter to which he referred was evidently that sent by the Albanian Central Committee on October 12.)

Unlike Mikoyan, however, Suslov made no allusion, direct or indirect, to Chou's criticism of Khrushchev for raising the Albanian issue at the party congress. He thus demonstrated a desire to keep the Albanian issue within bounds and not to allow it to contribute to the exacerbation of the Sino–Soviet

[244] Ibid., p. 19.
[245] Ibid. See also Linden, p. 113.
[246] *CDSP*, XIII/51, p. 19.
[247] Ibid.
[248] Ibid.

dispute. Since Suslov's special area of responsibility within the collective leadership was that of relations with the foreign communist and workers' parties, he would normally have been the second member of the three-man panel chosen to conduct talks with Chou En-lai for the purpose of attempting to prevent an open break. The substitution of Mikoyan for Suslov on the panel ensured the victory of Khrushchev's point of view and was no doubt made with that purpose in view.

Suslov's account of the new Party Program is valuable as representing the views of one of the top party leaders most directly responsible for its formulation. In a brilliant analysis Carl Linden has singled out some of the passages in Suslov's congress speech which make it possible to identify several points of theory on which he and Khrushchev differed in their approach. For example, whereas Khrushchev had shown a tendency to postulate not only the ending of the dictatorship of the proletariat in the Soviet Union but also the initiation of the process of the "withering away of the state," Suslov ". . . offered the thesis that the dictatorship had spread from the U.S.S.R. to many countries and had become the decisive force in world history; thus he projected an expanding, not a declining, role for the dictatorship concept. The Suslov thesis conveyed the image of militant prosecution of the class struggle on a world scale that was out of tune with Khrushchev's détente strategy."[249]

In Suslov's vision of the future, Khrushchev's new "state of the entire people," which was to take the place of the dictatorship of the proletariat, bore a suspiciously close resemblance to its immediate predecessor. For example, with regard to "criminal manifestations," Suslov warned that "It would be naive"

> . . . to count on simply letting matters take their own course in this respect and to tolerate unjustified liberalism, of which officials of our administrative agencies are frequently guilty. [!] Utilizing all the necessary means of education and persuasion and the force of the community against infringers of the law, *the state of the entire people must also unwaveringly apply means of coercion—its punitive sword*—against malicious and dangerous criminals, hooligans, plunderers of socialist property, loafers, parasites *and other antisocial elements that hinder the people from building communism.*[250]

In a formulation strikingly reminiscent of Stalin's discredited thesis that the nearer the Soviet state approaches socialism the more intense would become the resistance of the forces of opposition and therefore the greater the need for strengthening the organs of repression, Suslov declared that: "The tasks of strengthening socialist legality *increase* in the period of the full-scale building of communism."[251]

---

[249]Linden, p. 111.

[250]*CDSP*, XIII/51, p. 20; emphasis supplied. The expression "punitive sword" is a euphemism for the secret police, which uses the emblem of a flaming sword on its insignia.

[251]Ibid.; emphasis supplied.

Suslov's congress speech makes it possible to define his position on a number of controversial questions confronting the party leadership with a fair degree of precision. His restrained treatment of the Antiparty Group showed that on this issue he was willing to carry out the requirements of party discipline but nothing more. He displayed far more spirit in his condemnation of the Albanian leadership: whenever Suslov's Russian nationalism was touched, he was sure to respond. But he had no wish to embroil relations with the Chinese if it could be avoided. On the central themes of the new Party Program he alluded to differences of opinion within the leadership, but came out in support of several controversial positions sponsored by Khrushchev, even though he put his own Suslovian gloss on them.

On the strength of his congress speech, therefore, Suslov could not be ranked as either a firm and committed supporter of Khrushchev or his irreconcilable opponent. Rather he was a power in his own right, willing and able to defend his own position on controversial questions, but differing from Kozlov in his lack of any personal aspirations for supreme power.

Suslov's violently nationalist reaction to the Albanian challenge was a vital element in providing Khrushchev with a majority in the Presidium for his strategy of bringing this issue out into the open at the congress. Just as Khrushchev had been able to pick up support for his renewed attack on the Antiparty Group from men like Spiridonov and Mazurov who were not his followers on other issues, so he was able to add a powerful ally for his attack on the Albanians, thanks to Suslov's emotional reaction to the Albanians' obstreperousness.

The morning session of October 21 was brought to a close with short speeches by the remaining heads of ruling foreign communist parties, those of Bulgaria, North Korea, North Vietnam, and Outer Mongolia. TODOR ZHIVKOV, first secretary of the Bulgarian CP, the first speaker in this group, lined up formally behind the CPSU on the Albanian issue[252] and contrived to find a new superlative in praise of Khrushchev, whom he called "the most outstanding Marxist–Leninist of our time." But Zhivkov's effusiveness betrayed a symptomatic hankering for the old Stalinist ways rather than sincere support of Khrushchev as a liberalizing innovator; developments in Bulgaria after the congress were to show that the Bulgarian party leaders felt no enthusiasm for carrying out in their own party the logical consequences of the renewed assault on Stalin.

Thus far not a single speaker at the congress had taken the Chinese side in the controversy which Chou's speech had precipitated. The next two speakers, however—the first after Chou to represent Asian communist parties—broke with this precedent, KIM IL–SUNG, chairman of the (North) Korean Party of Labor, not only avoided joining in the condemnation of the Albanian leadership but pointedly pledged his party's continuing support for the "unity of the

[252]*Sten. ot.*, 1: 536.

socialist camp" and for the strengthening of its cooperation "with the peoples of the Soviet Union *and of all other socialist countries.*"[253]

Repeating the delicate balancing act which North Korea had performed in July, Kim cited *both* the North Korean–Soviet and North Korean–Chinese Treaties of Friendship, Cooperation and Mutual Aid as ". . . an enormous contribution to the defence of the security of the Korean people from imperialist aggression and the strengthening of peace in the Far East and in the entire world, in the consolidation of the unity and solidarity of the entire socialist camp."[254]

The most revealing indication of Kim's position, however, came in an exceptionally bellicose pledge of support for the hard line in Soviet foreign policy vis-à-vis the West:

> At the present time the conclusion of a peace treaty with Germany is *the most acute problem, which must be resolved without delay.* . . . The imperialist nations of the West have raised a military fuss around the German problem and are openly threatening peace in the entire world. In this situation the measures adopted recently by the Soviet government for the suppression of the provocative actions of the imperialists and the defense of the security of the Soviet Union and the entire socialist camp are *absolutely correct and necessary*, and *we support them fully and completely.*[255]

In voicing this support, Kim was deliberately taking sides in the power struggle within the CPSU leadership, a subject on which Kozlov's visit to Pyongyang in September had no doubt proved enlightening.

Like Kim, North Vietnam's HO CHI MINH, chairman of the Central Committee of the (North) Vietnam Party of Labor, avoided any reference to the Albanian question, thus supporting the Chinese position. But Ho's speech was far less one-sided, far more diplomatic, than Kim's, in large part because he skirted nearly all the controversial issues which confronted the international communist movement. On the question of the timing of the entry into the Promised Land of communism, Ho voiced a rather touching faith in Soviet benevolence: ". . . we believe profoundly that when communism will have been built in the Soviet Union, the construction of socialism will also have been completed and we will proceed to communism."[256]

The final speaker at the morning session of October 21, and the last of the heads of ruling parties to address the congress, was YUMZHAGIIN TSEDENBAL, first secretary of the Mongolian People's Revolutionary party. Despite Outer Mongolia's close proximity to and long historical association with China (some might say because of these very factors), the communist leaders in that country had usually taken a line in support of the Soviet Union as the Sino–Soviet conflict gathered momentum. Tsedenbal's congress speech

[253]Ibid., p. 543; emphasis supplied.
[254]Ibid.
[255]Ibid., p. 541; emphasis supplied.
[256]Ibid., p. 545.

showed the continuation of this tendency. Breaking ranks with his Asian colleagues, Tsedenbal condemned the "erroneous line of the leadership of the Albanian Party of Labor which is causing harm to our common cause and most of all to the national interests of the Albanian people."[257]

At the end of the ninth congress session, the tally sheet on the Albanian issue was heavily weighted in favor of the Soviet position and against the Chinese, indicating that Khrushchev's gamble was paying off. Only two foreign guest speakers, those representing the parties of North Korea and North Vietnam, had supported the Chinese position by failing to condemn the Albanian party leaders, while some of the most powerful figures in the CPSU itself—Brezhnev, Mikoyan, Suslov—had added new fuel to the anti-Albanian blaze lit by Khrushchev.

*　　*　　*

The tenth congress session, on the evening of October 21, led off with speeches by three foreign party leaders—BLAS ROCA for Cuba, DIPA AIDIT for Indonesia, and AJOY GHOSH for India. Of the three, only Blas Roca came out in support of the CPSU position by explicitly condemning the Albanian party leadership; Aidit and Ghosh said nothing on the subject, thereby signifying their support for the Chinese position. The outlines were thus beginning to emerge of a fateful split of the international communist movement along geographical lines, with a bloc of Asian communist parties, grouped around Peking, confronting a Western bloc centered on Moscow.

The fourth speaker at the tenth session was another worker, and a woman to boot: MARIA I. ROZHNEVA, assistant foreman at a textile factory in the Moscow oblast. In addition to serving as an example of the party's grassroots membership and its appeal for women, Mme. Rozhneva had the function of furthering the Khrushchev line by rendering personal thanks to "dear Nikita Sergeevich Khrushchev" for leading the struggle against the Antiparty Group and by stressing the importance of raising the quality of consumer goods. Since Mme. Rozhneva's opportunity to address the congress must be recognized (in view of her low standing in the party) as a sign that she was regarded as a loyal follower of Khrushchev (in a later speech to the congress, on October 27, Khrushchev was to single her out for mention as an exemplary worker), her failure to support the call for expulsion of the Antiparty Group leaders from the party would seem to indicate that at this stage of the congress proceedings this demand had not yet become a rallying cry for the pro-Khrushchev forces.

The most important speaker at the tenth session was the party's leading expert on economic management, ALEKSEI N. KOSYGIN (born 1904, party member since 1927), first deputy chairman of the USSR Council of Ministers and full member of the Presidium (both since May 4, 1960; Kosygin had also been a member of the Politburo in the period 1948–52).

---

[257]Ibid., p. 550.

A man of businesslike conciseness, Kosygin defined his position on the major internal political question at the very outset of his speech: "The restoration by the party of Leninist norms of party life and Leninist principles of leadership, the thorough elimination [*preodolenie do kontsa*] of the negative consequences of the cult of personality, have called forth an unprecedented upsurge of creative initiative and activity of our people, the true makers of history, and have inspired millions of people to great and glorious accomplishments."[258]

Thus for Kosygin the internal political conflict in the party was a closed issue, something which had been carried through to the end. It was in this spirit that he treated the subject of the Antiparty Group. For Kosygin, it would seem, there was no question of the group's members being guilty of crimes or acts of repression; the only misdeeds to which he called attention were errors of judgment in economic management: "They considered that the socialist style of economic administration was characterized purely and simply by centralization. The stand the members of the antiparty group took on the solution of economic problems was often dictated not by economic or technical advisability but by considerations of personal prestige. They stifled any helpful initiative. This gave rise to intolerable conditions for work. These actions did tremendous harm to the national economy."[259]

If this was all that was at issue, the question might well be asked, why spoil the festive mood of the congress by raking up these unpleasant matters once more? To forestall awkward questions of that kind, Kosygin had a ready explanation:

> It is not because the antiparty group constitutes a force at the present time or a danger to our party in its work, that we are speaking about them at our congress. *Our party is stronger and more unified than ever.* It is solidly united around its Central Committee headed by that staunch Leninist Nikita Sergeevich Khrushchev [*prolonged applause*]. But we are doing this to show the party and the people once again what the cult of the individual leads to, what irreparable harm the antiparty group could have done the party and the state. We want the lessons of history never to be forgotten.[260]

On *this* subject, clearly, Kosygin did feel strongly, for he added: "We must and will do everything possible to see to it that *from now on there is no place in our party or our society for a cult of the individual*, that its sprouts and roots are thoroughly destroyed."[261]

---

[258]Ibid., p. 574; emphasis supplied. The translation in *CDSP*, XIII/51, p. 22, misleadingly implies that the "negative consequences of the cult of the individual" were still "being overcome."

[259]*CDSP*, XIII/51, p. 23.

[260]Ibid.; emphasis supplied.

[261]Ibid.; emphasis supplied.

There was only one figure in the party against whom such words could be directed, and the obvious anti-Khrushchev tendency in Kosygin's warnings against a new cult of personality is in full accord with the extremely restrained terms in his speech which he applied to the First Secretary. "Staunch Leninist" was as far as he went in his praise of Khrushchev, though he commended him for his initiative in undertaking various urgently needed economic reforms.

On the Albanian issue Kosygin stayed well within the lines delineated by previous speakers, but made no effort to minimize the current actuality of the problem. He failed to follow Mikoyan, however, in rebuffing the Chinese criticism of Khrushchev for raising the issue at the congress.

The remainder of Kosygin's speech dealt with his area of expertise, the planning and administration of the Soviet economy. Animating his tables, charts, and statistics on Soviet economic development was the persistent theme of the economic rivalry between the Soviet Union and the United States, and, while he avoided any premature boasting à la Khrushchev, he showed himself equally convinced of the eventual victory of the Soviet Union in this field of competition.

One of the party's medium-level functionaries followed Kosygin to the rostrum: GEORGII I. VOROB'EV (born 1914, party member since 1939), first secretary of the party committee for the Krasnodar krai (since July 1960), and member of the Bureau for the RSFSR (since 1959). Vorob'ev was a specialist in agriculture who had clashed with Khrushchev on several occasions and who had worked for a number of years in Leningrad under F. R. Kozlov. Since he added nothing new on the subject of the Antiparty Group and failed to support the call for expulsion of its leaders, the reason for giving him the floor was obscure; perhaps the purpose was to provide extended coverage of agricultural problems at the congress.

More significant was the last speech of the evening, delivered by YAKOV N. ZAROBIAN (born 1908, party member since 1932), first secretary of the Armenian Communist party (since December 28, 1960). Unusual interest attaches to Zarobian's speech because he falls into a rather special category: like Rashidov, Kunaev, and Akhundov, he was a non-Russian Union Republic party boss; like Rasulov, however, he owed his elevation to that rank to the personal intervention of F. R. Kozlov. It is significant, therefore, that Zarobian followed the pattern set early by Rasulov by voicing warm praise for Khrushchev as well as sharp condemnation of the Antiparty Group, including support for the demand for the ousting of one member of the group, Malenkov, from the party. Zarobian's speech therefore tends to confirm the suspicion created by Rasulov's that staunch support of Khrushchev on this issue might be designed to conceal the speaker's political links with Kozlov. It is noteworthy, furthermore, that both Zarobian and Rasulov directed their fire against Malenkov, since there is good reason to believe that for Kozlov too, Malenkov was the principal culprit among the Antiparty Group leaders.

Gilpatric discloses U.S. military predominance (October 21)

Some of the speakers at the congress—Suslov, for example—portrayed the peoples of the capitalist nations as following its proceedings with baited breath. While it is doubtful that many of the Western nations' inhabitants were in reality particularly concerned with what was taking place in Moscow, one key group of Western officials—President Kennedy and his top foreign policy advisers—did study the congress reports with close attention.

On the evening of the opening day of the congress, without waiting for the published text of Khrushchev's report for the Central Committee, the White House issued a statement condemning Soviet plans to test a 50-megaton nuclear bomb—plans which had only just been revealed by Khrushchev. Further evidence of the care with which top U.S. officials were following events in Moscow came on the following day, at a news conference held by Secretary of State Rusk. Rusk opened the conference by saying: "I know that you will wish to know whether I have any comments on Chairman Khrushchev's speech of yesterday."[262] He then singled out for special attention the passage in which Khrushchev had withdrawn the deadline on signature of a German peace treaty, observing cautiously that the statement might "serve to reduce tension somewhat." Later in the conference, Rusk disclosed the source of the information available to U.S. officials on which the White House statement on Soviet test plans had been based: ". . . the information which we have comes from Mr. Khrushchev's speech, and, quite frankly, I have not had the official transcript of that portion of the speech in front of me yet. I have a copy of a broadcast in English to the United Kingdom."[263]

When the full text of Khrushchev's Report for the Central Committee was published in *Pravda* and *Izvestiia* on October 18, one passage in particular was certain to attract the President's close attention. Defining the world balance of power, Khrushchev had said: "We believe that the forces of socialism, all the forces that stand for peace, are today *more powerful* than the aggressive imperialist forces. But even if one agreed with the President of the United States that our forces are equal—he said this quite recently—it would plainly be unwise to threaten war. The fact that *equality is conceded* should lead to the drawing of appropriate conclusions. Nowadays it is dangerous to pursue a 'position of strength' policy."[264]

Khrushchev had gone on to state categorically that "A German peace treaty must and will be signed, with or without the Western powers," and that "The status of West Berlin will also be normalized on the basis of this treaty: West Berlin will be a free, demilitarized city."[265] He had thus made it clear that in his mind Western acceptance of the Soviet demands on Germany was ren-

[262]*DSB*, 45 (1961): 746.
[263]Ibid., p. 749
[264]*CSP IV*, p. 51; emphasis supplied.
[265]Ibid.

dered more likely because of the alleged shift in the world power balance favoring the Soviet Union.

True, Khrushchev had then gone on to lift the deadline on signing a German peace treaty, but this softening of his attitude appeared to be counterbalanced a little later on when he disclosed plans to end the current Soviet nuclear test series with a 50-megaton bomb. The prevailing view in U.S. policymaking circles was that in so doing he was pursuing a strategy of intimidation and threats. Adlai Stevenson, for example, in a speech in the United Nations on October 19, citing Khrushchev's references to a 100-megaton bomb, said: "*With no apparent motives except intimidation and terror*, Chairman Khrushchev boasted of 100-megaton bombs."[266] As Rusk observed with regard to Khrushchev's speech: "In some aspects it seems to be quite moderate in tone, and in some other aspects it was quite uncompromising in tone."[267]

In Kennedy's view, and that of some of his advisers, Khrushchev's expressed conviction that the world military balance now favored the Soviet bloc—a view which they knew to be erroneous—was a major cause for the assertive behavior manifested by the Soviet Union in the Berlin crisis. The subject had come up at the President's news conference on October 11, when a reporter asked: "There have been charges that we have not adequately maintained the strength or the credibility of our nuclear deterrent and that we also have not fully convinced the leaders of the Soviet Union that we are determined to meet force with force in Berlin or elsewhere. What is your reaction to those charges?"[268]

In reply, Kennedy offered a quick survey of the military build-up carried out since his administration took office:

Since January, we have added more than $6 billion to the national defense budget, which is more than a 14-percent increase over the previous budget. In strategic forces, which are the nuclear forces, we have ordered a 50-percent increase in the number of Polaris submarines to be on station—battle station—by the end of 1964; a 50-percent increase in the number of strategic bombers on 15-minute ground alert at the end of runways, which is already in effect; a 100-percent increase in our capacity to produce Minuteman missiles against the day when that production capacity may be needed, and a similar increase in Skybolt and other programs which affect our strategic arm.

Now to strengthen our nonnuclear forces—and I think this is important—we have called up two additional divisions and many thousands more—particularly in the air; we've increased by 75 percent our modern long-range airlift capacity; we've increased our antiguerrilla forces by 150 percent; we've stepped up the delivery of the M–14 rifle from a maximum of 9,000 a month to 44,000 a month and taken other steps to bring the Army, Navy,

---

[266] *DSB*, 45 (1961): 816; emphasis supplied.

[267] Ibid., p. 753.

[268] *JFK, 1961*, p. 658.

and Marine units to full strength in terms of manpower and equipment. And we still have some way to go.[269]

Impressive though the figures were, however, they did not in themselves constitute a direct reply to the questions: (1) of the real military balance between the Soviet Union and the United States and (2) of Khrushchev's understanding of the facts. Thus when Khrushchev in his October 17 speech continued to speak confidently of a shift in world power favoring the Soviet Union and its allies, it seemed clear that Kennedy's words of October 11 had made no impression on him. And when Khrushchev went on to add his impromptu revelation about Soviet plans to explode a 50-megaton bomb, Washington felt the need to make the real situation crystal clear. Not to do so, in Kennedy's view, carried the risk that the Soviets, whether or not they believed the situation to be as depicted by Khrushchev, might force matters in the Berlin crisis to the point of a direct military confrontation.

The opportunity to make an authoritative statement on the subject was ready to hand. Roswell Gilpatric, the under secretary of defense, was scheduled to make a speech to the Business Council, a civic group in Hot Springs, Virginia, on October 21. The speech which Gilpatric gave marks a major turning point in Soviet–U.S. relations and therefore merits close attention. It will be convenient to consider separately (1) the speech itself, (2) the evidence that it was an expression of official U.S. policy, and (3) the purpose the speech was intended to serve.

At the outset of his speech Gilpatric defined the goal of the administration's policy in military affairs: "The President was determined that our strategic power must be sufficient to deter any deliberate nuclear attack on this country or its allies by being able to survive a first strike by the enemy with sufficient arms to penetrate his defenses and inflict unacceptable losses upon him."[270]

Gilpatric then moved quickly to the immediate focus of U.S. military policy, the conflict with the Soviets over Berlin. Berlin, he said,

> . . . is the emergency of the moment, because the Soviets have chosen to make it so. We have responded immediately, with our western allies, by reinforcing our garrisons in that beleaguered city. We have called up some 150,000 reservists, increased our draft calls and extended the time in service of many who are already in uniform. These are the so-called quick-fix measures which we have invoked to improve the western tactical position in Berlin *and remind the Soviets* that the city is not an open invitation to that variety of aggression which has been described as the salami, or one slice at a time, method.[271]

[269]Ibid., pp. 658–59.

[270]*Documents on Disarmament, 1961*, p. 543; full text, pp. 542–50, citing a Department of Defense press release.

[271]Ibid., p. 544; emphasis supplied.

Behind these stop-gap measures, Gilpatric continued, lay the fundamental question of the real military balance, concerning which he expressed confidence based on "a sober appreciation of the relative military power of the two sides," and which he implied the Soviets also recognized: "We doubt that the Soviet leadership has in fact any less realistic views, although this may not be always apparent from their extravagant claims."[272]

Coolly and methodically, Gilpatric proceeded to spell out the realities of U.S. military power:

> The fact is that this nation has a nuclear retaliatory force of such lethal power that an enemy move which brought it into play would be an act of self-destruction on his part. The U.S. has today hundreds of manned intercontinental bombers capable of reaching the Soviet Union, including 600 heavy bombers and many more medium bombers equally capable of intercontinental operations because of our highly developed in-flight refueling techniques and world-wide base structure. The U.S. also has 6 Polaris submarines at sea carrying a total of 96 missiles, and dozens of intercontinental ballistic missiles. Our carrier strike forces and land-based theater forces could deliver additional hundreds of megatons. The total number of our nuclear delivery vehicles, tactical as well as strategic, is in the tens of thousands; and of course, we have more than one warhead for each vehicle.[273]

Even if they resorted to a surprise attack, Gilpatric continued, the Soviets could not hope for victory:

> Our forces are so deployed and protected that a sneak attack could not effectively disarm us. The destructive power which the United States could bring to bear even after a Soviet surprise attack upon our forces would be as great as—perhaps greater than—the total undamaged force which the enemy can threaten to launch against the United States in a first strike. In short, *we have a second strike capability which is at least as extensive as what the Soviets can deliver by striking first.* Therefore, we are confident that the Soviets will not provoke a major nuclear conflict.[274]

With regard to announced Soviet plans to explode a 50-megaton bomb, Gilpatric ruled out the possibility that genuine military considerations might be involved, and observed: "It is therefore quite clear that *the Russians' primary purpose is terror.* With the customary Soviet heavy-handedness, the timing has been chosen with one eye on Berlin and the other on the 22nd Party Congress. Perhaps this is also the Soviet Union's answer to the discordant voice from its populous neighbor to the south [i.e., communist China]."[275]

[272]Ibid.
[273]Ibid., pp. 544–45.
[274]Ibid., p. 545; emphasis supplied.
[275]Ibid.; emphasis supplied.

Though the United States considered the superbomb to be militarily purposeless, it was nevertheless taking additional measures in response to the Soviet military build-up, Gilpatric continued: ". . . we must and do take seriously the Soviet Union's military technology and the likelihood of future improvements in its nuclear strike posture. We are therefore increasing the survivability of our retaliatory forces by programs of hardening, concealment and mobility."[276]

Having dealt with the "formidable" weapons that "form the backbone of our deterrent strength," Gilpatric gave his listeners an outline of the military measures currently under way in the field of "conventional non-nuclear arms" and tactical nuclear weapons. In conclusion he voiced the firm resolve of the United States to take up arms rather than yield to Soviet demands: "The United States does not seek to resolve disputes by violence. But if forceful interference with our rights and obligations should lead to violent conflict—as it well might—the United States does not intend to be defeated."[277]

Available information on the genesis of Gilpatric's speech is scanty; neither Sorensen, Schlesinger, nor Salinger mentions it. A Washington reporter, Elie Abel, states that it was Gilpatric's own idea to give the speech, but notes that it received advance clearance from the President as well as from Rusk and McGeorge Bundy.[278]

In view of Kennedy's acute concern with the Berlin crisis, the U.S.–Soviet strategic balance, and Khrushchev's claims of strategic equality with the United States, however, it appears more likely that the initiative for the speech came from the President himself. At the very least, he welcomed the idea of its being made and lent it his full support.

As to the administration's explicit backing for Gilpatric, the record is clear. In releasing the text of the speech the Pentagon stressed that it had been cleared "at the highest level."[279] In a TV program, "Issues and Answers," on October 22, Rusk gave the speech his explicit endorsement. "Mr. Gilpatric," said Rusk, ". . . was making *an official statement*; it was a well-considered statement, and it was based upon the facts. These are the facts in the present situation. We are not dealing in the world these days from a position of weakness."[280] Rusk went on to assume joint personal responsibility for the speech: "I went over the speech with Mr. Gilpatric, and he and I discussed it before he made it."[281]

[276]Ibid.

[277]Ibid., p. 549.

[278]Elie Abel, *The Missile Crisis* (Philadelphia and New York: Lippincott, 1966), p. 38. Kaufmann, p. 323, misdates the speech Oct. 10, and misses its connection with Khrushchev's report to the party congress.

[279]John Scali in *DSB*, 45 (1961): 802. See also David Lawrence, *NYHT*, Oct. 24, 1961, p. 25.

[280]*DSB*, 45 (1961): 801; emphasis supplied.

[281]Ibid., p. 802.

If one of the principal purposes of the speech, however, was to convey a clear and unequivocal message about the U.S.–Soviet military balance to the Soviet leadership, why did the President not deliver the speech himself? Hugh Sidey, *Time's* White House correspondent, throws an indirect though revealing light on that question by quoting Kennedy's answer to a similar question put to him at the time of the Cuban missile crisis: "When I get up and say those things it sounds too belligerent."[282] Thus the decision was taken to reply to Khrushchev's claim of strategic parity with the United States authoritatively, fully, and categorically, but not provocatively.

The clearest available statement of Washington's purpose in authorizing the Gilpatric speech was provided in Rusk's TV interview on October 22. The crux of the Soviet–U.S. confrontation over Berlin, Rusk made it clear, was the problem of strategic balance:

> . . . when you are in problems of negotiation, the question inevitably comes up from time to time whether you are negotiating from a position of strength or of weakness or whether you have cause to be nervous or confident. The point is that the United States and its allies are strong. Mr. Khrushchev must know that we are strong, and *he does know that we are strong* and that, when we talk about exploratory talks or we talk about contacts with the Soviet Government on one or another point, this is no problem that turns on whether we feel that we are weak or not. We are not weak.[283]

What about Khrushchev's claim that the United States and the Soviets are "equal" in power, and his further claim that Kennedy had conceded this to be a fact, a reporter asked. Rusk's answer was an attempt to strip away the semantic confusion on which Khrushchev was relying to conceal the real situation:

> Well, I think when we use this word "equal" what is meant there is that in this confrontation of two great power blocs each side has a capacity to inflict very great damage upon the other. Therefore in terms of handling the relationships between the two power blocs, all responsible governments need to take that into account and not act irresponsibly or frivolously or not suppose that they can press in upon the vital interests of the other side without incurring very great risks. So there is an ability to inflict very great damage on both sides, but that does not necessarily mean that in the total situation the two situations are equal.[284]

Rusk explicitly discounted the possibility that Khrushchev might believe in his public claims: "I don't believe that Mr. Khrushchev is under any illusion about the strength of the West . . . ," but then proceeded to show that he himself still labored under an illusion about the relationship between Moscow and

---

[282]Sidey, p. 266.
[283]*DSB*, 45 (1961): 802; emphasis supplied.
[284]Ibid.

Peking: ". . . nor are we under any illusion about *the strength of the Sino-Soviet bloc.*"[285]

Gilpatric's speech presented a formidable challenge to the Soviet leadership. It threatened seriously to undermine the concept of world politics on which they based their optimistic forecasts, and with it their confident prediction that the Soviet Union would enter the stage of communism within twenty years. The speech also called into question the image of the United States drawn in speeches at the Soviet congress, in terms both of its relative strength and its leaders' purposes vis-à-vis the Soviet Union.

From the Soviet viewpoint, therefore, it was essential that an authoritative rebuttal to Gilpatric be delivered from the floor of the party congress as soon as possible. The obvious choice for speaker was the Soviet minister of defense, Marshal Rodion Ya. Malinovsky. We have already seen that the structural pattern of the congress indicates that Malinovsky's speech was moved up to an earlier position in the schedule than had originally been planned. The decision to do so was probably taken on Sunday, October 22, the day on which reports of Gilpatric's speech became available in Moscow. As we shall see, that decision was not the only one reached by the Soviet leadership on that date.

The concealed conflict (October 22)

For the great majority of congress delegates, Sunday, October 22, was a day of respite from the steady round of congress speeches, a welcome opportunity to explore the Soviet capital or relax in its parks and squares. For the top Soviet leaders, however, October 22 was a working day as crowded and demanding as any of the congress sessions. A number of urgent problems demanded their immediate attention, and the decisions they reached gave rise in turn to new complications.

We have already noted three of the subjects on the agenda: the procedural conflict with China over the Soviet–Albanian dispute, the strategic conflict with the United States over the world balance of power, and the organizational conflict in the United Nations over the choice of a successor to Dag Hammarskjöld. It is likely that decisions on all three of these problems were taken on October 22.

a) The discussion between Chou En-lai and a small group of Soviet leaders—Khrushchev, Mikoyan, and Kozlov—was the top item on the agenda. We know the result of the discussion from its public outcome—Chou's departure from Moscow on the 23rd, with more than a week of the congress still to go. It is clear, therefore, that the Soviet leadership showed no willingness to make the concessions which would have been required to avoid an open break with Peking. The outcome could have been predicted from an analysis of the composi-

---

[285]Ibid.; emphasis supplied. By this time Khrushchev's Oct. 17 speech, in which he launched the attack on Albania, and Chou's reply on Oct. 19 had been published. For further comment by Rusk on Sino–Soviet relations, see ibid., p. 804.

tion of the Soviet group. Khrushchev's position was a foregone conclusion, while Mikoyan had made it clear in his congress speech on October 20 that he rejected Chou's protest. That left Kozlov as the lone proponent of more cordial relations with the Chinese. Outnumbered two to one, Kozlov was unable to prevent a hardening of the Soviet attitude.

b) To reply to Gilpatric, Marshal Malinovsky was commissioned to prepare a speech strongly reaffirming Soviet strategic power in terms suitable for supporting the leadership's claims for strategic parity with the West, and his place in the congress schedule was moved up to the earliest suitable position, the evening session of October 23.

c) An important step toward resolution of the organizational crisis in the United Nations was taken on Monday, October 23, when Zorin accepted a compromise formula proposed by Stevenson under which the acting secretary general to be appointed would reach decisions "in a spirit of mutual understanding" with his principal subordinates. According to a dispatch from U.N. headquarters on the day this compromise was reached: "It was understood that Mr. Zorin's acceptance of the United States position was in accordance with *new instructions received from Moscow over the weekend.*"[286]

In all three of these decisions the paramount influence of Khrushchev is manifest. But what of Kozlov? He had not yet spoken out at the party congress on any of the major issues confronting it, and it was to be another six days before he finally addressed the delegates. It is not at all difficult, however, to deduce Kozlov's reactions to the course the congress had taken thus far, especially Khrushchev's denunciation of the Albanian leadership and the open break with Peking to which this action led.

Blocked from giving public expressions to his views, facing a congress organizationally dominated by Khrushchev and with his own followers debarred from speaking, sharply critical of the foreign policy line advocated by Khrushchev, Kozlov was left with but one path open to him—clandestine, conspiratorial opposition. The fact that by temperament, training, and inclination he would naturally have chosen this path anyway helped to determine the course of events.

On the evening of October 22 an American official in West Berlin, Allen Lightner, U.S. deputy chief of mission, drove with his wife through the Friedrichstrasse checkpoint in the direction of East Berlin.[287] It had long been the accepted practice in the divided city for U.S. civilian officials to make trips into the Eastern sector by car without presenting identification papers to the East German border guards (Volkspolizei). The official license plates had served to identify the car's occupants, and no challenge had hitherto been presented by the Volkspolizei. This right of unchallenged access to East Berlin on the part of U.S. civilian officials was one of the few remaining vestiges of the original postwar unity of the city under four-power control.

---

[286]*NYT*, Oct. 24, 1961, p. 9; emphasis supplied.

[287]For an account of the Oct. 22 incident, see Smith, *Defense of Berlin*, pp. 319–20.

On the evening of October 22, however, the East German police broke sharply with established practice and demanded that Lightner present identification papers before proceeding. On his refusal to comply with the demand, the Volkspolizei blocked his access into the eastern sector. When Lightner requested to see a Russian officer, the Volkspolizei replied that henceforth all persons in civilian clothes entering "the capital of the German Democratic Republic" would have to present identification papers to authorities representing the GDR. Lightner refused to comply with this demand, and after nearly an hour's unsuccessful wait for the East Germans to clear the way drove back to the checkpoint.

Waiting for him at the sector boundary was a U.S. officer, Lieutenant Colonel Sabolyk, with a small detachment of picked troops; within a short time the group was joined by two medium tanks and two armored personnel carriers. Lightner now made a second trip through the checkpoint toward East Berlin, alone this time, and the scene was replayed: Lightner's car was stopped, the Volkspolizei demanded to see his identification, he refused and requested to see a Soviet officer, the Volkspolizei rejected the request and blocked his way. This time, however, the scene ended differently. After Lightner had waited for half an hour, Colonel Sabolyk ordered a squad to escort Lightner's car through the barricade. Smith graphically describes what happenened next: "With bayonets fixed, the eight men of the battle group moved out smartly, took up positions flanking the car, and then walked slowly but firmly beyond the East German barrier into East Berlin. The *Vopos* [Volkspolizei] made no effort to interfere. Lightner drove on for a block, turned around and came back. Again the car was stopped. Again the eight-man escort moved out and conduct[ed] him back through the barrier. The East German police sullenly stepped aside."[288]

To make sure the point was grasped, Lightner made still a third trip into the eastern sector: "This time his car was allowed to proceed by the East Germans uninspected. After driving about a mile through East Berlin Lightner returned through the checkpoint, again without difficulty."[289]

The precipitating factor in the October 22 incident was the innovation on the part of the East German border police in demanding to see identification papers from a U.S. civilian official driving an automobile carrying U.S. license plates. This innovation was squarely in line with the position taken in Ulbricht's October 20 speech to the CPSU congress that the Western powers "now recognize the existence of two German states." The purpose behind the Volkspolizei's actions was to force the United States to acknowledge the authority of the East German regime in East Berlin. Conversely, the issue at stake as the Americans saw it was to deny the competence of the East German regime in the eastern sector of Berlin and thereby to assert the continuation of Soviet responsibility in that area.

[288]Ibid., p. 320.
[289]Ibid., p. 321.

Under whose orders did the Volkspolizei take their precedent-breaking action on the evening of October 22? The *Survey of International Affairs* comments that the action constituted a break in the previous pattern of events "which is difficult properly to explain."[290] Ulbricht's congress speech of October 19, however, leaves little doubt that the innovation had his personal approval. It was the manifestation in action of the policy he had advocated in his speech.

Was Ulbricht acting entirely on his own? Did his distaste for Khrushchev's withdrawal of the 1961 deadline for signing a German peace treaty lead him to strike out in Berlin in the hope of precipitating a showdown with the Western powers which might end in their complete exclusion from the city?

It is highly doubtful that Ulbricht would have taken such a risky step if he knew that the Soviet leadership was solidly united behind Khrushchev in his new policy of easing tensions in Berlin. Ulbricht was an experienced communist politician, a veteran of decades of rough-and-tumble fighting in the struggle not merely for power but for sheer survival. His position as East German political boss was totally dependent on continuing Soviet political, diplomatic, and military support. Under these circumstances the possibility can be ruled out that Ulbricht was acting impulsively, out of pique, in authorizing the crisis-precipitating innovation of the Volkspolizei on October 22. He must have had the assurance of support from someone high in the Soviet leadership.

The signs point unmistakably to Kozlov. Blocked from the opportunity to present his views on the congress floor, either in person or through his followers, smarting under the sharp affront which had just been administered to his ideological ally Chou En-lai, contemptuous of what he regarded as Khrushchev's weakness in the face of Western power, Kozlov would be in a receptive mood to listen to Ulbricht's arguments that the opportunity for direct action, for finally precipitating the Berlin showdown which Khrushchev was trying to avoid, lay in their hands. It is even likely that the initiative came from Kozlov. In any case, he and Ulbricht saw eye to eye on the policy to be pursued.

The coincidence in timing between the break with China and the outbreak of the new crisis in Berlin tells its own story. We are never likely to get documentary proof of the link between these events—very likely no such proof will ever turn up. After all, why should the conspirators commit their plans to paper? A few words from Kozlov to Ulbricht was all that was needed.

That the incident involving Mr. Lightner did not, however, represent simply the irresponsible action of a local Volkspolizei detachment but enjoyed official GDR backing was shown on the morning of Monday, October 23, when the East German legislature passed an ordinance requiring all foreigners entering East Berlin to present identification.[291] That the East German action in

---

[290]*SIA*, 1961, p. 271.

[291]*NYT*, Oct. 26, 1961, p. 3; Smith, *Defense of Berlin*, p. 321. According to a subsequent oral clarification, Western military personnel were exempt from the order.

turn had the approval of someone high in the Soviet hierarchy was shown by the fact that the new crisis in Berlin was not resolved until October 28. If Ulbricht had been nothing but the obedient tool of a Soviet leadership united behind Khrushchev, the crisis would either never have arisen in the first place or, having arisen, would have been promptly ended by orders to the Volkspolizei to return to their previous procedure.

Malinovsky replies to Gilpatric (October 23)

The eleventh session of the congress, which convened at 10 A.M. on the morning of Monday, October 23, continued the pattern established in the preceding four sessions, in that the list of speakers included one Presidium member (D. S. Poliansky), several Union Republic party bosses (A. Yu. Snechkus of Lithuania and T. Usubaliev of Kirghiziia) and a group of foreign CP leaders. For good measure, a woman worker (Valentina Gaganova) and a regional party boss (A. P. Shitikov, first secretary of Khabarovsk kraikom) were thrown in.

By now the underlying pattern of the congress had been established in the form of two basic questions. For speakers representing the CPSU, the crucial question was: What attitude do you take toward the proposal for the expulsion from the party of the leaders of the Antiparty Group? For foreign CP leaders the question was: What attitude does your party take in the dispute between the CPSU and the Albanian Party of Labor?

Judged on the basis of their response to these questions, the speeches at the eleventh session presented no surprises. The five foreign CP leaders who led off the session split along geographical lines, in accordance with the precedent established earlier, with SANZO NOSAKA for the Japanese CP maintaining silence on the Albanian question, thus lining up behind Peking, while the four Western CP leaders, representing the parties of the United States, West Germany, Spain, and Finland, threw their support to Moscow by condemning the Albanian leadership in varying degrees of firmness. Khrushchev's presence was signified in the protocols by the use of the long ritual embrace formula.

On the basis of his party career, which included technical training in agriculture, followed by years of service in the party apparatus, marked by a steady upward climb due as much to his own abilities as to the patronage of Khrushchev, several students of Soviet politics have rated DMITRI S. POLIANSKY (born 1917, party member since 1939) as a moderately loyal supporter of Khrushchev but with a tendency toward independence in his political allegiance. On this occasion, however, Poliansky came through with solid support for the First Secretary, especially with regard to his conduct of Soviet foreign policy. By structuring his speech so that his comments on the Antiparty Group came at the end, Poliansky introduced an element of tension which was heightened by the new details he revealed. After a general condemnation of the group, whose leaders, he charged, "opposed literally all measures of the

Party on every major question of domestic and foreign policy,"[292] Poliansky narrowed down the focus of his attack to Molotov personally. Having first demolished Molotov's claims to expertise in the field of agriculture, Poliansky took up his "incorrect positions in foreign policy":

> He opposed the Central Committee's efforts to get out of the blind alleys in foreign policy that had developed by that time as a result of Stalin's subjective approach to many international matters.
>
> Being unable to interpret new phenomena of life correctly, he turned out to be completely under the sway of dogmatism. Considering himself a theoretician, the farther he went, the more he confused *and confuses* elementary Leninist propositions, and *he even contradicts himself.* If one speaks about people who are incapable of applying the Leninist teaching, *this is true above all of Molotov.* He long ago departed from creative Leninism and became a hopeless conservative.[293]

Noteworthy here was Poliansky's emphasis on the current relevance of Molotov's views in foreign policy. Otherwise, however, he was still content to deal in generalities; there was as yet little sense of urgency in condemning Molotov's errors in this area.

Much more personal in tone was the attack on poor old Voroshilov to whom Poliansky next turned his attention. Addressing his remarks directly to the veteran army and party official who was seated on the dais along with the other members of the congress presidium, Poliansky warned him: "So, Comrade Voroshilov, don't pretend to be an innocent Ivan. You must bear full responsibility for your antiparty deeds, like the antiparty group."[294] But after this assault Poliansky backed off, without having voiced a specific demand for expulsion of the Antiparty Group leaders from the party.

*   *   *

The parade of foreign CP leaders to the congress rostrum continued at the outset of the evening session of October 23. As before, Khrushchev was on hand to exchange "warm greetings" with each speaker at the end of his speech. He had reason to be pleased: the balance was in his favor, four parties lining up in support of the Soviet position on Albania (representatives of the parties of Chile, Iraq, Portugal, and Austria) as against two abstainers (Algeria and Great Britain). But the appearance of two Western parties in the pro-Chinese column was an ominous warning that the split in the international communist movement could not be confined to Asia.

The Presidium speaker for the evening was N. G. IGNATOV (born 1901, party member since 1923), deputy chairman of the Council of Ministers of the USSR (since May 1960). In his long and varied career Ignatov had worked in the army, the secret police, the party apparatus, and the govern-

---

[292] *Pravda*, Oct. 24, 1961; *CDSP*, XIII/52, p. 22.
[293] *CDSP*, XIII/52, p. 22; emphasis supplied.
[294] Ibid., p. 23.

ment. Politically he had shown a marked tendency to support Khrushchev and an equally strong antipathy for Khrushchev's defeated rival, Malenkov; significant also was the fact that in the reshuffle of party posts carried through following Stalin's death, Ignatov had replaced F. R. Kozlov as party leader in Leningrad.

As was to be expected from a man with such a background, Ignatov joined vigorously in the attack on the Antiparty Group. Picking up Poliansky's lead, Ignatov emphasized the current relevance of Molotov's erroneous views on Soviet foreign policy: "Molotov arrogantly considered himself, *and still considers himself*, an expert on all aspects of international and domestic life. But it is a well-known fact that Molotov was *and remains* muddleheaded in his understanding of international relations and the country's internal development. . . . Molotov was *and remains* a hopeless dogmatist who has lost all notion of reality."[295]

Like Poliansky, however, Ignatov gave no specific evidence of where Molotov's views on foreign policy were wrong. Much more vivid and immediate was his account of the clash between the Antiparty Group and Khrushchev in June 1957. With liberal assists from Khrushchev himself, Ignatov gave the congress delegates the fullest and most graphic account yet presented to the party of how the struggle had been waged, and in so doing he contributed to the attack on Voroshilov by charging that he had served as the Antiparty Group's agent in the effort to keep Khrushchev from meeting with the members of the Central Committee.

On the question of expulsion, Ignatov took a forthright stand: "I second the suggestions made from this rostrum by delegates to the Twenty-Second Congress that Molotov, Kaganovich and Malenkov be expelled from the party, and I consider these suggestions absolutely proper."[296] Ignatov's stalwart support of the First Secretary was not enough, however, to safeguard his political position; at the end of the congress he was dropped from membership in the Presidium.

The final speaker of the evening of October 23 was Marshal RODION Ya. MALINOVSKY (born 1898, party member since 1926). Shortly after the October 1957 Central Committee plenum, at which Marshal Zhukov was dropped from the Presidium, Malinovsky had replaced Zhukov as minister of defense, a promotion which most Western observers attributed to Malinovsky's record of solid support for Khrushchev and to the long personal association between the two men, dating back to their common service in the Red Army during the Battle of Stalingrad.

At the outset of his speech Malinovsky signified his continuing allegiance to the First Secretary by unusually warm praise, calling him "the true Leninist, the outstanding leader of the party and government, dear Nikita Sergeevich Khrushchev."[297] Malinovsky defined the main theme of his speech as the con-

[295] *Pravda*, Oct. 25, 1961; *CDSP*, XIV/1, p. 18; emphasis supplied.
[296] *CDSP*, XIV/1, p. 18.
[297] *Sten. ot.*, 2: 109.

flict between the advancing world of socialism and the decrepit, doomed world of capitalism. The ultimate victory of socialism was historically inevitable, Malinovsky claimed, but he warned that

> . . . in its death throes, outworn capitalism threatens mankind with frightful calamities.
>
> The imperialist powers are hatching mad plans of armed attack on the Soviet Union and the other socialist states. Under various hypocritical pretexts they are rejecting the Soviet proposals for general and complete disarmament and are continuously increasing the power of their armed forces. They are threatening to reply with force to our just proposals for the conclusion of a German peace treaty [Malinovsky called it a "peaceful German treaty"] and the liquidation on that basis of the abnormal situation which has arisen in West Berlin.[298]

To indicate the seriousness of the situation, Malinovsky gave his listeners some sobering figures on the U.S. military build-up:

> . . . the U.S. President has increased the military budget by more than $6,000,000,000, i.e., 14%. He has promised by the end of 1964 to increase the number of Polaris-armed atomic submarines by 50%, to increase by 50% the number of strategic bombers on the runways and ready to take off 15 minutes after the alert; and to double the number of Minuteman missiles. He is increasing the numerical strength of the ground forces, bringing the production of rifles up from 9,000 to 44,000 a month, and increasing by 150% the troops for combating the guerrilla movements in oppressed countries.[299]

But Malinovsky implied that even with this build-up, the United States was still inferior to the Soviet Union in military power: "And all this is being done, as he [Kennedy] puts it, 'to achieve a balance with the Soviet Union'."[300] As to Soviet military measures, Malinovsky portrayed them as purely defensive:

> As a move in response to the intensified practical preparations for war being made by the Western countries with the "Berlin crisis" as the pretext, the Party Central Committee and the Soviet government were obliged to carry out a number of measures, which you know of, to strengthen the defense capacity and security of the U.S.S.R. The reduction of the armed forces that had been planned and was in process was temporarily halted; defense expenditures were increased somewhat; the regular demobilization from the army and navy to the reserve of noncommissioned officers and men who had completed their tour of active service was temporarily put off; nuclear weapons tests are being conducted.[301]

As the basis for the tasks set for the Soviet armed forces, Malinovsky cited the "historic" speech by Khrushchev to the Supreme Soviet in January

[298]Ibid., pp. 109–10.
[299]*Pravda*, Oct. 25, 1961; *CDSP*, XIV/1, p. 19.
[300]*CDSP*, XIV/1, p. 19.
[301]Ibid.

1960, and he underlined the importance of the party leadership for the armed forces by giving Khrushchev the rarely used title, "supreme commander-in-chief." In broad but graphic terms Malinovsky sketched a picture of future war as seen by Soviet military thinkers: "The world war of the future, if not prevented, will assume an unprecedentedly destructive character. It will result in the deaths of hundreds of millions of people, and whole countries will be turned into lifeless, ash-covered deserts."[302] Victory in a war waged with atomic weapons, Malinovsky contended, would require huge armies:

> Although nuclear weapons will hold the decisive place in a future war, we are nevertheless coming to the conclusion that *final victory over an aggressor* can be achieved only through combined operations by all branches of the armed forces. We are therefore devoting due attention to the perfection of weapons of all types, teaching our forces how to use them skillfully and to achieve *a decisive victory over the aggressor* [*applause*]. We also believe that under modern conditions any future war would be waged, despite the enormous losses, by mass, many-millions-strong armed forces.[303]

The Soviet leadership's concern with Western atomic power was candidly admitted: "The Presidium of the party Central Committee and the Soviet government have called upon us to pay special attention to the initial phase of a possible war. The reason why this phase is important is that the very first massed nuclear blows can to an enormous extent predetermine the whole subsequent course of the war and result in such losses in the rear and in the armed forces that the people and country will find themselves in an exceptionally difficult situation."[304]

Malinovsky explicitly ruled out the possibility that the Western powers' military build-up might have a defensive purpose: "A realistic assessment of the picture would lead one to believe that *what the imperialists are preparing is a surprise nuclear attack on the U.S.S.R. and the socialist countries.* Hence Soviet military doctrine regards it as the most important, the pre-eminent, the first-priority task of the armed forces to be in a state of constant readiness for effectively repulsing a surprise attack by the enemy and thwarting his criminal designs."[305]

Despite the frightful devastation which a nuclear war would entail, however, Malinovsky predicted that socialism would emerge victorious from such a war: "We are deeply convinced that in this war, if the capitalists force it on us, *the socialist camp will win, while capitalism will be destroyed forever.*"[306]

In language reminiscent of Khrushchev's statements during the summer, Malinovsky threatened England and West Germany with total destruction: "You must understand, madmen, that it would take really very few multimega-

---

[302] Ibid.
[303] Ibid., pp. 19–20; emphasis supplied.
[304] Ibid., p. 20.
[305] Ibid.; emphasis supplied.
[306] *Sten. ot.*, 2: 113; emphasis supplied.

ton nuclear bombs to wipe out your small and densely populated countries and kill you instantly in your lairs!"[307]

Having sketched an apocalyptic vision of thermonuclear war as a suitable background, Malinovsky was now ready to take on the challenging task of replying to Gilpatric. "On October 21 of this year," he said, "—quite recently, that is—U.S. Deputy Secretary of Defense Roswell Gilpatric addressed a meeting of the Business Council in Virginia, presumably not without President Kennedy's knowledge, and, brandishing the might of the United States, threatened us with force. What is there to say to this latest threat, to this petty speech? Only one thing: The threat does not frighten us! [*Stormy applause.*]"[308]

Malinovsky found it necessary to say a good deal more than that, however. His tactics called for ignoring completely the main lines of Gilpatric's argument—that the United States feared a surprise attack by the Soviet Union and that, to reduce the temptation among Soviet policymakers to launch such an attack, it was maintaining sufficient military power to take the full force of a first strike and still have enough reserve power to deal a devastating blow in return. As Malinovsky presented matters, Gilpatric's speech was nothing more than the bragging of a bully trying to pick a fight.

Malinovsky nevertheless attempted to minimize the damaging implications for Soviet strategy of the figures for U.S. military strength cited by Gilpatric by impugning the basis of U.S. strategic estimates as erroneous:

> The American experts use as the unit for their estimates a warhead of only five megatons. But as you already know, we have nuclear warheads with yields ranging from 20 to 30 to 100 megatons, and our ballistic rockets have given such a splendid account of themselves that nobody can have any doubt as to their ability to lift these warheads and deliver them to any spot on the globe from which an attack might be made on the Soviet Union and the other socialist countries [*stormy applause*]. In the light of these more precise data, the American experts must obviously make fundamental corrections in their estimates with respect both to the yield of the nuclear warheads and to the number that the Soviet Union has at its disposal.[309]

And again Malinovsky threatened America's allies with destruction: "Countries that make their territory available to the aggressor for military bases and missile sites should also give this some serious thought. These countries are small in size and have a high population density; the outbreak of a nuclear war would be the sheerest calamity for them."[310]

This concluded Malinovsky's formal response to Gilpatric's speech, even though he had not really come to grips with the problems it raised for Soviet military planners. Most of the remainder of his speech consisted of a review of

[307]Ibid.; the protocols record "stormy applause."
[308]*CDSP*, XIV/1, p. 20.
[309]Ibid.
[310]Ibid.

the existing state of the Soviet armed forces, so portrayed as to make them seem invincible, and bristling with threats, explicit or implied, of the devastation these forces were capable of wreaking on an adversary.

Toward the close of his address Malinovsky made his contribution to the renewed attack on the Antiparty Group. "We military men," he said,

> . . . have a special grievance against the members of the antiparty group. I see in this auditorium prominent military leaders who were innocently imprisoned. All army communists unanimously and with special fervor approve the crushing defeat of the antiparty group of Molotov, Malenkov, Kaganovich, Voroshilov, Bulganin, Pervukhin, and Saburov and heartily thank the Central Committee of our party for its firm Leninist line in fighting the antiparty group, and above all we thank Nikita Sergeevich Khrushchev, that outstanding champion of the restoration of Leninist principles and norms in the guidance of the party and state.[311]

Ignoring the proposal to expel the leaders of the group from the party, however, Malinovsky continued with a brief reference to the downfall of Marshal Zhukov, whom he accused of having "displayed adventurism and a Bonapartist ambition for personal power."[312] The moral to be drawn from Zhukov's fate, obviously, was the need for the armed forces to be fully under party control, and Malinovsky was careful to draw the moral explicitly.

Only toward the very end of his strikingly belligerent speech did Malinovsky briefly, almost as an afterthought, sound the note of peace: "Comrades! The Soviet Union is a peaceful country; we threaten no one and are exerting all our efforts to defend peace on earth. But the disasters of the last war, which claimed so many victims and brought so much suffering, are fresh in our minds, in the minds of all Soviet people. We have no right, therefore, to forget for a single instant the harsh lessons of that war, the savage nature of imperialism, and we are obliged to keep our powder dry."[313]

Malinovsky's speech may have served to reassure the congress delegates about the adequacy of Soviet military power, but it cannot have fulfilled the same function as far as the party leadership was concerned. The disquieting facts presented by Gilpatric remained unanswered; the challenge of American military power, and the obstacle this power constituted to the further extension of communist influence, had not been met.

Gilpatric's speech had served to put the Soviet leadership on notice with regard to the facts about U.S. military strength and all they implied for the world strategic balance. The basic question remained, however, whether the U.S. leadership had the will to use that strength, if necessary, to block Soviet plans in Germany. There were those in the communist world—Kozlov, Ulbricht, Chou, Hoxha, Kim—who believed the U.S. leaders lacked that will. For men harboring this belief, only a direct confrontation of naked military force could

[311]Ibid., p. 21.
[312]Ibid., p. 22.
[313]Ibid.

serve as a fully satisfactory test. They were about to have the confrontation they wanted.

The Presidium decides to continue the Soviet nuclear test series (October 24, morning)

The adverse reaction of world public opinion to the Soviet announcement of the resumption of nuclear testing at the end of August had been to a considerable extent dissipated by the U.S. action in following suit less than a week later. The widespread feeling that both sides were equally responsible for the nuclear arms race found expression in a draft resolution submitted by India in the U.N. General Assembly on October 16 which called on "the Powers concerned . . . to refrain from further test explosions pending the conclusion of the necessary agreements in regard to tests or general and complete disarmament."[314]

Khrushchev's disclosure on the following day, however, that the Soviet Union intended to detonate a 50-megaton bomb had the effect of reviving the outcry against the Soviet test program. Sensing the impending swing in world public opinion, the White House promptly issued a statement calling on the Soviet Union to "reconsider this decision, if in fact it has been made," and stressing the "mass of radioactive fallout" which would be added to "that which has been unleashed in recent weeks" (above, p. 370).

On October 20, six nations—Denmark, Canada, Iceland, Japan, Norway, and Sweden—submitted a joint resolution in the General Assembly "solemnly appealing" to the Soviet Union to abandon its plan to explode the 50-megaton bomb.[315] Subsequently Iran and Pakistan joined the original sponsors of the resolution.[316]

Apparently unmoved by the rising ground swell of criticism abroad, the Soviets on October 23 carried out a 30-megaton blast, the largest explosion thus far in their current series, as well as the largest hitherto set off on earth.[317]

The Soviets' explosion of the 30-megaton bomb on October 23 touched off a new wave of protest throughout the world. Those who denounced the action included the veteran British philosopher Bertrand Russell and Queen Elizabeth II. India's Prime Minister Nehru called the explosion "a horrible thing," and said he was "deeply pained and shocked." In a cable to Khrushchev, Swedish Premier Tage Erlander appealed for the immediate cancellation of further "horror" tests.[318] Other letters protesting the blast and Soviet plans for even larger explosions came from Japanese Premier Ikeda, Ethiopia's Emperor Haile Selassie, and Ghana's President Kwame Nkrumah.

[314] *Documents on Disarmament, 1961*, p. 539.

[315] Kathleen Teltsch, *NYT*, Oct. 21, 1961, p. 1.

[316] United Nations, Office of Public Information, *The United Nations and Disarmament 1945–1965* (New York: United Nations, 1967), p. 102.

[317] *NYT*, Oct. 24, 1961, p. 1.

[318] *NYT*, Oct. 25, 1961, p. 1.

In the existing state of our knowledge it must remain an open question whether the explosion of the 30-megaton bomb on October 23 represented merely the routine continuation of previously formulated plans or was the result of a specific decision reached by the collective leadership on October 22. No such uncertainty, however, attaches to the Presidium decision, reached on the morning of October 24, to continue the Soviet nuclear test series to its planned conclusion, despite the by now nearly universal condemnation of it abroad. The evidence is indirect but clear.

It will be recalled that the congress protocols indicate Khrushchev's absence from the first half of the morning session of October 24 (above, p. 298). This period, then, is one of those during which the Presidium may have held a meeting. A clearcut indication that it did meet and that it voted to continue the test series, notwithstanding the adverse reaction to it abroad, is provided by a reply which Khrushchev sent on October 24 to some of the prominent figures who had sent him messages of protest. On October 27 *Pravda* published an exchange of letters on the Soviet tests between Nkrumah and Khrushchev; the latter's reply was dated October 24, and it was stated that he had sent identical letters to Ikeda, Haile Selassie, John Collins, a group of British members of the Labour party, and Dr. Linus Pauling, the American nuclear physicist.[319]

In his letter Nkrumah described: ". . . how profoundly disturbed I was by the news that the U.S.S.R. government intends not only to continue nuclear tests but even to detonate a 50-megaton hydrogen bomb in the very near future."[320] Nkrumah expressed the hope that: ". . . it may be possible at least to postpone these tests until new attempts are undertaken to ensure a general agreement on the banning of nuclear weapon tests."[321]

He concluded his short letter with a fervent plea for a change in Soviet plans: "I ask you to put an end to this in the interests of mankind."[322]

Khrushchev's response to Nkrumah and others contained most of the themes already familiar from his speeches and writings on the subject of nuclear testing and need not be quoted here.[323] The most significant feature of the letter is its date, October 24, and the evidence this provides that a decision of the Presidium was taken on that date to continue the Soviet test series to the end.

Taking into account the Soviet leadership's standard operating procedure of requiring the loser in a split decision to defend publicly the majority line (compare the case of Kozlov's speech at Pyongyang), Khrushchev's October 24 letter provides the valuable additional information that he had advocated halt-

[319]*Pravda*, Oct. 27, 1961, p. 1; *CDSP*, XIII/43, pp. 26–27.

[320]*CDSP*, XIII/43, p. 26.

[321]Ibid.

[322]Ibid. The text of Nkrumah's letter as published in *New Times*, no. 45, Nov. 5, 1961, differs significantly in this passage, indicating a desire to tone down Nkrumah's words: "In the interests of humanity I ask you *to make a start on this*" (emphasis supplied).

[323]*Pravda*, Oct. 27, 1961, p. 1; condensed translation, *CDSP*, XIII/43, p. 27; full translation, *New Times*, no. 45, Nov. 5, 1961, pp. 33–36.

ing the tests, or at least the elimination of the 50-megaton superbomb from the plans. On this basis, working back to Khrushchev's impromptu announcement of the plans to test the 50-megaton bomb in his congress speech on October 17, we can provide a tentative explanation for his motives in taking that action: his aim was not, as most foreign observers believed, to intimidate the West, but to provoke precisely the kind of world public reaction which did in fact occur, for the purpose of compelling the Presidium to reconsider its decision to carry out the testing of the 50-megaton bomb, in the hope of getting it to reverse the decision.

The world did not have to wait until October 26, however, when Radio Moscow broadcast the text of Khrushchev's reply to Nkrumah,[324] to learn that the Soviet Union had decided to rebuff the protests and continue with its announced plans. On October 25 Japanese Foreign Minister Zentaro Kosaka handed the Soviet chargé d'affaires in Tokyo, Sergei P. Suzdalov, what the press described as "a strong note" condemning the Soviet tests and rejecting the justifications for them advanced in Khrushchev's letter to Ikeda of the 24th.[325]

Meanwhile the worldwide storm of protest continued to mount, finding its most vocal channel in the debate in the U.N. General Assembly. On October 25 the Political Committee of the General Assembly voted 75–10, with one abstention, to appeal to the Soviet Union to call off its scheduled 50-megaton blast.[326]

On October 27 the full General Assembly, by an overwhelming majority (87 in favor, 11 opposed, one abstention) passed a resolution "solemnly appealing" to the Soviet Union to call off its plans to test the 50-megaton bomb.[327] By a companion resolution passed by a vote of 74–0–17, the General Assembly endorsed a report of the U.N. Scientific Committee dealing with the effects of atomic radiation from fallout.[328]

Undeterred, the Soviet Union on October 31—the final day of the Twenty-second CPSU Congress—carried out the explosion of the 50-megaton bomb according to plan. In actual fact, the bomb's yield was considerably higher than 50 megatons, and its potential destructive power twice as great. According to Jacobson and Stein: "Subsequent evaluations estimated its yield as 58 megatons, but Hans Bethe, who headed the AEC panel which evaluated the Soviet test series, pointed out that had the fusion materials been encased in uranium rather than lead, its yield would have been 100 megatons or more."[329]

[324]*NYT*, Oct. 27, 1961, p. 15.

[325]*NYT*, Oct. 26, 1961, p. 12.

[326]Kathleen Teltsch, *NYT*, Oct. 26, 1961, p. 1. The Soviet bloc and Cuba voted against the resolution, Mali abstained, and fifteen members of the 101-man committee were absent when the vote was taken.

[327]General Assembly Resolution 1632 (XVI); text, *Documents on Disarmament, 1961*, p. 552.

[328]General Assembly Resolution 1629 (XVI); text, ibid., pp. 550–52.

[329]Jacobson and Stein, p. 284, quoting a speech by Dr. Bethe at Cornell University on Jan. 5, 1962, as reprinted in the *Congressional Record* (1962), pp. A1397–99.

Khrushchev's intergovernmental correspondence on the Soviet nuclear tests continued into early November, with replies to Swedish Premier Tage Erlander on November 5 and to Japanese Premier Ikeda on November 9. Prominent in these replies was the note of regret at the need to carry out the Soviet tests. In his reply to Ikeda, for example, Khrushchev wrote: "We resumed nuclear tests with aching heart and after prolonged reflection."[330] In the message to Erlander the point was made even more strongly: "I want only to emphasize once more that we took this step only after prolonged reflection and not without heart-ache, not without a feeling of grief understandable to all who value the ideals of safeguarding peace between peoples."[331] If one accepts the evidence pointing to Khrushchev's role in the Soviet leadership debate on the test series as an opponent of continuing the series to the end, then these expressions of regret may be taken at their face value rather than as sheer hypocrisy.

The question of Khrushchev's attitude toward the Soviet nuclear tests is complicated, however, by apparently trustworthy reports of a passage in his final speech to the congress which does not appear in the official protocols. According to an unsigned *New York Times* report from Washington, on October 31: "Premier Khrushchev was reported to have told a restricted meeting of the Communist Party congress that the explosion [of the 50-megaton bomb] 'proved somewhat bigger than the fifty megatons that the scientists had calculated.' The Soviet leader was said to have joked about the 'mistake' by declaring that 'we shall not punish them [the scientists] for it,' a comment that was reported to have drawn laughter and applause."[332]

Taking the historical record as a whole, the salient feature in Khrushchev's attitude toward atomic testing is his distinct lack of enthusiasm, which found expression in his repeated emphasis on the "forced" character of the Soviet test series. The excised passage in his October 31 speech is not enough in itself to alter this picture significantly, although it does serve as a useful reminder of the complexity of Khrushchev's psychological make-up and the ambivalence of his attitude on a number of questions.

The most eloquent comment on the Soviet 50-megaton bomb came from Nehru. "When I heard that the Soviet Union had exploded this bomb," he said in an address delivered at ceremonies marking the laying of the cornerstone of a hospital in Delhi: ". . . I was most dismayed. It is a very wrong thing and there is no justification for such an action. No argument whatsoever can possibly be used to justify a wrong of such magnitude."[333]

Nehru flatly rejected the Soviet defense of the decision to carry out the test: "The argument that these tests were carried out for their own protection and safety is wrong."[334] Drawing on traditional Hindu moral precepts, Nehru con-

[330]*International Affairs* 12 (Moscow: Dec., 1961): 3.

[331]Ibid., p. 5.

[332]*NYT*, Nov. 1, 1961, p. 1. Presumably the report was based on a Radio Moscow broadcast. See also Schwartz, p. viii.

[333]*Documents on Disarmament, 1961*, p. 554.

[334]Ibid.

demned the tests as an unmitigated evil: "Not only do they pollute the atmosphere of the world we live in, but they also pollute the minds of men and carry the world to the side of destruction. Russia has, by its action, done something that the United Nations and in fact the entire world was against and begged it to refrain from. It is a bad thing to happen."[335]

Disregarding the moral factor, however, as well as the closely related issue of the genetic danger represented by the Soviet nuclear bombs, the question may be asked whether the Soviet decision to carry out its 1961 test series was justified in terms of the strategic goals it was designed to attain.

The best commentary on this aspect of the problem is provided by the *Survey of International Affairs*, which ranks the bomb series as one of the major factors in contributing to the setbacks experienced by the Soviet Union in its foreign policy initiatives in 1961. The *Survey* sums up the evidence in a judicious evaluation:

> The year saw what amounted to a bid for world hegemony by the Soviet leadership in four separate areas, in control of the United Nations, in control of the arms race, in a break-out of the Eurasian land-mass into Africa, and in the control of central Europe. . . . By the end of the year it was clear that this bid had been defeated, and that despite the unsettled nature of the major problems which had occupied the world's statesmen during the year, the Soviet Union had again been forced into the defensive, and a direct trial of strength between the great powers been avoided.
>
> The main factors in the defeat of the Soviet bid seem in retrospect to have been partly personal and partly inherent in the nature of contemporary power politics, in the paradox of a totality of power so great as to prevent its use by any of those possessing it, and the decreasing degree to which its immensity could influence or terrify public opinion. *The biggest miscalculation in this field seemed to have been that of the Soviet Union in embarking on a programme of nuclear testing* designed mainly to play on the fears of the European public, but the effects of which, because of that public's ultimate inability to believe in the reality of the threat, only rebounded to the Soviet Union's disadvantage, so that *the months of the Soviet nuclear tests were those in which the Soviet lost ground in each of the areas in which its influence was engaged.*[336]

Marking time (October 24, morning and evening; October 25, morning)

Midway through its schedule the Twenty-second Congress seemed to be slowing down. The thirteenth session, on the morning of October 24, was the first for which the protocols indicate Khrushchev's absence by using the short form for the ritual of greetings with foreign speakers. (We have already suggested the reason for this absence.)

Otherwise the thirteenth session conformed to the pattern established earlier, with speeches by a Presidium member (N. A. Mukhitdinov), a Union

[335]Ibid.
[336]*SIA, 1961*, p. 295; emphasis supplied.

Republic party boss (A. Ya. Pel'she of Latvia), and a group of foreign delegates (from Argentina, Greece, Syria, and Guinea). In addition the session heard from a writer (M. A. Sholokhov), the Soviet youth chief (S. P. Pavlov), and a rising party ideologist (L. F. Il'ichev).

By the fourteenth session, on the evening of October 24, the pattern was beginning to break down. There was still a speech by a Presidium member (N. M Shvernik), but none by a Union Republic party boss, even though there was still one, I. I. Bodiul of Moldavia, who had not been heard from. The session led off with the usual parade of foreign speakers (representing parties from Ghana, Mali, Norway, Belgium, and Uruguay), and then continued with a kolkhoz chairman (V. V. Grachev), following which came Shvernik's turn. The last three speakers of the evening were party officials: Boris N. Ponomarev, head of the International Department in the party Central Committee, Andrei P. Kirilenko, first secretary of the Sverdlovsk obkom and candidate member of the Presidium, and Grigorii G. Abramov, first secretary of the Moscow obkom. This time Khrushchev's presence was indicated in the protocols by use of the long formula for greetings to foreign speakers.

Bodiul's turn came on the morning of October 25, at the fifteenth session, and if he felt a sense of wounded dignity in bringing up the tail of the procession of Union Republic party bosses, he could console himself with the reflection that he was at any rate the most prominent speaker at a distinctly lacklustre session. In addition to Bodiul, the fifteenth session heard from the usual handful of foreign delegation chiefs (those of Venezuela, Denmark, The Netherlands, Colombia, Australia, and Lebanon). Instead of giving the floor to some of the many upper-level party officials who had not yet been heard from, however, the congress organizers filled out the session with a Leningrad worker (V. A. Smirnov), a factory director (V. V. Krotov), the head of the Bashkir obkom (Z. N. Nuriev), a mining foreman (A. A. Kol'chik), and an encyclopedia editor (F. N. Petrov).

The morning of October 25 was the first time during which Khrushchev's absence during the entire session was indicated in the protocols.

The thirty-two speeches made during these three sessions did not contribute significantly to the resolution of any of the major problems facing the congress, and for our present purposes can be dealt with in summary, even statistical form. The foreign guest speakers can be divided into geographical blocs. The two representatives of Middle East CP's (Bakdash for Syria and Shawi for Lebanon) both supported the CPSU in its criticism of the Albanian party leadership, as did the CP representatives from Latin America (Codovilla for Argentina, Arismendi for Uruguay, Faria for Venezuela, and Vieira for Colombia). The kind of pressure being applied behind the scenes was rather naïvely revealed by Arismendi when he said: "*We consider it our duty to announce from this tribunal* that we condemn the position taken by the leadership of the Albanian Party of Labor."[337]

As to Africa, the speaker from Mali also lined up behind Moscow on the Albanian issue. (The speakers for the Guinean and Ghanaian delegations did

[337]*Sten. ot.*, 2: 203; emphasis supplied.

not represent communist parties and were therefore exempt from the requirement to state their position on this question.)

A jolt for Khrushchev, however, was the disappointing performance by the Western European and British Commonwealth speakers. Those representing the CP's of Norway, Belgium, Denmark, Canada, and Australia maintained silence on the Albanian issue, while only two in this group, the representatives of the CP's of Greece and The Netherlands, spoke in favor of the Soviet position.

One must be cautious, however, in interpreting these data: silence at the congress on the Albanian question cannot automatically be equated with sympathy for the Chinese position and insubordination to the Soviets. Two weeks after the congress one of the communist parties whose spokesman had abstained on the Albanian question at the congress, that of Denmark, moved over into the pro-Soviet column by publishing an editorial criticizing the Albanian leadership.[338] Similarly Tim Buck, the general secretary of the Canadian CP, who failed to join the anti-Albanian chorus at the congress, made amends by contributing an article to *Pravda*, on November 18, which "made explicit the Soviet threat of expelling Albania from the Soviet camp."[339] Either the Canadian and Danish CP's changed their views on the Soviet–Albanian conflict after the congress, therefore, or—more probably—they failed to react promptly to the signals contained in earlier congress speeches and to whatever pressures were being applied behind the scenes. These examples indicate that the foreign delegations probably did not have much advance warning that the Albanian issue would be raised at the congress in the form of a test question.

The party officials who spoke at the thirteenth, fourteenth, and fifteenth sessions fall into three groups: Presidium members or candidate members (Mukhitdinov, Shvernik, and Kirilenko); Union Republic party bosses (Pel'she and Bodiul); and party officials (Ponomarev, Il'ichev, and Abramov). Tabulation of their responses to the question of expulsion of the Antiparty Group leaders produces an interesting pattern.

Of the three Presidium members who spoke, two, Shvernik (born 1888, party member since 1905) and Kirilenko (born 1906, party member since 1931), gave their full support to the demand for expulsion. By contrast, Mukhitdinov (born 1917, party member since 1942), a Central Asian party official by origin (he had been first secretary of the Uzbek CP before being raised to the Secretariat and Presidium in June 1957), omitted any call for expulsion. This retreat into prudent silence on a key issue was a poor return for the patronage by Khrushchev to which Mukhitdinov largely owed his elevation to the central

---

[338]"Albanian leaders on a dangerous course," reprinted in *Pravda*, Nov. 14, 1961, from *Land og Volk* (Copenhagen), Nov. 13, 1961, cited in Griffith, *Albania*, p. 112. The Norwegian Communists may well have been responding to a signal from the Hungarian party newspaper as relayed by *Pravda*. See "On a dangerous course. 'Nepszabadsag' on the policy of the leadership of the APG [Albanian Party of Labor]," *Pravda*, Nov. 11, 1961, p. 4.

[339]Ibid., p. 113.

policymaking bodies of the party, and it is not surprising, therefore, that Mukhitdinov was dropped from both the Presidium and the Secretariat at the end of the congress. On the other hand, Kirilenko's strong support for the demand for expulsion, while it was not enough to enable him to retain his post as a candidate member of the Presidium at the end of the congress, may have helped prepare the way for his astonishing return in glory six months later, when he was brought back into the Presidium as a full member—one of the rare and noteworthy exceptions to the general rule in Soviet politics, "They never come back."

As to the three party officials, Il'ichev, Ponomarev, and Abramov, each of them supported the demand for expulsion, as did the Nobel Prize laureate Mikhail Sholokhov, in a speech which reverted to the form of a dialogue with Khrushchev (thus signaling the First Secretary's return for the second half of the thirteenth session).

Quite conspicuous, therefore, was the intransigence on the expulsion question displayed by SERGEI P. PAVLOV (born 1929, party member since 1954), the first secretary of the Komsomol (since March 1959). The strong support given Khrushchev by the Soviet youth organization at the time of the Kremlin power struggle in 1956–57 had been a major factor in assuring his victory over the Antiparty Group, and it was a matter for serious concern to him, therefore, that the Komsomol chief's speech at the Twenty-second Congress clearly indicated his distaste for the current internal and foreign policy initiatives of the First Secretary. Pavlov did this not only by slighting the expulsion question but also by voicing enthusiastic support for the Soviet resumption of nuclear testing.

The debate on Soviet foreign policy (October 25, evening)

To open the sixteenth session on the evening of October 25, the congress organizers continued their methodical progress down through the list of foreign delegations, turning over the rostrum to party leaders from Ceylon, Morocco, Mexico, Cyprus, Ecuador, and Iran. Despite their geographical diversity, the guest speakers on this occasion performed with exemplary discipline, each speaker in turn avowing his party's support for the Soviet position in its dispute with the Albanian party leadership, although the representatives from Ceylon, Morocco, and Mexico did so only in a rather perfunctory way.

The first Soviet speaker of the evening was IVAN A. KAIROV, president of the Academy of Pedagogical Sciences of the RSFSR. Since Kairov was not a party functionary, he was absolved from the necessity for taking a public stand on the question of expulsion of the leaders of the Antiparty Group; neither that subject nor the dispute with Albania was touched on in his speech, which dealt mainly with questions of teacher training, a field in which he asserted that "dear Nikita Sergeevich" had made valuable contributions.

The high point of the sixteenth session was a matched pair of speeches deal-ing mainly with questions of Soviet foreign policy. ANDREI A. GROMYKO (born 1909, party member since 1931), the Soviet foreign minister (since Feb-ruary 1957), led off with what was in effect the official foreign policy report to the congress by the ranking government official in that field. Gromyko's speech clearly stamps him as a hard-liner on Soviet policy vis-à-vis the West and, at best, as a reluctant follower of Khrushchev in the latter's pursuit of peaceful coexistence.

With the very minimum of words and no mention of specific individuals, Gromyko at the outset performed the duty, evidently distasteful to him, of condemning the Antiparty Group: "In the period since the Twentieth Party Congress our Central Committee has done enormous work in uniting party forces and exposing the renegades, the factionalists, who were trying to push the party and the country off the Leninist path in both domestic and foreign policy."[340] Neither here nor at any later point in his speech, however, did Gromyko specify in what way these faceless "renegades and factionalists" had tried to swerve the party and government from "the Leninist path" in foreign policy. Nowhere did he refer to Molotov by name or criticize the foreign policy line which he advocated—a strange omission, one would think, in what was officially the chief report to the congress on Soviet foreign policy.

As though to make up for his near silence on the Antiparty Group, Gromyko was generous with his praise for Khrushchev, whose name, he asserted, was linked with that of Lenin in the minds of all who cherished peace. But the peace Gromyko had in mind was clearly not one based on Soviet–Western con-ciliation. Early in his speech he launched into an enthusiastic encomium of "brave little Cuba," which he said had become "one of the Soviet people's best friends."[341] He went on to voice unshakable solidarity with communist China: "As is the case wherever the fight for peace is in progress, we con-stantly feel our friend and ally, the Chinese People's Republic, at our elbow in that organization [the United Nations]. Regardless of whether or not the representatives of people's China are seated alongside us at the international conference table, our peoples are traveling the same road, and *there is no power on earth that can disrupt the ranks of the socialist states*."[342] Since Gromyko nowhere in his lengthy speech referred to Albania, this assertion amounted to a programmatic declaration of independence from Khrushchev's foreign policy line. That this was the correct interpretation to be placed on Gromyko's words was amply confirmed in later passages of his speech.

As a participant in the June 1961 meeting at Vienna between Kennedy and Khrushchev, Gromyko felt called upon to give the delegates his personal im-pressions of that meeting. "It is hard to say," he stated,

[340]*Sten. ot.*, 2: 333; *CDSP*, XIV/4, p. 24.
[341]*CDSP*, XIV/4, p. 24.
[342]Ibid.; emphasis supplied.

... how historians, looking back on the meeting in Vienna, may describe it. But it is no exaggeration to say that it was one of the outstanding events of our time. It was only necessary to have been an eyewitness to what took place in Vienna for one to be left with a lifelong imprint of this event in which one had occasion to be a participant.

Our party and all our people should know that at the conference table in Vienna the interests of the Soviet state and the whole socialist camp, the interests of *all who want to erect a secure barrier against the unleashing of aggressive wars in Europe*, the interests of peace between peoples were upheld with a revolutionary fervor, firmness and skill worthy of the party of the immortal Lenin, worthy of our people.[343]

There was about this curiously impersonal verdict (why wasn't Gromyko able to bring himself to name Khrushchev?) an air of grudging approval, as of a strict schoolmaster reporting on an unruly and unpredictable pupil. Evidently, in Gromyko's judgment, Khrushchev had achieved a passing grade in the test which the Vienna meeting represented; he, Gromyko, was present as an eyewitness to certify to the fact.

It was when he came to the question of Germany, however, that Gromyko showed most clearly his independence and critical attitude toward the policies of his party and government chief. The single most important foreign policy statement made at the Twenty-second Congress was Khrushchev's announcement in his opening speech that the 1961 deadline on signing a peace treaty with Germany had been lifted. At no point in his report on Soviet foreign policy, however, did Foreign Minister Gromyko endorse this step toward a relaxation of Soviet–Western tension; rather, he came as close as party discipline allowed to stating his outright opposition to this move. "The Soviet Union," he asserted,

... is a great world power and at the same time a great European power. The fate of our country, of our people, is closely intertwined with the fate of the other European peoples. It is precisely here, in the very center of the European continent, that German militarism has sunk its roots, giving rise to both world wars. That is why the question of the strengthening of the security of this region of the world has always been at the center of the attention of the Central Committee of our party, of the Soviet government. That is why the Soviet government *is now raising* with such strength and sharpness the question of the necessity of carrying out, by means of *the conclusion of a German peace treaty*, such measures as would keep in check the militarism in Western Germany which is raising its head.[344]

Gromyko seemed barely able to restrain his hatred of West Germany:

The Soviet people is entitled to present West Germany with a bill, which has still by no means been paid in full, for the misfortunes and destruction caused by the Hitlerite invaders on our soil, for the plundered national

---

[343]Ibid.; emphasis supplied. Note Gromyko's use of the wall metaphor.
[344]*Sten. ot.*, 2: 338; emphasis supplied.

wealth and for the merciless exploitation of our people carried off to Germany in the war years [*prolonged applause*].

The Soviet people can without any difficulty rouse in themselves a feeling of enmity and anger toward West Germany: they have but to think back on the crimes of the Hitlerite invaders [*applause*].[345]

Gromyko was careful, of course, to draw a sharp distinction between West Germany, whose policies he found virtually indistinguishable from those of Hitler, and the communist regime in East Germany, which he portrayed as a reliable friend of the Soviet Union and a staunch defender of the cause of peace.

The closest Gromyko came to endorsing Khrushchev's action in lifting the deadline on a German peace treaty was the grudging admission that ". . . we formed the impression after recent talks with U.S. and British statesmen that the Western powers showed a certain understanding of the situation and that they were inclined to seek a solution to the German problem and the question of West Berlin on a mutually acceptable basis."[346] But instead of continuing with an expression of support for Khrushchev's line, Gromyko immediately called it into question: "Yet things have been happening that are hard to reconcile with a desire to facilitate agreement. The question of the German peace treaty is being presented in the Western press on an altogether unrealistic plane. Is this the force of inertia or something else?"[347]

Gromyko ended this section of his speech with yet another assertion of the Soviet government's determination to sign a German peace treaty: "If, however, it should prove impossible to conclude a German peace treaty on an agreed basis, the Soviet Union, in company with many other countries, will sign a peace treaty with the German Democratic Republic."[348] All that was lacking was the 1961 deadline for this action, and Khrushchev had effectively seen to the lifting of that.

On the subject of Soviet–U.S. relations Gromyko managed to sound a little more cordial, and he provided some quotations from his talks with Rusk which are worth citing for their documentary value:

In one of his recent talks with us, U.S. Secretary of State Rusk, expressing the U.S. government's viewpoint with regard to the situation that had developed in Europe and Germany, stated: "We all understand that N. S. Khrushchev and J. Kennedy would not like to go down in history as the statesmen who were presiding at a time of global catastrophe. *The problem of security in the world is therefore of equal concern to the Soviet Union and the United States*, as the world's two greatest powers."

This was a good, sensible statement. On behalf of our Central Committee and the Soviet government, we replied to it as follows: "If we were to

[345]*CDSP*, XVI/4, p. 25.
[346]Ibid.
[347]Ibid.
[348]Ibid.

succeed, on a basis acceptable to both the Soviet Union and the United States, in solving the question of writing finis to the second world war and the questions resulting from this, it would be a great contribution to the cause of peace and the development of relations between our countries. The Soviet government urges that N. S. Khrushchev and J. Kennedy preside over *an abrupt shift in the world situation* toward eliminating the threat of war and radically changing the state of Soviet–American relations [*applause*]. The peoples of the Soviet Union and the United States and of all other countries would be deeply grateful for this to the leaders of our states, for they would reap the fruits of this great victory" [*applause*].

Rusk stated that he fully shared the Soviet government's aspirations for peace, and on behalf of the American government he expressed the hope that ways would be found to ensure world peace. We really are, he said, the two great powers, and the strongest. We do have allies, but much depends on what Washington and Moscow do. This, too, is a sound judgment, and we can only welcome it if U.S. actions in the sphere of foreign policy have this orientation [*applause*].[349]

Gromyko immediately proceeded, however, to stress two points which could scarcely be regarded as contributions to better U.S.–Soviet relations: first, that capitalism was historically doomed to extinction in its competition with socialism, and second, that the Western leaders were bluffing when they expressed a willingness to use atomic weapons if necessary to defend their position in West Berlin. "One marvels," said Gromyko,

> . . . at the reckless statements we sometimes hear, coming from the banks of the Rhine one moment, the next moment from the banks of the Seine, and the next from the Thames, that the West is not afraid even of atomic war. What heroes! The people who come out with statements of this kind are undaunted, you see, by the bottomless furnace of nuclear-missile war, but their knees shake at the prospect of concluding a German peace treaty.
>
> What is most interesting is that the "heroes" who would have one believe that they do not dread nuclear war know themselves that this is just empty bravado. We, too, know that they are not telling the truth. And they in turn know that we've seen through them and are well aware that they are not telling the truth, and still there's no stopping them.[350]

Gromyko's purpose, it is plain, was to make his contribution to the test of nerves currently under way between the Soviet leadership and the West by attempting to undermine Western fortitude, and he continued, in accordance with a poker player's logic, by praising the steady nerves of the Soviet leadership and people:

> If their [the Western leaders'] purpose is to gamble on making us nervous, our advice to them is to realize, at long last, that blackmail does not work on Soviet people, their nerves will not break. These are the nerves of people who were not shaken in the cruel years of the Great Patriotic War [World

[349]Ibid.; emphasis supplied.
[350]Ibid.

War II] in the face of mortal danger, who were able to grind up and convert into dust the most powerful armed forces which an aggressor ever controlled. These are the nerves of people who lit the fires of the Seven-Year Plan, which are visible from all the continents of the earth, people with staunch will and courage who have undertaken such grandiose tasks as the transformation of society on communist principles.[351]

Why this great emphasis on the steady nerves of the Soviets, coupled with an attempt to undermine the West's confidence and will power? It is certainly not mere coincidence that only a few hours before Gromyko addressed the congress the acute crisis in Berlin, which had been building up ever since the East German border guards introduced their procedural innovation of October 22, had reached the danger point, and that a massive test of will power between the Soviet and American leadership had been joined.

With the personal approval of President Kennedy, to whom General Lucius Clay had carried his request for authorization, the U.S. commandant in Berlin, Major General Albert Watson II, on the morning of October 25 had delivered a protest to his Soviet counterpart, Col. A. I. Solov'ev, concerning the continuing East German interference with official U.S. missions into East Berlin.[352] The Soviet Commandant, however, had rejected the protest on the grounds that the decrees of the East German regime "are binding on access to East Berlin."[353]

Assured of support at the highest level, the U.S. military authorities in Berlin now repeated on a larger scale the tactical maneuver which had worked effectively at the outbreak of the crisis. To quote Smith:

At 10:30 A.M. an American vehicle with two mission representatives attempted to enter East Berlin. When the *Vopos* [East German police] refused to allow the car to pass, twelve U.S. military policemen escorted it through. Forty-five minutes later ten M–48 medium tanks lumbered up to Checkpoint Charlie and took up positions. Twice more that day American cars were escorted through the East Berlin checkpoint by military police. The East Germans, chagrined and humiliated, made no effort to interfere.[354]

Thus Gromyko's impugning of Western staunchness and his praise of the steadfastness of Soviet nerves had a direct, immediate relevance to the threatening situation in Berlin, even though he gave no overt indication of awareness of what was taking place there. And unless the congress delegates to whom he was speaking had been listening clandestinely to Western broadcasts, he could assume their ignorance of the new turn in the Berlin crisis, for the Soviet press was still maintaining a tight-lipped silence on the subject.

[351]*Sten. ot.*, 2: 345–46.

[352]Smith, *Defense of Berlin*, p. 321. The source for the statement that the U.S. protest had Kennedy's personal approval is General Clay.

[353]Gerd Wilcke, *NYT*, Oct. 26, 1961, p. 3, citing a communiqué issued by the U.S. mission.

[354]Smith, *Defense of Berlin*, p. 322.

Appropriately, Gromyko continued with an attempt to bolster Defense Minister Malinovsky's claims for Soviet military power, calling on this basis for a "reasonable" attitude on the part of the Western powers: "But what follows from this [Malinovsky's] speech? That our illustrious army possesses a formidable weapon that well serves the interests of safeguarding the security of the Soviet people and of our friends. This leads to an important conclusion one would think the statesmen of the major Western powers ought to draw: The thought of settling disputes by force of arms must be renounced, threats must be renounced, and *agreements must be reached on all outstanding issues.*"[355]

Gromyko brought his speech to a close by adroitly comparing Khrushchev's Virgin Lands program in Soviet agriculture with his innovations in Soviet foreign policy and by appearing to assert that the First Secretary was personally responsible for the direction of Soviet foreign policy: "The generator of the energy and ideas which enrich and advance our foreign policy is the Central Committee of the party and Comrade N. S. Khrushchev personally, who [plural] carry out the immediate leadership of the entire foreign policy activity of the Soviet government."[356] But all this was mere window-dressing; when it came to specific issues, Gromyko's speech showed no willingness to support Khrushchev's innovations in foreign policy.

Gromyko's speech to the Twenty-second Congress, in what it omitted, what it said, and the way it was said, enables us to identify him as a leading member of the hard-line faction in the Soviet leadership. In an essay published in 1962 I suggested that the time might come when the Soviet Foreign Ministry could serve as an instrument of mediation between an ideologically ossified Soviet leadership and the outside world. It did not then occur to me that the reverse situation might equally well occur, in which a leadership intent on breaking the Stalinist mold of Soviet foreign policy would encounter stubborn resistance from a Foreign Minister who tenaciously clung to the outlook and perspective of the Stalinist past. Yet this is exactly the situation which had developed at the time of the Twenty-second Congress. Short of openly defying Khrushchev, Gromyko was doing his level best to precipitate the very confrontation with the Western powers in Berlin which it was Khrushchev's concern to avoid.

Faced with this stubborn intransigence on the part of his Foreign Minister, Khrushchev resorted to a characteristic maneuver. If he could not force Gromyko to support his line in foreign policy, he could at least attempt to neutralize the effect of Gromyko's speech by following it immediately with an antidote. And that is exactly what he did.

The final speaker at the evening session on October 25 was PAVEL A. SATIUKOV (born 1911, party member since 1939), editor-in-chief of *Pravda* (since 1956). Concerning Satiukov's political allegiance the record is clear

---

[355]*CDSP*, XIV/4, p. 26; emphasis supplied.
[356]*Sten. ot.*, 2: 347.

and unambiguous: he was a loyal follower of Khrushchev, who had served on more than one occasion as a member of the entourage which accompanied the First Secretary on his foreign expeditions. (Satiukov was a member of Khrushchev's party on the latter's visit to the United States in 1959 and again on the trip to Paris for the abortive summit conference of May 1960.)

The choice of Satiukov as the speaker to follow Gromyko reflected this closeness to Khrushchev, for Satiukov gave what amounted to a straight Khrushchev-line speech on Soviet foreign policy. It is also relevant that Satiukov, as the editor-in-chief of *Pravda*, was in a far better position than the great majority of the congress delegates to know the facts about the ominous crisis which was building up in Berlin.

Customarily a congress speech by a "specialist" such as Satiukov would be concerned chiefly with recent developments in the speaker's area of competence. Satiukov's speech did in fact contain a section of this kind, in which he presented statistical data on the growth of Soviet newspaper circulation, cited Lenin on the ideological importance of the press, and so forth. Clearly, however, it was not for the sake of material of this kind that Satiukov had been assigned the task of following Gromyko to the speaker's rostrum. The main purpose of his speech was to combat the critics of Khrushchev's foreign policy line and to champion the cause of peaceful coexistence.

At the very outset Satiukov revealed the seriousness of his purpose by hailing the "great unity and solidarity" of the party—usually a reliable pointer to the fact that the infighting in the party leadership has reached an acute stage. After an introductory section in which he paid his respects to the new Party Program, Satiukov plunged into a discussion of the power struggle between Khrushchev and the Antiparty Group. But where earlier speakers had dwelt on the bloody crimes of individual members of the group, Satiukov portrayed the struggle as one between clearcut and sharply opposed principles:

> In the course of this struggle there came into direct conflict two approaches, opposite in principle, with regard to the solution of urgent questions. One approach, the Leninist, revolutionary, creative [one], was carried into effect by the Leninist Central Committee of the Party. The other approach was the anti-Leninist, dogmatist, revisionist [one], which was defended by the factionalists, the zealous defenders of the cult of personality. . . .
>
> The members of the antiparty group rejected everything planned by the Central Committee, everything which proceeded from the demands of life, from the experience of communist construction. These were attacks, not merely *against the innovatory course of the party in general*, against its general line.[357]

Extending his criticism of the Antiparty Group's position backward in time, Satiukov linked their views with those of Stalin in his later years: "For years on end no party congresses or plenary sessions of the Central Committee were

[357]Ibid., p. 349; emphasis supplied.

convened. The most active party figures were unable, had not the right, to speak about the problems being raised by life itself. And if someone did try to broach such matters, he was rudely cut short."[358]

Except for a passing swipe at Kaganovich, Satiukov centered the brunt of his attack on Molotov, whom he called "the ideological inspirer of the anti-party group." Systematically, Satiukov set himself to destroy Molotov's reputation as a theorist. First, as to Molotov's "arrogant" claim to be "well-nigh the sole interpreter of Leninist doctrine," Satiukov grudgingly admitted that "Molotov did work under Lenin," but then continued, ". . . the plain truth of the matter is that he had no grounds for making excessive claims. As we know, in not one of Lenin's speeches nor in his 'Testament' addressed in 1922 to the regular party congress is Molotov mentioned at all among the prominent party figures of the period. Nowhere and at no time did Lenin say anything about Molotov's 'services in the area of theory,' either. He said nothing because there were no such services."[359] Satiukov proceeded to quote from a stinging letter addressed to Molotov by Lenin in 1922 in which Lenin charged that the section of the Central Committee for which Molotov was responsible was being "thoroughly bungled as a result of obtuse bureaucracy." Digging further back into party history, Satiukov produced a party document from July 1920 in which a resolution of a province executive committee in Nizhny Novgorod (Gorky) had censured Molotov and another party official for "lack of proper tact and, more important, the factual groundlessness of the accusations [made by the two officials being criticized] and completely inadmissible demagogy."[360]

Moving ahead to the 1930's, Satiukov charged that Molotov, as chairman of the Council of People's Commissars from 1930 to 1941, had been "guilty of flagrant violations of revolutionary legality." Molotov's report on "wrecking and sabotage" to the famous "long plenum" of the party Central Committee in February–March 1937, Satiukov asserted, had served, along with Stalin's report to the plenum, ". . . as the theoretical justification for the mass repression against party, state, and economic cadres."[361] In other words, Molotov shared with Stalin responsibility for the unleashing of the terrible Great Purge.

Jumping ahead once again, Satiukov brought his dossier on Molotov's misdeeds down to the immediate past: "The delegates to the Twenty-Second Congress should know that in October of this year, just before the congress opened, Molotov sent a letter to the Central Committee. Without having a word to say about his subversive factionalist work against the Leninist Party and against the decisions of its Twentieth Congress, he tries afresh in this letter to pose as an interpreter of Leninism and again attacks the Central Committee and the draft Program of the CPSU."[362]

[358]*CDSP*, XIV/4, p. 27.
[359]Ibid.
[360]Ibid., pp. 27–28.
[361]Ibid., p. 28.
[362]Ibid.

Since Satiukov's critique of Molotov's letter constitutes our most authoritative source for its content (the letter not having been published in the Soviet Union), it is worth quoting at length:

> ... Molotov claims the new Program is antirevolutionary in spirit. This slanderous, shameful statement of Molotov's indicates that he has broken with the party, has broken with Leninism [*applause*].
> Molotov declares in his letter that the draft Program fails, you see, to coordinate communist construction in the U.S.S.R. with the prospects for the revolutionary struggle of the working class in capitalist countries, with the prospects for socialist revolution on an international scale. . . . Molotov goes so far as to make monstrous allegations that the draft Program sidesteps the difficulties in the struggle for communism and orients the Party and the people toward a continued advance to communism by the countries of the socialist commonwealth without revolutionary struggle. His contentions lead to the conclusion that *it is impossible to continue the advance to communism without the most serious political conflicts with the imperialist countries, and hence without war.*[363]

With a fervor which betrayed all too clearly the urgency with which he viewed the issue, Satiukov proceeded to hurl a direct defiance against Molotov: "We say to Molotov: No, the Communist Party of the Soviet Union has been and is doing everything possible to ensure peace for the Soviet people, the people who are building communism [*stormy applause*]. The Leninist principle of peaceful coexistence has been and remains our general line in foreign policy. This is plainly stated in the new Program, and the party will pursue this line consistently."[364]

As is customary in communist polemics, Satiukov bolstered his arguments by selected quotations from Lenin, in which the party's Founding Father gave voice to such Khrushchevian concepts as the revolutionary influence exerted by the Soviet Union in world affairs through its economic successes and the need for peaceful coexistence between states with different social systems.

Obsessively, however, Satiukov came back to his most serious charge against Molotov, that the policies advocated by the latter raised the risk of war: "The question arises as to what Molotov has in mind in wanting to jostle us from the position of peaceful coexistence. *He is trying to shove us onto the path of adventures, the path of war.* The party will not have this! This is not the teaching of Lenin, and we would not be Leninist *if we heeded the Molotovs.*"[365]

The Molotovs! It appeared, then, that the fallen leader was not alone in his views. Satiukov wisely refrained from specifying who the other "Molotovs" might be, just as he omitted any reference to the growing crisis in Berlin which had broken out as the result of the initiative taken by those who shared Molotov's views on foreign policy. But like Gromyko's suspicious harping on

---

[363] Ibid.; emphasis supplied.
[364] Ibid.
[365] Ibid.; emphasis supplied.

the theme of the steadiness of Soviet nerves, Satiukov's impassioned rejection of Molotov's foreign policy line makes sense only when viewed in the context of the very real threat of war which had arisen in Berlin while the congress was in session.

It remained now for Satiukov to clinch his case by supporting the demand for Molotov's expulsion from the party, and he did so in unusually colorful language: "[Our party] rejects the slanderous fabrications and attacks of an envenomed Molotov, who has grown politically blind, gone totally bankrupt, and has exposed himself as a factionalist and plotter. People of this kind, who have taken to fighting the Leninist general line of the party, have no place in our party's ranks!"[366]

For good measure, Satiukov added a demand for the expulsion from the party of his predecessor as editor-in-chief of *Pravda*, Dmitri S. Shepilov, the man who had "joined" the Antiparty Group (i.e., who had switched sides in the factional struggle) and whom Satiukov now tried to bury under a heap of such choice epithets as "careerist," "political schemer," "double-dealer," "tale-bearer," and "political prostitute."

To bring his speech to an orderly close, Satiukov-the-journalist gave in truncated form a report on the state of Soviet journalism.

Like Gromyko, Satiukov omitted any reference to Albania in his speech. The two silences on this crucial question, however, had diametrically opposed meanings. For Gromyko to fail to mention the Albanian question in the official report on Soviet foreign policy was to signify publicly his disapproval of Khrushchev's action in criticizing the Albanian party leadership, especially since he went out of his way to affirm the unshakable solidarity between the Soviet Union and communist China.

Satiukov's silence on the Albanian question served a different goal. His explicit and unqualified condemnation of Molotov's line in foreign policy showed clearly enough that he also condemned the foreign policy views of the Albanian leadership (and of the Chinese communists). Khrushchev's strategy, however, called for linking the attack on the Albanian leadership with the renewed assault on Stalin's cult of personality, leaving unstated (though implied) the graver issue of the dispute over foreign policy which had helped drive deeper the wedge between Moscow and Tirana (and between Moscow and Peking). Khrushchev's purpose in this maneuver was to portray his brand of peaceful coexistence as something which enjoyed the unanimous support of the Communist party of the Soviet Union, as well as of the overwhelming majority of parties outside the Soviet Union. Thus, in omitting any reference to Albania in the context of foreign policy, Satiukov was simply following Khrushchev's own lead.

Shelepin digs into the archives (October 26, morning)

The seventeenth session of the congress, on the morning of October 26, was the first since October 19 at which there was no speech by a Union Republic

[366] Ibid.

party boss, the tally in that category being now complete. The session heard instead from V. E. Dymshits, first deputy chairman of the Soviet State Planning Commission (Gosplan), the first of the regular group of governmental officials to address the congress. The session also heard from the oldest member of the Presidium and Secretariat, Otto V. Kuusinen, as well as from a party ideologist and editor (N. N. Semënov) and a medium-level party functionary (A. M. Shkol'nikov). By far the most sensational speech delivered at the session, however, was that of Aleksandr N. Shelepin, chairman of the Committee of State Security (KGB—the secret police).

To open the seventeenth session the usual half-dozen short speeches were delivered by heads of foreign party delegations (those of Martinique, Israel, Jordan, New Zealand, Switzerland, and Guadeloupe). From Khrushchev's point of view this was a highly unsatisfactory group: only S. Mikunis (general secretary of the Israeli CP) and Fuad Nassar (general secretary of the Jordanian CP) voiced support for his criticism of the Albanian party leadership. (Later, one of the remaining four, who maintained silence on the Albanian issue at the congress, changed his vote by contributing an article critical of Albania to *Pravda*.)[367]

At any event, Khrushchev was not present in person to hear these speeches: the protocols indicate his absence from at least the first part of the session by employing the short form of the ritual embrace formula, and he did not make his presence known during the remainder of the session.

The speech by N. N. SEMËNOV (born 1896, party member since 1947), chairman of the Board of the All-Union Society for the Dissemination of Political and Scientific Knowledge and the first Soviet scientist to win the Nobel Prize (in physics, 1956), extolled Khrushchev's contributions to the field of scientific research. Semënov credited Khrushchev with having taken the initiative leading not only to the reorganization of the Soviet Academy of Sciences but also to the establishment of the State Committee for Coordinating Scientific Research. By overcoming the Stalin cult, Semënov asserted, the party had released "a tempestuous flood of creative initiative on the part of our people," and for this service he expressed the "boundless" gratitude of Soviet scientists, along with that of the entire Soviet people, to Khrushchev, whom he hailed as "a true friend and organizer of Soviet science." Semënov contributed to the Khrushchev theme of rivalry with the United States by asserting that Soviet science already surpassed that of America "in a number of decisive spheres," and that: "The time is not far off when our country will occupy first place in all basic spheres of knowledge."[368]

The speech by OTTO V. KUUSINEN (born 1881, party member since 1904), deserves fairly close attention, despite its length and ideological ponderousness, because it shows how even a member of the collective leadership who customarily rendered Khrushchev close support on internal issues could continue to view the field of foreign policy and international relations from a dogmatic ideological position.

---

[367] *Pravda*, Dec. 17, 1961, cited in Griffith, *Albania*, p. 318.
[368] *Pravda*, Oct. 27, 1961; *CDSP*, XIV/4, p. 29.

Like many congress speakers, Kuusinen began by praising the new Party Program, credit for the development of which he assigned personally to Khrushchev: ". . . the working out of the new party Program was directly supervised by such a leader of the Leninist type as Nikita Sergeevich Khrushchev [*stormy applause*]."[369] Kuusinen went even further, however, claiming canonical authority for the new program, which he said "creatively enriches the general observations of Marx and Lenin about the transition to communism."[370]

When he turned to foreign policy, however, Kuusinen revealed all too clearly how hard it was for him to follow Khrushchev in his departures from party orthodoxy. Kuusinen devoted a great deal of attention to "American imperialism," which he portrayed as the direct heir to an earlier "contender for world domination—Hitlerite Germany." Dominated by their class instincts, Kuusinen charged, the Western imperialists, through NATO, were preparing "an aggressive war against the socialist countries." In order to mask their intentions, however, ". . . the NATO leaders are preparing to lay the blame for starting a war on the Soviet Union."[371] Kuusinen flatly ruled out the possibility that the leaders of the Western powers might have any valid reason to fear Soviet intentions: "Even broad bourgeois circles are compelled to acknowledge that the Soviet Union does not intend to attack anyone."[372] West Germany was being rearmed, in Kuusinen's view, ". . . due to the fact that the American imperialists are assigning the Bundeswehr [West German army] troops the role of striking force in Western Europe."[373]

Here, however, Kuusinen introduced a certain degree of shading into his black-and-white picture of Western policy: "We are far from regarding the entire present-day bourgeoisie as something unitary and homogeneous. It does not have and cannot have a single policy, especially on such a decisive question as that of war and peace. Hence the two trends in the foreign policy of the imperialist states."[374] Correctly, Kuusinen attributed this differentiation to Khrushchev:

> . . . Comrade Nikita Sergeevich Khrushchev has mentioned these trends many times in his speeches. One trend is belligerent and aggressive. It is supported by the most frantic circles of the imperialist bourgeoisie, which count on the force of arms to mend the shaky affairs of world capitalism. The other trend is a moderately sober one, supported by the circles of the bourgeoisie that realize the danger for capitalism itself of a new war, and that are prepared to accept in some form the principle of peaceful coexistence.[375]

[369]*CDSP*, XIV/4, p. 29.
[370]*Sten. ot.*, 2: 381.
[371]*Pravda*, Oct. 27, 1961; *CDSP*, XIV/4, p. 31.
[372]*CDSP*, XIV/4, p. 31.
[373]Ibid., p. 32.
[374]Ibid.
[375]Ibid.

But Kuusinen conspicuously failed to draw any operational conclusions from the postulated existence of a "moderately sober trend" in the governments of the Western powers, and concluded this section of his speech by affirming the need both for maintaining "the utmost vigilance" and for "strengthening the defense might" of the Soviet state.

Turning to the "economic competition between the two systems," Kuusinen depicted capitalism as blind, greedy, and doomed to extinction. The American disarmament proposals he explained away as a forced move to attempt to match the Soviet initiative: "There was nothing else for them to do: comrade Nikita Sergeevich Khrushchev had so boxed them in with the Soviet government's proposals that they had to raise their hands."[376]

Kuusinen next took up the alleged "unity of the party and international solidarity." Like Satiukov, he ringingly affirmed that: ". . . Our party has come to its Twenty-Second Congress united as never before."[377] But then, like Satiukov, he went on to reveal just how badly split the party leadership had been in the recent past, before the defeat of the Antiparty Group, all of whose members he specified by name. When it came to the question of expulsion, however, Kuusinen balked, substituting a weaker form of condemnation: "I fully agree with the comrades who have *severely condemned* the antiparty activity of the above-named factionalists."[378] Strikingly different from Satiukov's contention that the focal point of the struggle had been a conflict of principles was Kuusinen's assertion that the central issue had been nothing but the question of raw power:

> In the course of my long life I have many times had the opportunity to participate in the party's struggle against various kinds of opposition factions—Trotskyites, Zinovievites, Bukharinites and others. Usually each of these factions began the struggle against the party by proclaiming political differences. But it soon became clear that *the main thing for them was not political arguments but seizing power.* They always placed their own personal ambition and striving for power above the cause of the working class, the cause of socialism and communism.[379]

True, Kuusinen continued, the Antiparty Group had claimed to stand for certain policies, but the core of their position was nothing but obscurantist obstructionism: "Of course, the members of this group also had political motives for their factionalist activity: they opposed everything new and creative in the party's policy, they were against eliminating the consequences of the cult of the individual, and so on. In general they rebelled against the Leninist line of the party leadership."[380] Kuusinen brought the issue down to a personal

[376]Ibid.
[377]Ibid., p. 33.
[378]Ibid.; emphasis supplied.
[379]Ibid.; emphasis supplied.
[380]Ibid.

struggle to oust Khrushchev: ". . . even at the very beginning it came to light that *the chief aspiration of the group was to remove Comrade Nikita Sergeevich Khrushchev,* continuer of the cause of Lenin, from the Presidium of the Central Committee and to take full leadership into their own hands."[381]

Kuusinen took note of the polemical writings of Molotov, to which Satiukov had given prominent attention, but only to ridicule them:

> The factionalists of 1957, as distinguished from the previous antiparty groups, did not even have any written political platform. Molotov apparently noticed this "omission" only later. This is why he has recently engaged in writing notes that unscrupulously distort the Leninist line of the party Central Committee and *basely slander the political position of Comrade Khrushchev.* In essence, Molotov is trying to concoct a kind of sectarian platform for his further antiparty profiteering.[382]

At this point Kuusinen lifted a corner of the veil hiding the real point at issue—the near identity between the foreign policy line advocated by Molotov and that of the Albanian and Chinese parties—by adding: "He [Molotov] apparently has decided to stir up the waters in order to try later on to catch a fish in these muddy waters. Perhaps the bait will be swallowed by some bony sprat [*laughter*], if not here in home reservoirs, then at least *somewhere in foreign waters* [*stir in the hall; laughter*]."[383]

Satiukov, by his reference to "the Molotovs" in the party, had revealed that the former leader's foreign policy views still enjoyed support within the present party leadership. To this revelation Kuusinen now added the disclosure that Molotov's views also encountered a sympathetic reception "somewhere in foreign waters." Taken together, these two calculated indiscretions illuminate the real conflict over foreign policy which was raging both in the CPSU and in the international communist movement, a conflict which Molotov's unpublished letter to the Central Committee had served to dramatize.

The most Kuusinen was willing to offer concretely, however, was a half-hearted expression of support for the demand for expulsion of Molotov from the party: "It seems to me—and I think that you too, comrade delegates, are of the same opinion—that our Leninist party has no need for such an incorrigible and malicious political profiteer in its ranks."[384]

He showed much greater enthusiasm in his support of Khrushchev's criticism of the Albanian leadership, adding some new details to the list of misdeeds with which they were charged. And without openly admitting that a conflict over foreign policy lay at the center of the Soviet-Albanian dispute, he put the dispute in the general context of international affairs by saying: "The Albanian leaders themselves claim that they are nevertheless opponents of imperialism. *In words this may be so,* but their deeds only play into the hands

[381]Ibid.; emphasis supplied.
[382]Ibid.; emphasis supplied.
[383]Ibid.; emphasis supplied.
[384]Ibid.

of the imperialists. After all, the imperialists seek nothing so much as a split in the socialist camp."[385] Kuusinen thus implied that he agreed with what the Albanian leaders said about international affairs and criticized only their insubordination to the Soviet party. He went on to reject the Chinese criticism of Khrushchev for raising the Albanian issue at the congress: "What are we to do—encourage such conduct, ignore it at our congress, or even pat the slanderers and schismatics on the back? This would mean rejecting our duty to defend the international solidarity of the socialist camp."[386]

For all his personal praise of Khrushchev, however, Kuusinen had not contributed much to the First Secretary's struggle for acceptance of his line in foreign policy. Kuusinen was too senior a figure in the party, however, simply to trail along behind Khrushchev on a subject on which he had his own strongly rooted convictions. Usually a reliable supporter of Khrushchev's innovations in domestic policy, Kuusinen retained the mental outlook of an old Comintern stalwart in his views on foreign policy. It was for that reason, no doubt, that unlike Satiukov he had no substantive criticism to offer of Molotov's foreign policy line; for that reason, too, he implied that he found nothing objectionable in the formulation of the Albanian party leadership's foreign policy views. As his speech showed, Kuusinen himself, in his analysis of the motives and actions of the Western powers, was much closer to the Molotov–Albanian–Chinese view than he was to that of Khrushchev. If he nevertheless supported Khrushchev against his internal and foreign opponents, it was from personal reasons rather than from sincere ideological conviction.

The speech of VENIAMIN E. DYMSHITS (born 1910, party member since 1937), first deputy chairman of Gosplan (since 1961), dealt mainly with construction in the USSR, a field which Dymshits called "the question of questions" as far as economic growth was concerned, and one which he said Khrushchev "loves . . . and knows in detail."[387] Dymshits credited Khrushchev with having defended with "courage and vigor" the policy of reorganizing the management of industry and construction against the "old, obsolete forms that hindered the development of the productive forces of Soviet society" and against "the factionalists, who were detached from life and who sullied themselves with disgraceful, vile deeds which evoke a feeling of anger and indignation."[388] But he implied that the defeat of the Antiparty Group (the members of which he identified neither individually nor collectively) was an accomplished fact, and made no demand for their expulsion from the party.

Two of the major themes of Soviet internal politics, the attack on Stalin's cult of personality and Khrushchev's fight against the Antiparty Group, dominated the speech by ALEKSANDR N. SHELEPIN (born 1918, party member since 1940), head of the Committee of State Security (since December 1958).

---

[385]Ibid.; emphasis supplied.
[386]Ibid.
[387]*Sten. ot.*, 2: 392; *CDSP*, XIV/4, p. 33.
[388]*CDSP*, XIV/4, p. 33.

In any highly centralized modern state such as the Soviet Union the relationship between the political leadership and the head of the security police is a matter of vital concern. The founder of the Soviet secret police, Feliks Dzerzhinsky, had established as the fundamental maxim on which the work of the organization was based the principle that its highest duty was to carry out any and all tasks assigned to it by the political leadership, fully, unquestioningly, and without regard to hindrances of any sort. Complete devotion to the will of the leadership, whether it be embodied in a single figure or a collective group, was in theory the basic law under which the Soviet secret police carried on its widely ramified activities.

What if the leadership became split into contending factions, however? Where then would the loyalty and duty of the secret police lie? If such a situation arose, the secret police would be forced to choose sides, thereby acquiring a stake in the outcome of the power struggle and a quasi-independent role of its own in policy formulation.

The career of Aleksandr Shelepin provides some vivid illustrations of these general propositions. Before becoming chief of the KGB, Shelepin had served as first secretary of the Komsomol from 1952 to 1958 and in that capacity had thrown the full backing of the Soviet youth organization behind Khrushchev in his controversial but challenging program of assimilating the Virgin Lands, in which tens of thousands of Soviet young people volunteered for or were assigned to construction jobs in the harsh pioneering conditions of the unmastered steppe country of Kazakhstan and western Siberia.[389] As the power struggle between Khrushchev and the Antiparty Group mounted toward a climax in 1956 and early 1957, Shelepin kept the Komsomol firmly in line behind Khrushchev, resisting the tempting offers made him by the factionalists.

Shelepin's reward for having chosen the winning side came in December 1958, when he was appointed chairman of the KGB. Most Western observers at the time saw this appointment as a move by Khrushchev to strengthen his personal grip on the crucially important apparatus of repression and to reassert party primacy in the secret police, returning it to the purity of Dzerzhinsky's original concept of the relations which should exist between the police and the party leadership.

Viewing Shelepin's career in perspective, however, it is clear that this analysis was incorrect, plausible though it may have seemed at the time. Significant events from three periods in Shelepin's career indicate that whomever his political and ideological loyalty was directed toward, it was not Khrushchev. First, in his years as a rising young Komsomol official in Moscow (1940–52), Shelepin appears to have been linked with a faction in the party leadership in which Khrushchev played at most a peripheral role. Second, as head of the secret police between 1958 and 1961, Shelepin showed a strong tendency to undercut Khrushchev's foreign policy line by actions designed to impede

[389]See my biographical sketch of Shelepin in George W. Simmonds, ed., *Soviet Leaders* (New York: Crowell, 1967), pp. 87–95.

any rapprochement between the Soviet Union and the Western powers. And third, in the summer and early autumn of 1964, Shelepin and his hand-picked successor as chief of the KGB, Vladimir Semichastny, threw their clandestine support to the coalition which was preparing the overthrow of Khrushchev.

Against this background, it should occasion no surprise that Shelepin's speech to the Twenty-second Congress was a masterpiece of dissimulation, in which skillful phrasing and sensational details helped obscure the fact that the speaker was withholding support from the policies of his chief.

Shelepin opened with a lurid portrayal of the dangers which Western military and intelligence agencies, especially the U.S. Department of Defense and the CIA, represented to Soviet security. The policies of the U.S. government, Shelepin charged, were being more and more determined by "the adventurist course of these agencies."[390] Unlike Kuusinen, who for all his ideological rigidity had been willing to admit the existence of "two tendencies" in the leadership of the Western powers, Shelepin found not a single redeeming trait in the policies of the West.

The core of Shelepin's speech consisted of a graphic, often sensational, account of some episodes from the Great Purge and of the personal responsibility for the Terror borne by Molotov, Malenkov, Kaganovich, and Voroshilov. Unlike most earlier speakers, however, Shelepin extended his accusations to Stalin himself, linking him with the still unsolved mystery of the assassination of Sergei Kirov in December 1934: "Stalin and his intimates Molotov and Kaganovich used the murder of Sergei Mironovich Kirov as an excuse for organizing reprisals against people who were objectionable to them, prominent state figures."[391]

For any serious study of the Great Purge, Shelepin's report, based as it evidently was on documentary evidence from the secret police archives, constitutes an indispensable course. For our present purposes, however, its most significant aspect was the response Shelepin gave to the question of expulsion for the Antiparty Group leaders. As chief of the secret police his position on this question would help determine how it would be answered by the congress. If he unequivocally supported the demand, approval would be virtually certain; if he openly opposed expulsion or maintained silence on the question, it would be dead.

Shelepin's response to the question of expulsion was neither silence nor outright rejection, but a conditional approval, skillfully worded so as to sound firm but on closer inspection evasive and thus, in the final analysis, negative. Shelepin began this crucial passage with bold phrases: "I must declare at this congress, with a full sense of responsibility for the statement, that several members of the antiparty group, and above all Molotov, have thus far failed to draw the proper conclusions from this grim lesson, are behaving badly, double-dealing with the party and holding to their old views."[392] Thus it was mere adherence to "old views" and failure to make a clean breast of their misdeeds before the party, not the group's actual crimes, which Shelepin had in mind. His recommendation for corrective action was correspondingly mild: "The time has therefore come for the Party Central Committee's Party Control Committee *to consider calling the members of the antiparty group to the strictest account*. And in this matter I fully support the proposals made by the delegates who have spoken before me."[393]

Instead of calling for the group leaders' expulsion, thus, Shelepin was introducing a bureaucratic nuance, the significance of which has been well brought out by Tatu: ". . . recourse to the KPK [Party Control Committee] meant playing for time. As a stop-gap measure, this would prevent a surprise vote by the congress and would instead steer the matter into a maze of bureaucratic procedure."[394] And this is exactly what happened. Tatu relates that when he asked Khrushchev several weeks after the congress whether Molotov was still a member of the party, Khrushchev, "with some irritation, replied, 'Why don't you ask Shvernik [chairman of the Party Control Committee]? He's taking care of it'."[395]

With one of the principal tasks of his speech accomplished, Shelepin endeavored to minimize the effect abroad of the sordid revelations he had just presented to the delegates. Denying widespread Western speculation that the renewal of the attack on the Antiparty Group betokened the existence of some concealed but still active opposition in the party, Shelepin said:

> The antiparty group is not being talked about at our congress because it represents a danger to the party today. It does not! The members of the antiparty group are political corpses, who, far from representing any danger, do not even represent a shadow of a danger. We are talking about these factionalists with the purpose of once more laying bare their true complexion, of once more underlining the full extent of their nothingness as compared with the greatness of what the party and people have accomplished since the Twentieth Congress, with the truly breath-taking horizons being opened up to us by the magnificent new Program of the CPSU![396]

Showing the skill of a trained dialectician (and a dialectician's disregard for common sense and ordinary logic), Shelepin alleged that the very fact that the struggle against the Antiparty Group was being discussed at the congress proved that the party was united as never before:

> The discussion at our congress of the activities of the antiparty group is convincing evidence of the strengthened unity and monolithic solidarity of the party, is still further conclusive proof that the party is firmly pursuing a

[392]Ibid., p. 36.
[393]Ibid.; emphasis supplied.
[394]Tatu, pp. 163–64.
[395]Ibid., p. 164.
[396]*CDSP*, XIV/4, p. 36.

Leninist course, undeviatingly observing Leninist norms and principles in party and state leadership.

This extended discussion at our congress demonstrates with new forcefulness the maturity of the Communist Party and reinforces the confidence of the Soviet people that the grave abuses that flourished in the period of the cult of the individual will never, never recur in our country, in our party! [*Prolonged applause*].[397]

Shelepin devoted the final section of his speech to a report on the secret police. The dominant theme here was the re-establishment of "the true Leninist style" in the work of the state security agencies and of the close and cordial working relations which existed between the KGB, the party, and the Soviet people. Counterbalancing Shelepin's claim that "Soviet laws are the most humane in the world" was his undisguised threat of "stern" repression for all "internal enemies."[398]

A sharp and revealing contrast to Shelepin's equivocation on the expulsion question was provided by the final speaker at the seventeenth session, ALEKSEI M. SHKOL'NIKOV (born 1914, party member since 1940), first secretary of the Stalingrad obkom (since November 1960).

An ardent proponent of better material conditions for the Soviet collective farmers, Shkol'nikov showed himself on this occasion to be a staunch supporter of Khrushchev in the party factional struggle. Almost alone among congress speakers Shkol'nikov faced squarely the prospect of what victory by the Antiparty Group would have meant: "It must be said outright: If the antiparty group had succeeded in seizing power in the party and country, the methods of leadership that prevailed in the period of the cult of the individual, with all their severe consequences, would have been revived."[399]

For his special target Shkol'nikov singled out Voroshilov, whom he accused of having committed "grave crimes" and whom he called on to ". . . thank the Central Committee, bow his head before the party, and ask its forgiveness for his crimes."[400]

Briskly and without equivocation, Shkol'nikov took his stand on the question of expulsion: "As for Molotov, Kaganovich and Malenkov, they should be immediately expelled from the party. There is no room for them in our Leninist party."[401]

The Presidium weighs the fate of the Antiparty Group (October 26, evening)

Shkol'nikov's sharp personal attack on Voroshilov indicates that the old party warhorse was still stubbornly resisting the pressure being applied to

[397] Ibid.
[398] Ibid., p. 37.
[399] *Pravda*, Oct. 28, 1961; *CDSP*, XIV/5, p. 17.
[400] *CDSP*, XIV/5, p. 17.
[401] Ibid.

make him sign a statement admitting his complicity in the anti-Khrushchev conspiracy of 1956–57. At some point on October 26, Voroshilov's resistance was finally broken down, since a written statement bearing his signature and the date, October 26, was read for him at the morning session of the following day. Khrushchev, as we have seen, was absent from at least the first half of the morning session on October 26, and may well have been absent for the entire session; he also missed the first half at least of the evening session, and probably the entire session. We can therefore postulate a meeting of the Presidium on the 26th, and probably several closely linked sessions, at which the fate of Voroshilov, and probably that of other members of the Antiparty Group, was discussed. The decision on Voroshilov must have come *after* the morning session, since both Shelepin and Shkol'nikov at that time implied that the issue was still open.

In his statement to the congress Voroshilov dealt only with questions of internal policy. He signified his full acceptance of Khrushchev's report for the Central Committee (the speech of October 17), and called the new Party Program "a document of the greatest significance" and "the credo both of our party and the entire Soviet people," thereby dissociating himself from Molotov's attack on the program as "un-Leninist."

Voroshilov's confession was less than total, however. He claimed to have been associated with the anti-Khrushchev group only at its inception, and without fully realizing its factional nature:

> Yes, I admitted and admit that at the beginning of the struggle against this group I supported certain erroneous, harmful statements by some of its members, but I had no idea of its factionalist activities until their true face was exposed and they themselves admitted their factionalist activity in the course of examination of the conduct of these "cliquists" at the June 1957 plenary session of the party Central Committee. After this I immediately stated that I had never known about this, had never joined any group and had never had any dealings or associations with this sort of people.[402]

Voroshilov went on to "resolutely condemn" the "factionalist activity" of the Antiparty Group, and in the final paragraph of his statement stoutly denied that he had actually been a member of the group: "Throughout my fifty-eight years in the ranks of our glorious Communist Party I have never, nowhere, and under no circumstances retreated from the Statute and Program requirements and norms for the members of our party, have never betrayed the great principles of Marxism–Leninism, have never participated and will never participate in antiparty—whatever they may be called—groupings."[403]

For a confession, this was meager indeed, but it represented the best Khrushchev and his followers were able to achieve. Clearly, Khrushchev was being blocked in the effort to enlarge his disciplinary powers. Unable to reach his avowed targets—Molotov, Malenkov, and Kaganovich—he stood even less

[402]*Sten. ot.*, 2: 553; *CDSP*, XIII/46, p. 31.
[403]*CDSP*, XIII/46, p. 31.

chance of exerting control over the real challenger to his power and prerogatives, Frol Kozlov.

*   *   *

The eighteenth session on the evening of October 26 was the weakest yet provided by the congress organizers. The by now customary half-dozen speeches by heads of foreign delegations were evenly divided on the Albanian issue: party officials from Tunisia, Turkey, and Bolivia supported the CPSU's criticism of the Albanian leaders, while those from South Africa, Burma, and Malaya avoided taking a stand. Khrushchev's absence from the session was indicated in the protocols by the use of the short form of the ritual embrace formula.

The first Soviet speaker of the evening was FIKHRIAT A. TABEEV (born 1928, party member since 1951), first secretary of the Tatar obkom (since 1960). His total silence on the question of expulsion for the Antiparty Group leaders did not hinder his election to the Central Committee at the end of the congress. Obviously, then, he was neither a Khrushchev supporter nor dependent on Khrushchev's patronage for political advancement. The fact that such a relatively obscure party functionary, and an anti-Khrushchevite to boot, was given the opportunity to speak at the congress may be taken as an indication that the hitherto almost unbroken dominance of the congress by the First Secretary's supporters was being successfully challenged.

Tabeev was followed to the speaker's rostrum by an even more obscure individual, GEORGI A. NALIVAIKO, director of the Altai Scientific Agricultural Research Institute. Nalivaiko's speech dealt almost exclusively with technical problems of agriculture, and while he assured "dear Nikita Sergeevich" that: ". . . crop rotations saturated with corn are already yielding twice the output of field and livestock products as fallow-grassland crop rotations . . .,"[404] he had nothing to say on any of the basic issues facing the congress—Stalin's cult of personality, the Antiparty Group, or the dispute with the Albanians. Appropriately, after the congress he sank back into the obscurity from which he had momentarily been raised.

The pace picked up noticeably with the next speaker, PËTR N. POSPELOV (born 1898, party member since 1916), director of the Institute of Marxism–Leninism (1949–52 and again since March 1961), candidate member of the Presidium (since 1957). Pospelov's position on the factional split confronting the congress had been defined in his earlier career. Despite long service in the propaganda and ideological departments of the party hierarchy under Stalin, Pospelov had supported Khrushchev in the June 1957 showdown with the Antiparty Group and had gone on to praise Khrushchev as a communist theorist at the Twenty-first CPSU Congress in 1959.

In his speech to the Twenty-second Congress, Pospelov took the final step in the path blazed earlier by Satiukov, directly linking Molotov's attack

---

[404]*Sten. ot.*, 2: 450–51; *CDSP*, XIV/5, p. 19.

on the new Party Program with the Albanian party's criticism of Soviet foreign policy. "At this greatest turning point in history," said Pospelov, ". . . there have appeared miserable renegades, falsely calling themselves Marxists, who are trying to oppose our Program with anti-Leninist, unworthy and slanderous attacks. *These are the Albanian leaders and the chief ideologist of the schismatic antiparty group, Molotov.*"[405]

Pospelov left his listeners in no doubt that in his view, Molotov's greatest error was his rejection of the doctrine of peaceful coexistence: "Molotov, showing himself to be an unprincipled double-dealer, began opposing not only condemnation of the Stalin cult, not only the party's policy of eliminating the consequences of the cult of the individual and developing socialist democracy. *Molotov opposed the major fundamental proposition of the Twentieth Party Congress concerning the possibility of averting a new world war in the present epoch.*"[406]

Without directly quoting from Molotov's unpublished letter to the Central Committee, Pospelov identified as one of its principal points an attack on that passage in the new program which asserted that: "It is not through war with other countries but by the example of a more perfect organization of society, by the flowering of productive forces, the creation of all the conditions for the happiness and well-being of man, that the ideas of communism are winning the minds and hearts of the masses."[407]

"Molotov," Pospelov continued, ". . . slanderously asserts that this proposition of the Program is in deep conflict with the revolutionary essence of the Marxist–Leninist teaching. Actually, Molotov only demonstrates his own departure from Leninism, or else his ignorance, his failure to understand the fundamentals of Leninist revolutionary theory and the Leninist method."[408]

Pospelov accused Molotov of asserting that war is an indispensable means for the further extension of communism: "It turns out, according to Molotov, that it is precisely *through war* that we must win over hundreds of millions of people to the side of communism! But this is precisely what our enemies want to impute to us; it is the same 'big lie' about the Soviet Union's supposed intentions of promoting the spread of communism to other countries by means of war rather than by force of example that is spread by imperialist propaganda."[409]

As principal custodian of the party's ideological heritage, Pospelov brought up an imposing battery of citations from Lenin to prove that Molotov's position was ". . . a direct thrust at the fundamental propositions of Leninism; it is stupid, factionalist stubbornness, the desire to counterpose at all costs his own rotten, anti-Leninist, factionalist line to the Party's Leninist course."[410]

[405]*CDSP*, XIV/5, p. 19; emphasis supplied.
[406]Ibid.; emphasis supplied.
[407]Ibid.
[408]Ibid.
[409]Ibid., p. 20; emphasis in the original.
[410]Ibid.

Showing none of the political circumspection which had marked Shelepin's speech, Pospelov gave his answer to the question of expulsion in the most uncompromising terms yet heard at the congress:

> Surely our great party cannot tolerate in its ranks renegades and schismatics who impudently oppose the major propositions of Leninism, the Leninist course of our party and the great new program of our party, this now generally recognized Manifesto of the Communist Party of our epoch. Many delegates to the congress were right in saying that Molotov, Malenkov and Kaganovich cannot be members of our great Leninist party. There is no doubt that the Twenty-Second Congress will unanimously approve the proposal of a number of delegations to exclude these schismatics and factionalists from the party's ranks [*applause*]. They should be held responsible *both for their criminal actions during the period of the Stalin cult and for the attempt to counterpose their own antiparty, anti-Leninist line*, dangerous and harmful to the cause of communism, to the party's Leninist course![411]

Pospelov thus for the first time linked the crimes committed by the Antiparty Group leaders with their doctrinal errors, and on that dual basis demanded their expulsion from the party. The strength of his political convictions was no substitute, however, for political astuteness, and at the end of the congress Pospelov had to pay for his brashness by losing his post as candidate member of the Presidium.

Having condemned Molotov's views and given his answer to the question of expulsion, Pospelov turned to the Albanian issue. Here he had the advantage of recent firsthand experience, for he had led the CPSU delegation to the Fourth Congress of the Albanian Party of Labor in February 1961. The Albanian congress, he said, had made ". . . a painful impression both on us and on the delegations of the fraternal parties. The congress became a rowdy, noisy, importunate demonstration of the cult of the individual alien to Marxism–Leninism, a demonstration of incredible self-adulation of the Albanian Party of Labor, which supposedly never had made and never would make any mistakes."[412]

Alarmed by a number of glaring instances of direct anti-Soviet attacks by prominent Albanian officials, the CPSU delegation, at the end of the Albanian congress (February 21) had handed the Albanian leaders a "protest and warning" which Pospelov now quoted verbatim. In giving the congress the full text of this previously unpublished document, Pospelov provided an essential piece of evidence on the development of the Soviet–Albanian rift.

The concluding section of Pospelov's speech was a report to the congress on the work of the Institute of Marxism–Leninism, noteworthy in the present context for its assertion that capitalism, approaching its inevitable doom, ". . . carries on unrestrained propaganda of war and it regards the arms race as the ultimate resort in mending its shaky affairs."[413]

[411] Ibid.; emphasis supplied.
[412] Ibid.
[413] Ibid., p. 21.

Thus Pospelov, like Kuusinen, proved unable to free himself from the doctrinaire ideological ballast of Marxist–Leninist theory, despite his recognition of the imperative need for better Soviet–Western relations and his condemnation of Molotov's foreign policy views. But Pospelov, unlike Kuusinen, stopped short of charging the West with actually plotting an aggressive war.

The congress speech by ALEKSEI I. ADZHUBEI (born 1924, party member since 1954), editor-in-chief of *Izvestiia* (since 1959) and son-in-law of Khrushchev (since the early 1950's), was no match intellectually either for that of Pospelov or for the speech given on the preceding evening by Adzhubei's fellow journalist-editor, Pavel Satiukov.

Adzhubei has been described by an American press official who knew him well, Pierre Salinger, as lacking in subtlety and "arrogant most of the time and a braggart when the vodka was flowing."[414] The coarseness of intellectual fiber implied in Salinger's characterization was much in evidence in Adzhubei's congress speech. He revelled in name-dropping, dwelling with obvious satisfaction on his personal contacts with President Kennedy. On the subject of the Antiparty Group he accused the factionalists of taking "anti-Leninist" positions, but made no effort to define what a genuinely Leninist position would be. His only significant contribution to the discussion was the disclosure (perhaps inadvertent) that Molotov's pre-congress letter to the Central Committee had now been made available to the congress delegates: "We now see, too, that they [the Antiparty Group leaders] have not accepted the Twentieth Congress, and *we now know from Molotov's letter* that they do not accept the Twenty-Second Party Congress either."[415]

Avoiding any discussion of the principles at issue, Adzhubei seized on Molotov's opposition to extensive contacts between Soviet officials and those of Western nations as an excuse to launch into a highly personalized, anecdotal account of his travels abroad in the company of his powerful father-in-law. Far from trying to build up Khrushchev's reputation as a party theorist, however, as earlier speakers had done, Adzhubei seemed to take special satisfaction in singling out those episodes in Khrushchev's foreign journeys—the shoe-thumping tantrum at the United Nations in September 1960, for example—which showed Khrushchev at his most boorish, holding them up as specimens of how communist spokesmen abroad should behave. From his speech Adzhubei's attitude toward the West emerged as an unsavory mixture of envy, suspicion, distrust, and sneaking admiration.

Somehow, in his eagerness to portray himself as a participant in great events, Adzhubei neglected to perform some of the elementary duties which his client position vis-à-vis Khrushchev entailed. He said nothing, for example, about the demand for expulsion of the Antiparty Group leaders; he avoided the subject of peaceful coexistence and Molotov's doctrinal errors in

---

[414]Salinger, p. 183.
[415]*Pravda*, Oct. 28, 1961; *CDSP*, XIV/5, p. 21; emphasis supplied. Cf. Tatu, p. 146.

the field of foreign policy; and he overlooked the Albanian question entirely. All in all, Adzhubei's congress performance added little to the luster of Khrushchev's position.

The final speech at the eighteenth session was delivered by the second Soviet cosmonaut, GHERMAN S. TITOV (party member since August 7, 1961). Despite its comparative brevity, Titov's speech scored some useful points for Khrushchev: the advanced state of the Soviet space program as compared with that of the United States; the allegedly selfish and purely personal aspirations harbored by American astronauts, as contrasted with the lofty idealism inspiring Soviet space explorers; and the great contribution to the Soviet space program made by Khrushchev personally. He and Gagarin (the first Soviet cosmonaut), said Titov, ". . . are very proud that Nikita Sergeevich has called us 'celestial brothers.' I must say in confidence that among us cosmonauts we call Nikita Sergeevich our 'space father' [*lively stir in the hall; stormy applause*]. We constantly feel the concern of the party, its Central Committee, and Nikita Sergeevich Khrushchev personally for us cosmonauts and for the conquest of space [*stormy applause*]."[416]

Titov made no bones about the close ties between the Soviet space program and the Soviet armed forces. He himself, he disclosed, had been trained as a fighter pilot, and he said that while future Soviet space ships would be manned by navigators, engineers, and various kinds of specialists, ". . . at the present time it is more expedient to prepare cosmonauts from fighter pilots—it is cheaper, quicker, and more dependable."[417] In passing, Titov hailed the greatly increased fire power of Soviet aviation, which he claimed had resulted from the development of new types of guided missiles.

* * *

While the eighteenth session was being held in Moscow, the crisis in Berlin was approaching a showdown. Up until the evening of October 26, the Soviet military command in East Germany had been sticking to the position that the conflict was one in which they were not directly involved; any complaints the U.S. command might have over the changed procedures at the sector checkpoint, in their view, must be taken up with the appropriate authorities in the East German regime.

Faced with the steady pressure of Western military power, however, backed up by Kennedy's unflinching determination, the Soviet military authorities on the evening of October 26 prepared to abandon the pretense that they had no direct responsibility for the situation in Berlin. In a dispatch filed late on the 26th, *New York Times* correspondent Sydney Gruson reported that: "Thirty-three Soviet medium tanks, manned by Soviet troops, moved into the center of East Berlin tonight."[418]

[416]*CDSP*, XIV/5, p. 24.

[417]*Sten. ot.*, 3: 483. The protocols record "merry animation in the chamber" and "stormy applause."

[418]*NYT*, Oct. 26, 1961, p. 1. See also Smith, *Defense of Berlin*, p. 332.

Notwithstanding the heightening of tension which the action represented, it was the first sign that the Soviet-made crisis in Berlin was on the way to resolution. Since the Soviet command in East Germany had previously resisted all attempts to make them admit their responsibility for East Berlin, the movement of the tanks was an action which could only have been taken on instructions from Moscow. It was a sign that the Presidium was at last assuming direct charge of Soviet policy in the Berlin crisis.

The razor's edge (October 27, morning and afternoon)

For some reason the congress organizers interrupted the orderly procession of foreign guest speakers to the rostrum in drawing up their plans for the nineteenth session, on the morning of October 27, even though there were quite a few suitable candidates still to be heard from. The historian is thus deprived of the indication of Khrushchev's presence at or absence from the session provided by the use of one or the other variant of the ritual embrace formula in the protocols. One possible clue to his whereabouts is the fact that the only party official to address the session, M. T. Yefremov, apostrophized Khrushchev directly in a way which implied that he was present in person. Yefremov was the third speaker at the session, which was interrupted by a thirty-minute break after the speech by I. T. Novikov, the fifth speaker.

Khrushchev and the other members of the Presidium may therefore have been absent either from the entire session or at least from the second half. It seems highly probable that they did in fact skip part or all of the sessions, since there were a number of urgent problems requiring their attention, and and there is evidence that several crucial decisions were reached at about this time.

Of the nine speakers at the session, three were USSR ministers—B. P. Beshchev, minister of railways, I. T. Novikov, minister of electric power stations, and M. A. Ol'shansky, minister of agriculture. Two were academic functionaries: V. A. Kucherenko, president of the Academy of Architecture, and B. V. Ioganson, president of the Academy of Arts. There were two editors: N. M. Gribachev, poet, reactionary, and editor of *Sovetskii Soiuz*, and A. T. Tvardovsky, poet, liberal, and editor of *Novyi mir*, as well as a writer, A. Ye. Korneichuk. Only one speaker at the session represented the party hierarchy, Mikhail T. Yefremov.

YEFREMOV (born 1911, party member since 1932) was first secretary of Cheliabinsk obkom (since March 1961), a post to which he had been transferred (in effect, a demotion) from his previous job as chief of the Central Committee's Section for Party Organs of the RSFSR after the fall of Aristov in January 1961. In his speech Yefremov made clear his strong personal attachment to Khrushchev, whom he addressed directly: ". . . for this great contribution to the theory of Marxism–Leninism [the new Party Program], all Soviet people, yes, and not only Soviet people but all progressive mankind, are grateful to the Central Committee of the Communist Party of the Soviet Union, *are grateful to you, Nikita Sergeevich*, and will always be grateful."[419] Unless we assume that Yefremov delivered his speech unchanged from a written text prepared in advance, this would strongly imply that Khrushchev was present during the first half of the morning session on October 27.

In his account of the Antiparty Group's misdeeds Yefremov touched all the bases: "They opposed an advance in agriculture and the development of the virgin lands, they opposed the reorganization of the management of industry and construction, *they opposed the new course in our state's foreign policy. They were against everything* that in an unprecedentedly short period brought to our homeland new strength, a new flourishing."[420]

Appropriately, Yefremov showed no hesitation in supporting the demand for expulsion of the group's leaders: "I fully support the proposal that Molotov, Malenkov and Kaganovich be excluded from the party. Their actions were against the party, against the people. There is no room for them in the ranks of our Leninist party!"[421]

Since none of the other speakers at the nineteenth session carried much weight in the councils of the party, we can dispose of their speeches in summary fashion. Like Yefremov, each of the three ministers supported the demand for expulsion of the leaders of the Antiparty Group, usually to the accompaniment of graphic accounts of the havoc they had wrought in the speaker's area of expertise. Kaganovich was singled out by Beshchev as especially culpable, Malenkov by Novikov. The two academic functionaries maintained silence on the question of expulsion, although Kucherenko provided some additional details on the harmful influence exerted by Kaganovich in the field of construction. Neither of the two editors so much as mentioned the Antiparty Group, Gribachev because he was too reactionary, Tvardovsky because he was too liberal (he showed a pronounced distaste for anything which might be construed as contributing to Khrushchev's cult of personality). By way of compensation, the writer, Aleksandr Korneichuk, not only called for the expulsion of Molotov, Malenkov, and Kaganovich but added to the list the name of Shepilov, for whom he invented a new epithet: "Shepilov-who-crawled-to-them" (instead of the standard form, "Shepilov-who-joined-them"). To make matters complete, Korneichuk also attacked the Albanian party leadership for their continuing adherence to the cult of the individual.

The self-accusatory statement by Voroshilov, which we have already analyzed (above, p. 414), was read to the delegates following Korneichuk's speech, bringing the nineteenth session to a close.

Before the session adjourned it heard an announcement that Khrushchev would address the delegates that evening with concluding remarks, implying

---

[419]*Sten. ot.*, 2: 502; emphasis supplied.
[420]*Pravda*, Oct. 28, 1961; *CDSP*, XIV/6, p. 11; emphasis supplied.
[421]*CDSP*, XIV/6, p. 11.

that the lengthy discussion of the two reports he had presented at the outset of the congress was now closed.

*   *   *

On October 27, according to a report in the *New York Times*, U.S. Ambassador Llewellyn Thompson met with Soviet Foreign Minister Andrei Gromyko and lodged an oral protest "against the attempt of East German border guards to check the documents of United States citizens entering East Berlin."[422] In response: "Mr. Gromyko immediately countered with a protest against what he described as 'provocative' actions of United States military policemen in crossing the East Berlin border."[423]

Clearly, therefore, Gromyko had as yet received no instructions from the Presidium calling for a change in policy and was free to follow his own hard line in the Berlin crisis. At the sector boundary in Berlin, meanwhile, U.S. military police were carrying through another trip into the eastern sector, ignoring both the obstructions of the East German police and Gromyko's counterprotest.[424]

That afternoon, at about the time the twentieth session of the congress was getting under way in Moscow, ten Soviet tanks moved up to the sector boundary in Berlin and took up positions facing the West.[425] Like the earlier assembly of Soviet tanks in East Berlin, the movement to the border clearly implied a preceding top-level decision in Moscow authorizing the action. The logical deduction is that a decision to authorize the move was reached by the Presidium on the morning of October 27, probably while the congress was in session; was transmitted to the Soviet high command in East Germany with a minimum of delay, and was acted on during the early hours of the evening.

In terms of the poker-playing analogy cited at the outset of our analysis of the Berlin crisis (above, pp. 1–2), the action represented a last stubborn effort on the part of the Soviets to win the game by bluff, putting on a bold display of force and self-confidence. Viewed from the other side of the border, however, the action had a different significance. To General Lucius Clay, Kennedy's personal representative in West Berlin, the movement of the Soviet tanks was a vindication of his assertion of the continuing validity of four-power rule in Berlin. At a hastily called press conference on the evening of October 27 General Clay stated: "The fiction that it was the East Germans who were responsible for trying to prevent Allied access to East Berlin is now destroyed. . . . The fact that the Soviet tanks appeared on the scene proves that the harassments which were taking place at Friedrichstrasse [the border check point] were not those of the self-styled East German government but ordered by its Soviet masters."[426]

[422]*NYT*, Oct. 28, 1961, p. 1.
[423]Ibid.
[424]Smith, *Defense of Berlin*, p. 322.
[425]Ibid., p. 323.
[426]Ibid.

All through the long, drizzling autumn night the Soviet tanks stuck to the positions they had taken, a mere 75 yards from the sector boundary line along which a formation of American tanks had earlier established itself. For sixteen hours the tense confrontation continued, into the early morning hours of October 28. Finally, at 10:30 A.M., Berlin time, on October 28 the Soviet tanks turned and moved back into eastern Berlin; half an hour later the American tanks pulled back from their positions on the sector border. The supreme test of will-power in the Berlin crisis of 1961 had ended.

While the game in Berlin was being played out to the end, the congress in the Kremlin was hearing from the party's two most powerful leaders. On the evening of October 27 Khrushchev addressed the twentieth session of the congress and on the following morning, at long last, Frol Kozlov delivered his report on the new Party Statutes.

Khrushchev extends the attack on Stalin and the Albanians (October 27, evening)

For its twentieth session the congress reverted to the pattern of its opening days: Khrushchev dominated the session as the sole speaker, presenting his "Concluding Remarks" and thus bringing to an end the discussion of the reports for the Central Committee and on the new Party Program which he had delivered earlier. Although his speech on this occasion occupied only part of the available time, Khrushchev remained to the end of the session, at its close receiving the gift of an honorary necktie from a group of members of the Young Pioneers (the Soviet organization for grade-school children). In between these events the session got through some paper work: a resolution (*postanovlenie*) was unanimously adopted approving the domestic and foreign policies outlined in Khrushchev's report for the Central Committee; a commission was established, with Khrushchev as chairman, to prepare a more extensive draft resolution (*rezoliutsiia*) on the report for the CC, as well as to consider additions and changes in the draft Party Program; and the report for the Central Auditing Commission, which Gorkin had presented at the second session, was approved—unanimously, of course.

Khrushchev's "Concluding Remarks" on October 27 represented not merely the continuation of the line marked out in his two earlier speeches to the congress but, in a number of respects, an extension and deepening of it. At the outset he claimed total support from the congress and the party for the projected building of communism under the new Party Program and affirmed that the congress had been ". . . a most striking demonstration of the unity of our Leninist party and of the solidarity of all the Soviet people in their support of it."[427]

If the congress had given the appearance of unity, of course, it was only because Khrushchev's supporters had seen to it that few voices representing the internal opposition could be heard. Even more flagrantly in conflict with

---

[427] *Pravda*, Oct. 29, 1961; *CDSP*, XIII/46, p. 22.

the facts was Khrushchev's claim that the speeches and greetings to the congress from foreign parties "... have reflected the great unity that exists in the ranks of the world communist movement and have once again demonstrated that *the Leninist policy of our party is approved and supported by all Marxist–Leninist parties.*"[428] Ignoring both his own attack on the Albanian party leadership and Chou En-lai's sharp reproof to him for that action, Khrushchev claimed that: "The speeches delivered at our congress by the leaders of the communist and workers' parties of the countries in the socialist camp have shown that the fraternal parties are unanimously committed to the Declaration of 1957 and the Statement of 1960. *The socialist camp has once more demonstrated the monolithic solidarity of its ranks* and the growth and cohesion of the forces of world socialism."[429]

After this brazenly mendacious start, Khrushchev turned to questions of foreign policy, dwelling at length on the Soviet proposal for conclusion of a German peace treaty and advancing once again all the old familiar arguments in support of such a move. With scant regard for continuity, however, he suddenly reverted to his action in lifting the year-end deadline for signing a peace treaty, "if the Western powers show a willingness to settle the German problem."[430] "What counts most," he continued, "is not the particular date but a businesslike and honest settlement of the question."[431]

On the subject of the Soviet resumption of atomic tests, Khrushchev again repeated well-worn Soviet arguments justifying the action, with stress on its forced nature, but showed at the same time a candid appreciation of the real reasons for the unfavorable reaction the tests had evoked abroad, in particular the widespread fear of genetic damage resulting from radioactive fallout.

A lengthy and again thoroughly routine explanation of the need for peaceful coexistence followed, in the course of which Khrushchev avoided citing the real reasons why such a policy represented a vital necessity for the Soviet Union—U.S. military power—and instead substituted another of his bold-faced deceptions: "At present the world socialist system is mightier than the imperialist countries militarily as well."[432] Even Marshal Malinovsky, speaking on behalf of the Soviet armed forces, had avoided making such a flat statement, knowing as he did its falsity.

The claim of Soviet military superiority over the West was necessary to Khrushchev's argument, however, since on it he based his assertion that it was this factor, not any qualities of sobriety, wisdom, or genuine concern for humanity's survival on the part of the "imperialists" which explained their hesitation thus far to attack the Soviet Union and its allies. "Today," said

---

[428]*CDSP*, XIII/46, p. 22; emphasis supplied.
[429]Ibid., p. 23; emphasis supplied.
[430]Ibid.
[431]Ibid., p. 24.
[432]Ibid., p. 25.

Khrushchev, ". . . the imperialists are compelled—not so much by their reasonableness as by the instinct of self-preservation, if it can be put that way—to face up to their inability to squeeze, rob and enslave all others with impunity. Imperialism is being forced to reckon with the mighty forces that today block its way. The imperialists realize that if they unleash a world war, the imperialist system so hated by the people will inevitably perish in it."[433]

It was because of this relationship of forces in the world strategic balance, Khrushchev asserted, that peaceful coexistence had become a matter of "vital importance," and it was their failure to understand this truth which constituted the basic error of the "hopeless dogmatists" such as "the diehard Molotov."

Khrushchev's apparently boundless capacity for self-deception—one of the salient characteristics of his complex psychology—was never more in evidence than in this first section of his "Concluding Remarks." In the short space of less than a quarter of an hour he had ignored or denied the realities (to put as polite an interpretation on the matter as possible) with regard to three of the most important problems confronting the Soviet party and government: the deep political split in the party leadership, the steadily widening gulf between the CPSU and the Albanian and Chinese parties, which was threatening to tear asunder the international communist movement, and the overwhelming predominance of U.S. military power, which made a mockery of Khrushchev's claims for Soviet military superiority.

Charitably regarded, this opening section of Khrushchev's October 27 speech represented a valiant effort on his part to keep up his own courage and that of his followers in the face of the appalling difficulties in which the party found itself as the result of policies for which he bore the major responsibility. It was not, however, this labored and unconvincing defense of his stewardship which made the October 27 speech a landmark in the history of the CPSU, but the middle section of the speech, in which Khrushchev dropped any pretense of unity in the party and the international communist movement in order to deliver a slashing attack on some of his enemies at home and abroad.

Khrushchev began with the Albanian party leadership. And whereas previously, in speaking of the CPSU's position in the international communist movement he had been content to reaffirm hackneyed and unconvincing protestations of unity, now he cast off all restraint and lodged charges so bitter, so reckless, and so insulting that it seemed he was taking a perverse delight in the destruction of international communist amity.

The Albanian leadership, he implied, had suddenly shifted from feigned friendship with the Soviet party to undisguised hostility in order to carry out a betrayal comparable to that of Christ by Judas, and for similar motives: "Presumably they [the Albanian leaders] expect in this way to lay the groundwork for earning handouts from the imperialists. The imperialists are always willing to pay thirty pieces of silver to those who cause a split in the ranks

[433]Ibid.

of the communists. But pieces of silver have never brought anyone anything but dishonor and shame."[434]

Dropping the polite fiction on which all concerned had hitherto tacitly agreed, Khrushchev openly and with barbed sarcasm linked his two major enemies in the international communist movement, the party leaderships in Albania and China:

> Comrade Chou En-lai, head of the delegation of the Communist Party of China, voiced concern in his speech over our having openly raised the issue of Albanian–Soviet relations at the congress. As far as we can see, his statement primarily reflects alarm lest the present state of our relations with the Albanian Party of Labor affect the solidarity of the socialist camp. We share the anxiety of our Chinese friends and appreciate their concern for the strengthening of unity. If the Chinese comrades wish to apply their efforts to normalizing the Albanian Party of Labor's relations with the fraternal parties, it is doubtful whether there is anyone better able to facilitate accomplishment of this purpose than the Communist Party of China. This would really redound to the benefit of the Albanian Party of Labor and accord with the interests of the entire commonwealth of socialist countries.[435]

Continuing his earlier policy of attacking the Albanians for their alleged refusal to follow the CPSU in its condemnation of Stalin's cult of personality, while ignoring their criticism of his policy of peaceful coexistence vis-à-vis the Western powers, Khrushchev depicted internal conditions in communist Albania as a veritable reign of terror.

Not content with generalities, however, Khrushchev, in a sensational passage deliberately calculated to evoke a gut response from his audience, charged the Albanians with having condemned and executed a pregnant woman, Liri Gega, a former member of the Albanian Politburo for whom the Central Committee of the CPSU had unsuccessfully interceded.

Stepping up the pace of his attack, Khrushchev reached the ultimate insult one communist leader can hurl at another when he openly called for a popular uprising in Albania to overthrow the regime headed by Enver Hoxha: ". . . we are certain the time will come when the Albanian Communists and the Albanian people will have their say, and then the Albanian leaders will have to answer for the harm they have done their country, their people, and the cause of socialist construction in Albania."[436]

To bring this section of his speech to a more sober close, Khrushchev added a formal and obviously superficial condemnation of the "revisionism" which he said had "found expression in the program of the Yugoslav League of Communists," thus implying that the ferocious attack he had just mounted on the Albanian leaders for their "dogmatism" was simply part of the impartiality which the CPSU leadership meted out to other parties.

[434]Ibid., p. 26.
[435]Ibid.
[436]Ibid.

Having dragged his dispute with Albania and China down to a level of un-precedented bitterness and vituperation, Khrushchev turned with undi-minished zeal to the condemnation of his dead or defeated internal foes, Stalin and the Antiparty Group. Prominent at the outset of this section of his speech was the tell-tale emphasis on "the monolithic unity of the Leninist party," and on its "complete unity and solidarity."[437] But he quickly amended this asser-tion by admitting that "different opinions" could appear in the party, "espe-cially during transitional stages."[438] As an example of the proper Leninist way to deal with such occurrences, he cited Lenin's "great magnanimity" in rein-stating Zinoviev and Kamenev in the party leadership after their "betrayal of the cause of the revolution" by having publicly opposed Lenin's plans for the seizure of power by the Bolshevik party in November 1917.

This "magnanimity" Khrushchev contrasted with Stalin's behavior under similar circumstances:

> In the years following Lenin's death, the Leninist norms of party life were grossly distorted in the conditions of the Stalin cult. Stalin elevated limita-tions on inner-party and Soviet democracy to the status of norms of inner-party and state life. He crudely flouted the Leninist principles of leadership and permitted arbitrariness and abuses of power.
> Stalin could look at a comrade sitting at the same table with him and say: "Your eyes are shifty today," after which it could be assumed that the comrade whose eyes were supposedly shifty was under suspicion.[439]

Members of the Antiparty Group, Khrushchev said, had "categorically objected" to the proposal to discuss the "question of abuses of power in the period of the cult of personality" at the Twentieth Party Congress. But though their resistance had been overcome at that time, ". . . even after the congress, the factionalists continued their struggle and obstructed in every possible way the clarification of the question of abuses of power, fearing that their role as accomplices in the mass repressions would come to light."[440]

Thus the full story of Stalin's crimes remained to be told, and Khrushchev proceeded to tell, if not the full story, at least more of it than had been told at any previous party congress. Without beating around the bush he began his account at the focal point in the history of Stalin's purges, the assassination of Sergei Kirov in December 1934. It is true that Shelepin had touched on this crime in his speech on the preceding day, but Khrushchev went much further, providing previously unknown details of the highly suspicious circumstances surrounding both the assassination itself and the investigation of it which fol-lowed. Raising more questions than he answered, Khrushchev revealed that "a thorough study of this complex case is under way." No results of the study, however, have been published thus far, and Khrushchev's fall from power in

[437]Ibid., p. 27.
[438]Ibid.
[439]Ibid.
[440]Ibid.

October 1964 effectively prevented the emergence of any further revelations in regard to Kirov's assassination, his successors having shown no inclination to continue the investigation. Khrushchev's October 27 speech thus remains the fullest and most suggestive treatment of the subject thus far offered by any Soviet official.

The fact that Khrushchev chose to come back to a subject with which the secret police chief had dealt only a day earlier raises the suspicion that he was undertaking himself the performance of a task which had been assigned to Shelepin, but which the latter had discharged only imperfectly. Confirming this hunch is Khrushchev's observation, a little further on: "You have heard Comrade Shelepin's speech. He told the congress many things, but *needless to say he told by no means all that has now come to light.*"[441]

Khrushchev charged the leaders of the Antiparty Group not only with having opposed a full and honest disclosure of the crimes of Stalin and his associates (including, of course, their own) but of being willing to commit similar crimes in the future once they attained power: "Molotov said that in large matters there may be bad things and good. He justified the actions that had taken place in the period of the cult of the individual and claimed that *such actions are possible* and that *their repetition in the future is possible.*"[442] And this was the man, Khrushchev asserted, whom the group had selected for the position of leadership after their victory.

Now well launched on what Tatu correctly describes as "the public version" of his "'secret report' to the Twentieth Congress,"[443] Khrushchev proceeded to rake out previously unknown details of Stalin's purges, giving particular attention to the slaughter of the Soviet military high command. For the first time he revealed to a Soviet audience the fact—long known to Western historians—that the charges on which Marshal Tukhachevsky and other Red Army leaders were tried and executed in 1937 were based in part on forgeries concocted by the Nazi intelligence service.

Speaking on behalf of a group of "Old Bolsheviks" who he said had written to the congress, Khrushchev brought his account of Stalin's crimes to a close by proposing that "a monument should be erected in Moscow to the memory of comrades [i.e., party members] who fell victim to arbitrary rule."[444] Just as in his secret speech to the Twentieth Party Congress, however, Khrushchev showed no concern for the millions of *nonparty* victims who perished under Stalin. Nor has the proposed monument been erected.

To conclude his discussion of the Antiparty Group, Khrushchev took up Voroshilov's part in the factional conspiracy, depicting the aged and widely respected marshal as a willing dupe of the conspirators who, however, deserved lenience both because of his long service to the party and the state and

---

[441]Ibid.; emphasis supplied.
[442]Ibid.; emphasis supplied.
[443]Tatu, p. 150.
[444]*CDSP*, XIII/46, p. 29.

because he had broken away from the anti-Khrushchev faction at the time of the June 1957 Central Committee plenum.

There followed a section in which Khrushchev extolled with curious warmth the principle of collective leadership, going out of his way to warn against any tendency in the party to overemphasize his own role:

> In many speeches at the congress, and not infrequently in our press as well, when mention is made of the activity of our party's Central Committee a certain special emphasis is placed on me personally, and my role in carrying out major party and government measures is underlined.
>
> I understand the kind feelings guiding these comrades. Allow me, however, to emphasize emphatically that everything that is said about me should be said about the Central Committee of our Leninist party and about the Presidium of the Central Committee [*stormy, prolonged applause*]. *Not one major measure, not one responsible pronouncement has been carried out upon anyone's personal directive; they have all been the result of collective deliberation and collective decision* [*stormy applause*].[445]

Khrushchev even included the speech he was delivering in this general observation, thus making it clear that he was speaking on behalf of the entire Presidium in thus minimizing his own personal role.

Even in the struggle against the Antiparty Group, Khrushchev continued, the prominence given him personally as the group's chief target was merely the result of the fact that the party had given him its confidence: "Speaking against the course set by the Twentieth Congress, the schismatics concentrated their main fire against Khrushchev, who did not suit them. Why against Khrushchev? Well, because Khrushchev had been promoted by the will of the party to the post of First Secretary of the Central Committee."[446] Any cult of the individual, he insisted, was alien to Marxism–Leninism, although "Marxist–Leninists have always recognized and will continue to recognize the authority of leaders."[447]

Thus far what Khrushchev had to say was standard communist doctrine, although admittedly there was something rather odd in his choosing this particular occasion—toward the end of a congress which he and his supporters had almost totally dominated—to utter these truisms. Khrushchev went on, however, to inveigh against leaders who forgot their responsibility to the party and the people, and here, though his observations might look superficially like a mere continuation of his earlier warnings against the danger of a renewal of the cult of personality, on closer inspection a new and different note can be detected. This passage, Khrushchev's final word of advice to the congress, merits close attention, for in it he made the only guarded hints he permitted himself at the congress alluding to the real challenge to his position, preroga-

---

[445]Ibid., p. 30; emphasis supplied.
[446]Ibid.
[447]Ibid.

tives, and power which Kozlov and like-minded members of the party were offering.

"It is wrong, comrades," Khrushchev said, ". . . it is simply impossible to permit the inception and development of instances when the merited prestige of an individual may assume forms in which *he fancies that everything is permissible to him and that he no longer has need of the collective.* In such a case *this individual may stop listening to the voices of other comrades* who have been advanced to leadership, just as he was, *and may begin suppressing them.*"[448]

Read in the light of the Soviet rearmament measures of late August, this passage, with its clearly implied warning that the continuation of such practices might lead to the re-establishment of the blood purge in the party (the reference to "suppressing" other comrades) makes sense as a veiled allusion to Kozlov, especially when one takes into account Kozlov's well-known association with the organs of repression both in the Leningrad Case and in the Doctors' Plot.

In the concluding section of his speech Khrushchev tried to rekindle in his audience a mood of confident, optimistic anticipation of the glorious future awaiting them in the building of a communist society under the new Party Program. There can have been few of the delegates, however, who could so quickly and easily shake off the impressions of shock, conflict, and struggle which had been the dominant motifs of his speech.

Taken as a whole, the October 27 speech reveals a man operating under tremendous emotional pressure, working off his frustration and fury against dead men and enemies abroad or defeated because his most dangerous foes were too threatening and too powerful to be attacked openly. Part of the emotional tension which is such a striking characteristic of the speech, moreover, must be explained by the fact that it was delivered at a time when the speaker knew that the question of an atomic war was trembling in the balance, with the very survival of the Soviet Union dependent on the sobriety, good will, and judgment of those whom Khrushchev, in the speech, depicted as incurably aggressive imperialists. The acute Berlin confrontation, as Khrushchev well knew, was the result more of Soviet aggressiveness than of the unyielding Western response. By resisting Soviet pressure in Berlin, Kennedy was in fact rendering the most direct service possible to Khrushchev in his struggle against his internal foes, since a capitulation by the West in Berlin at this point would have meant the validation of the entire policy of pressure and blackmail against the West which Kozlov and like-minded associates had tried to establish as the Soviet foreign policy line.

Kozlov reports on the new Party Statutes (October 28)

The twenty-first session of the congress convened at 10 A.M. on October 28 to hear Frol Kozlov report on the new Party Statutes. Following Kozlov's speech, the delegates took a thirty-minute intermission and then reassembled

[448]Ibid., p. 31; emphasis supplied.

for the second half of the session. The first speakers after the break were half a dozen heads of foreign delegations; in reporting their speeches, the protocols indicate Khrushchev's absence in the customary way. There is no indication in the protocols, however, as to whether or not Khrushchev was present to hear Kozlov's report. In view of its importance, and the deductions as to a conflict in the Soviet leadership which the delegates would inevitably have drawn if he had stayed away while it was being delivered, we can assume that he was present during the first half of the session. In any case, the Presidium is not likely to have met while Kozlov was speaking, since his presence at a Presidium meeting would be essential.

While the congress was meeting in Moscow, the armored confrontation along the sector boundary line in Berlin ended shortly after 10:30 A.M., Berlin time (12:30 P.M., Moscow time), with the withdrawal of the Soviet tanks.[449] The resolution of the acute crisis in Berlin thus came at about the time of the intermission following the delivery of Kozlov's report. At approximately the same time *Pravda* was publishing the first account in the Soviet press of the Berlin crisis which had been building up since October 22.

Kozlov was a past master at manipulating communist terminology, skilled in the art of conveying implications by the use of subtle nuances in the way he varied the standard formulas. Since he was also a factionalist fighting for supreme power, however, he was usually careful to avoid too overt a correspondence between the terms he employed and the facts to which they alluded. Reading a speech by Kozlov therefore calls for close attention and intensive analysis. Repeatedly one has the feeling that Kozlov is trying to convey an esoteric meaning to informed listeners, but that he has so effectively covered his traces that positive identification of his meaning is difficult. In his October 28 report, however, Kozlov's political passions at times almost overmastered his conspiratorial instincts, so that in more than one passage the real meaning of what he is saying can be grasped fairly readily—provided, that is, one pays due attention to the context within which the report was delivered.

Kozlov opened with praise for the new Party Program, which he described as ". . . the fruit of the collective creative thought of the whole party and of its Leninist Central Committee headed by Comrade N. S. Khrushchev. His creative approach to theory, his close contact with life and his ability to give correct expression to the fundamental interests of the people stamp Comrade N. S. Khrushchev as a true Leninist, as an outstanding political figure and Marxist–Leninist theorist."[450]

Not in keeping, one would think, with Khrushchev's warning only the evening before not to exaggerate his personal role in party affairs. Was Kozlov so devoted a follower of Khrushchev that he deliberately ignored this warning? The remainder of his speech rules out this possibility.

The opening section of Kozlov's report, headed "The building of communism and the enhancement of the title of party member," consisted largely of smooth-sounding platitudes which neither convey much of significance nor

[449]Smith, *Defense of Berlin*, p. 323.
[450]*Pravda*, Oct. 29, 1961; *CDSP*, XIII/47, p. 9.

repay detailed analysis. The pace quickened, however, when Kozlov moved on to a discussion of the communist principle of criticism and self-criticism—always a convenient pretext for working off covert grudges and giving veiled expression to personal animosities. As usual, of course, Kozlov was circumspect. Who, for example, was the target of the following critique? "When an official stops seeing his own shortcomings and mistakes and is uncritical in appraising the results of his work, he becomes conceited and complacent, lives in the past and loses perspective. When his shortcomings and mistakes are pointed out to such an official, he treats the remarks of his comrades in a manner unbecoming a member of the party and all too often takes the course of *suppressing criticism*."[451]

Kozlov supplied an answer to the question of identification by dragging out from obscurity a certain "comrade Gasparian," former first secretary of the Artashat raikom in Armenia, who, he charged, had ". . . ordered an issue of the raion newspaper to be withdrawn and destroyed for the sole reason that it carried an editorial that in the most general terms called upon the delegates to a raion party conference to criticize shortcomings in the work of the raikom."[452] (It will be recalled that the Armenian party organization had been subjected during the past year to an unusually extensive purge, initiated by Kozlov.)

It was certainly not, however, merely to hold up to public disfavor an obscure and disgraced provincial official that Kozlov had introduced the subject of criticism and self-criticism, as he showed by his marked reluctance to move on to other topics. "A communist," he continued,

> . . . is called upon to rebuff firmly *any attempts to suppress criticism* and to resist any actions detrimental to the party and the state. We must everywhere establish conditions that will enable a party member to exercise freely *the right to criticize any communist regardless of the position he holds*. The draft Party Statutes not only proclaim this right for a party member but guarantee it. "Persons guilty of suppressing criticism or persecuting anyone for criticism," says the draft, "must be held to strict party responsibility, *up to and including expulsion from the ranks of the CPSU*."[453]

With these words Kozlov defined the first of his conditions justifying expulsion from the party: suppression of criticism. More ominously, Kozlov's words raised the dread spectre of a party purge, a spectre which no one familiar with his past career could dismiss as an idle threat. Would he drop the subject at this point or strengthen it by the use of more specific detail?

For three paragraphs of opaque generalizations Kozlov kept his listeners in suspense; then he set up his next target with two rhetorically balanced statements: "Be truthful and honest, observe party and state discipline strictly, and serve your people faithfully—this is what the party demands of every communist and of any party leader. . . . Unfortunately, we still come across facts

---

[451]*CDSP*, XIII/47, p. 9; emphasis supplied.
[452]Ibid.
[453]Ibid.; emphasis supplied.

when some officials forget this indisputable truth and take the course of deceiving the party and state."454

Kozlov was now ready to reveal his second target, a group of more highly placed officials in another Union Republic party organization which he had recently purged:

Take, for instance, the former leaders of the Tadzhik party organization—Ul'dzhabaev, Dodkhudoev, and Obnosov. Having proved incapable of insuring the further development of the republic's economy, especially cotton growing, *they resorted to antiparty acts* that to all intents and purposes constituted fraud. To conceal their political bankruptcy and at the same time make it appear that they were marching in step with life, these sorry excuses for leaders went in for hoodwinking and account padding. The republic was failing to meet the state plan for cotton procurements, but its leaders, having lost all shame and conscience, reported that the plan had been met ahead of schedule. They implanted servility and toadyism in the organization, trod inner-party democracy underfoot, and violated state laws.455

Modestly omitting to mention his own part in the purge of the Tadzhik party leadership, Kozlov presented matters as though the Tadzhiks themselves had risen to the occasion—with an assist from the CPSU Central Committee: "It must be pointed out that the party organization of Tadzhikistan proved equal to the situation. After investigating the state of affairs in the republic, with the help of the Central Committee of the CPSU, *it denounced the antiparty behavior* of the former leaders, and, as you know, a plenum of the Central Committee of the Communist Party of Tadzhikistan dismissed them from their positions and *expelled them from the party*."456

Two observations may be offered on this passage: first, by renewing the attack on Khrushchev's friend and supporter, the former Tadzhik First Secretary Tursunbai Ul'dzhabaev, Kozlov was providing a clear indication that beneath its ideology and rhetoric his speech was to be a slashing, partisan, factional effort. Second, by placing the case of the Tadzhik "antiparty" officials close to the beginning of his speech, Kozlov was completing his criteria for expulsion from the party; not criminal actions, not murder, but "dishonesty" and the suppression of criticism.

To make sure his listeners had grasped the point Kozlov repeated it a few paragraphs further on: "Our position will continue to be that *expulsion from the party*, the highest party penalty, should be resorted to only in the case of *people who are really unworthy of being in the party*."457

And again, Kozlov reiterated the theme of the need to criticize dishonest party leaders: "The people will not stand for deception and untruth! Only that communist, only that party leader who is honest and truthful is respected by

454Ibid.
455Ibid.; emphasis supplied.
456Ibid.; emphasis supplied.
457Ibid.; emphasis supplied.

the masses. Only such a leader works boldly and confidently. He does not fear *just criticism of his actions* but on the contrary regards criticism as help and support from the masses."[458]

Turning to the "further development of inner-party democracy," Kozlov extolled collective leadership as "the highest principle of party leadership," one which, he said, ". . . guarantees the party and all its bodies against *unilateral, subjective decisions and actions*."[459] But here Kozlov introduced a significant qualification: "Needless to say, collective leadership in no way lessens *the personal responsibility of a party worker* for matters entrusted to him, *for the execution of collectively adopted decisions*."[460]

Was this Kozlov's reply to Khrushchev's implied reproach, in his "Concluding Remarks" the night before, to those party members who "fancy that everything is permissible to them and that they no longer have need of the collective"? As so often in a Kozlov speech, one has the impression of a definite esoteric point being made, but in a way which eludes precise identification.

As Kozlov proceeded, however, the real target of his concealed barbs and allusions began gradually to take on greater solidity. A perceptible note of sarcasm crept into his tone when he took up the provision in the new statutes calling for the periodic renewal of membership of party bodies, from the CPSU Central Committee and its Presidium down to the basic level of party organization. "The need to introduce these important new provisions," said Kozlov, ". . . is demonstrated profoundly and comprehensively in Nikita Sergeevich Khrushchev's report on the draft Program of the CPSU."[461]

The statement is ambiguous: it could mean either that Khrushchev, in his report, had "demonstrated profoundly and comprehensively" the need to introduce the changes in question, or it could imply, subversively, that *the report itself* constituted an example of the kind of situation which made the replacement of outworn leaders necessary. One notes, also, Kozlov's reference to the First Secretary by his full name, without the honorary appellation, "comrade"—a usage which we have already seen in the congress speech of Walter Ulbricht.

Of particular interest, in view of Kozlov's republic-busting purges in Armenia and Tadhizkistan, was the position adopted in his report on the problems of factionalism and decentralization in the party. It was not to be expected, of course, that he would openly sanction the kind of subversive activities he had been engaging in; rather one would expect him to affirm strongly the need for centralization in the party and vehemently to condemn any form of factionalism. One does, in fact, find such affirmation and condemnation in his report to the congress. It is a different story, however, when one turns to the statutes themselves. As Leonard Schapiro was the first to point out, the

---

[458] Ibid.; emphasis supplied.
[459] Ibid.; emphasis supplied.
[460] Ibid.; emphasis supplied.
[461] Ibid.

new statutes eliminate a provision (article 42 in the old statutes) under which personnel changes at the level of Union Republic first secretary required the approval of the full CPSU Central Committee.[462] The new statutes therefore actually *facilitated* the kind of purge which Kozlov had carried out in Armenia and Tadzhikistan, and thereby *increased* the possibility that an internal opposition faction could successfully build a political base.

To conceal these implications of the statutes, Kozlov went out of his way to reaffirm the continuing need in the CPSU for measures to prevent the formation and development of factions. "During the discussion of the draft Statutes," he said, ". . . the following questions were asked: Does not the monolithic unity of the CPSU and of Soviet society as a whole exclude the possibility of any divisive activity within the party's ranks? Under present circumstances, need the Statutes contain any formal guarantees against factionalism and clique activity?"

And he supplied the unequivocal answer:

Yes, comrades, such guarantees are needed. To be sure, there is no social base left in Soviet society that could feed opportunistic currents in the party. But the sources of ideological waverings on the part of particular individuals or groups have not yet been entirely eliminated. *Some persons may fall under the influence of bourgeois propaganda from the outside.* Others, having failed to comprehend the dialectics of society's development and having turned, in Comrade N. S. Khrushchev's wonderful expression, into dying embers, will have nothing to do with anything new and go on clinging to old dogmas that have been toppled by life.[463]

By a logical association of ideas this brought Kozlov to the subject of the Antiparty Group. His list of charges against the group, all of whose members he specified by name, began with their opposition to the changes in the party line introduced at the Twentieth Party Congress. After the 1956 congress, Kozlov asserted, these individuals had formed a clandestine factional conspiracy in order to "seize the leadership of the party and country and alter the party's policy."[464] In itself this charge, if substantiated, would have merited expulsion from the party, for under the new statutes, "All manifestations of factionalism and group activity are incompatible with Marxist–Leninist party principles and with party membership."[465] As we shall see presently, however, Kozlov failed to draw this conclusion.

On the subjects of the group's alleged crimes and acts of illegal repression, Kozlov resorted to generalities and euphemisms: "Facts have been disclosed

---

[462]Leonard Schapiro, "The Party's New Rules," *Problems of Communism*, vol. 11, no. 1 (Jan.–Feb. 1962): 351. For the text of the article in question, see Jan F. Triska, ed., *Soviet Communism: Programs and Rules* (San Francisco: Chandler, 1962), p. 181 (hereinafter cited as Triska).

[463]*CDSP*, XIII/47, p. 11; emphasis supplied. Note the linking of ideas with Khrushchev's name.

[464]Ibid.

[465]Triska, pp. 155–56.

and set forth attesting that Molotov, Kaganovich, and Malenkov *had a hand in the destruction* of many altogether innocent people, including prominent party figures and statesmen, and that *by their careerist policy and their departure from Marxism–Leninism they contributed to the establishment and flourishing of the cult of the individual.*"[466]

"Even now," Kozlov continued, ". . . the organizers of the antiparty group are still endeavoring to uphold their pernicious views. Molotov has been showing particular zeal in this respect. *He has even gone so far as to describe the new program of the CPSU as antirevolutionary in spirit.* . . . This declaration of Molotov's is in effect a challenge to our whole party and to the Twenty-Second Congress of the CPSU, which has given its unanimous approval to the new program."[467] From the rostrum of the congress, Kozlov thus contrived to insert into the official record the charge, which he ascribed to Molotov, that the new program was "antirevolutionary" in spirit. Exactly the same charge would later be made by the Chinese communists.

In his discussion of the purge in Tadzhikistan, Kozlov had already set forth his recommendations for dealing with "antiparty" actions—the "highest party penalty," expulsion from the party. What Kozlov euphemistically referred to as the "unsavory deeds" with which the leaders of the Antiparty Group were charged (of which there was ample documentary proof, as Shelepin had shown), by any normal standard of justice ought to have weighed far heavier in the scales than the falsification of figures on cotton production, the most serious charge Kozlov had been able to level against Ul'dzhabaev and the other former Tadzhik party leaders. There was an important difference, however, between the individuals convicted of "antiparty" actions in Tadzhikistan and the Antiparty Group; the former included a close friend and supporter of Khrushchev, whereas the latter had as its avowed purpose his overthrow. This difference explains why Kozlov reached different conclusions in the two cases.

For Ul'dzhabaev and his associates the penalty meted out by Kozlov personally was expulsion from the party, a penalty he reserved for those "who are really unworthy of being in the party." When it came to Molotov, Malenkov, and Kaganovich, however, Kozlov's answer to the question of expulsion was even more clearly an evasion of the issue than Shelepin's handing of the case over to the Party Control Committee. "I share the opinion of those delegates who have spoken here," said Kozlov, ". . . that Molotov, Kaganovich, and Malenkov *should be called to strict account before the party and the people* for all their antiparty, criminal acts."[468]

Under the party statutes, a party member cannot be prosecuted in the regular courts for criminal acts; expulsion from the party is a formal prerequisite.[469] By failing to endorse the proposal for expulsion, therefore, Kozlov

---

[466]*CDSP*, XIII/47, p. 11; emphasis supplied.

[467]Ibid.; emphasis supplied.

[468]Ibid.; emphasis supplied.

[469]Art. 13 of the 1952 statutes, art. 12 of the new. Triska, p. 166.

was leaving open the possibility that the leaders of the Antiparty Group might get off scot-free in spite of their direct complicity in the purges; after all, they could always plead that they had carried out their bloody deeds in line of party discipline. (This, incidentally, is why it was essential for Khrushchev to pin the label of "criminal" on Stalin himself, in order to eliminate the defense by the Antiparty Group leaders that they had been acting on legitimate party orders.)

For all his half-heartedness, however, Kozlov had finally toed the line, uttering the crucial word, "criminal," to characterize the Antiparty Group's deeds. It seemed to be far more difficult for him to show any real enthusiasm for the criticism of the Albanian party leadership. His technique for dealing with this problem was simple but ingenious: he attributed to Khrushchev the criticism he advanced, thus preserving the appearance of loyalty to the leadership's decision on the Albanian issue while at the same time dissociating himself from any personal responsibility for the substance of the charges. The key sentence in this section of his report was the opening one, in which he said: "Comrades! In the Central Committee's report to the congress and yesterday in his concluding remarks, *Nikita Sergeevich Khrushchev stated* that recently, *without any cause on the part of the Communist Party of the Soviet Union or its leadership,* the leaders of the Albanian Party of Labor have abruptly altered their political policy and taken the course of sharply impairing relations with our party, with the Soviet Union, and with other socialist countries."[470]

Having introduced Khrushchev (note the ironic form of designation) as the authority for his charges, Kozlov could feel free to set forth the standard set of grievances against the Albanians. It was noteworthy, however, that in so doing he avoided adding any fresh details to what had already been presented to the congress by earlier speakers. Kozlov also expressed guarded approval for the party's (i.e., Khrushchev's) action in airing its dispute with the Albanians at the congress, thus associating himself with the rejection of Chou's criticism of Khrushchev. It will be recalled, however, that when the Chinese delegation to the congress left Moscow on October 30, Kozlov was the only member of the Presidium who accompanied them to the airport. His support for party policy in the Albanian dispute cannot, therefore, be taken as proof that he approved the split with Albania or China, any more than his reluctant criticism of the Antiparty Group indicates sincere support of Khrushchev on that question.

In evaluating Kozlov's position on these two key issues, it is essential to take into account the timing of his speech. For a party official to offer support to Khrushchev in the early days of the congress had an entirely different meaning from similar action taken in the congress's twelfth day. Kozlov was the last full member of the Presidium to address the congress, and there was a full day's interval—October 27—between his speech and that of his fellow-member of the Presidium, Otto Kuusinen, during which no Presidium member

[470]*CDSP*, XIII/47, p. 13; emphasis supplied.

spoke. As we shall see presently, there is reason to believe that the Presidium had formally adopted positions on these two key issues on October 27, i.e., *before* Kozlov addressed the congress. This being the case, Kozlov's speech cannot be cited as evidence of his loyalty to Khrushchev; rather it represented the performance of his duty as a party member obligated to support the decisions reached by the collective leadership.

For the remainder of Kozlov's report, which concerned itself primarily with technical questions of party organization, we can limit ourselves to consideration of a few salient passages. Kozlov's firm belief in the need for organizational discipline and ideological purity in the party's ranks was well known. The following passage is therefore to be read as ironical: "What we need is a reduction of the apparatus of the party agencies and an increase in the ranks of the party *aktiv* [non-professional party aides]. The party agencies, *says Nikita Sergeevich Khrushchev,* should have more and more commissions, departments instructors, and secretaries of raikoms and gorkoms, working on an unpaid basis."[471] The implication is clear: Khrushchev is threatening to dilute the party and weaken its organization with his recommendations for "democratizing" it.

Kozlov, the advocate of top priority for the Soviet armed forces, spoke out openly in the following passage: "The Communist Party regards as its sacred duty concern for strengthening the U.S.S.R.'s defense capacity; the party considers its leadership to be the keystone in the development and organization of the armed forces."[472]

The same point was made again a little further on: "Everyone knows that our party regards the defense of the socialist homeland and the strengthening of the U.S.S.R.'s defenses as the sacred duty of the party and of the Soviet people as a whole, as an essential condition for the preservation and consolidation of peace all over the world, and regards the struggle for peace among nations as its paramount task."[473]

Toward the end of his report Kozlov dealt directly with the touchy subject of a new party purge. His own record as a close supporter of two of the last purge actions undertaken under Stalin—the Leningrad Case (1949) and the abortive Doctors' Plot (1952–53)—was known to the entire party, and Kozlov was therefore lying when he implied that there had been no purge in the party since the Eighteenth Party Congress in 1939: "As we know, the party deemed it necessary as far back as its Eighteenth Congress to renounce the mass purges. . . . Since that time twenty-two years have elapsed. Socialism has triumphed fully and conclusively in the country, and the U.S.S.R. has entered the period of the full-scale building of communism. Is there any need, under the circumstances, to revive the party purges?"

Kozlov's answer to this ominous question was none too reassuring: "The purges were necessary in a setting of acute class struggle in the country. To-

[471]Ibid., p. 15; emphasis supplied.
[472]Ibid.
[473]Ibid., p. 16.

day, in the period of the full-scale building of communism, when indestructible moral and political unity of the whole people has been established in the country, there is no need for a measure of this kind. So strong is the party ideologically and organizationally that *persons who violate the Program and Statutes can be cleared out of its ranks without purges [prolonged applause]*."[474]

The threat of punitive action, reinforced by recollections of the ouster of Ul'dzhabaev et al., was abundantly clear, even if the dread word "purge" had been explicitly disavowed.

The manner in which Kozlov's report was carried by the two leading Soviet newspapers is an essential factor to be considered in evaluating its significance. *Pravda* and *Izvestiia* ran the full text of the speech in their issues of October 29, filling pages 3 and 4 in both newspapers; a photograph of Kozlov was prominently displayed at the top center of page 3 in both papers. On pages 1 and 2 of the same issue, both papers carried the full text of Khrushchev's "Concluding Remarks" of October 27, *but without any photograph*. This small but significant distinction did not escape notice in Moscow. An alert Western reporter, Rowland Evans, Jr., filed a dispatch from the Soviet capital entitled, "The Moscow Story: 'Downgrading' Mr. Khrushchev," in which he stated that

> A deliberate and highly significant effort to downgrade Soviet Premier Nikita S. Khrushchev's personal power and prestige appears to be under way here in the Twenty-Second Soviet Communist Party Congress, in the opinion of some Western observers on the scene. . . .
> A sharp turn in the past few days away from the practice of extolling the Soviet Premier has become all too obvious. Some experienced observers here believe the sudden change is the result of a collective decision of a powerful group in the Presidium of the Central Committee, possibly headed by Frol R. Kozlov, who ranks second to Mr. Khrushchev in the Soviet leadership.[475]

As evidence, Evans cited three items in his "bill of particulars": First, Khrushchev himself, in his speech of October 27, ". . . went far out of his usual path to say explicitly that every action for which he had been praised in the first ten days of the congress was in reality the result of 'collective' leadership—of the Presidium, the Central Committee and other 'elected' party units from top to bottom."[476] Second, Adzhubei, in his speech on October 26, had ". . . astonished some observers here by listing two separate groups of members of the Presidium who, he said, should share credit with Mr. Khrushchev for undertaking arduous trips abroad in the interest of the Soviet Union."[477] Third, Evans cited the form in which *Pravda* and *Izvestiia* carried

[474]Ibid.; emphasis supplied.
[475]*NYHT*, Oct. 30, 1961, p. 1.
[476]Ibid.
[477]Ibid. In my opinion, Adzhubei's speech was not part of the campaign to downgrade Khrushchev; its primary motive was self-aggrandizement.

Kozlov's speech and added: "Seemingly insignificant occurrences like the display of a picture are given large significance here [in Moscow] as revealing implications of what may be going on behind the scenes."[478]

At the time Evans filed his story (October 29) the results of the elections to the central bodies of the party had not yet been made public; it was only on November 1 that *Pravda* and *Izvestiia* disclosed that at the plenum of the newly elected Central Committee, held at the close of the congress (October 31), Kozlov for the first time was officially confirmed in the second position in the party, a fact conveyed by the listing of the members of the new Secretariat, which placed Kozlov's name immediately after that of Khrushchev, the first secretary, and ahead of the names of the other members of the Secretariat, out of alphabetical order.[479]

This development clinches the evidence for the enhancement of Kozlov's power and status toward the end of the congress, and taken in conjunction with his congress speech and that of Khrushchev on October 27, makes it clear that this meant a scaling-down of Khrushchev's power.

* * *

We must now consider the relationship between these developments and the acute crisis which had developed as the result of the confrontation of U.S. and Soviet tanks along the sector boundary in Berlin. This confrontation, as we have seen, began at about the time when the delegates were assembling to hear Khrushchev's "Concluding Remarks," on the evening of October 27, and ended with the withdrawal of the Soviet tanks shortly after Kozlov had finished delivering his report on the new Party Statutes on the morning of October 28.

There were a number of internal themes linking Khrushchev's speech of October 27 and that of Kozlov on October 28, especially the emphasis in both on the paramount need for collective leadership. In several passages Kozlov seems to be replying to or commenting on points made by Khrushchev the preceding evening.

Taking all these facts into account, we can reconstruct the course of events as follows: bitterly opposed to Khrushchev's line on foreign policy, especially as regards Soviet relations with the West and with Albania and China, and finding himself and his supporters outmaneuvered and silenced at the congress, Kozlov, with the help of his friend and ally Ulbricht and the support of the Soviet military command in East Germany, provoked a confrontation with the West by challenging existing Western rights in Berlin. As tension there mounted, Kozlov held out for either a shift in the foreign policy line of the CPSU or a strengthening of his own position in the hierarchy of the party. Khrushchev first attempted to meet the challenge by having Satiukov remind the congress of the Soviet Union's imperative need for

---

[478] Ibid.

[479] *Pravda* and *Izv.*, Nov. 1, 1961, p. 2; *CDSP*, XIII/44, p. 20.

peace (Gromyko being unwilling to lend his voice to the support of Khrushchev's conciliatory policy in Germany), but Kozlov and his allies responded by stepping up the pressure, moving Soviet tanks into East Berlin on the evening of October 26.

Kozlov refused to deliver his report to the congress until his terms had been met, and by October 27, as a result of this boycott, the congress had been brought virtually to a standstill: the anomalous and aberrant pattern of the morning session on the 27th (no speech by a Presidium member, no foreign guest speakers) shows that it was a hurriedly improvised session designed to conceal the breakdown of the schedule. It was at this point that we can most logically place the crucial meeting of the Presidium which resolved the crisis; the fact that an announcement was made at the end of the morning session stating that Khrushchev would present his "Concluding Remarks" that evening constitutes a confirmation of this deduction.

The Presidium must therefore have met on the morning of October 27 for the purpose of ending the split in the leadership, restoring unity of command, and laying down an agreed policy on the principal unresolved issues. Khrushchev was therefore on solid ground in stating that his "Concluding Remarks" had the sanction of the Presidium. The following appear to have been the major points decided:

1. Support of the renewed attack on the Antiparty Group was made a matter of party discipline, binding on every member of the Presidium. Kozlov was therefore forced to include a passage condemning the group in his report on the new Party Statutes.

Khrushchev was unable, however, to get Presidium sanction for his proposal to oust the leaders of the Antiparty Group, Molotov, Kaganovich, and Malenkov. Here the resistance of moderates like Kosygin and Mikoyan, who usually supported Khrushchev's line but who feared granting him disciplinary power over members of the leadership group, proved decisive.

2. Support for Khrushchev's condemnation of the Albanian party leadership and rejection of Chinese criticism of this act were also made matters of party discipline. Kozlov therefore had no choice but to express his approval for these measures, even though he found a means, as we have seen, to do so in such a way that his real views could be deduced without undue difficulty.

3. As his reward for these forced concessions to Khrushchev and as his price for calling back the Soviet tanks in Berlin, Kozlov demanded (a) that Khrushchev explicitly disavow the rapidly burgeoning cult of personality which was being built up around him and (b) that Kozlov's own position as the No. 2 man in the party be formally acknowledged and explicitly recognized in the elections held at the end of the congress. These conditions, as we know, were met.

4. As a sop to Kozlov and the hard-line faction in the party, the Foreign Ministry, and the armed forces, and to minimize the impression of Soviet weakness which a pull-back in Berlin might convey to Western observers, it was decided to mount a diplomatic offensive against the Soviet Union's

small and isolated Western neighbor, Finland. This maneuver was duly launched a few days later (October 30) with the dispatch of a note to the Finnish government requesting consultation on "measures to insure the defense of the frontier of the two countries against the threat of an attack by West Germany and its allies."[480] For good measure, the Soviet nuclear test series was still in progress, and the 50-megaton bomb was just about ready to go (it was set off on the 30th).

The Soviet tank alert in East Berlin was maintained until 10:30 A.M. on October 28, i.e., until word could be received there that Kozlov had delivered his report and, by including in it the necessary minimum verbal support for the agreed policies of the leadership on the Antiparty Group and Albania, had signified his acceptance of party discipline. Once that fact was clear, there was no reason for the Soviet military command in East Berlin to continue the confrontation there.

The acute crisis in the party leadership thus ended with the restoration of a measure of harmony and the preservation of the image of unity which the CPSU strives to present to the outside world. The ragged edges of the compromise were visible if one looked for them closely enough, but, as so often in the past, the Soviet leadership was helped in its efforts to deceive the outside world by the readiness of foreign observers to be deceived. Typical in this respect were the editorials and news reports carried by the West's most powerful and influential newspaper, the *New York Times*. In an editorial on October 30, the *Times* asserted that: "The features of Soviet totalitarianism today are clearly apparent. There is the one-party dictatorship organized in the hierarchical pattern, which means in practice that *the edict of Nikita Khrushchev is law*."[481] The *Times* said nothing about the evidence for a "downgrading" of Khrushchev's position toward the end of the congress. Instead, it portrayed him as the unchallenged master of the party. In a story reporting the election of the new central bodies of the CPSU, the *Times's* Moscow correspondent, Theodore Shabad, began by stating that: "Premier Khrushchev emerged today from the final session of the Twenty-Second Congress of the Communist Party as firmly as ever in control of the party leadership."[482] Then, with no effort at transition, the story continued: "An election of members of the party's ruling body also confirmed Frol R. Kozlov as undisputed second-in-command and heir apparent to the 67-year-old Mr. Khrushchev."[483]

It was not until a week later that the *Times* published a cautious demurral to this view of Soviet politics, in the form of a dispatch from London in which Drew Middleton reported that: "Several developments support the view that Mr. Khrushchev's personal position in the upper levels of the party has been

[480]*NYT*, Oct. 30, 1961, p. 1; text, ibid., Oct. 31, 1961, p. 12.
[481]"Khrushchev wars on Stalinists," *NYT*, Oct. 30, 1961, p. 28; emphasis supplied.
[482]*NYT*, Nov. 1, 1961, p. 1.
[483]Ibid.

reduced. . . . For the first time there is a Deputy, Frol R. Kozlov, in the party Secretariat—in other words, an alternative leader."[484]

It was to be a long time, however, before Western observers began to realize just how deep the split in the Soviet leadership really was.

The restoration of unity in the Kremlin had been achieved at a heavy price. The split between Moscow and Tirana and between Moscow and Peking had been deepened, possibly beyond the possibility of bridging, and for the first time had been openly acknowledged and extended to the international communist movement as a whole. In the field of international relations, the bitter Soviet struggle for power had had the effect of bringing the great powers to the very brink of nuclear catastrophe, where the preservation of peace hung on the fragile thread of the steady nerves of Soviet and American tank crews and their commanding officers. Only a profound belief in the basically peaceful intentions of the Western leaders—the exact opposite of what Khrushchev and other Soviet officials were affirming at the Moscow congress—could have justified this perilous flirting with disaster.

The price for maintaining the pretence of unity in the deeply divided Soviet leadership, therefore, was the projection outward of that division into the major arenas of international relations. It was a price which the entire world had to pay in one form or another.

*   *   *

The remainder of the morning session of the congress on October 28 and the entire evening session which followed can be dealt with in summary form. During this period ten foreign guest speakers addressed the congress, five in the second half of the morning session, five at the conclusion of the evening session. Viewed from the standpoint of their response to the question of Albania, these speakers conformed fairly closely to the pattern established earlier. Like the speakers who had represented the communist parties of Denmark and Norway, those who now took the rostrum on behalf of parties in Sweden and Iceland maintained silence on the Albanian issue. This does not necessarily mean, however, that they intended thereby to signify their disapproval of CPSU policy; we have already seen that the parties of Denmark and Norway subsequently came out in support of Soviet policy, even though the representatives of both parties in their speeches at the congress ignored the Albanian issue. It is noteworthy that the speaker for Sweden (Hilding Hagberg, chairman of the Swedish Communist party), went to unusual lengths in his personal praise of Khrushchev.[485]

Six of the speakers at these two sessions represented Latin American communist parties, and of these only one (Juan Ducoudrai, secretary of the National Socialist Party of the Dominican Republic) failed to support the Soviet position on Albania; all the others (representing parties in Brazil, Costa Rica,

[484]*NYT*, Nov. 8, 1961, p. 2.
[485]*Sten. ot.*, 3: 33.

Peru, El Salvador, and Panama) expressed some form of approval for the Soviet condemnation of the Albanian party leadership.

While these individuals were speaking the protocols indicate Khrushchev's absence by employing the short form of the ritual embrace formula, even though one of them (Paul Vergès, first secretary of the Communist Party of Réunion) appeared to be addressing Khrushchev directly.[486] The height of absurdity was reached at the end of the speech by the final foreign guest speaker, R. Castellanos, secretary of the Panamanian Communist party, who had brought with him a peasant's sombrero to present to Khrushchev as a gift (everyone was familiar with the First Secretary's fondness for exotic headgear) but who, in Khrushchev's absence, was reduced to the meaningless gesture of presenting it to the Presidium of the congress.[487]

The group of foreign guest speakers also included representatives from communist parties in the Sudan and Réunion, both of whom spoke in support of the CPSU in its dispute with the Albanian party leadership.

Turning to the category of CPSU officials, seven *apparatchiki* addressed the congress during these two sessions, each offering both a *compte rendu* for his or her own region and a commentary on Kozlov's report. On the test question of the proposal to expel the leaders of the Antiparty Group, the speeches of these officials faithfully mirrored the split in the party: Three supported the proposal, three avoided taking a stand on it, thus rejecting it, and one straddled the issue by the use of a compromise formula. It will be convenient to consider the speeches of these delegates in the order in which they spoke.

1) IVAN P. KAZANETS (born 1918, party member since 1944), second secretary of the CP Ukraine (since 1960), praised the "colossal importance" of Khrushchev's trips to the Donbas mining region, but maintained silence on the question of expulsion. Kazanets's coolness toward Khrushchev on this issue may be related to the divergence of their professional interests. Trained in the field of ferrous metallurgy, Kazanets had good cause to differ with Khrushchev over the question of economic priorities. (In 1965, after Khrushchev's fall, Kazanets was appointed USSR minister of ferrous metallurgy.)

2) NIKOLAI G. YEGORYCHEV (born 1920, party member since 1942), second secretary of the Moscow gorkom (since February 1961), achieved a record at the Twenty-second Congress by voicing support for *both* the expulsion of the Antiparty Group leaders and the party's condemnation of the Albanian party leadership (the latter issue was clearly not one on which party officials below the Presidium level were required to take a stand). For good measure Yegorychev threw in the only explicit approval forthcoming at the congress for Khrushchev's proposal to erect a monument to innocent party and state officials who had perished in the purges.[488] This tendency to over-

[486]Ibid., p. 103.

[487]Ibid., p. 113.

[488]Ibid., pp. 53–54; *CDSP*, XIV/7, pp. 5–6.

achievement makes Yegorychev a rather interesting figure, and his subsequent party career confirms the impression that he was an impulsive individual inclined to take up extreme positions in support of causes championed by one party leader or another. By the time the Twenty-third CPSU Congress met in March 1966, however, Yegorychev had lost his enthusiasm for bringing the crimes of the Stalin era to the attention of the party.[489] In the reshuffle which followed the Arab defeat in the Six-Day War in June 1967, Yegorychev was ousted from his party job (by that time he had risen to first secretary of the Moscow gorkom), under conditions which indicate that he had made the cardinal error of criticizing the Soviet policies which helped contribute to that debacle.[490] Yegorychev found it difficult to recover from this setback to his career, and his appointment as Soviet ambassador to Denmark in April 1970, indicates that he may have finally sunk into limbo.[491]

3) VASILII S. TOLSTIKOV (born 1917, party member since 1948), second secretary of the Leningrad gorkom (since 1960), spoke only briefly on the subject of the Antiparty Group and made no reference to the proposal for expulsion of its leaders; he said nothing in praise of Khrushchev, but extolled collective leadership and praised the new Party Statutes as a "Leninist" document. This behavior is consistent with Tolstikov's later career, which shows him to have been close politically to F. R. Kozlov, to whom he may have owed his start in the party apparatus.[492]

When Spiridonov lost his post as first secretary of the Leningrad obkom in April 1962, Tolstikov moved up to replace him.[493] He retained this position until September 1970, when he was relieved of his duties at a plenum supervised by M. A. Suslov in order to assume the position of Soviet ambassador to Peking.[494]

4) SALCHAK K. TOKA (born 1901, party member since 1919), first secretary of the Tuva obkom (since 1944), was a veteran non-Russian party organizer in one of the Soviet Union's middle Asian borderlands. Toka had headed the party organization in the Tuva obkom since its establishment in 1944, and before that time had served for twelve years as the first secretary of the Tuva People's Revolutionary party which helped pave the way for the absorption of Tuva into the RSFSR in 1944. This was his first opportunity to address a CPSU congress, and he used the occasion to praise the party's policy on the national question, giving special attention to Khrushchev's sponsorship of the Virgin Lands program, an action which he credited with having transformed Tuva from a grain-importing into a grain-exporting region.[495]

[489]Linden, p. 223.
[490]Victor Zorza in the *Washington Post*, July 2, 1967, p. A-17, and Tatu, p. 533.
[491]*NYT*, Apr. 12, 1970, p. 10.
[492]See Tatu, pp. 223 and 333-34.
[493]Ibid., p. 233.
[494]*NYT*, Sept. 17, 1970, p. 8.
[495]*Sten. ot.*, 3: 76.

The honor of addressing the congress which was extended to Toka probably is to be explained on the ground of the strategic importance of the area he represented rather than his personal stature in the party. A week before the opening of the congress a Soviet government decree had raised the Tuva Autonomous Region to the status of an Autonomous Soviet Socialist Republic, an upgrading which may be related to the developing Sino–Soviet dispute in the sense that it betokened a concern on the part of the Soviet leadership with strengthening the inner-Asian border regions of the USSR.[496] In continuation of this policy a decree of the RSFSR Council of Ministers promulgated on October 25, only a few days before the session at which Toka spoke, provided for economic aid to Tuva in its conversion into an ASSR.[497]

Toka's position on the question of expulsion of the leaders of the Antiparty Group is of special interest not only because he supported the proposal unequivocally but also because of the grounds on which he based his stand. "The draft of the new Party Statutes," Toka pointed out, ". . . quite rightly states: 'Any manifestation of factionalism or clique activity is incompatible with Marxist–Leninist party principles and with party membership.' I agree with the comrades who have proposed expelling these renegades from the party."[498] By citing the draft statutes which Kozlov had introduced to the congress, Toka was in effect implying a reproach to Kozlov for not having applied to the Antiparty Group leaders the penalty explicitly provided by the statutes for the kind of activity in which they had engaged.

It was perhaps to mitigate the effect of the pro-Khrushchev tone of his speech and to take out a little reinsurance that Toka included a passage expressing enthusiastic approval for the "measures adopted by [the Central Committee of the party and the Soviet government] for the strengthening of the defense might of our beloved Motherland."[499] In any case Toka's career was not harmed by his speech; at the end of the congress he was re-elected a candidate member of the Central Committee, and when he turned sixty a few months later he was awarded the Order of Lenin "for his services to the Soviet state."[500]

5) OL'GA P. KOLCHINA (born 1918, party member since 1946), second secretary of the Moscow obkom (since 1960), was the second of two women party officials to address the congress, Mme. Furtseva having been the first. In her speech Mme. Kolchina gave what was perhaps the most thoughtful evaluation offered at the congress of the psychological impact produced by the revelations which had been made there and at the Twentieth Congress in

[496]An RSFSR decree announcing the conversion was passed on Oct. 9, 1961, and confirmed by a USSR decree on the following day. See *Pravda*, Oct. 11, 1961, p. 1; *CDSP*, XIII/41, pp. 29–30. See also *NYT*, Oct. 12, 1961, p. 6.

[497]For a reference to the decree, see Toka's speech, *Sten. ot.*, 3: 78.

[498]*CDSP*, XIV/7, p. 9.

[499]*Sten. ot.*, 3: 74.

[500]*Pravda*, Dec. 15, 1961, p. 2; *CDSP*, XIII/50, p. 28.

1956 about the crimes committed by Stalin and his associates. "It is not easy," Mme. Kolchina said,

> . . . to carry out a reappraisal of certain views, certain concepts. But what became known at the Twentieth Congress of the party about Stalin's cult of personality and its grave consequences, the additional materials and facts about which we have heard here, at this congress, in the reports of comrade N. S. Khrushchev, in the speeches of members of the Presidium of the Central Committee and of many delegates, forces us to abandon completely many old evaluations, ideas, and concepts.
>
> Expressing the will and thoughts of all communists, we unanimously condemn and brand with shame the actions of the antiparty factionalist group and unanimously endorse the opinion of many of the delegates that Molotov, Kaganovich and Malenkov, whose black deeds disgraced the great and bright name of communist, have no place in the Leninist party![501]

Mme. Kolchina thus reacted in the way Khrushchev presumably hoped all the delegates to the congress would, and her reward for this support was election to the position of candidate member of the Central Committee at the end of the congress.

6) VASILII Ye. CHERNYSHEV (born 1908, party member since 1928), first secretary of the Maritime kraikom (since 1959), had passed the early phase of his career in the Belorussian party organization. In his congress speech Chernyshev manifested a distinct aloofness toward Khrushchev, disposing of both the cult of personality and the Antiparty Group in one crisp sentence which omitted any call for expulsion of the group's leaders.[502] Chernyshev expressed gratitude to Khrushchev for his aid to the Maritime krai, but astutely balanced this homage by equal praise for Kozlov's report on the new Party Statutes.[503] When he came to specifying high-ranking party visitors who had visited his remote bailiwick, Chernyshev included not only Khrushchev and Kozlov but also Kosygin, Mikoyan, and Poliansky.[504]

Chernyshev's career data suggest that his patronage ties were with Mazurov (party boss in Belorussia for many years) and Kosygin (at a later period), rather than with either Khrushchev or Kozlov.[505]

In its sharp contrast to the preceding speech by Mme. Kolchina, Chernyshev's congress speech shows the stubborn, unyielding opposition typical of many congress delegates to Khrushchev's efforts to evoke an emotional groundswell with his disclosure of the crimes of Stalin and other former party leaders.

---

[501]*Sten. ot.*, 3: 79; partial translation, *CDSP*, XIV/7, p. 9.

[502]*Sten. ot.*, 3: 86; *CDSP*, XIV/7, p. 10.

[503]*Sten. ot.*, 3: 86–87.

[504]Ibid., p. 89.

[505]See Chernyshev's obituary in *Pravda*, Nov. 14, 1969, p. 3; *CDSP*, XXI/46, p. 27, and Christian Duevel, "Some puzzling thoughts at Chernyshev's tombstone," Radio Liberty dispatch, Nov. 21, 1969.

7) ALEKSANDR V. BASOV (born 1912, party member since 1945), first secretary of the Rostov obkom (since 1960), distinguished himself by inventing new superlatives in praise of Khrushchev: ". . . the outstanding Marxist–Leninist, the ardent fighter for the happiness of the peoples, who has raised to a height never before attained the immortal banner of the great Lenin, comrade N. S. Khrushchev."[506] In rather questionable taste, one would think, after Khrushchev's call for an end to panegyrics addressed to him. But when it came to the test question of expulsion, Basov hedged, taking cover behind the elastic formula previously employed for the same purpose by Kozlov: "We fully support the suggestion voiced by delegates to the congress that the organizers of the antiparty group—Molotov, Malenkov, and Kaganovich, and Shepilov, who joined them—*be called to strict account before the party*."[507] After this, it scarcely mattered that Basov added an additional paragraph of unrestrained praise for Khrushchev's "tireless energy, governmental wisdom, organizational talent, [and] closeness to the people."[508]

The ambivalence of Basov's attitude toward Khrushchev, which his fulsome praise could not entirely hide, was to emerge openly at a plenum of the CPSU Central Committee in early March 1962, when he opposed Khrushchev's advocacy of the maintenance of private garden plots on Soviet collective farms.[509] No doubt as the direct result of this clash, Basov subsequently lost his post as first secretary of the Rostov obkom.[510] Temporarily raised to a higher position after Khrushchev's overthrow (he was appointed RSFSR minister of agriculture in March 1965), Basov held that job for only nine months before being relegated to diplomatic exile by appointment as ambassador to Rumania in December 1965.[511]

To complete our account of the congress sessions held on October 28 we must take note of the speech by one of the party's most important officials, Marshal FILIPP I. GOLIKOV (born 1900, party member since 1918), head of the Main Political Administration (MPA) (since January 1958), the party's watchdog agency charged with ensuring the loyalty and political indoctrination of the Soviet armed forces.

At the outset of his speech Golikov gave a fairly clear indication of his position in the party leadership dispute by mentioning without comment Kozlov's recent visit to armed forces installations in the Soviet Far East and then pointedly following this with a much fuller reference to the travels in the USSR and abroad of Khrushchev, "with all his exceptionally strenuous activity."[512]

[506]*Sten. ot.*, 3: 94.

[507]Ibid., p. 100; *CDSP*, XIV/7, p. 12; emphasis supplied.

[508]*Sten. ot.*, 3: 100.

[509]See Ploss, p. 192.

[510]Ibid., p. 259, citing *Pravda*, Aug. 16, 1962.

[511]Michel Tatu, *Le Pouvoir en U.R.S.S., du Déclin de Khrouchtchev à la Direction Collective* (Paris: Bernard Grasset, 1967), p. 538. Hereinafter cited as Tatu, *Le pouvoir*. The English translation of Tatu's book is defective at this point (Tatu, p. 496).

[512]*Sten. ot.*, 3: 66.

With regard to the party's struggle against the cult of the individual and the Antiparty Group, Golikov asserted that the communists in the armed forces had been "the steadfast support of our Leninist Central Committee," and he assured the congress delegates that they would continue to provide "monolithic support."[513] With soldierly directness Golikov took his stand on the question of expulsion: "The opinion voiced by congress delegates that there is no room in the party for the leaders of the antiparty group I consider to be very well-founded, and I second it."[514]

Golikov went on to give a valuable account of the Central Committee plenum held in late October 1957, at which Marshal G. K. Zhukov was ousted from his position as candidate member of the Presidium on charges of "Bonapartism," and then continued with a description of the changes introduced into the work of the MPA following Zhukov's fall, changes which he himself had been primarily responsible for sponsoring.

In the context of the present study an unusually interesting passage in Golikov's speech was one in which he took up the subject of military relations between the Soviet Union and its Western allies during World War II. Having cited a testimony by Edward R. Stettinius as to the importance of the Soviet war effort for allied victory, Golikov went on to contrast this with a recent statement by a prominent U.S. official: "Mention should be made, I think, of the height of cynicism, the supreme insult to the memory of millions of people who died heroically in the struggle with fascism, in a statement by U.S. Vice President Johnson. Only recently, on August 20, he made bold to say the following in West Berlin, having the German revanchists in mind: 'The Western powers—the U.S.A., France, and Britain—have never had better or more courageous allies'."[515]

Golikov refrained, however, from drawing any far-reaching conclusions about U.S. policies or intentions from this isolated example, and he followed it immediately with further tributes to the Soviet war effort in World War II made by Franklin Roosevelt and Winston Churchill, leaving his audience with the impression of the feasibility and value of military collaboration between the armed forces of the Soviet Union and those of the Western powers. Nowhere in his speech did Golikov allude to existing tension between the Soviets and the West in Berlin, nor did he make any reference to the rearmament measures which had been undertaken by the Soviet government in late August.

The cleansing of the mausoleum (October 30, morning)

Thus far only seven party officials had been given the opportunity to address the congress on the subject of Kozlov's report on the new Party Statutes, as compared with nearly sixty who had spoken on the subject of Khrushchev's

[513]Ibid.; *CDSP*, XIV/7, p. 7.
[514]*CDSP*, XIV/7, p. 7.
[515]Ibid., p. 8.

reports. Clearly, further discussion of the statutes was the logical topic for the next session of the congress, which met on the morning of Monday, October 30. (The delegates took a holiday on Sunday, October 29.)

Instead, the twenty-third session opened with an episode which, as we have already noted, is recognizable on purely formal grounds as an interruption to the normal congress schedule. Five delegates, three of them prominent party officials who had already delivered major reports, joined forces to present a strongly emotional plea for removing the embalmed corpse of Stalin from the Mausoleum on Red Square which it shared with the venerated ashes of Lenin. In a congress marked by unexpected turns and twists, this episode stands out as the most bizarre surprise of all.

At the outset of the twenty-third session the chairman, N. M. Shvernik, announced that "certain delegations" had requested an opportunity to speak. "The Presidium of the congress," Shvernik continued, "has deemed it possible to satisfy these requests."[516]

With this introduction the campaign to cleanse the mausoleum got under way. I. V. SPIRIDONOV, first secretary of the Leningrad obkom, who had been one of the first party officials to speak in the discussion of Khrushchev's reports, led off with a short but hard-hitting speech dealing mainly with the enormous harm done to the Leningrad party organization by the purges carried out in the years after the assassination of Kirov (1934–38) and in the postwar years (1949–50).

Spiridonov declared that the Leningrad obkom delegation ". . . has received the decisions of meetings of the working people of the Kirov Plant (the former Putilov Plant) in Leningrad and the Neva Lenin Machine-Building Plant . . . in which the Leningraders propose that Stalin's remains be moved to another place [*Shouts in the hall: 'Right!' Stormy applause*]."[517] Acting on these suggestions, and speaking "on behalf of the Leningrad party organization and the working people of Leningrad," Spiridonov submitted the proposal ". . . that Stalin's remains be removed from the Vladimir Il'ich Lenin Mausoleum to another place, and this be done as soon as possible [*Shouts in the hall: 'Right!' Stormy, prolonged applause*]."[518]

Spiridonov was followed by P. N. DEMICHEV, first secretary of the Moscow gorkom, who like Spiridonov had been among the first party officials to address the congress. In his first speech Demichev had implied that the struggle against the Antiparty Group was a closed chapter and that no further penalty was required for its leaders (above, p. 336). Demichev's first speech, however, was delivered before the campaign to oust the Antiparty Group leaders had been properly launched, and it is likely that the restraint he displayed on that occasion reflected caution in moving into risky and untested territory rather than lack of conviction. When he addressed the congress for

[516]*Sten. ot.*, 3: 114.
[517]Ibid., p. 115; *CDSP*, XIV/7, p. 12.
[518]*CDSP*, XIV/7, p. 12.

the second time, Demichev showed himself to be one of the most ardent proponents of expulsion for the Antiparty Group leaders.

In the opening sentence of his short speech Demichev announced that the Moscow delegation, on behalf of the communists of the Soviet capital, ". . . wholly and completely supports the proposal of the Leningrad delegation concerning the removal of the sarcophagus with the body of J. V. Stalin from the Mausoleum."[519]

As the principal reason for this action, Demichev cited Khrushchev's "Concluding Remarks," thus indicating that Khrushchev had achieved some success in his efforts to shock the delegates into dramatic action condemning Stalin's crimes. To show that the proposal enjoyed grass-roots support, Demichev cited a resolution to this effect which he said had been "unanimously adopted [at] a meeting of the workers, engineers, and technicians of the Vladimir Il'ich plant," and added, "Many such resolutions could be cited."[520] Spiridonov, too, had referred to meetings held in factories at which the workers had advanced the proposal to remove Stalin's body from the mausoleum, a fact which helps substantiate a rumor which Tatu reports as having circulated on the preceding day (Sunday, October 29), "that such a proposal had been made at factory meetings in Moscow."[521]

The third speaker in the discussion on the mausoleum was not a party official but a member of the governmental hierarchy, GIVI D. DZHAVA-KHISHVILI (born 1912, party member since 1940), chairman of the Council of Ministers of the Georgian SSR (since 1953). (It is true that Dzhavakhishvili had served earlier in the party apparatus, but in the post-Stalin years his work had been mainly in the government.) From the standpoint of political strategy, it was, of course, highly desirable that the campaign to remove Stalin's body should receive the support of a prominent political figure from the dead dictator's home territory, Georgia. The logical and most authoritative candidate for this purpose would have been the first secretary of the Georgian CP, V. P. Mzhavanadze. Mzhavanadze is sometimes regarded as having been a protégé and follower of Khrushchev, on the strength of his long years of service in the Ukrainian party organization at a time when Khrushchev was party boss in that republic. Mzhavanadze's speech to the congress (above, pp. 346–47), however, showed that he felt little warmth toward the First Secretary, and his failure to join the campaign to throw out Stalin's corpse reinforces this impression. Like many older party stalwarts, Mzhavanadze was inclined to be nostalgic for the good old days of Stalinism, a fact which no doubt contributed to his estrangement from Khrushchev.

In his brief speech Dzhavakhishvili added fresh details about the harmful effects of Stalin's purges, identifying by name some half dozen party officials in Georgia whom it had been necessary to rehabilitate posthumously,

---

[519]*Sten. ot.*, 3: 116.

[520]*CDSP*, XIV/7, p. 13.

[521]Tatu, *Le Pouvoir*, p. 164. The translation is defective at this point (Tatu, p. 158).

and referring without elaboration to the "Mingrelian case," which despite the obscurity which still hangs over it, he described as "known to everyone."[522] The Georgian party organization, he said, "fully approves and supports the proposals of the Leningrad and Moscow delegations on moving Stalin's remains from the mausoleum to some other place."[523]

For their fourth speaker the organizers of the campaign to cleanse the mausoleum came up with a surprise, an obscure figure from the party's past named DORA A. LAZURKINA (party member since 1902), a pensioner who belonged to the Leningrad party organization. As one who had known Lenin personally in the years before the revolution, Mme. Lazurkina opened with reminiscences of her encounters with Lenin in Geneva, which, she said, had made her feel "as if I had grown wings."[524] Moving ahead to the years of the Great Purge, Mme. Lazurkina described the circumstances under which she, as a member of the Leningrad obkom in 1937, had been arrested and imprisoned after having tried in vain to defend the party loyalty of a fellow Old Bolshevik who had been denounced by Andrei Zhdanov, at that time party boss in Leningrad. Through seventeen years of exile, she said, she had maintained faith in Stalin, but this faith was finally shattered at the time of the Twentieth Party Congress in 1956 when for the first time she "learned the hard truth about Stalin."[525]

In her analysis of the harm Stalin had done the party, Mme. Lazurkina showed herself to be a sensitive and perceptive observer of the changes which overtook the Leninist norms of party life under Stalin. "The great evil caused by Stalin," she said, ". . . consists not only in the fact that many of our best people perished, not only in the fact that arbitrary actions were committed and innocent people were shot and imprisoned without trial. This was not all. The entire atmosphere that was created in the party at that time was totally at variance with the spirit of Lenin. It was out of harmony with the spirit of Lenin."[526] Graphically Mme. Lazurkina described the conditions which existed in the party in 1937, the year the Great Purge took on its mass character: "Fear, which was uncharacteristic of us Leninists, prevailed. People slandered one another, they lost their faith, they even slandered themselves. Lists of innocent people who were to be arrested were drawn up. We were beaten so that we would slander others. We were given these lists and forced to sign them. They promised to release us and threatened: 'If you don't sign, we'll torture you!'"[527]

When Mme. Lazurkina went on to support the proposal to remove Stalin's body from the mausoleum, Khrushchev himself broke in to shout, "Right!,"[528] thereby revealing the intense personal interest he took in the proceedings.

[522]*Sten. ot.*, 3: 118; *CDSP*, XIV/7, p. 13.
[523]*CDSP*, XIV/7, p. 13.
[524]Ibid.
[525]Ibid.
[526]Ibid.
[527]Ibid.
[528]Ibid., p. 14.

Mme. Lazurkina saved her most sensational effect for the end. "Comrades," she said, ". . . I have always carried Il'ich [Lenin] in my heart, always, in the most difficult moments. The only reason I survived is that Il'ich was in my heart, and I sought his advice, as it were [*applause*]. Yesterday I asked Il'ich for advice and it was as if he stood before me alive and said: 'I do not like being next to Stalin, who inflicted so much harm on the party.' [*stormy, prolonged applause*]."[529]

Historians have always been interested in tracing the obscure process whereby a religious belief grows up around the cult of a dead hero, and for the light it casts on this problem Mme. Lazurkina's speech deserves a place in any history of the Soviet Communist party. More noteworthy for our present purposes was her disclosure that the séance at which she had consulted Lenin's spirit took place "yesterday," i.e., Sunday, October 29—another indication that the campaign to "cleanse" the mausoleum was a hurriedly improvised affair, the organizers of which took advantage of the break in the congress schedule caused by the end of the week.

To bring the mausoleum "cleansing" operation to a quick and successful close, N. V. PODGORNY, first secretary of the Ukrainian CP, in his second congress speech introduced a formal resolution on behalf of the Leningrad and Moscow delegations and the communist parties of the Ukraine and Georgia providing (1) that the mausoleum in Red Square should henceforward be designated "the Vladimir Il'ich Lenin Mausoleum," and (2) that the continued retention there of Stalin's sarcophagus should be recognized as "unsuitable, . . . since the serious violations by Stalin of Lenin's behests, the abuses of power, the mass repressions against Soviet people and other actions in the period of the cult of the individual make it impossible to leave the coffin with his body in the V. I. Lenin Mausoleum."[530]

Shvernik, as the presiding officer at the session, immediately put Podgorny's motion to a vote by show of cards, and it was carried unanimously.[531] Tatu's comment on the vote is apt: "It is true that everyone voted for it, including the members of the Presidium; but, in a public meeting there was hardly any alternative, short of violating a tradition of several decades' standing."[532]

By the use of emotional shock tactics, therefore, the small group of those advocating "cleansing" of the mausoleum, who obviously enjoyed Khrushchev's lively support, had achieved a symbolic triumph over the dead Stalin. That Khrushchev's purpose in the appeal to the delegates' emotions was to strengthen his disciplinary powers as well as to reinforce the lesson of the party's condemnation of Stalin's cult of personality is indicated by the position taken by the ten party members who addressed the twenty-third session *after* the vote on the mausoleum. As Table 7 indicates, nine out of ten of the speak-

[529]Ibid.
[530]Ibid.
[531]*Sten. ot.*, 3: 123.
[532]Tatu, p. 158.

Table 7.   Speakers at Morning Session, October 30

Speaker	Position on Ex-pulsion of Leaders of Antiparty Group	Position on Removal of Stalin's Body
A. V. Georgiev (first secretary, Altai kraikom)	supports proposal	supports proposal
N. N. Rodionov (second secretary, CP Kazakhstan)	supports proposal	supports proposal
A. I. Shibaev (first secretary, Saratov obkom)	supports proposal	supports proposal
P. A. Leonov (secretary, Sakhalin obkom)	supports proposal	maintains silence
Z. T. Serdiuk (first deputy chairman, Party Control Committee)	supports proposal	supports proposal
Yu. M. Vecherova (worker, Ivanovo)	supports proposal	supports proposal
F. S. Goriachev (first secretary, Novosibirsk obkom)	supports proposal	supports proposal
S. N. Shchetinin (first secretary, Irkutsk obkom)	supports proposal	maintains silence
V. I. Gubanov (kolkhoz party secretary)	supports proposal	supports proposal
V. A. Kochetov (editor, *Oktiabr'*)	maintains silence	maintains silence

ers on this occasion, most of whom represented party committees, supported the demand for expulsion of the Antiparty Group leaders, while seven out of ten also expressed approval of the proposal for the removal of Stalin's body (for which *all* the delegates at the session had just voted). This was a higher percentage of speakers in support of the proposal for expulsion of the Anti-party Group leaders than had been achieved at any earlier session of the congress.

With the adoption of the vote on the mausoleum, the general level of interest in congress speeches drops off sharply, and we can omit detailed analysis of most of the speeches presented at the session. Three of the speeches, however, deserve attention for the light they cast on the struggle for power in the party, as well as on other matters.

The political career of NIKOLAI N. RODIONOV (born 1915, party member since 1944), second secretary of the Kazakhstan Communist party (since January 1960), presents a complex pattern which has given rise to sharply conflicting evaluations of his political affiliation among Western analysts. The basic facts are not in dispute: Rodionov received his technical training in the field of ferrous metallurgy and spent most of the 1940's, including the war years, working as an engineer-technician in the Magnitogorsk metallurgical combine and in a Leningrad research institute. From 1948 to 1960 he held posts in the Leningrad party organization, rising to the post of first secretary of the Leningrad gorkom during the period 1957–60. In mid-January 1961, however, he was transferred to the Kazakh CP organization as its second secretary; the plenum of the Kazakh CP Central Committee at which this "election" was formalized was supervised by Leonid I. Brezhnev, at that time in charge of cadre assignments in the Union Republics as a member of the Secretariat. (Brezhnev was released from this post at the Central Committee plenum in mid-July 1960, and was replaced by F. R. Kozlov.)

Rodionov remained in the Kazakhstan party post until late December 1962, when he was relieved of his duties "in connection with another assignment" at a plenum supervised by Kozlov. He was next heard from back in Leningrad, as deputy chairman of the Leningrad Council of the National Economy (sovnarkhoz). His readmittance to the party apparatus came in October 1965, when he was elected first secretary of the Cheliabinsk obkom. It was as a delegate from that organization that he attended the Twenty-third CPSU Congress in March 1966, where his solid standing in the party was indicated both by the opportunity afforded him to address the congress[533] and by his promotion to full membership in the Central Committee.

Rodionov's 1966 congress speech, which was marked by outspoken praise for Brezhnev and support of his policies as first secretary, provides a useful clue to his party loyalties. The problem has raised some difficulties, primarily because of Rodionov's long association with the Leningrad party organization and his background in ferrous metallurgy. Since these two traits, especially in combination, usually serve as reliable pointers to a patron-client relationship with F. R. Kozlov for the period of the 1950's and early 1960's, a number of Western analysts have assumed that Rodionov was a supporter of Kozlov, and have interpreted his career on that basis. Before offering a different solution of the problem, it will be useful to look at the substance of Rodionov's 1961 congress speech.

The most noteworthy aspect of the speech was not its mawkishly lyrical praise of Khrushchev (a characteristic passage read, "The party knows

---

[533]*XXIII S"ezd Kommunisticheskoi Partii Sovetskogo Soiuza 29 marta–8 aprelia 1966 goda. Stenograficheskii otchet*, 2 vols. (Moscow: Politizdat, 1966), 1: 598–604.

that where comrade Khrushchev is, there is truth and progress, life and happiness"), nor his assertion, outdoing even Mme. Lazurkina, that Lenin was "literally alive, standing before us, calling [us] to follow him," but the unusual vigor with which he renewed the assault on the Antiparty Group. In his indictment of the group Rodionov left no room for compromise:

> The participants in the antiparty group have been called dogmatists. This is correct. But what they tried to do in June 1957 was not dogmatism. It was banditry, it was robbery in broad daylight. And for robbery it is necessary to answer with the full severity of the law. They were preparing to inflict a grievous wound on the party, they had set their sights on the very heart of the people—on the Leninist leadership of the Central Committee. This cannot be forgiven them. Molotov, Kaganovich, and Malenkov, about whose base actions delegates to the congress have spoken with such anger, used their presence in the Presidium of the Central Committee not in the interests of the party but in order to satisfy their own selfish, careerist lust. They have absolutely nothing in common ideologically with the party; the hands of these adventurists are stained with the sacred blood of the best sons of the people.[534]

Rodionov continued with a bitter, highly personal attack on Voroshilov (the only member of the Antiparty Group actually present at the congress), whom he warned against misinterpreting the "magnanimity" shown him by the party: ". . . we all want Comrade Voroshilov to understand and evaluate this as pardon granted him by the party and not as an underestimation of his sins. Comrade Voroshilov was in the same den with the antiparty beast, and he did not stray in there by accident, as he has tried to make out in his statement to the congress. One can err on certain particular questions, although even this is not good, but one cannot err when it is a matter of the fate of the party and of its honor."[535]

In drawing a picture of what would have happened if the Antiparty Group had been victorious, Rodionov went further than any previous speaker: ". . . we are all aware that if the antiparty group had gained the upper hand in June 1957, they would not have reckoned with either age or past services, and many delegates to the congress would have been missing from this hall today. Cruel new repressions would have befallen our party, and many devoted communists would have been thrown in prison and destroyed. A victory of the antiparty group promised terrible calamities."[536]

For having saved the party from these calamities, said Rodionov, "we delegates to the Twenty-second Congress . . . say again and again: Thank you, a big thank you to Nikita Sergeevich Khrushchev for the great courage he has displayed in defending the interests of the party."

On the question of expulsion, Rodionov was explicit: "Proceeding from the Leninist instructions concerning the necessity of protecting the firmness,

[534]*Sten. ot.*, 3:130; *CDSP*, XIV/7, pp. 14–15.

[535]Ibid., p. 15.

[536]Ibid.

steadfastness and purity of the party and *from the provision in the draft of the new Statutes that any manifestation of factionalism and clique activity is incompatible with Marxist-Leninist party spirit and with membership in the party*, we declare: There is no room for the antiparty group in our glorious Communist Party."[537] Thus Rodionov, like Toka the night before, cited the new Party Statutes as the basis for the demand for expulsion of the Antiparty Group leaders, an implicit reproof to Kozlov who had failed to make this connection in his report to the congress. It is noteworthy, incidentally, that on the few occasions when Rodionov cited Kozlov by name in his speech, he added nothing by way of praise or commendation.

Rodionov was equally forthright on the question of "cleansing" the mausoleum: "Comrade delegates! The delegation of the Kazakhstan party organization, together with the entire congress, ardently supports *the proposal of the Leningraders* that Stalin's body be removed from the mausoleum. This is correct. Stalin's remains should not profane *the sacred feelings people experience when they come to see Lenin* [*applause*]. Justice demands that Stalin's remains be moved to another place. This reflects the view of all communists."[538]

The partisan vigor of Rodionov's attack on the Antiparty Group, on Voroshilov, and on Stalin, makes the correct identification of his political loyalties a matter of some importance for the correct understanding of the relationship of forces in the struggle for power in the party. If he was a client of Kozlov, as Sidney Ploss, for example, assumes,[539] then his congress speech would force us to modify sharply the view of Kozlov's own position on these matters which we have presented.[540]

Taking into account Rodionov's career as a whole, his attitude toward Kozlov can be recognized as one of mutual hostility rather than patronage and support. It is true that the two men served together for a number of years in the Leningrad party organization, but Rodionov's transfer from that organization to the Kazakhstan CP in January 1960 was in no sense a promotion, while his removal from the Kazakhstan job in December 1962—at Kozlov's instigation—was unmistakably a demotion. Not until after Kozlov's death, in December 1964, was the way open for Rodionov's re-entry into the party apparatus.

Clearly, then, the ups and downs of Rodionov's career do not indicate a harmonious working relationship between him and Kozlov. Rodionov's strong support for Brezhnev at the 1966 congress, and Brezhnev's presence at the Kazakhstan CP plenum in January 1960 which elected him second secretary, point toward the solution of the problem. Whatever his original relationship

---

[537] Ibid.; emphasis supplied.

[538] Ibid.; emphasis supplied.

[539] Ploss, p. 181, says of Rodionov that his "professional training and career background linked him with Kozlov," and on p. 254 characterizes him as a "Kozlovite."

[540] Similarly Robert Conquest, *Russia After Khrushchev* (New York: Praeger, 1965), p. 156, identifies Rodionov as a member of the "Leningrad machine under Kozlov." Linden, p. 124, more cautiously calls Rodionov "a figure with connections in high places."

with Kozlov may have been, it is clear that by early 1960 the two men were no longer allies. The appointment to the Kazakhstan party post, with Brezhnev's assistance, introduced a new patron for Rodionov, to whom he subsequently rendered support. The dismissal from his Kazakhstan post in December 1962 came at a time when Kozlov was strongly reasserting his influence in party appointments.[541]

As to the reason for Rodionov's hostility to Kozlov, it may have had its origin in Kozlov's participation in the Leningrad Case. Rodionov's strong emotional rejection of purges in general is clear from his 1961 congress speech. It may also be relevant that one of the prominent victims in the Leningrad case was M. I. Rodionov, whose ouster from the post of chairman of the Council of Ministers of the RSFSR was reported by *Izvestiia* on March 13, 1949.[542]

In a number of respects the speech by ZINOVII R. SERDIUK (born 1903, party member since 1925), first deputy chairman of the Party Control Committee (probably since May 1961), reads like a continuation and extension of Khrushchev's "Concluding Remarks." Revealing a firsthand knowledge of the party archives, Serdiuk cited unpublished documents directly implicating Molotov and Kaganovich in the mass repressions carried out during the Great Purge, and strengthened Khrushchev's hints at high-level connivance in the assassination of Kirov. As we have seen, Serdiuk supported the proposals for expulsion of the Antiparty Group leaders and for the removal of Stalin's corpse. It appears likely that if Khrushchev had been able to arrange for Serdiuk's appointment as chairman of the Party Control Committee instead of merely its first deputy chairman, under Shvernik, the expulsion of Molotov, Malenkov, and Kaganovich would have been carried out without delay.

The final speaker at the twenty-third session was a hard-line writer, VSEVOLOD A. KOCHETOV (born 1912, party member since 1944), editor-in-chief of the neo-Stalinist literary journal, *Oktiabr'*.[543]

Kochetov had already defined his position, both on questions of literary criticism and on Soviet policy vis-à-vis the West, before he spoke at the congress. In the aftermath of the U–2 crisis in May 1960, for example, he had contributed an article to *Pravda* criticizing as naive the policy of seeking better relations with the United States, and had gone so far as to apply the term "simpleton" to those who believed in the goodwill of President Eisenhower, a criticism which all too obviously could be applied to Khrushchev.[544]

[541]For a valuable analysis of Rodionov's career in the light of the feud between Kozlov and Brezhnev, see Tatu, pp. 514–15.

[542]Robert Conquest, *Power and Policy in the U.S.S.R. The Study of Soviet Dynasties* (New York: St. Martin's Press, 1961), p. 95. I do not know whether the two Rodionovs were related.

[543]The date of Kochetov's appointment to this position is uncertain. Tatu, p. 65, dates it to "the beginning of 1961." According to *Sten. ot.*, 3: 181, L. N. Yefremov introduced Kochetov as "writer, editor-in-chief of the journal *Oktiabr'*," but in the list of delegates (ibid., p. 451), Kochetov's occupation is given simply as "writer."

[544]Tatu, pp. 65–66.

Against this background it should come as no surprise that Kochetov's congress speech was an unyielding defense of the hard-line position in literature, coupled with a blanket indictment of the contemporary literature of the West as "bedroom-and-brandy literary rubbish," or that he failed to support either the proposal for expulsion of the Antiparty Group leaders or the proposal for the removal of Stalin's body. Taken as a whole, Kochetov's speech is fully consistent with a comment by Tatu: "In Moscow literary circles, Kozlov was spoken of as Kochetov's protector."[545]

It would probably be a mistake, nevertheless, to read any special significance into the fact that the final speaker in the congress discussion was a follower of Kozlov, thus bringing that part of the congress's work to a close on a distinctly anti-Khrushchev note. The fact is that by the time Kochetov finished speaking it was already well into the afternoon (the abnormal length of the twenty-third session was obviously due to the insertion at its outset of the discussion about the mausoleum). According to L. N. Yefremov, who presided over the second half of the session, sixty-five delegates had requested permission to address the congress in the discussion on Kozlov's report, and although only eighteen had done so thus far, Yefremov introduced a motion to end the discussion at that point, a motion which was promptly carried by unanimous vote. Kozlov himself, Yefremov indicated, had waived his right to deliver a concluding speech.[546]

It was unusual for the chairmanship of a congress session to change hands after an intermission, as was the case in the twenty-third session. Shvernik, however, who presided over the first half of the session, was a member of the Presidium, and this may well have been the reason why a substitute had to be found for him after the intermission. Khrushchev, as we have seen, made his presence known during the first half of the session by an interjection during the speech by Mme. Lazurkina, but the protocols provide no evidence for his presence during the second half. A meeting of the party leadership at this time would appear logical in view of the urgent need to prepare for the election to the new Central Committee and other party bodies which was the sole item on the agenda for the evening of October 30.

The elections to the party's central bodies and changes in the party leadership (October 30, evening, and October 31, morning and evening)

The twenty-fourth session of the congress, on the evening of October 30, was a closed one, at which the delegates cast their votes for the new Central Committee and Central Auditing Commission of the party. The results of the voting were presented the next morning by P. N. Demichev. Following the reading of their names, Khrushchev in a brief statement congratulated the newly elected party officials, hailed the "unity and monolithic solidarity" of

[545]Ibid., footnote, p. 282.
[546]*Sten. ot.*, 3: 189.

the party, and assured the delegates that the new Central Committee would exert every effort to justify the confidence of the party and of the people.

It is not possible to present here a detailed analysis of the composition of the new central party bodies, valuable though such an analysis would be for the light it would throw on political currents in the party. From the standpoint of Khrushchev's position it will be sufficient to point out that it was the Central Committee elected at the Twenty-second Congress which sustained the action by the conspiratorial faction which ousted Khrushchev from power in October 1964, thus forming a striking contrast to the events of June 1957, when a plenum of the CC which had been elected at the Twentieth Congress in 1956 sustained Khrushchev in his battle against the coalition headed by Molotov, Malenkov, and Kaganovich.[547]

The real pay-off in the internal struggle for power in the party came at the evening session of October 31, the final session of the congress, when Khrushchev announced the composition of the new Presidium, Secretariat, and other central organs. Despite his apparent satisfaction, the results added up to a setback for him and a gain for Kozlov and his allies. In the Presidium, Khrushchev lost three faithful supporters: Ignatov, Mukhitdinov, and Mme. Furtseva. In the Secretariat, Kozlov himself made the greatest gain, winning official recognition as second-in-command, directly under Khrushchev, and thus by official acknowledgement the next in line of succession.

The other changes in the Secretariat reflect a complicated process of bargaining, with gains for one faction balanced more or less adequately by those of another. The old Secretariat, which had emerged from the changes of the spring and summer of 1960, was composed of five men: Khrushchev, Kozlov, Kuusinen, Mukhitdinov, and Suslov. One of these men—Mukhitdinov —was dropped, thus making it abundantly clear that his ouster from the Presidium represented a real disgrace, not merely a readjustment of functions. Five new secretaries were added, making the new Secretariat almost double the size of the old. On the face of it the new men appeared to represent a gain for Khrushchev. Two of the newcomers, Demichev and Il'ichev, are clearly to be regarded as Khrushchev supporters at this time, and a third, Spiridonov, had performed useful services for Khrushchev at the congress in his attack on the Antiparty Group and his strong support for the removal of Stalin's body. Despite Spiridonov's Leningrad connections, therefore, Khrushchev may well have regarded him at this time as a dependable follower; it is true that certain ambiguities and hesitancies in the position taken by Spiridonov at the congress might suggest that his loyalties were divided and that his Leningrad-heavy-industry background really made him more of a Kozlovite than a Khrushchevite. But the disclosure of Spiridonov's true political allegiance lay six months in the future at the time of the Twenty-second Congress.

The position of Shelepin, another new member of the Secretariat, was ambiguous. His appointment, in December 1958, as chief of the secret police

---

[547]For a directly contrary view, see Tatu, p. 188.

was generally regarded abroad as evidence that Khrushchev was putting in his own hand-picked man to ensure reliable control of this vitally important power center. Taking the long view of Shelepin's career, however, one can see that he had been playing a double game all along, in which apparent loyalty to Khrushchev masked an active policy of sabotaging his foreign policy initiatives and building up positions of strength from which eventually to challenge and overthrow him.

The one unmistakably non-Khrushchev or even anti-Khrushchev appointee to the new Secretariat was Boris Ponomarev, a party ideologist who was Suslov's inseparable companion and associate. With Ponomarev an almost overt oppositionist, and with Spiridonov and Shelepin likely to oppose Khrushchev on key issues, the gains for the First Secretary in the Secretariat were more apparent than real.

The Party Program, Statutes, and other documents adopted at the congress

It was through intensive study of the documents adopted at the Twenty-second Congress that Western analysts first came to recognize that the congress did not, as was widely believed at the time, represent a routine political victory for Khrushchev, but, on the contrary, signified a defeat for him. Since the task of analyzing the party documents has already been performed adequately by a number of scholars, it will not be necessary to go into the problem in detail, especially since the results of the study are fully compatible with the analysis which has been presented here.

The characteristic common to nearly all the documents adopted by the congress is the modification or abandonment of policy innovations which can be identified as representing the views of Khrushchev on a number of key issues of internal and foreign policy. These changes fall into four major categories: (1) those concerned with questions of Soviet economic policy, especially the problem of resource allocation; (2) those concerned with the struggle for power in the party, including the question of Stalin's cult of personality, the mass repressions during the purges, and the Antiparty Group; (3) those concerned with the split in the international communist movement resulting from the Soviet–Albanian and Soviet–Chinese disputes; and (4) those concerned with Soviet policy toward the West. A few examples from each category will illustrate the prevailing trend.

1) The question of economic priorities[548]

In the draft of the Party Program as published in *Pravda* on July 30, 1961, the party's position on the role of heavy industry in the Soviet economy was defined as follows: "The CPSU will continue to give unflagging attention to

---

[548]For a thorough and highly illuminating discussion of this problem and its historical background, see ibid., pp. 164–75.

the growth of heavy industry, which ensures the development of the country's productive forces and defense capacity. *In the new period of the Soviet Union's development*, heavy industry must so grow that on the basis of technological progress it can ensure the expansion of branches of the economy producing consumer goods in order to meet ever more fully the requirements of the people."[549]

Note the key Khrushchev concept that the Soviet economy has entered a "new period," in which the principal function of heavy industry becomes the expansion of those sectors of industry producing goods for the consumer. Now observe how this concept has been eliminated in the official text of the party program as adopted by the Twenty-second Congress: "The CPSU will continue to give unflagging attention to the growth of heavy industry *and its technical progress. The chief task of heavy industry is to ensure fully the needs of the country's defense* and the development of branches of the economy producing consumer goods in order to satisfy better and more fully the requirements of the people, the vital needs of Soviet man, and to ensure the development of the country's productive forces."[550]

Not only has the concept of a "new period" been eliminated, but the further development of heavy industry "and its technical progress" has been assigned an absolute value. Foremost in the list of functions of heavy industry, in the final text, is the satisfaction of military production, with consumer goods relegated to a secondary position (to have eliminated it entirely would have been too crass a demonstration of the anti-Khrushchev bias which underlay the revision of the program, as well as poor public relations).

The significance of the elimination of the "new period" concept has been well analyzed by Carl Linden: "He [Khrushchev] had used the idea as the underpinning for his arguments that the time was ripe for redefining the roles of heavy and light industry and for reorienting heavy industry itself more and more toward consumer goals."[551]

Closely related to this setback for Khrushchev on the role of heavy industry was the addition of a paragraph to the party statutes providing that one of the duties of every party member was "... *to help in every way to strengthen the defense might of the U.S.S.R.*, to wage a tireless struggle for peace and friendship among peoples."[552] By this addition the advocates of an unrestricted Soviet arms build-up succeeded in making support of this policy the binding duty of each party member. At the same time the addition provided a retrospective justification of the Soviet military measures of late August, including the resumption of nuclear testing. By making support of this policy a party duty, the congress put a formidable new obstacle in the path of Khrushchev's efforts to readjust Soviet budgetary expenditures for the benefit of agriculture and the consumer.

[549]*CSP IV*, p. 16; emphasis supplied.
[550]Ibid., pp. 15–16; emphasis supplied.
[551]Linden, pp. 130–31.
[552]*CSP IV*, p. 35; emphasis supplied.

2) The question of power relationships in the party

Khrushchev's drive to enhance his disciplinary powers had ended in failure. Despite all the evidence presented to it about the crimes committed by Stalin and the Antiparty Group, the Twenty-second Congress had failed to approve the proposal for the group leaders' expulsion from the party. Backed by the moderates in the party leadership, the opponents of Khrushchev on this issue were able to prevent him from bringing it to a direct vote at the congress; if he had succeeded in this maneuver, his success with the proposal to re-bury Stalin's corpse might well have been repeated.

In the resolution adopted by the congress on Khrushchev's report for the Central Committee, the problem of the Antiparty Group was treated as a closed issue: "Having cast aside the unprincipled factionalists, plotters and careerists, the party closed ranks still more tightly, strengthened its ties with the people and mobilized all its forces for the successful implementation of its general line."[553] The resolution said nothing about the crimes committed by Stalin, resorting to euphemisms the strongest of which, as Tatu has pointed out,[554] were "abuse of power," "mistakes," "distortions," and "methods alien to the spirit of Leninism."[555] It also firmly closed the door on any further investigation of the circumstances surrounding the assassination of Kirov and other guilty secrets from the party's bloody past by stating flatly that, "The party has told the people *the whole truth* about the abuses of power in the period of the cult of the individual."[556] This statement was in striking contrast to Khrushchev's promise, in his "Concluding Remarks" on October 27, that "as long as we continue to work we can and must find out many things and tell the truth to the party and people,"[557] as well as to Serdiuk's assertion that the investigation of the Kirov assassination "has not yet been completed."[558]

As to the crimes of the members of the Antiparty Group, the resolution limited itself to condemning their resistance to the innovations in party policy introduced at the Twentieth Party Congress. Voroshilov, whom Khrushchev and others had identified as a full member of the group, was not included in the list of members given in the congress resolution, but instead was credited with having helped the party by his switch at the time of the June 1957 CC plenum; no mention was made of Khrushchev's attack on him at the congress or of his own confession.[559]

3) The question of international communist relations

Khrushchev failed to carry the congress with him in his condemnation of the Albanian party leadership and his linking of the Soviet–Albanian dispute

[553]Ibid., p. 226.
[554]Tatu, p. 155.
[555]*CSP IV*, p. 226.
[556]Ibid.; emphasis supplied.
[557]Ibid., p. 197.
[558]Ibid., p. 217.
[559]See Linden, pp. 126, 128–29, and Tatu, pp. 155–56.

with the conflict between Moscow and Peking. The evidence on this point is cogently summed up by Carl Linden:

> It [the congress resolution] failed to second Khrushchev's public exposure of the Peking–Tirana alliance or his condemnation of the Albanian leaders as beyond redemption. Instead it referred to Khrushchev's original call to the Albanian leaders to return to unity, which had explicit Central Committee approval. Further, the resolution did not repeat the defense of the propriety of the public attack on the Albanians given by Khrushchev and others and which was a clear rebuff of Chou En-lai's complaint on this score. Incorporation of this challenge to the Chinese in the resolution would have amounted to putting the whole authority of the Congress behind it. Moreover, the resolution avoided repeating the charges of nationalism, "sectarianism" and "dogmatism" raised against the Albanians at the congress sessions. It simply criticized them for "erroneous views" and actions counter to the 1957 and 1960 Communist conferences and dubbed these views as "dissident."[560]

4) The question of Soviet–Western relations

The degree to which Khrushchev failed to carry the congress and the party with him can be gauged most fully from those sections of the resolution adopted by the congress on his report for the Central Committee which deal with questions of Soviet foreign policy. In one paragraph the resolution set forth an unimpeachable Khrushchevian position:

> As a result of the fundamental shift in favor of socialism in the balance of forces in the world arena, the policy of peaceful coexistence of states with different social systems has acquired an even firmer foundation. The principle of the peaceful coexistence of states with different social systems, which was enunciated by V. I. Lenin and constitutes the basis of the Soviet Union's foreign policy, has won broad recognition as the way to preserve peace and prevent a new world war. Under present circumstances there is a prospect of ensuring peaceful coexistence over the entire period within which the social and political problems today dividing mankind should find their solution. The situation is so developing that even before the complete victory of socialism on earth, while capitalism remains in part of the world, it will actually be possible to exclude world war from the life of society.[561]

This formulation, however, was immediately followed and largely nullified by a bellicose paragraph which left virtually no room for accommodation or rapprochement between the Soviet Union and the West. (It is noteworthy that nowhere did the resolution refer to Khrushchev's move toward a relaxation of tension in Berlin by dropping the deadline on a peace treaty

---

[560]Linden, pp. 132–33. For the passage on Albania in the congress resolution, see *CSP IV*, p. 222.

[561]*CSP IV*, p. 223.

with Germany, or to his references to the possibility of fruitful negotiations between the Soviet Union and the Western powers over Germany.)

"At the same time," the resolution stated,

> . . . it must be remembered that the foreign policy of the imperialist states is shaped by the class interests of monopoly capital, in which aggression and war are organically inherent. As long as imperialism lasts, there will be soil for aggressive wars. *International imperialism, American imperialism above all, represents the chief danger to world peace. It is making preparations for the most ghastly crime against mankind—a thermonuclear world war.* The imperialists have created a dangerous situation in the center of Europe, threatening war in response to the proposal of the Soviet Union and other peace-loving countries that an end be put to the vestiges of the Second World War, a German peace treaty concluded and the status of West Berlin normalized. The forces of reaction have time and again placed world peace in jeopardy in recent years, and they have not ceased their attempts to exacerbate the international situation and bring mankind to the brink of war. *A higher degree of vigilance than ever is today demanded of the peoples.*[562]

The anti-Khrushchev, anti-Western temper of the congress in the field of foreign policy was reflected most clearly in the following paragraph of the resolution, which explicitly sanctioned the recent measures of military build-up taken by the Soviet government: "The congress considers the measures taken by the Central Committee and the Soviet Government for further strengthening our homeland's defense capacity to be *timely, sound, and necessary.* As long as imperialist aggressors exist, we must be on the alert, keep our powder dry, and improve the defenses of the socialist countries [and of] their armed forces."[563]

Taken in conjunction with the corresponding changes in the program and statutes, as well as with the enhancement of Kozlov's stature in the party leadership, this section of the resolution reveals the true character of the congress and makes plain Khrushchev's failure either to win support for his policies or to consolidate his position.

The withering away of the Berlin crisis

With the conclusion of the Twenty-second Congress the way was finally clear for the dying away of the Berlin crisis of 1961. The Soviet game had been played out to its ultimate conclusion: the threat to the viability of East Germany had been removed by the building of the Berlin Wall; the series of Soviet nuclear tests had been carried out with only minor modifications; there had even been a direct military confrontation in Berlin for the benefit of the hard-liners in the Soviet leadership.

---

[562]Ibid.; emphasis supplied.
[563]Ibid.; emphasis supplied.

In the formulation of Soviet foreign policy, therefore, Khrushchev was now freed of the constraints which had been imposed by the collective leadership on his freedom of action. This release was not accompanied, however, by any strengthening of his internal political position; on the contrary, the new power structure in the leading bodies of the CPSU, established at the end of the Twenty-second Congress, represented additional limitations on his power. As to Berlin, there had been no solution of the problem, nor meaningful negotiations between the Soviets and the Western powers. At a more fundamental level, the question of the Soviet–American strategic balance remained unresolved.

Nothing had really been settled, therefore, either in the international conflict over Berlin or in the internal struggle for power in the Kremlin. In both spheres what had been achieved was at best no more than the tacit consent of the principal contestants to suspend hostilities for the time being. The situation was fraught with the certainty of renewed conflict once the temporary lull had come to an end.

Blocked from finding their natural outlet in the areas of direct concern, the powerful tensions wracking the Soviet leadership exploded with redoubled fury in the only direction available to them, the international communist movement. In a rapid succession of increasingly hostile moves on both sides, the Soviet dispute with Albania mounted to a precedent-breaking climax in early December, with the formal rupture of diplomatic relations between the two states.[564]

The period following the Twenty-second Congress was therefore marked by an unusually high degree of instability and inconsistency in Soviet internal and foreign policy. Typical was the vacillation over the question of what to do with the leaders of the Antiparty Group. Some party organizations, that of Belorussia, for example, continued the campaign for their expulsion from the party.[565] The Soviet Academy of Sciences, headed by Khrushchev's admirer M. V. Keldysh, revealed that Molotov had been expelled from his post as an honorary academician as far back as March 26, 1959, and that Shepilov had been dropped as a corresponding member.[566] Yet no formal action was publicly announced and in January 1962 Molotov, who had been called back to Moscow in late November, was barred from returning to his post with the Atomic Energy Commission in Vienna after an unseemly display of clumsiness and lack of coordination between spokesmen for the Foreign Ministry and the Soviet press.[567]

Beneath the surface confusion a process of regrouping was going on, a shaking down of the CPSU leadership in preparation for a renewal of the

[564]For a detailed account of this phase of the Soviet–Albanian conflict, see Griffith, *Albania*, pp. 111–21.

[565]*Sovetskaia Belorussiia*, Nov. 15, 1961.

[566]*Izv.*, Nov. 17, 1961; *CDSP*, XIII/46, p. 49.

[567]Tatu, pp. 211–12.

power conflict. Viewed in the context of Soviet–American relations, the months from early November 1961 to mid-March 1962 can best be understood as the incubation period of the decision by the Soviet leadership to try a renewed challenge to U.S. strategic superiority, this time not in Berlin but in Cuba. Since that complex and highly important development falls outside the limits of the present study, we shall confine our discussion to those events in the post-congress period which served to mark the end of the Berlin crisis in 1961.

At the Kremlin reception marking the anniversary of the Bolshevik Revolution on November 7, Khrushchev sought out the West German ambassador, Hans Kroll, to express his desire for an improvement in Soviet–West German relations. At the end of their brief discussion, in which Foreign Minister Gromyko took part, Khrushchev invited Kroll to visit him in the Kremlin a few days later.

During the ensuing talk, which took place on November 9, Khrushchev told Kroll that "... *the final reconciliation of the German and Soviet peoples would mean the crowning of my life work in the field of foreign policy. I would be happy if I could achieve this work of reconciliation personally with your Federal Chancellor.*"[568]

There was no immediate follow-up from the Soviets to this fervent declaration, though rumors about it and leaks to the press kicked up a considerable fuss in relations between Bonn and the Western allies. If anything, Soviet policy toward West Germany in the following weeks seemed directed toward fanning West German animosity, with threatening gestures from Ulbricht (November 26 and 30), an ill-considered Soviet propaganda attack on West German General Adolf Heusinger (December 12), and belligerent utterances by Soviet Ambassador to the United States Menshikov (December 11 and 17).

By late December the evidence of disunity in the Soviet leadership was so strong that the party theoretical journal, *Kommunist*, found it necessary to publish an article denying that the party was "threatened by any split whatever." Significantly, the same issue of *Kommunist* included an article affirming that "peaceful coexistence is the general line of Soviet foreign policy."[569]

On the same day on which this revealing issue of *Kommunist* was sent to the press, December 26, a meeting of the Secretariat was held at which Kozlov demanded stringent penalties for peasants accused of damaging agricultural machinery.[570]   But this foray by Kozlov into Khrushchev's special field, agriculture, was followed almost immediately by a series of counterstrokes in

[568]Kroll, p. 527; emphasis in the original.

[569](1) S. Mezentsev, F. Petrenko, and G. Shitarëv (all members of the editorial board of *Kommunist*), "The party and the building of communism," *Kommunist* 18 (1961): 17–29 (quote at p. 24); see also Linden, p. 136. (2) A. Popov and A. Sergeev, "Peaceful coexistence—the general line of Soviet foreign policy," *Kommunist* 18 (1961): 54–62; see also Griffith, *Albania*, p. 138.

[570]Ploss, p. 241.

foreign policy which bear the unmistakable imprint of the First Secretary's initiative.

As we have seen, Soviet Ambassador to the United States Menshikov was a charter member of the hard-line faction on Soviet policy toward the West. He had been an enthusiastic supporter of the drive for signature of a German peace treaty in 1961, and as late as December 11 was still insisting on the full withdrawal of Western occupation forces from West Berlin, categorically ruling out the possibility of negotiations until this demand was met.[571] It was therefore a direct blow at the hard-line faction when Menshikov was replaced as ambassador to the United States by a man more amenable to Khrushchev's policies, Anatoly F. Dobrynin, who had served as a technical consultant to Khrushchev in the latter's conversations with U.S. Ambassador Llewellyn Thompson in early April 1961.

Washington's *agrément* to Dobrynin was given on December 27,[572] indicating that the Soviet decision to recall Menshikov was made shortly before that date. Menshikov's stubborn refusal to contribute to the moderation of Soviet policy on Berlin was reason enough for Khrushchev to wish him replaced. That his recall represented a reprimand and a disgrace was indicated by the sharp fall in influence his new position carried with it: early in January 1962 he was named foreign minister of the RSFSR, a meaningless post carrying prestige but no power to influence policy. Nor did he ever regain a position of influence: he was kept in the RSFSR post until his retirement on pension in September 1968.[573]

Coinciding with Menshikov's recall came a new step in Khrushchev's personal campaign for better Soviet relations with West Germany. On December 27 the head of the German Department of the Soviet foreign ministry, Ivan I. Il'ichev, gave West German Ambassador Kroll a memorandum containing ". . . ideas and considerations about the general world political situation, with special reference to the German question and the possibility of a step-by-step improvement in Soviet–German relations."[574] Oddly enough, the paper contained neither a signature nor a date, though its tone and content identified it unmistakably as the work of Khrushchev.[575]

It seemed, however, that Il'ichev had bungled his instructions. "Khrushchev later told me," Kroll reports, ". . . that the memorandum had been thought of as the working basis for our next discussion, to which he wished to invite me immediately after the turn of the year, and therefore had been intended only for me personally."[576] Not having been so informed by Il'ichev,

[571]*NYT*, Dec. 12, 1961, p. 1; *SIA, 1961*, pp. 279–80.

[572]*NYT*, Dec. 28, 1961, p. 9.

[573]*Sovetskaia Rossiia*, Sept. 12, 1968, cited in Radio Liberty dispatch, Nov. 13, 1968.

[574]Kroll, pp. 537–38.

[575]Text in *Europa Archiv*, Folge 3/1962, pp. D59–D70, citing *Bulletin des Presse- und Informationsamtes der Bundesregierung*, no. 6, Jan. 10, 1962.

[576]Kroll, p. 538.

however, Kroll treated the memorandum with all the respect due an official state document, and forwarded it to the Foreign Office in Bonn with a recommendation to take it "very seriously." Almost at once word of its existence leaked out, and on January 10 the West German government published the full text.

Since the memorandum was never officially acknowledged by the Soviet government (the Soviet press ignored it), and since it played no significant role in the subsequent development of Soviet–West German relations, its chief importance lies in the insight it provides into Khrushchev's unorthodox procedures and what would later be characterized as his "hare-brained schemes" in the realm of Soviet foreign policy.

The memorandum sought to flatter West Germany, to sow the seeds of distrust between the Federal Republic and its Western allies, and to portray West Germany and the Soviet Union as natural partners, especially in economic development. The withdrawal of Bonn from NATO and its turn toward a policy of friendship with Moscow appeared to be the principal goals toward which the memorandum was directed. On the specific issues of the Berlin question it had nothing new to offer, unless one could take seriously its statement that: "We have nothing against the most active contacts between the Federal Republic and West Berlin in the economic, *political*, and cultural spheres."[577]

These two events—the recall of Menshikov and the unsigned memorandum of December 27—mark the muffled close of the Berlin crisis of 1961. The change in the ambassadorship removed from a key post one of the leading architects of the policy which had led to the Soviet Berlin campaign of 1961, while Khrushchev's unsigned and unauthorized memorandum showed that he had recovered some degree of freedom of action, if not in the formulation of Soviet foreign policy, at least in the power to express his own independent views.

The time had not yet come, however, for a real shift in Soviet policy on Berlin and the German question, since the underlying problem—the Soviet–American strategic imbalance—had not yet been squarely faced by the Soviet leadership. It took the Cuban missile crisis of 1962 to settle that question, if not for all time, then at least for the period of Khrushchev's rule. Appropriately, the final echo of the Berlin crisis of 1961 came in January 1963, as part of the aftermath of the Cuban missile crisis.

In that month Khrushchev journeyed to East Berlin to take part in the Sixth Congress of the Socialist Unity party (SED). In his major speech to the congress, delivered on January 16, he offered a defense of Soviet policy in the Berlin crisis of 1961, particularly the decision to build the Berlin Wall, under the curious guise of a conversation between an American journalist and his Soviet colleague. The American, said Khrushchev,

---

[577] *Europa Archiv*, Folge 3/1962, p. D68; emphasis supplied. The standard Soviet position was that West Berlin must be fully separate from the Federal Republic in the political sphere.

. . . remarked to a Soviet journalist: "On August 13 you seem to have obtained everything you wanted to get through conclusion of a German peace treaty." Objected the Soviet journalist: "No, a peace treaty has not been signed and, consequently, this is not quite the case." Then the American said: "True, a peace treaty has not been signed, but *you have almost completely attained the goal that you pursued in insisting on its conclusion.* You have closed the border, you have cut off the access of the West to the German Democratic Republic. Thus even before signing a peace treaty you have obtained what you sought and what you wanted to get through concluding this treaty.

"And, having got what you wanted," continued the American journalist, "you have also gained the opportunity to step on the corns of the West. The lanes of access to West Berlin through the territory of the German Democratic Republic are such corns. As long as there are no firm international obligations regulating access, it depends in general on the government of the German Democratic Republic, which can always intensify or relax the pressure if it chooses to do so."[578]

"Not everything here is exact," Khrushchev observed prudently, "but the American journalist comes close to the truth."

Our ally and friend, the German Democratic Republic, has obtained what every sovereign state requires, the right to control its borders and to take measures against those who would try to weaken the socialist system of the German Democratic Republic. This is a big common gain for all the countries of socialism party to the Warsaw Pact. And now, if one takes the question from the standpoint of the most immediate interests of the socialist countries, the problem of concluding a German peace treaty does indeed stand differently than before the defensive measures were taken on the German Democratic Republic's border with West Berlin.[579]

In effect, therefore, Khrushchev was telling his East German audience (including Ulbricht) to be content with the strengthening of their state which resulted from the building of the Berlin Wall, and not to harbor any thoughts of challenging the West's military power by force of arms. Later in his speech, Khrushchev supplied the other half of the strategic equation by arguing that nuclear war between the great powers must be avoided at all costs. For once, he even admitted that the socialist nations, too, would suffer irreparable losses in such a war:

There is no doubt that if a thermonuclear war were unleashed by the imperialist maniacs, the capitalist system that gave rise to the war would perish in it. But would the socialist countries and the cause of the struggle for socialism throughout the world gain from a world thermonuclear catastrophe? Only people who deliberately close their eyes to the facts can think this. As far as the Marxist–Leninists are concerned, they cannot think in terms of a communist civilization built upon the ruins of the world's cultural

[578] *Pravda* and *Izv.*, Jan. 17, 1963; *CDSP*, XV/3, p. 6; emphasis supplied.
[579] *CDSP*, XV/3, p. 6.

centers, on ravaged earth contaminated by thermonuclear fallout. This is not to mention the fact that for many people there would be no question of socialism at all, since they would have been removed from the face of our planet.[580]

Khrushchev's immediate target in making this assertion was the leadership of the Albanian party, but it was aimed equally at the Chinese communists and at those who sympathized with them in the international communist movement—and in the Communist party of the Soviet Union itself.

Glossary*

aktiv: Full-time party officials for whom party employment is a career, as contrasted with rank-and-file party members whose principal occupation is in a nonparty position.

Antiparty Group: A group of party and government leaders who tried to oust Khrushchev from his position as First Secretary in the period between the Twentieth Congress in February 1956 and the June 1957 plenum of the CC. The leaders of the group were G. M. Malenkov, V. M. Molotov, and L. M. Kaganovich, and it also included N. A. Bulganin, K. Ye. Voroshilov, M. G. Pervukhin, M. Z. Saburov, and D. T. Shepilov (always stigmatized in official party accounts as "Shepilov-who-joined-them").

apparatus (Russian: *apparat*): The full-time professional staff of the party; the party bureaucracy.

Armenian purge: On December 28, 1960, a plenum of the Armenian party CC was held at which S. A. Tovmasian was replaced as First Secretary by Ya. N. Zarobian. F. R. Kozlov supervised the plenum and gave a speech which was not reported in the Soviet press. At the next plenum of the Armenian party CC, held on February 10, 1961, sweeping changes in the leading party organs were carried through. The Armenian purge was completed in March 1961, with the removal of S. L. Tumanian, the last remaining member of the former party secretariat.

Available evidence indicates that the Armenian purge was a factional move by Kozlov designed to weaken Khrushchev's political base by seizing control of one of the Union Republic party organizations. Exactly the same pattern was to be followed in the Tadzhik purge (q.v.) a few months later.

Bundesrat: The upper house of the West German legislature, representing the constituent states (*Länder*) of the Federal Republic, including West Berlin.

Bundestag: The lower house of the West German legislature, elected by popular suffrage. It elects the chancellor, passes all legislation, and ratifies major treaties.

---

*As used herein, "party" refers to the Communist party of the Soviet Union; "CC" refers to the Central Committee of the party.

473

Bundeswehr: The army of the Federal Republic of Germany, established in 1954 and subsequently incorporated into the NATO military command.

Bureau for the RSFSR: An agency of the CC established on February 27, 1956, immediately following the Twentieth Congress, to supervise and control party affairs in the RSFSR. Khrushchev served as its chairman from its establishment to his overthrow in October 1964. It was abolished at the Twenty-third Congress in 1966, the first held after Khrushchev's fall.

CC (Central Committee. Russian: *Tsentral'nyi komitet,* abbreviated TsK): The governing body of the party between congresses. Under the 1961 party rules the CC:

> directs the entire work of the Party in the interval between Congresses, represents the Party in its relations with other parties, organizations and institutions, sets up various Party institutions and directs their activities, appoints the editors of central press organs under its control and confirms the appointment of the editors of the Party organs of big local organizations, organizes and manages enterprises of a public character, distributes the forces and resources of the Party, and manages the central funds.
>
> The Central Committee guides the work of the central Soviet and public organizations through the Party groups within them.[1]

At the Twentieth Congress in 1956, a CC of 133 full and 122 candidate members was elected; these figures were raised to 175 and 155 respectively at the Twenty-second Congress in 1961.

CENTO: The Central Treaty Organization, established in 1955 by Turkey, Iraq, the United Kingdom, Pakistan, and Iran (Iraq withdrew in 1959). The United States participates but is not a member; in 1959 it entered into bilateral defense agreements with Turkey, Iran, and Pakistan. Also known as the Baghdad Pact, the designation of the treaty of February 24, 1955, between Turkey and Iraq, which served as the nucleus of the organization.

Central Auditing Commission (*Tsentral'naia revizionnaia komissiia,* abbreviated TsRK): A body elected by the party congress. Under the 1961 party rules the TsRK "(a) investigates whether affairs are handled expeditiously and properly by the central bodies of the Party and whether the apparatus of the Secretariat of the Central Committee is working smoothly, and (b) audits the accounts of the treasury and the enterprises of the Central Committee of the Party."[2] At congresses of the party the chairman of the TsRK customarily presents a report concerning the party's fiscal operations and the size and efficiency of its membership and apparatus.

Comintern: The Third (Communist) International, established in 1919 and dissolved in 1943.

congress: The highest organ of the party. Under the 1961 party rules the congress:

> a. Hears and acts on the reports of the Central Committee of the party, of the Central Auditing Commission, and of the other central organizations;
> b. Revises and amends the Program and Rules of the party;
> c. Determines the tactical line of the party on major questions of current policy;

---

[1]Triska, pp. 175–76.
[2]Ibid., p. 176.

d. Elects the Central Committee of the Communist Party of the Soviet Union and the Central Auditing Commission.[3]

Under the 1961 rules, regular party congresses are to be convened at least once every four years. Congresses are numbered from the First, which met in Minsk in 1898.

"cult of personality" or "cult of the individual" (*kul't lichnosti*): The term employed by the party to designate the period of Stalin's arbitrary one-man rule.

"doctors' plot": An alleged conspiracy by a group of Kremlin physicians, predominantly Jewish, to eliminate prominent party, government, and military leaders by deliberately prescribing faulty medical treatment for them. The "plot," which was apparently intended as the opening move in a new large-scale purge, was announced by *Pravda* on January 13, 1953. After Stalin's death it was officially admitted that the "plot" had been concocted by the secret police with the use of "impermissible means of investigation" (i.e., torture) to extract confessions from the accused physicians.

Of the members of the Soviet collective leadership in 1961, the one most closely linked with the "doctors' plot" was Frol Kozlov: an article by him calling for heightened vigilance against internal and foreign enemies was published shortly before the official announcement of the "plot."[4]

"dogmatism": The tendency to adhere slavishly to the letter of the Marxist-Leninist sacred scriptures as a guide to current policy rather than make rational adjustments to changing conditions within the general framework of Marxist-Leninist principles. In the Sino-Soviet conflict the term was applied to the policies advocated by the Chinese Communists and their Albanian allies by Khrushchev and the Soviet leadership. The opposite of "revisionism," q.v.

Federal Republic of Germany (FRG; German: *Bundesrepublik Deutschlands*): The government of Western Germany, established September 21, 1949, on the territory of the three Western Zones of Occupation of post–1945 Germany (those of the United Kingdom, the United States, and France). Capital, de jure: Berlin; de facto: Bonn.

First Secretary: The head of the party Secretariat (q.v.), elected by and in principle responsible to the CC. Each non-Russian Union Republic party organization, e.g., that of Armenia, "elects" its own First Secretary, on the designation of and subject to the control of the all-Union Secretariat, which may remove him and name someone else to the post. In principle, the Union Republic First Secretary wields power in the given party organization comparable to that of the party First Secretary at the all-Union level; in practice, political control in the non-Russian republics is usually concentrated in the hands not of the First Secretary, customarily a native of the given republic, but of the Second Secretary, a Russian.

Geneva Conference of 1954: An international conference held at Geneva, Switzerland, between April and July 1954, for the purposes of reunifying Korea and restoring peace to the states of Indochina—Vietnam, Laos, and Cambodia. The

[3]Ibid., pp. 174–75.

[4]F. Kozlov, "Political Vigilance Is the Duty of a Party Member," *Kommunist* 1 (1953): 46–58.

chief participants were the Soviet Union, Great Britain, France, the United States, the Chinese People's Republic, representatives of North and South Korea, Vietnam, the Vietminh (representing the Democratic Republic of Vietnam), Laos, and Cambodia.

Geneva conference on Laos: Following the establishment of a cease-fire in Laos in early May 1961, a fourteen-nation conference met in Geneva to establish a neutral, unified Laotian government. Among the delegates were the three leading contenders for power in Laos, Princes Souvanna Phouma, Souphanouvong, and Boun Oum.

Geneva disarmament conferences: In the period preceding the Berlin crisis of 1961 the following international conferences on disarmament were being held in Geneva: (a) a ten-nation conference on general disarmament; (b) U.S.-British-Soviet negotiations on a nuclear test ban agreement; and (c) U.S.-Soviet negotiations on the prevention of surprise attack. In addition, U.S.-Soviet talks on disarmament were held (though not at Geneva) in the period March-September 1961.

GDR (German Democratic Republic; German: *Deutsche Demokratische Republik*, abbreviated DDR): The government of East Germany, established October 7, 1949, in what had been the Soviet Zone of Occupation. Capital: East Berlin (Pankow).

gorkom (short for *gorodskoi komitet*): A party committee in a city (*gorod*) or town.

KGB (*Komitet Gosudarstvennoi Bezopasnosti*, Committee of State Security): The Soviet secret police, charged with both internal security and espionage and other clandestine activities abroad.

kolkhoz (short for *kollektivnoe khoziaistvo*): A collective farm, the basic unit in Soviet collectivized agriculture.

Kommandatura: (1) The four-power authority for the governing of Berlin, established in accordance with the Allied agreement of June 5, 1945, on control machinery in Germany with representatives of the United Kingdom, the United States, the Soviet Union, and France; reorganized on a three-power basis December 21, 1948, following the walkout of the Soviet representative.

(2) The Soviet control authority in East Berlin, established after the break-up of the four-power body.

Komsomol (*Vsesoiuznyi Leninskii Kommunisticheskii Soiuz Molodëzhi*, All-Union Leninist Communist League of Youth): The Soviet political organization for young people between the ages of fourteen and twenty-eight.

kraikom (short for *kraevoi komitet*): a party committee in a krai (territory), an administrative subdivision corresponding to an oblast.

"Leningrad case": A purge of the Leningrad party and government apparatus carried out in 1949. Frol Kozlov, who was sent to Leningrad as a party organizer in the Kirov metallurgical plant at the beginning of the purge, evidently played a key role in the "Leningrad case."

Main Political Administration: The Military Department of the CC, which is also a branch of the Soviet Defense Ministry. Its function is to ensure the political reliability and loyalty of the armed forces.

NATO: The North Atlantic Treaty Organization, established April 4, 1949, by Belgium, Canada, Denmark, France, Iceland, Italy, Luxembourg, the Netherlands, Norway, Portugal, the United Kingdom, and the United States. Greece and Turkey joined in 1952, the Federal Republic of Germany in 1955.

obkom (short for *oblastnoi komitet*): A party committee in an oblast—a province, region, or district (the principal administrative subdivision below the republic level in the Soviet Union).

Party Control Committee (*Komitet Partiinogo Kontrolia*, abbreviated KPK): The party's disciplinary organ, set up by the CC to supervise members' conduct, take action against those who violate its discipline, rules, or moral code, and review appeals against expulsion orders.

plenum: A full meeting (i.e., one attended by a quorum) of a legislative or other body, e.g., of the CC. Plenums of party CC's at Union Republic level may be supervised by a visiting official of the central party apparatus empowered to make both policy and personnel changes (*see* Armenian purge; Tadzhik purge).

Presidium (Politburo): The highest policy-making body of the party, formed by and, in principle, answerable to the CC, but in practice virtually autonomous. Established at the Eighth Congress in 1919, under the designation "Politburo" (short for Political Bureau), the body was redesignated "Presidium" at the Nineteenth Congress in October 1952, but reverted to "Politburo" at the Twenty-third Congress in 1966.

At the onset of the Berlin crisis of 1961 the Presidium included the following full members: Brezhnev, Furtseva, Ignatov, Khrushchev, Kosygin, Kozlov, Kuusinen, Mikoyan, Mikhitdinov, Podgorny, Poliansky, Shvernik, and Suslov. Madame Furtseva, Ignatov, and Mukhitdinov were dropped from the new Presidium elected at a CC plenum immediately following the Twenty-second Congress.

raikom (short for *raionnyi komitet*): A party committee in a raion (city district or borough).

Rapacki Plan: A proposal laid before the Twelfth Session of the U.N. General Assembly on October 2, 1957, by Polish Foreign Minister Adam Rapacki and elaborated in a Polish government memorandum of February 14, 1958. The plan, which enjoyed Soviet support, called for the establishment of a nuclear-free zone in Central Europe, to include Poland, Czechoslovakia, and the two German states.

revanchism (from the Russian *revansh*, revenge; the English spelling reflects the French original, *revanche*): The doctrine, imputed by Soviet spokesmen to West German policy-makers, of revenge against the Soviet Union and its allies for Germany's defeat in World War II.

"revisionism": The tendency to deviate from the basic principles of Marxism-Leninism, especially in the direction of so-called "bourgeois liberalism." In the Sino-Soviet dispute the term was applied by the Communist Chinese and Albanian party leaders to Khrushchev and his followers in the Soviet leadership, as well as to the Yugoslav communists.

RSFSR (Russian Soviet Federative Socialist Republic): The Russian republic, the largest, most populous, and most influential of the 15 Union Republics which constitute the Soviet Union.

SEATO: The Southeast Asia Treaty Organization, established by treaty on September 8, 1954, among Australia, France, New Zealand, Pakistan, the Philippines, Thailand, the United Kingdom, and the United States. By a subsequent protocol, military protection was extended by SEATO to the Republic of Vietnam (South Vietnam) and the kingdoms of Cambodia and Laos.

Secretariat: The organizational control center of the party, responsible for the assignment, promotion, transfer, or demotion of party members. At the onset of the Berlin crisis of 1961 the Secretariat consisted of the following members: Khrushchev, First Secretary; Kozlov, Kuusinen, Mukhitdinov, and Suslov. At a CC plenum held immediately following the Twenty-second Congress in October 1961 a new Secretariat was elected with the following members: Khrushchev, First Secretary; Kozlov (listed immediately following Khrushchev, out of alphabetical order, and therefore ranked as Second Secretary); Demichev, Il'ichev, Kuusinen, Ponomarev, Spiridonov, Shelepin, and Suslov.

SED (*Sozialistische Einheitspartei Deutschlands*, Socialist Unity party of Germany): The Communist party of East Germany, formed by a forced merger between the Communist and Socialist parties of Germany in the Soviet Zone of Occupation in April 1946.

Sputnik: An earth-circling artificial satellite. The first Sputnik, a 184-lb. satellite carrying a radio transmitter and batteries, was orbited by the Soviets on October 4, 1957.

Tadzhik purge: At a plenum of the Tadzhik party CC on April 11–12, 1961, a drastic purge of the party leadership was carried out under the supervision of F. R. Kozlov, who made a speech which was not reported in the Soviet press. Like the Armenian purge (q.v.), the Tadzhik purge was evidently part of a factional drive spearheaded by Kozlov to weaken Khrushchev's political base.

troika: A three-man body, a triumvirate, a form which the Soviets for a time demanded as a replacement for the secretary-general of the U.N., to include representatives of the three principal groups of nations into which, in the Soviet view, the world was divided—the Western nations, the Soviet bloc, and the neutral or uncommitted nations, with each of the three members empowered to veto the actions of the other two.

When the three-power test-ban negotiations at Geneva were resumed in March 1961, the Soviets extended their demand for a troika to the control board under discussion for monitoring possible violations of a nuclear test-ban agreement.

Volkskammer: The legislative body of the German Democratic Republic, based on communist-style elections.

Volkspolizei ("People's Police," popularly abbreviated "Vopos"): The army of East Germany, thinly disguised as a police force and charged with responsibility, inter alia, for border security.

Warsaw Pact: A multilateral treaty signed at Warsaw on May 14, 1955, by the Soviet Union and seven of its East European ally-satellites: Albania, Bulgaria, Czechoslovakia, the GDR, Hungary, Poland, and Romania. The member-states of the Warsaw Pact contribute contingents to a common military force, the commander of which, by treaty, is always a Soviet officer.

Young Pioneers, or Pioneers (Russian designation: *Pionerskaia Organizatsiia imeni V. I. Lenina*, Pioneer Organization Named for V. I. Lenin): The Soviet social and political organization for children between the ages of ten and fifteen.

List of Works Cited*

Abel, Elie. *The Missile Crisis*. Philadelphia and New York: Lippincott, 1966.

Alexeyev, A. "Once more about the structure of the U.N. executive agencies," *International Affairs* 8 (Moscow, 1961): 35–40.

Becker, Abraham S. "Soviet Military Outlays Since 1955." Santa Monica: RAND Corp., 1964.

Biddleford, James (pseudonym of Sidney I. Ploss). "Deadlock in the party presidium," *New Leader*, vol. 44, no. 35, October 16, 1961, pp. 19–22.

Bloomfield, Lincoln P., Clemens, Walter C., Griffiths, Franklin. *Khrushchev and the Arms Race: Soviet Interest in Arms Control and Disarmament 1954–1964*. Cambridge, Mass.: M.I.T. Press, 1966.

Conquest, Robert. *Power and Policy in the U.S.S.R. The Study of Soviet Dynastics*. New York: St. Martin's Press, 1961.

———. *Russia After Khrushchev*. New York: Praeger, 1965.

Cousins, Norman. "President Kennedy and the Russian fable," *Saturday Review*, January 9, 1971, pp. 20–21.

Current Digest of the Soviet Press.

Current Soviet Policies IV: The Documentary Record of the Twenty-Second Congress of the Communist Party of the Soviet Union. New York: Columbia University Press, 1962.

Dallin, Alexander. *The Soviet Union at the United Nations*. New York: Praeger, 1962.

Dean, Arthur H. *Test Ban and Disarmament. The Path of the Negotiations*. New York and Evanston: Harper and Row, 1966.

Deutscher, Isaac. "The Sino-Soviet Truce Breaks Down," in *Russia, China, and the West: A Contemporary Chronicle, 1953–1966*, edited by Fred Halliday. Baltimore: Penguin Books, 1970. Cited from the *Washington Post*, July 5, 1961, pp. A–1, A–6.

Dodd, Thomas. "N-bomb: Ideal weapon for defense," *U.S. News and World Report*, vol. 51, no. 3, July 17, 1961, pp. 48–50.

*The full bibliographical information is given in the footnotes only the first time a work is mentioned in the book. (See *Abbreviations of Works Most Frequently Cited*, p. 485.)

XX S"ezd Kommunisticheskoi Partii Sovetskogo Soiuza 14–25 fevralia 1956 goda. Stenograficheskii otchet. 2 vols. Moscow: Gospolitizdat, 1956.

XXII S"ezd Kommunisticheskoi Partii Sovetskogo Soiuza 17–31 oktiabria 1961 goda. Stenograficheskii otchet, 3 vols. Moscow: Gospolitizdat, 1962.

XXIII S"ezd Kommunisticheskoi Partii Sovetskogo Soiuza 29 marta–8 aprelia 1966 goda. Stenograficheskii otchet, 2 vols. Moscow: Politizdat, 1966.

Europa Archiv, Folge 3/1962.

Facts on File, 1961.

Fitzsimons, Louise. *The Kennedy Doctrine.* New York: Random House, 1972.

Gallagher, Matthew P. "Military manpower: A case study," *Problems of Communism,* vol. 13, no. 3 (May–June 1964):56.

Griffith, William E. *Albania and the Sino–Soviet Rift.* Cambridge, Mass.: M.I.T. Press, 1963.

––––––. *The Sino–Soviet Rift.* Cambridge, Mass.: M.I.T. Press, 1964.

Hodnett, Grey, "Khrushchev and party-state control," in Alexander Dallin and Alan F. Westin, eds., *Politics in the Soviet Union: 7 Cases.* New York: Harcourt, Brace and World, 1966.

Hoeffding, Oleg. "Sino-Soviet Economic Relations 1958–1962." Santa Monica: RAND Corp., 1963.

Horelick, Arnold, and Rush, Myron L. *Strategic Power and Soviet Foreign Policy.* Chicago: University of Chicago Press, 1966.

Izvestiia (listed in chronological order):

K. Perevoshchikov and N. Polianov, "Dorogu blagorazumiiu" [Make way for common sense], June 6, 1961, pp. 1–2.

"Idti po puti mira" [Follow the path of peace], June 8, 1961, p. 1.

"Gettisberg diktuet Belomu Domu?" [Is Gettysburg dictating to the White House?], August 17, 1961, p. 2.

V. Silant'ev, "Anglichane ne khotiat voevat'" [Englishmen do not wish to fight], August 26, 1961, p. 2.

"V interesakh bezopasnosti" [In the interests of security], September 3, 1961, p. 4.

P. Visimov, "Uralskii arsenal" [Urals arsenal], September 6, 1961, p. 1.

I. Lysenko and M. Krishton, "Kukuruzu na zerno ubiraem razdel'no" [We harvest the seed-corn separately], September 6, 1961, p. 3.

V. Nariakov, "Meniu iz sta bliud. Kukuruza na obedennom stole" [Menu of 100 dishes—corn at the dinner table], September 8, 1961, p. 6.

"Vozmozhnye preemniki Khammarshel'da" [Possible successors to Hammarskjöld], September 21, 1961, p. 4.

Jacobson, Harold K., and Stein, Eric. *Diplomats, Scientists and Politicians. The United States and the Nuclear Test Ban Negotiations.* Ann Arbor: University of Michigan Press, 1966.

Johnson, Haynes, et al. *The Bay of Pigs: The Leaders' Story of Brigade 2506.* New York: Norton, 1964.

Kaufmann, William W. *The McNamara Strategy.* New York: Harper and Row. 1964.

Keesing's Contemporary Archives (1961):18223.

Khrushchev, N. S. *Kommunizm—mir i schast'e narodam,* 2 vols. Moscow: Gospolitizdat, 1962.

––––––. *Stroitel'stvo Kommunizma v SSSR i razvitie sel'skogo khoziaistva,* 8 vols. Moscow: Gospolitizdat, 1962–64.

Klass, Philip J. "Keeping the nuclear peace: spies in the sky," *New York Times Magazine,* Sept. 3, 1972, pp. 7, 31–32, 35–36.

Korovin, E. "Time for reform," *New Times,* no. 39, September 27, 1961, pp. 7–8.

Kozlov, F. "Politicheskaia bditel'nost'—obiazannost' chlena partii" [Political vigilance is the duty of a party member], *Kommunist* 1 (1953):46–58.

Krasnaia Zvezda (listed in chronological order).

Col. I. Alekseev, "Vozdushnye koridory—ne dlia revanshistov!" [The air corridors are not for revanchists], September 9, 1961, p. 5.

Marshal K. S. Moskalenko, "Raketnye voiska na strazhe bezopasnosti Rodiny" [Rocket troops on guard over the security of the Motherland], September 13, 1961, p. 3.

K. Vershinin, "Voenno-vozdushnye sily sumeiut postoiat' za Rodinu" [The Military Air Force is able to stand up for the Motherland], September 16, 1961, p. 2.

A. S. Zhadov, "Sukhoputnye voiska v boevoi gotovnosti" [The land forces are in readiness], September 20, 1961, p. 2.

S. S. Biriuzov, "Zorkie strazhi sovetskogo neba" [Vigilant guards of the Soviet sky], September 22, 1961, p. 2.

A. G. Golovko, "Voennye moriaki vsegda gotovy k zashchite otechestva" [The Marines are always ready for the defense of the Fatherland], September 29, 1961, p. 2.

Lt. Col. A. Kascheev and Maj. S. Vladimirov, "O chëm umolchal Prezident SShA. Kolonizatory 'usmiriaiut' Yuzhnyi V'etnam" [What the U.S. President did not mention—Colonialists "pacify" South Vietnam], September 29, 1961, p. 4.

Kroll, Hans. *Lebenserinnerungen eines Botschafters.* Cologne and Berlin: Kiepenheuer und Witsch, 1967.

Linden, Carl A. *Khrushchev and the Soviet Leadership 1957–1964.* Baltimore: The Johns Hopkins Press, 1966.

_____, "Khrushchev and the Party Battle," *Problems of Communism*, vol. 12, no 5 (September–October 1963):27–35.

McDermott, Geoffrey. *Berlin: Success of a Mission?* New York and Evanston: Harper and Row, 1963.

Mezentsev, S., Petrenko, F., Shitarëv, G. "Partiia i stroitel'stvo kommunizma" [The party and the building of communism], *Kommunist* 18 (1961):17–29.

Mosely, Philip E. "Soviet myths and realities," *Foreign Affairs*, vol. 39, no. 3 (April 1961):341–54.

Nimitz, Nancy. "Soviet Expenditures and Scientific Research." Santa Monica: RAND Corp., 1963.

Plenum Tsentral'nogo Komiteta Kommunisticheskoi Partii Sovetskogo Soiuza 24–26 marta 1965 goda. Stenograficheskii otchet. Moscow: Izdatel'stvo Politicheskoi Literatury, 1965.

Ploss, Sidney I. *Conflict and Decision-making in Soviet Russia: A Case Study of Agricultural Policy 1953–1963.* Princeton: Princeton University Press, 1965.

Popov, A., and Sergeev, A. "Mirnoe sosuschchestvovanie—general'nyi kurs sovetskoi vneshnei politiki" [Peaceful coexistence—the general line of Soviet foreign policy], *Kommunist* 18 (1961):54–62.

Popov, I., and Tomashpol'skii, L. "Kitaiskii narod stroit sotsializma" [The Chinese people are building socialism], *Ekonomicheskaia Gazeta*, June 10, 1961, p. 4.

Pravda (listed in chronological order).

Vladimir Orlov, "Pero zhar-ptitsy" [The fire-bird's feather], July 2, 1961, p. 3.

"Mify i deistvitel'nost'. Driu Pirson o germanskom voprose" [Myths and realities. Drew Pearson on the German question], August 15, 1961, p. 6.

"Glavnaia ekonomicheskaia zadacha partii i naroda" [The main economic task of the party and the people], August 22, 1961, p. 1.

Vl. Kuznetsov, "Novyi udar po provokatoram" [New blow at provocateurs], August 24, 1961, p. 5.

"Volia miroliubivykh narodov nepokolebima" [The will of the peace-loving peoples is unflinching], August 28, 1961, p. 1.

V. Tiukov, "Dlia blaga sovetskikh liudei" [For the benefit of the Soviet people], August 31, 1961, p. 3.

O. Orestov, "Prestupnaia igra s ognem" [Criminal playing with fire], September 6, 1961, p. 5.

I. Vorob'ev and V. Zhuravskii, "Sto bliud iz kukuruzy" [One hundred dishes from corn], September 7, 1971, p. 6.

R. Ya. Malinovskii, "Zashchita sotsialisticheskogo otechestva—nash sviash-chennyi dolg" [The defense of the socialist Fatherland is our sacred duty], September 14, 1961, pp. 3–4.

"Vremia i sobytiia—protiv SShA. Stat'ia Driu Pirsona" [Time and events are against the U.S.A. Article by Drew Pearson], September 21, 1961, p. 5.

Ye. Litoshko and B. Strel'nikov, "V dobryi put'" [Good luck], November 5, 1961, p. 6.

"Po opasnomu puti. 'Nepsabadshag' o politike rukovodstva APG" [On a dangerous course. "Nepszabadsag" on the policy of the leadership of the APG (Albanian Party of Labor)], November 11, 1961, p. 4.

"Gazeta 'Land og folk' o deistviiakh albanskikh rukovoditelei" [The newspaper "Land og Folk" on the actions of the Albanian leaders], November 14, 1961, p. 3.

Rigby, Thomas H., "How strong is the leader?", *Problems of Communism*, vol. 11, no. 5 (September–October 1962): 1–8.

―――. "The extent and limits of authority (a rejoinder to Mr. Linden)," ibid., vol. 12, no. 5 (September–October 1963): 27–35.

Rovere, Richard H. "Letter from Washington," *New Yorker*, vol. 37, no. 25, August 5, 1961, p. 32.

Royal Institute of International Affairs. *Documents on International Affairs, 1961.* London: Oxford University Press, 1965.

Salinger, Pierre. *With Kennedy.* New York: Doubleday, 1966.

Schapiro, Leonard. "The party's new rules," *Problems of Communism*, vol. 11, no. 1 (January–February 1962): 351.

Schick, Jack M. *The Berlin Crisis 1958–1962.* Philadelphia: University of Pennsylvania Press, 1972.

Schlesinger, Arthur M., Jr. *A Thousand Days: John F. Kennedy in the White House*, Boston: Houghton Mifflin; Cambridge, Mass.: The Riverside Press, 1965.

Schwartz, Harry, ed. *Russia Enters the 1960s. A Documentary Report on the 22nd Congress of the Communist Party of the Soviet Union.* Philadelphia and New York: Lippincott, 1962.

Sidey, Hugh. *John F. Kennedy, President.* New York: Atheneum, 1963.

Sidorov, A.. and Shitarëv, G. "Lenin i s"ezdy partii" [Lenin and party congresses], *Kommunist* 15 (1961): 92–101.

Simmonds, George W., ed. *Soviet Leaders.* New York: Crowell, 1967.

Slusser, Robert M. "America, China, and the Hydra-Headed Opposition," in Peter H. Juviler and Henry W. Morton, eds., *Soviet Policy-Making. Studies of Communism in Transition.* New York: Praeger, 1967.

―――. "The Presidium Meeting of February 1961: A Reconstruction," in Alexander and Janet Rabinowitch, with Ladis K. D. Kristof, eds., *Revolution and Politics in Russia: Essays in Memory of B. I. Nicolaevsky.* Bloomington: Indiana University Press, 1972.

————. "The Role of the Foreign Ministry," in Ivo J. Lederer, ed., *Russian Foreign Policy: Essays in Historical Perspective*. New Haven and London: Yale University Press, 1962.

Smith, Jean Edward. *The Defense of Berlin*. Baltimore: The Johns Hopkins Press, 1963.

Sorensen, Theodore C. *Kennedy*. New York and Evanston: Harper and Row, 1965.

Spravochnik partiinogo rabotnika. Vypusk chetvertyi. Moscow: Gospolitizdat, 1963.

Tatu, Michel. *Le Pouvoir en U.R.S.S., du Déclin de Khrouchtchev à la Direction Collective*. Paris: Bernard Grasset, 1967.

————. *Power in the Kremlin, From Khrushchev to Kosygin*. New York: Viking Press, 1968.

Thomson, James C., Jr. "How could Vietnam happen? An autopsy," *Atlantic*, vol. 221, no. 4 (April 1968):48.

Triska, Jan F., ed. *Soviet Communism: Programs and Rules*. San Francisco: Chandler, 1962.

United Kingdom. *Documents About the Future of Germany (Including Berlin), June to July 1961*. London: H.M.S.O., 1961, Cmnd. 1451.

————. *Selected Documents on Germany and the Question of Berlin 1944–1961*. London: H.M.S.O., 1961, Cmnd. 1552.

United Nations, Office of Public Information. *The United Nations and Disarmament 1945–1965*. New York: United Nations, 1967.

U.S. Arms Control and Disarmament Agency. *Documents on Disarmament, 1961*. Washington, D.C.: G.P.O., 1962.

U.S. Congress, Joint Economic Committee, 87th Congress, 2nd session. *Dimensions of Soviet Economic Power*. Washington, D.C.: G.P.O., 1962.

U.S., *Department of State Bulletin*, 45 (1961).

U.S. Department of State. *American Foreign Policy: Current Documents, 1961*. Washington, D.C.: G.P.O., 1965.

U.S., Office of the Federal Register. *John F. Kennedy. Containing the Public Messages, Speeches, and Statements of the President, January 20 to December 31, 1961*. Washington, D.C.: G.P.O., 1962.

U.S. Senate, Committee on Foreign Relations. *Documents on Germany, 1944–1961*. Washington, D.C.: G.P.O., 1961.

Vakhabov, A. "Kollegial'nost'—vysshii printsip partiinogo rukovodstva. S teoreticheskoi konferentsii v g. Chirchike" [Collegiality is the highest principle of party leadership. From the theoretical conference in Chirchik], *Pravda Vostoka*, June 16, 1961, p. 3.

Vneocherednoi XXI S"ezd Kommunisticheskoi Partii Sovetskogo Soiuza 27 ianvaria—5 fevralia 1959 goda. 2 vols. Moscow: Gospolitizdat, 1959.

Vneshniaia Torgovlia 5 (1961): 11–12, 17–18.

Vneshniaia politika Sovetskogo Soiuza i mezhdunarodnye Otnosheniia. Sbornik dokumentov, 1961 god. Moscow: Izdatel'stvo Instituta Mezhdunarodnykh Otnoshenii, 1962.

Voss, Earl H. *Nuclear Ambush. The Test-ban Trap*. Chicago: Regnery, 1963.

Walton, Richard F. *Cold War and Counterrevolution: The Foreign Policy of John F. Kennedy*. New York: Viking Press, 1972.

Watt, D. C. *Survey of International Affairs, 1961*. London: Oxford University Press, 1965.

Wesson, Robert G. *Soviet Foreign Policy in Perspective*. Homewood, Ill.: Dorsey Press, 1969.

Yezhegodnik Bol'shoi Sovetskoi Entsiklopedii, 1961. Moscow: Sovetskaia Entsiklopediia, 1961.

Zagoria, Donald S. *The Sino-Soviet Conflict 1956-1961.* Princeton: Princeton University Press, 1962.

Abbreviations of Works
Most Frequently Cited

AFP, 1961   U.S. Department of State, *American Foreign Policy: Current Documents, 1961.* Washington, D.C.: G.P.O., 1965.

BSE, 1961   *Yezhegodnik Bol'shoi Sovetskoi Entsiklopedii.* Moscow: Sovetskaia Entsiklopediia, 1961.

CDSP   *Current Digest of the Soviet Press.*

Cmnd. 1451   United Kingdom. *Documents about the Future of Germany (including Berlin), June to July 1961.* London: H.M.S.O., 1961, Cmnd. 1451.

Cmnd. 1552   United Kingdom. *Selected Documents on Germany and the Question of Berlin 1944–1961.* London: H.M.S.O., 1961, Cmnd. 1552.

CSP IV   *Current Soviet Policies IV: The Documentary Record of the Twenty-second Congress of the Communist Party of the Soviet Union.* New York: Columbia University Press, 1962.

Dallin   Dallin, Alexander. *The Soviet Union at the United Nations.* New York: Praeger, 1962.

Dean   Dean, Arthur H. *Test Ban and Disarmament. The Path of the Negotiations.* New York and Evanston: Harper and Row, 1966.

DIA, 1961   Royal Institute of International Affairs. *Documents on International Affairs, 1961.* London: Oxford University Press, 1965.

Documents on Disarmament, 1961   U.S. Arms Control and Disarmament Agency. *Documents on Disarmament, 1961.* Washington, D.C.: G.P.O., 1962.

485

Documents on Germany	U.S. Senate, Committee on Foreign Relations. *Documents on Germany, 1944–1961.* Washington, D.C.: G.P.O., 1961.
DSB	U.S., *Department of State Bulletin.*
Griffith, *Albania*	Griffith, William E. *Albania and the Sino–Soviet Rift.* Cambridge, Mass.: M.I.T. Press, 1963.
Horelick and Rush	Horelick, Arnold, and Rush, Myron L. *Strategic Power and Soviet Foreign Policy.* Chicago: University of Chicago Press, 1966.
Izv.	*Izvestiia.*
Jacobson and Stein	Jacobson, Harold K., and Stein, Eric. *Diplomats, Scientists and Politicians. The United States and the Nuclear Test Ban Negotiations.* Ann Arbor: University of Michigan Press, 1966.
JFK, 1961	U.S., Office of the Federal Register. *John F. Kennedy. Containing the Public Messages, Speeches, and Statements of the President, January 20 to December 31, 1961.* Washington, D.C.: G.P.O., 1962.
Kaufmann	Kaufmann, William W. *The McNamara Strategy.* New York: Harper and Row, 1964.
Khrushchev, *Kommunizm*	Khrushchev, N. S. *Kommunizm—mir i schast'e narodam,* 2 vols. Moscow: Gospolitizdat, 1962.
Khrushchev, *Stroitel'stvo*	Khrushchev, N. S., *Stroitel'stvo Kommunizma v SSSR i razvitie sel'skogo khoziaistva,* 8 vols. Moscow: Gospolitizdat, 1962–64.
Kroll	Kroll, Hans. *Lebenserinnerungen eines Botschafters.* Cologne and Berlin: Kiepenheuer und Witsch, 1967.
Linden	Linden, Carl A. *Khrushchev and the Soviet Leadership 1957–1964.* Baltimore: The Johns Hopkins Press, 1966.
NYHT	*New York Herald Tribune.*
NYT	*New York Times.*
Ploss	Ploss, Sidney I. *Conflict and Decision-making in Soviet Russia: A Case Study of Agricultural Policy 1953–1963.* Princeton: Princeton University Press, 1965.
Salinger	Salinger, Pierre. *With Kennedy.* New York: Doubleday, 1966.
Schlesinger	Schlesinger, Arthur M., Jr. *A Thousand Days: John F. Kennedy in the White House.* Boston: Houghton Mifflin; Cambridge, Mass.: The Riverside Press, 1965.

Schwartz	Schwartz, Harry, ed. *Russia Enters the 1960s. A Documentary Report on the 22nd Congress of the Communist Party of the Soviet Union.* Philadelphia and New York: Lippincott, 1962.
SIA, 1961	Watt, D. C. *Survey of International Affairs, 1961.* London: Oxford University Press, 1965.
Sidey	Sidey, Hugh. *John F. Kennedy, President.* New York: Atheneum, 1963.
Smith, *Defense of Berlin*	Smith, Jean Edward. *The Defense of Berlin.* Baltimore: The Johns Hopkins Press, 1963.
Sorensen	Sorensen, Theodore C. *Kennedy.* New York and Evanston: Harper and Row, 1965.
Sten. ot.	*XXII S"ezd Kommunisticheskoi Partii Sovetskogo Soiuza 17–31 oktiabria 1961 goda. Stenograficheskii otchet*, 3 vols. Moscow: Gospolitizdat, 1962.
Sten. ot., 1956	*XX S"ezd Kommunisticheskoi Partii Sovetskogo Soiuza 14–25 fevralia 1956 goda. Stenograficheskii otchet.* 2 vols. Moscow: Gospolitizdat, 1956.
Sten. ot., 1959	*Vneocherednoi XXI S"ezd Kommunisticheskoi Partii Sovetskogo Soiuza 27 ianvaria—5 fevralia 1959 goda. Stenograficheskii otchet.* 2 vols. Moscow: Gospolitizdat, 1959.
Sten. ot., 1966	*XXIII S"ezd Kommunisticheskoi Partii Sovetskogo Soiuza 17–31 oktiabria 1961 goda. Stenograficheskii otchet.* 2 vols. Moscow: Gospolitizdat, 1966.
Tatu	Tatu, Michel. *Power in the Kremlin, From Khrushchev to Kosygin.* New York: Viking Press, 1968.
Tatu, *Le Pouvoir*	Tatu, Michel. *Le Pouvoir en U.R.S.S., du Déclin de Khrouchtchev à la Direction Collective.* Paris: Bernard Grasset, 1967.
Triska	Triska, Jan F., ed. *Soviet Communism: Programs and Rules.* San Francisco: Chandler, 1962.
VPSS, 1961	*Vneshniaia politika Sovetskogo Soiuza i mezhdunarodnye otnosheniia. Sbornik dokumentov, 1961 god.* Moscow: Izdatel'stvo Instituta Mezhdunarodnykh Otnoshenii, 1962.
Zagoria	Zagoria, Donald S. *The Sino-Soviet Conflict 1956–1961.* Princeton: Princeton University Press, 1962.

Acknowledgments

This book has been a long time in the making, and my obligations are numerous. My deepest debt is to the late Professor Philip E. Mosely, whose unfailing help and support enabled me to continue my work. His untimely death was a tremendous loss to American scholarship, but his achievements are of fundamental importance and they will loom still larger as time passes and their true dimensions become better known.

I am grateful to the following institutions which have provided research grants in support of my work: The Relm Foundation; the American Philosophical Society; the Humanities Fund, Inc.; and the Johns Hopkins University Faculty Research Grants. Some of the basic work was done under a year's appointment (1966–67) as a visiting scholar at the Russian Institute, Columbia University; I am indebted to the very capable staff of the Russian Institute, and especially to its then director, Professor Alexander Dallin, for this opportunity. I am grateful to Professor Alfred D. Chandler, Jr., former chairman of the Department of History, the Johns Hopkins University, for enabling me to take sabbatical leave at a critical time. My thanks go also to Professor Zbigniew K. Brzezinski, director of the Research Institute on Communist Affairs, for assistance while I was working at Columbia University.

In November 1968 the Research Seminar on Communist Affairs at Columbia provided an opportunity for me to present my analysis of the Twenty-second Congress of the Communist Party of the Soviet Union to what was, I fear, a fairly skeptical audience; I am grateful to Professor Marshall D. Shulman, director of the Russian Institute, for helping to arrange this presentation, to Mr. Paul Borsuk for his work as rapporteur, and to the participants in the seminar for their stimulating questions, comments, and objections.

Most of the research and writing was carried out at the Milton S. Eisenhower Library of the Johns Hopkins University. Mr. John Berthel, librarian, and his hard-working and devoted staff met every request for help promptly, sympathetically, and efficiently. At the Library of Congress, Dr. Paul L. Horecky, then associate director, now director of the Slavic and Central European

Division, not only helped me locate obscure publications but also lent a sympathetic ear to my analysis of recent Soviet history. I have also used the Butler Library at Columbia University, the Lenin Library in Moscow, the New York Public Library, the University of Michigan Library, and the Michigan State University Library, and I am grateful to their staffs for help rendered.

Vital assistance was provided by the research department of Radio Liberty, Munich, in particular by its knowledgeable director, Dr. Albert Boiter; its assistant director, Mr. Peter Dornan, a valued friend and a fine scholar; and Mr. Christian Duevel, whose writings, were they better known, would ensure him recognition as one of the best informed and most penetrating analysts of Soviet affairs now at work.

Among the fellow-scholars who have contributed in one way or another to completion of the task, I express my gratitude to Professors Seweryn D. Bialer, Jerome D. Gilison, George Ginsburgs, Grey Hodnett, Michael Luther, and Jay Sorenson. Professor Stephen F. Cohen has been a constant source of information, insight, and challenge. An Americanist and a good friend, Professor Kenneth S. Lynn, volunteered to read the lengthy typescript and helped thereby to smooth the way for publication.

For encouragement to work in the challenging but difficult field of recent Soviet history I am grateful to Professors Peter H. Juviler and Henry W. Morton, who gallantly accepted an essay I wrote on recent Soviet foreign policy for a volume they were preparing on Soviet policy-formulation; this exploratory and in part speculative essay served as the pilot project for the longer, deeper, and larger work of which the present volume, in concept, forms a part. Professor Morton also kindly arranged a seminar of Manhattan-based scholars in the spring of 1967 at which I presented some of my conclusions and discussed briefly the procedures and principles on which the work is based.

I wish to thank Mr. Jack Goellner, editorial director of The Johns Hopkins University Press, for his encouragement, enthusiasm, and confidence. I am grateful also to Mr. Harold Ingle, director of the Press, for his steady support and interest, and to Mrs. Nancy Gallienne, who as my editor was a model of helpfulness and tact. The demanding task of typing the lengthy manuscript was admirably performed by Mrs. Catherine Grover. Several secretarial aides in the Department of History, the Johns Hopkins University, helped as needed; to all of them I am grateful.

Over the seemingly endless years during which the book was taking shape, my wife, Elizabeth, provided help and understanding for which I can never adequately thank her. So too, in their various ways, did our children, Ginny, Paul, and Jim. "Big Jim"—Dr. James Tape, our son-in-law—was one of the earliest members of my captive audience, and I am grateful for his patience, interest, and confidence in the ultimate outcome. I owe an enormous debt of gratitude to my uncle, Professor Jean Paul Slusser, for vital moral and material support and for an intelligent and critical evaluation of the book, much of which he read in manuscript. Another uncle, Professor Herbert R. Slusser, with his wife Lois, has been a numinous figure in my personal world as far back as I can remember; he, too, has served as a sounding-board for some of my fine-spun theories. And I cannot omit to mention with gratitude the late Mrs. Helen C. Wadsworth and her sister, Miss Alice E. Woodman, to both of whom I owe more than I can ever repay.

The usual disclaimer—that the final responsibility for the work in question rests with its author, and that the many people who have helped him are blameless for its faults or errors—is true in the most literal sense in the case of the present book. The help I have received in no way diminishes my responsibility for what I recognize to be, in part, highly unorthodox conclusions. The fact that some of those who helped me have tended to question my findings and look askance at my methods serves only to deepen my gratitude to them.

ROBERT M. SLUSSER

Washington, D. C., November 1963—
East Lansing, Michigan, September 1972

SUBJECT INDEX

NAME INDEX

503

The Johns Hopkins University Press

This book was composed in Times Roman text and Univers display
by Jones Composition Company from a design by Edward Scott. It was
printed by Universal Lithographers, Inc. on S. D. Warren's 60-lb.
Sebago, in a text shade, regular finish and bound by L. H. Jenkins, Inc.
The cloth edition was bound in Joanna Arrestox.

Library of Congress Cataloging in Publication Data

Slusser, Robert M.
    The Berlin crisis of 1961.

    Bibliography: p.
    1. Berlin wall (1961-   ) 2. Berlin question
(1945-   ) 3. Khrushchev, Nikita Sergeevich, 1894-
1971.   4. World politics—1955-1965.   5. Kommunisti-
cheskaia partiia Sovetskago Soiuza.   22. S"ezd, Moscow,
1961.
DD881.S52   943'.155'087   72-4025
ISBN 0-8018-1404-9